Racism
in the
United States

Also available in
Bibliographies and Indexes in Ethnic Studies

Annotated Bibliography of Puerto Rican Bibliographies
Fay Fowlie-Flores, compiler

RACISM
IN THE
UNITED STATES

A Comprehensive
Classified Bibliography

Compiled by MEYER WEINBERG

Bibliographies and Indexes in Ethnic Studies, Number 2

GREENWOOD PRESS
New York • Westport, Connecticut • London

Library of Congress Cataloging-in-Publication Data

Racism in the United States : a comprehensive classified bibliography
/ compiled by Meyer Weinberg.
     p. cm. — (Bibliographies and indexes in ethnic studies, ISSN
1046-7882 ; no. 2)
     ISBN 0-313-27390-1 (lib. bdg. : alk. paper)
     1. Racism—United States—Bibliography. 2. Minorities—United
States—Bibliography. 3. United States—Race relations—
Bibliography. I. Weinberg, Meyer, 1920- . II. Series.
Z1361.E4R34   1990
[E184.A1]
016.973'04—dc20   89-78118

British Library Cataloguing in Publication Data is available.

Library of Congress Catalog Card Number: 89-78118
ISBN: 0-313-27390-1
ISSN: 1046-7882

First published in 1990

Greenwood Press, 88 Post Road West, Westport, CT 06881
An imprint of Greenwood Publishing Group, Inc.

Printed in the United States of America

The paper used in this book complies with the
Permanent Paper Standard issued by the National
Information Standards Organization (Z39.48-1984).

10 9 8 7 6 5 4 3 2 1

To
Sarge Korman Ruck

Contents

Introduction

This is the most comprehensive, book-length bibliography of racism in the United States. Wherever possible it lists materials produced by persons belonging to a minority. Because racism is a phenomenon of long standing, historical references are plentiful, but, at the same time, the recent past is covered in detail. In addition to racism, references dealing with sexism and antisemitism are listed. They resemble racism in reducing human individuals to abstract "others," and deny the equal humanity of large groups of people. All three of these forms of dehumanization often interact.

Racism is frequently viewed as a mode of oppression or group denial of rights, many times in the context of governmental affairs. Cruel personal treatment is highlighted. All these conceptions may well be warranted, but exploitation, especially of an economic variety, is just as significant. Yet, the ordinary literature of the subject does not always reflect the fact. The present collection attempts to rectify this customary omission or underevaluation.

In addition, racism is too often presented as a happenstance affair or as an unthinking reaction by persons long socialized against certain groups, entirely passing it over as deliberate racism, arising out of conscious calculation of advantage by some groups over others. Many efforts to gain political or economic points are of this variety, sometimes summarized as "divide and rule." Seemingly spontaneous "racial" episodes may turn out to be elaborately-designed political or economic ventures.

In the last few years racism and antisemitism have been in the news, especially when occurring in educational institutions. How ready are schools and colleges for campaigns against these scourges? Not very, unfortunately.

School people are educated and trained in university curricula that carefully avoid discussing topics such as racism. U.S. history texts rarely mention the term or analyze its development. Yet, it is one of the most fundamental trends in American life and history. In sociology and psychology courses "prejudice" or "cultural deprivation" is misleadingly treated as an equivalent of racism. Educational researchers also avoid concern with racism. The standard educational journals ignore the subject. Evidently there is a broad consensus among educational researchers on the unimportance of racism. This constitutes a formidable barrier to remedial action.

Many educators think that multicultural education automatically takes care of racism. A review of textbooks and educational literature reveals no such thing. Most multicultural material deals wholly with the cultural distinctiveness of various groups and little more. Rarely is sustained attention given to the realities of systematic discrimination against the same group that also happens to utilize quaint clothing, fascinating toys, delightful fairy tales, and delicious food. Responding to racist attacks and defamation is also part of the culture of minority groups in the United States.

Racism resists being decomposed into an individual prejudice and treated merely as an unfortunate difference among a number of isolated individuals. Racism is always collective. Prejudiced individuals may join the large movement, but they do not cause it. The point, sometimes difficult to grasp, is fundamental.

When Frederick Douglass, a fugitive slave and Black abolitionist, escaped to England he wrote a friend in Boston that in England skin color brought neither privilege nor penalty. Accordingly, racism is a system of privilege and penalty. The privileges may be better housing, employment, education, and health standards; the penalties, less adequate conditions in all these areas of living. At the heart of the system are mechanisms to allocate privilege and penalty. These mechanisms are staffed by individuals, to be sure. However, the system would collapse if individuals operated the system according to personal whim. Stability of the system depends on the creation of allocative mechanisms that operate institutionally, rather than by individual preference.

In a system of institutional racism privileges and penalties are allocated by decisions that seem automatic and impersonal rather than deliberate and personal. During the 1920s, for example, officials of Ohio University wished to stop the enrollment of out-of-state Blacks but wanted to avoid the reputation of being racist. The change was accomplished by adopting a rule that no out-of-state student would be accepted who was ineligible to attend her or his own state university. Since all southern state universities barred Blacks, this meant that no southern Blacks could attend Ohio University either. Hereafter, out-of-state Black applicants to Ohio University would be excluded by an impersonal, institutional rule rather than by an act of an official who personally found Blacks hateful. Conceivably, a Black might now be excluded from the school even by an official who personally adored Blacks but who was obliged to follow through.

Institutional racism is thus a product of deliberate human decision. Over time, however, its origins may be forgotten, and it takes on the appearance of a supra human process. Those who justify this racism either profit from it or regard the traditional as appropriate. A combination of both reasons can lead even otherwise enlightened persons to defend institutional racism.

The form of institutional racism that is most effective has the least visible connection with an individual's decision making. As Henry David Thoreau wrote in another context: "The longer the lever, the less perceptible its motion" (Autumn, p. 121). If the racist act seems part of ordinary, everyday procedure, not chargeable to this or that individual, it is highly effective. To search out the human agency in institutional racism is very difficult, although not impossible. Occasionally it resembles an onion: Layers of institutional procedures and traditions to be unpeeled and interrelated historically with motives and interests of directing powers.

Institutionalized racism expresses the vested interests of a dominant group; dominant because of its superior economic and political power. As Thorstein Veblen perceived a vested interest is a commercialized right to something for nothing. Institutionalizing racism rewards those in charge and their supporters. The right to a superior education simply because of a prior position of power is difficult to justify in its own terms. Justification seeks loftier grounds such as high test scores or inherent worth as embodied in racist doctrine.

Racism consists centrally of two facets: First, a belief in the inherent superiority of some people and the inherent inferiority of others; and second, the acceptance of distributing goods and services -- let alone respect -- in accordance with such judgments of unequal worth. Some theorists have contended persons may exemplify either of the two facets without the other. It would seem sounder to expect both to be present in racist action.

How is the silence of institutional racism related to the ruckus of individual racism? Unbeknown to their respective practitioners -- who are frequently separated by social and economic circumstances -- they are mutually supportive. Gatekeepers in institutionally racist structures are not really unaware of the price excluded persons pay for their exclusion; nor is the crude violence of a swastika-daubing entirely unconnected with the overwhelming institutional exclusion of Jews from certain employments. Institutional racism prepares the ground for personal racism while personal racism helps sustain institutional racism.

To eliminate institutional racism, we must first deinstitutionalize it. The very features that were created to privilege some and penalize others need to be countered decisively. Affirmative action, for example, aims to destroy a long-standing preference for whites and males. Its purpose is not to create a new privileged class. Instead, it provides breathing space to create a new fairness in employment. Minorities and women are assured first call for some jobs that they were historically denied because they were of the "wrong" race or sex. This new situation is expected to be monitored by the government authorities until the handicap is counteracted. From this point on a presumably fairer distribution of employment would exist.

Deinstitutionalization of racism cannot result merely from changing personal opinions of individuals in an organization. Rather, a new fundamental purpose must infuse the basic operations of the institution. To bring about such a change might require pressure brought by minority and women's groups, by government, by labor unions, and by lawsuits. The more powerful the institution, the more numerous the means to resist change. Not only that; racist institutions frequently support others like themselves. An institutionally racist public school system will line up with a dominant, institutionally racist political party. An institutionally racist housing industry will align itself with an institutionally racist banking industry; loans will be made more readily for segregated than for integrated housing.

None of these racist institutions can be expected to lead a campaign against institutionalized racism, especially in areas where their own material interests are involved. Together, these, and many others, constitute a powerful combine of vested interests. They cannot be expected to welcome change; indeed, they can be depended upon to resist it. Slavery was a prime racist institution, supported not only by owners of slaves but also by large-scale wholesale merchants and bankers in the North who profited from shipping and financing the cotton crop. It took a civil war to deinstitutionalize slavery. During the past 25 years, many features of the Jim Crow system of racial discrimination have been dismantled. This was one of the great achievements of the Civil Rights movement. Much racism remains to be deinstitutionalized, as can be seen by the contents of this volume.

More than four out of five Americans are white. But it is racism, not numbers, that makes the United States a "white man's country." Even the way we try to oppose racism is sometimes infected with racism.

In educational circles, for example, it is widely accepted that "minority problems" should be dealt with in their designated localities, meaning in schools attended by minority children. Thus, in schools with many minorities, one can expect to find minority insignia that presumably raise the self-esteem of minority students. Mexican national holidays are celebrated in schools of the U.S. Southwest. Occasionally, courses in Mexican-American history are taught. Or, in other cities Black history month is a major event. If in all these schools white students happen to be in attendance, all the better. These mind-opening programs are regarded as unnecessary in schools enrolling no minority students. No minority students, no problem.

But what is the problem? Overwhelmingly, whites, not minorities, are the bearers of racism. According to public opinion studies, a sizable minority of Ivy League alumni still believe whites are born superior in intelligence to Blacks. About a third of white Chicagoans express similar views. What are schools in the United States doing to counteract this personal racism?

Very broadly speaking minority students are a measurable part of enrollment in about 3,000 of the country's 15,000 or so school districts. The 12,000 districts are more or less white. There is no Black history month, no Mexican-American history courses in these schools. These are perfect breeding-grounds for personal racism or what is known simply as racial prejudice.

The sources of such sentiments in white schools are racially-biased textbooks, curricula, teachers and staff, let alone community attitudes imported into the classroom through television, press, church, and home. Racism does not require the physical presence of minorities. In fact, in their absence, stereotypes prosper.

Some racists relate bitter personal experiences with Blacks or Hispanics. Far more pervasive, however, is a brand of racism that arises from the real stuff of stereotypes -- fabricated reality based on imagined hurts. Minorities become mere "others" and are viewed as dangerous, threatening, and illicit.

Many educators, and others, opt for color-blindness in the hope that ugly realities will wither away from inattention. Perhaps the ugliness would wither if students and others learned to what they should be inattentive. "Doing what comes naturally" in a racist order, on the other hand, guarantees the perpetuation of racism. In the prejudiced school, separateness buttresses the development of racist ideology.

We cannot seriously claim to deal with racism without confronting the doctrine of white supremacy. This holds for all schools, whether or not minority students are present. It is true as well for all-minority schools. The most detailed account of Black life is of little use unless the student also comes to understand the falsehood of white supremacy. Clearly, where detailed knowledge of Black life and history coexists with a belief in white supremacy, the result can only be a demeaning paternalism and patronization.

Some years ago, a Black magazine published a series of articles on the theme: When should I tell my children what problems to expect in life because of their race? The accounts were a chilling commentary on inhumanity in American life. American educators, especially those in all-white schools, might well undertake a parallel task and help white parents explore the problems that will arise from their children developing a false sense of superiority arising from the privilege of the white race. This includes denigration of the alleged inferior.

Education on racism should be viewed as an extension of rather than a substitute for multicultural education. If educators restrict their instruction to distinctive dances and foods of minorities, they will encourage a view of such people as quaint and interesting but as not engaging in "real history" such as whites in America do by acting in politics, writing books, and working at jobs. On the other hand, to speak only of racism is to engender a view of minority people merely as victims who lack institutions and cultural practices of their own.

Prejudice becomes racism when linked with an ideology of treating others as inferiors, of advocating discriminatory deprivation of education, housing, jobs, and much else. Prejudice need never become racism. Indeed, for many years -- especially during centuries of ancient history -- it is difficult to document the existence even of racial prejudice. This was also true where Blacks and whites worked side by side. In early colonial times, during the 17th and 18th centuries, it took many years until full-scale racism was enacted into the slave codes. By 1776 or thereabouts, for example, nearly every colonial code equated "Black" with "slave." The legal history of slavery in this country is filled with instances of racist doctrine that developed over time.

While institutional racism may endow whites with privileges, the distribution of power remains largely unchanged in the general class structure. Under institutional racism, oppression and exploitation of some whites by other whites continue. Inequality in the distribution of wealth, income, and chances in life endures. Poorer and more powerless whites may support the class structure because it allows them to possess minor privileges over minorities. The ruling class supports the class structure out of its own self-interest. It opposes general equality principally because its own sweeping privileges would then necessarily end. Least of all is class structure ideologically pro-white. The history of the United States suggests as much.

Knowledge about the role of racism in U.S. life and history is essential. But racism must not be offered as a ready-made explanation of every problem that afflicts minority people. Recently, two historians have suggested the danger in pursuing this road. In dealing with the rise of the New South, 1865-1900, Harold D. Woodman declares: "Anything that explains everything in the end explains nothing."[1] Racism undoubtedly played a role in economic, political, social and other conflicts during this period. Its precise role, however, depended on how it, in turn, was affected by historical circumstances, contemporary political movements, and other factors. Not racism pure and simple, but racism in all its complexity must be studied. A comparable caution comes from Eric Foner, author of a new detailed history of the Reconstruction years, 1863-1877. He notes that "instead of viewing racism as a deus ex machina that independently explains the course of events and Reconstruction's demise, I view it as an intrinsic part of the process of historical development, which affected and was affected by changes in the social and political order."[2]

By no means are these historians slighting the issue of racism. Indeed, Foner's index may be the first in a U.S. general historical work to have extensive entries under the term. Few historians bother to deal

---

[1] Harold D. Woodman, "Economic Reconstruction and the Rise of the New South, 1865-1900," p. 260 in John B. Boles and Evelyn Thomas Nolen (eds.), Interpreting Southern History. (Baton Rouge: Louisiana State University Press, 1987).

[2] Eric Foner, Reconstruction. America's Unfinished Revolution. 1863-1877. (New York: Harper and Row, 1988), p. xxvi.

frontally with racism and fewer still want to call attention in indexes to the fact that they have done so. The very complexity and bulk of the present bibliography, however, attest to the need to go beyond mere mentions of racism.

References in this volume consist of published articles, books, monographs, printed congressional and executive hearings and reports, theses and dissertations, research reports on specific institutions and practices, as well as selected accounts by investigative journalists and writers. Items are annotated when the titles are not self-explanatory. Eighty-seven subject headings are used and nearly each section of the work as a whole is thoroughly cross-referenced. An author index closes the work.

One section contains highly selected references on racism in countries other than the United States. The purpose is to give the reader an opportunity to view racism comparatively, thus highlighting both the distinctive and the common elements of racism in the United States and elsewhere. There is no effort to be comprehensive in this section.

I wish to thank Donna Goodleaf and Kim Holder, my research assistants, for their aid in many ways. The reference staff of the library at the University of Massachusetts, Amherst, was, as usual, cooperative and helpful. Betty Craker, Karen Morris, and Ivette Palacin typed the final manuscript with high intelligence and resourcefulness. The Office of the Provost, University of Massachusetts, Amherst, kindly supplied part of the secretarial funds.

Racism
in the
United States

1. Affirmative Action

Resolved, that it is the duty of abolitionists to give encouragement to colored youth in obtaining a knowledge of trades and professions in preference to the whites.

- Resolution before the annual meeting of the Middlesex County Anti-Slavery Society, October 10, 1838, Liberator, November 23, 1838.

A Decade of New Opportunity, Affirmative Action in the 1970s. Washington, D.C.: Potomac Institute, December 1984.

Abram, M. B. Affirmative Action: Fair Shakers and Social Engineers. Harvard Law Review 99 (April 1986):1312-26.

Affirmative Action: A Symposium. Iowa Law Review 72 (January 1987):255-85.

Affirmative Action: Cure or Contradiction? A Symposium. Center Magazine (November-December 1987):20-25.

Amott, T. and J. Mattaei. The Promise of Comparable Worth: A Socialist-Feminist Perspective. Socialist Review 18 (April-June 1988):101-17.

Auerbach, Carl A. The Silent Opposition of Professors and Graduate Students to Preferential Action Programs: 1969-1975. Minnesota Law Review 72 (June 1988):1233-80.

Bakke, Weber, and Affirmative Action. New York: The Rockefeller Foundation, December 1979.

Bates, T. Impact of Preferential Procurement Policies on Minority-Owned Businesses. Review of Black Political Economy 14 (Summer 1985).

Beeson, R. M. Desegregation and Affirmative Action in Higher Education in Oklahoma: A Historical Case Study. Doctoral dissertation, Oklahoma State University, 1986. UMO # 8701016.

Belfer, Roberta. Affirmative Action and the Anti-Defamation League, 1964 to 1978. Master's thesis, Concordia University (Canada), 1985.

Bell, D. A., Jr. The Final Report: How Affirmative Action at Harvard Was Transformed from 1988 Tragedy to 1990 Triumph. Cambridge, MA: Harvard Law School, 1988.

Bell, D. A., Jr. Preferential Affirmative Action. Harvard Civil Rights - Civil Liberties Law Review 16 (Winter 1982):855-873.

Bell, D. A., Jr. Application of the Tipping Point Principle to Law Faculty Hiring Policies. Nova Law Journal 10 (Winter 1986):855-873.

Berger, Joseph. The Bakke Case 10 Years Later: Mixed Realities. New

1

York *Times* July 13, 1988.

Bielby, W. T. Modern Prejudice and Institutional Barriers to Equal
    Employment Opportunity for Minorities. *Journal of Social Issues* 43
    (1987):79-84.

Boxill, B. R. *Blacks and Social Justice*. Totowa, NJ, 1984.

Braddock, J. H. and J. M. McPartland. How Minorities Continue to be
    Excluded from Equal Employment Opportunities: Research on Labor
    Market and Institutional Barriers. *Journal of Social Issues* 43
    (1987):5-39.

Braddock, J. H. and J. M. McPartland. Social Science Evidence and
    Affirmative Action Policies: A Reply to the Commentators. *Journal
    of Social Issues* 43 (1987):133-43.

Brimelow, P. A Man Alone [Thomas Sowell, Affirmative Action]. *Forbes*
    (August 24, 1987):40-41, 44, 46.

Brown, C. The Federal Attack on Labor Market Discrimination: The Mouse
    that Roared? In: Ronald G. Ehrenberg (ed.), *Research in Labor
    Economics*. Greenwich, CT: JAI Press, 1982.

Burbridge, L. C. Changes in Equal Employment. In: Gilbert Ware (ed.),
    From the Black Bar. Voices for Equal Justice, pp. 262-81. New York:
    Putnam, 1986.

Butterfield, Bruce. Labor's Affirmative Action Pledge. *Boston Globe*
    November 22, 1988. [Minority and women apprentices in Boston].

Clague, Monique W. The Affirmative Action Showdown of 1986: Implications
    for Higher Education. *Journal of College and University Law* 14
    (Fall 1987):171-257.

Clague, Monique W. Voluntary Affirmative Action Plans in Public
    Education: Anticipating a Supreme Court Decision. *Journal of Law
    and Education* 14 (July 1985):309-48.

Clarke, Deborah J. Constitutional Law: Employment Discrimination -
    Emerging Judicial Standards for Careful Construction of Affirmative
    Action Remedies. *Oklahoma Law Review* 41 (Summer 1988):289-313.

Cohen, C. Naked Racial Preference. *Commentary* 81 (March 1986):24-31.

Combs, M. W. and J. Gruhl (eds.) *Affirmative Action: Theory, Analysis
    and Prospects*. Jefferson, NC: McFarland, 1986.

Comer, J. P. and J. E. Coleman. Quotas, Race and Justice. *New York Times*
    March 17, 1974. [Two articles].

Connor, L. A. *The Impact of Affirmative Action on the Employment
    Practices in Pennsylvania's State System of Higher Education, 1974-
    1984*. Doctoral dissertation, University of Pittsburgh, 1985. UMO #
    8600634.

2

Cooper, K. J. 30 Schools But Few Black Professors [Boston area colleges
    and universities]. <u>Boston</u> <u>Globe</u> April 28, 1983.

Cooper, K. J. At UMass: A Director with Clout [Affirmative action hiring
    at UMass, Boston]. <u>Boston</u> <u>Globe</u> April 28, 1983.

Culp, J. M. and G. Loury. The Impact of Affirmative Action on Equal
    Opportunity: A New Look. <u>In</u>: <u>Bakke, Weber, and Affirmative Action</u>,
    pp. 124-36. New York: Rockefeller Foundation, December 1979.

Davis, G. <u>Affirmative Action Implementation in Illinois Public State</u>
    <u>Universities.</u> Doctoral dissertation, Illinois State University,
    1986. UMO # 8626589.

Davitt, M. H. <u>The Effect of Federal Affirmative Action Policies on Hiring</u>
    <u>Practices of a Local Education Agency</u> [California district, 1973-
    1983]. Doctoral dissertation, University of California, Riverside,
    1983. UMO # 832417.

Deutsch, C. H. The Ax Falls on Equal Opportunity [Sharp reduction in
    corporate affirmative action programs headed by Black executives].
    <u>New York Times</u> January 4, 1987.

Duncan, M. L. The Future of Affirmative Action: A Jurisprudential/Legal
    Critique. <u>Harvard Civil Rights/Civil Liberties Law Review</u> (Summer
    1982):503-53.

Dunlap, J. <u>A Study of the Conflict between Seniority Rights and the Anti-</u>
    <u>Discrimination Goals of Title VII and Affirmative Action</u>. Doctoral
    dissertation, Pepperdine University, 1986]. UMO # 8710914.

Edwards, H. T. Affirmative Action or Reverse Discrimination: The Head
    and Tail of 'Weber'. <u>Creighton Law Review</u> 13 (Spring 1980):713-768.

Ezorsky, Gertrude. In Affirmative Action Numbers Count. <u>New Politics</u> 1
    (Summer 1987):35-37. [See below, H. Hill, 1987].

Farmer, J. Affirmative Action: Problems and Prospects. <u>Trotter</u>
    <u>Institute Review</u> (UMass Boston) 1 (Winter 1987):4-9.

Farnham, Alan. Holding Firm on Affirmative Action. <u>Fortune</u> (March 14,
    1989):87-88.

Feagin, J. R. Changing Black Americans to Fit a Racist System? <u>Journal</u>
    <u>of Social Issues</u> 43 (1987):85-89.

Feild, J. <u>Affirmative Action: A Fresh Look at the Record Twenty-Two</u>
    <u>Years After the Beginning</u>. Washington, D.C.: Center for National
    Policy Review, 1984.

Fisher, A. B. Businessmen Like to Hire by the Numbers. [Affirmative
    action]. <u>Fortune</u> (September 16, 1985):26-30.

Fleming, J. E. and others. <u>The Case for Affirmative Action for Blacks in</u>

3

Higher Education. Washington, D.C.: Howard University Press, 1978.

Fox-Genovese, E. Women's Rights, Affirmative Action, and the Myth of
   Individualism. George Washington Law Review 54 (January-March
   1986):338-74.

Fullinwider, R. K. The Reverse Discrimination Controversy: A Moral and
   Legal Analysis. Rowman and Littlefield, 1980.

Gelb, Hal. Should Equal Opportunity Apply on the Stage? New York Times
   August 28, 1988.

Gelbspan, R. Minorities Aren't Hired for Top Jobs, Leaders Say
   [Minorities in industry in Boston area]. Boston Globe January 12,
   1986.

Giampetro, Andrea and Nancy Kubasek. Individualism in America and Its
   Implications for Affirmative Action. Journal of Contemporary Law 14
   (Fall 1988):165-94.

Glazer, N. Affirmative Discrimination: Ethnic Inequality and Public
   Policy. New York: Basic Books, 1975.

Glazer, N. The Affirmative Action Stalemate. Public Interest (Winter
   1988):99-114.

Goering, John M. Resolute Ignorance or Political Straw Man? Society 25
   (January-February 1988):67-70.

Goldman, A. H. Justice and Reverse Discrimination. Princeton, NJ:
   Princeton University Press, 1979.

Gould, S. H. and P. L. Van Den Berghe. Particularism in Sociology
   Departments' Hiring Practices. Race 15 (January 1, 1973):106-111.

Greene, Kathanne W. Compensation and Redistribution: The Use of
   Competing Principles of Justice in the U.S. Supreme Court's
   Affirmative Action Decisions. Doctoral dissertation, University of
   Utah, 1988. UMO # 8814801.

Griswold, E. N. and others. Racial Preferences and Scarce Resources:
   Implications of the 'Bakke' Case. Washington University Law
   Quarterly 1 (Winter 1979):55-111.

Gross, B. R. (ed.) Reverse Discrimination. Prometheus, 1977.

Hammerman, H. Education and Equal Employment Opportunity. In: A Decade
   of New Opportunity, Affirmative Action in the 1970s. Washington,
   D.C.: Potomac Institute, October 1984.

Harvey, J. C. The Reagan Administration and Affirmative Action in Four
   Major Cities: Detroit, Boston, New Orleans and Memphis. Thurgood
   Marshall Law Review 9 (Fall 1983):1-16.

Hawkins, W. G. The Myth and Reality of Affirmative Action: A Study of

4

Affirmative Actions at the U.S. Military Academy, West Point from 1970-1977. Master's thesis, New York State University at Binghampton, 1985.

Heins, M. Cutting the Mustard: Affirmative Action and the Nature of Excellence [Boston University]. Boston: Faber and Faber, 1987.

Hernandez, Peggy. Many Chances to Dispute Malones [Issue of misrepresentation of race in affirmative action]. Boston Globe November 7, 1988.

Hicks, Jonathan. Blacks in Business Get a Tantalizing Glimpse of the Top. New York Times August 7, 1988.

Hill, Herbert. The Equal Employment Opportunity Acts of 1964 and 1972: A Critical Analysis of the Legislative History and Administration of the Law. Industrial Relations Law Journal 2 (Spring 1977):1-96.

Hill, Herbert. Preferential Hiring: Correcting the Demerit System. Social Policy (July-August 1973):96-102.

Hill, Herbert. Race and Ethnicity in Organized Labor: The Historical Sources of Resistance to Affirmative Action. In: Winston A. Van Horne and Thomas V. Tonnesen (eds.), Ethnicity and the Work Force. Milwaukee, WI: University of Wisconsin System American Ethnic Studies Coordinating Committee/Urban Corridor Consortium, 1985.

Hill, Herbert. Race, Ethnicity and Organized Labor: The Opposition to Affirmative Action. New Politics (Winter 1987):31-83.

Hills, D. M. An Affirmative Action, Equal Opportunity Employer: Perception and Implementation of the Term by Search Committees at Two Public Universities. Doctoral dissertation, University of Maryland, 1987. UMO # 872545.

Hook, S. Rationalizations for Reverse Discrimination. New Perspectives 17 (Winter 1985):9-11.

Jackson, C. Affirmative Action in Los Angeles County: The Continuing Invisibility of Hispanics. Doctoral dissertation, University of Southern California, 1981.

Jacobson, C. K. Black Support for Affirmative Action Programs. Phylon 44 (December 1983):299-311.

Jencks, C. Affirmative Action for Blacks: Past, Present, and Future. American Behavioral Scientist 28 (July-August 1985):731-60.

Jones, J. E., Jr. The Bugaboo of Employment Quotas. Wisconsin Law Review (1970):341-403.

Josey, E. J. Can Affirmative Action Succeed? The Black Caucus of ALA Surveys Minority Librarians in 22 Leading Libraries. Library Journal 100 (January 1, 1975):28-31.

Katz, I. and H. M. Proshansky. Rethinking Affirmative Action. _Journal of Social Issues_ 43 (1987):99-104.

Keith, S. N. and others. Effects of Affirmative Action in Medical Schools. _New England Journal of Medicine_ December 12, 1985.

Kellough, James E. _Federal Equal Employment Opportunity Policy and Numerical Goals and Timetables: An Impact Assessment_. Doctoral dissertation, Miami University, 1987. UMO # 8806170.

Kennedy, R. Persuasion and Distrust: A Comment on the Affirmative Action Debate. _Harvard Law Review_ 99 (April 1986):1327-46.

Kilson, M. L. In Defence of Affirmative Action: The American Case. _New Community_ 10 (Spring 1983):464-69.

King, N. Minority-Hiring Fight at Harvard [The Law School]. _Boston Globe_ November 17, 1982.

Kluegel, J. R. The Bases of Contemporary Affirmative Action Attitudes: Effects of Self-Interest, Racial Affect, and Stratification Beliefs on Whites' Views. _Social Forces_ (March 1983):707-824.

Lawrence, C. R., III. Education for Black Power in the Eighties: Present Day Implications of the 'Bakke' Decision. _National Black Law Journal_ 10 (Winter 1987):58-63.

Leonard, J. S. _Does Affirmative Action Work?_ Doctoral dissertation, Harvard University, 1983. UMO # 8311895.

Leonard, J. S. The Impact of Affirmative Action on Employment. _Journal of Labor Economics_ 2 (October 1984).

Leonard, J. S. What Promises Are Worth: The Impact of Affirmative Action Goals. _Journal of Human Resources_ 20 (Winter 1985).

Leonard, J. S. What Was Affirmative Action? _American Economic Review_ 76 (May 1986).

Livingston, J. C. _Fair Game? Inequality and Affirmative Action_. W.H. Freeman, 1979.

Loury, G. C. Why Preferential Admission Is Not Enough For Blacks. _Chronicle of Higher Education_ March 25, 1987.

Luzipho, D. S. _An Examination of the Reagan Administration's Policy on Affirmative Action_. Master's thesis, Atlanta University, 1986.

Lynch, F. R. Affirmative Action, the Media, and the Public. _American Behavioral Scientist_ 28 (July-August 1985):807-27.

Lynch, F. R. and others. Affirmative Action: Past, Present and Future. _American Behavioral Scientist_ 28 (July-August 1985):721-843.

Malveaux, J. M. Shifts in the Employment and Occupational Status of Black

Americans in a Period of Affirmative Action. In: Bakke, Weber, and Affirmative Action, pp. 137-169. New York: Rockefeller Foundation, December 1979.

Marrifold, E. M. Implementation of Affirmative Action Plans for Equal Employment Opportunity in Public School Districts of the Commonwealth of Pennsylvania. Doctoral dissertation, Unniversity of Pittsburgh, 1980. UMO # 8028115.

Morris, A. A. New Light on Racial Affirmative Action. U.C. Davis Law Review 20 (Winter 1987):219-71.

Murray, C. Affirmative Racism. New Republic (December 31, 1984):18-23.

Nacoste, R. W. Social Psychology and Affirmative Action: The Importance of Process in Policy Analysis. Journal of Social Issues 43 (1987):127-32.

Neili, R. Ethnic Tribalism and the Revolt Against Human Personhood: What's Wrong With Affirmative Action. This World (Fall 1987):59-78.

Nenno, Barbara A. Faculty Search Committees and Affirmative Action Policy. Doctoral dissertation, University of Colorado, 1988. UMO # 8819690.

Nxumalo, O. E. H. M. Case Study of the Implementation of Affirmative Action in the Faculty of Arts and Sciences at Harvard University. Doctoral dissertation, Harvard University, 1986. UMO # 8704580.

O'Neill, T. J. Bakke and the Politics of Equality: Friends and Foes in the Classroom of Litigation. Middletown, CT: Wesleyan University Press, 1984.

Parker, K. E. Ideas, Affirmative Action and the Ideal University. Nova Law Journal 10 (Winter 1986):761-77.

Pettigrew, T. F. and J. Martin. The Fruits of Critical Discussion: A Reply to the Commentators. Journal of Social Issues 43 (1987):45-46.

Phillips, Robert H. Equal Employment Opportunity, Affirmative Action, Mayoral Initiatives and Bureaucratic Responses: The Case of Detroit. Doctoral dissertation, Wayne State University, 1987. UMO # 8809126.

Reid, H. O., Sr. Assault on Affirmative Action: The Delusion of a Color-Blind America. Howard Law Journal 23 (1980):381-428.

Reynolds, Pamela. 10 Years Later, Bakke Case Is Still Hotly Disputed. Boston Globe June 28, 1988. [1st of two articles].

Rhee, F. Black Faculty and Tenure [Duke University]. Duke Chronicle February 16, 1984.

Rucker, R. E. and J. D. Bailey. The Fall and Demise of Affirmative Action. In: Samuel K. Gove and Thomas W. Stauffer (eds.), Political

Controversies in Higher Education. Westport, CT: Greenwood, 1986.

Scalia, A. and others. Affirmative Action: Panel Presentation and Discussion. _Federal Rules Decisions_ 114 (May 1987):442-69.

Schwartz, H. The 1986 and 1987 Affirmative Action Cases: It's All Over but the Shouting. _Michigan Law Review_ 86 (December 1987).

Sedler, R. A. Beyond Bakke: The Constitution and Redressing the Social History of Racism. _Harvard Civil Rights-Civil Liberties Law Review_ 14 (Spring 1979):133-71.

Shanor, Charles A. Affirmative Action in EEOC Litigation. _Georgia Law Review_ 21 (Summer 1987):1059-94.

Slocum, A. A. (ed.) _Allan Bakke versus Regents of the University of California_, 6 vols. Dobbs Ferry, NY: Oceana Publications, 1978.

Smith, J. C., Jr. Review: Affirmative Action. _Howard Law Journal_ 27 (Spring 1984):495-522.

Smith, M. L. The Handy Myth of Reverse Racism. _Cleveland Plain Dealer_ May 6, 1983.

Smith, R. Affirmative Action in Extremis. _Wayne Law Review_ 16 (July 1980).

Smothers, Ronald. Affirmative Action Booms in Atlanta. _New York Times_ January 27, 1989.

Sowell, T. Racism, Quotas and the Front Door. _Wall Street Journal_ July 28, 1978.

Sowell, T. 'Weber', 'Bakke', and the Presuppositions of Affirmative Action. _Wayne Law Review_ 26 (July 1980):1309-36.

Stone, J. Equal Protection in Special Admission Programs: Forward from 'Bakke'. _Hastings Constitutional Law Quarterly_ 6 (Spring 1979):719-50.

Takaki, R. The Myth of Ethnicity: Scholarship of the Anti-Affirmative Action Backlash. _Journal of Ethnic Studies_ 10 (Spring 1982):17-42.

Thalberg, I. Themes in the Reverse-Discrimination Debate. _Ethics_ 91 (October 1980).

Tribe, L. H. In What Vision of the Constitution Must the Law Be Colorblind? _John Marshall Law Review_ 20 (Winter 1986):201-07.

Tribe, L. H. Perspectives on 'Bakke': Equal Protection, Procedural Fairness, or Structural Justice? _Harvard Law Review_ 92 (February 1979):664-77.

U.S. Commission on Civil Rights. _Affirmative Action in the 1980s: Dismantling the Process of Discrimination_. Washington, D.C.: The

Commission, November 1982.

U.S. Commission on Civil Rights. Consultations on the Affirmative Action
    Statement of the U.S. Commission on Civil Rights, vol. 2,
    Washington, D.C.: The Commission, 1982.

U.S. Commission on Civil Rights, Massachusetts Advisory Committee.
    Teacher Layoff, Seniority and Affirmative Action. Washington, D.C.:
    The Commission, May 1982.

U.S. Congress, 97th, 1st session, House of Representatives, Committee On
    Education and Labor, Subcommittee On Employment Opportunities.
    Oversight Hearings on Equal Employment Opportunity and Affirmative
    Action: Hearings ..., 2 vols. Washington, D.C.: GPO, 1982.

U.S. Congress, 97th, 1st session, House of Representatives, Committee On
    Education and Labor, Subcommittee On Employment Opprotunities.
    Report on Affirmative Action and the Federal Enforcement of Equal
    Opportunity Employment Laws. Washington, D.C.: GPO, 1982.

U.S. Congress, 97th, 1st session, Senate, Committee On the Judiciary,
    Subcommitte on the Constitution. Affirmative Action and Equal
    Protection: Hearings ... Washington, D.C.: GPO, 1983.

U.S. Congress, 98th, 2nd session, House of Representatives, Committee On
    Education and Labor, Subcommittee On Employment Opportunities. The
    State of Affirmative Action in the Federal Government: Staff Report.
    Washington, D.C.: GPO, 1984.

University of California. Report on the University's Employee
    Affirmative Action Programs, 1980-1982. Berkeley, CA: Office of the
    Vice President - Academic and Staff Personnel Relations, June 1982.

Weatherspoon, F. D. Equal Employment Opportunity and Affirmative Action:
    A Sourcebook. New York: Garland, 1985.

Weiss, R. J. Affirmative Action: A Brief History. Journal of Intergroup
    Relations (Summer 1987):40-53.

Wilkerson, Isabel. Discordant Notes in Detroit: Music and Affirmative
    Action [Detroit Symphony Orchestra]. New York Times March 5, 1989.

Wolkinson, Benjamin W. Blacks, Unions, and the EEOC: A Study of
    Administrative Futility. Lexington, MA: Lexington Books, 1973.

Woo, D. Myths of Affirmative Action. Daily Californian (University of
    California, Berkeley) June 22, 1983.

Affirmative Action Bibliography

Brousseau, B. and C. Klein (comps.) Affirmative Action, Equal Employment
    Opportunity in the Criminal Justice System: A Selected Bibliography.
    Washington, D.C.: National Institute of Justice, 1980.

Swanson, K. (comp.) *Affirmative Action and Preferential Admissions in Higher Education: An Annotated Bibliography.* Metuchen, NJ: Scarecrow Press, 1981.

[See also sections 20 and 44]

2. Africa

> *Leading American Negroes are ... widely ignorant of the history and present situation in Africa and indifferent to the fate of African Negroes. This represents a great change from the past ... Negro authors and scholars have shied away from the subject which in the twenties and thirties was their preserve.*
>
> - W. E. B. Du Bois, "Africa and the American Negro Intelligentsia," 1954.

Ako, Edward O. The African Inspiration of the Black Arts Movement. Diogenes 135 (1986):93-104.

Asante, M. K. and A. L. Smith. The Afrocentric Idea. Philadelphia, PA: Temple University Press, 1987.

Austin, A. D., (ed.) African Muslims in Antebellum America: A Sourcebook. New York: Garland, 1981.

Collier, Eugenia. The African Presence in Afro-American Literary Criticism. Obsidian 6 (Winter 1980):30-55.

Cromwell, Adelaide M. (ed.) Dynamics of the African/Afro-American Connection. Washington, D.C.: Howard University Press, 1988.

Crowley, D., (ed.) African Folklore in the New World. Austin: University of Texas Press, 1977.

Drake, St. Clair. Negro Americans and the African Interest. In: John P. Davies (ed.), The American Negro Reference Book. Englewood Cliffs, NJ: Prentice-Hall, 1968.

Du Bois, W. E. B. Africa and the American Negro Intelligentsia. Presence Africaine vol. (December 1954-January 1955).

Herskovits, Melville J. The Myth of the Negro Past. New York: Harper and Row, 1941.

Herskovits, Melville J. What Has Africa Given America? New Republic (September 4, 1935):92-94.

Howard, L. C. A Note on New England Whaling and Africa Before 1860. Negro History Bulletin 22 (1958):13-15.

Jackson, W. Melville Herskovits and the Search for Afro-American Culture. In: George W. Stocking, Jr. (ed.), Malinowski, Rivers, Benedict, and Others .... Madison: University of Wisconsin Press, 1987.

Jones, F. White Racism and Africanity in the Development of Afro-American Communities. In: Institutional Racism and Community Competence, pp. 67-74. Oscar A. Barbarin and others, (eds.) Washington, D.C.: GPO,

1982.

Long, Richard A. Some Backgrounds for African Continuity Studies.
    Journal of African Studies 2 (1975-1976):561-68.

Magubane, Bernard. The Ties that Bind: African-American Consciousness of
    Africa. Trenton, NJ: Africa World Press, 1987.

Normandy, E. L. Black American and U.S. Policy toward Africa: Two Case
    Studies from the Pre-World War II Period. Doctoral dissertation,
    University of South Carolina, 1987. UMO # 8724860.

Rafua, Leonara. The Black Arts Movement: The African-American
    Community's Answer to Cultural Imperialism. Nigerian Theatre Journal
    1 (1984):103-09.

Roediger, D. R. The Meaning of Africa for the American Slave. Journal of
    Ethnic Studies 4 (1977):1-15.

Simmons, Donald C. Possible West African Sources for the American Negro
    Dozens. Journal of American Folklore 76 (October-December 1963).

Stuckey, Sterling. 'I Want to Be African': Paul Robeson and the Ends of
    Nationalist Theory and Practice, 1941-1945. Massachusetts Review 17
    (Spring 1976).

Stuckey, Sterling. Slave Culture. Nationalist Theory and the Foundation
    of Black America. New York: Oxford University Press, 1987.

Twining, Mary and Keith Baird (eds.) Sea Island Roots: African Presence
    in the Carolinas and Georgia. Trenton, NJ: Africa World Press.

Williams, Lorraine A. Africa and the Afro-American Experience: Eight
    Essays. Washington, D.C.: Howard University Press, 1977.

Work, M. M. The African Medicine Man. Southern Workman 36 (October
    1907):561-64.

Work, M. N. An African System of Writing. Southern Workman 37 (October
    1908):518-26.

Work, M. N. The African Family as an Institution. Southern Workman 38
    (June-August 1909):319-97, 343-53 and 433-40.

Work, M. N. African Agriculture. Southern Workman 39 (November-December
    1910):613-18.

Work, M. N. African Agriculture. Southern Workman 40 (January-Febuary
    1911):37-42, 79-87.

3. Anti-racism

Put the question nakedly to the American people today, whether they are prepared for the entire and full recognition of the colored man's equality in this country, and you would be voted down ten to one.

- Charles L. Remond, *Liberator*, May 26, 1865.

Adedeji, M. Crossing the Colorline: Three Decades of the United Packinghouse Workers of America's Crusade Against Racism in the Trans- Mississippi West, 1936-1968 [Texas, Oklahoma, Louisiana, Arkansas, New Mexico and South Kansas]. Doctoral dissertation, North Texas State University, 1978. UMO # 7824626.

Adler, E. A Small Beginning. An Assessment of the First Five Years of the Programme to Combat Racism. Geneva: World Council of Churches, 1974.

Aptheker, H. The History of Anti-Racism in the United States. Black Scholar 6 (January-February 1975):16-22.

Ben-Tovim, G. The Struggle Against Racism: Theoretical and Strategic Perspectives. Marxism Today vol. 22 (January 1, 1978).

Boggs, J. and G. L. Boggs. Uprooting Racists and Racism in the U.S. Negro Digest 19 (January 1970):20-22.

Chesler, M. A. Creating and Maintaining Interracial Coalitions. In: Benjamin P. Bowser and Raymond G. Hunt (eds.), Impacts of Racism on White Americans, pp. 217-244. Beverly Hills, CA: Sage, 1981.

Downs, A. Racism in America and How to Combat It. U.S. Commission on Civil Rights Clearinghouse Publication. Washington, D.C.: GPO, 1970.

Draft Programme for 10 Years of Action Against Racialism A UNESCO Memorandum. Patterns of Prejudice 6 (September-October):21-24.

Ferrell, C. L. Nightmare and Dream: Antilynching in Congress, 1917-1921. New York: Garland, 1976.

Forman, J. The Indivisible Struggle Against Racism, Apartheid and Colonialism. Position Paper on SNCC delivered at the International Seminar... in Lusaka, Zambia, July 24-August 4, 1967. List Mailing (January 1, 1967).

French, Desiree. Fighting Racism, Sexism at Work. Boston Globe August 21, 1988.

Garofalo, R. Rocking Against Racism in Massachusetts. One Two Three Four: A Rock 'n' Roll Quarterly 3 (Autumn 1986):75-86.

Gutierrez, J. A. A Gringo Manual on How to Handle Mexicans. Crystal
    City, TX: Wintergarden Publishing House, 1974.

Hyatt, M. Franz Boas and the Struggle for Black Equality: The Dynamics of
    Ethnicity. Perspectives in American History vol. 2 (1985).

Institute of Race Relations. Antiracist Not Multicultural Education.
    Race and Class 22 (Summer 1980):81-83.

Johut, R. G. Racism and Its Elimination. U.N. Institute for Training and
    Research, New York.

Jones, Donald. If I Were a White Man. Common Sense 13 (December
    1944):429-31.

Kahn-Tietz, L. Becoming Anti-racist: A Psychological Process. Master's
    thesis, Pacific Oaks College, 1986.

Katz, Phyllis A. and Dalmas A. Taylor (eds.) Eliminating Racism:
    Profiles in Controversy. New York: Plenum Press, 1988.

Ladner, W. W. and J. A. Ladner. Defusing Race: Development Since the
    Kerner Report. In: Benjamin P. Bowser and Raymond G. Hunt
    (eds.),Impacts of Racism on White Americans, pp. 51-69. Beverly
    Hills, CA: Sage, 1981.

Lawton, J. H. 'Alternative': Student Dialogue Attacks Racism. Catholic
    Educational Review (November 1968).

Lester, Julius. Black and White - Together. Salmagundi 81 (December 1,
    1988).

Lewis, Russell. Anti-Racism: A Mania Exposed. London: Quartet, 1988.
    [Great Britain].

Liskofsky, S. The U.N. Declaration on the Elimination of Religious
    Intolerance and Discrimination: Historical and Legal Perspectives.
    In: James E. Wood, Jr. (ed.), Religion and the State: Essays in Honor
    of Leo Pfeffer. Waco, TX: Baylor University Press, 1985.

Love, S. N. Carolina Indians' Protest of Racism Gains Wide Support.
    Militant April 1, 1988.

Mullard, C. The Educational Management and Demanagement of Racism.
    Education Policy Bulletin 10 (1982):21-40.

Pollack, Andy. Activists Discuss Antiracist Unity. Against the Current
    3 (November-December 1988):7. [Conference in mid-October 1988].

Programme of Action for the Second Decade to Combat Racism and Racial
    Discrimination. Objective: Justice 16 (June 1984):1-17.

Sivanandan, A. A Different Hunger: Writings on Black Resistance. London:
    Pluto Press, 1982.

Sivanandan, A. Challenging Racism--A Strategy for the 1980s. <u>Searchlight</u> (May 1983).

Smith, D. E. Racism--What Is Our Responsibility? <u>Society-Societe</u> 2 (1978):4.

United Nations Program for a Decade for Action to Combat Racism and Racial Discrimination. <u>Objective: Justice</u> 5 (October-December 1973):21-25.

Weinberger, G. <u>Gegen Rassismus und Rassendiskriminierung--Kampfdekade der UNO</u>. Berlin.

Welsing, F. L. C. Building A World Without Racism. <u>Integrateducation</u> 13 (January-February 1975):20-26.

Young, R. P. <u>Societal Change and the Evolution of American Race Relations</u> [Decline of racism]. Doctoral dissertation, Stanford University, 1979. UMO # 8006374.

Young, W. M. <u>Beyond Racism: Building an Open Society</u>. New York: McGraw Hill, 1969.

[See also sections 59 and 80]

15

4. Antisemitism in the U.S.

The supertragedy of this war is the treatment of the Jews in Germany. There has been nothing comparable to this in modern history. Yet its technique and its reasoning have been based upon a race philosophy similar to that which dominated both Great Britain and the United States in relation to colored people.

    - W. E. B. Du Bois, "Prospect of a World Without Race Conflict," 1944.

The American Experience - The American Priest [film]. New York: Anti-Defamation League, 1989. [Antisemitic Catholic priest, Charles Coughlin, 1930s and early 1940s].

Appel, J., and A. Selma. Anti-Semitism in American Caricature. Society (November-December 1986):78-83.

Aronsfeld, C. C. Spotlight on the Liberty Lobby: An Aspect of American Antisemitism. Research Report (Institute of Jewish Affairs) 3 (March 1983).

Avineri, S. Soured Promise [The Pollard Affair and antisemitism in the U.S.A.]. Jerusalem Post March 10, 1987.

Baldwin, James. Negroes Are Antisemitic Because They're Anti-White. New York Times Magazine April 9, 1967.

Banta, Martha. [Ezra] Pound and Antisemitism. American Literary History 1 (March 1989).

Bard, Mitchell. Can a Jew be President? Midstream 34 (November 1988):7-11.

Baskin, S. Raising the Ivy Covered Walls: Jews and Universities, 1916-1923. Stanford Quarterly Review (Winter 1972):20-29.

Bayor, R. H. Klans, Coughlinites and Aryan Nations: Patterns of American Anti-Semitism in the Twentieth Century. American Jewish History 76 (December 1986):181-96.

Berquist, J. M. The Concept of Nativism in Historical Study Since Strangers in the Land [Book by John Higham]. American Jewish History 76 (December 1986):125-41.

Biale, J. J'Accuse: American Jews and L'Affaire Pollard. Tikkun 2 (1987):10-12.

Bliven, Bruce. Salesmen of Anti-Semitism. New Republic (November 17, 1947).

Boas, R. P. Jew-Baiting in America. Atlantic Monthly (May 1921):663-4.

Boxerman, B. A. Rise of Anti-Semitism in St. Louis, 1933-1945.
    YIVO Annual of Jewish Social Science 14 (1969):251-69.

Brickman, William W. (comp.) The Jewish Community in America. New York.

Burt, R. A. Two Jewish Justices. Outcasts in the Promised Land [Louis D.
    Brandeis and Felix Frankfurter]. University of California Press,
    Berkeley.

Buchsbaum, Tamar. A Note on Antisemitism in Admissions at Dartmouth.
    Jewish Social Studies 49 (Winter 1987):79-84.

Chyet, S. F. The Political Rights of Jews in the United States:
    1776-1840. American Jewish Archives 10 (April 1958):14-75.

Colgan, C. A. Warner Brothers' Crusade Against the Third Reich:
    A Study of Anti-Nazi Activism and Film Production, 1933-1941.
    Doctoral dissertation, University of Southern California, 1985.
    [Micrographics Dept., Doheny Library, USC, Los Angeles, CA
    90089-0182].

Cook, J. G. The Racists: Anti-Semitism amid the Magnolias. In: The
    Segregationists, pp. 149-186. New York: Appleton-Century-Crafts.

Davis, L. J. Ballad of an American Terrorist [Robert Jay Mathews, author
    of The Turner Diaries and member of neo-Nazi National Alliance and of
    Christian Identity]. Harper's (July 1986):53-60, 62.

Deutsch, A. Racial Bars in American Medicine. PM September 15, 1947.

Dinnerstein, L. Anti-Semitism Exposed and Attacked, 1945-1950. American
    Jewish History 71 (September 1981):134-149.

Dinnerstein, L. Antisemitism in the United States Today. Patterns of
    Prejudice 22 (Autumn 1988):3-14.

Dinnerstein, L. Uneasy at Home. Antisemitism and the American Jewish
    Experience. New York: Columbia University Press, 1987.

Dinnerstein, L. and D. Reimers. Strangers in the Land: Then and Now.
    American Jewish History 76 (December 1986):107-16.

Dobkowski, M. N. A Historical Survey of Justice of Anti-Semitism in
    America Prior to World War II. In: Herbert Hirsch and Jack D. Spiro
    (eds.), Persistent Prejudice: Perspectives on Anti-Semitism.
    Fairfax, VA: George Mason University Press, 1988.

Dobkowski, M. N. The Tarnished Dream: The Basis of American Anti-
    Semitism. Westport, CT: Greenwood Press.

Dodson, D. W. Religious Prejudice in Colleges. American Mercury (July
    1946):5-13.

Douglas, Kirk. The Ragman's Son. An Autobiography. New York: Simon and

Schuster, 1988.

Domhoff, G. W. and R. L. Zweigenhaft. Jews in the Corporate Establishment. New York Times April 24, 1983.

Evans, H. W. The Klan's Fight for Americanism [Attacks Jews in the U.S.]. North American Review 223 (1925):33-63.

Feingold, H. L. Finding a Conceptual Framework for the Study of American Antisemitism. Jewish Social Studies 47 (Fall 1985):313-26.

Fisher, S. G. Alien Degradation of American Character. Forum 14 (1892-3):608-15.

Flory, Wendy S. The Pound Problem. In: Daniel Hoffman (ed.), Ezra Pound and William Carlos Williams: The University of Pennsylvania Conference Papers, pp. 107-27. Philadelphia, PA: University of Pennsylvania Press, 1983.

Forster, Arnold. Square One: The Memoirs of a True Freedom Fighter's Life-long Struggle Against Anti-Semitism, Domestic and Foreign. New York: Donald I. Fine, 1988.

Friedlander, H. and E. M. McCarrick. The Extradition of Nazi Criminals: Ryan, Artukovic, and Demjanjuk. Simon Wiesenthal Center Annual 4 (1987):65-98.

Friedlander, H. and E. M. McCarrick. Nazi Criminals in the United States: The Fedorenko Case. Simon Wiesenthal Center Annual 2 (1985):63-93.

Friedlander, H. and E. M. McCarrick. Nazi Criminals in the United States: Denaturalization after Fedorenko. Simon Wiesenthal Center Annual 3 (1986):47-85.

Frondorf, Shirley. The Death of a "Jewish American Princess": The True Story of a Victim on Trial. New York: Villard Books, 1988.

Garwood, D. D. Gerald Burton Winrod and the Republican Senatorial Primary of 1938 [Kansas]. Master's thesis, Emporia State University, 1981.

Gerber, D. A. (ed.) Antisemitism in American History. Urbana: University of Illinois Press.

Gertz, E. Odyssey of a Barbarian: The Biography of George Sylvester Viereck. Buffalo, NY: Promethus Books.

Gilbert, A. Jews, Prejudice and Catholic Practice. In: Phillip Scharper (ed.), American Catholics. New York:

Glock, C. Y. and R. Stark. Christian Beliefs and Anti-Semitism. New York: Harper & Row.

Gornick, Vivian. Twice an Outsider: On Being Jewish and a Woman. Tikkun 4 (March-April 1989):29-31, 123-25

Handlin, O. and M. F. Handlin. The Acquisition of Political and Social Rights by the Jews in the United States, 1654-1954. AJYB 56 (1955).

Handlin, O. and M. F. Handlin. Danger in Discord; Origins of Anti-Semitism in the United States (third edition).

Hapgood, N. Do Americans Dislike Jews? Harper' Weekly (August-November 1915).

Harrie, Dan. Silent No More. Hadassah Magazine (March 1989):10-13. [Kootenai County, northern Idaho].

Harrison, Don. Jews and the Culture Revival of Philadelphia. In: Murray Friedman (ed.), Philadelphia Jewish Life, 1940-1985. Ardmore, PA: 1986.

Hentoff, N. Blacks and Jews: An Interview with Julius Lester. Evergreen Review (April 1965).

Higham, C. American Swastika. Garden City, NY: Doubleday.

Higham, J. The Strange Career of 'Strangers in the Land' [His own book]. American Jewish History 76 (December 1986):214-26.

Hook, S. Anti-Semitism in the Academy: Some Pages of the Past. Midstream 26 (1979).

Hunt, L. U.S. Cover-up of Nazi Scientists. Bulletin of the Atomic Scientists (April 1985):16-24.

James Baldwin on Blacks and Jews. Transcript of a Lecture Delivered on February 28, 1984 at the University of Massachusetts at Amherst. Amherst: W.E.B. Du Bois Department of Afro-American Studies, University of Massachusetts, March 1988.

Jick, L. A. The Holocaust. Its Use and Abuse within the American Public. Yad Vashem Studies 14 (1981).

Kaganoff, N. M. Judaic Americana. American Jewish History 76 (December 1986):227-55.

Karp, A. Haven and Home: A History of the Jews in America. New York: Schocken.

Kaufman, Alan. '1933-1988'. Anti-Semitism in America. Jewish Frontier 55 (November-December 1988):7-12.

Kellman, Steven G. The Last Temptation of Christ: Blaming the Jews. Midstream 34 (December 1988):33-37.

Kent, G. O. Klaus Barbie, the United States Government, and the Beginning of the Cold War. Simon Wiesenthal Center Annual 3 (1986):261-76.

Kolodny, R. L. Catholics and Father Coughlin: Misremembering the Past. *Patterns of Prejudice* 19 (October 1985):15-25.

Kraut, A. M. Silent Strangers: Germs, Genes, and Nativism in John Higham's 'Strangers in the Land'. *American Jewish History* 76 (December 1986):142-58.

Krefetz, G. *Jews and Money: The Myth and the Reality*. New Haven, CT: Ticknor and Fields, 1982.

Larson, R. Toward an Understanding of Totalitarianism and Antisemitism. *Midwest Quarterly* 28 (Winter 1987):161-75.

Ledeboer, S. C. The Man Who Would be Hitler: William Dudley Pelley and the Silver Legion. *California History* 65 (June 1986):126-36, 154-5.

Levine, D. O. *The American College and the Culture of Aspiration, 1915-1940* [Deals with antisemitism]. Ithaca, NY: Cornell University Press.

Levinger, L. J. *Antisemitism in the United States: Its History and Causes*. New York: Bloch, 1925.

Liberty Lobby and the Carto Network [Willis Carto, founder of Liberty Lobby, and his antisemitic policies]. *ADL Facts* (Winter 1982):5-19.

Marcus, Jacob R. (comp.) *An Index of Scientific Articles on American Jewish History*. Cincinnati, OH.

McWilliams, C. *A Mask for Privilege: Anti-Semitism in America*. Boston: Little Brown.

Meyer, W. H., Jr. Anti-Semitism in American Literature: Its Hypervisual/Hyperverbal Roots. *North Dakota Quarterly* 55 (Winter 1987):100-17.

Modras, Ronald. Father Coughlin and the Jews: A Broadcast Remebered. *America* (March 11, 1989):219-22.

Montagu, M. F. A. Anti-Semitism in the Academic World. *Chicago Jewish Forum* 4 (Summer 1946):221-222.

Morais, N. Jewish Ostracism in America. *North American Review* vol. 133 (1881).

Morse, S. The Christianization of America: How Serious a Threat? *Jewish Monthly* (January 1987):19-22, 27-28.

Oren, D. A. *Joining the Club. A History of Jews and Yale*. New Haven, CT: Yale University Press.

Platt, I. *League for Human Rights: Cleveland Jewry's Fight against Naziism*. Master's thesis, Cleveland State University, 1977.

Pollack, N. The Myth of Populist Anti-Semitism. *American Historical*

Review 68 (1962/63):76-80.

Raab, E. High Anxiety [Rising antisemitism in the USA?]. Present Tense
    15 (January-February 1988):46-49.

Rabinowitz, Howard N. Nativism, Bigotry and Anti-Semitism in the South.
    American Jewish History 77 (March 1988):437-51.

Rapp, M. G. An Historical Overview of Anti-Semitism in Minnesota, 1920-
    1960 - With Particular Emphasis on Minneapolis and St. Paul.
    Doctoral dissertation, University of Minnesota, 1977. UMO #
    7726152.

Ribuffo, L. P. Henry Ford and 'The International Jew'. In: Jonathan D.
    Sarna (ed.), The American Jewish Experience. New York: Holmes and
    Meier.

Ricks, Christopher. T.S. Eliot and Prejudice. London: Faber, 1988.
    [Antisemitism].

Rose, L. B. The Secret Life of Sarah Lawrence [The history of Jewish
    quotas at Sarah Lawrence College]. Commentary 75 (May 1983):52-56.

Rosovsky, N. and Others. The Jewish Experience at Harvard and
    Radcliffe. Cambridge, MA: Harvard University Press.

Roth, P. My Life as a Boy. New York Times October 18, 1987.

Sarna, J. D. Anti-Semitism and American History. Commentary (March
    1981):42-7.

Sanua, Marianne. Stages in the Development of Jewish Life at Princeton
    University. American Jewish History 76 (June 1987):391-415.

Schapper, M. U. The Jews and the Post-War Reaction After 1918. Jewish
    Life 9 (April 1955).

Schappes, M. U. Anti-Semitism and Reaction, 1795-1800. PAJHS 38
    (December 1948):109.

Schmier, L. Anti-Semitic Uprising in Thomas County, Georgia: An Act
    Unbecoming. Civil War Times Illustrated 23 (October 1984):23-25.

Schwartz, B. The Jewish Prayer for the Government in America. American
    Jewish History 76 (March 1987):334-39.

Shaffer, R. Jews, Reds, and Violets: Anti-Semitism and Anti-radicalism
    at New York University, 1916-1929. Journal of Ethnic Studies 15
    (Summer 1987):47-83.

Shapiro, Edward S. Anti-Semitism: Denying the Obvious. Congress Monthly
    (January 1989):7-9.

Shapiro, Edward S. The Approach of War: Congressional Isolationism and
    Anti-Semitism, 1939-1941. American Jewish History 74 (September

1984):45-65.

Shapiro, Edward S. John Higham and American Anti-Semitism [Referring to author of 'Strangers in the Land'. *American Jewish History* 76 (December 1986):201-13.

Simons, Howard. *Jewish Times. Voices of the American Jewish Experience.* Boston: Houghton Mifflin, 1988.

Smith, G. L. K. *In:* Elva M. Smith and Charles F. Robertson (eds.), *Beseiged Patriot: Autobiographical Episodes Exposing Communism, Traitorism and Zionism from the Life of Gerald L. K. Smith.* Eureka Springs, AR: Elva M. Smith Foundation.

Spaights, E. and Others. Attitude of Black Collegians toward Jews and Economic Matters. *College Student Journal* 19 (Summer 1985):118-22.

Starr, H. The Affair at Harvard. *Menorah Journal* 8 (October 1922):263-76.

Strong, D. S. *Organized Anti-Semitism in America.* 2nd ed. Washington, D.C.: American Council on Public Affairs.

Strong, D. S. *Anti-Revolutionary, Antisemitic Organizations in the United States Since 1933.* Chicago.

Synnott, M. G. Anti-Semitism and American Universities: Did Quotas Follow the Jews? *In* David A. Gerber (ed.), *Anti-Semitism in American History.* Urbana: University of Illinois Press.

Tobin, Gary A. Jewish Perceptions of Antisemitism and Antisemitic Perceptions of Jews. *Stud. Contemp. Jewry* 4 (1988):210-31.

Tress, Madeleine and Ellen Cantarow. The Undeniability of Anti-Semitism. *Middle East Report* (January-February 1989):3, 47. [An exchange of views].

Twain, Mark. *Concerning the Jews.* New York: Anti-Defamation League.

U.S. Congress, 81st, 2nd session, House of Representatives, 'Congressional Record,' 1950, 96,; Part 13 Yiddish Communism versus Christian Civilization. [By Rep. John E. Rankin, Miss.].

Volkman, E. *A Legacy of Hate: Anti-Semitism in America.* New York: Watts.

Wechsler, H. S. The Rationale for Restriction: Ethnicity and College Admission in America, 1910-1980 [Esp. Jews]. *American Quarterly* 35 (Winter 1984):643-67.

Weil, F. D. The Variable, Effects of Education on Liberal Attitudes: A Comparative-historical Analysis of Anti-Semitism Using Public Opinion Survey Data. *American Sociologial Review* 50 (August 1985):458-74.

Weingarten, I. *The Image of the Jew in the American Periodical Press, 1881-1921.* Doctoral dissertation, New York University, 1980. UMO #

8017536.

Weinstein, J. J.   Jewish Students at Columbia.   Menorah Journal   22
    (1934).

Williams, B. J.   Anti-Semitism and Shreveport, Louisiana: The Situation in
    the 1920s.   Louisiana History   21 (Fall 1989):387-98.

Winkowski, Robert B.   The American Catholic Press as an Instrument of
    Social Education in the Emergence of Nazism.   Doctoral dissertation,
    Boston University, 1988.   UMO # 8801601.

Wolfson, A.   The Boston Jewish Community and the Rise of Nazism, 1933-
    1939.   Jewish Social Studies   48 (Summer-Fall 1986):305-14.

Wrong, D. H.   The Rise and Decline of Anti-Semitism in America.   In: Peter
    I. Rose (ed.), The Ghetto and Beyond. Essays on Jewish Life in
    America, pp. 313-34. New York: Random House.

Yankelovich, Skelly; White, Inc.   Anti-Semitism in the United States. Vol
    I: The Summary Report.   New York: American Jewish Committee, July
    1981.

[See also section 8]

5. Athletics

When black [boxer] Jack Johnson beat a white man at a white man's game before an audience of a hundred millions, with what mingled motive did those millions, from the United Society of Christian Endeavor to the hoodlums of the nation, join hand to shout "Shame!"

- W. E. B. Du Bois, "The Souls of White Folk," 1910.

Allen, William B. Rhodes. Handicapping, or Slowing the Pace of Integration. New Perspectives 19 (Winter 1988):19-24. [Proposition 48, NCAA].

Ashe, Arthur R., Jr. and others. A Hard Road to Glory. 3 vols. New York: Warner, 1988. [History of the black athlete in the U.S. since 1619].

Becker, R. Black Athletes Disillusioned [Amherst College]. Amherst Student May 11, 1981.

Berryman, J. W. Early Black Leadership in Collegiate Football: Massachusetts as a Pioneer. Historical Journal of Massachusetts 9 (June 1981):17-28.

Bey, L. W. Impact of Desegregation on Selected Aspects of the Athletic Programs of the Traditionally Black Institutions in the Central Intercollegiate Athletic Association. Doctoral dissertation, Temple University, 1985. UMO # 8521050.

Borges, R. Black QBs: A History of Crossed Signals. Boston Globe January 25, 1988.

Bourdieu, Pierre. Sport and Social Class. Social Science Information 17 (1978).

Braddock, J. H., II. Race, Athletics, and Educational Attainment: Dispelling the Myths. Youth and Society 12 (March 1981):335-50.

Bruce, J. The Kansas City Monarchs: Champions of Black Baseball. University Press of Kansas, 1985.

Burna, Clarence E. Position Occupancy Patterns as a Function of Race: The National Football League Draft, 1968-1983. Doctoral dissertation, University of Montana, 1988. UMO # 8809069.

Chalk, O. Black College Sport [History of Black athletes in colleges]. New York: Dodd Mead, 1976.

Chu, Donald. The Character of American Higher Education and Intercollegiate Sport. Albany: State University of New York Press, 1988.

Churchill, W. and others. An Historical Overview of Twentieth Century Native American Athletics. Indian Historian 12 (1979):22-33.

Cohen, A. S. Tackling Sports Racism [Relative lack of Black athletes in sports program at Harvard University]. Harvard Crimson October 29, 1982.

De Venzio, D. Rip-Off U.: The Annual Theft and Exploitation of Major College Revenue Producing Student-Athletes. Charlotte, NC: Fool Court Press, 1985.

Du Bois, W. E. B. As the Crow Flies [Black boxers]. Crisis 36 (August 1929):257.

Dupont, K. P. 40 Years Later [Three articles on Blacks in organized baseball]. Boston Globe May 17-19, 1987.

Eason, A. J. The Philosophy, Impact, and Contributions of Alonzo Smith "Jake" Gaither to Black Athletes, Football, and Florida Agricultural and Mechanical University. Doctoral dissertation, Florida State University, 1987. UMO # 8711716.

Edwards, H. Academic Expectations and Black Athletes. Education Week June 4, 1986.

Edwards, H. Educating Black Athletes. Atlantic Monthly 252 (August 1982):31-38.

Edwards, H. Interview. Zeta Magazine 1 (April 1988):66-69.

Edwards, H. The Myth of the Racially Superior Athlete. Intellectual Digest 44 (1972):32-38.

Edwards, H. The Revolt of the Black Athlete. New York: Free Press, 1969.

Eitzen, D. S. and D. A. Purdy. The Academic Preparation and Achievement of Black and White Collegiate Athletes. Journal of Sport and Social Issues 10 (Winter-Spring 1986):15-29.

Eitzen, D. S., and N. R. Yetman. Immune from Racism? [Discrimination against Blacks in sports]. Civil Rights Digest 9 (Winter 1977):3-13.

Frazier, B. A. The Current Socio-economic Status of Black Football and Basketball Athletes Who Enrolled as Freshmen at Bethune-Cookman College and Florida A & M University During the Years 1965-1970. Doctoral dissertation, Florida State University, 1979.

Goldberg, Steven. Poverty Doesn't Make Blacks Better Athletes [letter]. New York Times April 15, 1989.

Golden, D. Dr. J's UMass Residency [Julius Erving at University of Massachusetts, Amherst, 1968-1971]. Boston Globe Magazine November 1, 1987.

Goodwin, M. CBS Dismisses Snyder [Racist remarks on Black athletes by Jimmy (the Greek) Snyder]. New York Times January 17, 1988.

Green, R. L. and others. Black Athletes: Educational, Economic, and Political Considerations. Journal of Non-White Concerns 3 (October 1974):6-38.

Green, T. S. and others. Black Women in Sport. ERIC ED 220 437.

Green, R. L. and others. Blacks in the Big Ten. Integrated Education (May-June 1972):32-39.

Hart-Nibbrig, N. E. and C. Cottingham. The Political Economy of College Sports. Lexington, MA: Lexington Books, 1986.

Hilliard, D. C. Heroes in Black and White: The Meanings of Racism in American Sports. Proceedings-Annual Meeting of the Association for the Anthropological Study of Play. 7 (1981):38-49.

Hoose, Phillip M. Necessities: Racial Barriers in American Sports. New York: Random House, 1989.

Jackson, R. We Have a Serious Problem That Isn't Going Away. Sports Illustrated May 11, 1987.

Jaher, F. C. White American Views Jack Johnson, Joe Louis, and Muhammed Ali. In: Donald Spivey (ed.), Sport in America: New Historical Pespectives. Westport, CT: Greenwood, 1985.

Johnson, Joseph, John Slaughter, and Tony Osborne. [Three interviews on NCAA's Proposition 48]. New Perspectives 19 (Winter 1988), 4-5, 10-14.

Jones, Terry. Racial Practices in Baseball Management. Black Scholar 18 (May-June 1987):16-24.

Jordan, J. Physiological and Anthropometrical Comparisons of Negroes and Whites. Journal of Health, Physical Education, and Recreation (November-December 1969):93-99.

Kahn, L. M. and P. D. Sherer. Racial Differences in Professional Basketball Players' Compensation. Journal of Labor Economics 6 (January 1988).

Kimble, M. Black Athletes: Student, or Just 'Meat'? [University of Arizona]. Tucson Daily Citizen December 5, 1980.

Kjeldsen, E. K. M. Integration of Minorities into Olympic Sport in Canada and the USA. Journal of Sport and Social Issues vol. 8 (Summer-Fall).

Kountze, M. Fifty Sports Years Along Memory Lane. [Black athletes in Greater Boston area]. Sports History, Mystic Valley Press, Medford, MA 21 Locisic Street, Medford, MA 02155.

Krieger, Dave. For Black Athletes, Life Can Be Tough in Boulder. Rocky Mountain News May 15, 1988. [University of Colorado, Boulder].

Lapchick, Richard E. Broken Promises: Racism in American Sports. St. New York: St. Martin's/Marek, 1984.

Lapchick, Richard E. The Student Athlete. New Perspectives 19 (Winter 1988):35-45.

Lawson, H. A. Physical Education and Sport in the Black Community: The Hidden Perspective. Journal of Negro Education 48 (Spring 1979):187-95.

Lipsyte, R. An Outsider Joins the Team [Harry Edwards, Major League Baseball's representative of affirmative action]. New York Times Magazine May 22, 1988.

Littwin, M. Black Athletes in Salt Lake City-Act of Faith. Los Angeles Times December 24, 1980.

Mangan, J. A. The Games Ethic and Imperialism. London: Viking, 1986.

Markmann, Joseph M. A Note on Discrimination by Race in Professional Basketball. American Economist 20 (Spring 1976):65-67.

McCormick, Robert E. and Roger E. Meimers. Sacred Cows, Competition, and Racial Discrimination. New Perspectives 19 (Winter 1988):47-52.

Mogull, Robert G. Football Salaries and Race: Some Empirical Evidence. Industrial Relations 12 (February 1973):109-12.

Mogull, Robert G. Salary Discrimination in Major League Baseball. Review of Black Political Economy 5 (Spring 1975).

Olson, J. and others. The Black Athletes: A Shameful Story: The Myth of Integration in American Sport. New York: Time-Life Books, 1968.

Parks, J. E. The Development of All-Black Basektball Teams in Topeka High School, 1929-1949. 1982.

Peterson, R. W. Only the Ball Was White.

Petr, Todd A. Bylaw 5-1-(j): A Historical Perspective [Proposition 48, NCAA]. New Perspectives 19 (Winter 1988):15-18.

Pomerantz, G. In NFL, Black Assistants Still Waiting for Chance To Become Head Coaches. Washington Post December 27, 1985.

Roberts, Randy. Papa Jack: Jack Johnson and the Era of White Hopes. New York: Free Press, 1983.

Rockwood, Charles E. and Ephriam Asher. Racial Discrimination in Professional Basketball Revisted. AMerican Economist 20 (Spring 1976):59-64. [See Markmann, above].

Ruben, D. Changing Courts [Len Elmore, former National Basketball Association player, graduates from Harvard Law School]. Boston Globe Magazine June 14, 1987.

Ruck, R. Sandlot Seasons: Sport in Black Pittsburgh. Urbana: University of Illinois Press, 1987.

Sailes, G. A. A Socioeconomic Explanation of Black Sports Participation Patterns. Western Journal of Black Studies 11 (Winter 1987):164-67.

Sammone, J. T. Beyond the Ring: The Role of Boxing. Urbana: University of Illinois Press, 1988.

Scott, J. The White Olympics. Ramparts 6 (May 1968):54-61.

Scully, Gerald W. Economic Discrimination in Professional Sports. Law and Contemporary Problems 38 (Winter-Spring 1973):67-84.

Simons, B. We Shall Overcome (Eventually). Professional Sports Journal (February 1980):47-52.

Soiles, Gary. Guest Editorial: The Exploitation of the Black Athlete: Some Alternative Solutions. Journal of Negro Education 55 (Fall 1986):439-42.

Spivey, D. The Black Athlete in Big-time Intercollegiate Sports, 1941-1968. Phylon 44 (June 1983):116-25.

Spivey, D., Ed. Black Conscousness and Olympic Protest Movement, 1964-1980. In: Sport in America: New Historical Perspectives. Westport, CT: Greenwood, 1985.

Thomsen, Ian. Thomas: I'm Not a Racist [Isiah Thomas, basketball player with Detroit Pistons]. Boston Globe May 28, 1988.

Underwood, J. On the Playground. Life 11 (Spring 1988):102-108.

U.S. Congress, Ninety-Seventh, Second Session, House of Representatives, Committee On Education and Labor, Subcommittee On Employment Opportunities. Oversight Hearing on Equal Employment Opportunity in the National Football League: Hearing ... Washington, D.C.: GPO, 1982.

Weaver, Warren, Jr. [John] Thompson to Leave Bench in Protest on [Athletic] Scholarships. New York Times January 14, 1989. [Georgetown University basketball coach].

Whiteside, Larry. Fading Dreams. Boston Globe November 15, 1988. [Minority development in organized baseball].

Wiggins, D. K. Peter Jackson and the Elusive Heavyweight Championship: A Black Athlete's Struggle Against the Late Nineteenth Century Color-Line. Journal of Sports History 12 (Summer 1985):143-68.

61 (November 1932):449-69.

Williams, C. H. Twenty Years' Work of the C.I.A.A. [Colored Inter-
Collegiate Athletic Association]. Southern Workman 61 (February
1932):65-76.

Wolf, M. Boxing and the Black Man during the Gilded Age. Master's
thesis, Western Michigan University, 1978.

Wynes, C. E. 'Alexander the Great,' Bridge Builder [Black civil
engineer and football player at State University of Iowa]. Palimpsest
66 (May-June 1985):78-86.

Yasser, R. The Black Athletes' Equal Protecction Case against the
NCAA's New Academic Standards. Gonzaga Law Review 19 (Winter
1983):83-103.

Athletics Bibliography

Davis, L. G. and B. S. Daniels. Black Athletes in the U.S.: A
Bibliography of Books, Articles, Autobiographies, and Biographies on
Profesional Black Athletes in the U.S., 1800-1981. Westport, CT:
Greenwood, 1981.

Janis, L. (comp.) Annotated Bibliography on Minority Women in
Athletics. ERIC ED L46 010.

6. Autobiography and Biography

*The success of such a man as Frederick Douglass is worth more to
the race than a pile of resolutions and speeches as high as
Bunker Hill monument. Had it not been for the Abolitionists,
the brilliant genius of Mr. Douglass would probably have died
with him. All honor to those noble men and women, who had the
courage to do what they did!*

- John S. Rock, Liberator, August 15, 1862.

Aaron, H. L. and F. Bisher. Aaron r.f. [Hank Aaron] (revised edition).
New York: Crowell, 1974.

Adamic, L. Laughing in the Jungle: The Autobiography of an Immigrant in
America, 1932.

Adeleke, R. O. Martin Robison Delany and the Black Struggle for
Freedom. Doctoral dissertation, University of Western Ontario,
1985.

Albert, O. V. R. The House of Bondage or Charlotte Brooks and Other
Slaves. New York: Oxford University Press, 1988. Reprint.

Ali, M. and R. Durham. The Greatest: My Own Story. New York: Random
House, 1975.

Anderson, J. A. Philip Randolph: A Biographical Portrait. New York:
Harcourt Brace Jovanovich, 1972.

Anderson, R. B. From Mother's Aid Child to University Professor. The
Autobiography of an American Black Woman. Iowa City: School of
Social Work, University of Iowa, June 1985.

Angelou, M. I Know Why the Caged Bird Sings. New York: Random House,
1969.

Armstrong, Gregory. The Dragon Has Come: The Last Fourteen Months in the
Life of George Jackson. New York: Harper and Row, 1974.

Atkins, J. A. The Age of Jim Crow [Autobiography]. New York: Vantage
Press, 1964.

Backett, R. J. M. Beating Against the Barriers. Biographical Essays in
Nineteenth-Century Afro-American History. Baton Rouge: Louisiana
State University Press, .

Balanoff, E. The Gary School Crisis of the 1950s: A Personal Memoir.
Indiana Magazine of History 83 (March 1987):65-73.

Baldwin, J. Autobiographical Notes. New York: Knopf, 1953.

Ballard, A. B. One More Day's Journey. The Story of a Family and a

People. New York: McGraw-Hill, 1984.

Baraka, I. A. The Autobiography of LeRoi Jones/Amiri Baraka. New York: Freundlich, 1984.

Bates, D. The Long Shadow of Little Rock: A Memoir. New York: David McKay Co., 1962.

Bedini, S. A. The Life of Benjamin Banneker. New York: Scribners, 1972.

Bennet, K. Kaibah: Recollection of a Navajo Girlhood. Los Angeles: Western Lore Press, 1964.

Berry, L. H. I Wouldn't Take Nothin' for My Journey. Chicago: Johnson, 1981.

Blackett, R. J. M. Beating Against the Barriers. Biographical Essays in Nineteenth-Cenury Afro-American History. Baton Rouge: Louisiana State University Press, 1980.

Blackman, Margaret B. Sadie Brower Neakok, An Inupiaq Woman. Seattle: University of Washington Press, 1989. [Barrow and North Slope, Alaska].

Blassingame, J. W. The Frederick Douglass Papers: Series One: Speeches, Debates, and Interviews. Vol. I: 1841-46. New Haven, CT: Yale University Press, 1980.

Bonnin, G. S. An Indian Teacher Among Indians. Atlantic Monthly 85 (March 1900):381-6.

Bonnin, G. S. Impressions of an Indian Childhood. Atlantic Monthly 85 (January 1900):34-47.

Bonnin, G. S. School Days of an Indian Girl. Atlantic Monthly 85 (February 1900):185-94.

Braithwaite, W. S. B. The William Stanley Braithwaite Reader. Ann Arbor, MI: University of Michigan Press, 1972.

Brock, Euline W. Thomas W. Cardozo: Fallible Black Reconstruction Leader. Journal of Southern History 47 (May 1981):183-206.

Brooks, Amanda Lee. Captain Paul Cuffe (1759-1817) and the Crown Colony of Sierra Leone: The Liminality of the Free Black. Doctoral dissertation, University of Chicago, 1988.

Brown, C. S. (ed.) Ready from Within: Septima Clark and the Civil Rights Movement. Navarro, CA: Wild Trees, 1986.

Brown, H. R. Die, Nigger, Die. New York: Dial, 1969.

Brown, H. Q. and others. Homespun Heroines and Other Women of Distinction [About 60 Black women]. New York: Oxford University Press, 1988 (orig. 1926).

Buaken, M. I Have Lived with the American People [Filipino-American autobiography]. Caldwell, Idaho: 1948.

Buckley, G. L. The Hornes: An American Family [Brooklyn, New York]. New York: Knopf, 1986.

Bulosan, C. America Is in the Heart: A Personal History [Filipino-American autobiography]. 1946.

Calderon, E. and L. R. Teel. Erma: A Black Woman Remembers: 1912-1980. New York: Random House, 1981.

Campanella, R. It's Good to Be Alive. Boston: Little, Brown, 1959.

Carroll, D. and R. Firestone. Diahann: An Autobiography. Boston: Little, Brown, 1986.

Cayton, H. R. Long Old Road. New York: Trident, 1965.

Charles, C. Roy Wilkins, the NAACP and the Early Struggle for Civil Rights. Towards the Biography of a Man and a Movement, 1901-1939. Doctoral dissertation, Cornell University, 1981. UMO # 8111001.

Clark, S. Echo In My Soul. New York: Dutton, 1962.

Comer, J. P. Beyond Black and White. New York: Quadrangle, 1972.

Cooper, W. F. Claude McKay, Rebel Sojourner in the Harlem Renaissance. Baton Rouge: Louisiana State University Press, 1986.

Coppin, F. J. Reminiscences of School Life, and Hints on Teaching. Philadelphia, PA: African Methodist Episcopal Book Concern, 1913.

Costanzo, A. Surprizing Narrative: Olaudah Equiano and the Beginnings of Black Autobiography. Westport, CT: Greenwood, 1987.

Cotton, E. E. A Spark for My People. The Sociological Autobiography of a Negro Teacher. New York: Exposition, 1954.

Dailey, M. C., Jr., and E. D. Washington. The Evolution of Doxey A. Wilkerson, 1935-1945. Freedomways 25 (Summer 1985):101-15.

Davis, A. Y. Angela Davis: An Autobiography. New York: Random House, 1974.

Davis, Benjamin J., Jr. Communist Councilmen from Harlem: Autobiographical Notes Writen in a Federal Penitentiary. New York: International Publishers, 1969.

Davis, Sammy, Jr., Jane Boyar and Burt Boyar. Why Me? The Sammy Davis Jr. Story. New York: Farrar, Straus & Giroux, 1989.

Douglass, F. Life and Times of Frederick Douglass. Hartford, CT: Park Publishing Co., 1882 (Revised 1892).

Douglass, F. My Bondage and My Freedom. New York: 1855.

Douglass, F. Narrative of Frederick Douglass. Boston: 1845.

Drake, S. C. Dr. W.E.B. Du Bois: A Life Lived Experimentally and Self-Documented. Contributions in Black Studies 8 (1986-1987)111-34.

Du Bois, S. G. His Day Is Marching On: A Memoir of W.E.B. Du Bois. Philadelphia, PA: Lippincott, 1971.

Du Bois, W. E. B. The Autobiography of W.E.B. Du Bois. New York: International Publishers, 1968.

Duberman, Martin B. Paul Robeson. A Biography. New York: Knopf, 1989.

Dudley, David L. "The Trouble I've Seen": Visions and Revisions of Bondage, Flight, and Freedom in Black American Autobiography. Doctoral dissertation, Louisiana State University, 1988. UMO # 8819934.

Earley, Charity Adams. One Woman's Army. A Black Officer Remembers the WAC. College Station, TX: Texas A & M University Press, 1989.

Edwards, H. The Struggle that Must Be: An Autobiography. New York: Macmillan, 1980.

Evans, G. 'Incorrigible Integrationist' Kenneth Clark Reflects on a Lifetime of Question-Asking. Chronicle of Higher Education May 21, 1986.

Farmer, J. Lay Bare the Heart: An Autobiography of the Civil Rights Movement. Arbor House, 1985.

Faulkner, A. O. and others. When I Was Comin' Up: An Oral History of Aged Blacks. Hamden, CT: Archon Books, 1982.

Foner, P. S. (ed.) Paul Robeson Speaks. Writings, Speeches, Interviews, 1918-1974. New York: Brunner/Mazel, 1978.

Forman, J. The Making of Black Revolutionaries: A Personal Account. New York: Macmillan, 1972.

Forman, J. Sammy Younge, Jr. New York: Grove Press, 1968.

Franklin, J. H. George Washington Williams. A Biography. Chicago: University of Chicago Press, 1985.

Frazier, E. F. My Most Humiliating Jim Crow Experience. Negro Digest 4 (November 1945).

Fultz, M. A 'Quintessential American': Horace Mann Bond, 1924-1939. Harvard Educational Review 55 (November 1985):416-42.

Gabbin, J. V. Sterling A. Brown: Building the Black Aesthetic Tradition.

Westport, CT: Greenwood Press, 1985.

Galarza, E. <u>Barrio Boy</u>. Notre Dame, IN: University of Notre Dame Press, 1971.

Garrow, D. J. <u>Bearing the Cross. Martin Luther King, Jr., and the Southern Christian Leadership Conference</u>. New York: Morrow, 1986.

Gaston, A. G. <u>Green Power: The Successful Way of A.G. Gaston</u>. Birmingham, AL: Southern University Press, 1968.

Gayle, A., Jr. <u>Wayward Child: A Personal Odyssey</u>. Garden City, NY: Anchor Books/Doubleday, 1977.

Gingras, L. <u>Growing Up Indian: Stories from the Life of Louie Gingras, an 82 Year Old Kootenai Indian</u>. ERIC ED 184787.

Giroux, V. A., Jr. The Rise of Theodore G. Bilbo (1908-1932). <u>Journal of Mississippi History</u> 43 (August 1981):180-209.

Goldman, P. <u>The Death and Life of Malcolm X</u> (second edition). Urbana, IL: University of Illinois Press, 1979.

Gorman, K. L. <u>Martin Robison Delany: The Chatham Years</u>. Master's thesis, Arizona State University, Tempe, 1988.

Graymont, B. (ed.) <u>Fighting Tuscarora. The Autobiography of Chief Clinton Richard</u>. Syracuse, NY: Syracuse University Press, 1973.

Gregory, D. and R. Lipsyte. <u>Nigger: An Autobiography</u>. New York: Dutton, 1964.

Grimke, C. F. <u>The Journals of Charlotte Forten Grimke</u>. Stevenson, Brenda, (ed.) New York: Oxford University Press, 1988 (reprint).

Gunther, L. A., III. <u>Flamin' Tongue: The Rise of Adam Clayton Powell, Jr., 1908-1941</u>. Doctoral dissertation, Columbia University, 1985. UMO # 8604627.

Gwaltney, J. L. On Going Home Again - Some Reflections of a Native Anthropologist. <u>Phylon</u> 37 (September):236-42.

Gwaltney, J. L. (ed.) <u>Drylongso: A Self-Portrait of Black America</u>. New York: Random House, 1980.

Haley, J. H. <u>Charles N. Hunter and Race Relations in North Carolina</u> [Born a slave circa 1851]. Chapel Hill, NC: University of North Carolina Press, 1987.

Halila née El Agrebi, Sonad. <u>The Intellectual Development and Diplomatic Career of Ralph J. Bunche: The Afro-American, Africanist, and Internationalist</u>. Doctoral dissertation, University of Southern California, 1988.

Hanchett, C. M. George Boyder Vas Rhon, 1824-1878: Black Educator, Poet,

Fighter for Equal Rights (2 parts). W. Pa. Hist. Mag. 68 (July-October 1985):205-19, 333-49.

Harding, V. Recalling the Inconvenient Hero: Reflections on the Last Years of Martin Luther King, Jr. Union Seminary Quarterly Review 40 (January 1986):53-68.

Harlan, L. R. Booker T. Washington, 2 vols. New York: Oxford University Press, 1972-1983.

Harlan, L. R. and others. The Booker T. Washington Papers. Urbana. IL: University of Illinois Press.

Harley, Sharon. Mary Church Terrell: Genteel Militant. In: Leon Litwack and August Meier (eds.), Black Leaders of the Nineteenth Century. Urbana: University of Illinois Press, 1988.

Haskins, Jim and N. R. Mitgang. Mr. Bojangles. The Biography of Bill Robinson. New York: Morrow, 1988.

Hastings, R. J. A Nickel's Worth of Skim Milk: A Boy's View of the Great Depression [1930s]. Carbondale, IL: Southern Illinois University Press, 1986 (orig. 1972).

Haywood, H. Black Bolshevik: An Autobiography of an Afro-American Communist. Chicago: Liberator Press, 1978.

Hedgeman, A. A. The Trumpet Sounds: A Memoir of Negro Leadership. New York: Holt, 1964.

Heiss, G. G. The Public Career of David Walker: The Antebellum Years. Master's thesis, University of Arkansas, 1982.

Herndon, A. Let Me Live. New York: Random House, 1937.

Hill, R. A. and B. Bair. Marcus Garvey: Life and Lessons. Berkeley, CA: University of California Press, 1987.

Himes, C. B. The Quality of Hurt: The Autobiography of Chester Himes, vol. 1. Garden City, NY: Doubleday, 1972.

Holland, E. I. M. The Autobiography of a Parader Without a Permit [Includes author's own autobiography, in Miss.]. Doctoral dissertation, University of Minnesota, 1986. UMO # 8620190.

Holte, J. C. The Ethnic I: A Sourcebook for Ethnic-American Autobiography. Westport, CT: Praeger, 1988.

Horne, G. C. Black and Red: W.E.B. Du Bois and the Cold War, 1944-1963. Doctoral dissertation, Columbia University, 1984. UMO # 8427412.

Howe, P. J. and A. Reid. The Failed Dreams of Lonnie Gilchrist. Boston Globe April 18, 1988.

Hudson, Clenora F. Emmett Till: The Impetus for the Modern Civil Rights

Movement. Doctoral dissertation, University of Iowa, 1988. UMO # 8815090.

Hufford, Larry. Chicano Challenged American To Live Its Ideas. _National Catholic Reporter_ July 15, 1988. [Willie Velasquez, Texas].

Hughes, L. M. _The Big Sea: An Autobiography_. New York: Knopf, 1940.

Hurston, Z. N. _Dust Tracks on a Road: An Autobiography_ (new edition). Urbana, IL: University of Illinois Press, 1985.

Hyun, Peter. _Mansei! The Making of a Korean American_. Honolulu: University of Hawaii Press, 1986.

Jacobs, H. _Incidents in the Life of a Slave Girl_. New York: Oxford University Press, 1988 (orig. 1861).

James, C. L. R. George Jackson. _Radical America_ 5 (November-December 1971):51-56.

James, C. L. R. Paul Robeson: Black Star. _In: Spheres of Existence_, pp. 256-64. Westport, CT: Lawrence Hill & Co., 1980 (orig. November 1970).

Johnson, A. P. _A Study of the Life and Work of a Pioneer Black Educator: John W. Davis_. Doctoral dissertation, Rutgers University, 1987. UMO # 8727322.

Johnson, J. _Jack Johnson Is a Dandy: An Autobiography_. New York: Signet, 1970.

Johnson, J. W. _Along this Way: The Autobiography of James Weldon Johnson_. New York: Viking, 1933.

Kahapes, A. N. _Alika, the Hawaiian_, Vol. I [Memoir]. New York: Vantage Press, 1987.

Kahn, R. M. The Political Ideology of Martin Delany. _Journal of Black Studies_ 14 (June 1984):415-40.

Keckley, E. _Behind the Scenes. Or, Thirty Years a Slave, and Four Years in the White House_. New York: Oxford University Press, 1988 (reprint).

King, M. _Freedom Song. A Personal Story of the 1960s Civil Rights Movement_ [SNCC]. New York: Morrow, 1987.

Kingston, M. H. _The Woman Warrior: Memoirs of a Girlhood among Ghosts_. New York: 1976.

Lacy, L. A. _The Rise and Fall of a Proper Negro. An Autobiography_. New York: Macmillan, 1970.

Larison, C. W. _Silvia Dubois, a Biography of the Slav Who Whipt Her Mistres and Gand Her Fredom_. [Edited and translated by Jared C.

Lobdell.] New York: Oxford University Press, 1988 (reprint).

Lester, J. All Is Well. New York: Morrow, 1976.

Levesque, George A. Boston's Black Brahmin: Dr. John S. Rock. Civil War
     History 26 (December 1980):337-42.

Lewis, D. L. King: A Biography (second edition). Urbana. IL:
     University of Illinois Press, 1978.

Li, Ling-Ai. Life Is for a Long Time: A Chinese Hawaiian Memoir. New
     York: Hastings House, 1972.

Lightfoot, Sara Lawrence. Balm in Gilead. Journey of a Healer.
     Cambridge, MA: Addison-Wesley, 1988. [Biography of Dr. Margaret
     Morgan Lawrence, a black psychoanalyst].

Lipitz, George. A Life in the Struggle: Ivory Perry and the Culture of
     Opposition. Philadelphia, PA: Temple University Press, 1989.

Litwack, Leon F. and August Meier (eds.) Black Leaders of the Nineteenth
     Century, Urbana: University of Illinois Press, 1988.

Logan, R. W. and M. R. Winston. Dictionary of American Negro Biography.
     New York: Norton, 1983.

Lowe, P. Father and Glorious Descendant. Boston: 1943. [Autobiography
     by Chinese American].

Lynch, J. R. Reminiscences of an Active Life: The Autobiography of John
     Roy Lynch. Chicago: University of Chicago Press, 1970.

Lynn, C. J. There Is a Fountain: The Autobiography of a Civil Rights
     Lawyer. Westport, CT: Hill, 1978.

Malcolm X. with A. Haley. The Autobiography of Malcolm X. New York:
     Grove, 1965.

Mandel, B. J. The Didactic Achievement of Malcolm X's Autobiography.
     Afro-American Studies 2 (March 1972)269-74.

Masters, I. The Life and Legacy of Oliver Brown. Doctoral dissertation,
     University of Oklahoma, 1981. [Topeka, Kansas].

Mays, B. E. Born to Rebel: An Autobiography. New York: Scribners,
     1971.

McClain, L. A Foot in Each World: Essays and Articles by Leanita
     McClain. Evanston, IL: Northwestern University Press, 1987.

McCunn, Rutheanne Lum. Chinese American Portraits. Personal Histories
     1828-1988. San Francisco, CA: Chronicle, 1988.

McGovern, J. R. Black Eagle: General Daniel "Chappie" James, Jr.
     Alabama: University of Alabama Press, 1985.

McMurry, L. O. Recorder of the Black Experience: A Biography of Monroe Nathan Work. Baton Rouge: Lousiana State University Press, 1985.

McNeil, G. R. Groundwork: Charles Hamilton Houston and the Struggle for Civil Rights. Philadelphia, PA: University of Pennsylvania Press, 1983.

McPherson, D. A. Order Out of Chaos: The Autobiographical Works of Maya Angelou. Doctoral dissertation, University of Iowa, 1986. UMO # 8622797.

Molek, M. Immigrant Woman. Dover, DE: 1976. [Autobiography of a Slovene immigrant].

Moody, Anne. Coming of Age in Mississippi. New York: Dial, 1968.

Moore, J. T. Pride Against Prejudice: The Biography of Larry Doby. Westport, CT: Greenwood, 1988.

Moss, Alfred. Alexander Crummell: Black Nationalist and Apostle of Western Civilization. In: Leon Litwack and August Meier (eds.), Black Leaders of the Nineteenth Century. Ubana, IL: University of Illinois Press, 1988.

Motley, W. F. The Diaries of Willard Motley. Klinkowitz, Jerome (ed.) Ames, IA: Iowa State University Press, 1979.

Murray, P. Proud Shoes: The Story of an American Family. New York: Harper and Row, 1987.

Neary, J. Julian Bond. Black Rebel. Biography. New York: Morrow, 1971.

Neilson, M. C. Even in Mississippi: A Biography of Robert Clark. Master's thesis, University of Mississippi, 1986.

Newby, Robert. The Making of a Class-Conscious 'Race Man'. Critical Sociology (Summer 1988).

Newton, H. Revolutionary Suicide. New York: Harcourt Brace Jovanovich, 1973.

Norris, C. and S. D. Washington. The Last of the Scottsboro Boys: An Autobiography. New York: Putnam's, 1979.

Oates, S. B. Let the Trumpet Sound: The Life of Martin Luther King, Jr. New York: Harper and Row, 1982.

Ofari, E. 'Let Your Motto be Resistance': The Life and Thought of Henry Highland Garnet. Boston: Beacon Press, 1972.

Okimoto, Daniel. American in Disguise. Philadelphia, PA: Lippincott, 1971.

Ovington, Mary White. The Walls Came Tumbling Down. New York: Harcourt, Brace, 1947.

Padilla, Genaro M. The Recovery of Chicano Nineteenth-century Autobiography. American Quarterly 40 (1988)286-306.

Painter, N. I. The Narrative of Hosea Hudson: His Life as a Negro Communist in the South. Cambridge, MA: Harvard University Press, 1979.

Parker, Dorothy R. Choosing Indian Identity: A Biography of D'Arcy McMickle. Doctoral dissertation, University of New Mexico, 1988. UMO # 8820690.

Patterson, William L. The Man Who Cried Genocide. New York: International Publishers, 1971.

Payne, Charles Edward. Paul Robeson: A Psychobiographical Study of the Emotional Development of a Controversial Protest Leader [Until age 42]. Doctoral dissertation, Northwestern University, 1987. UMO # 8729031.

Perry, J. B. Hubert Henry Harrison. 'The Father of Harlem Radicalism': The Early Years - 1883 through the Founding of the Liberty League and the Voice in 1917. Doctoral dissertation, Columbia University, 1986. UMO # 8610803.

Pickens, W. Bursting Bonds. Boston: Jordan and Moore Press, 1929.

Pickens, W. The Heir of Slaves: An Autobiography. Boston: Pilgrim Press, 1911.

Porter, J. N. Black-Jewish Relations: Some Notes on Cross-Cultural Research Plus a Selected Annotated Bibliography. International Review of Sociology (September 1971):1-9.

Powell, A. C. Adam. New York: Dial, 1979.

Prince, M. and others. Six Women's Slaves Narratives. New York: Oxford University Press, 1988 (orig 1831 to c. 1891).

Rigsby, Gregory U. Alexander Crummell: Pioneer in Nineteenth-Century Pan-African Thought. Westport, CT: Greenwood, 1987.

Robeson, P. L. Here I Stand. New York: Othello Associates, 1958.

Robeson, P. L. I Don't Want to be White. Chicago Defender January 26, 1935.

Robinson, J. I Never Had It Made. New York: Putnam's, 1972.

Rosengarten, T. All God's Dangers. [Nate Shaw] New York: Knopf, 1974.

Russell, K. K. Growing Up with Privilege and Prejudice [Daughter of Bill Russell, Boston Celtic star of 1950s-1960s]. New York Times

Magazine June 14, 1987.

Scally, A., Jr. _Carter G. Woodson: A Bio-Bibliography_. Westport, CT:
     Greenwood, 1985.

Schor, J. S. _Henry Highland Garnet: A Voice of Black Radicalism in the
     Nineteenth Century_. Westport, CT: Greenwood, 1977.

Schuyler, G. S. _Black and Conservative: Autobiography_. New Rochelle,
     NY: Arlington House, 1966.

Seale, B. _A Lonely Rage: The Autobiography of Bobby Seale_. New York:
     Times Books, 1977.

Sellers, C. and R. Terrell. _The River of No Return: The Autobiography of
     a Black Militant and the Life and Death of SNCC_. New York: Morrow,
     1973.

Shakur, A. _Assata: An Autobiography_. Westport, CT: Lawrence Hill,
     1987.

Shinsei, K. _Imin no Aiwa: Sad Tale of an Immigrant_. [Okinawan immigrant
     to U.S.] Translated by Ben Kobashigawa. Los Angeles: 1978.

Simmons, L. W. (ed.) _Sun Chief, the Autobiography of a Hopi Indian_. New
     Haven, CT: Yale University Press, 1942.

Smith, A. _An Autobiography. The Story of the Lord' Dealings with Mrs.
     Amanda Smith the Colored Evangelist_. [Written by Black author] New
     York: Oxford University Press, 1988 (orig. 1893).

Smith, V. _Self-Discovery and Authority in Afro-American Narrative_.
     Cambridge, MA: Harvard University Press, 1987.

Starobin, R. S. (ed.) _Blacks in Bondage: Letters of American Slaves_.
     New York: New Viewpoints, 1974.

Stewart, M. W., Jr., J. Lee, A. J. Foote and V. W. Broughton. _Spiritual
     Narratives_ [Four autobiographical narratives]. New York: Oxford
     University Press, 1988 (orig. between 1835 and 19070.

Swann, Brian and Arnold Krupat (eds.) _I Tell You Now. Autobiographical
     Essays by Native American Writers_. Lincoln: University of Nebraska
     Press, 1987.

Taiz, L. _Race and the Politics of Culture: The Rise and Fall of Paul
     Robeson_. Master's thesis, San Francisco State University, 1983.

Tarry, E. _The Third Door: The Autobiography of an American Negro Woman_.
     New York: McKay, 1955.

Terrell, M. E. C. _A Colored Woman in a White World_. Washington, D.C.:
     Ransdell, 1940.

Thompson, E. B. _American Daughter_. Chicago, IL: University of Chicago

Press, 1946.

Travis, D. J. An Autobiography of Black Chicago. Chicago, IL: Urban
    Research Institute, 1981.

Trees, D. How Columbus and I Discovered America: The Life and Adventures
    of an Immigrant [Serbian Immigrant]. Grosse Pointe, MI: 1965.

Truth, S. Sojourner Truth's Narrative. Boston: Author, 1875.

Tuchman, H. L. Negro-Jewish Relations: A Bibliography Covering Materials
    Published from January 1960 through May 1968. Hebrew College
    Library, Brookline, MA.

Turner, Darwin T. (ed.) The Wayward and the Seeking: A Collection of
    Writings by Jean Toomer. Washington, D.C.: Howard University Press,
    1980.

Turner, W. Burghardt and Joyce Moore Turner (eds.) Richard B. Moore,
    Caribbean Militant in Harlem. Collectd Writings 1920-1972.
    Bloomington: Indiana University Press, 1985.

Walker, Margaret. Richard Wright: Daemonic Genius. New York:
    Warner/Amistad, 1989.

Washington, B. T. Up From Slavery. New York: Doubleday, Page, 1901.

Welch, A. A Narrative of the Early Days and Remembrance of Occola
    Nikkanochee. Gainesville, FL: University Presses of Florida, 1977.

Wells, I. B. Crusade for Justice: The Autobiography of Ida B. Wells.
    Chicago, IL: University of Chicago Press, 1970.

Wilkins, R. A Man's life. New York: Simon and Schuster, 1982.

Wilkins, R. Standing Fast. New York: Viking Press, 1982.

Williams, Harry M., Jr. When Black Is Right: The Life and Writings of
    George S. Schuyler. Doctoral dissertation, Brown University, 1988.
    UMO # 8822613.

Williams, M. D. Childhood in an Urban Black Ghetto: Two Life Histories.
    In: Joseph M. Hawes (ed.), Growing Up in America: Children in
    Historical Perspective. Urbana: University of Illinois, 1985.

Wong, M. D. Fifth Chinese Daughter. New York, 1950.

Wright, R. N. Black Boy: A Record of Childhood and Youth. New York:
    Harper and Row, 1945.

Yates, James. Mississippi to Madrid: Memoir of a Black American in the
    Abraham Lincoln Brigade. Open Hadd Publishing, 1989.

Yoneda, K. G. Ganbatte. Sixty-year Struggle of a Kiber Worker [Leader
    in American Communist Party]. Los Angeles, CA: Asian American

Studies Center, University of California, 1983.

Autobiography and Biography Bibliography

Andrews, William L. (comp.) Annotated Bibliography of Afro-American Biography, Beginnings to 1930. Resources for American Literary Study 12 (Autumn 1982)119-33.

Brignano, R. C. (comp.) Black Americans in Autobiography: An Annotated Bibliography of Autobiographies and Autobiographical Books Written Since the Civil War (revised edition). Durham, NC: Duke University Press, 1984.

Davis, L. G. (comp.) A Paul Robeson Research Guide: A Selected Annotated Bibliography. Westport, CT: Greenwood, 1982.

Ethnic Biography and Autobiography [Bibliography]. MELUS 9 (Summer 1982):entire issue.

Johnson, T. V. (comp.) Malcolm X. A Comprehensive Annotated Bibliography. New York: Garland, 1986.

Pyatt, S. E. (comp.) Martin Luther King, Jr.: An Annotated Bibliography. Westport, CT: Greenwood, 1986.

7. Black Towns

[Black] town promoters asked members of the race to join them in order to gain economic independence and enjoy the benefits of unrestrained freedom while proving to the dominant society that blacks were ... capable of governing their own affairs.

- Norman L. Crockett, The Black Towns, p. 182.

Bethel, E. R. Promiseland: A Century of Life in a Negro Community [All-Black town in S.C.]. Philadelphia, PA: Temple University Press.

Biddle, W. L. and G. Geis. Racial Self-Fulfillment and the Rise of an All-Negro Community in Oklahoma. Phylon 18 (1957):247-60.

Bittle, William and Gilbert Geis. Racial Self-fulfillment and the Rise of an All-Negro Community in Oklahoma. Phylon 17 (3rd quarter 1957):247-60.

Boynton, M. Springtown New Jersey: Explorations in the History and Culture of a Black Rural Community. Doctoral dissertation, University of Pennsylvania, 1986. UMO # 8614769.

Cimbala, Paul A. A Black Colony in Dougherty County: The Freedmen's Bureau and the Failure of Reconstruction in Southwest Georgia. Journal of South West Georgia History 4 (Fall 1986):72-89.

Crockett, N. L. The Black Towns [Five towns: Langston, Clearview, and Boley, Okla.; Nicodemus, Kansas; and Mound Bayou, Miss.]. University Press of Kansas.

Du Bois, W. E. B. Men of the Month [On all-Black towns]. Crisis 19 (January 1920):126-127.

Ernst, R. T. Growth Development and Isolation of an All-Black City: Kinlock, Missouri. In: Robert T. Ernst and Lawrence Hugg (eds.), Black America, pp. 368-88. Garden City, NY: Doubleday.

Fine, G. A. The Pinkston Settlement: An Historical and Social Psychological Investigation of the Contact Hypothesis [Indiana]. Phylon 40 (September 1979):229-242.

Frazier, Ian. Great Plains - III. New Yorker (March 6, 1989):41-44. [Nicodemus, Kansas, population ca. 50, a black town founded in 1877].

Geismar, J. H. The Archaeology of Social Disintegration in Skunk Hollow: A Nineteenth-Century Rural Black Community [New Jersey]. New York: Academic Press.

Gloster, R. Oklahoma's Black Towns Banding Together in Effort to Improve Economics. Daily Oklahoman March 8, 1981.

Hamilton, K. M. Townsite Speculation and the Origin of Boley, Oklahoma.

Chroniles of Oklahoma 55 (1977):180-9.

Hamilton, K. M. Black Town Promotion and Development on the Middle
    Border, 1877-1914. Doctoral dissertation, Washington University,
    1978. UMO # 7911489.

Hamilton, K. M. The Origins and Early Promotion of Nicodemus: A Pre-
    Exodus, All-Black Town. Kansas History 5 (Winter 1982):220-42.

Harris, A. Dearfield, a Negro Ghost Town in Weld County, Colorado. Negro
    History Bulletin 27 (1963):38-0.

Hermann, J. S. The Pursuit of a Dream [Davis Bend and Mound Bayou].
    New York: Oxford University Press.

Hill, M. C. The All-Negro Communities of Oklahoma: The Natural History of
    a Social Movement. Journal of Negro History 31 (1946):254-68.

Hill, M. C. The All-Negro Society in Oklahoma. Doctoral dissertation,
    University of Chicago, 1946.

James, F. Decline and Fall of Freedmen's Village in Arlington, Virginia.
    Negro History Bulletin 37 (1974):247-50.

James, F. The Establishment of Freedmen's Village in Arlington, Virginia.
    Negro History Bulletin 33 (1970):90-93.

Kenney, C. The Aftershock of a Radical Notion [First of two articles on
    1986 proposal to form a separate Black city in Boston called
    Mandela]. Boston Globe Magazine April 12, 1987.

Love, R. Community in Transition: A Study of Mound Bayou, Mississippi.
    Doctoral dissertation, Boston University, 1982. UMO # 8221017.

Meier, A. Booker T. Washington and the Town of Mound Bayou. Phylon 15
    (1954):396-401.

Mobley, J. A. In the Shadow of White Society: Princeville, a Black Town
    in North Carolina, 1865-1915. North Carolina Historical Review 63
    (July 1986):340-84.

Norris, M. E., Jr. Dearfield, Colorado-The Evolution of a Rural Black
    Settlement: An Historical Geography of Black Colonization on the
    Great Plains. Doctoral dissertation, University of Colorado, 1980.
    UMO # 8021613.

Reidy, Joseph P. 'Coming from the Shadow of the Past': The Transition
    from Slavery to Freedom at Freedmen's Village, 1863-1900. Virginia
    Magazine of History and Biography 95 (October 1987):403-28.

Rose, H. M. The All-Black Town: Suburban Prototype or Rural Slum: In
    Harlan Hahn (ed.), People and Politics in Urban Society, pp. 397-431.
    Beverly Hills, CA: Sage.

Rose, H. M. The All-Negro Town: Its Evolution and Function. Geographical

Review 55 (July 1965):262-381.

Simmons, W. J. _Johnson's Crossing: An Institutional Analysis of a Rural Black Community_ [Northeast Florida]. Doctoral dissertation, University of Florida, 1981. UMO # 8203722.

Taylor, H. L., Jr. _The Building of a Black Industrial Suburb: The Lincoln Heights, Ohio Story_ [Suburb of Cincinnati]. Doctoral dissertation, State Univ. of New York at Buffalo, 1979. UMO # 8005721.

Tolson, Arthur L. _The History of Langston, Oklahoma: 1890-1950_. Master's thesis, Oklahoma A & M College, 1952.

Walter, I. and J. E. Kramer. Political Autonomy and Economic Dependence in an All-Negro Municipality [Kinloch, MO]. _American Journal of Economics and Sociology_ 28 (1969):225-48.

White, M. M. _'We Lived On an Island': An Afro-American Family and Community in Rural Virginia, 1865-1940_. Doctoral dissertation, University of Texas, 1983. UMO # 8329888.

Woodard, J. E. Vernon: An All Negro Town in Southeastern Oklahoma. _Negro History Bulletin_ 27 (1964):115-16.

8. Blacks and Jews

It is not only that antisemitism is immoral - though that alone is enough. It is used to divide Negro and Jew, who have effectively collaborated in the struggle for justice. It injures Negroes because it upholds the doctrine of racism which they have the greatest stake in destroying.

- Martin Luther King, Jr., "Negroes, Jews, Israel and Anti-Semitism," January 1968.

Aberbach, M. The Negro in Jewish Tradition. Herzl Institute Bulletin 3 (May 7, 1967):1-6.

Albernathy, A. T. The Jew and Negro Being a Study of the Jewish Ancestry from an Impartial Standpoint. Moravian Falls, NC: Dixie Publishing Co.

Anti-Defamation League, Civil Rights Division Louis Farrakhan. An Update. ADL Facts 30 (Spring 1985).

Bandler, K. Farrakhan on the Campus: Challenges Facing Jewish Students. Israel Horizons (January-February 1986):15-17.

Baraka, A. Confessions of a Former Anti-Semite. Village Voice December 17, 1980.

Berger, G. Black Jews in America: A Documentary with Commentary. New York: Comm. on Synagogue Rels. Fed. of Jewish Philanthropies of NY, 1979.

Berman, Paul. [Jesse] Jackson and the Jewish Left. Tikkun 3 (July-August 1988):53-55.

Berson, L. E. The Negroes and the Jews. New York: Random House.

Berube, M. R. and M. Gittell (eds.) Confrontation at Ocean Hill-Brownsville: The New York School Strikes of 1968. New York: Praeger.

Black Group Celebrates Judaism as True Heritage [Ethiopian Hebrews, N.Y.C.]. New York Times May 29, 1985.

Black Power, Foul and Fragrant [Louis Farrakhan]. Economist (October 22, 1985:25-6.

Bond, Horace Mann. Negro Attitudes Towards Jews. Jewish Social Studies (January 1965).

Brackman, H. D. The Ebb and Flow of Conflict: A History of Black-Jewish Relations Through 1900. Doctoral dissertation, University of California, 1977.

Brackman, Harold. Mirror of Conflict: The Black Press and Major Issues
    of Jewish Concern. Los Angeles, CA: Simon Wiesenthal Center, 1988.

Brent, Jonathan. Political Perversity in Chicago. New Republic August 8
    and 15, 1988. [Antisemitism of Steve Cokely].

Burnell, J. B. Conflicting Jewish Attitudes to Affirmative Action.
    Patterns of Prejudice 15 (July 1981):19-28.

Capeci, D. J., Jr. Black-Jewish Relations in Wartime Detroit: The Marsh,
    Loving, Wolf Surveys and the Race Riot of 1943. Jewish Social
    Studies 47 (Fall 1985):221-42.

Carson, C., Jr. Blacks and Jews in the Civil Rights Movement.
    In: Joseph R. Washington (ed.), Jews in Black Perspectives: A
    Dialogue. Rutherford, NJ: Fairleigh Dickinson University, 1984.

Cohen, K. O. Black-Jewish Relations in 1984: A Survey of Black U.S.
    Congressmen. Patterns of Prejudice 19 (April 1985):3-18.

Cohen, K. O. Jesse Jackson on Black-Jewish Relations (interview).
    Patterns of Prejudice 20 (October 1986):43-45.

Cohen, O. Problems in Intergroup Relations: Negro Anti-Semitism
    in the United States. Toward Cultural Democracy (April 1970):110-16.

Cowett, M. Birmingham's Rabbi: Morris Newfield and Alabama, 1895-1940.
    Alabama: University of Alabama Press.

Daum, A. Blacks and Jews: Repairing the Rift. Pioneer Woman (November-
    December 1985).

Didion, Joan. Letter from Los Angeles. New Yorker April 24, 1989.
    [Jews and Blacks in Los Angeles politics].

Diner, H. R. In the Almost Promised Land: Jewish Leaders and Blacks,
    1915-1935. Doctoral dissertation, University of Illinois, 1975.

Diner, H. R. In the Almost Promised Land: American Jews and Blacks,
    1915-1935. Westport, CT: Greenwood, 1977.

Dinnerstein, L. The Origins of Black Anti-Semitism in America. American
    Jewish Archives 38 (November 1986):113-22.

Dinnerstein, L. (ed.) Jews in the South. Baton Rouge: Louisiana State
    University Press.

Dreyfuss, J. Such Good Friends, Blacks and Jews in Conflict. Village
    Voice August 27, 1979.

Drimmer, Melvin. On the Contrary, Blacks and Jews Remain Friends. New
    York Times April 15, 1989 (op-ed page).

Du Bois, W. E. B. The Case for the Jews [Palestine]. Chicago Star May
    8, 1948.

Du Bois, W. E. B. [Denunciation of Antisemitism among some Blacks]. Amsterdam News October 5, 1940.

Du Bois, W. E. B. [Jewish] Organization. Crisis 9 (March 1915):235.

Du Bois, W. E. B. The Jews. Crisis 30 (May 1933):117.

Du Bois, W. E. B. The Negro and the Warsaw Ghetto. Jewish Life 6 (May 1952):14-15.

Du Bois, W. E. B. The Souls of Black Folk. Chicago: McClurg, 1903.

Epstein, Joseph. Racial Perversity in Chicago. Commentary (December 1988):27-35.

Louis Farrakhan: In His Own Words. ADL Special Report (October 1985):1-11.

Fein, L. The Awkward Alliance [Blacks and Jews]. Moment (January-February 1986):18-20.

Foner, P. S. Black-Jewish Relations in the Opening Years of the 20th Century. Phylon (4th Quarter 1975):359-67.

Foner, P. S. (ed.) W.E.B. Du Bois Speaks ... 1920-1963. New York: Pathfinder Press, 1970.

Frank, S. The Future of Black/Jewish Relations. New Menorah 9 (1987).

Geltman, M. The Confrontation: Black Power, Anti-Semitism, and the Myth of Integration. Englewood Cliffs, NJ: Prentice-Hall.

Ginsberg, Y. Jewish Attitudes toward Black Neighbors in Boston and London. Ethnicity 8 (June 1981):206-218.

Green, Nancy L. Juifs et Noirs aux Etats-Unis: La Rupture d'une 'alliance naturelle'. Annales 42 (March-April 1987):445-64.

Gross, Barry. 'Intellectual Overlordship': Blacks, Jews and Native Son. Journal of Ethnic Studies 5 (Fall 1977):51-59.

Harap, L. Anti-Negroism Among Jews. Negro Quarterly 1 (Summer 1942):105-11.

Harap, L. Dramatic Encounters: The Jewish Presence in Twentieth-Century American Drama, Poetry, and Humor and the Black-Jewish Literary Relationship. Westport, CT: Greenwood.

Hertzberg, S. Southern Jews and their Encounter with Blacks: Atlanta, 1850-1915. Atlanta Historical Review 23 (Fall 1979):7-24.

Hyatt, M. Franz Boas and the Struggle for Black Equality: The Dynamics of Ethnicity. Perspectives in American History 2 (1985) 269-95.

Israel, E. L. Jew Hatred Among Negroes. Crisis (February 1936).

Joravsky, Ben. Blacks and Jews in Chicago. Tikkun 3 (September-October 1988):38-40.

Kaufman, Jonathan. Black-Jewish Dynamic Follows Jackson in N.Y. Boston Globe April 10, 1988.

Kaufman, Jonathan. Blacks and Jews: An Historical Perspective. Tikkun 3 (July-August 1988):42-44, 92-94.

Kaufman, Jonathan. Tense Times for Blacks, Jews. Boston Globe December 4, 1988.

Kaufman, Jonathan. Too Young to March with Martin Luther King. Boston Globe Magazine August 21, 1988. [Donna Brazile].

King, Martin Luther, Jr. Of Riots and Wrongs Against the Jews. SCLC Newsletter (July-August 1964).

King, Martin Luther, Jr. Of Riots and Wrongs Against Jews. Jewish Currents 18 (November 1964).

King, Martin Luther, Jr. Negroes, Jews, Israel, and Anti-Semitism. Jewish Currents 21 (January 1968).

Klug, Brian. Springtime in Chicago: A Pattern of Politics and Prejudice. Patterns of Prejudice 22 (Autumn 1988):36-46.

Korn, B. W. Jews and Negro Slavery in the Old South, 1780-1865. Elkins Park, PA: Reform Congregation Keneseth Israel

Korn, B. W. Jews and Negro Slavery in the Old South, 1789-1865. AJHQ 50 (March 1961).

Korn, B. W. (ed.) The Jews of the Confederacy: Docoments. American Jewish Archives 8 (April 1961):3-90.

Korn, B. W. (ed.) The Jews of the Union: Documents. American Jewish Archives 8 (November 1961):131-230.

Kramer, M. Blacks and Jews: How Wide the Rift [N.Y.C.]. New York (February 4, 1985):26-32.

Kramer, M. The Charmer [Louis Farrakhan]. New York (October 7, 1985):16, 19-20.

Kramer, M. Loud and Clear. New York (October 21, 1985):22-23.

Kurapka, David. Hate Story. New Republic (May 30, 1988):19-21. [Louis Farrakhan].

Labovitz, S. Attitudes Toward Blacks Among Jews: Historical Antecedents and Current Concerns. Doctoral dissertation, University of Pennsylvania, 1972.

Lambert, Frederick J. and others. Chicago's Black-Jewish Divisions Made Worse. New York Times August 9, 1988. [Series of letters].

Lester, J. The Time Has Come [Louis Farrakhan]. New Republic (October 28, 1985):11-12.

Levine, N. Ocean Hill-Brownsville: A Case History of Schools in Crisis. New York: Popular Library

Lewis, D. L. Parallels and Divergences: Assimilationist Strategies of Afro-American and Jewish Elites from 1910 to the Early 1930s. Journal of American History 71 (1984).

Lipset, S. M. Blacks and Jews: How Much Bias? Public Opinion (July-August 1987):4-5, 57-58.

[Louis] Farrakhan Rides the Wave of Black Anger. In These Times October 19, 1988.

Marx, Robert J. Black-Jewish Relations in Chicago. Jewish Current November 1988.

Muwakkil, S. Neo-Nazi Rally Boosts Farrakhan's Audience. In These Times July 9, 1986.

Perry, H. L. and R. B. White. The Post-Civil Rights Transformation of the Relationship Between Blacks and Jews in the United States. Phylon 47 (Spring 1986):51-60.

Plax, M. J. Jews and Blacks in Dialogue. Midstream 28 (January 1982):10-17.

Polos, N. C. Black Anti-Semitism in Twentieth-Century America: Historical Myth or Reality? American Jewish Archives 27 (April 1975):8-31.

Price, I. B. Black Responses to Anti-Semitism: Negroes and Jews in New York, 1880 to World War II. Doctoral dissertation, University of New Mexico, 1973.

Rampersad, Arnold. Langston Hughes's Fine Clothes to the Jew. Callaloo 9 (Winter 1986).

Rapoport, L. The Day of 'The Charmer' [Louis Farrakhan]. Jerusalem Post November 15, 1985.

Reddick, L. D. Anti-Semitism Among Negroes. Negro Quarterly (Summer 1942).

Robeson, P. Bonds of Brotherhood. Jewish Life 9 (November 1954):13-14.

Ruchames, L. The Abolitionists and the Jews. Publications of the American Jewish Historical Society (December 1952):131-55.

Shankman, A. Friend or Foe? Southern Afro-Americans View the Jew, 1880-

1935. In: Nathan M. Kaganoff and Melvin G. Urofsky (eds.), 'Turn to the South': Essays on Southern Jewry. Charlottesville, VA.

Silberg, F. B. Black/Jewish Relations: A Prologue. Jewish Spectator (Winter 1986):19-22.

Silberman, C. E. Affinity and Confrontation: The Lessons of the Holocaust Have Bearing on the Relations Between Blacks and Jews. Anti-Defamation League Bulletin 34 (January 1977):5-6.

Smothers, Ronald. Conference Discussing Relations of Blacks and Jews Yields a Clash. New York Times April 9, 1989.

Starosta, W. J. and L. Coleman. Jesse Jacksons's 'Hymietown' Apology: A Case Study of Interethnic Rhetorical Analysis. In: Young Yun Kim (ed.), Interethnic Communication: Current Research. Newbury Park, CA: Sage.

Stemons, J. S. As Victims to Victims: An American Negro Laments with Jews. New York: Fortuny's, 1941.

Stern, Sol. Jesse's Jews. New Republic (June 20, 1988).

Strickland, William. We Can Overcome: The Black-Jewish Rift. Tikkun 3 (July-August 1988):49-52.

Toll, W. Pluralism and Moral Force in the Black-Jewish Dialogue. American Jewish History (September 1987):87-105.

Ungor, A. The Jew and the Negro. Conservative Judaism 13 (Fall 1958):1-34.

Washington, J. R., Jr. (ed.) Jews in Black Perspective: A Dialogue. Rutherford, NJ: Fairleigh Dickinson University Press.

Wedlock, L. The Reaction of Negro Publications and Organizations to German Anti-Semitism. Master's thesis, Howard University, 1942.

Weinstein, Jacob Joseph. A Comparative Study of the Persecution of the Jew and the Negro. Hebrew Union College rabbinic thesis, 1929.

Weisbord, R. G. and R. Kazarian, Jr. Israel and Black America: The Moshe Dayan Incident Revisited. Jewish Frontier 49 (November 1982):10-12.

Weisbord, R. G. and R. Kazarian, Jr. Israel in the Black American Perspective. Westport, CT: Greenwood.

Weisbord, R. G. and A. Stein. Bittersweet Encounter: The Afro-American and the American Jew. Westport, CT: Negro Universities Press.

Weitz, M. Black Attitudes to Jews in the United States from World War II to 1976. Doctoral dissertation, Yeshiva University, 1977.

Whiteman, M. Jews in the Antislavery Movement. In: Introduction to the

Kidnapped and the Ransomed: The Narrative of Peter and Vina Still. Philadelphia: The Jewish Publication Society of America,

Wilkerson, D. A. Negroes and Jews: Interdependent. Jewish Currents 23 (September 1969):11-15.

Williams, O. R., Jr. Historical Impressions of Black-Jewish Relations Prior to World War II. Negro History Bulletin 40 (July-August 1977):728-731.

Williams, P. N. Moses and Afro-Americans. Religion and Intellectual Life 4 (Winter 1987):11-15.

Zucker, B. Black Americans' Reaction to the Persecution of European Jews. In: Henry Friedlander and others (eds.), Simon Wiesenthal Center Annual, Vol. 3. White Plains, NY: Kraus International Publications.

Blacks and Jews Bibliography

Davis, L. G. Black-Jewish Relations in the United States, 1752-1984. A Selected Bibliography. Westport, CT: Greenwood.

Levtow, P. Black-Jewish Relations in the U.S.: A Selected Annotated List of Books, Pamphlets, and Articles. New York: American Jewish Committee.

[See also section 4]

9. Business

[When I was a schoolboy] if a colored person went to collect a bill, he was inquired of, "Can you write your name?" Now it is taken for granted.

- George T. Downing, president, Convention of the Colored Citizens of New England, <u>Liberator</u>, August 19, 1859.

Abner, D. Negro Life Insurer: A Historical Perspective, 1883-1930. <u>Asa T. Spaulding</u> <u>Insurance</u> <u>Journal</u> 1 (1981-82):1-12.

Abraham, J. M. Black Business in Baltimore: 1850-1981. <u>In</u>: Jaki Hall (ed.), <u>The</u> <u>Black</u> <u>Pages</u>. Baltimore, MD: Jaki Hall Enterprise, 1981.

Alexander, M. <u>The</u> <u>Black</u> <u>Entrepreneur</u> <u>in</u> <u>the</u> <u>Trucking</u> <u>Industry</u>. Master's thesis, Ball State University, 1985.

Alexander, R. J. Negro Business in Atlanta. <u>Southern</u> <u>Economic</u> <u>Journal</u> 17 (April 1951):451-64.

Ando, F. H. An Analysis of the Formation and Failure Rates of Minority-owned Firms. <u>Review</u> <u>of</u> <u>Black</u> <u>Political</u> <u>Economy</u> 15 (Fall 1986).

Auster, E. R. Owner and Organizational Characteristics of Black- and White-Owned Businesses: Self-Employed Blacks Had Less Training, Fewer Resources, Less Profits, but Had Similar Survival Rates. <u>American</u> <u>Journal</u> <u>of</u> <u>Economics</u> <u>and</u> <u>Sociology</u> 47 (July 1988).

Bailey, R. W. <u>Black</u> <u>Business</u> <u>Enterprise:</u> <u>Historical</u> <u>and</u> <u>Contemporary</u> <u>Perspectives</u>. New York: Basic Books, 1971.

Bates, T. <u>Black</u> <u>Capitalism:</u> <u>A</u> <u>Quantitative</u> <u>Analysis</u>. New York: Praeger, 1973.

Bates, T. The Potentials of Black Capitalism. <u>Public</u> <u>Policy</u> 21 (1973):135-48.

Bates, T. M. and W. Bradford. <u>Financing</u> <u>Black</u> <u>Economic</u> <u>Development</u> [Banking]. New York: Academic Press, 1979.

Bluestone, B. Black Capitalism: The Path to Black Liberation? <u>Review</u> <u>of</u> <u>Radical</u> <u>Political</u> <u>Economics</u> (May 1969):36-55.

Bonacich, Edna. 'Making It' in America: A Social Evolution of the Ethics of Immigrant Entrepreneurship. <u>Sociological</u> <u>Perspectives</u> 30 (October 1987):446-66.

Bonacich, Edna. The Social Costs of Immigrant Entrepreunership [Koreans in the U.S.]. <u>Amerasia</u> <u>Journal</u> 14 (1988):119-28.

Brimmer, A. F. The Black Banks: An Assessment of Performance and Prospects. <u>Journal</u> <u>of</u> <u>Finance</u> 26 (May 1971):379-405.

Brimmer, A. F. Profit versus Pride: The Trouble with Black Capitalism.
    Nation's Business (May 1969):78-79.

Brimmer, A. F., and H. S. Terrell. The Economic Potential of Black
    Capitalism. Black Politician 2 (1971):19-23, 78-87.

Carlisle, R. Black-Owned Shipping Before Marcus Garvey. American Neptune
    35 (1975):197-206.

Chavers-Wright, M. The Guarantee: P.W. Chavers, Banker, Entrepreneur,
    Philanthropist in Chicago's Black Belt of the Twenties. New York:
    Wright-Armstead Associates, 1985. [2410 Barker Avenue, Bronx, NY
    10467].

Cole, J. R. and others. Black Banks: A Survey and Analysis of the
    Literature. Review of Black Political Economy 14 (Summer 1985):29-
    50.

Cole, F. A., Jr. Black Economic Development. Chicago: Nelson Hall,
    1975.

Cole, F. A., Jr. Financial Institutions and Black Entrepreneurships.
    Journal of Black Studies 3 (1973):329-49.

Collins, Sharon M. Pathways to the Top: Black Mobility in the Business
    World. Doctoral dissertation, Northwestern University, 1988. UMO #
    8822966.

Cross, T. L. Black Capitalism. New York: Atheneum, 1969.

Days, D. S., III. Fullilove [Affirmative action for minority business
    enterprise]. Yale Law Journal 96 (January 1987):453-85.

Deutsch, C. H. Still on the Outside Looking In [Blacks and Hispanics in
    business]. New York Times July 5, 1987.

Dubery, S. Black's Preference for Black Professionals, Businessmen and
    Religious Leaders. Public Opinion Quarterly (September 20,
    1970):113-16.

Du Bois, W. E. B. Black Banks and White in Memphis. Crisis 35 (May
    1928):154, 173-4.

Du Bois, W. E. B. Business as a Public Service. Crisis 36 (November
    1929):374-5, 392.

Du Bois, W. E. B. [On Black businessmen]. Amsterdam News October 10,
    1942.

Du Bois, W. E. B. The Negro Bank. Crisis 23 (April 1922):253-4.

Du Bois, W. E. B. Postscript [On Dunbar National Bank]. Crisis 35
    (November 1928):381-2.

Du Bois, W. E. B. (ed.) The Negro in Business. Atlanta: Atlanta University Press, 1899.

Du Bois, W. E. B. [What are banks for?]. Chicago Defender March 10, 1945.

Fitzgerald, J. In Banks, Blacks' Progress Is Slow. Boston Globe April 26, 1983.

Frappier, J. Chase Goes to Harlem: Financing Black Capitalism. Monthly Review 28 (1977):20-33 .

Fratoe, F. A. A Sociological Analysis of Minority Business. Review of Black Political Economy p. 15 (Fall 1986).

Geller, S. M. Black Men and Businessmen: The Growing Awareness of a Social Responsibility. Kennikat: 1974.

George, N. Where Did Our Love Go? The Rise and Fall of the Motown Sound. New York: St. Martin's Press, 1986.

Gilbert, A. L. The Comptroller of the Currency and the Freedmen's Savings Bank [Bankruptcy in 1874]. Journal of Negro History 57 (1972):125-43.

Gilbreath, Kent. Business Development on the Navajo Reservation. New Mexico Business Education 25 (March 1972):3-10.

Green, T. L. Junius R. Lewis and the Golden Chest Mining Company. Colorado Magazine 50 (1973):24-40.

Greenberg, S. B. Business Enterprise in a Racial Order. Politics and Society 6 (1976):213-40.

Handy, J. W., III. A Macro Analysis of Firm Formation and Firm Failure in the Black-owned Business Sector. Doctoral dissertation, Georgia State University, 1985. UMO # 8618218.

Harmon, J. H. and others. The Negro as a Business Man. 1929.

Harris, A. L. The Negro as Capitalist: A Study of Banking and Business Among American Negroes. New York, 1970 (orig. 1936).

Henderson, A. B. Herman E. Perry and Black Enterprise in Atlanta, 1908-1925. Business History Review 61 (Summer 1987).

Hicks, J. P. Black Professionals Refashion their Careers [Blacks employed in large corporations leaving for positions in Black-owned firms or to open their own businesses]. New York Times November 29, 1985.

Higgs, R. Participation of Blacks and Immigrants in the American Merchant Class, 1890-1910: Demographic Relations. Explorations in Economic History 13 (1976):153-64.

Hitchcock, F. G. Black Music and Popular Culture: Atlantic Records,

1947-1964. Master's thesis, University of Texas, 1978.

Horton, Hayward. A Demographic Analysis of Black Entrepreneurs. Doctoral dissertation, Pennsylvania State University, 1987. UMO # 8728020.

Hypps, I. C. Changes in Business Attitudes and Activities of the Negro in the United States since 1619. Doctoral dissertation, New York University, 1944.

Irons, E. D. Black Banking - Problems and Prospects. Journal of Finance 26 (May 1971):407-25.

Irons, E. D. Black Entrepreneurship: Its Rationale, Its Problems, Its Prospects. Phylon (March 1976):12-25.

Irons, E. D. Positive View of Black Capitalism. Bankers Magazine (Spring 1970):43-47.

Jackson, G. B. and D. W. Davis. The Industrial History of the Negro Race of the United States. Richmond, VA: The Virginia Press, 1908.

Jackson, L. J. The Development of Black Business in Texas, 1919-1969: From a Houston Perspective. Master's thesis, Texas Tech University, 1978.

Johnson, John H. with Lerone Bennett, Jr. Succeeding Against the Odds. New York: Warner Books, 1989. [Publisher of Ebony Magazine].

Joint Center for Political Studies. Black Business Enterprise: A Statistical Portrait. Washington, D.C.: The Center, 1983.

Kim, Illsoo. A New Theoretical Perspective on Asian Enterprises. Amerasia Journal 14 (1988):xi-xiv.

Lancaster, E. M. A Guide to Negro Marketing Information. Washington, D.C.: Business & Defense Services Administration, U.S. Dept. of Commerce, 1966.

Light, I. H. Ethnic Enterprise in America: Business and Welfare among Chinese, Japanese, and Blacks. Berkeley, CA: University of California Press, 1972.

Lindley, J. T. and others. Racial Discrimination in the Provision of Financial Services. American Economic Review 74 (September 1984).

Ma, L. Eve Armentrout. The Big Business Ventures of Chinese in North America, 1850-1930. In: The Chinese American Experience. San Francisco, CA: 1984.

Marable, M. Black Capitalism: Entrepreneurs, Consumers and the Historical Evolution of the Black Market. In: How Capitalism Underdeveloped Black America, pp. 133-67. Boston: South End Press, 1983.

Marshall, J. The Status of Black Business Franchising in Michigan. In: The State of Black Michigan: 1987, pp. 27-39. East Lansing, MI:

Urban Affairs Programs, Michigan State University, 1987.

McCareins, A. Survival in a Male Establishment: Black Women in
    Middle Management Positions in the Banking Industry. The Program on
    Women, Northwestern University, Evanston, IL.

Milloy, C. Sweet Inspiration [Sugar Puddin' dolls]. Washington Post
    November 30, 1986.

Min, Pyong Gap. Ethnic Business Enterprise: Korean Small Business in
    Atlanta. Staten Island, NY: Center for Migration Studies, 1988.

Murphy, E. L. Minority Business in Manufacturing. Review of Black
    Political Economy 4 (1974):31-46.

Oak, V. V. The Negro's Adventure in General Business. Westport, CT:
    Negro Universities Press, 1949.

Ofari, E. The Myth of Black Capitalism. New York: Monthly Review Press,
    1970.

Osborne, Alfred E., Jr. and Michael E. Granfield. The Potential of Black
    Capitalism Perspective. Pubic Policy 24 (Fall 1976):529-44.

Osthaus, C. L. Freedman, Philanthrophy, and Fraud: A History of the
    Freedman's Savings Bank. Urbana, IL: University of Illinois Press,
    1976.

Osthaus, C. R. The Rise and Fall of Jesse Binga, Black Financier.
    Journal of Negro History 58 (January 1973):39-60.

Parent, W. A Liberal Legacy: Blacks Blaming Themselves for Economic
    Failures. Journal of Black Studies 16 (September 1985).

Pierce, J. A. Negro Business and Business Education. Westport, CT:
    Negro Universities Press, orig. 1947.

Puth, R. C. Supreme Life: The History of a Negro Life Insurance
    Company. Doctoral dissertation, Northwestern University, 1967.

Puth, R. C. Supreme Life: The History of a Negro Life Insurance
    Company, 1919-1962. Business History Review 43 (1969):1-20.

Shanks, Hershel. Connections. Howard Squadron's Wedtech Troubles
    [Exploitation of minority-owned business]. Moment 14 (March 1989).

Simmons, C. W. Maggie Lena Walker and the Consolidated Bank and Trust
    Company [Richmond, VA]. Negro History Bulletin 38 (1975):345-9.

Spencer, C. A. Black Benevolent Societies and the Development of Black
    Insurance Companies in Nineteenth Century Alabama. Phylon 46 (Fall
    1985):251-61.

Stenzler, Y. Maryland Districts Restructure Procedures to Meet Minority
    Purchasing Goal. School Business Affairs 46 (August 1980):22-23.

Swinton, D. H. and J. Handy. The Determinants of the Growth of Black
    Owned Businesses: A Preliminary Analysis. Atlanta: Southern
    Center for Studies in Public Policy, Clark College, 1984.

Tate, C. Brimmer and Black Capitalism: An Analysis. Review of Black
    Political Economy (Spring-Summer 1970):84-90.

Thieblot, A. J., Jr. and L. P. Fletcher. Negro Employment in Finance: A
    Study of Racial Policies in Banking and Insurance. Philadelphia, PA:
    University of Pennsylvania Press, 1970.

Thomas, B. C. A Nineteenth Century Black Operated Shipyard, 1866-1884:
    Reflections Upon Its Inception and Ownership. Journal of Negro
    History 59 (1984):1-12.

Tolson, A. L. Historical and Modern Trends in Black Capitalism. Black
    Scholar 6 (1975):8-14.

Tucker, D. M. Black Pride and Negro Business in the 1920s: George
    Washington Lee of Memphis. Business History Review 43 (Winter
    1969):435-51.

Vowels, R. C. Atlanta Negro Business and the New Black Bourgeoisie.
    Atlanta Historical Bulletin 21 (Spring 1977):48-63.

Walker, J. E. K. Racism, Slavery, and Free Enterprise: Black
    Entrepreneurship in the United States before the Civil War. Business
    History Review 60 (Autumn 1986):343-82.

Washington, B. T. Proceedings of the National Negro Business League.
    Boston: J. R. Hamm, 1900.

Washington, B. T. The Negro in Business. New York: AMS Press, 1971
    [orig. 1907].

Weare, W. B. Black Business in the New South: The North Carolina Mutual
    Life Insurance Company, 1898-1935. Doctoral dissertation,
    University of North Carolina, 1970.

Weems, Robert E., Jr. The History of the Chicago Metropolitan Mutual
    Insurance Company: An Examination of Business as a Black Community
    Institution. Doctoral dissertation, University of Wisconsin, 1987.
    UMO # 8801507.

Wright, R. E. 'Black Capitalism.' Toward Controlled Development of Black
    America. Negro Digest (December 1969).

Business Bibliography

Barry, T. E. and others. Marketing and the Black Consumer: An Annotated
    Bibliography. Chicago: American Marketing Association, 1976.

58

Davis, L. G. Black Business, Employment, Economics and Finance in Urban
   America: A Selective Bibliography. [Exchange Bibliography No. 629].
   Monticello, IL: Council of Planning Librarians, 1974.

Davis, L. G. Black Capitalism in Urban America. [Exchange Bibliography
   No. 630]. Monticello, IL: Council of Planning Librarians, 1974.

Gilbert, A. L. and T. H. Countee, Jr. Black Banks. Bulletin of
   Bibliography 28 (April-June 1972):60-72.

Halliday, T. Y. The Negro in the Field of Business: An Annotated
   Bibliography (third edition). Washington, D.C.: Institute for
   Minority Business Education, Howard University, 1975.

Hill, G. H. Black Business and Economics. A Selected Bibliography. New
   York: Garland, 1985.

Minority Business Enterprise: A Bibliography. Washington, D.C. Office
   of Minority Business Enterprise, U.S. Dept. of Commerce, 1973.

The Negro in Business: A Bibliography, 1935. Washington, D.C.: Negro
   Affairs Division, U.S. Dept. of Commerce, 1935.

Pressley, M. M. Selected Bibliography of Readings and References
   Regarding Marketing to Black America. [Exchange Bibliography No.
   671]. Monticello, IL: Council of Planning Librarians, 1974.

Winters, W. R., Jr. and others. Minority Enterprise and Marketing: An
   Annotated Bibliography. Monticello, IL: Council of Planning
   Librarians, 1971.

10. Children, Effects on

The day will dawn when mother must explain gently but clearly why the little girls next door do not want to play with 'niggers'; what the real cause of the teachers' unsympathetic attitude, and how people may ride in the backs of streetcars and the smoker end of trains, and still be people, honest high-minded souls.

- W. E. B. Du Bois, "Of Children," 1912.

Aboud, F. Children and Prejudice. The Development of Ethnic Awareness and Identity. New York: Blackwell, 1988.

Alexander, R. What is a Racist Book. Interracial Books for Children 3 (Autumn 1970).

Arnold, M. C. The Effects of Racial Identity on Self-Concept in Interracial Children. Doctoral dissertation, Saint Louis University, 1984. UMO # 8418608.

Balch, P. and K. Paulsen. Methodology for the Study of the Development of Racism [Preschool children]. ERIC ED 210 412.

Banfield, B. How Racism Takes Root. UNESCO Courier March 1979.

Banks, J. A. Reducing Prejudice in Students: Theory, Research, and Strategies. February 3, 1982. ERIC ED 215 930.

Barsh, R. L. Indian Child Welfare Act of 1978: A Critical Analysis. Hastings Law Journal 31 (1980).

Becker, J. Racism in Children's and Young People's Literature in the Western World. Journal of Peace Research (1973).

Berry, G. L., and C. Mitchell-Kernan. Television and the Socialization of the Minority Child. New York: Academic Press, 1982.

Beuf, A. H. Red Children in White America [Native American children]. Philadelphia, PA: University of Pennsylvania Press, 1977.

Bidol, P. M. 'A Rap on Race' - A Mini-Lecture on Racism Awareness. Interracial Books for Children 5 (1974):9-10.

Bock, R. D. and E. G. J. Moore. Advantage and Disadvantage: A Profile of American Youth. Hillsdale, NJ: L. Erlbawm Associates, 1986.

Boyd, B. M. Growing Up Racist. Village Voice August 5-11, 1981.

CIBC Racism and Sexism Resource Center for Educators. Human and Anti-Human Values in Children's Books, 1976. [Racism and Sexism Resource Center for Educators, 1841 Broadway].

Comer, J. P. Black Children in a Racist Society. <u>Current</u> 162 (1974):53-56.

Committee for Economic Development <u>Children in Need: Investment Strategies for the Educationally Disadvantaged</u>. New York: CED, 1987.

Cramer, J. Your Kids Are the Target When the Klan Comes Along. <u>American School Board Journal</u> 169 (May 1982):23-27.

The Crime of Being a Chicano Child. <u>Ideal</u> February 1, 1970.

Da Costa, G. A. Orphans and Outlaws: Some Impacts of Racism. <u>Multiculturalism</u> 2 (1978):4-7.

Darlington, R. B. Long-term Effects of Preschool Programs. <u>In</u>: Ulric Neisser (ed.), <u>The School Achievement of Minority Children</u>. Hillsdale, NJ: Erlbaum, 1986.

Davis, Allison. The Socialization of the American Negro Child. <u>Journal of Negro Education</u> 8 (July 1939).

Derrick, E. W. Effects of Evacuation of Japanese American Youth. <u>School Review</u> 55 (June 1947):356-62.

Dieterich, D. Racism, Sexism in Children's Literature. <u>Reading Teacher</u> 28 (December 1974):346-349.

Edelman, M. W. <u>A Call for Action to Make Our Nation Safe for Children: A Briefing Book on the Status of American Children in 1988</u>. Washington, D.C.: Children's Defense Fund, 1988.

Gates, D. and others. Lessons in Cruelty. ["How we teach children about the dark side of human history"]. <u>Newsweek</u> May 30, 1988.

Gibbs, Jewelle T. <u>Young, Black and Male in America</u>. Dover, MA: Auburn House, 1988.

Gibbs, Jewelle T., Larke N. Huang, and others. <u>Children of Color. Psychological Interventions with Minority Youth</u>. San Francisco, CA: Jossey-Bass, 1989.

Gibson, E. G. <u>The Black Image in Children's Fiction: A Content Analysis of Racist Content, Black Experience and Primary Audience in Children's Books Published Between 1950-1970 and 1971-1982</u>. Doctoral dissertation, Temple University, 1985. UMO # 852108.

Gladwin, T., and A. Saidin. <u>Slaves of the White Myth: The Psychology of Neocolonialism</u>. Atlantic Highlands, NJ: Humanities Press, 1980.

Hale-Berson, J. Cultural Context for Child Care in the Black Community. <u>In</u>: Jeffrey Lande, Sandra Scarr and Nina Guzenhauser (eds.), <u>Caring for Children. Challenge to America</u>. Hillsdale, NJ: Erlbaum, 1989.

Hall, S. Teaching Race. <u>Early Child Development and Care</u> 10 (1983):259-273.

Harris, A. _A World Unsuspected: Portraits of Southern Childhood_. Chapel Hill, NC: University of North Carolina Press, 1987.

Kafka, S. _I Will Always Stay Me: Writings of Migrant Children_. Austin: Texas Monthly Press, 1982.

Klein, G. _Reading Into Racism. Bias in Children's Literature and Learning Materials_. London: Routledge and Kegan Paul, 1986.

Kunjufu, J. _Countering the Conspiracy to Destroy Black Boys_, 2 vols. (Revised edition). Chicago: African American Images, 1985.

Larrick, N. The All-White World of Children's Books. _Saturday Review_ (September 1965).

Larson, R. G. Racism in Kindergarten? _Elementary School Journal_ 69 (1969):180-185.

Lattimer, B. I. Children's Books and Racism. _Black Scholar_ 4 (May-June 1973):21-27.

Lightfoot, C. Racism in U.S. School Textbooks. _Political Affairs_ 52 (June 1973):17-29.

Lubek, S. _Sandbox Society. Early Education in Black and White America - A Comparative Ethnography_. Philadelphia, PA: Falmer Press, 1985.

MacCann, D. and G. Woodward (eds.) _The Black American in Books for Children: Readings in Racism_ (second edition). Metuchen, NJ: Scarecrow Press, 1985.

MacCann, D. and G. Woodward (eds.) _Cultural Conformity in Books for Children: Further Readings in Racism_. Metuchen, NJ: Scarecrow Press, 1977.

Madsen. Jane M. Historical Images of the Black Child in Children's Literature and Their Contemporary Reflections. _Minority Views_ 4 (Fall 1980)1-36.

March, C. C., Jr. Old Assumptions and New Packages: Racism Educational Models, and Black Children. _Young Children_ 33 (September 1978):45-51.

McAdoo, H. P. and J. L. McAdoo (eds.) _Black Children. Social, Educational, and Parental Environments_. Newbury Park, CA: Sage, 1985.

McLaurin, M. A. _Separate Pasts: Growing Up White in the Segregated South_. Athens, GA: University of Georgia Press, 1987.

McLoyd, V. C. and S. M. Randolph. Secular Trends in the Study of Afro-American Children: A Review of Child Development [1936-1980]. _Monographs of the Society for Research in Child Development_ 50

Morgan, T. The World Ahead, Black Parents Prepare Their Children for Pride and Prejudice. New York Times Magazine (October 27, 1985).

Nieto, S. Self-Affirmation or Self-destruction: The Image of Puerto Ricans in Children's Literature Written in English. In: Asela Rodriguez de Laguna (ed.), Images and Identities. The Puerto Rican in Two World Contexts. New Brunswick, NJ: Transaction Books, 1987.

Orphanages: Racial Lines Divide Many [Oxford, N.C.]. New York Times November 28, 1986.

Phinney, Jean S. and Mary Jane Rotheram. Children's Ethnic Socialization. Pluralism and Development. Newbury Park, CA: Sage, 1987.

Pierce, C. M. Poverty and Racism as They Affect Children. In: I. N. Berlin (ed.), Advocacy for Child Mental Health. New York: Brunner/Mazel, 1975.

Porter, C. P. Socialization, Black School-age Children and the Color Case Hierarchy. Doctoral dissertation, University of Arizona, 1985. UMO # 8522821.

Powell, G. and others. The Psychological Development of Minority Group Children. Larchmont, NY: Brunner/Mazel, 1983.

Preiswerk, R. (ed.) The Slant of the Pen. Racism in Children's BOoks. Geneva: World Council of Churches, 1979.

Racism and the Black Child. Multicultural Teaching 1 (1983):45-48.

Racism in Children's and School Textbooks. Programme to Combat Racism, World Council of Churches, Geneva.

Racist and Sexist Images in Children's Books [Papers on Children's Literature No. 1]. Writers and Readers Publishing Cooperative, n.d., London.

Rawson, A. Racism in Children's Books, 1980. English Language Centre, Tile Kiln Lane, London N13, England.

Richardson, B. B. Racism and Childrearing: A Study of Black Mothers. Doctoral dissertation, Claremont Graduate School, 1981.

Rosenberg, M. B. Living in Two Worlds: The Story of Bi-racial Children. New York: Lathrop, Lee and Shepard Books, 1986.

Sexism and Racism: Different Issues? Interracial Books for Children 5 (1974):11.

Simmons, P. Handling Racist Incident: A Case History. Interracial Books for Children Bulletin 11, nos. 3-4 (1980).

Sims, R. Shadow and Substance. Afro-American Experience in Contemporary Children's Fiction. Urbana, IL: National Council of Teachers of English, 1982.

Sims, R. Children's Books about Blacks: A Mid-Eighties Status Report. In: G. Sernick (ed.), <u>Children's</u> <u>Literature</u> <u>Review</u>, pp. 8-14. Detroit, MI: Gale, 1985.

Sisters Desert 'Racist Institution' [St. Raymond's Elementary School, Detroit, MI]. <u>America</u> (February 1971).

Spencer, M. Black Children's Ethnic Identity Formation: Risk and Resilience of Castelike Minorities. <u>In</u>: Mary Jane Rotheram (ed.), <u>Children's</u> <u>Ethnic</u> <u>Socialization:</u> <u>Pluralism</u> <u>and</u> <u>Development</u>. Newbury Park, CA: Sage, 1987.

Spurlock, J. Some Consequences of Racism for Children. <u>In</u>: Charles V. Willie, Bernard M. Kramer and Bertram S. Brown (eds.), <u>Racism</u> <u>and</u> <u>Mental</u> <u>Health</u>, pp. 147-163. Pittsburgh, PA: University of Pittsburgh Press, 1973.

Spurlock, J. Development of Self-concept in Afro-American Children. <u>Hospital</u> <u>and</u> <u>Community</u> <u>Psychiatry</u> 37 (January 1986):66-70.

Sung, B. L. <u>The</u> <u>Adjustment</u> <u>of</u> <u>Chinese</u> <u>Immigrant</u> <u>Children</u> <u>in</u> <u>New</u> <u>York</u> <u>City</u>. Staten Island, NY: Center for Migration Studies, 1987.

Tait, J. W. <u>Some</u> <u>Aspects</u> <u>of</u> <u>the</u> <u>Effect</u> <u>of</u> <u>the</u> <u>Dominant</u> <u>American</u> <u>Culture</u> <u>Upon</u> <u>Children</u> <u>of</u> <u>Italian-born</u> <u>Parents</u>. New York: Columbia University Press, 1942.

Trentadue, J. C. and M. A. DeMontigny. The Indian Child Welfare Act of 1978: A Practioner's Perspective. <u>North</u> <u>Dakota</u> <u>Law</u> <u>Review</u> 62 (Fall 1986):487-537.

Uribe, O., Jr. and J. S Martinez. <u>Analyzing</u> <u>Children's</u> <u>Books</u> <u>from</u> <u>a</u> <u>Chicano</u> <u>Perspective</u>, 1975. ERIC ED 129 458.

Webb, G. B. <u>An</u> <u>Analysis</u> <u>of</u> <u>Change</u> <u>in</u> <u>Sociocultural</u> <u>Integration</u> <u>Symbolism</u> <u>in</u> <u>a</u> <u>Sample</u> <u>of</u> <u>Middle</u> <u>and</u> <u>Secondary</u> <u>School</u> <u>American</u> <u>History</u> <u>Textbooks</u>. Doctoral dissertation, George Peabody College for Teachers. UMO # 8619643.

West, H. I. Telling a Black Child About Racism. <u>Washington</u> <u>Post</u> September 9, 1973.

Yazzie, N. G. Development of Indian Child is Different. <u>Navajo</u> <u>Times</u> 19 (May 4, 1978):10, 38.

Yuill, P. Little Black Sambo: The Continuing Controversy. <u>School</u> <u>Library</u> <u>Journal</u> 22 (March 1976):71-75.

Zelizer, V. A. <u>Pricing</u> <u>the</u> <u>Priceless</u> <u>Child.</u> <u>The</u> <u>Changing</u> <u>Social</u> <u>Value</u> <u>of</u> <u>Children</u>. New York: Basic Books, 1985.

11. Citizenship

*... My ancestors ... baked bread for George Washington's troops
when they crossed the Delaware, and my own father was a slave.
I stand here struggling for the rights of my people to be full
citizens in this country and they are not.*

> \- Paul Robeson, "The House Un-American Activities
> Committee," 1956.

Baker, Ray Stannard. Following the Color Line: American Negro
    Citizenship in the Progressive Era. New York: Doubleday, Page,
    1908.

Berry, Mary F. Military Necessity and Civil Rights Policy: Black
    Citizenship and the Constitution, 1861-1868. Port Washington, NY:
    1977.

Carter, E., II. A 'Wild Irishman' under Every Federalist's Bed:
    Naturalization in Philadelphia, 1789-1806. Pennsylvania Magazine of
    History and Biography 94 (1970):331-46.

Douglass, F. Citizenship of Colored Americans. Douglass' Monthly
    (February 1863).

Du Bois, W. E. B. (editorial supervisor). An Appeal to the World: A
    Statement on the Denial of Human Rights to Minorities in the Case of
    Citizens of Negro Descent in the United States of America and an
    Appeal to the United Nations for Redress. New York: NAACP, 1947.

Du Bois, W. E. B. The Negro Citizen. In: Charles S. Johnson (ed.), The
    Negro in American Civilization, pp. 461-70. New York: Holt, 1930.

Gerson, L. L. The Hyphenate in Recent American Politics and Diplomacy.
    Lawrence, KS.

Harrington, M. Loyalties: Dual and Divided. In: Stephan Thernstrom
    (ed.), Harvard Encyclopedia of American Ethnic Groups, pp. 676-86.
    Cambridge, MA: Harvard University Press.

Hirabayashi, L. R. and J. A. Hirabayashi. A Reconsideration of the
    United States Military's Role in the Violation of Japanese-American
    Citizenship Rights. In: Winston A. van Horne (ed.), Ethnicity and
    War. Milwaukee, WI: Amer. Ethnic Studies Coord. Comm., Urb. Corridor
    Consort. U.Wis.Sys.

Ichioka, Y. The Early Japanese Immigrant Quest for Citizenship: The
    Background of the 1922 Ozawa Case. Amerasia Journal 4 (1977):1-22.

Karst, Kenneth L. Belonging to America. Equal Citizenship and the
    Constitution. New Haven, CT: Yale University Press, 1989.

Kettner, J. H. The Development of American Citizenship, 1608-1870.

Chapel Hill, NC: University of North Carolina Press, 1978.

King, Richard H. Citizenship and Self-respect: The Experience of
     Politics in the Civil Rights Movement. _Journal of American Studies_
     2 (April 1988):7-24.

Langston, J. M. _Freedom and Citizenship_. Washington, D.C.

McGovney, D. O. American Citizenship [Racial factors]. _Columbia Law
     Review_ 11 (1911):231-50, 326-47.

McGovney, D. O. Race Discrimination in Naturalization. _Iowa Law Bulletin_
     8 (1923):129-61, 211-44.

O'Brien, John T. _From Bondage to Citizenship: The Richmond Black
     Community, 1865-1867_. Doctoral dissertation, University of
     Rochester, 1974.

Oldendorf, S. B. _Highlander Folk School and the South Carolina Sea Island
     Citizenship Schools: Implications for the Social Studies_ [1957-1961].
     Doctoral dissertation, University of Kentucky, 1987. UMO # 8715945.

Pierce, E. L. _Enfranchisement and Citizenship_. Boston: Roberts Bros.

Schweninger, L. Black Citizenship and the Republican Party in
     Reconstruction Alabama. _Alabama Review_ 29 (April 1976):83-101.

Spahr, C. B. The Negro As a Citizen. _Outlook_ 62 (July 1, 1899):490-99.

Ueda, R. Naturalization and Citizenship. _In_: Stephan Thernstrom (ed.),
     Harvard Encyclopedia of American Ethnic Groups, pp. 734-48.
     Cambridge, MA: Harvard University Press.

Walters, R. White Nationalism in the United States. _Without Prejudice_
     1 (Fall 1987).

Woodson, C. G. Fifty Years of Negro Citizenship as Qualified by the
     United States Supreme Court. _Journal of Negro History_ 6 (1921).

Young, B. D. The American Indian: Citizenship Captivity. _Saturday Review_
     48 (December 11, 1965):25.

12. Civil Rights

The overwhelming lesson of the civil rights movement which found expression in Black Power was that racism was not an aberration of the American way of life. It was the American way of life.

- Julius Lester, Race Relations Reporter, September 1974 (emphasis added).

Abernathy, R. The Nonviolent Movement: The Past, the Present, and the Future. In: Rhoda L. Goldstein (ed.), Black Life and Culture in the United States, pp. 180-209. New York: Crowell, 1971.

Adams, P. L. Fighting for Democracy in St. Louis: Civil Rights during World War II. Missouri Historical Review 80 (October 1985):58-75.

Alvarez Gonzalez, Jose J. La proteccion de los derechos humanos en Puerto Rico. Revista Juridica de la Universidad de Puerto Rico 57 (Winter-Spring 1988):133-81.

Anderson, A. B., and G. W. Pickering. Confronting the Color Line. The Broken Promise of the Civil Rights Movement in Chicago. Athens, GA: University of Georgia Press, 1986.

Bardolph, Richard (ed.) The Civil Rights Record: Black Americans and the Law, 1840-1970. New York: Cornell, 1970.

Baxter, Gregory W. Analysis of Casehandling under Section 706 (c) of the Civil Rights Act of 1964. Doctoral dissertation, Nova University, 1988. UMO # 8812787.

Beardslee, W. R. The Way Out Must Lead In: Life Histories in the Civil Rights Movement. Atlanta, GA: Center for Research in Social Change, Emory University, 1977.

Benjamin, Playthell. Jive at Five. Village Voice July 19, 1988. [Al Sharpton, Alton Maddox, Vernon Mason and civil rights in New York City].

Blackstock, N. Labor Struggles in the Changing South. The Impact of the Civil Rights Movement. International Socialist Review (September 1979):15-20.

Bland, R. W. The Collective Struggle for Negro Rights: 1915-1940. North Carolina Central Law Review 2 (Spring 1970).

Blassingame, J. W. The Revolution that Never Was. The Civil Rights Movement, 1950-1980. Perspective 14 (September 1982):3-15.

Blumberg, R. L. Civil Rights: The 1960s Freedom Struggle. Boston: Twayne, 1984.

Branch, Taylor. Parting the Waters: America in the King Years, 1954-

1963. New York: Simon and Schuster, 1988.

Brauer, C. M. (ed.) Civil Rights During the Kennedy Administration [47 microfilm reels]. Frederick, MD: University Publications of America, 1987.

Bridges, R. D. Equality Deferred: Civil Rights for Illinois Blacks, 1865-1885. Journal of the Illinois State Historical Society 74 (Spring 1981):82-108.

Brown, Ira V. Pennsylvania and the Rights of the Negro, 1865-1887. Pennsylvania History 28 (January 1961):45-57.

Bullock, C., III and C. Lamb (eds.) Implementation of Civil Rights Policy. Monterey, CA: Brooks/Cole Publishing Co., 1984.

Cantarow, E., and S. G. O'Malley. Ella Baker: Organizing for Civil Rights. In: Moving the Mountain, pp. 52-93. Old Westbury, NY: Feminist Press, 1980.

Carmichael, S. Toward Black Liberation. Massachusetts Review 7 (Autumn 1966):639-51.

Carson, C. In Struggle: SNCC and the Black Awakening of the 1960's. Cambridge, MA: Harvard University Press, 1981.

Chambers, E. W. We Have Marched, We Have Cried, We Have Prayed. Ebony (April 1968).

Chandler, Robert J. Friends in Time of Need: Republicans and Black Civil Rights in California During the Civil War Era. Arizona and the West 22 (Winter 1982):319-40.

Citizen's Commission on Civil Rights. One Nation, Indivisible. Washington, D.C.: The Commission, 1989. [Charges lack of civil rights enforcement].

Clark, K. B. The Civil Rights Movement: Momentum and Organization. Daedalus 95 (Winter 1966):239-67.

Clark, K. B. and K. Clark-Harris. What Do Blacks Really Want? Ebony (January 1985).

Cluster, D. They Should Have Served that Cup of Coffee: Seven Radicals Remember the 60s. Boston: South End Press, 1979.

Colburn, D. R. Racial Change and Community Crisis: St. Augustine, Florida, 1877- 1980. New York: Columbia University Press, 1985.

Cooper, J. P., Jr. The Rise of George C. Wallace: Alabama Politics and Policy, 1958-1966. [Doctoral dissertation, Vanderbilt University, 1987] UMO # 8714420.

Crawford, Vicki L. "We Shall Not Be Moved": Black Female Activists in the Mississippi Civil Rights Movement, 1960-1965. Doctoral dissertation, Emory University, 1987. UMO # 8803286.

Du Bois, W. E. B. Civil Rights Legislation before and after the Passage
of the 14th Amendment. Lawyers' Guild Review 6 (November-December
1946):640-42.

Du Bois, W. E. B. 'Negro Is Still Slave,' Declares Prof. Du Bois.
Cincinnati Times-Star December 5, 1910.

Dykstra, R. R. White Man, Black Laws: Territorial Iowans and Civil
Rights, 1838- 1843. Annals of Iowa 46 (Fall 1982):403-40.

Eagles, C. W. (ed.) The Civil Rights Movement in America: Essays.
Jackson: University Press of Mississippi, 1986.

Edley, C., Jr. The Moral Foundations of Civil Rights Policy. New York:
1986.

Edwards, H. Black Students. New York: Free Press, 1970.

Fager, C. E. Uncertain Resurrection: The Poor People's Washington
Campaign. Grand Rapids, MI: Eerdmans, 1969.

Farmer, J. Where Does the Civil Rights Movement Stand Today? Humanist
(November-December 1985):5-10.

Garofalo, Reebee. The Impact of the Civil Rights Movement on Popular
Music. Radical America 21 (November-December 1987), mailed March
1989.

Garrow, D. J. Black Civil Rights During the Eisenhower Administration.
Constitutional Commentary 3 (Summer 1986):601-13.

Garrow, D. J. Protest at Selma: Martin Luther King, Jr. and the Voting
Rights Act of 1965. New Haven, CT: Yale University Press, 1978.

Gerlach, E. Status of Civil Rights in Texas, Vol. II: An Employment
Profile in San Antonio, 1968-1978. A Case Study. January 1980. ERIC
ED 188 820.

Gilliam, R. White Racism and the Civil Rights Movement. Yale Review 62
(June 1973):520-543.

Glen, John M. Highlander. No Ordinary School, 1932-1962. Lexington:
University Press, of Kentucky, 1988.

Godwin, John L. The Case of the Wilmington Ten: From Civil Rights to
Black Nationalism, 1898 to 1980. Master's thesis, University of
South Carolina, 1988.

Grossman, E. The Unhappy History of Civil Rights Legislation [Laws of
1870s]. Michigan Law Review 50 (1952):1333-43.

Haines, H. H. Black Radicalization and the Funding of Civil Rights: 1957-
1970. Social Problems 32 (October 1984):31-43.

Haines, H. H. Black Radicals and the Civil Rights Mainstream, 1954-1970. Knoxville, TN: University of Tennessee Press, 1988.

Hamilton, C. V. The Politics of Civil Rights. New York: Random House, 1968.

Hardin, S. C. Civil Rights and White Resistance in the Black Belt: A Case Study of Marengo County, Alabama, 1954-1956. Master's thesis, University of South Alabama, 1987. UMO # MA 1330983.

Harding, S. Reconstructing Order through Action: Jim Crow and the Southern Civil Rights Movement. In: Charles C. Bright and Susan Harding (eds.), Statemaking and Social Movements: Essays in History and Theory. Ann Arbor: University of Michigan Press, 1984.

Harrison, E. Civil Rights in Texas [Series of articles]. Fort Worth Star-Telegram June 19-22, 1982.

Harvey, J. C. Black Civil Rights During the Johnson Administration. Jackson: University and College Press of Mississippi, 1973.

Hoffman, E. D. The Genesis of the Modern Movement for Equal Rights in South Carolina, 1930-1939. Journal of Negro History 44 (October 1959):346-69.

Jackson, M. C., Jr. The Status of Civil Rights in Michigan. In: Frances S. Thomas (ed.) The State of Black Michigan: 1987. East Lansing, MI: Urban Affairs Programs, Michigan State University, 1987.

Jaffe, A. Grenada, Mississippi. New South 21 (Fall 1966):15-28.

Juhnke, W. E. (ed.) President Truman's Committee on Civil Rights [10 microfilm reels]. Frederick, MD: University Publications of America, 1987.

Kaczorowski, R. J. To Begin the Nation Anew: Congress, Citizenship, and Civil Rights after the Civil War. American Historical Review 92 (February 1987):45-68.

Lawson, S. F., (ed.) Civil Rights During the Johnson Administration [41 microfilm reels]. Frederick, MD: University Publications of America, 1987.

Lewis, D. L. Martin Luther King, Jr., and the Promise of Nonviolent Populism. In: John Hope Franklin and August Meier (eds.), Black Leaders of the Twentieth Century, pp. 277-303. Urbana: University of Illinois Press, 1982.

Lim, G. Edison Uno, Nisei Civil Rights Advocate: A Profile. Integrateducation 15 (October-November 1977).

Lytle, Clifford. The History of the Civil Rights Bill of 1964. Journal of Negro History 51 (1966):275-96.

Marable, Manning. _Race, Reform, and Rebellion. The Second Reconstruction in Black America, 1945-1982_. Jackson, MI: University Press of Mississippi, 1984.

Matusow, A. J. From Civil Rights to Black Power: The Case of SNCC, 1960-1966. _In_: Barton J. Bernstein and Allen J. Matusow (eds.), _Twentieth Century America: Recent Interpretations_, Rev. ed., pp. 494-521. New York: Harcourt Brace Jovanovich, 1972.

McAdam, Doug. The Decline of the Civil Rights Movement. _In_: Jo Freeman (ed.), _Social Movements of the Sixties and Seventies_, pp. 298-319. New York: Longman, 1983.

McAdam, Doug. _Freedom Summer_ [Mississippi, 1964]. New York: Oxford University Press, 1989.

McClain, Charles J., Jr. The Chinese Struggle for Civil Rights in Nineteenth Century America; The First Phase, 1850-1870. _California Law Review_ 72 (1984):529-68.

McClure, P. The Erosion of Civil Rights Enforcement. _Black Scholar_ 17 (May-June 1986):10-18.

McCoy, D. R., and R. T. Ruetten. The Civil Rights Movement: 1940-1954. _Midwest Quarterly_ 11 (October 1969):11-34.

McElhone, P. S. _The Civil Right Activities of the Louisville Branch of the National Association for the Advancement of Colored People: 1914-1960_. Master's thesis, University of Louisville, 1976. UMO # 1309200.

McPherson, James Alan. Burning Memories, Mississippi 1963. _New York Times_ January 14, 1989.

Meier, A. and E. Rudwick. _CORE: A Study in the Civil Rights Movement 1942-1968_. New York: Oxford, 1973.

Meier, A. and E. Rudwick. _Congress of Racial Equality Papers, 1959-1976_ [80 microfilm reels]. Frederick, MD: University Publications of America, 1987.

Morris, A. D. Black Southern Student Sit-In Movement: An Analysis of Internal Organization. _American Sociological Review_ 46 (December 1981):744-67.

Morris, A. D. _The Origins of the Civil Rights Movement_. New York: Free Press, 1984.

Moses, B. Mississippi: 1961-1962. _Liberation_ 14 (January 1970):7-17.

Murray, Hugh. Change in the South. _Journal of Ethnic Studies_ 16 (Summer 1988):119-36.

Myrdal, Gunnar. Social Trends in America and Strategic Approaches to the Negro Problem. _Phylon_ 9 (1948):196-214.

Namorato, M. V. (ed.) Have We Overcome? Race Relations Since Brown.
MI: University Press of Mississippi, 1979.

Nash, D. Inside the Sit-Ins and Freedom Rides. In: Mathew Ahmann (ed.),
The New Negro, pp. 43-60. Notre Dame, IN: Fides Publishers, 1961.

Norrell, R. J. Reaping the Whirlwind: The Civil Rights Movement in
Tuskegee. New York: Knopf, 1985.

O'Dell, J. H. Climin' Jacob's Ladder: The Life and Times of the Freedom
Movement. Freedomways 9 (Winter 1969):7-13.

O'Dell, J. H. On the Transition from Civil Rights to Civil Equality.
Freedomways 18 (Fourth Quarter 1978).

Oral Histories of the Johnson Administration [763 microfiches]. Frederick,
MD: University Publications of America, 1986.

Orum, A. M. Black Students in Protest: A Study of the Origins of the
Black Student Movement. Washington, D.C.: American Sociological
Association, 1973.

Panetta, L. E., and P. Gall. Bring Us Together. The Nixon Team and the
Civil Right Retreat. Philadelphia, PA: Lippincott, 1971.

Peake, T. Keeping the Dream Alive: A History of the Southern Leadership
Conference from King to the 1980s. New York: Peter Lang, 1987.

Peck, James. Freedom Rides - 1947 and 1961. In: A. P. Hare and H. H.
Blumberg (eds.), Nonviolent Direct Action. American Cases: Social
Psychological Analyses. Washington, D.C.: Corpus Books, 1968.

Petrof, J. V. The Effect of Student Boycotts upon the Purchasing Habits
of Negro Families in Atlanta, Georgia. Phylon 24 (1963):266-70.

President's Commission On Campus Unrest. The Black Student Movement, pp.
91-116, In: The Report ...Campus Unrest. Washington, D.C.: GPO,
1970.

Project, G. P. L. O. H. Greensboro Sit-ins. Southern Exposure 9 (Spring
1981):23-28.

Przybyszewski, Linda C. A. Judge Lorenzo Sawyer and the Chinese: Civil
Rights Decisions in the Ninth Circuit. W. Legal Hist. 1 (Winter-
Spring 1988):23-56.

Raines, H. My Soul Is Rested: Movement Days in the Deep South
Remembered. Penguin, 1983.

Redding, S. The Black Youth movement. American Scholar (Autumn
1969).

Rollins, J. Part of a Whole: The Interdependence of the Civil Rights
Movement and Other Social Movements. Phylon 47 (Spring 1986):61-70.

Romo, R. George I. Sanchez and the Civil Rights Movement. La Raza Law Journal 1 (Fall 1986):342-62.

Rose, Kenneth W. The Politics of Social Reform in Cleveland, 1945-1967: Civil Rights, Welfare Rights, and the Response of Civic Leaders. Doctoral dissertation, Case Western Reserve University, 1988. UMO # 881957.

Ruben, David. Veterans of Southern Wars. Boston Globe Magazine June 19, 1988. [Reunion of Student Nonviolent Coordinating Committee (SNCC)].

Rustin, B. Down the Line. Chicago: Quadrangle Books, 1971.

Salter, John R., Jr. Jackson, Mississippi: An American Chronicle of Struggle and Schism. Melbourne, FL: Robert E. Krieger, 1987. [1962-1963].

Schmid, Carol L. The Supreme Court, Civil Rights and Racial Equality: A Sociological Interpretation. Research in Law, Deviance and Social Control 9 (1988):63-84.

Sellers, Cleveland L., Jr. The Civil Rights Movement [1954-1968]. Doctoral dissertation, University of North Carolina at Greensboro, 1987. UMO # 8803795.

Sitkoff, H. The Civil Rights Movement in the 20th Century. New York: Praeger, 1974.

Sitkoff, H. A New Deal for Blacks: The Emergence of Civil Rights as a National Issue. New York: Oxford, 1978.

Sowell, T. Civil Rights: Rhetoric or Reality. New York: Morrow, 1984.

Stevans, L. K. and others. Civil Rights Legislation and Racial Employment Differentials. Review of Black Political Economy 13 (Winter 1984-85).

The Student Protest Movement: A Recapitulation. Atlanta: Southern Regional Council, September 29, 1961.

U.S. Commission On Civil Rights, Iowa Advisory Committee. Implementation of Federal Civil Rights Laws in Iowa: Non-discrimination in the Block Grants and Minority Business Participation. Washington, D.C.: The Commission, September 1983.

U.S. Commission On Civil Rights, Montana, North Dakota, and Committees, South Dakota Advisory. Indian Civil Rights Issues in Montana, North Dakota, and South Dakota. Washington, D.C.: The Commission, 1974.

U.S. Commission On Civil Rights, Texas State Advisory Committee. Texas - the State of Civil Rights Ten Years Later, 1968-1978. A Report. Washington, D.C.: GPO, 1980.

Von Hoffman, N. Mississippi Notebook. New York: David White, 1965.

Washington Council of Lawyers. Reagan Civil Rights: The First Twenty Months. <u>Human Rights Annual</u> 1 (1983):117-71.

Watters, P. <u>Down to Now: Reflections on the Southern Civil Rights Movement</u>. New York: Pantheon, 1971.

Winfrey, R. H. <u>Civil Rights and the American Indian: Through the 1960s</u>. Doctoral dissertation, University of Oklahoma, 1986. UMO # 8617416.

Woodward, C. V. What Happened to the Civil Rights Movement? <u>Harper's</u> (January 1967).

Civil Rights Bibliography

Hill, G. H. <u>Civil Rights Organizations and Leaders. An Annotated Bibliography</u>. New York: Garland, 1986.

[See also sections 1, 32, 34, and 44]

13. Class Structure

The colored group is not yet divided into capitalists and laborers. There are only the beginnings of such a division ... Today to a very large extent our laborers are our capitalists and our capitalists are our laborers. Our small class of well-to-do men have come to affluence largely through manual toil and have never been physically or mentally separated from the toilers. Our professional classes are sons and daughters of porters, washerwomen, and laborers.

- W. E. B. Du Bois, "The Class Struggle," 1921.

Abu-Amr, A. Racism and Class National Struggle. Master's thesis, Howard University, 1982.

Altschuler, G. C. Race, Ethnicity, and Class in American Social Thought, 1865-1919. Arlington Heights, IL: Harlan Davidson, Inc., 1982.

Anderson, S. E. Black Students: Racial Consciousness and the Class Struggle, 1960-1976. Black Scholar 8 (January-February 1977):35-43.

Barrera, M. Race and Class in the Southwest: A Theory of Racial Inequality. Notre Dame, IN: University of Notre Dame Press, 1979.

Barsh, R. L. Plains Indian Agrarianism and Class Conflict. Great Plains Quarterly 7 (1987):83-90.

Beatty, J. A Cultural Encounter [Middle class Blacks]. Boston Globe Magazine November 17, 1985.

Bennett, L., Jr. Black Bourgeoisie Revisited. Ebony 28 (August 1973):50-55.

Bernstein, R. 20 Years After the Kerner Report: Three Societies, All Separate. New York Times February 29, 1988.

Billingham, G. L. A Study of Social Class Differentiation in the Afro-American Community. Doctoral dissertation, New York University, 1963.

Blumberg, P. Inequality in an Age of Decline. New York: Oxford University Press, 1980.

Bonacich, E. Class Approaches to Ethnicity and Race. Insurgent Sociologist 10 (Fall 1980):9-23.

Borrego, J. G. Capitalist Accumulation and Revolutionary Accumulation: The Context for Chicano Struggle. Doctoral dissertation, University of California, Berkeley, 1978. UMO # 7904383.

Boston, Thomas D. Race, Class and Conservatism. Winchester, MA: Unwin Hyman, 1988.

Bragg, Pa,. The Role of the Black Middle Class. California Aggie (UC Davis) May 9, 1988.

Burton, O. V. Class, Conflict, and Consensus: Antebellum Southern Community Studies. Westport, CT.: Greenwood, 1982.

Bussard, Robert L. The 'Dangerous Class' of Marx and Engels: The Rise of the Idea of the Lumpenproletariat. History of European Ideas 8 (1987):675-92.

Campos, R., and Others. Puerto Rico: identidad nacional y clases sociales. Rio Piedras: Huracan, 1979.

Cannon, L. W., and R. Vanneman. Class Perceptions in the Black Community. Memphis, TN: Center for Research on Women, Memphis State University, 1984.

Carrion, J. M. The Petty Bourgeoisie in Puerto Rico. Doctoral dissertation, Rutgers University, 1978. UMO # 7910371.

Carson, E. D. The Black Underclass Concept: Self-Help vs. Government Intervention. American Economic Review 76 (May 1986).

Chang, H. Race and Class. In: P. Leim and E. Montague (eds.), Toward a Marxist Theory of Racism: Two Essays by Harry Chang. Review of Radical Political Economics 17 (1985):34-45.

Chang, W. B. C. The Myth of Chinese Success in Hawaii. Hawaii Pono 1 (October 1971):59-76.

Clark, K. B. The Black Plight. Race or Class? New York Times Magazine October 5, 1980.

Clymer, A. Poll Links Economic Slide to Social Divisiveness. New York Times June 27, 1980.

Colasanto, D., and L. Williams. The Changing Dynamics of Race and Class [Nationwide survey of August 1986]. Public Opinion (January-February 1987):50-53.

Collins, S. M. The Making of the Black Middle Class. Social Problems 30 (1983):369-82.

Collins, S. Racism and Class: A Response to Vincente Navarro. Monthly Review 39 (June 1987):19-27 [See Vicente Navarro, below].

Cook, T. D. and T. R. Curtain. The Mainstream and the Underclass: Why Are the Differences So Salient and the Similarities So Unobtrusive? In: John C. Masters and William P. Smith (eds.), Social Comparison, Social Justice, and Relative Deprivation. Hillsdale, NJ: Lawrence Erlbaum Associates, 1987.

Dalphin, J. The Persistence of Social Inequality in America. Cambridge, MA: Schenkman, 1982.

Danziger, Sheldon and Peter Gottschalk. Earnings Inequality, the Spatial Concentration of Poverty, and the Underclass. American Economic Review 77 (May 1987):211-15.

Darity, William, Jr. Equal Opportunity, Equal Results, and Social Hierarchy. Praxis International 7 (July 1987):174-85.

Dawson, M. C. Race and Class in the Formation of Afro-American Political Attitudes: 1972-1983. Doctoral dissertation, Harvard University, 1986. UMO # 8620452.

Day, V. K. Y. 'My Family is Me': Women's Kin Networks and Social Power in a Black Sea Island Community [South Carolina]. Doctoral dissertation, Rutgers University, 1986. UMO # 8620025.

Denantes, F. Racisme et 'classe ouvriere'. Project 80 (December 1973):1233-1240.

Du Bois, W. E. B. [Black and white working class against poverty and race hate]. Pittsburgh Courier April 24, 1937.

Du Bois, W. E. B. [Divisions among Black people]. Pittsburgh Courier July 4, 1936.

Du Bois, W. E. B. The Economic Future of the Negro. Publications of the American Economic Association [Series 3] 7 (1906):219-42. [The historic rise of economic classes among Negro Americans].

Du Bois, W. E. B. Our Class Struggle [In "Postscript"]. Crisis 40 (July 1933):164-5.

Du Bois, W. E. B. The Present Leadership of American Negroes [Review of "Black Bourgeoisie" by E. Franklin Frazier]. Freedom May 20, 1957.

Du Bois, W. E. B. Race in America [Racism as elitism and class oppression]. Boston Transcript February 21, 1904.

Du Bois, W. E. B. [Race problem and the labor problem]. Pittsburgh Courier November 14 and 21, 1936.

Du Bois, W. E. B. [Social classes among Blacks]. Amsterdam News April 11, 1942.

Dunn, M. The Cities' Black Poor: America's Angry Untouchables. Los Angeles Times August 24, 1980.

Durant, T. J., Jr. and J. S. Louden. The Black Middle Class in America: Historical and Contemporary Perspectives. Phylon 47 (Winter 1986):253-63.

Duster, Troy. Social Implications of the 'New' Black Urban Underclass. Black Scholar 19 (May-June 1988):2-9.

Duster, Troy. The Structure of Privilege and Its Universe of Discourse.

American _Sociologist_ 11 (May 1976):73-78.

Ellison, R. W. When Does a Black Join the Middle Class? _Los Angeles
Times_ January 29, 1975.

Erie, S. P. Public Policy and Black Economic Polarization. _In_: Ray C.
Rist (ed.), _Policy Studies Review Annual, Vol. 6_. Beverly Hill, CA:
Sage, 1982.

Farley, R., and S. M. Bianchi. _Social and Economic Polarization: Is It
Occurring Among Blacks?_ September 1982. ERIC ED 223 743.

Feiner, S. F. Property Relations and Class Relations in Genovese and the
Modes of Production Controversy. _Cambridge Journal of Economics_ 10
(March 1986).

Flynn, C. L., Jr. _White Land, Black Labor, Caste and Class in Late
Nineteenth-Century Georgia_. Baton Rouge: Louisiana State
University, 1983.

Frazier, E. F. _Black Bourgeoisie: The Rise of a New Middle Class in the
United States_. New York: Macmillan, 1962 (orig. 1957).

Frazier, E. F. The Negro Middle Class and Desegregation. _Social Problems_
4 (April 1957):291-301.

Frazier, E. F. Occupational Classes among Negroes in Cities. _American
Journal of Sociology_ 35 (March 1930):718-38.

Freeman, A. Race and Class: The Dilemma of Liberal Reform. _Yale Law
Journal_ (Fall 1981).

Freeman, R. B. _Black Elite: The New Market for Highly Qualified Black
Americans_. New York: McGraw-Hill, 1976.

Garcia, H. D. C. _Chicano Social Class, Assimilation, and Nationalism_, 2
vols. Doctoral dissertation, Yale University, 1980. UMO # 8024801.

Gatewood, Willard B., Jr. Aristocrats of Color: South and North. The
Black Elite, 1880-1920. _Journal of Southern History_ 54 (1988):3-20.

George, Hermon, Jr. Black America, the 'Underclass' and the Subordination
Process. _Black Scholar_ 19 (May-June 1988):44-54.

Gershman, C. The Black Plight. Race or Class? _New York Times Magazine_
October 5, 1980 [See also Kenneth B. Clark].

Glasgow, D. G. _The Black Underclass: Poverty, Unemployment, and
Entrapment of Ghetto Youth_. San Francisco, CA: Jossey-Bass, 1980.

Graebener, J. _Klassengesellschaft und Rassismus_. Düsseldorf, West
Germany: Bertelsmann Universitätsverlag, 1971.

Green, D. S., and E. Smith. W.E.B. Du Bois and the Concept of Race and
Class. _Phylon_ 44 (December 1983):262-72.

Grizarry, A. Economic Relations for Class Reproductions: The Class of Puerto Ricans. Doctoral dissertation, City University of New York, 1983. UMO # 8401903.

Gutierrez, Ramon A. Unraveling America's Hispanic Past: Internal Stratification and Class Boundaries. Aztlan 17 (Spring 1986):79-101.

Haley, C. T. To Do Good and Do Well: Middle Class Blacks and the Depression, Philadelphia, 1929-1941. Doctoral dissertation, SUNY at Binghampton, 1980. UMO # 8016647.

Handy, K. M. Race and Class Consciousness among Southern Blacks. Sociological Spectrum 4 (1984):383-404.

Hill, R. C. Race, Class and the State: The Metropolitan Enclave System in the United States [Detroit]. Insurgent Sociologist 10 (Fall 1980):45-59.

Hirata, L. C. Toward a Political Economy of Chinese America: A Study of Property Ownership in Los Angeles Chinatown. Amerasia Journal 3 (Summer 1975):76-96.

Hudgins, J. L. Changes in Solidarity and Stratification among Black Americans. Doctoral dissertation, Duke University, 1987. UMO # 8718419.

Hur, K. K. and L. W. Jeffres. Communication, Ethnicity, and Stratification: A Review for Research Directives, Hypotheses and Generalizations. In: B. Dervin and M. J. Voigt (eds.), Progress in Communication Sciences, Vol. 6, pp. 47-76. Norwood, NJ: Ablex, 1985.

Jackman, M. R., and R. W. Jackman. Class Awareness in the United States. Berkeley, CA: University of California Press, 1983.

Jameson, J. F. The Revolution and the Status of Persons. In: The American Revolution Considered as a Social Movement, pp. 3-26. Princeton, NJ: Princeton University Press, 1926.

Jencks, Christopher. Deadly Neighborhoods: How the Underclass Has Been Misunderstood. New Republic (June 1988):23-32.

Johnson, T. V. Marxism-Leninism and the 'Underclass'. Political Affairs 65 (September 1986):13-19.

Kaelble, H. Historical Research on Social Mobility [Translated by Ingrid Noakes]. New York: Columbia University Press, 1981.

Kaelble, H. Social Mobility in the 19th and 20th Centuries: Europe and America in Comparative Perspective. New York: St. Martin's Press, 1986.

Kalmar, K. L. Southern Black Elites and the New Deal: A Case Study of

Savannah, Georgia. <u>Georgia</u> <u>Historical</u> <u>Quarterly</u> 65 (Winter 1981):341-55.

Katznelson, I. <u>City</u> <u>Trenches:</u> <u>Urban</u> <u>Politics</u> <u>and</u> <u>the</u> <u>Patterning</u> <u>of</u> <u>Class</u> <u>in</u> <u>the</u> <u>United</u> <u>States</u>. New York: Pantheon, 1981.

Kemp, K. A. Race, Ethnicity, Class and Urban Spatial Conflict: Chicago as a Crucial Test Case. <u>Urban</u> <u>Studies</u> 23 (June 1986).

Kilson, M. Black Social Classes and Intergenerational Poverty. <u>Public</u> <u>Interest</u> 64 (Summer 1981):58-78.

Kilson, M. D. D. B. Afro-American Social Structure, 1790-1970. <u>In</u>: Martin L. Kilson and Robert J. Rotberg (eds.), <u>The</u> <u>African</u> <u>Diaspora</u>, pp. 414-458. Cambridge, MA: Harvard University Press, 1976..

Kronus, S. <u>The</u> <u>Black</u> <u>Middle</u> <u>Class</u>. Columbus, OH: Merrill, 1971.

Kulikoff, A. L. The Origins of Afro-American Society in Tidewater Maryland and Virginia, 1700-1790. <u>William</u> <u>and</u> <u>Mary</u> <u>Quarterly</u> 35 (1978):226-59.

Landry, B. Growth of the Black Middle Class in the 1960s. <u>Urban</u> <u>League</u> <u>Review</u> 3 (Winter 1978):68-82.

Landry, B. <u>The</u> <u>New</u> <u>Black</u> <u>Middle</u> <u>Class</u>. Berkeley, CA: University of California Press, 1987.

Lapham, L. H. <u>Money</u> <u>and</u> <u>Class</u> <u>in</u> <u>America.</u> <u>Notes</u> <u>and</u> <u>Observations</u> <u>on</u> <u>Our</u> <u>Civil</u> <u>Religion</u>. New York: Weidenfeld & Nicolson, 1988.

Laslett, Michael. Inter-Racial Violence: Conflicts of Class and Culture. <u>Minority</u> <u>Trendsletter</u> 1 (September-October 1987).

Leading Black Neighborhoods [Black middle and upper-middle class areas]. <u>Black</u> <u>Enterprise</u> 5 (December 1974):25-33, 61.

Leahy, R. L. (ed.) The Development of the Conception of Social Class. <u>In</u>: <u>The</u> <u>Child's</u> <u>Construction</u> <u>of</u> <u>Social</u> <u>Inequality</u>, pp. 79-107. New York: Academic Press, 1983.

Leba, J. K. and others. <u>The</u> <u>Vietnamese</u> <u>Entrepreneurs</u> <u>in</u> <u>the</u> <u>U.S.A.:</u> <u>The</u> <u>First</u> <u>Decade</u>. Houston, TX: Zieleks, 1985.

Leonard, J. S. <u>Splitting</u> <u>Blacks?</u> <u>Affirmative</u> <u>Action</u> <u>and</u> <u>Earnings</u> <u>Inequality</u> <u>Within</u> <u>and</u> <u>Across</u> <u>Races</u>. National Bureau of Economic Research, 1984.

Lester, J. On Becoming American: Reflections on the Black Middle Class. <u>Race</u> <u>Relations</u> <u>Reporter</u> 5 (September 1974):11-14.

Levison, A. The Divided Working Class. <u>Nation</u> May 1, 1972.

Levy, Frank. <u>How</u> <u>Big</u> <u>Is</u> <u>the</u> <u>American</u> <u>Underclass?</u> Working Paper No. 0090-1. Washington, D.C.: Urban Institute, 1977.

Logan, R. W. The Hiatus - A Great Negro Middle Class. Southern Workman (December 1929).

Loury, G. C. and others. Moving Up at Last? [Blacks in the middle class]. Harper's (February 1987):35-39, 42-46.

Magnet, Myron. America's Underclass: What To Do? Fortune (May 11, 1987):130-50.

Maharidge, D. Journey to Nowhere: The Saga of the New Underclass. Garden City, NY: Doubleday, 1985.

Major, G. H. and D. E. Saunders. Black Society. Chicago: Johnson Publishing Co., 1977.

Malveaux, Julianne. Race, Class, and Black Poverty. Black Scholar 19 (May-June 1988):18-21.

Marable, M. Beyond the Race-Class Dilemma [Followed by commentary by Roger Wilkins, Nathan Huggins, Herbert G. Gutman, Aryeh Neier, Herbert Hill and Hulbert H. James]. Nation 232 (April 11, 1981).

Martin, T. C.L.R. James and the Race/Class Question. Race 14 (October 1972):183-193.

McBridge, D., and M. H. Little. The Afro-American Elite, 1930-40: A Historical Profile. Phylon 42 (Summer 1981):105-19.

McFate, Katherine. Defining the Underclass. Focus (Joint Center for Political Studies) (June 1987):5-7.

Meier, A. Some Observatioons on the Negro Middle Class. Crisis (October 1957).

Meier, A. and D. Lewis. History of the Negro Upper Class in Atlanta, Georgia, 1890-1958. Journal of Negro Education 28 (Spring 1959):128-39.

Moore, J. W. Minorities in the American Class System. Daedalus 110 (Spring 1981):275-299.

Morgan, G. Class Theory and the Structural Location of Black Workers. Insurgent Sociologist 10 (Winter 1981):21-34.

Moriarity, J. Holyoke's Hispanics Span Economic Spectrum [Mass.]. Springfield Republican July 24, 1983.

Morrissey, M. Ethnic Stratification and the Study of Chicanos. Journal of Ethnic Studies 10 (Winter 1983):71-99.

Mullings, Leith. Ethnicity and Stratification in the Urban United States. In: Marvin J. Berlowitz and Ronald S. Edari (eds.), Racism and the Denial of Human Rights: Beyond Ethnicity, pp. 21-38. Minneapolis, MN: MEP Publications, 1984.

Mullins, E. I. and P. Sites. The Origins of Contemporary Eminent Black Americans. American Sociological Review 49 (October 1984):672-84.

Muraskin, W. A. Middle-Class Blacks in a White Society: Prince Hall Freemasonry in America. Berkeley, CA: University of California Press, 1975.

Nathan, Richard. Will The Underclass Always be with Us? Society (March-April 1987):57-62.

Navarro, V. The Rainbow Coalition and the Challenge of Class. Monthly Review 39 (June 1987):19-27 [See Sheila Collins, above].

Newman, Katherine S. Falling from Grace. The Experience of Downward Mobility in the American Middle Class. New York: Free Press, 1988.

Oblinger, C. D. Alms for Oblivion: The Making of a Black Underclass in Southeastern Pennsylvania, 1780-1860. In: John E. Bodnar (ed.), The Ethnic Experience in Pennsylvania, pp. 94-119. Lewisburg, PA: Bucknell University Press, 1973.

Oestreicher, R. J. Changing Class Relations in Detroit: 1880-1900. In: James W. Soltow (ed.), Essays in Economic and Business History. East Lansing, MI: Graduate School of Business Administration, Michigan State University, 1979.

Oestreicher, R. J. Fragmentation. Working People and Class Consciousness in Detroit. 1875-1900. Urbana, IL: University of Illinois Press, 1985.

Orans, M. Race and Class Conflict in Crosscultural Perspective. Urban Affairs Annual Reviews 5 (1971):1-68.

Pettigrew, T. F. Race and Class in the 1980s: An Interactive View. Daedalus 110 (Spring 1981):233-55.

Polenberg, R. One Nation Divisible: Class, Race, and Ethnicity in the U.S. Since 1938. New York: Viking, 1980.

Pollack, Andy. Critique of William J. Wilson. The Ignored Significance of Class. Against the Current 3 (September-October 1988):7-8. 44-51.

Pomerantz, L. The Chinese Bourgeoisie and the Anti-Chinese Movement in the United States, 1850-1905. Amerasia Journal 11 (Spring-Summer 1984):1-34.

Proctor, Samuel D. Survival Techniques and the Black Middle Class. In: Rhoda L. Goldstein (ed.), Black Life and Culture in the United States, pp. 281-85. New York: 1971.

Proctor, W. G., Jr. The Ambiguous Auction Block [Social stratification of Blacks in Ga.]. Georgia Review 23 (1969):63-71.

Pyatt, R. A., Jr. Excluded from the Board [Absence of Blacks from boards of directors of firms in Washington, D.C. metropolitan area]. Washington Post January 21, 1986.

Race, Sex and Class: A Statement from England. Interracial Books for Children 5 (1974):6.

Reischauer, Robert D. The Size and Characteristics of the Underclass. Washington, D.C.: Brookings, 1987.

Resnick, S. and R. Wolff. Power, Property and Class. In: Paul Zarembka (ed.), Research in Political Economy, Vol. 9. Greenwich, CT: JAI Press, 1986.

Rex, John. The Ghetto and the Underclass: Essays on Race and Social Policy. Aldeshot: Avebury, 1988.

Ricketts, E. R. and I. V. Sawhill. Defining and Measuring the Underclass. Journal of Policy Analysis and Management 7 (Winter 1988):316-25.

Rose, S. J. Social Stratification in the United States: An Analytical Guidebook. Baltimore, MD: Social Graphics Co., 1983.

Rosenberg, J. An Interview with William Julius Wilson. Democratic Left 14 (September-October 1986):27-30.

Sampson, W. A. New Insights on Black Middle-Class Mobility. Urban League Review 5 (Summer 1980):21-41.

Sampson, W. A., and P. Rossi. Race and Family Social Standing. American Sociological Review 40 (1975):201-214.

Scott, J. The Black Bourgeoisie and Black Power. Black Scholar 4 (January 1973):12-18.

Seligman, Adam. The American System of Stratification: Some Notes Towards Understanding Its Symbolic and Institutional Concomitants. In: S. N. Eisenblatt and others (eds.), Centre Formation, Protest Movements, and Class Structure in Europe and the United States. New York: New York University Press, 1987.

Shulman, S. Race, Class and Occupational Stratification: A Critique of William J. Wilson's "The Declining Significance of Race". Review of Radical Political Economics 13 (Fall 1981):21-31.

Sites, P. and E. I. Mullins. The American Black Elite, 1930-1978. Phylon 46 (Fall 1985):269-80.

Spriggs, W. E. The Virginia Farmers' Alliance: A Case Study in Race and Class Identity. Journal of Negro History 44 (1979):191-204.

Steedman, C. K. Landscape for a Good Woman: A Story of Two Lives. New Brunswick, NJ: Rutgers University, 1987.

Steele, S. On Being Black and Middle Class. Commentary 85 (January

1988):42-47.

Steinberg, S. The Ethnic Myth: Race, Ethnicity and Class in American
    Society. New York: Atheneum, 1981.

Szymanski, A. Race, Sex, and the U.S. Working Class. Social Problems 21
    (June 1974):706-25.

Thomas, M. E. and M. Hughes. The Continuing Significance of Race: A
    Study of Race, Class, and Quality of Life in America. American
    Sociological Review (December 1986):830-41.

Thomas, R. W. Working-class and Lower-class Origins of Black Culture:
    Class Formation and the Division of Black Cultural Labor. Minority
    Voices 1 (Fall 1977):81-103.

The Black Middle Class. Business Week (March 14, 1988):62-64.

Thompson, D. C. A Black Elite: A Profile of Graduates of UNCF Colleges.
    Westport, CT: Greenwood, 1986.

Tribune, Chicago. The American Millstone: An Examination of the Nation's
    Permanent Underclass [Chicago]. Chicago: Contemporary Books, 1986.

Turner, J. Implications of Class Conflict and Racial Cleavage for the
    U.S. Black Community. Review of Black Political Economy 6 (Winter
    1976):133-44.

Valentine, C. A. Voluntary Ethnicity and Social Change: Classism,
    Racism, Marginality, Mobility, and Revolution with Special Reference
    to Afro-American and Other Third World People. Journal of Ethnic
    Studies 3 (Spring 1975):1-27.

Vowels, R. C. Atlanta Negro Business and the New Black Bourgeoisie.
    Atlanta Historical Bulletin 21 (Spring 1977):48-63.

Watts, J. G. I'm Not Bourgeois, I'm Black [The poor in Harlem]. Village
    Voice December 17, 1980.

Watts, R. A. Vernon Jordan and the Black Bourgeoisie: Failing to Help
    Those Who Need Help Most. Harvard Crimson October 30, 1981.

Wenger, M. G. State Responses to Afro-American Rebellion: Internal Neo-
    Colonialism and the Rise of a New Black Petite Bourgeoisie.
    Insurgent Sociologist 10 (Fall 1980):61-72.

Whitman, D. The Class Conflict Behind the Miami Riot. USA Today 109
    (November 1980).

Wiener, Jonathan M. Class Structure and Economic Development in the
    American South, 1865-1955. American Historical Review 84 (October
    1979):970-92.

Williams, J. Education and Race: The Racialisation of Class Inequalities?
    British Journal of Sociology of Education 7 (1986):135-154.

Williams, J. The Black Elite. Why the Ranks of Washington's Well-Off and
    Powerful Blacks Are Swelling. Washington Post Magazine January 4,
    1981.

Willson, J. Sketches of the Higher Classes of Coloured Society in
    Phildelphia. Philadelphia, PA: Merrihew Thompson, 1841.

Wilson, W. J. Class Conflict and Jim Crow Segregation in the Postbellum
    South. Pacific Sociol. Review 19 (1976):431-46.

Wilson, W. J. Cycles of Deprivation and the Underclass Debate. Social
    Service Review   (December 1985).

Wilson, W. J. The Declining Significance of Race: Blacks and Changing
    American Institutions (second edition). Chicago: University of
    Chicago Press, 1980.

Wilson, W. J. Some Reflections on Race, Class, and Public Policy. Urban
    League Review 5 (Summer 1980):7-20.

Wilson, W. J. The Truly Disadvantaged: The Inner City, the Underclass,
    and Public Policy. Chicago: University of Chicago Press, 1987.

Wilson, W. J. The Urban Underclass. In: Leslie Dunbar (ed.), Minority
    Report, pp. 118-51. New York: Pantheon, 1984.

Wilson, W. J. (ed.) The Ghetto Underclass: Social Science
    Perspectives. Newbury Park, CA: Sage, 1989.

Winch, J. Philadelphia's Black Elite: Activism, Accommodation, and the
    Struggle for Autonomy, 1787-1848. Philadelphia, PA: 1980.

Wolfe, M. R. The Appalachian Reality: Ethnic and Class Diversity. E.
    Tenn. Hist. Soc. Publ. 52-53 (1980-81):40-60.

Wong, B. Social Stratification, Adoptive Strategies, and the Chinese
    Community in New York City. Urban Life 5 (April 1976):33-52.

Woodard, M. D. The Dimensions of the Afro-American Social Structure: The
    Post Civil Rights Era [Class Structure - Chicago]. Doctoral
    dissertation, University of Chicago, 1984.

Work, M. N. Problems of Adjustment and Class in the South. Social Forces
    16 (October 1937):108-117.

[See also sections 23, 24, 54, and 83]

14. Collective Self-defense

The historical reality of race relations ... is that whites have never altered their institutions primarily for benefit of blacks ... The hopes for racial justice have always depended upon the blacks themselves.

- Edgar J. McManus, Black Bondage in the North (1973)

Abbott, Martin. Freedom's Cry: Negroes and Their Meetings in South Carolina, 1865-1869. Phylon 20 (Fall 1959).

Akard, W. K. Wocante Tinza: A History of the American Indian Movement. Doctoral dissertation, Ball State University, 1987. UMO # 8727165.

Aleander, R. P. The National Bar Association. National Bar Journal 1 (1941):1-15.

Allsup, C. The American G.I. Forum: Origins and Evolution. Austin: University of Texas Press, 1982.

Bacote, C. A. Negro Proscriptions, Protests, and Proposed Solutions in Georgia, 1880-1908. Journal of Southern History (November 1959).

Bland, R. W. The Collective Struggle for Negro Rights: 1915-1940. North Carolina Central Law Review 2 (Spring 1970).

Bracey, John and others (eds.) American Slavery: The Question of Resistance. Belmont, CA: 1971.

Carson, E. D. The Charitable Activities of Black Americans: A Portrait of Self- help? Review of Black Political Economy 15 (Winter 1987).

Chandler, C. R. The Mexican American Protest Movement in Texas. Doctoral dissertation, Tulane University, 1968.

Cullinane, M. The Filipino Federation of America: The Prewar Years, 1925-1940 - An Overview. Crossroads: An Interdisciplinary Journal of Southeast Asian Studies 1 (February 1983):74-85.

Dann, M. Black Populism: A Study of the Colored Farmers' Alliance Through 1891. Journal of Ethnic Studies 2 (1974):58-71.

Eisenberg, B. Only for the Bourgeois? James Weldon Johnson and the NAACP, 1916-1930. Phylon 43 (June 1982):110-24.

Fairclough, A. The Preachers and the People: The Origins and Early Years of the Southern Christian Leadership Conference, 1955-1959. Journal of Southern History 52 (August 1986):403-40.

Foner, Philip S. and George E. Walker (eds.) Proceedings of the Black State Conventions, 1840-1865. 2 vols. Philadelphia, PA: Temple University Press, 1979.

Foner, Philip S. and George E. Walker (eds.) Proceedings of the Black
     National and State Conventions, 1865-1900. Philadelphia, PA: Temple
     University Press, 1986.

Franklin, V. P. Black Self-Determination. Westport, CT: Lawrence Hill,
     1984.

Garcia, R. A. The Chicano Movement and the Mexican American Community,
     1972-1978 An Interpretive Essay. Socialist Review 8 (July-October
     1978):117-36.

Garfinkel, H. When Negroes March: The March on Washington Movement in
     the Organizational Politics for FEPC. Glencol, IL: Free Press,
     1959.

Grant, D. L. The Anti-lynching Reform Movement: 1883-1932. San
     Francisco, CA: Rand E Associates, 1977.

Guillemin, J. American Indian Resistance and Protest. In: Ted R. Gurr
     (ed.), Violence in America, II (third edition). Newbury Park, CA:
     Sage, 1989.

Harding, V. The Other American Revolution. Atlanta: Institute of the
     Black World, 1980.

Hine, W. C. The 1867 Charleston Streetcar Sit-ins: A Case of Successful
     Black Protest. South Carolina Historical Magazine 77 (April
     1976):110-14.

Hirabayashi, J. and others. Pan-Indianism in the Urban Setting. In:
     Thomas Weaver and Douglas White (eds.), The Anthropology of Urban
     Environments. Washington, D.C.: 1972.

Horne, G. Communist Front? The Civil Rights Congress, 1946-1956.
     Rutherford, NJ: Fairleigh Dickinson University Press, 1987.

Hosokawa, B. JACL in Quest of Justice [Japanese American Citizens
     League]. New York: Morrow, 1982.

Jackman, N. R. Collective Protest in Relocation Centers. American Journal
     of Sociology 63 (November 1957):256-72.

Jackson, J. J. Our Association, 'Where It's At, Baby!' [President,
     Association of Social and Behavioral Sciences; formerly Association
     of Social Science Teachers]. Journal of Social and Behavioral
     Sciences 15 (Fall 1969):53-60.

Josephy, A. M., Jr. Red Power: The American Indian's Fight for Freedom.
     New York: 1970.

Juan, E. S., Jr. In the Belly of the Monster: The Filipino Revolt in the
     U.S. Praxis 1 (1976).

Kellogg, C. F. NAACP: A History of the National Association for the

Advancement of Colored People, Vol. I: 1909-1920. Baltimore, MD: Johns Hopkins University Press, 1967.

Lee, J. R. E. The National Association of Teachers of Colored Youths. Voice of the Negro 2 (June 1905):381-85.

Martin, C. H. The Civil Rights Congress and Southern Black Defendants. Georgia Historical Quarterly 71 (Spring 1987):25-52.

Martinez, S., E. Longeaux and Vasquez. Viva La Raza: The Struggle of the Mexican-American People. New York: Doubleday.

Mazon, M. The Zoot-Suit Riots: The Psychology of Symbolic Annihilation. Austin: University of Texas Press, 1984.

McMillan, E. [Interview; President of national NAACP]. Peoples' Daily World August 21, 1986.

Meier, A. and J. Bracey. The Anti-Lynching Campaign, 1912-1955, part 7 of Papers of the NAACP. New Parts on Educational Equality, Voting Rights, Housing, the Scottsboro Case, and Anti-Lynching [65 microfilm reels]. Frederick, MD: University Publications of America, 1987.

Meier, A. and Elliot Rudwick. The Origins of Nonviolent Direct Action in Afro-American Protest: A Note on Historical Discontinuities. In: August Meier and Elliot Rudwick, Along the Color Line. Explorations in the Black Experience, pp. 307-404. Urbana, IL: University of Illinois Press, 1976.

Minick, Marc A. Antecedents of Solidarity in Black Middleton. Doctoral dissertation, Virginia Commonwealth University, 1987. UMO # 8728352.

Moore, J. T. A Search for Equality: The National Urban League, 1910-1961. Pennsylvania State University Press, 1981.

Morales, R. F. Makibaka: The Filipino American Struggle. Los Angeles: Mountainview Publishers, 1974.

Morris, A. Black Southern Student Sit-In Movement: An Analysis of Internal Organization. American Sociological Review 46 (December 1981):744-67.

Naison, M. D. Black Agrarian Radicalism in the Great Depression: The Threads of a Lost Tradition [Alabama Sharecroppers Union & Southern Tenant Farmers Union]. Journal of Ethnic Studies 1 (1973):47-65.

O'Brien, J. T. Reconstruction in Richmond: White Restoration and Black Protest, April-June 1865. Virginia Magazine of History and Biography 89 (July 1981):259-81.

Olzak, S. Have the Causes of Ethnic Collective Action Changed Over a Hundred Years? Evidence from the 1870s and 1880s and the 1970s. Technical Report 87-6. Ithaca, NY: Cornell University, 1987.

Peake, T. R. Keeping the Dream Alive. A History of the Southern

Christian Leadership Conference from King to the Nineteen-Eighties.
New York: Peter Lang, 1987.

Reed, Christopher R. Organized Racial Reform in Chicago during the
Progressive Era: The Chicago NAACP, 1910-1920. Michigan Historical
Review 14 (Spring 1988):75-99.

Reed, L. The Southern Conference for Human Welfare and the Southern
Conference Educational Fund, 1938-1963. Doctoral dissertation,
Indiana University, 1986. UMO # 8617789.

Richards, J. G. The Southern Negro Youth Congress: A History. [Doctoral
dissertation, University of Cincinnati, 1987] UMO # 8722073.

Rigsby, G. U. Alexander Crummell: Pioneer in Nineteenth-century Pan-
African Thought. Westport, CT: Greenwood, 1987.

Rosenbaum, R. J. Mexicano Resistance in the Southwest: 'The Sacred Right
of Self- Preservation'. Austin: University of Texas Press, 1981.

Sierra, C. M. The Political Transformation of a Minority Organization:
The Council of La Raza, 1965-1980. Doctoral dissertation, Stanford
University, 1983. UMO # 8314492.

Sim, Y. A Chinaman's Chance in Civil Rights Demonstration: A Case Study
[New York City Chinatown demonstration of April 1975]. ERIC ED 190
604.

Stoper, E. The Student Nonviolent Coordinating Committee: Rise and Fall
of a Redemptive Organization. Journal of Black Studies 8 (September
1977):13-34.

Streater, J. B., Jr. The National Negro Congress: 1936-1947. Doctoral
dissertation, University of Cincinnati, 1981.

Takahashi, J. Japanese American Responses to Race Relations: The
Formation of Nisei Perspectives [Japanese American Citizens League].
Amerasia Journal 9 (1982):29-57.

Talbot, A. K., Jr. The Virginia Teachers Association: Establishment and
Background. Negro History Bulletin 45 (January-March 1982):8-10.

Thomas, M. B. The Uses of Expectancy Theory and the Theory of Learned
Helplessness in Building upon Strengths of Ethnic Minorities: The
Black Experience in the United States. International Journal for the
Advancement of Counseling 9 (1986):371-79.

Thornton, J. M. Challenge and Response in the Montgomery Bus Boycott of
1955-56. Alabama Review 33 (July 1980):163-235.

Trask, Haunani-Kay. The Birth of the Modern Hawaiian Movement: Kalama
Valley, Oahu. Hawaiian Journal of History 21 (1987):126-53.

U.S. Congress, 94th, 2nd session, Senate Committee on the Judiciary,
Subcommittee on Internal Security. Revolutionary Activities Within

the United States: The American Indian Movement. Washington, D.C.:
     GPO, 1976.

Velez, G. A. A Study of the Historical Development of the Congress of
     Filipino American Citizens. Doctoral dissertation, Rutgers
     University, 1983. UMO # 8325920.

Wax, D. D. 'The Great Risque We Run': The Aftermath of Slave Rebellion
     at Stono, South Carolina, 1739-1745. Journal of Negro History 67
     (Summer 1982):136-47.

Wesley, C. H. History of Sigma Pi Phi, First of the Negro-American Greek
     Letter Fraternities. Washington, D.C.: Association for the Study of
     Negro Life and Slavery, 1954.

Whittel, G. Students' Role in the Struggle [Second national conference of
     the Student Organization for Black Unity, April 1-4, 1971, Frogmore,
     SC]. SOBU Newsletter 1 (April 17, 1971).

Wittner, L. S. The National Negro Congress: A Reassessment. American
     Quarterly 20 (Winter 1970):883-901.

Work, M. N. Self-Help among the Negroes. Survey (August 7, 1909):616-
     18.

Work, M. N. Secret Societies as Factors in the Social and Economic Life
     of the Negro. Proceedings of the Southern Sociological Congress
     (1916).

Yette, S. F. The Choice: The Issue of Black Survival in America. New
     York: Putnam's, 1971.

Collective Self-defense Bibliography

Davis, L. G. A History of Black Self-Help Organizations and Institutions
     in the U.S., 1776-1976: A Working Bibliography. [Exchange
     Bibliography No. 1207.] Monticello, IL: Council of Planning
     Librarians, 1977.

Graham, J. D. Negro Protest in America, 1900-1955: A Bibliographic
     Guide. South Atlantic Quarterly 67 (Winter 1968):94-107.

[See also sections 12, 55, and 82]

15. Colonialism

*Colonies, we call them, these places where 'niggers' are cheap
and the earth is rich; they are those outlands where like a
swarm of hungry locusts white masters may settle to be served as
kings; may wield the lash of slave drivers, may rape girls and
wives, grow rich as Croesus and send homeward a golden stream.*

- W. E. B. Du Bois, "Of the Culture of White Folk," 1917.

Ahearn, Wilbert H. The Cox Plan of Reconstruction: A Case Study in
    Ideology and Race Relations. Civil War History 16 (December
    1970):293-308. [Proposal to colonize U.S. blacks in their own
    territory].

Alatas, S. H. The Myth of the Lazy Native. Edinburgh: Edinburgh
    University Press,1977.

Almaguer, Tomas. Toward the Study of Chicano Colonialism. Aztlan 2
    (Spring 1971):7-22.

America's Exiles: Indian Colonization in Oklahoma. Chronicles of Oklahoma
    54 (Spring 1976):entire issue.

Asad, Talal (ed.), Anthropology and the Colonial Encounter. London:
    Itasca Press, 1973.

Bee, R., and R. Ginagerich. Colonialism, Classes, and Ethnic Identity:
    Native Americans and the National Political Economy. Comparative
    International Development 12 (1977):70-93.

Bennett, L., Jr. System. Internal Colonialism Structures Black, White
    Relations in America. Ebony 27 (April 1972):33-42.

Bertung, J. An Appraisal of Functionalist Theories in Relation to Race
    and Colonial Societies. In: Sociological Theories: Race and
    Colonialism, pp. 183-210. Paris: UNESCO, 1980.

Blauner, R. Internal Colonialism and Ghetto Revolt. Social Problems
    16 (Spring 1969):393-408.

Blauner, R. Racial Oppression in America. New York: Harper and Row,
    1972.

Boahen, A. A. African Pespectives on Colonialism. Baltimore, MD: Johns
    Hopkins University Press, 1987.

Bonilla, E. S. Requiem Por Una Cultura: Ensayos Sobre la Socilizacion el
    Puertorriqueno en Su Cultura y en Ambito del Poder Colonial. Rio
    Piedras: Editorial Edil, .

Braddock, J. H., II. Colonialism, Education, and Black Students: A
    Social-Psychological Analysis. Doctoral dissertation, Florida State

University, 1973. UMO # 7409479.

Braddock, J. H., II. Internal Colonialism and Black American Education. *Western Journal of Black Studies* 2 (Spring 1978):24-33.

Campos, R., and F. Bonilla. *La economia politica de la relacion colonial: la experiencia puertorriquena.* New York: Centro de Estudios Puertorriquenos, CUNY, 1979.

Cheboksarov, N. N. Critical Analysis of Racism and Colonialism. *In: Sociological Theories: Race and Colonialism*, pp. 347-382. Paris: UNESCO, 1980.

Chisholm, S. The Black As a Colonized Man. *Afro-American Studies* 1 (May 1970):1-10.

Cho, C. K. From Assimilationism to Internal Colonialism: Theories of Racial Inequality. *Critical Perspective of Third World America* 1 (Fall 1983):238-60.

Churchill, W. Indigenous Peoples of the United States: A Struggle Against Internal Colonialism. *Black Scholar* 16 (January-February 1985):29-35.

Churchill, Ward. Literature and the Colonization of the American Indian. *Journal of Ethnic Studies* 10 (Fall 1982):37-56.

Cintron Ortez, R. A Colonial Experience: Schools in Puerto Rico as Agents of Domination. *Critical Anthropology* 2 (Spring 1972):104-12.

Cleaver, E. *Revolution in the White Mother Country and National Liberation in the Black Colony.* Oakland, CA: Black Panther Party, 1968.

Clignet, R. Sociologie de la colonisation americaine en territoire indien. *Cahiers internationaux de sociologie* 20 (1956):61-89.

Colorado, Pamela. *Native American Alcoholism: A Issue of Survival.* Doctoral dissertation, Brandeis University, 1986. UMO # 8722511.

Cubano, Astrid. *Trade and Politics in Nineteenth Century Puerto Rico.* Doctoral dissertation, Princeton University, 1988. UMO # 8819192.

Del Valle, M. Puerto Rico before the United States Supreme Court. *Revista Juridica de la Universidad Interamericana de Puerto Rico* 19 (September-December 1984):13-81.

Ernst, K. Racialism, Racialist Ideology, and Colonialism, Past and Preent. *In: Sociological Theories: Race and Colonialism*, pp. 453-474. Paris: UNESCO, 1980.

Fausz, F. J. The Invasion of Virginia: Indians, Colonialism and the Conquest of Cant: A Review Essay on Anglo-Indian Relations in the Chesapeake. *Virginia Magazine of History and Biography* 95 (April 1987):133-56.

Conquest of Cant: A Review Essay on Anglo-Indian Relations in the Chesapeake. _Virginia Magazine of History and Biography_ 95 (April 1987):133-56.

Flores, G. Race and Culture in the Internal Colony: Keeping the Chicano in His Place. _In_: Frank Bonilla and Robert Girling (eds.), _Structurees of Dependency_, pp. 189-213. Nairobi, CA: Nairobi Bookstore, 1973.

Gaines, Judith. Warrior in the Modern World. _Boston Globe Magazine_ August 28, 1988. [Mescalero Apache nation].

Gladwin, T., and A. Saidin. _Slaves of the White Myth: The Psychology of Neocolonialism_.

Hall, S. Race, Articulation and Societies Structured in Dominance. _In_: _Sociological Theories: Race and Colonialism_, pp. 304-345. Paris: UNESCO, 1980.

Hall, Thomas. The Transformation of the Mexican Northwest into the American Southwest: Three Paths of Internal Development. _In_: Francisco O. Ramirez (ed.), _Rethinking the Nineteenth Century: Contradictions and Movements_. Westport, CT: Greenwood, 1988.

Hamilton, Charles V. Conflict, Race and System - Transformation in the United States. _Journal of International Affairs_ 23 (1969):106-18.

Haywood, Harry. _Negro Liberation_. New York: International Publishers, 1948.

Hernandez-Marquez, R. The Puerto Rican Industrial Policy Debate of 1940-1947: The Limits of Dependent Colonial Growth. _Berkeley Planning Journal_ 3 (1986):76-104.

Hershel, Helene J. Colonialism Reconsidered: An Analysis of Socioeconomic and Cultural Factors Affecting the Mental Health of Hawaiians. _Humanity and Society_ 10 (November 1986):448-68.

Indian Law Resource Center. U.S. Colonialism and the Hopi Nation. _Akwesasne Notes_ 11 (May 1979):13-17.

Iverson, K. Civilization and Assimilation in the Colonized Schooling of Native Americans. _In_: Philip G. Altbach and Gail P. Kelly (eds.), _Education and Colonialism_, pp. 149-80. New York: Longman, 1978.

Kagiwada, G. Beyond Internal Colonialism: Reflections from the Japanese American Experience. _Humboldt Journal of Social Relations_ 10 (Fall/Winter 1982/83):177-203.

Kwo, W. H. Colonized Status of Asian-Americans. _Ethnic Groups_ 3 (1981):227-51.

Lamphere, L. The Internal Colonization of the Navajo People. _Southwest Economy and Society_ 1 (Spring 1976):6-14.

Martinez, O. J. The Chicanos of El Paso: A Case of Changing Colonization. (May 1977) ERIC ED 153 780.

Martinez, R. Internal Colonialism: A Reconceptualization of Race Relations in the United States. Humboldt Journal of Social Relations 10.

McClurken, James M. We Wish to be Civilized: Ottawa-American political Contests on the Michigan Frontier. 2 vols. Doctoral dissertation, Michigan State University, 1988. UMO # 8814879.

Mintz, S. W. (ed.) Slavery Colonialism, and Racism. New York: Norton, 1975.

Mizio, E. Puerto Rican Social Workers and Racism. Social Casework 53 (1973)267-72.

Moore, J. W. Colonialism: The Case of the Mexican Americans. Social Problems 17 (1970):463-72.

Murguia, E. Assimilation, Colonialism and the Mexican American People. Austin: University of Texas Press, 1975.

Nelson, Anne. Murder under Two Flags: The U.S., Puerto Rico, and the Cerro Maravilla Cover-up. Boston: Ticknor and Fields, 1986.

O'Dell, J. H. Colonialism and the Negro American Experience. Freedomways (Fall 1966).

O'Dell, J. H. A Special Variety of Colonialism. Freedomways (Winter 1967).

Omvedt, G. Towards a Theory of Colonialism. Insurgent Sociologist 3 (Spring 1973):1-24.

Ornelas, C. and others. Decolonizing the Interpretation of the Chicano Political Experience. Los Angeles: Chicano Studies Center, University of California, 1975.

Ortez, R. C. A Colonial Experience: Schools in Puerto Rico as Agents of Domination. Critical Anthropology 2 (Spring 1972):104-12.

Pool, C. G. The Process of Dependency: An Ethnohistorical Study of the Political Economy of the Wichita Reservation, 1867-1901. Doctoral dissertation, University of Oklahoma, 1987. UMO # 8713829.

Puerto Rico: Class Struggle and National Liberation. Latin American Perspectives 3 (Summer 1976):entire issue.

Puryear, J. M. Only the United States Can Decolonize Puerto Rico. R. Interam. 12 (Winter 1982-83):490-95.

Rex, J. Race, Colonialism and the City. London: Routledge and Kegan Paul, 1973.

Rodriguez, Victor M. External and Internal Factors in the Organization of Production and Labor in the Sugar Industry of Puerto Rico, 1860-1934. Doctoral dissertation, University of California, Irvine, 1987. UMO # 8803618.

Ross, R. (ed.) Racism and Colonialism: Essays on Ideology and Social Structure. Boston: Kluwer, 1982.

Schement, J. R. and L. A. Singleton. Spanish Language Radio in the Southwest: A Case of Media Colonialism (April 1978). ERIC ED 157 130.

Seda Bonilla E. Requiem Por Una Cultura: Ensayos Sobre la Socilizacion el Puertorriqueno en Su Cultura y en Ambito del Poder Colonial. Rio Piedras: Editorial Edil, 1970.

Snipp, C. M. The Changing Political and Economic Status of the American Indians: From Captive Nations to Internal Colonies. American Journal of Economics and Sociology 45 (1986):145-58.

Solomon, M. Black Critics of Colonialism and the Cold War. In: Thomas G. Patteron (ed.), Cold War Critics. New York, 1971.

Souder-Jaffery, Laura. A Not So Perfect Union: Federal Territorial Relations between the United States and Guam. Pakistan Journal of American Studies 5 (March 1987):57-81.

Staples, R. Race and Colonialism: The Domestic Case in Theory and Practice. Black Scholar 7 (June 1976):37-40.

Staples, R. The Urban Plantation, Racism and Colonialism in the Post-Civil Rights Era. Oakland, CA: Black Scholar Press, 1988.

Sturner, J. The Political Sociology of Racism and Systematic Oppression: Internal Colonialism as a Paradigm for Socioeconomic Analysis. Stud. Afric. 1 (Fall 1979):294-314.

Suarez, Manuel. Requiem on Cerro Maravilla: The Police Murders in Puerto Rico and the U.S. Government Cover-up. Waterfront Press, 1987.

Tabb, W. K. Capitalism, Colonialism, and Racism. Review of Radical Political Economy 3 (Summer 1971):90-106.

Task, H. Hawaiians, American Colonization, and the Quest for Independence. Social Proes in Hawaii 31 (1984-85).

The Institute of the Black World. Education and Black Struggle: Notes from the Colonized World. Cambridge, MA: Harvard Educational Review.

Thomas, P. A Neo-rican in Puerto Rico: Or Coming Home. In: Asela Rodriguez de Laguna (ed.), Images and Identities. The Puerto Rican in Two World Contexts, pp. 153-156. New Burnswick, NJ: Transaction Books, 1987.

in Two World Contexts, pp. 153-156. New Burnswick, NJ: Transaction Books, 1987.

Thomas, R. K. Colonialism: Classic and Internal. [Native American reservations]. New University Thought 4 (Winter 1966-67):37-44.

Trask, H. Hawaiians, American Colonization, and the Quest for Independence. Social Process in Hawaii 31 (1984-85).

Turner, J. Black America: 'Colonial Economy Under Siege'. First World 1 (March-April 1977):7-9.

Turner, T. S. Anthropology and the Politics of Indigenous Peoples' Struggles. Cambridge Anthropology 5 (1979):1-43.

U.S. Commission On Civil Rights. The Navajo Nation: An American Colony. Washington, D.C.: The Commission, September 1975.

Volk, R. W. An Historical Analysis of the Functions and Reproduction of the Navajo Reservation. Doctoral dissertation, University of Illinois, 1987. UMO # 8721776.

Warrior, C. Poverty, Community, and Power. New University Thought (Summer 1965).

Wilkie, M. E. Colonials, Marginals and Immigrants: Contributions to a Theory of Ethnic Stratification. Comparative Studies in Society and History 19 (January 1977):67-95.

Zapata-Oliveras, Carlos R. Puerto Rico - United States Relations, 1898-1945. Horizontes 30 (October 1985 and April 1987):105-36.

16. Community Development

*What are we doing, ourselves, for the elevation of our
people, as a body? Are not too many of us satisfied
with taking care of No. ONE?*

    - Colored American, January 2, 1838.

Berndt, H. E. New Rulers in the Ghetto: The Community Development
    Corporation and Urban Poverty. Westport, CT: Greenwood, 1977.

Blackwell, J. E. The Black Community: Diversity and Unity (2nd edition).
    New York: Harper & Row, 1985.

Blea, I. I. Bessemer: A Sociological Perspective of a Chicano Barrio.
    Doctoral dissertation, University of Colorado, 1980. UMO # 8113944.

Burton, O. V. Toward a New South? Studies in Post-Civil War Southern
    Communities. Westport, CT: Greenwood, 1982.

Cummings, J. Chinatown in Country in Crossfire [Locke, California]. New
    York Times January 5, 1988.

Davis, D. Against the Odds: Postbellum Growth and Development in a
    Southern Black Urban Community, 1865-1900 [Memphis]. Doctoral
    dissertation, SUNY at Binghampton, 1987. UMO # 8720656.

Davis, F. Problems of Economic Growth in the Black Community: Some
    Alternative Hypotheses. Review of Black Political Economy 1
    (1971):75-107.

Du Bois, W. E. B. [Building good all-Black neighborhoods]. Amsterdam News
    November 1, 1941.

Du Bois, W. E. B. The Upbuilding of Black Durham. World's Work 23
    (January 1912):334-8.

Durrill, Wayne. K. Producing Poverty: Local Government and Economic
    Development in a New South County, 1874-1884. Journal of American
    History 71 (March 1984):764-81.

Garcia, M. H. Adaptation Strategies of the Los Angeles Black Community,
    1883-1919. Doctoral dissertation, University of California, Irvine,
    1985. UMO # 8603244.

Gibson, J. Ghetto Economic Development. New Ways of Giving Non-Whites the
    Business? Civil Rights Digest (Spring 1969).

Gillenkirk, J. and J. Motlow. Bitter Melon-Stories from the Last Rural
    Chinese Town in America, 1987.

Goston, M. and M. Kennedy. Blueprint for Tomorrow. The Fight for
    Community Control in Boston's Black and Latino Neighborhoods. Radical

America   20 (September-October 1986):7-22.

Henderson, William L. and Larry Ledebur. Programs for the Economic
    Development of the American Negro Community: The Moderate Approach.
    American Journal of Economic Sociology 30 (January 1971):27-45.

House, Roger. Blacks in Boston Seek to Secede. _Nation_ November 7, 1988.
    [Mandela].

Johnson, D. R. and Others. _The Politics of San Antonio: Community_
    Progress, and Power. Lincoln: University of Nebraska Press, 1983.

Kennedy, M. and C. Tilly. The Mandela Campaign: A Summary [A proposal to
    incorporate an area in Roxbury, Boston as a separate municipality].
    Radical America 20 (September-October 1986):23-25.

King, M. _Chain of Change. Struggles for Black Community Development_.
    Boston: South End Press, 1981.

Kwong, P. _The New Chinatown_. New York: Hill & Wang, 1987.

Lane, J. B. and E. J. Escobar. _Forging a Community. The Latino in_
    Northwest Indiana 1919-1975. Bloomington, IN: Indiana University
    Press, 1987.

Levitan, S. E. and Others. _Economic Opportunity in the Ghetto: The_
    Partnership of Government and Business. Baltimore, MD: Johns
    Hopkins University Press, 1970.

Lewis, Diane E. Roxbury's Rebirth Brings New Hope and Old Fears. _Boston_
    Globe June 12, 1988. [First of three articles on Boston's black
    community].

Logan, E. W. and D. A. Frate. The Struggle for Black Community
    Development in Holmes County, Mississippi: Internal Efforts, External
    Support, and the Role of Science. _In: The Extended Family_, pp. 3-
    20. The Hague: Mouton, 1978.

Miller, B. H. _Blacks in Winston-Salem, North Carolina 1895-1920:_
    Community Development in an Era of Benevolent Paternalism. Doctoral
    dissertation, Duke University, 1981. UMO # 8212967.

Nash, G. B. _Forging Freedom. The Formation of Philadelphia's Black_
    Community, 1720-1840. Cambridge, MA: Harvard University Press,
    1988.

Parker, R. D. The Black Community in a Company Town: Alcoa, Tennessee,
    1919-1939. _In:_ William H. Turner and Edward J. Cabbell (eds.),
    Blacks in Appalachia. Lexington: University of Kentucky Press, 1985.

Perry, S. E. _Building a Model Black Community. The Roxbury Action_
    Program. New Brunswick, NJ: Transaction Publishers, 1978.

Puryear, A. and C. West. _Black Enterprise, Inc._ [Bedford-Stuyvesant
    Restoration Corp.]. Garden City: Anchor Press/Doubleday, 1973.

Robbins, F. W. A World-Within-a-World: Black Nashville, 1880-1915.
    Doctoral dissertation, University of Arkansas, 1980. UMO # 8026015.

Summerville, J. The City and the Slum: 'Black Bottom' in the Development
    of South Nashville. Tennessee Historical Quarteerly 40 (Summer
    1981):182-192.

Taylor, H. L. On Slavery's Fringe: City-building and Black Community
    Development in Cincinnati, 1800-1850. Ohio History 95 (Winter-
    Spring 1986):5-33.

Terrell, B. and C. Turner. Community and Kinship, History and Control.
    Two Community Activists Talk About Boston's Future. Radical America
    20 (September-October 1986):27-39.

U.S. Commission On Civil Rights. Greater Baltimore Commitment: A Study of
    Urban Minority Economic Development. Washington, D.C.: The
    Commission, May 1983.

Vietorisz, T. and B. Harrison. The Economic Development of Harlem. New
    York: Praeger, 1970.

Weaver, Garrett. The Development of the Black Durham Community, 1880-
    1915. Doctoral dissertation, University of North Carolina, Chapel
    Hill, 1987. UMO # 8722355.

Community Development Bibliography

Browne, R. S. Black Economic Development: A Bibliography. New York:
    Afram Associates, 1970.

Contant, F. Community Development Corporations: An Annotated
    Bibliography. [Exchange Bibliography No. 530.] Monticello, IL:
    Council of Planning Librarians, 1974.

Davis, F. G. The Economics of Black Community Development: An Analysis
    and Program for Autonomous Growth and Development. University Press
    of America, 1976 (orig. 1972).

Williams, D. E. The Political Economy of Black Community Development: A
    Research Bibliography. [Exchange Bibliography No. 457.] Monticello,
    IL: Council of Planning Librarians, 1973.

17. Concentration Camps

[At the concentration camp in Tule Lake, California] in the afternoon, I went to American school which began with all of the children standing up to pledge allegiance to the flag of the United States.

- Isao Fujimoto, "The Failure of Democracy in a Time of Crisis. The War-Time Internment of the Japanese Americans and Its Relevance Today," September 1969.

Armor, John and Peter Wright. Manzanar. New York: Times Books, 1989. [Photographs by Ansel Adams].

Bailey, P. City in the Sun: The Japanese Concentration Camp at Poston, Arizona. Los Angeles, CA: Westernlore Press, 1971.

Bearden, R. E. The Internment of Japanese Americans in Arkansas 1942-1945. Master's thesis, University of Arkansas, Fayetteville, 1985.

Bosworth, A. R. America's Concentration Camps. New York: Norton, 1967.

Broom, L. and J. I. Kitsuse. The Managed Casualty: The Japanese American Family in World War II. Berkeley, CA: 1956.

Christgau, J. 'Enemies': World War II Alien Internment. Ames, IA: Iowa State University Press, 1985.

Daniels, R. Concentration Camps USA. New York: Holt, 1971.

Daniels, Roger. The Forced Migrations of West Coast Japanese Americans, 1942-1946: A Quantitative Note. In: Roger Daniels (ed.), Japanese Americans: From Relocation to Redress. Salt Lake City: University of Utah Press, 1986.

Daniels, R. The Japanese Experience in North America: An Essay in Comparative Racism. In: N. Brian Winchester (ed.), The Japanese Experience in North America: Papers and Proceedings. Alberta: University of Lethbride, 1977.

Daniels, R. The Politics of Prejudice. Berkeley, CA: 1962.

Daniels, R. and others. Japanese Americans from Relocation to Redress. Salt Lake City: University of Utah Press, 1986.

Daniels, Roger (ed.) American Concentration Camps. A Documentary History of the Relocation and Incarceration of Japanese Americans, 1942-1946. 9 vols. New York: Garland, 1989. [Archival materials].

Drinnon, R. Keeper of Concentration Campus. Dillon S. Myer and American Racism. Berkeley, CA: University of California Press, 1987.

Gesensway, D., and M. Roseman. Beyond Words. Images from America's

Concentration Camps. Ithaca, NY: Cornell University Press, 1988.

Girdner, A., and A. Loftis. The Great Betrayal. New York: 1969.

Hansen, A. A. Cultural Politics in the Gila Relocation Center, 1942-1943. Arizona West 27 (Winter 1985):327-62.

Hansen, A. A. and D. A. Hacker. The Manzanar Riot: An Ethnic Perspective. Amerasia Journal 2 (Fall 1974):112-57.

Hedepath, W. America's Concentration Camps: The Rumors and the Realities. Look May 28, 1968.

Hersey, John. Behind Barbed Wire. New York Times Magazine September 11, 1988.

Hohri, William. Repairing America: An Account of the Movement for Japanese American Redress. Pullman, WA: Washington State University Press, 1988.

Irons, Peter. Justice at War. The Inside Story of the Japanese American Internment. New York: Oxford University Press, 1983.

Irons, Peter. Race and the Constitution: The Case of the Japanese American Internment. This Constitution 13 (Winter 1986):18-26.

Irons, Peter and Ken Masugi. Japanese Americans During World War II. New Perspectives 18 (Winter-Spring 1986):2-13.

Iyeki, M. H. The Japanese American Coram Nobis Cases: Exposing the Myth of Disloyalty. Review of Law and Social Change 13 (1984-1985):199-221.

James, T. The Education of Japanese Americans at Tule Lake, 1942-1946. Pacific Historical Review 56 (February 1987):25-58.

Kaminaga, Y. Social Change through Legal Means: A Case Study of the Japanese American Legal Movement. Doctoral dissertation, University of California, San Diego, 1987. UMO # 8712288.

Leonard, Kevin A. The Changing Pace of Racism: Japanese Americans and Politics in California, 1943-1946. Master's thesis, University of California, Davis, 1988.

McKay, Nellie. Japanese American Women's Internment Camp Poetry. American Literary History 1 (March 1989).

Modell, J. (ed) The Kikuchi Diary: Chronicles from an American Concentration Camp. Urbana, IL: University of Illinois Press, 1973.

Nakasone-Huey, Nancy N. In Simple Justice: The Japanese-American Evacuation Claims Act of 1948. Doctoral dissertation, University of Southern California, 1986.

Oishi, Gene. In Search of Hiroshi: A Japanese-American Odyssey.

Rutland, VT: Tuttle, 1988.

Okamura, R. Y. The American Concentration Camps: A Cover-up through Euphemistic Terminology. Journal of Ethnic Studies 10 (Fall 1982):95-109.

Okihiro, G. Y. Japanese Resistance in America's Concentration Camps: A Reevaluation. Amerasia Journal 2 (Fall 1973):20-34.

Okihiro, G. Y. and J. Aly. The Press, Japanese Americans, and the Concentration Campus. Phylon 44 (March 1983):66-80.

Olmstead, T. Nikkei Internment: The Perspective of Two Oregon Weekly Newspapers. Oregon Historical Quarterly 85 (Spring 1984):4-32.

Papers of the U.S. Commission on Wartime Relocation and Internment of Civilians Part 1 Numerical File Archive [35 microfilm reels]. Frederick, MD: University Publications of America, 1987.

Prows, Suzanne M. Santa Anita Assembly Center for the Japanese, Acadia, California, 1942. Master's thesis, University of San Diego, 1988.

Ringle, K. The Untold Story of One Man's Fight for the Nisei [About Lt. Cmdr. Kenneth Duval Ringle]. Los Angeles Times December 6, 1981.

Russell, Andrew. A Fortunate Few: Japanese Americans in Southern Nevada, 1905-1945. Nevada Historical Society Quarterly 31 (Spring 1988):32-52.

Spicer, E. H. and Others. Impounded People. Japanese-Americans in the Relocation Centers. Tucson: University of Arizona Press, 1969.

Spickard, P. R. The Nisei Assume Power: The Japanese Citizens League, 1941-1942. Pacific Historical Review 52 (May 1983):147-74.

Starn, O. Engineering Internment: Anthropologists and the War Relocation Authority. American Ethnologist 13 (November 1986):700-20.

Sundquist, Eric J. The Japanese-American Internment: A Reappraisal. American Scholar 57 (Autumn 1988):529-47.

Suzuki, B. M. Concentration Camps-American Style: The Role of the W.R.A. Master's thesis, California State University, Sacramento, 1977.

Suzuki, L. E. Ministry in the Assembly and Relocation Centers of World War II. Berkeley, CA: Yardbird Publishers, 1979.

Taylor, S. C. Japanese Americans and Keetley Farms: Utah's Relocation Colony. Utah Historical Quarterly 54 (Fall 1986):328-44.

ten Broeck, J. and Others. Prejudice, War, and the Constitution [Internment of Japanese Americans]. Berkeley, CA: University of California Press, 1954.

Thomas, D. The Salvage [Internment of Japanese-Americans]. Berkeley, CA:

University of California Press, 1952.

Thomas, D. and R. S. Nishcinoto. The Spoilage. Berkeley, CA:
    University of California Press, 1946.

Tipton-Schutte, M. K. Editorial Individualism: Orange County's Daily
    Press Response to the Removal and Return of California's Japanese
    Americans in World War II. Master's thesis, California State
    University, 1979. UMO # 1313560.

U.S. Commission of Wartime Relocation and Internment of Civilians.
    Personal Justice Denied [Investigation of basis for Japanese-
    American claims for reparation payments for being confined to
    concentration camps]. Washington, D.C.: GPO, 1982.

Uchida, J. Journey to Topaz [Novel for younger readers about life in
    Japanese-American concentration camp]. Berkeley, CA: Creative Arts
    Books, 1985.

Wax, R. H. In and Out of the Tule Lake Segregation Center: Japanese
    Internment in the West, 1942-1945. Montana 37 (Spring 1987):12-25.

Weglyn, M. Years of Infamy: The Untold Story of America's Concentration
    Camps. New York, 1976.

Yatsushiro, T. Politics and Cultural Values: The World War II Japanese
    Relocation Centers and the United States Government. New York:
    Arno, 1979.

Yuki, Joyce. Concentration Camps in the U.S. California Aggie (U.C.
    Davis) June 6, 1988.

[See also sections 20, 32, 77, and 82]

18. Crime

*Murder may swagger, theft may rule, and prostituting flourish,
and the nation gives but spasmodic, intermittent, and lukewarm
attention. But let the murderer be black, or the thief brown or
the violator of womanhood have but a drop of Negro blood, and
the righteousness of the indignation sweeps the world. Nor
would this fact make the indignation less justifiable did not we
all know that it was blackness that was condemned, and not
crime.*

- W. E. B. Du Bois, "The Souls of Black Folk," 1903.

Acharya, S. The Underground Economy in the United States: Comment.
International Monetary Fund Staff Papers 31 (December 1984).

Austin, T. L. Does Where You Live Determine What You Get? A Case Study
of Misdemeanant Sentencing. Journal of Criminal Law & Criminology
76 (Summer 1985):490-571.

Ayers, E. L. Vengeance and Justice: Crime and Punishment in the
Nineteenth-Century American South. New York: Oxford, 1984.

Baker, David V. Race, Racism, and the Death Penalty in the United States:
An Historical, Theoretical, and Empirical Analysis. Doctoral
dissertation, University of California, Riverside, 1987. UMO #
8808633.

Barkan, S. E. Protesters on Trial: Criminal Justice in the Southern
Civil Rights and Vietnam Antiwar Movements. New Brunswick, NJ:
Rutgers University Press, 1985.

Bazelon, D. L. Questioning Authority-Justice and Criminal Law. New York:
Knopf, 1988.

Beeman, Perry. Panel Blasts D.M. Police for 'Racism'. Des Moines
Register November 18, 1988. [Des Moines, Iowa, Civil Service
Commission].

Blanks, R. S. (ed.) The Inequality of Justice: A Report on Crime and
the Administration of Justice in the Minority Community. January
1982. ERIC ED 218 384.

Blumstein, A. On the Racial Disproportionality of United States' Prison
Populations. Journal of Criminal Law & Criminology 73 (1982):1259-
81.

Bradmiller, L. L. and W. S. Walters. Seriousness of Sexual Assault
Charges: Influencing Factors. Criminal Justice & Behavior 12
(December 1985):463-84.

Brown, L. Southern Violence-Regional Problem or National Nemesis?
Legal Attitudes toward Southern Homicide in Historical Perspective.

Vanderbilt Law Review 32 (1979):225-50.

Buck, A. J. and others. The Natural Rate of Crime by Type of Community. _Review of Social Economy_ 43 (October 1985).

Calvin, A. D. Unemployment among Black Youths, Demographics, and Crime. _Crime and Delinquency_ 27 (April 1981):234-244.

Carson, C. S. The Underground Economy: An Introduction. _Survey of Current Business_ 64 (May and July 1984).

Curtis, L. A. Race and Violent Crime: Toward a New Policy. _In:_ Neil A. Weiner and Marvin E. Wolfgang (eds.), _Violent Crime, Violent Criminals_. Newbury park, CA: Sage, 1989.

Danziger, S. and D. Wheeler. The Economics of Crime: Punishment or Income Redistribution. _Review of Social Economy_ 33 (October 1975):113-31.

Davis, Mike and Sue Ruddick. Los Angeles: Civil Liberties between the Hammer and the Rock. _New Left Review_ 170 (July-August 1988):37-60.

Dobry, S. V. _Common Law and Civil Law Interactions: Their Effect on Migrants within the Americas_ [NYC]. Doctoral dissertation, Fordham University, 1987. UMO # 8714579.

Dorin, D. D. A Case Study of the Misuse of Social Science in Capital Punishment Cases: The Massachusetts Supreme Judicial Court's Finding of Racial Discrimination in _Watson_ (1980). _In:_ Kenneth C. Haas and James A. Inciardi (eds.), _Challenging Capital Punishment_. Newbury Park, CA: Sage, 1988.

Du Bois, W. E. B. _Some Notes on Negro Crime Particularly in Georgia_. Atlanta: Atlanta University Press, 1904.

Du Bois, W. E. B., and A. G. Dill. _Morals and Manners Among Negro Americans_. [Analysis of crime, pp. 36-50]. Atlanta: Atlanta University Press, 1913.

Dunbaugh, Frank M. Racially Disproportionate Rates of Incarceration in the United States. _Prison Law Monitor_ 1 (1979).

Flowers, Ronald B. _Minorities and Criminality_. Westport, CT: Greenwood, 1988.

Focus on Racism. _Crime and Social Justice_ 14 (1980):entire issue.

Gaertner, W. and A. Wenig. _The Economics of the Shadow Economy_. Berlin: Springer Verlag, 1985.

Goetting, A. Racism, Sexism, and Ageism in the Prison Community. _Federal Probation_ 49 (September 1985):10-22.

Goldberg, Stephanie B. _McClaskey_ Hit; Criminologist: Court Ignored 'Starkest' Race Bias Evidence. _ABA Journal_ 74 (October 1, 1988).

Greenberg, J., and Others. The Long Road Up from Barbarism: The Case Against Capital Punishment. Lexington, MA: Lexington Books, 1984.

Gross, Samuel R. and Robert Mauro. Death and Discrimination: Racial Disparities in Capital Sentencing. Boston: Northeastern University Press, 1988.

Gross, Samuel R. and Robert Mauro. Patterns of Death: An Analysis of Racial Disparities in Capital Sentencing and Homicide Victimization. Stanford Law Review 37 (November 1984):27-153.

Gurr, Ted Robert. Drowning in a Crime Wave. New York Times April 12, 1989.

Gyimah-Brempong, K. Empirical Models of Criminal Behavior: How Significant a Factor Is Race? Review of Black Political Economy 15 (Summer 1986).

Hacker, A. Black Crime. White Racism. New York Review of Books March 3, 1988.

Hannah, T. S. Racial Economic Inequality and General Economic Inequality as Predictors of Violent and Property Crime Rates in North Carolina. Master's thesis, North Carolina State University, Raleigh, 1985.

Harer, Miles D. Relative Deprivation and Crime: The Effects of Income Inequality on Black and White Arrest Rates. Doctoral dissertation, Pennsylvania State University, 1987. UMO # 8807790.

Hindus, M. S. Black Justice under White Law: Criminal Prosecutions of Blacks in Antebellum South Carolina. Journal of American History 63 (December 1976):575-99.

Howsen, M. Roy and Stephen B. Jarrell. Some Determinants of Property Crime: Economic Factors Influence Criminal Behavior but Cannot Completely Explain the Syndrome. American Journal of Economics and Sociology 46 (October 1987):445-57.

Humphrey, John A. and Timothy J. Fogarty. Race and Plea-Bargained Outcomes: A Research Note. Social Forces 66 (Sept. 1987)176-82.

Irwin, J. The Jail: Managing the Underclass in American Society. Berkeley, CA: University of California Press, 1985.

Jackson, Don. Police Embody Racism to My People. New York Times January 23, 1989. [Long Beach, CA].

Jacoby, Tamar with Lynda Wright. When Cops Act on a Hunch. Newsweek October 10, 1988.

Jennings, W. P., Jr. A Note on the Economics of Organized Crime. Eastern Economic Journal 10 (July-September 1984).

Johnson, S. L. Race and the Decision to Detain a Suspect. Yale Law

Journal 93 (December 1983):214-58.

Kaufman, Michael T. In 113th Precinct, Ambivalent to Police. New York Times November 7, 1988. [Issue of racism in NYC police force].

Kempf, K. L., and R. L. Austin. Older and More Recent Evidence on Racial Discrimination in Sentencing. Journal of Quantitative Criminology 2 (March 1986):29-48.

Kempton, Murray. The Briar Patch: The People of the State of New York v. Lummumba Shakur, et al. New York: Dutton, 1973.

Kerr, P. Chinese Crime Groups Rising to Prominence in New York. New York Times January 4, 1988.

Koch, E. I. Race, Crime, Prejudice, Fear. New York Times January 19, 1987.

Lane, R. Roots of Violence in Black Philadelphia: 1860-1900. Cambridge, MA: Harvard University Press, 1986.

Langan, P. A. Racism on Trial: New Evidence to Explain the Racial Composition of Prisons in the United States. Journal of Criminal Law & Criminology 76 (Fall 1985):666-83.

Langan, P. A. and L. A. Greenfield. The Prevalence of Imprisonment. Bureau of Justice Statistics Special Report July 1985. Justice Statistics Clearinghouse, National Criminal Justice Reference Service, Box 6000, Rockville, MD 20850].

Leger, R. G., and H. G. Barnes. Black Attitudes in Prison: A Sociological Analysis. Journal of Criminal Justice 14 (1986):105-22.

Lichtenstein, Alex. 'That Disposition to Theft, with Which They Have Been Branded': Moral Economy, Slave Management, and Law. Journal of Social History 22 (1988):413-40.

Macher, David J. Race, Statistics and the Death Penalty. Western State University Law Review 15 (Fall 1987):179-215.

Marable, Marable. Black Prisoners and Punishment in a Racist/Capitalist State. In: How Capitalism Underdeveloped Black America, pp. 105-30. Boston: South End Press, 1983.

Mattera, P. Off the Books: The Rise of the Underground Economy. New York: St. Martin's Press, 1985.

Mendez, G. A. The Role of Race and Ethnicity in the Incidence of Police Use of Deadly Force. New York: National Urban League, 1983.

Messner, S. F. and S. J. South. Economic Deprivation, Opportunity Structure and Robbery Victimization: Intra- and Interracial Patterns. Social Forces 64 (June 1986):975-91.

Miller, E. M. and L. H. Kleinman. Political Economy and the Social
    Control of Ethnic Crime. In: Lionel Maldonado and Joan Moore
    (eds.), Urban Ethnicity in the United States. Newbury Park, CA:
    Sage, 1985.

Minority Youth Incarceration and Crime. Crime and Delinquency 33 (April
    1987):entire issue.

Moore, H., Jr. and J. B. Moore. Some Reflections: On the Criminal
    Justice System, Prisons, and Repressions. In: Gilbert Ware (ed.),
    From the Black Bar. Voices for Equal Justice, pp. 32-44. New York:
    Putnam's, 1976.

Morris, Thomas D. Equality, 'Extraordinary Justice', and Criminal
    Justice: The South Carolina Experience, 1865-1866. South Carolina
    Historical Magazine 83 (January 1982):16-22.

Moss, D. C. Discrimination in Criminal Justice Administration. The
    Statistics of Death. American Bar Association Journal 73 (January
    1, 1987).

Myers, Martha and S. M. Talarico. The Social Contexts of Racial
    Discrimination in Sentencing. Social Problems 33 (February
    1986):236-51.

Myers, Samuel L., Jr. Employment and Crime: An Issue of Race. Urban
    League Review (Fall 1981).

Myers, Samuel L., Jr. Statistical Tests of Discrimination in Punishment.
    Journal of Quantitative Criminology 1 (June 1985):191-218.

Myers, Samuel L., Jr. and W. J. Sabol. Business Cycles and Racial
    Disparities in Punishment. Contemporary Policy Issues 7 (October
    1987).

Myers, Samuel L., Jr. and W. J. Sabol. Unemployment and Racial
    Differences in Imprisonment. Review of Black Political Economy 16
    (Summer-Fall).

Nelli, H. S. The Business of Crime: Italians and Syndicate Crime in the
    United States. New York: 1976.

Oloroso, A., Jr. Homicide Rate Can Be Cut: Requires Joint Preventive
    Programs. [Chicago area] Chicago Reporter 17 (February 1988):8-9,
    11.

Overby, A. Discrimination Against Minority Groups. In: Leon Radzinowicz
    and Marvin E. Wolfgang (eds.), The Criminal in the Arms of the Law,
    Vol. 2, pp. 569-81. New York: Basic Books, 1971.

Paternoster, R. and A. Kazyaka. Racial Considerations in Capital
    Punishment: The Failure of Evenhanded Justice. In: Kenneth C. Haas
    and James A. Inciardi (eds.), Challenging Capital Punishment.
    Newbury Park, CA: Sage, 1988.

Perry, Ronald W. The American Dilemma at Sea: Race and Incarceration in the Naval Justice System. Phylon 41 (Spring 1980):50-56.

Petersik, T. W. Legal Income Opportunity and Property Crime Participation. [Pittsburgh, 1980]. Doctoral dissertation, George Washington University, 1986. UMO # 8627835.

Pettiway, E. E. The Internal Structure of the Ghetto and the Criminal Commute. Journal of Black Studies 16 (December 1985).

Phillips, L. and H. L. Votey, Jr. Black Women, Economic Disadvantage, and Incentive to Crime. American Economic Review 74 (May 1984).

Phillips, L. and H. L. Votey, Jr. Crime Generation and Economic Opportunities for Youth. In: The Economics of Crime Control, Chapter 8. Beverly Hills, CA: Sage, 1981.

Pritchard, D. Race, Homicide and Newspapers [Milwaukee, 1981-1982]. Journalism Quarterly 62 (Autumn 1985):500-07.

Race and the Death Penalty. Southern University Law Review 14 (Fall 1987):20-53.

Race, Crime, and Culture. Crime and Social Justice. 20 (1983):entire issue.

Radelet, M. L. and G. L. Pierce. Race and Prosecutorial Discretion in Homicide Cases. Law & Society Review 19 (1985):587-621.

Reed, Ishmael. Living at Ground Zero. Image Magazine (San Francisco Chronicle Examiner) (March 13, 1988):11-30.

Reuter, P. The Organization of Illegal Markets: An Economic Analysis. Washington, D.C.: GPO, 1985.

Reynolds, H. The Economics of Prostitution. Springfield, IL: C.C. Thomas, 1985.

Riedel, M. and others. The Nature and Patterns of American Homicide. Washington, D.C.: GPO, 1985.

Roberts, Harrell B. The Inner World of the Black Juvenile Delinquent. Hillsdale, NJ: Lawrence Erlbaum Associates, 1987.

Roberts, S. Race and Crime: Beyond Statistics to Find Answers. [N.Y.C.]. New York Times July 27, 1987.

Robin, G. Do the Police Racially Discriminate Against Juvenile Offenders? The Police Chief 51 (February 1984):60-69.

Sarri, R. Gender and Race Differences in Criminal Justice Processing. Women's Studies International Forum 9 (1986):89-99.

Schmidt, J. C., Jr. Juries, Jurisdiction, and Race Discrimination: The Lost Promise of 'Strauder' v. 'West Virgina'. Texas Law Review 61

(May 1983):1401-1500.

Schwarz, Philip J. Twice Condemned: Slaves and the Criminal Laws of
    Virginia, 1705-1865. Baton Rouge: Louisiana State University Press,
    1988.

Shipp, E. R. At the Bar. To Be Black and a Prosecutor: Suspicion at the
    Office and Hostility at Home. New York Times August 26, 1988.

Smith, S. W. Judicial and Administrative Action to Avoid Racism in Post-
    Trial Criminal Practices and Procedures. In: Gilbert Ware (ed.),
    From the Black Bar. Voices for Equal Justice, pp. 151-64. New York:
    Putnam's, 1976.

Staples, R. White Racism, Black Crime and American Justice: An
    Application of the Colonial Model to Explain Crime and Race. Phylon
    36 (March 1975):14-22.

Steiner, Jesse F. and Roy M. Brown. North Carolina Chain Gang: A Study
    of Convict Road Work. Chapel Hill, NC: University of North Carolina
    Press, 1927.

Stevens, Edward W., Jr. Literacy, Law, and Social Order. DeKalb, IL:
    Northern Illinois University Press, 1988.

Stewart, D. O. The System on Trial; Racism, Discretion and the Will of
    the Court. [Crime] American Bar Association Journal 73 (July 1,
    1987):38.

Stout, D. S. The Lawyers of Death Row. New York Times Magazine February
    14, 1988.

Tanzi, V. The Underground Economy in the United States: Comment.
    International Monetary Fund Staff Papers 31 (December 1984).

Terry, Don. Black Fight for a Place Among the 'Finest'. New York Times
    November 19, 1988. [Black police officers in New York City].

The Underground Economy. American Owl 2 (November 1978).

U.S. Bureau of Justice Statistics. Time Served in Prison and on Parole.
    Washington, D.C.: U.S. Department of Justice, 1987.

U.S. Bureau of Justice Statistics. Criminal Victimization in the United
    States, 1985: A National Crime Survey Report. Washington, D.C.:
    U.S. Department of Justice, 1988.

U.S. Federal Bureau of Investigation. Crime in the United States.
    Washington, D.C.: GPO, 1988.

Viets, D. The Political Reality of Prisons. Contributions in Black
    Studies 2 (1978-1979).

Viscusi, W. K. Market Incentives for Criminal Behavior. In: Richard B.
    Freeman and Harry J. Holzer (eds.), The Black Youth Employment

Crisis Chicago, IL: University of Chicago Press, 1986.

Viscusi, W. K. The Risks and Rewards of Criminal Activity: A
    Comprehensive Test of Criminal Deterrence. Journal of Labor
    Economics 4 (July 1986).

Wallace, D. The Political Economy of Incarceration Trends in Late U.S.
    Capitalism: 1971-1977. Insurgent Sociologist 10 (1981):59-65.

Wiegand, R. B. Dimensions of the Shadow Economy. Doctoral dissertation,
    Vanderbilt University, 1984. UMO # 8522494.

Work, M. N. Negro Criminality in the South. Annals of the American
    Academy of Political and Social Sciences 49 (September 1913):74-80.

Yeager, M. Unemployment and Imprisonment. Journal of Criminal Law &
    Criminology 70 (1979).

Yee, Min S. The Melancholy History of Soledad Prison: In Which A Utopian
    Scheme Turns Bedlam New York: Harpers Magazine Press, 1973.

Zatz, Marjorie S. The Changing Forms of Racial/Ethnic Biases in
    Sentencing [Since 1930]. Journal of Research in Crime and
    Delinquency 24 (February 1987):69-92.

Zatz, M. S. Pleas, Priors, and Prison: Racial/Ethnic Differences in
    Sentencing. Social Science Research 14 (June 1985):169-93.

Crime Bibliography

Davis, L. G. Crime in the Black Community: An Exploratory Bibliography.
    [Exchange Bibliography No. 852.] Monticello, IL: Council of
    Planning Librarians, 1975.

Du Bois, W. E. B. A Select Bibliography of Negro Crime. In: Some Notes
    on Negro Crime Particularly in Georgia, pp. vi-viii. Atlanta:
    Atlanta University Press, 1904.

Schlachter, G. and P. R. Byrne. Crime and Punishment in America: A
    Historical Bibliography. Santa Barbara, CA: ABC-CLIO Information
    Services, 1984.

Wolfgang, M. E. and others. Criminal Violence and Race: A Selected
    Bibliography. Washington, D.C.: National Institute of Justice,
    1982.

[See also sections 29, 44, and 78]

19. Desegregation

We find another argument for equal education rights in the fact
that children learn more from each other than from their
teachers. ...

> - Sallie Holley, graduate of Oberlin College, testifying to
> the Rhode Island legislative committee on caste schools,
> Liberator, June 10, 1859.

Albert, Barb. Desegregation: Equality Eludes Us [Series of eight
    articles on desegregation in Indianapolis]. Indianapolis Star
    October 25, 1987+.

Allen, I. L. Variable White Ethnic Resistance to School Desegregation:
    Italian-American Parents in Three Connecticut Cities, 1966. In:
    William C. McCready (ed.), Culture, Ethnicity, and Identity. New
    York: Academic Press, 1983.

Alves, M. J. and C. V. Willie. Controlled Choice Assignments: A New and
    More Effective Approach to School Desegregation. Urban Review 19
    (1987):67-88.

Americans Finding Busing Much More Palatable Now [Poll by Louis Harris and
    Associates in Sept. 1988]. School Bus Fleet (April-May 1989).

Archbald, Douglas A. Magnet School, Voluntary Desegregation, and Public
    Choice Theory: Limits and Possibilities in a Big City School System
    [Milwaukee, WI]. Doctoral dissertation, University of Wisconsin,
    1988. UMO # 8810443.

Arias, M. B. and J. L. Bray. Equal Educational Opportunity and School
    Desegregation in Triethnic Districts. Denver, CO: Education
    Commission of the States, 1983.

Atkins, T. [Review of Anthony Lukas, 'Common Ground']. Social Policy
    (Winter 1986).

Baco, R. L. Issues in Desegregation and Bilingual Education: Mexican-
    American Opinions. Doctoral dissertation, United States
    International University, 1977. UMO # 7909503.

Bailey, Edwin Franklin. An Investigation of Teacher Expectations and
    Selected Potential Correlates in a Desegregated Public School System.
    Doctoral dissertation, Saint Louis University, 1988. UMO # 8816633.

Ballentine, A. G. School Desegregation: An Encore of Separate but Equal.
    Creighton Law Review 20 (Spring 1987):1055-92.

Barber, Bernard. Effective Social Research. Eight Cases in Economic,
    Political Science, and Sociology. New York: Russell Sage
    Foundation, 1989. [Desegregation, among other topics].

Barnes, C. A. Journey from Jim Crow: The Desegregation of Southern
    Transit. New York: Columbia University Press, 1983.

Bogira, S. Whatever Happened to School Desegregation? [Chicago public
    schools]. Reader January 29, 1988.

Braddock, J. H. School Desegregation and Black Assimilation. Journal of
    Social Issues 41 (Fall 1985):9-22.

Bruce, Mildred D. The Richmond School Board and the Desegregation of
    Richmond Public Schools, 1954 to 1971. Doctoral dissertation,
    College of William and Mary, 1988. UMO # 8813497.

Bullock, C. S., III. Defiance of the Law: School Discrimination before
    and after Desegregation [Georgia]. Urban Education 11 (October
    1976):239-62.

Casey, J. A. Effects of Desegregation: Relationship Among
    Human/Modifiable/Nonmodifiable Attributes and Frequency of
    Interracial Interactions of Blacks, Hispanics, Asians and Whites in
    Grades 1-12. Doctoral dissertation, University of San Francisco,
    1984. UMO # 8424806.

Center for National Policy Review. Why Must Northern School Systems
    Desegregate: A Summary of Federal Court Findings in Recent Cases. In:
    U.S. Congress, 97th, 1st session, House of Rep., Committee on
    the Judiciary, Subcomm. on Civil and Constitutional Rights. School
    Desegregation Hearings ... , pp. 261-92. [Cases updated July 1981].
    Washington, D.C.: GPO.

Coleman-Puckett, A. Student Achievement in Schools Desegregated by Court
    Order. Doctoral dissertation, University of Arizona, 1986. UMO #
    8704760.

Committee on Racial Equality. A Report on Racial/Ethnic Equity and
    Desegregation in Connecticut's Public Schools. Hartford, CT:
    Conecticut State Department of Education, January 1988.

Cooper, H. M. On the Social Psychology of Using Research: The Case of
    Desegregation and Black Achievement. ERIC ED 252 646.

Culbertson, M. May I Speak? Diary of a Crossover Teacher. [Edited by Sue
    Eakin]. Gretna, LA: Pelican Publishing Co., 1972.

Damico, S. B., and C. Sparks. Cross-group Contact Opportunities: Impact
    on Interpersonal Relationships in Desegregated Middle Schools.
    Sociology of Education 59 (April 1986):113-23.

Demeter, J. Lukas' Morality Play. Radical America 20 (September-October
    1986):61. [Critical comment on Anthony Lukas, 'Common Ground,' a
    portrayal of desegregation in Boston].

Di Bona, Joseph. The Resegregation of Schools in Small Towns and Rural
    Areas of North Carolina. Journal of Negro Education 57 (Winter
    1988):43-50.

Dr. [Henry E.] Garrett Teaches School Superintendent Neil V. Sullivan. *Citizen* (October 1967).

England, R. E. and D. R. Morgan. *Desegregating Big City Schools: Strategies, Outcomes, and Impacts*. New York: Associated Faculty Press, 1986.

Epstein, J. L. After the Bus Arrives: Resegregation in Desegregated Schools [Role of teacher attitudes]. *Journal of Social Issues* 41 (Fall 1985):23-43.

Fine, D. R. *When Leadership Fails: Desegregation and Demoralization in the San Francisco Schools*. New Brunswick, CT: Transaction Books, 1986.

Foderaro, Lisa W. In Yonkers [New York], a Measured Integration of School. *New York Times* September 25, 1988.

Fuerst, J. S. School Desegregation in the Hartford Connecticut Area: Four Methods. *Urban Education* 22 (April 1987):73-84.

Fuller, H. L. *The Impact of the Milwaukee Public School System's Desegregation Plan on Black Students and the Black Community (1976-1982)*. Doctoral dissertation, Marquette University, 1985. UMO # 8526784.

Gaillard, Frye. *The Dream Long Deferred*. Chapel Hill, NC: University of North Carolina Press, 1988. [Desegregation in Charlotte-Mecklenburg County, NC].

Garrett, H. E. *Children: Black and White* [How Classroom Desegregation Will Work]. Kilmarnock, VA: Patrick Henry Press, 1968. [Box 355, Kilmarnock, VA 22482].

Garrett, H. E. Garrett's Stuff. *Integrated Education* (March-April 1968):42.

Garrett, H. E. *How Classroom Desegregation Will Work*. Richmond, VA: Patrick Henry Press, 1965.

Giles, M., D. S. Gatlin and E. F. Cataldo. Racial and Class Prejudice: Their Relative Effects on Protest Against School Desegregation. *American Sociological Review* 41 (April 1976):280-288.

Green, J. Searching for 'Common Ground': A Review Essay [Extended critique of Anthony Lukas' 'Common Ground,' a portrayal of desegregation in Boston']. *Radical America* 20 (September-October 1986):44-60.

Hall, V. C. and Others. Behavior, Motivation, and Achievement in Desegregated Junior High School Science Classes. *Journal of Educational Psychology* 78 (1986):108-15.

Hirshon, Stanley P. Jazz, Segregation and Desegregation. *In*: William J.

Cooper, Jr. and others (eds.), A Master's Due: Essays in Honor of David
    Herbert Donald. Baton Rouge: Louisiana State University Press,
    1986.

Hood, Joye H. An Historical Study of Court-Ordered Integration in
    Metropolitan Nashville-Davidson County Schools. Doctoral
    dissertation, Tennessee State University, 1985. UMO # 8802609.

Jacoway, E. and D. R. Colburn (eds.) Southern Businessmen and
    Desegregation. Baton Rouge: Louisiana State University Press, 1982.

Jarrett, O. S. and L. C. Quay. Cross-racial Acceptance and Best Friend
    Choice: A Study of Kindergarteners and First Graders in Racially
    Balanced Classrooms. Urban Education 19 (1984):215-25.

Johnson, C. E. Black Student Participation in Extra-curricular Activities
    in Desegregated High Schools. Doctoral dissertation, Purdue
    University, 1985 UMO # 8529284.

Kleinman, Dena. School Bias: Town Looks for Answers. New York Times
    September 26, 1988. [Bloomfield, CT].

Kumagi, G. L. Politics of School Desegregation in the St. Paul Public
    Schools: The Decision-making Process. Doctoral dissertation,
    University of Minnesota, 1987. UMO # 8718653.

Landis, J. T. The Crawford Desegregation Suit in Los Angeles 1977-81: The
    Multiethnic Community versus Bustop. Doctoral dissertation,
    University of California, Los Angeles, 1984. UMO # 8428536.

Lines, P. M. Student Achievement in an Integrated Setting. Denver, CO:
    Education Commission of the States, 1983.

Lively, D. E. The Effectuation and Maintenance of Integrated Schools:
    Modern Problems in a Post-desegregation Society. Ohio State Law
    Journal 48 (Winter 1987):117-39.

Livesay, J. M. Domination and Legitimation in a Southern School District:
    The Reproduction of Racism in Black-White Relations. Doctoral
    dissertation, University of North Carolina, 1985. UMO # 8527300.

Lopez, Thomas S. Community Conflict and the Return to Neighborhood
    Schools in Norfolk, Virginia: Secession of Another Kind. Doctoral
    dissertation, Pennsylvania State University, 1988. UMO # 8818023.

McNeil, G. R. Community Initiative in the Desegregation of District of
    Columbia Schools, 1947-1954. Howard Law Journal 23 (1980):25-41.

Miller, N. Independent Meta-Analysis of the Effect of School
    Desegregation on Black Academic Achievement. ERIC ED 252629.

Miller, R. L. The Impact of Voluntary Busing on the Desegregation
    Experiences of Minority students in Five Connecticut Suburban
    Communities. Doctoral dissertation, University of Connecticut,
    1986. UMO # 8700067.

Obermanns, Richard and Louisa Oliver. New Dimensions in School and Housing Desegregation Policy for Ohio. Cleveland, OH: The Cuyahoga Plan of Ohio, Inc., December 1988.

Orduz, E. An Implementation Study of the Policy Prohibiting Within-School Segregation in a Large City School District [Chicago Public Schools]. Doctoral dissertation, University of Illinois at Chicago, 1987. UMO # 8712037.

Orfield, Gary. Desegregation of Black and Hispanic Students from 1968 to 1980. ERIC ED 221644.

Orfield, Gary. Racial Change in the U.S. School Enrollments, 1968-1984. Chicago: Department of Political Science, University of Chicago, 1986.

Orfield, Gary and Franklin Monfort. Are American Schools Resegregating in the Reagan Era? A Statistical Analysis of Segregation Levels from 1980-1984. Chicago: Department of Political Science, University of Chicago, 1986.

Powell, Gloria J. A Six-City Study of School Desegregation and Self-Concept among Afro-American Junior High School Students: A Preliminary Study with Implications for Mental Health. In: Barbara Ann Bass and others (eds.), The Afro-American Family, pp. 265-316. New York: Grune & Stratton, 1982.

Prager, J. and Others. School Desegregation Research: New Directions in Situational Analysis. New York: Plenum Press, 1986.

Rangel, Jesus. Bias Order Again Splits Jersey Town [School desegregation order in Hillside, NJ]. New York Times September 16, 1988.

Rosen, S. School Desegregation and the Chicano Community. ERIC ED 131974.

Rossell, Christine H. The Buffalo Controlled Choice Plan. Urban Education 22 (October 1987).

Salinas, G. Mexican-Americans and the Desegregation of Schools in the Southwest. Houston Law Review 8 (1971):925-51.

Sampson, W. A. Desegregation and Racial Tolerance in Academia. Journal of Negro Education 55 (Spring 1986):171-84.

School Desegregation and Black Achievement. Washington, D.C.: National Institute of Education, 1984.

Schoonover, Harold K., Jr. The Desegregation of the Plainfield, New Jersey Public Schools, 1962-1972: A Case Study. Doctoral dissertation, Rutgers University, 1988. UMO # 8813193.

Seltzer, Andrew. A Study of Achieving Black Students Attending an Integrated Elementary School. Doctoral dissertation, Rutgers

University, 1987. UMO # 8808233.

Scott, R. School Achievement and Desegregation: Is There a Linkage?
Mankind Quarterly 24 (1983):61-82.

Scott, R. Sex and Race Achievement Profiles in a Desegregated High School
in the Deep South. Mankind Quarterly 25 (Spring 1985):291-302.

Sears, D. O., and D. R. Kinder. Whites' Opposition to Busing: On
Conceptualizing and Operationalizing Group Conflict. Journal of
Pesonality and Social Psychology 48 (1985):1141-47.

Stephan, W. The Effects of School Desegregation: An Evaluation on 30
Years after 'Brown'. In: M. J. Saks and L. Saxe (eds.), Advances in
Applied Social Psychology. III, Hillsdale, NJ: Lawrence Erlbaum
Associates, 1986.

Sullivan, J. A. Equal Protection in the Post-Milliken Era: The Future of
Interdistrict Remedies in Desegregating Public Schools. Columbia
Human Rights Law Review 18 (Winter 1986):137-67.

Thornbrough, Emma Lou. Breaking Racial Barriers to Public Accommodations
in Indiana, 1935 to 1963. Indiana Magazine of History 83 (December
1987)301-43.

Ward, C. and R. Clark. Racism and the Desegregating Process: A
Mississippi Study. Jackson, MI: Educational Resources Center, 1970.

Washington, M. L. An Analysis of Educational Attitude of Black Youth
Within the Omaha Public School System. Doctoral dissertation,
University of Nebraska, 1985. UMO # 8521485.

Watson, C. W. The Helms-Johnston Amendment: A Congressional Effort to
Curb the Jurisdiction Cases. Howard Law Journal 26 (Fall 1983):1661-
77.

Watson, Diane E. The Effects of the Desegregation Controversy on Trustee
Governance in the Los Angeles Unified School District (1975-1980).
Doctoral dissertation, Claremont Graduate School, 1987. UMO #
8729393.

Weinberg, M. Improving Education in Desegregated Schools. In: Robert L.
Green (ed.), Metropolitan Desegregation New York: Plenum, 1985.

Welch, F. and Others. New Evidence on School Desegregation. Washington,
D.C.: U.S. Commission on Civil Rights, June 1987.

Weld, E. N. Racial Harmony: Putting It In Words. [4th and 5th grade
children's poetry on the desegregation experience in Boston] Boston
Globe January 17, 1988.

Whitfield, B. Conflict, Conflict Management and Their Applicability to
the St. Louis School Desegregation Controversy [St. Louis
metropolitan area]. Doctoral dissertation, State University of New
York at Buffalo, 1987. UMO # 8719767.

Wilson, F. D. The Impact of School Desegregation Programs on White Public-School Enrollment, 1968-1976. Sociology of Education 58 (1985):137-53.

Wortman, P. M. and F. B. Bryant. School Desegregation and Black Achievement: An Integrative Review. Sociological Methods and Resarch 13 (1985):289-324.

Wright, J. Skelly. Public School Desegregation: Legal Remedies for De Facto Segregation. In: Norman Dorsen (ed.), The Evolving Constitution: Essays on the Bill of Rights and the U.S. Supreme Court. Middletown, CT: Wesleyan University Press, 1987.

[See also sections 3, 12, 25, 26, 32, 44, 60, and 80]

20. Discrimination

Discrimination hinders the formation of ideals and the emerging of ability. But the doing away with discrimination will never settle these matters - rather, it opens the way for us to face the real problems of life.

> - W. E. B. Du Bois, "Can the Negro Expect Freedom by 1965?" (1947).

Alvarez, R., and Others. Discrimination in Organizations. San Francisco, CA: Jossey-Bass, 1979.

Arnold, H. E. Discrimination or Disintegration: Factors Affecting the Relative Earnings Position of Black Males during the 1960s and 1970s. Doctoral dissertation, Florida State University, 1986. UMO # 8625768.

Ashefelter, O. Racial Discrimination and Trade Unionism. Journal of Political Economy 80 (1972):435-64.

Ayres, B. Drummond, Jr. Maryland Shore Cited by Blacks In Cases of Bias. New York Times August 17, 1988.

Bahr, H. M., and Others. Discrimination against Urban Indians in Seattle. Indian Historian 5 (Winter 1972):4-11.

Belton, Robert. Causation in Employment Discrimination Law. Wayne Law Review 34 (Spring 1988):1235-1306.

Belz, H. The Freedman's Bureau Act of 1865 and the Principle of No Discrimination According to Color. Civil War History 21 (September 1975):197-217.

Berg, I. Racial Discrimination in Housing: A Study in Quest for Governmental Access by Minority Interest Groups 1945-1962. Doctoral dissertation, University of Florida, 1967. UMO # 6809511.

Bielby, W. T., and J. N. Baron. Men and Women at Work: Sex Segregation and Statistical Discrimination. American Journal of Sociology 91 (January 1986):759-99.

Black Owners' Suit Charges Burger King with Discrimination. New York Times October 19, 1988. [Associated Press story].

Blau, Francine and Marianne Ferber. Discrimination: Empirical Evidence from the United States. American Economic Review 77 (May 1987): 316-20.

Bloch, H. D. The Circle of Discrimination: An Economic and Social Study of the Black Man in New York. 1969.

Bloch, H. D. Craft Unions: A Link in the Circle of Negro Discrimination

[N.Y.C., 1866-1945]. Phylon 18 (1958):361-72.

Bloch, H. D. Discrimination Against the Negro in Employment in New York, 1920-1963. American Journal of Economics and Sociology 24 (1965):361-81.

Bloch, H. D. The New York City Negro and Occupational Eviction, 1860-1910. International Review of Social History 5 (1960):26-38.

Boch, H. D. Terence V. Powderly and Disguised Discrimination. American Journal of Economics and Sociology 33 (1974):145-60.

Boston, T. D. Race, Class and Conservatism. Winchester, MA: Unwin Hyman, 1988.

Boswell, T. E. Discrimination and Chinese Immigration. American Sociological Review 51 (June 1986):312-71.

Braddock, J. H., and J. M. McPartland. How Minorities Continue to Be Excluded from Equal Employment Opportunities: Research on Labor Market and Institutional Barriers. Baltimore, MD: Johns Hopkins University, Center for Social Organization of Schools, 1986.

Brown, C. The Federal Attack on Labor Market Discrimination: The Mouse that Roared? Cambridge, MA: National Bureau of Economic Research, 1981.

Brown, H. and D. Ford. An Exploratory Analysis of Discrimination in the Employment of Black MBA Graduates. Journal of Applied Psychology 62 (1977):50-56.

Brown, M. and P. Philips. Competition, Racism, and Hiring Practices among California Manufacturers, 1860-1882. Industrial and Labor Relations Review 40 (October 1986).

Buinghurst, N. G. The 'Descendants of Ham' in Zion: Discrimination Against Blacks Among the Shifting Mormon Frontier, 1830-1920. Nevada Historical Society Quarterly 24 (Winter 1981):298-318.

Bullard, R. D., and D. L. Tryman. Competition for Decent Housing: A Focus on Housing Discrimination Complaints in a Sunbelt City [Houston]. Journal of Ethnic Studies 7 (Winter 1980):51-63.

Burstein, Paul. Discrimination, Jobs, and Politics: The Struggle for Equal Employment Opportunity in the United States since the New Deal. Chicago: University of Chicago Press, 1985.

Caccavallo, F. M. Racial Discrimination: The Housing Market. American Economist 25 (Spring 1981).

Campbell, W. E. Profit, Prejudice, and Protest: Utility Competition and the Generation of Jim Crow Streetcars in Savannah, 1905-1907. Georgia Hist. Quarterly 70 (Summer 1986):197-231.

Carter, T. P. School Discrimination: The Mexican American Case. ERIC ED

048969.

Chestang, L. The Delivery of Child Welfare Services to Minority Group Children and their Families. In: Child Welfare Strategy in the Coming Years, pp. 169-94. Washington, D.C.: Department of Health, Education, and Welfare, 1978.

Christiansen, J. B. The Split Labor Market Theory and Filipino Exclusion: 1927-1934. Phylon 40 (Spring 1979):66-74.

Clark, D. The Irish in Philadelphia. Philadelphia, PA: 1974.

Close, M. M. Child Welfare and People of Color: Denial of Equal Access. Social Work Research and Abstracts 19 (Winter 1983):13-20.

Comanor, W. Racial Discrimination in American Industry. Economica 40 (November 1973):363-78.

Cotton, J. Discrimination and Favoritism in the U.S. Labor Market: The Cost to a Wage-Earner of Being Female and Black and the Benefit of Being Male and White. American Journal of Economics and Sociology 47 (January 1988).

Crosby, F., and Others. Recent Unobtrusive Studies of Black and White Discrimination and Prejudice: A Literature Review. Psychological Bulletin 87 (May 1980).

Cruz, J. R. Las relaciones raciales en Puerto Rico. Revista de Ciencias Sociales (1967).

Daniel, P. T. K. A History of Discrimination against Black Students in Chicago Secondary Schools. History of Education Quarterly 20 (Summer 1980):147-62.

Darity, W., Jr. The Theory of Racial Discrimination Revisited: Beyond the Ideology of Equality. Adherent 7 (December 1980).

Davila, A. E. Racial Earnings Differentials in Texas. Federal Reserve Bank of Dallas Economic Review (November 1984).

De Leon, A. They Called Them Greaser: Anglo Attitudes toward Mexicans in Texas, 1821-1900. Austin: University of Texas Press, 1983.

De Vise, P. Housing Discrimination in the Chicago Metropolitan Area: The Legacy of the 'Brown' Decision. De Paul Law Review 34 (Winter 1985):491-513.

Dewey, D. Southern Poverty and the Racial Division of Labor. New South 17 (May 1962).

Duvall, J. E., and R. N. Marguilies. Employment Discrimination [in 1986]. Mercer Law Review 38 (Summer 1987):1213-51.

Edelman, M. W. Portrait of Inequality. Black and White Children in America. Washington, D.C.: Childen's Defense Fund, 1980.

Ernst, R. Immigrant Life in New York City, 1825-1863. New York: 1965.

Feagin, J. R. Discrimination American Style. Englewood Cliffs, NJ: Prentice-Hall, 1984.

Feins, J. D., and Others. Final Report of a Study of Racial Discrimination in the Boston Housing Market. Cambridge, MA: Abt Associates, November 1981.

Freeman, A. D. Legitimizing Racial Discrimination Through Antidiscrimination Law: A Critical Review of Supreme Court Doctrine. Minnesota Law Review 62 (1978).

Freeman, R. B. Decline of Labor Market Discrimination and Economic Analysis [1890-1970]. American Economic Review 63 (1973):280-6.

Fremgen, J. P. Housing Discrimination: A Problem That Won't Go Away [Washington, D.C. metropolitan area]. Washington Post July 17, 1982.

Gilman, H. J. Economic Discrimination and Unemployment. American Economic Review (December 1965).

Gitelman, Howard M. 'No Irish Need Apply': Patterns and Responses to Ethnic Discrimination in the Labor Market. Labor History 14 (1973):56-68.

Glenn, N. D. Occupational Benefits to Whites from the Subordination of Negroes. American Sociological Review (June 1963).

Glenn, N. D. White Gains from Negro Subordination. Social Problems (Fall 1966).

Gold, D. E. Class Structure and the Economics of the Housing Problem: The Cause and Effects of Housing Market Discrimination, 2 vols. Doctoral dissertation, New School for Social Research, 1977. UMO # 7728210.

Gold, D. E. Housing Market Discrimination: Causes and Effects of Slum Formation. New York: Praeger, 1980.

Goode, V. Integration versus Integration: Race, Law and Economics in the Context of Housing Discrimination. Thurgood Marshall Law Review 11 (Spring 1986):363-80.

Gordon, D. M. and others. Segmented Work, Divided Workers: The Historical Transformation of Labor in the United States. New York: Cambridge University Press.

Gross, Samuel R. and Robert Mauro. Death and Discrimination: Racial Disparities in Capital Sentencing. Boston: Northeastern University, 1988.

Gwartney, J. Discrimination and Income Differentials. American Economic

Review 60 (June 1970):396-408.

Hakken, J. Discrimination Against Chicanos in the Dallas Rental Housing Market .... Washington, D.C.: Office of Policy Development and Research, U.S. Dept. of HUD, August 1979.

Hall, B. and others. Discrimination: Does It Exist Here? [Series of articles on Oskaloosa and Mahaska County, Iowa]. _Oskaloosa Herald_ July 6-14, 1982.

Hanafin, Teresa M. Atlanta. A Southern Attack on Skewed Lending [Discriminatory lending practices by city's banks]. _Boston Globe_ March 5, 1989.

Hannon, J. U. Ethnic Discrimination in a 19th Century Mining District: Michigan Copper Mines. _Explorations in Economic History_ 19 (January 1982):28-50.

Harding, R. R. Housing Discrimination as a Basis for Interdistrict School Desegregation Remedies. _Yale Law Journal_ 93 (December 1983):340-61.

Haywood, A. Can Theories of Intentional Wage Discrimination and Comparable Worth Help Black People? _National Black Law Journal_ 10 (Winter 1987):16-55.

Hefner, James A. The Illusion of Inclusion. In: Marguerite Ross Barnett and James A. Hefner (eds.), _Public Policy for the Black Community: Strategies and Perspectives_, pp. 257-70. Port Washington, NY: Alfred Publishing Co., 1976.

Hendon, W. S. Discrimination Against Negro Homeowners in Property Tax Assessment. _American Journal of Economics and Sociology_ 27 (1968):125-32.

Hewitt, W. L. Mexican Workers in Wyoming during World War II: Necessity, Discrimination and Protest. _Annals of Wyoming_ 54 (Fall 1982):20-33.

Higham, J. W. Social Discrimination Against Jews in America, 1830-1930. _American Jewish Historical Society Publication_ 47 (September 1957):1-33.

Hill, H. The New York City Terminal Market Controversy: A Case Study of Race, Labor, and Power. _Humanities in Society_ 6 (Fall 1983):351-91.

Hill, P. J. Relative Skill and Income Levels of Native and Foreign-born Workers in the United States. _Explorations in Economic History_ 12 (1975):47-60.

Hitt, M. A. and others. Discrimination in Industrial Employment: An Investigation of Race and Sex Bias Among Professions. _Work and Occupations_ 9 (May 1982):217-231.

Hoffman, J. _Racial Discrimination and Economic Development_. Lexington, MA: Lexington Books, 1975.

Holmes, M. S. The Blue Eagle as 'Jim Crow Bird': The NRA and Georgia's
    Black Workers. Journal of Negro History 57 (1972):276-83.

Honig, D. Worcester County, Maryland - A Dream Deferred [Discrimination
    in housing]. Howard Law Journal 27 (Winter 1984):91-143.

Houston, C. H. Foul Employment Practice on the Rails. In: Gilbert
    Ware (ed.), From the Black Bar. Voices for Equal Justice, pp. 230-
    43. New York: Putnam's, 1976.

Jefferson, A. W. Housing Discrimination and Community Response in North
    Lawndale (Chicago). Illinois 1948-1978. Doctoral dissertation, Duke
    University, 1979. UMO # 8003626.

Jencks, C. Discrimination and Thomas Sowell. New York Review of Books
    March 3, 1983.

Jjr, W. C. F., J. L. Olson, W. W. Malloy, and W. L. Boykin.
    Discrimination in Educational Placement and Referral.
    Integrateducation, XXI vol. 1-6 (January-December 1983).

Kain, J. F., and J. M. Quigley. Housing Markets and Racial
    Discrimination: A Microeconomic Analysis. New York: Columbia
    University Press, 1975.

Kamp, A. R. The History Behind 'Hansberry v. Lee' [Housing
    discrimination]. U.C. Davis Law Review 20 (Spring 1987):481-99.

Keith, D. J. Labor-Management Collusion Against Blacks. In: Gilbert
    Ware (ed.), From the Black Bar. Voices for Equal Justice, pp. 249-
    54. New York: Putnam's, 1976.

Kiker, B. F. and J. A. Heath. The Effect of Socio-economic Background on
    Earnings: A Comparison by Race. Economics of Education Review 4
    (1985).

King, Allan G. Labor Market Discrimination Against Black Women. Review
    of Black Political Economy 8 (Summer 1978):325-36.

Kirchheimer, A. The Woman Leading Fight against Dual Discrimination [Ms.
    Maria Jiminez Van Hoy, president, National Conference of Puerto Rican
    Women]. Boston Globe August 5, 1981.

Klausner, Samuel J. Anti-Semitism in the Executive Suite, Yesterday,
    Today and Tomorrow. Moment 13 (September 1988):32-39.

Klausner, Samuel J. Succeeding in Corporate America: The Experience of
    Jewish M.B.A's. New York: American Jewish Committee, 1988.

Kluegel, J. R. The Causes and Costs of Racial Exclusion from Job
    Authority. American Sociological Review 43 (June 1978):281-301.

Knoll, J. A. The Effect of Prejudice upon the Employment of Indians.
    Master's thesis, University of Idaho, 1947.

Krofcheck, M. D., and C. Jackson. The Chicano Experience with Nativism in
    Public Administration. Public Administration Review 34 (November-
    December 1974):534-39.

La Botz, D. Filipino Americans Deal with Racism. Chicago Defender
    September 20, 1980.

Landers, C. E., and P. L. Weaver. The Cost of Being Black, 1970: Some
    Preliminary Observations. Journal of Social and Behavioral Sciences
    20 (Fall 1974):120-29.

Lauren, Paul G. Power and Prejudice. The Politics and Diplomacy of
    Racial Discrimination. Boulder, CO: Westview, 1988.

Leonard, J. S. The Interaction of Residential Segregation and Employment
    Discrimination. Journal of Urban Economics 21 (May 1987).

Levin, Sharon G. and Stanford L. Levin. Profit Maximization and
    Discrimination. Industrial Organization Review 4 (1976):108-16.

Linder, M. Farm Workers and the Fair Labor Standards Act: Racial
    Discrimination in the New Deal. Texas Law Review 65 (June
    1987):1335-94.

Longres, J. F., Jr. Racism and Its Effects on Puerto Rican Continentals.
    Social Casework 55 (February 1974):67-75.

Luebben, R. A. Prejudice and Discrimination against Navajos in a Mining
    Community. In: Howard Bahr and others (eds.), Native Americans
    Today: Sociological Perspectives. New York: Harper & Row, 1972.

Lykes, M. B. Discriminating and Coping in the Lives of Black Women.
    Journal of Social Issues 39 (1983):79-100.

Lykes, M. B. Discrimination in the Lives of Older Black Women. ERIC ED
    244168.

Lyson, T. A. Race and Sex Segregation in the Occupational Structures of
    Southern Employers. Social Science Quarterly 34 (March 1985).

Marcus, L. R., and F. O. Smith. Black Faculty and Survival Systems
    [Discrimination against Black scientists in academe before World War
    II]. Integrateducation 17 (May-August 1979):31-36.

Margo, R. A. Race and Human Capital: Comment. American Economic Review
    76 (December 1986):[See James P. Smith, below].

Margo, R. A. Race Differences in Public School Expenditures:
    Disfranchisement and School Finance in Louisiana, 1890-1910. Social
    Science History (Winter 1982).

Marks, C. Split Labor Markets and Black-White Relations, 1865-1920.
    Phylon 42 (Winter 1981):293-308.

Marshall, F. R. The Economics of Racial Discrimination: A Survey. Journal of Economic Literature 12 (September 1974):849-71.

McGahey, R. and J. Jeffries. Minorities and the Labor Market. Twenty Years of Misguided Policy. Washington, D.C.: Joint Center for Political Studies, 1985.

McGovney, D. O. Race Discrimination in Naturalization. Iowa Law Bulletin 8 (1923):129-211.

Medoff, M. H. Discrimination and the Occupational Progress of Blacks since 1950. American Journal of Economics and Sociology 44 (July 1985):295-304.

Meeker, E. and J. Kan. Racial Discrimination and Occupational Attainment at the Turn of the Century. Explorations in Economic History 14 (July 1977):250-76.

Mindiola, T., Jr. Age and Income Discrimination Against Mexican Americans and Blacks in Texas, 1960 and 1970. Social Problems 27 (December 1979):196-208.

Mitchell, B. C. The Paddy Camps. The Irish of Lowell, 1821-61. Urbana, IL: University of Illinois Press, 1987.

Mitchell, Gail G. J. A Comparison of the Higher Level Thinking Skills of Black/White Students and the Influence of Selected Demographic Variables on their Placement in Programs for the Gifted. Doctoral dissertation, Ball State University, 1987. UMO # 8729829.

Mohl, Raymond A. and Neil Betten. Discrimination and Repatriation: Mexican Life in Gary. In: James B. Lane and Edward J. Escobar (eds.), Forging a Community: The Latino Experience in Northwest Indiana, 1919-1975. Bloomington, IN: Indiana University Press, 1987.

Montejano-Enriquez, D. The Making of a Racial Order: A Journey through Mexican Texas, 1848-1930. Doctoral dissertation, Yale University, 1977.

Montgomery, E. and W. Wascher. Race and Gender Wage Inequality in Services and Manufacturing. Industrial Relations 26 (Fall 1987):284-90.

Morrison, K. C. Federal Aid to Housing and Discrimination. Journal of Social and Behavioral Sciences 14 (Spring 1969):42-50.

Murayama, Y. The Disappearance of Racial Wage Discrimination toward Japanese Immigrant in the Pacific Northwest: 1890-1950. American Review (Tokyo) 18 (1984):232-34.

Nelson, S. C. Housing Discrimination and Black Employment Opportunities. Doctoral dissertation, Princeton University, 1976. UMO # 7623868.

Newburger, H. Recent Evidence on Discrimination in Housing. Washington,

D.C.: Office of Policy Development and Research, U.S. Dept. of HUD, 1984.

Nickel, J. W. Discrimination and Morally Relevant Characteristics. *Analysis* 32 (1972):113-114.

Niemi, A. W., Jr. Occupational/Educational Discrimination Against Black Men. *Journal of Black Studies* 9 (September 1978):87-92.

Nordheimer, J. Black Cubans: Apart in Two Worlds [Florida]. *New York Times* December 2, 1987.

Nordlie, P. G. *Measuring Changes in Institutional Racial Discrimination in the Army*. McLean, VA: Champion Press, 1974.

Novall, R. J. Caste in Steel: Jim Crow Careers in Birmingham. *Journal of American History* 73 (December 1986):669-94.

Ong, P. M. Chinese Labor in Early San Francisco: Racial Segmentation and Industrial Expansion. *Amerasia Journal* 8 (Spring-Summer 1981):69-92.

Palmore, E. and F. J. Whittington. Differential Trends Toward Equality Between Whites and Nonwhites. *Social Forces* 49 (September 1970):108-117.

Partsch, K. J. Elimination of Racial Discrimination in the Enjoyment of Civil and Political Rights. *Texas International Law Journal* 14 (Spring 1979):191-250.

Pascal, A. *Racial Discrimination in Economic Life*. Lexington, MA: D.C. Heath, 1972.

Penrose, E. R. *California Nativism: Organized Opposition to the Japanese, 1890-1913*. San Francisco, CA: R and E Research Associates, 1973.

Peterson, R. H. Anti-Mexican Nativism in California, 1848-1853: A Study of Cultural Conflict. *Southern California Quarterly* 62 (Winter 1980):309-27.

Pettigrew, T. F. (ed.) *Racial Discrimination in the United States*. New York: Harper & Row, 1975.

Philips, P. A Note on the Apparent Constancy of the Racial Wage Gap in New Jersey Manufacturing, 1902 to 1979. *Review of Black Political Economy* 13 (Spring 1985).

Polier, Justine Wise. Racial Discrimination. *Juvenile Justice in Double Jeopardy*. Hillsdale, NJ: Lawrence Erlbaum, 1989.

Ponder, H. An Example of the Alternative Cost Doctrine Applied to Racial Discrimination [Economic boycott]. *Journal of Negro Education* 35 (1966):42-7.

Poston, Dudley, L. Jr., and David Alvirez. On the Cost of Being a Mexican-American Worker. Social Science Quarterly 53 (March 1973):695-709.

Pottinger, J. S. Discrimination and Denial Due to National Origin [Esp. language rights]. Integrated Education 8 (July-August 1970).

Pratt, S. A. J. and A. Krishnaswami. Seminar on the Elimination of All Forms of Racial Discrimination. UN Document ST/RAD/HR/34. New York: United Nations, 1968.

Programme of Action for the Second Decade to Combat Racism and Racial Discrimination. Objective: Justice 16 (June 1984):1-17.

Prout, L. R. Racism, Cuban Style [Rejection of Black Cubans by other Cubans in Union City, NJ]. Village Voice September 2, 1981.

Quinn, Robert P. and others. The Chosen Few: A Study of Discrimination in Executive Selection. Ann Arbor, MI: Survey Research Center, University of Michigan, 1968.

Rabinowitz, H. N. From Exclusion to Segregation: Southern Race Relations, 1865-1890. Journal of American History 63 (September 1976):325-350.

Ragan, J. F., Jr. and C. H. Tremblay. Testing for Employee Discrimination by Race and Sex. Journal of Human Resources 23 (Winter 1988).

Research in Questions of Equity and Discrimination. In: Mary P. Martin and E. Michael Staman (eds.), The Practice of Institutional Research. ERIC ED 218992.

Register, C. A. Racial Employment and Earnings Differentials: The Impact of the Reagan Administration. Review of Black Political Economy 15 (Summer 1986).

Reich, M. Racial Inequality. A Political-Economic Analysis. Princeton, NJ: Princeton University Press, 1981.

Reissman, L. Housing Discrimination in New Orleans: Summary and Recommendations. New Orleans: Tulane Urban Studies Center, Tulane University, 1970.

Ringer, B. B. 'We the People' and Others: Duality and America's Treatment of Its Racial Minorities. New York: Methuen, 1983.

Roback, J. The Political Economy of Segregation: The Case of Segregated Streetcars. Journal of Economic History 46 (December 1986):893-917.

Roberts, C. A., and R. Higgs. Did Southern Farmers Discriminate? An Exchange. Agricultural History 49 (1975):441-7.

Rodriguez, C. E. Puerto Ricans: Between Black and White. In: Clara E. Rodriguez and others (eds.), The Puerto Rican Struggle, pp. 20-30. New York: Puerto Rican Migration Research Consortium, 1980.

Rodriguez, C. E. Prisms of Race and Class [Review essay on Thomas
    Sowell's 'Ethnic America,' as applied to Puerto Ricans]. Journal of
    Ethnic Studies 12 (Summer 1984):99-120.

Roemer, J. Divide and Conquer: Microfoundations of Marxiam Theory of
    Wage Discrimination. Bell Journal of Economics 10 (Autumn
    1979):695-705.

Salman, I. Referral of Mexican American Students to Special Education
    Services. Doctoral dissertation, University of Southern California,
    1987.

Santa Cruz, H. Special Study of Racial Discrimination in the Political,
    Economic, Social and Cultural Spheres. New York: United Nations
    June 1969, U.N. Document E/CN.4/Sub.2/301.

Schafer, R. Racial Discrimination in the Boston Housing Market. September
    1976. ERIC ED 170386.

Schafer, R. Racial Discrimination in the Boston Housing Market. Journal
    of Urban Economics 6 (1979):176-196.

Shenon, Philip. Hispanic F.B.I. Agents' Suit Reflects a Sense of
    Betrayal. New York Times September 11, 1988.

Schiller, B. R. The Economics of Poverty and Discrimination, (fourth
    edition). Englewood Cliffs, NJ: Prentice-Hall, 1984.

Schmidt, F. H. Job Caste in the Southwest. Industrial Relations 9
    (October 1969):100-10.

Seda Bonilla, E. El Desarollo Socio-Politico de la Poblacion Negra en
    Puerto Rico. In: Memorias del Primer Congreso de Minoritas
    Ethnicas. Panama: 1974.

Shapiro, D. Wage Differentials among Black, Hispanic, and White Young
    Men. Industrial and Labor Relations Review 37 (July 1984).

Shapiro, R. Discrimination and Community Mental Health. Challenging
    Institutional Racism. Civil Rights Digest 8 (Fall 1975):19-23.

Shelton, B. A. Racial Discrimination in Initial Labor Market Access.
    National Journal of Sociology 1 (1987):101-15.

Shergold, P. R. Relative Skill and Income Levels of Native and Foreign
    Born Workers: A Reexamination. Explorations in Economic History 13
    (1976):451-61.

Shulman, S. Changing Patterns of Labor Market Discrimination:
    Differentials in the Probability of Employment by Race and City.
    Doctoral dissertation, University of Massachusetts, 1984.

Shulman, S. Competition and Racial Discrimination: The Employment
    Effects of Reagan's Labor Market Policies. Review of Radical

129

Political Economics 16 (Winter 1984):111-28.

Shulman, S. Discrimination, Human Capital, and Black-White Unemployment:
    Evidence from Cities. Journal of Human Resources 22 (Summer 1987).

Siegel, P. M. On the Cost of Being a Negro. Sociological Inquiry 35
    (Winter 1965):41-57.

Slavin, S. L. Bias in U.S. Big Business Recruitment [Antisemitism].
    Patterns of Prejudice 10 (September-October 1976):22-25.

Smallwood, J. Perpetration of Caste: Black Agricultural Workers in
    Reconstruction Texas. Mid-America 61 (January 1979):5-23.

Smith, A. N. Blacks and the Los Angeles Municipal Transit System, 1941-
    1945. Urbanism Past & Present 6 (Winter-Spring 1980-81):25-31.

Smith, B. A. A Study of Racial Discrimination in Houston. In: J.
    Vernon Henderson (ed.), Research in Urban Economics, I. Greenwich,
    CT: JAI Press, 1981.

Smith, J. P. Race and Human Capital: Reply. American Economic Review
    76 (December 1986):[See Robert A. Margo, above].

Smith, M. Industrial Racial Wage Discrimination in the U.S. Industrial
    Relations (Winter 1979).

Smith, N. A. and Q. Taylor. Racial Discrimination in the Workplace: A
    Study of Two West Coast Cities During the 1940s [Portland, Oregon and
    Los Angeles, Calif.]. Journal of Ethnic Studies 8 (Spring 1980):35-
    54.

Smythe, H. M. The Concept 'Jim Crow'. Social Forces 7 (1948).

Sniderman, P. M., and M. S. Hagen. Race and Inequality: A Study in
    American Values. Chatham, NJ: Chatham House, 1985.

Sogrera, M. Racismo y Politica en Puerto Rico. Rio Piedras, PR:
    Editorial Edil.

Sowell, T. Markets and Minorities. New York: Basic Books, 1981.

Sowell, T. and L. D. Collins (eds.) American Ethnic Groups. Washington,
    D.C.: Urban Institute, 1978.

Steeh, C. A. G. Racial Discrimination in Alabama, 1870-1910. Doctoral
    dissertation, University of Michigan, 1975. UMO # 7520456.

Stehno, S. M. Differential Treatment of Minority Children in Service
    Systems. Social Work 27 (January 1985):39-45.

Streifford, W. M. Racial Economic Dualism in St. Louis. Review of Black
    Political Economy 4 (1974):63-82.

Surace, S. J. Achievement, Discrimination, and Mexican Americans.

Comparative _Studies_ _in_ _Society_ _and_ _History_ 24 (April 1982):315-39.

Szymanski, A. Racial Discrimination and White Gain. _American_
     Sociological _Review_ 41 (June 1976):403-414 [See W. Villemez, below].

Szymanski, A. Trends in Economic Discrimination against Blacks in the
     U.S. Working Class. _Review_ _of_ _Radical_ _Political_ _Economy_ 7 (Fall
     1975):1-21.

Tempest, R. Housing Bias: HUD Faulted for Inaction [Clarksville]. _Los_
     Angeles _Times_ January 23, 1984.

Terborg-Penn, R. Discrimination vs. Afro-American Women in the Woman's
     Movement, 1830-1920. _In_: Sharon Harley and Rosalyn Terborg-Penn
     (eds.), _The_ _Afro-American_ _Woman:_ _Struggles_ _and_ _Images_. Port
     Washington, NY: Kennikat Press, 1978.

Terrell, M. C. D.C. Discrimination. _Washington_ _Post_ September 14, 1952.

Terrell, M. C. What It Means to Be Colored in the Capital of the United
     States. _Independent_ January 24, 1907.

Thernstrom, S. _The_ _Other_ _Bostonians_. Cambridge, MA: Harvard University
     Press, 1973.

Thomas, C. Discrimination and Its Effects. _Integrateducation_ 21
     (January-December 1983):204-97.

Thompson, J. L. Discrimination, Jobs, and Politics: The Struggle for
     Equal Employment Opportunity in the United States since the New Deal.
     Michigan _Law_ _Review_ 85 (April-May 1987).

Torres, J. C. The Dilemma of White Skin [Skin color among Cubans in
     Little Havana, Miami]. _Village_ _Voice_ August 27, 1980.

Tuck, R. A. _Not_ _With_ _the_ _Fist_ [Discrimination against Mexican-Americans
     in San Bernardino, CA]. New York: Harcourt Brace, 1946.

Turner, C. B., and B. A. Turner. Racial Discrimination in Occupations,
     Perceived and Actual. _Phylon_ 42 (Winter 1981):322-334.

U.S. Commission On Civil Rights. _Discriminatory_ _Religous_ _Schools_ _and_ _Tax_
     Exempt _Status_. Washington, D.C.: The Commission, December 1982.

U.S. Commission On Civil Rights. Employment Discrimination Against the
     Chinese (testimony). _Integrateducation_ 12 (July-August 1974):19-20.

U.S. Commission On Civil Rights. _The_ _Mexican-American_ _Education_ _Study._
     Report _V:_ _Teachers_ _and_ _Students._ _Differences_ _in_ _Teacher_ _Interaction_
     with _Mexican_ _American_ _and_ _Anglo_ _Students_. Washington, D.C.: GPO,
     March 1973.

U.S.Congress, 96th, 1st Session, Joint Economic Committee. _The_ _Cost_ _of_
     Racial _Discrimination:_ _Hearing_ _..._ Washington, D.C.: GPO, 1980.

U.S. Department of Housing and Urban Development. Discrimination in the Dallas Rental Market. Washington, D.C.: GPO, .

Valente, J. Black Hispanics: Caught between Two Worlds [Washington, D.C. area]. Washington Post September 16, 1980.

Villamez, W. Black Subordination and White Economic Well-Being. American Sociological Review (October 1978):[See reply by Albert Szymanski in same issue].

Vinod, H. D. Measurement of Economic Distance between Blacks and Whites. Journal of Business and Economic Statistics 3 (January 1985).

Ward, Lewis B. The Ethics of Executive Selection. Harvard Business Review (March-April 1965).

Weisburd, Abe. Blacks Sue State Dept. on Bias. Guardian (N.Y.C.) November 5, 1986.

Williams, R. M. Capital, Competition,and Discrimination: A Reconsideration of Racial Earnings Inequality. Review of Radical Political Economics 19 (Summer 1987):1-15.

Withey, E. Discrimination in Private Employment in Puerto Rico. Revista Puertorriquena sobre los Derechos Humanos/Puerto Rican Journal of Human Rights 1 (August 1977):43-47.

Wong, M. G. The Cost of Being Chinese, Japanese, and Filipino in the United States: 1960, 1970, and 1976. Pacific Sociological Review 25 (January 1982):58-78.

Yinger, J. M. Economic Incentives, Institutions, and Racial Discrimination: The Case of Real Estate Brokers. Cambridge, MA: CPR Publications, Department of City and Regional Planning, Harvard University, Cambridge, MA, February 1978.

Yinger, J. M. Measuring Racial Discrimination with Fair Housing Audits: Caught in the Act. American Economic Review 76 (December 1986).

Discrimination Bibliography

Kadish, E. Discrimination in Employment: A Selective Bibliography. Law and Contemporary Problems 49 (Autumn 1986):211-35.

Siegel, J. A. (comp.) Racial Discrimination in Housing. Monticello, IL: Council of Planning Librarians, 1977.

[See also sections 6, 10, 12, 15, 17, 18, 29, 31, 32, 33, 34, 35, 37, 38, 40, 41, 42, 48, 50, 55, 73, 75, 77, 78, 79, and 83]

21. Documentaries

From 1908 on I was compiling a day by day record of what was taking place with reference to the Negro. Thus it became possible to answer in a factual manner questions relating to all matters concerning him.

- Monroe N. Work, February 7, 1940 in Linda O. McMurry, Recorder of the Black Experience. A Biography of Monroe Nathan Work, p. 71.

Aptheker, H. (ed.) A Documentary History of the Negro People in the United States, 3 vols.

Axtell, J. (ed.) The Indian Peoples of Eastern America: A Documentary History of the Sexes. New York: 1981.

Berlin, I. and others (eds.) Freedom. A Documentary History of Emancipation, 1861-1867. New York: Cambridge University Press, 1986-.

Feldstein, S. (ed.) The Poisoned Tongue. A Documentary History of American Racism and Prejudice. New York: Morrow, 1972.

Foner, P. S. and J. S. Allen (eds.) American Communism and Black Americans: A Documentary History, 1919-1929. Philadelphia, PA: Temple University Press, 1986.

Foner, P. S. and R. L. Lewis (eds.) The Black Worker: A Documentary History from Colonial Times to the Present, 8 vols. Philadelphia, PA: Temple University Press, 1978-1984.

Josephy, A. M., Jr. (ed.) Red Power. The American Indians' Fight for Freedom. Lincoln: University of Nebraska Press, 1985. [Documentary history, since 1960s].

La Gumina, S. J. Wop! A Documentary History of Anti-Italian Discrimination in the United States. San Francisco: Straight Arrow Books, 1973.

Lazerson, M. (ed.) American Education in the Twentieth Century: A Documentary History. New York: Teachers College Press, 1987.

Lerner, G. (ed.) Black Women in White America. A Documentary History. New York: Pantheon, 1972.

Mullin, M. (ed.) American Negro Slavery: A Documentary History. University of South Carolina Press, 1976.

Price, C. A. (ed.) Freedom Not Far Distant: A Documentary History of Afro-Americans in New Jersey. Newark: New Jersey Historical Society, 1980.

Rose, W. L. (ed.) A Documentary History of Slavery in North America.
    New York: Oxford University Press, 1976.

Rosenstiel, A. (ed.) Red and White: Indian Views of the White Man, 1492-
    1982. New York: Universe Books, 1983.

Selzer, M. (ed.) 'Kike!' A Documentary History of Anti-Semitism in
    America. New York: World, 1972.

Sernett, M. C. (ed.) Afro-American Religious History. A Documentary
    Witness. Durham, NC: Duke University Press, 1985.

Vogel, V. (ed.) This Country Was Ours. A Documentary History of The
    American Indian. New York: Harper & Row, 1972.

Weinberg, M. (ed.) America's Economic Heritage, 2 vols. Westport, CT:
    Greenwood, 1983.

Wu, C. T. (ed.) 'Chink!' A Documentary History of Anti-Chinese Prejudice
    in America. New York: World, 1972.

22. W. E. B. Du Bois

*... Dr. Du Bois took the lead in making the United States and
the world recognize that racial prejudice was not a mere matter
of Negroes being persecuted but was a cancer which poisoned the
whole civilization of the United States.*

- C. L. R. James, "Black Power" 1967.

Aptheker, H. (ed.) The Complete Published Works of W.E.B. Du Bois, 37
    vols. White Plains, NY: Kraus International Publications, 1986.

Aptheker, H. (ed.) The Correspondence of W.E.B. Du Bois, 3 vols.
    Amherst, MA: University of Massachusetts Press, 1973-1978.

Demarco, J. P. The Concept of Race in the Social Thought of W.E.B. Du
    Bois. Philosophical Forum 3 (Winter 1971-1972).

Dennis, R. M. Race, Structured Inequality and the Consequences of Racial
    Domination: The Sociology of W.E.B. Du Bois. In: V. Gordon (ed.),
    Lectures: Black Scholars on Black Issues, pp. 149-169. Washington,
    D.C.: University Press of America, 1979.

Drake, S. C. Dr. W.E.B. Du Bois: A Life Lived Experimentally and Self-
    Documented [The text of a speech delivered Feb. 26, 1964].
    Contributions in Black Studies 8 (1986-1987):111-34.

Du Bois, W. E. B. Against Racism: Unpublished Essays, Papers, Addresses,
    1867-1961 (Edited by Herbert Aptheker). Amherst, MA: University of
    Massachusetts, 1985.

Du Bois, W. E. B. Black America. In: Fred J. Ringel (ed.), America as
    Americans See It, pp. 140-155. New York: Literary Guild, 1932.

Du Bois, W. E. B. The Economic Revolution in the South. In: Booker T.
    Washington and W.E.B. Du Bois (eds.), The Negro in the South, 1907.

Du Bois, W. E. B. The Negro in America. In: Encyclopedia Americana,
    vol. 11. New York: Encyclopedia Americana Company, 1904.

Du Bois, W. E. B. The Negro in America Today. Freedom Jan. 16, 23, 30;
    Feb. 13; Mar. 5, 1956.

Du Bois, W. E. B. The Negro Race in the United States of America. In:
    G. Spiller (ed.), Papers in Inter-Racial Problems Communicated to the
    First Universal Races Congress Held at the University of London, July
    26-29, 1911, pp. 348-364. London: P. J. King & Son, 1911. [See
    1970 edition, edited by Aptheker].

Du Bois, W. E. B. L'Ouvrier negre en Amerique. Revue Economique
    Internationale (Brussels) 4 (November 1906):298-348.

Du Bois, W. E. B. The Segregated Negro World. World Tomorrow 6 (May

1923):136-8.

Du Bois, W. E. B. Slavery and Its Aftermath. _Dial_ 40 (May 1, 1906):294-5.

Harding, V. W.E.B. Du Bois and the Black Messianic Vision. _Freedomways_ (Winter 1969).

Harris, V. J. _The Brownies' Book: Challenge to the Selective Tradition in Childen's Literature_ [Prepared by W.E.B. Du Bois, 1920-1921]. Doctoral dissertation, University of Georgia, 1986. UMO # 8628882.

Hector, M. G. _Racism, Black Nationalism and W.E.B Du Bois: A Study of a Divided Soul_. Master's thesis, Emory University, 1980.

Marable, Manning. Peace and Black Liberation: The Contributions of W.E.B. Du Bois. _Science and Society_ 47 (Winter 1984):385-405.

Meade, H., II. _W.E.B. Du Bois and His Place in the Discussion of Racism_. Doctoral dissertation, University of Massachusetts at Amherst, 1987.

Nakamura, Masaka S. _Beyond "Cultural Deprivation": A View of Democracy of Culture_. Doctoral dissertation, Cornell University, 1988. UMO # 8804527.

Taylor, C. M. W.E.B. Du Bois's Challenge to Scientific Racism. _Journal of Black Studies_ 11 (June 1981):449-460.

Wilson, W. _A Syllabus for the Study of Selective Writings by W.E.B. Du Bois_. May 1970. ERIC ED 041974.

W. E. B. Du Bois Bibliography

Aptheker, H. (comp.) _Annotated Bibliography of the Published Writings of W.E.B. Du Bois_. Millwood, NY: Kraus-Thomson, 1973.

Partington, P. G. (comp.) _W.E.B. Du Bois: A Bibliography of His Published Writings_. Whittier, CA: Author, 1977.

23. Economic Standards

*In the whole realm of manufacturing under the factory system,
the Negro is excluded by the trades union and the deliberate and
widespread agreement of employers.*

- W. E. B. Du Bois, "Our Economic Future," May 1928.

Abeles, Schwartz, Hackel, and Silverblatt, Inc. The Chinatown Garment
    Study. New York: ILGWU, 1983.

Albelda, R. and others. Mink Coats Don't Trickle Down. The Economic
    Attack on Women and People of Color. Boston: South End Press, 1988.

Alvirez, D. Economic Exploitation among the Mexican Americans in Texas
    and New Mexico. In: Division of Education and Cultivation of the
    United Methodist Church 'Live a New Life', pp. 173-86. Cincinnati,
    OH: United Methodist Publishing House, 1972.

Anderson, B. E. Economic Patterns in Black America. In: James D.
    Williams (ed.), The State of Black America 1982, pp. 1-32. New York:
    National Urban League, January 1982.

Anderson, B. E., and P. H. Cottingham. The Elusive Quest for Economic
    Equality. Daedalus 110 (Spring 1981):257-274.

Anderson, B. E., and P. A. Wallace. Public Policy and Black Economic
    Progress: A Review of the Evidence. American Economic Review 65
    (1975):47-52.

Au Claire, P. A. Public Attitudes toward Social Welfare Expenditures.
    Social Work 29 (March-April 1984):139-44.

Azores-Gunter, Tania F. M. Status Achievement Patterns of Filipinos in
    the United States. Doctoral dissertation, University of California,
    Los Angeles, 1987. UMO # 8803683.

Barbanel, Josh. Crisis of the Welfare System: Seeking Benefits through
    Judges. New York Times August 29, 1988.

Barr, A. Occupational and Geographic Mobility in San Antonio, 1870-1900.
    Social Science Quarterly 51 (1970):396-403.

Beeghley, L. Living Poorly in America. New York: Praeger, 1983.

Berg, R. H. The Socio-economic Exploitation of Ethnicity on a Western
    Massachusetts Tobacco Farm. Dialectical Anthropology 5 (November
    1980).

Bernstein, R. America Still Haunted by Problems of Black Poor. New York
    Times January 17, 1988.

Bianchi, S. M. Household Composition and Racial Inequality. New

Brunswick, NJ: Rutgers University Press, 1981.

Bianchi, S. M. Measurement of Household Economic Well-Being. American Statistical Association Proceedings of the Social Statistics Section (1980):143-148.

Bianchi, S. M. Racial Differences in Per Capita Income, 1960-1976: The Importance of Household Size, Headship, and Labor Force Participation. Demography 17 (May 1980).

Biles, R. Memphis in the Great Depression. Knoxville: University of Tennessee Press, 1986.

Black, F. and others. The Mean Season: The Attack on the Welfare State. New York: Pantheon, 1987.

Blackwell, J. E. The Economic Status of Blacks in Boston. Trotter Institute Review (UMass Boston) 1 (Winter 1987):9-13.

Blackwell, J. E. Jobs, Income and Poverty: The Black Share of the New Boston. In: P. Clay (ed.), The Emerging Black Community of Boston, Boston: William Monroe Trotter Institute, UMass/Boston, 1985.

Blakey, G. T. Hard Times and New Deal in Kentucky 1929-1939. Lexington: University Press of Kentucky, 1986.

Bluestone, B. and B. Harrison. The Growth of Low-Wage Employment, 1963-86. American Economic Review 78 (May 1988).

Bonilla, F., and R. Campos. A Wealth of Poor: Puerto Ricans in the New Economic Order. Daedalus 110 (Spring 1980):133-76.

Borrero, I. M. Citizens in Limbo: An Economic Analysis of Puerto Ricans in the U.S. Doctoral dissertation, Brandeis University, 1987. UMO # 8722491.

Boxberger, Daniel L. Resource Allocation and Control on the Lummi Indian Reservation: A Century of Conflict and Change in the Salmon Fishery. Doctoral dissertation, University of British Columbia, 1986. [Northwest Washington State].

Braroe, N. W. Reciprocal Exploitation in an Indian-White Community. Southwestern Journal of Anthropology 31 (1965):166-78.

Brimmer, A. F. Economic Situation of Blacks in the United States. Federal Reserve Bulletin March 1972.

Brimmer, A. F. Economic Situation of Blacks in the United States. Review of Black Political Economy 2 (Summer 1972):35-54.

Brimmer, A. F. Trends, Prospects, and Strategies for Black Economic Progress. Review of Black Political Economy 14 (Spring 1986).

Brown, C. Black-White Earnings Ratios since the Civil Rights Act of 1964: The Importance of Labor Market Dropouts. _Quarterly Journal of Economics_ 99 (February 1984).

Brown, J. Larry. Hunger in the U.S. _Scientific American_ 258 (February 1987):37-41.

Brune, T. and E. Camacho. Chicago Became Blacker, Poorer in 1970s: Minorities Bear Brunt of Poverty Increase. _Chicago Reporter_ 12 (April 1983):1.

Bryce, H. J. Putting Black Economic Progress in Perspective. _Ebony_ 28 (August 1973):58-62.

Bullard, R. D. _Blacks in Boomtown: The Economics of Houston's Black Community_. April 1980. ERIC ED 194679.

Carballo, M. and M. J. Bane (eds.) _The State and the Poor in the 1980s_. [Massachusetts]. Boston: Auburn House, 1983.

Carling, A. Ethnicity and Exploitation. _New Left Review_ 160 (November-December 1986):58-61.

Carlson, Leonard A. and Caroline Swartz. The Earnings of Women and Ethnic Minorities, 1959-1979. _Industrial Labor Relations Review_ 41 (July 1988).

Center on Budget and Policy Priorities. _National Overview. Holes in the Safety Nets: Poverty Programs and Policies in the States_. 1988. Center on Budget and Policy Priorities, 236 Massachusetts Ave., N.E., Suite 305, Washington, D.C. 20002. [Available also are individual state reports].

Children's Defense Fund. _American Children in Poverty_. Washington, D.C: Children's Defense Fund, 1984.

Churchill, W., and W. La Duke. Radioactive Colonization and the Native American. _Socialist Review_ 15 (May-June 1985):95-119.

Clement, P. F. _Welfare and the Poor in the Nineteenth-Century City: Philadelphia, 1800-1854_. Cranbury, NJ: Fairleigh Dickinson University Press, 1985.

Collier, B. J., and L. Williams. The Economic Status of the Black Male: A Myth Exploded. _Journal of Black Studies_ 12 (June 1982):487-498.

Collins, C. (ed.) _Black Progress: Reality or Illusion?_ New York: Facts on File, 1985.

Cotton, J. P. Some Observations on 'Closing the Gap' [In re: James P. Smith and Finis Welch 'Closing the Gap: Forty Years of Economic Progress for Blacks (February 1986)]. _Trotter Institute Review_ (UMass Boston) 1 (Winter 1987):13-16.

Cray, R. E., Jr. White Welfare and Black Strategies: The Dynamics of

Race and Poor Relief in Early New York, 1700-1825. Slavery and
    Abolition 7 (1986):273-89.

Danziger, S. and P. Gottschalk. Earnings Inequality, the Spatial
    Concentration of Poverty, and the Underclass. American Economic
    Review 77 (May 1987).

Danziger, S. and R. Plotnick. The War on Income Poverty: Achievements
    and Failures. In: P. Sommers, (ed.), Welfare Reform in America.
    Hingham, MA: Martinus Nijhoff, 1982.

Danziger, S. and D. H. Weinberger, (eds.) Fighting Poverty: What Works
    and What Doesn't. Cambridge, MA: Harvard University Press, 1986.

Darden, J. T. Racial Dispartities in Michigan since the Civil Disorders
    of 1967: Summary and Conclusions. In: Frances S. Thomas (ed.), The
    State of Black Michigan: 1987, pp. 79-81. East Lansing, MI: Urban
    Affairs Programs, Michigan State University, 1987.

Darity, W. A., Jr. The Goal of Racial Economic Equality: A Critique.
    Journal of Ethnic Studies 10 (Winter 1983):51-70.

Darity, W. A., Jr. Illusions of Black Economic Progress. Review of Black
    Political Economy 10 (Winter 1980).

Darity, W. A., Jr. and S. L. Myers, Jr. Changes in Black-White Income
    Inequality, 1968-78: A Decade of Progress. Review of Black
    Political Economy 10 (Summer 1980):384-90.

Darity, W. A., Jr. and S. Myers, Jr. The Illusion of Black Progress:
    The 'Vintage Effect'. Urban League Review 5 (Summer 1980):54-
    65.

Day, Phyllis J. The New Poor in America: Isolationism in an
    International Political Economy. Social Work 34 (May 1989):227-33.

Dietz, James L. Economic History of Puerto Rico: Institutional Change
    and Capitalist Development. Princeton, NJ: Princeton University
    Press, 1987.

A Dream Deferred: The Economic Status of Black Americans. Washington,
    D.C.: Center for the Study of Social Policy, July 1983.

Du Bois Scores White Reign at Bryn Mawr. [Current economic conditons].
    Philadelphia Tribune April 30, 1931.

Du Bois, W. E. B. [Is poverty one's own fault?]. Chicago Defender
    January 20, 1945.

Du Bois, W. E. B. [Lessons in economics]. Amersterdam News June 20,
    1942.

Du Bois, W. E. B. Our Economic Future. Crisis 35 (May 1928):168-70.

Du Bois, W. E. B. Postscript. [On economic condition of Black people].

<u>Crisis</u> 36 (March 1929):93-4.

Du Bois, W. E. B. Postscript. [Economic situation]. <u>Crisis</u> 40 (April 1933):93-4.

Du Bois, W. E. B. The Economic Future of the Negro. <u>Publications</u> <u>of</u> <u>the</u> <u>American</u> <u>Economic</u> <u>Association</u> 7 (3rd series) (February 1906):219-42.

Du Bois, W. E. B. The Economics of Negro Emancipation in the United States. <u>Sociological</u> <u>Review</u> 4 (October 1911)303-13.

Du Bois, W. E. B. The Negro in the Black Belt: Some Social Sketches. <u>U.S.</u> <u>Dept.</u> <u>of</u> <u>Labor</u> <u>'Bulletin'</u> 4 (May 1899):401-417.

Du Bois, W. E. B. The Negro Since 1900. A Progress Report. <u>New</u> <u>York</u> <u>Times</u> <u>Magazine</u> November 21, 1948 (pp. 24, 54-58).

Du Bois, W. E. B. [Studying economics in high school]. <u>Chicago</u> <u>Globe</u> April 22, 1950.

Du Bois, W. E. B. The World and Us. [Blacks in economic depression]. <u>Crisis</u> 23 (January 1922):103-7.

Du Bois, W. E. B. (ed.) <u>Efforts</u> <u>for</u> <u>Social</u> <u>Betterment</u> <u>among</u> <u>Negro</u> <u>Americans</u>. Atlanta: Atlanta University Press, 1909.

Du Bois, W. E. B. and others. The Economic Position of the American Negro. American Economic Association <u>Publications</u> (3rd series) 1 (February 1905):216-221.

Dygert, H. and D. Shibata. Chinatown Sweatshops: Wage Law Violations in the Garment Industry. <u>University</u> <u>of</u> <u>California,</u> <u>Davis,</u> <u>Law</u> <u>Review</u> 8 (1975):63-83.

An Economic Bill of Rights. <u>Review</u> <u>of</u> <u>Black</u> <u>Political</u> <u>Economy</u> 3 (1972):1-41.

Ernst, R. The Economic Status of New York City Negroes, 1850-1853. <u>Negro</u> <u>History</u> <u>Bulletin</u> 12 (1949):131-2, 139-43.

Estrada, L. F., and Others. Chicanos in the United States: A History of Exploitation and Resistance. <u>Daedalus</u> 110 (Spring 1981):103-31.

Ezeani, E. Economic Conditions of Freed Black Slaves in the United States, 1870-1920. <u>Review</u> <u>of</u> <u>Black</u> <u>Political</u> <u>Economy</u> 8 (1977):104-18.

Ezekiel, R. S. <u>Voices</u> <u>from</u> <u>the</u> <u>Corner.</u> <u>Poverty</u> <u>and</u> <u>Racism</u> <u>in</u> <u>the</u> <u>Inner</u> <u>City</u> [Detroit]. Philadelphia, PA: Temple University Press, 1984.

Farley, R. The Quality of Life for Black Americans Twenty Years after the Civil Rights Revolution. <u>Milbank</u> <u>Quarterly</u> 65 (1987):9-34 (supplement).

Farley, R. Trends in Racial Inequalities: Have the Gains of the 1960s Disappeared in the 1970s? American Sociologial Review 42 (1977):189-208.

Farley, R. Three Steps Forward and Two Back? Recent Changes in the Social and Economic Status of Blacks. Ethnic and Racial Studies 8 (1985).

Farley, R., and W. R. Allen. The Color Line and the Quality of Life: Problem for the Twenty-first Century. New York: Russell Sage Foundation, 1987.

Farley, R., and S. M. Bianchi. The Growing Gap Between Blacks. American Demographics (July 1983):14-18.

Fisher, S. From Margin to Mainstream: The Social Progress of Black Americans. New York: Praeger, 1982.

Ford, A. M. The Political Economics of Rural Poverty in the South. Cambridge, MA: Harvard University Press, 1973.

The Forgotten Half: Non-College Youth in America. Youth & America's Future: The William T. Grant Foundation, Commission on Work, Family and Citizenship, 1988.

Fowler, B. B. Miracle in Gary: Negro Gropes Toward Economic Equality. Forum (September 1936):134-37.

Franklin, J. H. Public Welfare in the South During the Reconstruction Era, 1865-80. In: Frank R. Bruel and Steven J. Diner (eds.), Compassion and Responsibility Chicago, IL: University of Chicago Press, 1980.

Freeman, R. B. Have Black Labor Market Gains Been Permanent or Transitory? Cambridge, MA: Harvard Institute of Economic Research, 1981.

Gelfand, M. I. (ed.) The War on Poverty, 1964-1968. Part I: White House Central Files [16 microfilm reels]. Frederick, MD: University Publications of America, 1987.

Glassberg, E. Work, Wages and the Cost of Living, Ethnic Differences and the Poverty Line, Philadelphia, 1880. Pennsylvania History 46 (January 1979):17-58.

Gordon, L. A Brief Look at Blacks in Depression Mississippi, 1929-1934. Journal of Negro History 44 (1979):377-390.

Gorner, P. Industry and Racism. [About the research of John W. Work]. Chicago Tribune July 19, 1984.

Gotsch-Thomson, S. Correlates of Poverty: An Analysis of Demographic, Structural, and Individual Factors Related to Poverty in the Black-Belt Counties of Alabama. Review of Black Political Economy 13 (Winter 1984-85).

Gray, A. T. The Nature of the Black Economy: An Inquiry into the Constraints on Black Progress. Master's thesis, Virginia State University, 1985.

Gregory, K. D. Five Decades of Economic Trend in Black Detroit. Michigan Chronicle September 27, 1986.

Gregory, K. D. Trends in the Economic Status of Michigan Blacks since 1967. In: Frances S. Thomas (ed.), The State of Black Michigan: 1987, pp. 3-18. East Lansing, MI: Urban Affairs Programs, Michigan State University, 1987.

Griswold Del Castillo, R. Myth and Reality: Chicano Economic Mobility in Los Angeles, 1850-1880. Aztlan 6 (Summer 1975):151-71.

Gwartney, J., and T. S. McCaleb. Have Antipoverty Programs Increased Poverty? Cato Journal 5 (Spring-Summer 1985):1-16.

Hall, F. D. The Transition to Post-Industrialism and the Urban Underclass [1968-1982]. Doctoral dissertation, University of North Carolina, 1985. UMO # 8605598.

Hamilton, C. V. Social Policy and the Welfare of Black Americans: From Rights to Resources. Political Science Quarterly 101 (1986):239-55.

Hannon, J. U. Poverty in the Antebellum Northeast: The View from New York State's Poor Relief Rolls. Journal of Economic History 44 (December 1984):1007-32.

Hare, Bruce R. Structural Inequality and the Endangered Status of Black Youth. Journal of Negro Education 56 (Winter 1987):100-10.

Harris, D. J. Capitalist Exploitation and Black Labor: Some Conceptual Issues. Review of Black Political Economy 8 (Winter 1978).

Harris, Fred R. and Roger W. Wilkins (eds.) Quiet Riots: Race and Poverty in the United States. New York: Pantheon, 1988.

Harrison, B. Welfare Payments and the Reproduction of Low-Wage Workers and Secondary Jobs. Review of Radical Political Economics 11 (Summer 1979):1-16.

Hartmann, G. B. An Economic Analysis of Black Nashville. Doctoral dissertation, State University of New York at Albany, 1975.

Haveman, R. H. The War on Poverty and the Poor and the Nonpoor. Political Science Quarterly 102 (Spring 1985):65-78.

Haynes, M. A Century of Change: Negroes in the U.S. Economy, 1860-1960. Monthly Labor Review 85 (December 1962):1359-65.

Hendrickson, K. E., Jr. (ed.) Hard Times in Oklahoma: The Depression Years. Oklahoma City: Historical Society, 1983.

Herbers, J. Poverty Rate on Rise Even Before Recession [Williamsburg

County]. New York Times February 20, 1982.

Higgs, R. Competition and Coercion: Blacks in the American Economy, 1865-1914. New York: Cambridge University Press, 1976.

Hill, R. B. Benign Neglect Revisited: The Illusions of Black Progress. Washington, D.C.: National Urban League, 1973.

Hirschman, C., and M. G. Wong. Socioeconomic Gains of Asian Americans, Blacks, and Hispanics: 1960-1976. American Jurnal of Sociology 90 (1984):584-607.

Hogan, L. Principles of Black Political Economy. Boston: Routledge & Kegan Paul, 1984.

Hogan, L. (ed.) The State of the Black Economy. Transaction Books, 1980.

House, T. Some Economic Aspects of Blacks in Mobile, Alabama. Master's thesis, Atlanta University, 1980.

Hutchins, M. F. The History of Poor Law Legislation in Georgia, 1733-1919. Atlanta, GA: Cherokee Pub. Co., 1985.

Iatridis, D. S. New Social Deficit: Neoconservatism's Policy of Social Underdevelopment. Social Work 33 (January-February 1988):11-15.

Ijere, M. O. Survey of Afro-American Experience in the U.S. Economy. Hicksville, NY: Exposition, 1978.

In New York City, There Are Many Ways To Be Poor. New York Times March 5, 1989. Section E, p. 6

Irvin, A. W. Energy Development and the Effects of Mining on the Lakota Nation. Journal of Ethnic Studies 10 (Spring 1982):89-101.

Jencks, C. How Poor Are the Poor? New York Review of Books May 9, 1985.

Jjr, C. J. B., and T. Breiter. Hispanics on Welfare - the Facts and Figures. Agenda 7 (March-April 1977):4-10.

Johnson, C. S. The Economic Status of Negroes. Nashville, TN: Fisk University Press, 1933.

Johnson, S. Economic Well-being and Parity in the Marketplace: Two Measures of Black Progress, 1948-1979. Master's thesis, Vanderbilt University, 1982.

Jones, F. C. External Crosscurrents and Internal Diversity: An Assessment of Black Progres, 1960-1980. Daedalus 110 (Spring 1981):71-101.

Jones, Lewis W. and Everett S. Lee. Rural Blacks - A Vanishing Population. ERIC ED 126219.

144

Josephy, A. M., Jr. Now That the Buffalo's Gone: A Study of Today's
     American Indians. New York: Knopf, 1982.

Karger, Howard J. and David Stoesz. Welfare Reform: Maximum Feasible
     Exaggeration. Tikkun 4 (March/April 1989):23-35, 118-22.

Kessler, M. A. Economic Status of Nonwhite Workers, 1955-1962. Missouri
     Labor Review 86 (July 1963):780-8.

Kiefer, D. and P Philips. Doubts Regarding the Human Capital Theory of
     Racial Equality. Industrial Relations 27 (Spring 1988).

Kimmich, M. H. America's Children. Who Cares? Growing Needs and
     Declining Assistance in the Reagan Era. Washington, D.C.: Urban
     Institute Press, 1985.

Klausner, S. Z. Six Years in the Lives of the Impoverished: An
     Examination of the WIN Thesis [Camden, NJ]. May 1, 1978. ERIC ED
     163121.

Komisar, L. Down and Out in the USA: A History of Social Welfare. New
     York: Watts, 1977.

Koretz, D. and M. Ventresca. Poverty Among Children. Washington, D.C.:
     Congressional Budget Office, 1984.

Kornblum, W. Lumping the Poor. What Is the 'Underclass'? Dissent 31
     (Summer 1984):295-302.

Kornweibel, T., Jr. An Economic Profile of Black Life in the Twenties.
     Journal of Black Studies 6 (1976):307-20.

Lan, D. The Chinatown Sweatshops: Oppression and an Alternative.
     Amerasia Journal 1 (November 1971):40-57.

Latino Commission of Tri-State and others. Outlook: The Growing Latino
     Presence in the Tri-State Region. New York: The Commission, 1988.
     [NY,NJ, and CT],

Lazear, E. The Narrowing of Black-White Wage Differentials Is Illusory.
     American Economic Review 69 (September 1979).

Levitan, S. A. Still a Dream: The Changing Status of Blacks Since 1960.
     Cambridge, MA: Harvard University Press, 1975.

Litan, Robert E. and others (eds.) American Living Statistics.
     Washington, D.C.: Brookings, 1988.

Malveaux, Jeanne. The Economic Statuses of Black Families. In: Harriett
     P. McAdoo (ed.), Black Families. Newbury Park, CA: Sage, 1988.

Mariante, B. R. How Have They Fared in Paradise? A Reconnaissance of
     Life-style Indicators among Hawaiian Ethnic Groups. Ethnic Groups 5
     (1984):227-53.

Masters, S. Black-White Income Differentials: Empirical Studies and Policy. New York: Academic Press, 1975.

May, L. Poverty Hangs Over Black Miami Areas Like Shroud. Los Angeles Times June 19, 1983.

McCall, Cheryl. Life at Pine Ridge Bleak. Colorado Daily May 16, 1975.

McElvaine, R. S. (ed.) Down and Out in the Great Depression. Letters from the Forgotten Man. Chapel Hill: University of California Press, 1983.

Miller, K. Economic Handicap of the Negro in the North. Annals of the American Academy 27 (May 1906):543-50.

Miller, M., and R. Maril. Poverty in the Lower Rio Grande Valley of Texas: Historical and Contemporary Dimensions. College Station, TX: Texas Agricultural Experiment Station, February 1979.

Mohl, R. Poverty in New York, 1785-1825. New York, 1927.

Mooney, B. and others. Black and Poor in Atlanta. [Series of articles available in a single reprint]. Atlanta Constitution October 18-27, 1981.

Murphy, Sean. A New Middle Class Widens Gap with Poor. Boston Globe June 13, 1988. [Boston's black community].

Nee, J., and J. Sanders. The Road to Parity: Determinants of the Socioeconomic Achievements of Asian Americans. Ethnic and Racial Studies 8 (January 1985):75-93.

O'Hare, William P. Poverty in America: Trends and New Patterns. Population Bulletin 40 (1985)2-43 (entire issue).

On the Nature of Black Progress [letters]. Commentary 56 (August 1973):4-22.

Patterson, J. T. America's Struggle against Poverty, 1900-1980. Cambridge, MA: Harvard University Press, 1981.

Pearce, D., and P. McAdoo. Women and Children: Alone and in Poverty. Washington, D.C. Center for National Policy Review, Catholic University Law School, September 1981.

Pearce, D., and H. P. McAdoo. Women in Poverty: Toward a New Understanding of Work and Welfare. In: Thirteenth Final Report. Washington, D.C.: National Advisory Council on Economic Opportunity, 1981.

Perlo, V. Trends in the Economic Status of the Negro People. Science & Society 16 (Spring 1952):115-50.

Perlo, V. Economics of Racism: Roots of Black Inequality. New York: International, 1975.

Physician Task Force. Hunger in America: The Growing Epidemic. Middletown, CT: Wesleyan University Press, 1985.

Pinkney, A. The Myth of Black Progress. New York: Cambridge University Press, 1984.

Pitre, M. The Economic Philosophy of Martin L. King, Jr. Review of Black Political Economy 9 (Winter 1979):191-98.

Piven, F. F., and R. A. Cloward. The New Class War: Reagan's Attack on the Welfare State and Its Consequences. New York: Pantheon, 1982.

Pope, R. M. The Hungry Years: The Story of One Family's Struggle for Survival during the Great Depression. Circle Pines, MN: Bold Blue Jay Publications, 1982. [200 Moonlite Dr., Circle Pines, MN 55014].

Poverty Amidst Affluence. Bostonians the Boom Left Behind. [Series of articles]. Boston Globe Magazine December 15, 1985.

Precourt, W. E. Image of Appalachian Poverty. In: Appalachia and America. Lexington, KY: University Press of Kentucky, 1983.

The Problems of Insurance among Negroes Prior to the Civil War. Negro History Bulletin (November 1963):42-43.

Ram, R. Composite Indices [Quality of living, USA and elsewhere]. Journal of Development Economics 11 (1982).

Ransom, R. L. Growth and Welfare in the American South of the Nineteenth Century. Explorations in Economic History 16 (1979):207-236.

Raymond, R. Mobility and Economic Progress of Negro Americans during the 1940s. American Journnal of Economics and Sociology 28 (1969):337-50.

Reich, M. The Persistence of Racial Inequality in Urban Areas and Industries, 1950-1970. American Economic Review 70 (May 1980).

Reich, M. The Economic Impact in the Postwar Period. In: Benjamin P. Bowser and Raymond G. Hunt (eds.), Impacts of Racism on White Americans, pp. 165-176. Beverly Hills, CA: Sage, 1981.

Reid, J. Black America in the 1980s. December 1982 ERIC ED 224854.

Richan, W. Government Policies and Black Progress: The Role of Social Research in Public Policy Debates. Social Work 32 (July-August 1987):353-56.

Richards, E. Below the Line. Living Poor in America. New York: Consumers Union, 1988.

Robinson, J. L. (ed.) Living Hard: Southern Americans in the Great Depression. Washington, D.C.: University Press of America, 1981.

Rochin, R. I. Economic Deprivation of Chicanos - Continuing Neglect in the Seventies. *Aztlan* 4 (Spring 1973):85-102.

Rodgers, H. R., Jr. Black Americans and the Feminization of Poverty: The Intervening Effects of Unemployment. *Journal of Black Studies* 17 (June 1987):402-17.

Rodgers, H. R., Jr. *The Cost of Human Neglect*. Cambridge, MA: Harvard University Press, 1982.

Rogers, T. W. *A Geographic Analysis of Poverty in Mississippi*. April 1979 ERIC ED 182058.

Rosenbaum, R. H. *The Public Issues Handbook*. Westport, CT: Greenwood, 1983.

Ross, C. and others. The Level and Trend of Poverty in the United States, 1939-1979. *Demography* 24 (November 1987).

Salvo, J. J., and J. M. McNeil. *Lifetime Work Experience and Its Effect on Earnings: Retrospective Data from the 1979 Income Survey Development Program*. Washington, D.C.: GPO, 1984.

Sandefur, Gary D. and Arthur Sabamoto. American Indian Household Structure and Income. *Demography* 25 (February 1988).

Schram, Sanford F. and others. Child Poverty and Welfare Benefits: A Reassessment with State Data of the Claim that American Welfare Breeds Dependence. *American Journal of Economics and Sociology* 47 (October 1988):409-22.

Scott, A. Economic Support for Blacks in Philadelphia. In: *The State of Black Philadelphia, 1981*, pp. 101-112. Philadelphia, PA: Urban League of Philadelphia, 1981.

Seward, J. N. America's Economic Crisis: A Black Perspective. *Black Scholar* 5 (1974):2-12.

Shaikh, Anwar and Ertugrul Ahmet. The Welfare State and the Myth of the Social Wage. In: Robert Cherry and others (eds.), *The Imperiled Economy*, vol. 1. New York: Union for Radical Political Economics, 1988.

Shulman, S. Black Wage and Occupational Gains: A Reevaluation. *Review of Black Political Economy* 12 (1984):59-69.

Sisk, G. N. Social Aspects of the Alabama Black Belt, 1875-1917. *Mid-America* 37 (1955):31-47.

Skin, J. S. and I. Garfinkel. The Quality of Education and Cohort Variation in Black-White Earnings Differentials: Comment. *American Economic Review* 70 (March 1980):186-191.

Smeeding, T. P. and others. Comparative Well-being of Children and Elderly. *Contemporary Policy Issues* 5 (April 1987).

148

Smith, J. P. and F. Welch. Closing the Gap: Forty Years of Economic Progress for Blacks. Santa Monica, CA: Rand Corporation, 1986.

Smith, J. P. and F. Welch. Race and Poverty: A Forty Year Record. American Economic Review 77 (May 1987):152-58.

Snipp, C. M. American Indians and Natural Resource Development: Indigenous Peoples' Land, Now Sought After, Has Produced New Indian-White Problems. American Journal of Economics and Sociology 45 (October 1986):457-74.

Snyder, D. L. and J. C. Andersen. Competition for Water: The Issue of Native American Water Rights. Annals of Regional Science 22 (February 1988).

Sorkin, A. L. The Econommic and Social Status of the American Indian, 1940-1970. Journal of Negro Education 45 (Fall 1976):432-47.

Southern Regional Council. Hungry Children. Atlanta: 1967.

Spence, L. H. Creating An Underclass of the Poor in Boston. Boston Globe April 11, 1981.

Stillwaggon, E. M. Anti-Indian Agitation and Economic Interests. Monthly Review 33 (November 1981).

Stockman, L. V. Poverty and Hunger: A Pittsburgh Profile of Selected Neighborhoods. Doctoral dissertation, University of Pittsburgh, 1982. UMO # 8321644.

Taylor, B. After Twenty-five Years [Economic condition of Blacks in the U.S. since 1955]. Southern Exposure 9 (Spring 1981):120-124.

Thomas, M. E. Race, Class and the Quality of Life of Black People. Doctoral dissertation, Virginia Polytechnic Institute & State Univ. 1986. UMO # 8700125.

Tienda, M. and W. A. Diaz. Puerto Ricans' Special Problems. New York Times August 28, 1987.

Tobier, E. The Changing Face of Poverty. Trends in New York City's Population in Poverty, 1960-1990. New York: Community Service Society, November 1984.

Tolchin, Martin. Minority Poverty on Rise but White Poor Decline. New York Times September 1, 1988.

Toro, R. D. J. Historia Economica de Puerto Rico. Southwestern Publishing Co., 1982.

Trattner, W. I. From Poor Law to Welfare State: A History of Social Welfare in America (third edition). New York: Free Press, 1984.

Trattner, W. I. (ed.) Social Welfare or Social Control? Some Historical

Reflections on Regulating the Poor. Knoxville: University of
Tennessee Press, 1983.

Trennert, R. A. From Carlisle to Phoenix: The Rise and Fall of the
Indian Outing System, 1878-1930 [Indian students as cheap farm
labor]. Pacific Historical Review 52 (August 1983):267-91.

U.S. Bureau of Labor Statistics. Characteristics of the Population Below
the Poverty Level, 1983. Washington, D.C.: GPO, 1985.

U.S. Bureau of the Census. Money, Income, and Poverty Status in the
United States: 1987. Washington, D.C.: GPO, 1988.

U.S. Bureau of the Census. The Social and Economic Status of the Black
Population in the United States (1972). Washington, D.C.: GPO,
1973.

U.S. Commission On Civil Rights. The Economic Progress of Black Men in
America. Washington, D.C.: GPO, 1986.

U.S. Commission On Civil Rights. The Economic Status of Americans of
Asian Descent. Washington, D.C.: The Commission, 1988.

U.S. Commission On Civil Rights. The Economic Status of Americans of
Southern and Eastern European Ancestry. Washington, D.C.: The
Commission, October 1986.

U.S. Conference of Mayors. Hunger in American Cities. Washington, D.C.:
The Conference, June 1983.

U.S. Congress, Ninety-Eighth, First, House of Representatives, Committee On
the Budget, Task Force On Entitlements, Uncontrollables and Indexing.
Women and Children in Poverty: Hearing ... Washington, D.C.: GPO,
1984.

U.S. Congress, Ninety-Eighth, Second Session, House of Representatives,
Committee On Ways and Means, Subcommittee On Oversight and
Subcommittee on Public Assistance and Unemployment Compensation.
Families in Poverty: Changes in the 'Safety Net'. Washington, D.C.:
GPO, 1984.

U.S. Congress, Ninety-Ninth, First Session, House of Representatives,
Committee On Ways and Means. Children in Poverty. Washington, D.C.:
GPO, 1985.

U.S. Congress, Ninety-Ninth, First Session, House of Representatives,
Committee On Ways and Means, Subcommittee On Public Assistance and
Unemployment Compensation. Poverty and Hunger in America: Hearing
... Washington, D.C.: GPO, 1985.

U.S. Congressional Budget Office. Reducing Poverty Among Children.
Washington, D.C.: GPO, May 1985.

U.S. Department of Labor, Division of Negro Economics. The Negro at Work
during the World War and during Reconstruction. Washington, D.C.:

GPO, 1920.

Urban League of Greater New York. Status of Black New York '79. 1979
     ERIC ED 183641.

Vaughn-Cooke, D. The Economic Status of Black America - Is there a
     Recovery? In: James D. Williams (ed.), The State of Black America
     1984, pp. 1-23. New York: National Urban League, January 19, 1984.

Warner, D. C. (ed.) Toward New Human Rights: The Social Policies of the
     Kennedy and Johnson Administrations. Austin: University of Texas
     Press, 1977.

Weisskopf, T. The Current Economic Crisis in Historical Perspective.
     Socialist Review (May-June 1981).

Westcott, D. N. Blacks in the 1970s: Did They Scale the Job Ladder?
     Monthly Labor Review 105 (June 1982):29-38.

White, Richard. The Roots of Dependency, Subsistence, Environment, and
     Social Change Among the Choctaws, Pawnees, and Navajos. Lincoln:
     University of Nebraska Press, 1988.

Wilkerson, I. Growth of the Very Poor Is Focus of New Studies. New York
     Times December 20, 1987.

Williams, J. D. (ed.) The State of Black America 1980. January 22, 1980.
     ERIC ED 183692.

Williams, J. D. (ed.) The State of Black America 1982. New York:
     National Urban League, January 14, 1982, New York.

Williams, J. D. (ed.) The State of Black America 1984. New York:
     National Urban League, January 19, 1984.

Wilson, William Julius, Martin Kilson, and Adolph Reed, Jr. [Letters on
     Wilson's The Truly Disadvantaged]. Nation May 14, 1988.

Winkler, D. R. and W. D. Morgan. A Decline in Poverty in the United
     States, 1959-1974. Review of Social Economy 37 (October 1979).

Wodarski, J. S. and others. Reagan's AFDC Policy Changes: The Georgia
     Experience. Social Work 31 (July-August 1986):273-79.

Wolters, R. Negroes and the Great Depression: The Problem of Economic
     Recovery. Westport, CT: Greenwood, 1970.

Woodrum, E., and Others. Japanese American Economic Behavior: Its
     Types, Determinants, and Consequences. Social Forces 58 (June
     1980):1235-54.

Wyers, N. L. Economic Insecurity: Notes for Social Workers. Social Work
     33 (January-February 1988):18-22.

Young, T. R. Class Warfare in the 80s and 90s: Reaganomics and Social

Justice. <u>Wisconsin</u> <u>Sociologist</u> 25 (1988)68-75.

Zarefsky, D. <u>President</u> <u>Johnson's</u> <u>War</u> <u>on</u> <u>Poverty:</u> <u>Rhetoric</u> <u>and</u> <u>History</u>. University, AL: University of Alabama Press, 1986.

Economic Standards Bibliography

Banks, V. J. and others. <u>Research</u> <u>Data</u> <u>on</u> <u>Minority</u> <u>Groups:</u> <u>An</u> <u>Annotated</u> <u>Bibliography</u> <u>of</u> <u>Economic</u> <u>Research</u> <u>Service</u> <u>Reports,</u> <u>1955-</u> <u>1965</u>. Washington, D.C.: U.S. Department of Agriculture Economic Research Service, 1966.

Davis, L. G. <u>Poverty</u> <u>and</u> <u>the</u> <u>Black</u> <u>Community:</u> <u>A</u> <u>Preliminary</u> <u>Survey</u>. [Exchange Bibliography No. 965.] Monticello, IL: Council of Planning Librarians, 1975.

<u>Poverty,</u> <u>Rural</u> <u>Poverty,</u> <u>and</u> <u>Minority</u> <u>Groups</u> <u>Living</u> <u>in</u> <u>Rural</u> <u>Poverty:</u> <u>An</u> <u>Annotated</u> <u>Bibliography</u>. 1969. ERIC ED 041679.

[See also sections 9, 16, 20, 24, 27, 29, 33, 35, 39, 41, 42, 49, 54, 81, and 83]

24. Economics of Racism

The colored man [who is a sharecropper] is charged with
everything and credited with nothing. If a pig dies or the wind
blows the barn down and kills a sheep, the colored man must pay
for it, and if he dare question the farmers of the charge he is
ordered off the farm, and the Justice of the Peace says he has
violated the contract and cannot have his share of the crop.

- People's Advocate, December 1, 1883.

Aldrich, M. Capital Theory and Racism: From Laissez-Faire to the
    Eugenics Movement in the Career of Irving Fisher. Review of Radical
    Political Economics 7 (Fall 1975):33-42.

Aldrich, M. Progressive Economists and Scientific Racism: Walter Willcox
    and Black Americans, 1895-1910. Phylon 40 (Spring 1979):1-14.

Allen, R. L. Black Awakening in Capitalist America. Garden City:
    Doubleday, 1969.

Baran, P., and P. M. Sweezy. Monopoly Capitalism and Race Relations. In:
    Monopoly Capital. New York: Monthly Review Press, 1966.

Baron, H. M. Racial Domination in Advanced Capitalism: A Theory of
    Nationalism and Division in the Labor Market. In: R. C. Edwards and
    others (eds.), Labor Market Segmentation. Lexington: Heath, 1975.

Bloice, C. The Black Worker's Future under American Capitalism. Black
    Scholar 3 (May 1972):14-22.

Bloom, J. M. Class, Race, and the Civil Rights: The Changing Political
    Economy of Southern Racism. Bloomington: Indiana University Press,
    1986.

Bonacich, E. Middleman Minorities and Advanced Capitalism. Ethnic Groups
    2 (1980):211-219.

Cherry, R. Racial Thought and the Early Economics Profession. Review of
    Social Economy 34 (October 1976).

Cloutier, N. R. Who Gains from Racism? The Impact of Racial Inequality
    on White Income Distribution. Review of Social Economy 45 (October
    1987).

Cole, C. L. Chinese Exclusion: The Capitalist Perspective of the
    'Sacramento Union, 1850-1882'. California History 57 (Spring
    1978):8-31.

Du Bois, W. E. B. The Economic Aspects of Race Prejudice. Editorial
    Review (New York) 2 (May 1910):488-93.

Du Bois, W. E. B. [Economic history of American capitalism]. Chicago

Defender April 6, 13, and 20, 1946.

Du Bois, W. E. B. Negroes and the Crisis of Capitalism in the United
    States. _Monthly Review_ 4 (April 1953):478-85.

Ellison, R. An American Dilemma: A Review. _In_: _Shadow and Act_ [Written
    in 1944]. New York: New American Library, 1966.

Franklin, R. S. and S. Resnik. _The Political Economy of Racism_. New
    York: Holt, Rinehart, and Winston, 1973.

Gagala, K. L. _Racism in the Building Trade_ [Detroit and Chicago].
    Doctoral dissertation, Michigan State University, 1970.

Glenn, N. D. White Gains from Negro Subordination. _Social Problems_ 14
    (Fall 1966):159-78.

Good, P. The Bricks and Mortar of Racism [N.Y.C. building crafts]. _New
    York Times Magazine_ May 21, 1972.

Gorner, P. Industry and Racism. _Chicago Tribune_ July 19, 1984.

Greer, E. Racism and U.S. Steel, 1906-1976. _Radical America_ 10
    (September-October 1976):54-71.

Handlin, O. Does Economics Explain Racism. _Commentary_ 6 (July 1948):79-
    85.

Harrington, M. The Economics of Racism. _Commonweal_ 74 (July 7, 1961).

Harris, Abram L. The Economic Foundation of American Race Division.
    Social Forces 5 (1927):468-78.

Henderson, V. Race, Economics, and Public Policy. _Integrateducation_ 14
    (January-February 1976).

Hollister, F. Skin Color and Life Chances of Puerto Ricans. _Caribbean
    Studies_ 9 (October 1969).

Jorgensen, J. G. A Century of Political Economic Effects on American
    Indian Society, 1880-1980. _Journal of Ethnic Studies_ 6 (Fall
    1978):1-82.

Kent, C. A., and J. W. Johnson. _Indian Poverty in South Dakota_.
    Vermillion, SD: University of South Dakota, 1969. ERIC ED 042529.

Kirby, J. T. Black and White in the Rural South, 1915-1954. _Agricultural
    History_ 58 (July 1984):411-22.

Locke, Alain. The High Cost of Prejudice. _Forum_ 78 (1927):500-510.

Marable, Manning. _How Capitalism Underdeveloped Black America Problems in
    Race, Political Economy and Society_. Boston: South End Pres, 1983.

Naison, Mark. Marxism and Black Radicalism in America. _Radical America_

5 (May-June 1971):5-25.

Nearing, Scott. Black America. New York: Vanguard, 1929.

Nikolinakos, M. Notes on an Economic Theory of Racism. Race 14 (April 1973):365-381.

Olzak, Susan. Causes of Ethnic Conflict and Protest in Urban America, 1877-1889. Social Science Research 16 (June 1987):185-210.

Perlo, V. The Economics of Racism. U.S.A.: Roots of Black Poverty. New York: International Publishers, 1976.

Pitts, T. Racism and the U.S. Economy. PCR Information (World Council of Churches) 24 (1987):28-33.

Reese, J. E., and M. Fish. Economic Genocide: A Study of the Comanche, Kiowa, Cheyenne, and Arapaho. Negro Educational Review 24 (January-April 1973):86-103.

Reich, M. Changes in the Distribution of Benefits from Racism in the 1960s. Journal of Human Resources 16 (Spring 1981).

Reich, M. The Economic Impact in the Postwar Period. In: Benjamin P. Bowser and Raymond G. Hunt (eds.), Impacts of Racism on White Americans, pp. 165-176. Beverly Hills, CA: Sage, 1981.

Reich, M. Economic Theories of Racism. In: Martin Carnoy (ed.), Schooling in a Corporate Society. The Political Economy of Education in America, pp. 67-79. New York: McKay, 1972.

Reich, M. The Economics of Racism. In: David M. Gordon (ed.), Problems in Political Economy, pp. 107-113. Lexington: Lexington Books, 1971.

Riedesel, P. L. Racial Discrimination and White Economic Benefits. Social Science Quarterly 60 (June 1979):[See also reply by A. Szymanski].

Rozat, G. and R. Bartra. Racism and Capitalism. In: Sociological Theories: Race and Colonialism, pp. 287-304. Paris: UNESCO, 1980.

Sales, W., Jr. Capitalism Without Racism: Science or Fantasy. Black Scholar 9 (March 1978):23-34.

Schaefer, R. T. Racial Prejudice in a Capitalist State: What Has Happend to the American Creed? Phylon 47 (Fall 1986):192-198.

Schneiderman, L. Racism and Revenue-Sharing. Social Work 17 (May 1972):44-49.

Stanback, H. J. Racism, Black Labor, and the Giant Corporation. Doctoral dissertation, University of Massachusetts, 1980. UMO # 8101399.

Swan, J. H. Racism in Labor Markets (2 vols.). Doctoral dissertation,

Northwestern University, 1981. UMO # 8120020.

Szymanski, A. The Political Economy of Racism. In: Scott McNall (ed.),
    Political Economy. A Critique of American Society Glenview, IL:
    Scott, Foresman and Co., 1981.

Van Drimmelen, R. Racism and Economics - An Ecumenical Concern. PCR
    Information (World Council of Churches) 24 (1987):7-13.

Vowels, R. C. The Political Economy of American Racism - Nonblack
    Decision - Making and Black Economic Status. Review of Black
    Political Economy (Summer 1971):3-39.

Welsing, F. C. Black Survival Units and the Economy of the White
    Supremacy System. Journal of Afro-American Issues 3 (1975):266-278.

Wibich, M. and U. Winter. Kapitalismus und Indianer in den USA.
    Frankfurt: Verlag Marxistische Blätter, 1976.

Willhelm, S. The Demise of Black People in a White America: The
    Perpetration of Economic Racism. 1977. ERIC ED 139891.

Willhelm, S. Who Needs the Negro? Cambridge, MA: Schenkman, 1971.

Wright, N., Jr. The Economics of Race. American Journal of Economics
    and Sociology (January 1967).

[See also sections 13, 20, 23, 55, 68, and 76]

25. **Education:** **Elementary** **and** **Secondary**

If Negroes have done well in certain separate Negro schools, two
speculations arise: how much more might Negroes have done if
all their separate schools had been adequately equipped and
taught; and further, what might not the Negro pupil have done
if, without hurt or hindrance, the whole educational opportunity
of America had been open to him, without discrimination?

- W. E. B. Du Bois, "Pechstein and Pecksniff," 1929.

Abney, E. E. The Effects and Consequences of Desegregation on the
Professional Job Status of Black Public School Principals Employed in
Florida. Cross Reference 1 (May-June 1978):239-258.

Adams, D. W. Fundamental Considerations: The Deep Meaning of Native
American Schooling, 1880-1900. Harvard Educational Review 58
(February 1988):1-28.

Addo, Linda A. A Historical Analysis of the Impact of Selected Teachers
on Education for Blacks in Coastal South Carolina, 1862-1970.
Doctoral dissertation, University of North Carolina at Greensboro,
1988. UMO # 8824055.

Allen, Rosemary. Business Influence on School Board and City Politics....
Doctoral dissertation, Claremont Graduate School, 1988. UMO #
8811908.

Allsup, C. Education is Our Freedom: The American G.I. Forum and the
Mexican American School Segregation in Texas, 1948-1957. Aztlan 8
(Spring-Fall 1977):27-50.

Anderson, J. D. Education for Servitude: The Social Purpose of Schooling
in the Black South, 1870-1930. Doctoral dissertation, University of
Illinois, 1973.

Anderson, J. D. The Education of Blacks in the South, 1860-1935. Chapel
Hill, NC: University of North Carolina Press, 1988.

Anderson, J. D. Ex-Slaves and the Rise of Universal Education in the New
South, 1860-1880. In: Ronald K Goodenow and Arthur Q. White (eds.),
Education and the Rise of the New South. Boston: Hall, 1981.

Anderson, J. D. The Historical Development of Black Vocational Education.
In: Harvey Kantor and David Tyack (eds.), Work, Youth, and
Schooling, pp. 180-222. Stanford, CA: Stanford University Press,
1982.

An Important Message from the Knights of the Ku Klux Klan of California to
Public School Authorities and Teachers. The Kourier Magazine 9
(April 1933):10-11.

Arevalo, R., and J. A. Brown. Educational Abuse of Chicano Youths.

Social Work in Education 5 (1983):158-65.

Asian/Pacific American Concerns Staff. Asian/Pacific American Education Agenda for the 1980s. 1980. ERIC ED 199319.

Aspira, Inc. of New York. Racial and Ethnic High School Dropout Rates in New York City's Public Schools. New York: Aspira, Inc. of New York, 1983.

Aspira, Inc. Trends in Segregation of Hispanic Students in Major School Districts Having Large Hispanic Enrollment. (Desegregation and the Hispanic in America, 5 vols., 1979-1980). 1980. ERIC ED 190270-190275.

At S.I. School, Lessons in Curbing Racial Strife [New Dorp High School, Staten Island]. New York Times May 1, 1988.

Beek, N. The Vanishing Californians: The Education of Indians in the Nineteenth Century. Southern California Quarterly 69 (Spring 1987):33-50.

Beezer, B. Black Teachers' Salaries and the Federal Courts before 'Brown v. Board of Education: One Beginning for Equity'. Journal of Negro Education 55 (Spring 1986):200-13.

Bell, D. Control Not Color: The Real Issue in the Milwaukee Manifesto [North Division School District, Milwaukee, Wisconsin]. Milwaukee Journal September 30, 1987.

Bell, M. L., and C. V. Morsink. Quality and Equity in the Preparation of Black Teachers. Journal of Teacher Education 37 (1986):16-20.

Beltran, L. B. Mexican and Mexican American Adolescent Achievement in an Urban U.S. Community: Making It Through High School [Midwest]. Doctoral dissertation, Northwestern University, 1987. UMO # 8723619.

Berliner, David C. Meta-Comments: A Discussion of Critiques of L.M. Dunn's Monograph Bilingual Hispanic CHildren on the U.S. Mainland. Hispanic Journal of Behavioral Sciences 10 (September 1988):273-90.

Berman, E. H. The Politics of Literacy and Educational Underdevelopment in Kentucky. Comparative Education Review 22 (February 1978):15-33 [See critique by H. Dudley Plunkett, pp.134-142, and reply, 143-146].

Beverly, E. E. A Study of the Community Power Structure As It Relates to the Educational Decison-Making Process in a Small Suburban School District [Inkster]. Doctoral dissertation, University of Michigan, 1987. UMO # 8712073.

Bigjim, F. S. We Talk, You Yawn: A Discourse on Education in Alaska [Education of Eskimo and Indians]. Portland, OR: Press-22, 1985

Black, MacKnight. Minority Student Issues: Racial/Ethnic Data Collected by the National Center for Education Statistics Since 1969. Washington, D.C.: U.S. Dept. of Education, Office of Educational Research and Improvement, March 1989.

Blumenthal, Ralph and Sam Howe Verhover. Of Patronage and Profit: Tale of School Board 12. New York Times December 16, 1988.

Bond, H. M. The Curriculum and the Negro Child. Journal of Negro Education 4 (April 1935):159-68.

Bond, H. M. Negro Education in Alabama. A Study in Cotton and Steel. New York: Atheneum, 1969.

Branch, Eleanor. 'We Have to Work Together'. An Interview with Outgoing BUSD President Joe Gross. Berkeley Voice December 21, 1988. [Berkeley, California Public Schools].

Brodbelt, Bonita. At Goudy, the Future Dies Early. Chicago Tribune June 15, 1988. [First of a series of articles on Goudy Elementary School in Chicago].

Brodbelt, S. Disguised Racism in Public Schools. Educational Leadership 29 (May 1972):699-702.

Brousseau, Kate. L'education des Negres aux Etas Unis. Paris: 1904.

Brown, C. G. Twenty Years On: New Federal and State Roles to Achieve Equity in Education. Washington, D.C.: National Center for Policy Alternatives, 1987.

Brown, G. and others. The Condition of Education for Hispanic Americans. Washington, D.C.: National Center for Education Statistics, 1980.

Brown, P. L. A Century of "Separate But Equal" Education in Anne Arundel County. New York: Vantage Press, 1988.

Butchart, R. E. Northern Schools, Southern Blacks, and Reconstruction: Freedmen's Education, 1862-1875. Westport, CT: Greenwood, 1980.

Butchart, R. E. 'We Best Can Instruct Our Own People': New York African Americans in the Freedmen's Schools, 1861-1875. Afro-Americans in New York Life and History 12 (January 1988):27-49.

Canino, M. J. An Historical Review of the English Language Policy in Puerto Rico's Educational System 1898-1949. Doctoral dissertation, Harvard University, 1981. UMO # 8125472.

Carmody, Deirdre. Hispanic Dropout Rates Puzzling. New York Times August 17, 1988

Carpenter, J. Racism in American Education. Marquette University Education Review 6 (Spring 1975):5-19.

Carr, Edward W. A Study of Equity and Adequacy in the Virginia Public

School Finance System from 1979 to 1986. Doctoral dissertation, College of William and Mary, 1987. UMO # 8801203.

Carter, R. L. The NAACP's Legal Strategy against Segregated Education. Michigan Law Review 86 (May 1988).

Carter, T. P. Mexican-Americans in School: A History of Educational Neglect. New York: College Entrance examination Board, 1970.

Casserly, M. D. and J. R. Garrett. Beyond the Victim: New Avenues for Research on Racism in Education. Educational Theory 27 (Summer 1977):196-204.

Chicago Schools: 'Worst in America'. Chicago Tribune May 15, 1988 [First of a series of articles].

Chinn, P., and S. Hughes. Representation of Minority Students in Special Education Classes [1978+]. RASE: Remedial & Special Education 8 (July-August 1987):41-46.

Choy, R. K. H. The Racial and Ethnic Mix of Pupils and Resource Allocation: A Review of Some Methods of Analysis. August 1980. ERIC ED 194683.

Choy, R. K. H. and B. R. Gifford. Resource Allocation in a Segregated School System: The Case of Los Angeles. Journal of Education Finance 6 (Summer 1980):34-50.

Chun, Eva W. Sorting Black Students for Success and Failure: The Inequity of Ability and Grouping and Tracking. Urban League Review 11 (1987-88).

Cimbala, P. A. Making Good Yankees: The Freedmen's Bureau and Education in Reconstruction Georgia, 1865-1870. Atlanta Historical Journal 29 (Fall 1985):5-18.

Clark, R. and C. G. Ward (eds.) Racism and the Desegregating Process. Jackson, MS: Educational Resources Center, 1970.

Clayton, C. E. Successful High Schools for Blacks and Hispanics. In: Educational Standards, Testing, and Access. Princeton, NJ: Educational Testing Service, 1985.

Coffin, G. C. Desegregation-Integration-Racism. School Board Policies (Croft Educational Services) 7 (February 1972).

Cohen, Deborah L. Reform at 5: The Unfinished Agenda. Education Week February 1, 1989. [Center for Successful Child Development, The "Beethoven Project," Chicago].

Commission on Minority Participation in Education and American Life. One-Third of a Nation. Washington, D.C.: American Council on Education, 1988.

Comptroller General of the U.S. School Dropouts: The Extent and Nature of the Problem. Washington, D.C.: U.S. General Accounting Office, 1986.

Cooper, Annie. A Story Road: Black Education in Iowa, 1838-1860. Annals of Iowa 48 (Winter-Spring 1986):113-34.

Corbin, David. Class over Caste. [Black schooling in coal-mining areas] In: William H. Turner and Edward J. Cabbell (eds.), Blacks in Appalachia. Lexington, KY: University of Kentucky Press, 1985.

Cordasco, F. and E. Bucchioni (eds.) Puerto Rican Children in Mainland Schools. A Source Book for Teachers. Metuchen, NJ: Scarecrow Press, 1968.

Cremin, Lawrence A. American Education: The Metropolitan Experience, 1876-1988. New York: Harper and Row, 1988.

Crosby, E. W. The Nigger and the Narcissus (or Self-Awareness in Black Education). In: John F. Szwed (ed.), Black America, pp. 271-285. New York: Basic Books, 1970.

Cummins, Jim. Teachers Are Not Miracle Workers': Lloyd Dunn's Call for Hispanic Activism. Hispanic Journal of Behavioral Sciences 10 (September 1988):263-72.

Cuphone, E. B. Equal Educational Opportunities and Enrollment Patterns of Minority Students in Remedial Education. Doctoral dissertation, University of Massachusetts, 1986. UMO # 8701151.

Curtis, C. A. A Study of Private Education in a Black Community: The Concord Baptist Church Elementary School in Bedford-Stuyvesant. Doctoral dissertation Rutgers University, 1987. UMO # 8727313.

Davis, G. Racism and the School Curriculum Past and Present. Multicultural Teaching 1 (1983).

Davis, J. E. A Virginia Asset: The Virigina Industrial School for Colored Girls. Southern Workman 49 (August 1920):357-64.

Donato, R. In Struggle: Mexican Americans in the Pajaro Valley Schools, 1900-1979. Doctoral dissertation, Stanford University, 1987. UMO # 8722985.

Du Bois, W. E. B. The Burden of Negro Schooling. Independent 52 (July 18, 1901):1667-8.

Du Bois, W. E. B. The Cost of Education. Crisis 3 (November 1911).

Du Bois, W. E. B. The Negro Common School. Atlanta: Atlanta University Press, 1901.

Du Bois, W. E. B. Sociology and Industry in Southern Education. Voice of the Negro 4 (May 1907):170-5.

Du Bois, W. E. B. [Testimony] U.S. Congress, 75th, 1st session, House of

Representatives. In: Hearings on Federal Aid for the Support of Public Schools, pp. 284-295. Washington, D.C.: GPO, 1937.

Du Bois, W. E. B. [Testimony] U.S. Industrial Commission, Vol. 15. In: Immigration and Education, pp. 159-175. Washington, D.C.: GPO, 1901.

Du Bois, W. E. B. and A. G. Dill (eds.) The Common School and the Negro American. Atlanta: Atlanta University Press, 1911.

Dunn, Lloyd M. Bilingual Hispanic Children on the U.S. Mainland: A Review of Research on Their Cognitive, Linguistic, and Scholastic Development. Circle Pines, MN: American Guidance Service, 1987.

Dunn, Lloyd M. Has Dunn's Monograph Been Shot Down in Flames - Author Reactions to the Preceding Critiques of It. Hispanic Journal of Behavioral Sciences 10 (September 1988):301-23.

Evans, H. W. The Public School Problem in America ... Outlining Fully the Policies and the Program of the Knights of Ku Klux Klan Toward the Public School System. Atlanta, GA: 1924.

Fell, M. L. The Foundations of Nativism in American Textbooks, 1783-1860. Washington, D.C.: Catholic University of America Press, 1941.

Ferguson, Charles G. John Locke and the Education of the Poor. Doctoral dissertation, College of William and Mary, 1987. UMO # 8803968.

Fernandez, Ricardo R. (ed.) Achievement Testing: Science vs. Ideology. Hispanic Journal of Behavioral Sciences 10 (September 1988):entire issue. [Bilingual Hispanic children].

Fernandez, Ricardo R. and Gangjian Shu. School Dropouts. New Approaches to an Enduring Problem. Education and Urban Society 20 (August 1988):363-86. [Hispanic students and the schools].

Figueroa, P. M. E. and L. T. Swart. Teachers' and Pupils' Racist and Ethnocentric Frames of Reference: A Case Study. New Community 13 (Spring-Summer 1986):40-51. [Britain].

Fine, M. Why Urban Adolescents Drop Into and Out of Public High School. Teachers College Record 87 (Spring 1986):363-409.

Fossett, M., and O. R. Galle. Race, Sex, and Economic Returns to Education. Child and Youth Services Review 4 (1982):111-13.

Fuke, R. P. A School for Freed Labor: The Maryland 'Government Farms,' 1864-1866. Maryland Historian 26 (Spring-Summer 1985):11-23.

Garmoran, Adam and Mark Berends. The Effects of Stratification in Secondary Schools: Synthesis of Survey and Ethnographic Research. National Center on Effective Secondary Schools, Wisconsin Center for Education Research Document Service, Room 242, Educational Sciences Bldg., 1025 W. Johnson St., Madison, WI 53706, 1988.

Gerber, J. B. Southern White Schooling. 1880-1940. Doctoral
    dissertation, University of California, Davis, 1986. UMO # 8701687.

Gillerman, G. Sarah Roberts, Charles Summer, and the Idea of Equality
    [School segregation in Boston, 1850]. Boston Bar Journal 31
    (September-October 1987).

Ginzburg, A., and Others. A School Based Analysis of Inter- and
    Intradistrict Resource Allocation [2,636 elementary schools in New
    York state]. Washington, D.C.: AVI Policy Research, May 1, 1980.
    [1701 K Street, N.W., Washington, D.C. 20006].

Gonzalez, G. C. Segregation of Mexican Children in a Southern California
    City: The Legacy of Expansionism and the American Southwest [Santa
    Ana, CA, 1913-1948]. Western Historical Quarterly 16 :55-76.

Gonzalez, G. C. Racism, Education, and the Mexican Community in Los
    Angeles, 1920-30. Societas 4 (Autumn 1974):287-301.

González-Gómez, Juan. Case Study: The Aftermath of a Community Struggle
    for Bilingual Education in a Selected School District in
    Massachusetts [Worcester]. Doctoral dissertation, University of
    Massachusetts, 1988. UMO # 8813227.

Gorov, L. Children of Civic Leaders at Luther South: We're All Mixed
    [Luther South High School, private institution in Chicago]. Chicago
    Reporter 17 (April 1988):8-9.

Grant, G. The World We Created at Hamilton High. Cambridge, MA: Harvard
    University Press, 1988.

Grant, Linda (ed.) Minorities. Elementary School Journal 88 (May
    1988):441-570.

Green, R. L. Racism in American Education. Phi Delta Kappan 53 (January
    1972):274-276.

Green, W. J. Mathematics Placement, the Implementation of Racism in Our
    Schools. Integrateducation 18 (January-August 1980):40-41.

Gross, J. New York's School Chief: The View in Minneapolis [Richard R.
    Green]. New York Times January 7, 1988.

Gutman, Herbert G. Schools for Freedom: Post-Emancipation Origins of
    Afro-American Education. In: Ira Berlin (ed.), Power and Culture:
    Essays on the American Working Class, pp. 260-97. New York: 1987.

Hairston, L. B. A Study of Industrial Arts Education Programs in Virginia
    for Blacks: 1951-1969. Doctoral dissertation, Virginia Polytechnic
    Institute and State University, 1986. UMO # 8712380.

Hale, S. E. T. Foundations of Mainstreaming Mentally Handicapped
    Children: Social Control. Segregation, and Racism in Public
    Elementary Schools. Doctoral dissertation, University of
    Cincinnati, 1985. UMO # 8605499.

Hancock, Lynnell. Patronage Principals. <u>Village</u> <u>Voice</u> July 26, 1988.
[Politics in Community School Districts 10 and 12, South Bronx].

Hancock, Lynnell. The Teachers Union Connection. <u>Village</u> <u>Voice</u> December
27, 1988. [Community school boards scandal in New York City].

Hancock, Lynnell and others. Can the City's Schools Be Saved? <u>Village</u>
<u>Voice</u> September 20, 1988. [Series of articles about public schools
of NYC].

Harlan, L. R. <u>Separate</u> <u>and</u> <u>Unequal</u> <u>Public</u> <u>School</u> <u>Campaigns</u> <u>and</u> <u>Racism</u> <u>in</u>
<u>the</u> <u>Southern</u> <u>Seaboard</u> <u>States,</u> <u>1901-1915</u>. Chapel Hill, NC:
University of North Carolina Press, 1958.

Harris, C. V. Stability and Change in Discrimination against Black Public
Schools: Birmingham, Alabama, 1871-1931. <u>Journal</u> <u>of</u> <u>Southern</u>
<u>History</u> 51 (August 1985):373-416.

Harris, E. E. Prejudice and Other Social Factors in School Segregation.
<u>Journal</u> <u>of</u> <u>Negro</u> <u>Education</u> (Fall 1968).

Haycox, S. 'Races of a Questionable Type': Origins of the Jurisdiction
of the U.S. Bureau of Education in Alaska, 1867-1885. <u>Pacific</u>
<u>Northwest</u> <u>Quarterly</u> 75 (October 1984):156-63.

Hechinger, F. M. Toward Educating the Homeless. <u>New</u> <u>York</u> <u>Times</u> February
2, 1988.

Hendrick, I. G. Early Schooling for Children of Migrant Farmworkers in
California. The 1920s. <u>Aztlan</u> 8 (Fall 1977):11-26.

Hennessy, M. and others. <u>The</u> <u>Effects</u> <u>of</u> <u>Current</u> <u>and</u> <u>Alternative</u> <u>Intra-</u>
<u>District</u> <u>Allocation</u> <u>Procedures</u> <u>on</u> <u>Coverage</u> <u>of</u> <u>Disadvantaged</u> <u>Students</u>.
March 17, 1978. ERIC ED 198184.

Henningsen, V. W., III. <u>Reading,</u> <u>Writing,</u> <u>and</u> <u>Reindeer:</u> <u>The</u> <u>Development</u>
<u>of</u> <u>Federal</u> <u>Education</u> <u>in</u> <u>Alaska,</u> <u>1877-1920</u>. Doctoral dissertation,
Harvard University, 1987. UMO # 8722686.

Hentoff, Nat. Ocean Hill-Brownsville: A Time of Mourning or Redemption?
<u>Village</u> <u>Voice</u> September 20, 1988.

Hentoff, Nat. One Summer in Philadelphia, Mississippi. <u>Village</u> <u>Voice</u>
July 19, 1988. [Booker T. Washington High School, 1964].

Hirano-Nakaniski, M. The Extent and Relevance of Pre-High School
Attrition and Delayed Education for Hispanics. <u>Hispanic</u> <u>Journal</u> <u>of</u>
<u>Behavioral</u> <u>Sciences</u> 8 (March 1986):61-76.

Hirayama, K. K. Asian Children's Adaptation to Public Schools. <u>Social</u>
<u>Work</u> <u>in</u> <u>Education</u> 7 (Summer 1985):213-20.

Hispanic Policy Department Project. <u>Too</u> <u>Late</u> <u>To</u> <u>Patch:</u> <u>Reconsidering</u>
<u>Second-Chance</u> <u>Opportunities</u> <u>for</u> <u>Hispanic</u> <u>and</u> <u>Other</u> <u>Dropouts</u>.

Washington, D.C.: Hispanic Information Center, 1988.

Hoffer, Thomas B. High School Retention of Hispanic American Youth.
Chicago, IL: National Opinion Research Center, 1986.

Hogan, D. J. Class and Reform: School and Society in Chicago, 1880-1930.
Philadelphia, PA: University of Pennsylvania Press, 1985.

Hogan, D. J. Education and the Making of the Chicago Working Class, 1880-
1930. History of Education Quarterly 18 (Fall 1978):227-270.

Hornick, N. S. Anthony Benezet and the Africans' School: Toward a Theory
of Full Equality. Pennsylvania Magazine of History and Biography 99
(1975):299-421.

House, Ernest R. Jesse Jackson and the Politics of Charisma. The Rise
and Fall of the PUSH/Excel Program. Boulder, CO: Westview, 1988.

Hunt, Barbara J. The Public Education of Blacks in City of Pittsburgh,
1920-1950: Actions and Reactions of the Black Community in Its
Pursuit of Educational Equality. Doctoral dissertation, University
of Pittsburgh, 1987. UMO # 8810108.

Hunt, T. C. Sectionalism, Slavery, and Schooling in Antebellum Virginia.
West Virginia History 46 (1985-1986):125-36.

Hyams, B. K. School Teachers as Agents of Cultural Imperialism in
Territorial Hawaii. Journal of Pacific History 20 (July-October
1985):202-24.

Introducing Consequences in Public Education: Rewards and Intervention
[State takeover of academically-failing school districts]. In:
Capital Ideas (National Governors' Association). January 15, 1987.

Jacoway, E., and D. R. Colburn, (eds.) Southern Businessmen and
Desegregation. Baton Rouge: Louisiana State University Press, 1982.

James, T. Exile Within. The Schooling of Japanese Americans, 1942-1945.
Cambridge, MA: Harvard University Press, 1987.

Jerrems, R. L. Racism: Vector of Ghetto Education. Integrated Education
(July-August 1970):40-47.

Johnson, Dirk. Catholic Schools Reach Out to Serve Poor and to Borrow.
New York Times September 13, 1988. [Chicago].

Johnson, Dirk. A City's Unwelcome Lesson About Schools and Class. New
York Times April 2, 1989. [South Loop Elementary School, Chicago].

Johnson, Julie. Curriculum Seeks to Lift Blacks' Self Image. New York
Times March 8, 1989.

Jones, M. D. The American Missionary Association and the Beaufort, North
Carolina School Controversy, 1866-67 [Separate education for Black
freedmen and poor whites]. Phylon 48 (June 1987):103-11.

Jordan, E. C. The Impact of the Negro Organization Society on Public
    Support for Education in Virginia 1912-1950. Doctoral dissertation,
    University of Virginia, 1978. UMO # 7916270.

Jud, G. D. and D. G. Bennett. Public Schools and the Pattern of
    Intraurban Residential Mobility [Charlotte, N.C. and Los Angeles,
    CA]. Land Economics 62 (November 1986).

Kelly, M. E., and K. R. McConnochie. Compensatory Education: A Subtle
    Form of Racism? Australian Journal of Education 18 (March 1974):30-
    49.

King, W. M. Black Children, White Law: Black Efforts to Secure Public
    Education in Central City, Colorado, 1864-1869. Essays & Monographs
    Colo. Hist. (1984):55-79.

Kirsch, Irwin S. and Ann Jungeblut. Literacy: Profiles of America's
    Young Adults. Princeton, NJ: National Assessment of Educational
    Progress, 1986.

The Klan and the Public School. The Kourier Magazine 1 (May 1925):25-27.

Klan Boomed in School. New York Times December 8, 1924.

Klan Has Eye on Morton High, School Citizen Warns [Illinois]. The Kourier
    Magazine 9 (April 1933):18.

Klan Intervention on Schools is Cited. New York Times February 13, 1951.

Kluger, R. Simple Justice: The History of Brown v. Board of Education
    and Black America's Struggle for Equality. New York: Knopf, 1975.

Kousser, J. M. Making Separate Equal: Integration of Black and White
    School Funds in Kentucky. Journal of Interdisciplinary History 10
    (Winter 1980):399-428.

Kousser, J. M. Progressivism - For Middle Class Whites Only: North
    Carolina Education, 1880-1910. Journal of Southern History 46 (May
    1980):169-194.

Kousser, J. M. Separate But Not Equal: The Supreme Court's First
    Decision on Racial Discrimination in Schools ['Cumming v. School
    Board of Richmond County, Augusta, Georgia']. Journal of Southern
    History 46 (February 1980):17-44.

La Brecque, Ron. Something More Than Calculus [Jaime Escalante, Garfield
    High School, Los Angeles]. New York Times Education Life November
    6, 1988.

Lawson, E. Black Women Teachers of the Freedmen in the American
    Missionary Association. Oberlin, OH: Women's History Project,
    Oberlin College, 1981.

Leeper, R. R. (ed.) Dare to Care/Dare to Act. Racism and Education.

Washington, D.C.: Association for Supervision and Curriculum Development, 1971.

Leung, Edwin Pak-wah. The Education of Early Chinese Students in America. In: The Chinese American Experience: Papers from the Second National Conference on Chinese American Studies. San Francisco, CA: 1980.

Levidow, Les. 'Ability' Labeling as Racism. In: Dawn Gill and Les Levidow (eds.), Anti-Racist Science Teaching, pp. 233-67. London: Free Association Books, 1987.

Levin, B. K. Education of Children of Undocumented Immigrants: Teacher and Parent Perceptions and Expectations. Doctoral dissertation, University of Colorado, 1986. UMO # 8618971.

Levin, H. M. Education and Earnings of Blacks and the 'Brown' Decision. October 1979. ERIC ED 176374.

Lewis, M. D. Employment and Utilization of Negro Teachers in Selected Communities [Omaha]. Omaha, NE: Omaha Urban League, 1957.

Lewis, Neil A. New York City Weighs Scrapping Its High School Integration Policy. New York Times August 17, 1988.

Lickona, T. Moral Development in the Elementary School Classrooms. In: William M. Kurtines and Jacob Gewitz (eds.), Moral Behavior and Development. Advances in Theory, Research, and Application, vol. 1. Hillsdale, NJ: Erlbaum, 1989.

Loehr, Peter. The 'Urgent Need' for Minority Teachers. Education Week October 5, 1988.

Logan, Thomas N. The Opposition in the South to the Free-School System. Journal of Social Science 9 (January 1878):92-100.

Lomawaima, Kimberly T. "They Called It Prairie Light": Oral Histories from Chilocco Indian Agricultural Boarding School, 1920-1940. Doctoral dissertation, Stanford University, 1987. UMO # 8800979.

Low, V. The Unimpressible Race: A Century of Educational Struggle by the Chinese in San Francisco. San Francisco, CA: East/West Pub. Co., 1982.

Mallam, R. C. Academic Treatment of the Indian in Public School Texts and Literature. Journal of American Indian Education 13 (1973):14-19.

Marable, Manning. Booker T. Washington and the Political Economy of Black Education in the United States 1880-1915. Education with Production 4 (February 1986):10-37.

Marable, Manning. The Destruction of Black Education. In: How Capitalism Underdeveloped Black America, pp. 215-28. Boston: South End Press, 1983.

Marcus, L. R., and B. D. Stickney. Race and Education. The Unending Controversy. Springfield, IL: Thomas, 1981.

Margo, Robert A. Disfranchisement, School Finance, and the Economics of Segregated Schools in the United States South, 1890-1910. Doctoral dissertation, Harvard University, 1982. UMO # 8222668.

Margo, Robert A. Disenfranchisement, School Finance, and the Economics of Segregated Schools in the United States South, 1890-1910. New York: Garland, 1985.

Margo, Robert A. Educational Achievement in Segregated School Systems: The Effects of 'Separate-but-Equal'. American Economic Review 76 (September 1986):794-801.

Margo, Robert A. Race Differences in Public School Expenditures: Disfranchisement and School Finance in Louisiana, 1890-1910. Social Science History 6 (Winter 1982):9-33.

Margo, Robert A. Race, Educational Attainment, and the 1940 Census. Journal of Economic History 46 (March 1986):189-98.

Margo, Robert A. 'Teacher Salaries in Black and White': The South in 1910. Explorations in Economic History 21 (July 1984)):306-26.

Marshall, S. I. An Analysis of Trends and Conditions in School Districts with Black Superintendents and a Composite Profile of the Black Superintendent at His/Her Initial Appointment. Doctoral dissertation, Virginia Polytechnic Institute & State University, 1987. UMO # 8719030.

Masem, P. W. Resegregation: A Case Study of an Urban School District [Little Rock, 1957-1978]. Doctoral dissertation, George Peabody College for Teachers of Vanderbilt University, 1986. UMO # 8709411.

Matthews, Samuel. John Isom Gaines: The Architect of Black Public Education. Queen City Heritage 45 (Spring 1987):41-48.

May, Ernest M. Schools Can Nip Criminal Careers in the Bud [Letter]. New York Times January 31, 1989.

McCarthy, Cameron. Rethinking Liberal and Radical Perspectives on Racial Inequality in Schooling: Making the Case for Nonsynchrony. Harvard Educational Review 58 (August 1988):265-79.

McCaul, R. L. The Black Struggle for Public Schooling in Nineteenth-Century Illinois. Carbondale, IL: Southern Illinois University Press, 1987.

McCorry, J. J. Marcus Foster and the Oakland Public Schools. Leadership in an Urban Bureaucracy. Berkeley, CA: University of California Press, 1978.

McGehee, C. S. E. O. Tade, Freedman's Education, and the Failure of Reconstruction in Tennessee. Tenn. Hist. Quarterly 43 (Winter

1984):376-89.

McMorris, R. Not a Wave-Maker, Skinner's Achievements Ripple to Other Blacks [Interview with Eugene Skinner, first Black teacher employed in Omaha public schools]. Omaha World Herald May 26, 1979.

Mc Neil, Teresa B. St. Anthony's Indian School in San Diego, 1886-1907. Journal of San Diego History 34 (Summer 1988):187-200.

Meier, August and John Bracey (editorial advisers). The Campaign for Educational Equality, 1913-1950 (part 3). In: Papers of the NAACP. New Parts on Educational Equality, Voting Rights, Housing, the Scottsboro Case, and Anti-Lynching [43 microfilm reels]. Frederick, MD: University Publications of America, 1987.

Miller, D. A., III. The Influence of Sex, Race, and Attractiveness in the Recruitment and Selection of School Psychologists in the Public Schools. Doctoral dissertation, University of Iowa, 1979. UMO # 7928597.

Miller, D. E. The Limits of Schooling by Imposition: The Hopi Indians of Arizona. Doctoral dissertation, University of Tennessee, 1987. UMO # 8721290.

Mirikitani, Raymond T. A Longitudinal Study of Achievement in Hawaiian Public Elementary Schools, 1975-83. Doctoral dissertation, Stanford University, 1988. UMO # 8815027.

Molin, P. F. Changes in Organization and Governance of Indian Education Associated with the Indian Self-determination and Education Assistance Act (P. L. 93-638) of 1975 [Contract schools]. Doctoral dissertation, University of Minnesota, 1987. UMO # 8723835.

Monk, D. H. Toward a Multilevel Perspective on the Allocation of Educational Resources. Review of Educational Research 51 (Summer 1981):215-236.

Montague, W. 'Patience and Time': Allies for Change on King Cotton's Land [Black education in the public schools of Marengo County, Alabama]. Education Week February 17, 1988.

Moranian, S. E. Ethnocide in the Schoolhouse: Missionary Effort to Educate Indian Youth in Pre-reservation Wisconsin. Wisconsin Magazine of History 64 (Summer 1981):242-60.

Morgan, T. Bronx School Ordered Shut for Low Scores [J.H.S. 123, Throgs Neck section, Bronx]. New York Times August 10, 1987.

Morris, R. C. Reading, 'Riting, and Reconstruction: The Education of Freedmen in the South, 1861-1870. Chicago: University of Chicago Press, 1982.

Morton, F. J. Negro Educators for Negro Education. School and Society 24 (November 20, 1926):625-29.

Muwakkil, S. Educator Joe Clark's School of Hard Knocks [Paterson, NJ]. In These Times February 3, 1988.

National Black Child Development Institute. Budget Cuts and Black Children: A Response to the President's Budget for Fiscal Year 1983. Washington, D.C.: The Institute, 1982.

Navarro, R. Identity and Consensus in the Politics of Bilingual Education: The Case of California, 1967-1980. Doctoral dissertation, Stanford University, 1984. UMO # 8408334.

The Negro School Child in Atlanta. Atlanta: Citizen's Committee on Public Education, 1941.

Neill, D. M. The Struggles in the Boston Black Community for Equality and Quality in Public Education: 1959-1987. Doctoral dissertation, Harvard University, 1987. UMO # 8722693.

Neisser, U. (ed.) The School Achievement of Minority Children: New Perspectives. Hillsdale, NJ: Erlbaum, 1986.

Noah, T. Saving One High School [Orangeburg-Wilkinson High School, South Carolina]. Newsweek May 2, 1988.

Noboa, A. Hispanic Segregation Trends in School Districts with Hispanic Enrollment Above 5% and Exceeding a Total Student Enrollment of 3,000. April 21, 1980. ERIC ED 187784.

O'Neill, D. M., and P. Sepielli. Education in the United States: 1940-1983. Washington, D.C.: GPO, July 1985.

Oakes, Jeanne. Beyond Tracking. Educational Horizons 65 (Fall 1986):32-35.

Ogbu, J. U. Black Education: A Cultural Ecological Perspective. In: Harriette P. McAdoo (ed.), Black Families. Newbury Park, CA: Sage, 1988.

Ogbu, J. U. Class Stratification, Racial Stratification, and Schooling. In: Lois Weis (ed.), Class, Race, and Gender, pp. 163-82. Albany: University of New York Press, 1988.

Ogbu, J. U. The Consequences of the American Caste System. In: Ulric Neisser (ed.), The School Achievement of Minority Children. Hillsdale, NJ: Erlbaum, 1986.

Ogbu, J. U. Societal Forces as a Context of Ghetto Children's School Failure. In: Lynn Feagan and Dale C. Farran (eds.), The Language of Children Reared in Poverty, pp. 117-83. New York: Academic Press, 1982.

Olneck, M. R., and M. Lazerson. Education. In: Stephan Thernstrom (ed.), Harvard Encyclopedia of American Ethnic Groups, pp. 303-19. Cambridge, MA: Harvard University Press, 1980.

Orazem, P. F. Black-White Differences in Schooling Investment and Human Capital Production in Segregated Schools. American Economic Review 77 (September 1987).

Orfield, G. Must We Bus? Segregated Schools and National Policy. Washington, D.C.: Brookings Institution Press, 1978.

Orr, E. W. Twice as Less. Black English and the Performance of Black Students in Mathematics and Science. New York: Norton, 1987.

Orr, M. T. A Critical Examination of a Policy Process, OCR Review of New York City Schools [1972-1976]. Doctoral dissertation, Columbia University, 1979. UMO # 8009693.

Our Public Schools. The Kourier Magazine 4 (January 1928):12-19.

Our Public Schools: Klan's Attitude vs. Catholic Church's. The Kourier Magazine 11 (September 1934):1-3.

Page, R. Lower Track Classes at College-Preparatory High School: A Caricature of Educational Encounters. In: George and Louise Spindler (eds.), Interpretive Ethnography of Education at Home and Abroad. Hillsdale, NJ: Lawrence Erlbaum Associates, 1987.

Parish, Ralph and others. Knock at Any School. Phi Delta Kappan 70 (January 1989):386-94.

Parker, G. M., and W. O'Connor. Racism in the Schools. Training and Development Journal 24 (November 1970):27-32.

Parker, Lawrence J. Equity and Excellence in Education: The Fiscal and Legal Implications. Doctoral dissertation, University of Illinois, Urbana, 1987. UMO # 8803165.

Patton, J. O. The Black Community of Augusta and the Struggle for Ware High School 1880-1899. In: Vincent P. Franklin and James D. Anderson (eds.), New Perspectives in Black Educational History, pp. 45-59. Boston: Hall, 1978.

Payne, C. M. Getting What We Ask For: The Ambiguity of Success and Failure in Urban Education. Westport, CT: Greenwood, 1984.

Payne, C. M. Multicultural Education and Racism in American Schools. Theory Into Practice 23 (1984):124-31.

Perkins, L. M. The Black Female American Missionary Association Teacher in the South, 1861-1870. In: Jeffrey J. Crow and Flora J. Hatley (eds.), Black Americans in North Carolina and the South. Chapel Hill, NC: University of North Carolina Press, 1984.

Perlmann, Joel. Ethnic Differences. Schooling and Social Structure among the Irish, Italians, Jews, and Blacks in an American City, 1880-1935 [Providence, RI]. New York: Cambridge University Press, 1989.

R.I. Perspectives in American History 2 (1985).

Perry, Imani. A Black Student's Reflection on Public and Private Schools.
    Harvard Educational Review 58 (August 1988):332-36.

Peterson, P. E. The Politics of School Reform, 1870-1940. Chicago:
    University of Chicago Press, 1986.

Pinsky, M. Double Dealing in Plains, Georgia. Southern Exposure 7
    (Summer 1979):98-102.

Plisko, V. W. and J. D. Stern (eds.) The Condition of Education: 1985
    Edition. Washington, D.C.: National Center for Educational
    Statistics, 1985. [Contains school-achievement statistics of
    Hispanic children].

Poverty and Education in Chicago, 1980 [Data by White, Black, and Latino
    groups]. Chicago Reporter (Special Report) 12 (January 1983):4.

Powel, L. I. The Old Cedar School [KKK and the public schools].
    Troudale, OR: George Estes, 1922.

Powers, Brian A. Second Class Finish: The Effects of Rituals and
    Routines of a Working-Class High School. Doctoral dissertation,
    University of California, Berkeley, 1987. UMO # 8814022.

Prewitt Diaz, Joseph O. Assessment of Puerto Rican Children in Bilingual
    Education Programs in the United States: A Critique of Lloyd M.
    Dunn's Monograph. Hispanic Journal of Behavioral Sciences 10
    (September 1988):237-52.

Pritchett, J. B. North Carolina's Public Schools: Growth and Local
    Taxation. Social Science History 9 (Summer 1985).

Problems of Race and Ethnic Relations Among High School Youth: Part Two.
    International Journal of Group Tensions (Summer 1988):63-150,
    [entire issue].

Proctor, R., Jr. Racial Discrimination Against Black Teachers and Black
    Professionals in the Pittsburgh Public School System, 1834-1973.
    Doctoral dissertation, University of Pittsburgh, 1979. UMO # 7924678.

Punke, H. H. Racism and Inferior Education. Alabama Lawyer 32 (1971).

Quintero Alfaro, A. G. Educacion y cambio social en Puerto Rico: una
    epoca critica. Rio Piedras, PR: Editorial Edil, 1972.

Rabinowitz, H. N. Half a Loaf: The Shift from White to Black Teachers in
    the Negro Schools of the Urban South, 1865-1890. Journal of Southern
    History 40 (November 1974):565-594.

Rabkin, J. Behind the Tax-Exempt Schools Debate. Public Interest 68
    (Summer 1983):21-36.

Ralph, John. Improving Education for the Disadvantaged: Do We Know When

Ralph, John. Improving Education for the Disadvantaged: Do We Know When to Help? Phi Delta Kappan 70 (January 1989):395-401.

Rebell, M. A., and A. R. Block. Equality and Education: Federal Civil Rights Enforcement in the New York City School System. Princeton, NJ: Princeton University Press, 1985.

Reid, A. Images of Hatred Disturb Neighborhood [Agassiz Elementary School, Cambridge, MA]. Boston Globe January 6, 1988.

Reitz, C. Racism, Capitalism, and the Schools: Understanding Demographic Data and Educational change in Buffalo, New York (1930-1977). Urban Education 18 (1984):490-502.

Resnick, D. P. (ed.) Literacy in Historical Perspective. Washington, D.C.: Library of Congress, 1983.

Revere, A. L. B. A Description of Black Female School Superintendents. Doctoral dissertation, Miami University, 1985. UMO # 8526800.

Reynoso, Cruz. Educational Equity. UCLA Law Review 36 (October 1988):107-17.

Ribadeneira, Diego. Hispanics Demand a Better Effort by City Schools. Boston Globe November 21, 1988.

Richards, C. E. Race and Demographic Trends: The Employment of Minority Teachers in California Public Schools. Economics of Education Review 5 (1986).

Richards, C. E. and D. J. Encarnation. Teaching in Public and Private Schools: The Significance of Race. Educational Evaluation & Policy Analysis 8 (Fall 1986):237-52.

Rimer, S. Paterson Principal: A Man of Extremes [Joe Clark, Eastside High School, Paterson, NJ]. New York Times January 14, 1988.

Robb, C. Education [Part of series: "Poverty Amidst Affluence. Bostonians the Boom Left Behind"]. Boston Globe Magazine December 15, 1985.

Roberts, W. Legal Aspects of Bilingualism in Puerto Rico (1900-1952). Doctoral dissertation, Northwestern University, 1983. UMO # 8400727.

Robertson, W. Employment Opportunity in the Schools: Job Patterns of Minorities and Women in Public Elementary and Secondary Schools, 1975. Washington, D.C.: Equal Employment Opportunity Commission, 1977.

Rodkin, J. S. A Study of the Puerto Rican Migration to Lancaster, Pennsylvania and the Response of the Public School System. Doctoral dissertation, Temple University, 1987. UMO # 8716462.

Roos, Peter D. Bilingual Education: The Hispanic Response to Unequal Educational Opportunity. Law and Contemporary Problems 42 (Autumn

1978):111-40.

Rosenfeld, G. 'Shut Those Thick Lips': A Study of Slum Failure. New York: Holt, 1971.

Salmans, S. The Tracking Controversy. New York Times Education Life April 10, 1988.

Sandler, M. Equal Employment Opportunity Consciousness Among Arkansas Public School Districts. Journal of Negro Education 51 (Fall 1982):412-424.

San Miguel, Guadalupe, Jr. From a Dual to a Tri-Partite School System: The Origins and Development of Educational Segregation in Corpus Christi, Texas. Integrateducation 17 (September-December 1979):27-38.

San Miguel, Guadalupe, Jr. 'Let All of Them Take Head.' Mexicans and the Campaign for Educational Equality in Texas, 1910-1981. Austin: University of Texas Press, 1987.

San Miguel, Guadalupe, Jr. Status of the Historiography of Chicano Education: A Preliminary Analysis. History of Education Quarterly 26 (Winter 1986):523-36.

Santiago Santiago, I. A Community's Struggle for Equal Educational Opportunity: Aspira v. Board of Education. Princeton, NJ: Office for Minority Education, Educational Testing Service, 1978.

Schmidt, William E. Private Gifts to Public Schools Bring Questions of Fairness. New York Times December 27, 1988.

School in Oklahoma [K.K.K.]. Pittsburgh Courier October 6, 1923.

Schuck-Martino, Pedro O. An Interpretation of Economic Changes, Political Ideologies and Sociological Ideas in Educational Reform Policy in Puerto Rico: 1940-1960. Doctoral dissertation, Boston University, 1988. UMO # 8806755.

Search for Solutions. Chicago Sun-Times May 1, 1988. [First of a series of articles on the Chicago Public Schools].

Sedlacek, W. E., and G. C. Brooks, Jr. Racism in the Public Schools: A Model for Change. Journal of Non-White Concerns in Personnel and Guidance 1 (April 1973):133-143.

Shapiro, Svi. Capitalism at Risk: The Political Economy of the Educational Reports of 1983. Educational Theory 35 (Winter 1985):57-72.

Sherman, J. D. Financing Local Schools: The Impact of Desegregation. Policy Studies Journal (Summer 1979):701-707.

Sherman, J. D. School Desegregation and Financial Support for the Public Schools in Four Southern States [Alabama, Louisiana, Mississippi, and

South Carolina]. April 1981. ERIC ED 206746.

Sherman, J. D. Underfunding of Majority-Black School Districts in South Carolina. Washington, D.C.: Lawyers' Committee on Civil Right Under Law, October 1977.

Sherman, J. D., and P. S. Tomlinson. Impact of School Finance on Minorities: A Study of Seven Southern States. Journal of Law and Education 9 (July 1980):353-367.

Sherwood, G. H. The Oblates' Hundred and One Years [First Black sisterhood, to teach Black children, since 1829 in Baltimore]. New York: Macmillan, 1931.

Simmons, S. J. The Development of Schooling in Floyd County, Virginia, 1831-1900. Doctoral dissertation, Virginia Polytechnic Institute and State University, 1987. UMO # 8719058.

Simon, K. W. Tax-exempt Status of Racially Discriminatory Religious Schools. Tax Law Review 36 (Summer 1981):477-516.

Slaughter, Diana T. and Deborah J. Johnson (eds.) Visible Now: Blacks in Private Schools. Westport, CT: Greenwood, 1988.

Smith, Kitty Lou. An Exploration of the Beliefs, Values, and Attitudes of Black Students in Fairfax County. Doctoral dissertation, Virginia Polytechnic Institute and State University, 1987. UMO # 8802737.

Smith, M. C. The Creation of an Inner City District for Inner City Students: A Commentary [North Division School District, Milwaukee, Wisconsin]. Metropolitan Education 5 (Fall 1987):1-6.

Smith, R. K. The Economics of Education and Discrimination in the U.S. South: 1870-1910. Doctoral dissertation, University of Wisconsin, 1973. UMO # 7410269.

Smith, T. L. Immigrant Social Aspirations and American Education. American Quarterly 21 (1969):523-43.

Sparrow, F. Definitional Racism and Public Education. Forum (November-December 1972).

The Staff of the Chicago Tribune. Chicago Schools: 'Worst in America'. An Examination of the Public Schools that Fail Chicago. Chicago: The Chicago Tribune, 1988. [Reprint of series of articles that appeared May 15-29, 1988].

Stark, Irwin. The Invisible Island [Novel about schools of Harlem]. New York: Viking Press, 1948.

Stein, A. Educational Equality in the U.S.: The Emperor's Clothes. Science and Society 36 (Winter 1972):469-476.

Stones, M. E. School Administrator Attitudes and Racism. Integrated Education 11 (March-April 1973):54-59.

Storey, Laurie J. Manchester [N.H.] Schools' [Martin Luther] King Day Sparks Furor. Boston Globe December 11, 1988.

Streitmatter, J. L. Ethnic/Racial and Gender Equity in School Suspensions. High School Journal 69 (December 1985-January 1986):139-43.

Successful Schooling Policies, Practices, Programs. Journal of Negro Education 54 (Summer 1985):entire issue.

Sweat, E. F. Some Notes on the Role of Negroes in the Establishment of Public Schools in South Carolina. Phylon 22 (1961):161-6.

Talbot, A. K., Jr. History of the Virginia Teachers Association: 1940-1965. Doctoral dissertation, College of William and Mary, 1981. UMO # 8206544.

Talbot, A. K., Jr. The Virginia Teachers Association: Establishment and Background. Negro History Bulletin 45 (January-March 1982):8-10.

Task Force on the New York State Dropout Problem. Dropping Out of School in New York State: The Invisible People of Color. Albany, NY: African American Institute of the State University of New York, 1986.

Terris, D. Lonely Preppies [Black students in New England preparatory schools]. Boston Globe Magazine September 22, 1985.

Thomas, J. A. Resource Allocation in School Districts and Classrooms. Journal of Education Finance 5 (Winter 1980):246-261.

Thomas, William B. A Quantitative Study of Differentiated School Knowledge Transmission in Buffalo, 1918-1931. Journal of Negro Education 57 (Winter 1988):66-80.

Thompson, H. The Navajos' Long Walk for Education: A History of Navajo Education. Navajo Nation, AZ: Navajo Community College Press, 1975. [Tsaile, Navajo Nation, AZ 86556].

Tollett, K. S. The Right to Education. Reaganism, Reaganomics, or Human Capital? Washington, D.C.: Howard University, Institute for the Study of Educational Policy, 1983.

Tomlinson, S. Inexplicit Policies in Race and Education. Education Policy Bulletin 9 (Fall 1981):149-166.

Trennert, R. A., Jr. The Phoenix Indian School: Forced Assimilation in Arizona, 1891-1935. Norman, OK: University of Oklahoma Press, 1988.

Trueba, Henry T. Comments on L.M. Dunn's Bilingual Hispanic Children on the U.S. Mainland: A Review of Research on Their Cognitive, Linguistic, and Scholastic Development. Hispanic Journal of Behavioral Sciences 10 (September 1988):253-62.

Tyack, D. and R. Lowe. The Constitutional Moment: Reconstruction and

176

Black Education in the South. _American Journal of Education_ 94 (February 1986):236-56.

U.S. Commission On Civil Rights. _Mexican American Education Study_ (6 vols.). Washington, D.C : GPO, 1970-1974.

U.S. Congress, 97th, 2nd session, House of Representatives, Committee On the Judiciary, Subcommittee On Civil and Constitutional Rights. _IRS Tax Exemptions and Segregated Private Schools: Hearing ..._ Washington, D.C.: GPO, 1983.

U.S. Congress, 97th, 2nd session, Senate, Committee On Finance. _Legislation to Deny Tax Exemption to Racially Discriminatory Private Schools: Hearing ..._ Washington, D.C.: GPO, 1982.

U.S. Congress, Joint Committee On Taxation. _Background Relating to the Effect of Racially Discriminatory Policies on the Tax-Exempt Status of Private Schools_. Washington, D.C.: GPO, 1982.

Verhovek, S. H. Troubled Bronx School's Fate Now Rests With Students [JHS 123]. _New York Times_ November 18, 1987.

Waggoner, D. Undereducated Youth in Texas. A Study of Macro-Community Dropout Rates. _IDRA Newsletter (Intercultural Development Research Association)_ (March 1987).

Washington, D. E. Education of Freedmen and the Role of Self-Help in a Sea Island [St. Helena Island, S.C.] Setting. _Agricultural History_ 58 (July 1984):442-55.

Wasserman, M. Busing as a 'Cover Issue'-A Radical View. _Urban Review_ 6 (September-October 1972):6-11.

Watford, B. A. Racism in Suburban Schools. _Changing Education_ (Spring 1969).

Weinberg, Meyer. Education in Black Schools [Quality of education in all-Black schools]. _In: The Search for Quality Integrated Education_, pp. 112-26. Westport, CT: Greenwood, 1983.

Weinberg, Meyer. _Intra-District Inequalities, I and II_. March 1980. ERIC ED 193348 and 193350.

Weinberg, Meyer. School Desegregation and Planned Deprivation. _Integrateducation_ 13 (May-June 1975):112-15.

Weiss, Philip. The Education of Chancellor [Richard R.] Green [New York City Schools]. _New York Times Magazine_ December 4, 1988.

Wennersten, J. R. The Black School Teacher in Maryland-1930s. _Negro History Bulletin_ 38 (1975):370-3.

Westin, Richard B. _The State and Segregated Schools: Negro Public Education in North Carolina, 1863-1923_. Doctoral dissertation, Duke University, 1966.

White, K. B. The Alabama Freedmen's Bureau and Black Education: The Myth of Opportunity. Alabama Review 34 (April 1981):107-24.

Whiteside, Barbara J. T. A Study of the Structure, Norm and Folkways of the Educational Institutions of the Nation of Islam in the United States from 1932 to 1975. Doctoral dissertation, Wayne State University, 1987. UMO # 8809151.

Wilcove, M. J. The Dilemma of LA Schools. LA Weekly November 6, 1987. [Los Angeles, CA].

Wilkerson, I. 'Separate and Unequal': A View from the Bottom [Mark Jenkins, 15 year old, resident of Cabrini-Green Housing Project, Chicago]. New York Times March 1, 1988.

Williams, J. Puzzling Legacy of 1954. Washington Post May 17, 1979.

Williams, L. Short-Changing Equal Education [School finance in South]. Southern Exposure 7 (Summer 1979):103-106.

Willig, Ann C. A Case of Blaming the Victim: The Dunn Monograph on Bilingual Hispanic Chidren on the U.S. Mainland. Hispanic Journal of Behavioral Sciences 10 (September 1988):219-36.

Wilson, C. Racism in Education: A Black Position Paper [Presented at March 19, 1969 annual conference of the Association for Supervision and Curriculum Development]. Community (March-April 1969).

Wilson, J. M. P. An Appalling Waste. Factors Affecting the Development of Mexican- American Elementary School Students in Texas. Texas Observer August 23, 1963.

Wilson, R. The Educational Establishment. People Against Racism in Education 1 (June 1973).

Wnek, Cynthia A. Big Ben the Builder: School Construction - 1953-56. Doctoral dissertation, Loyola University of Chicago, 1988. UMO # 8817938. [Benjamin C. Willis, Superintendent in Chicago].

Woodson, C. S. Early Negro Education in West Virginia. Institute: West Virginia Collegiate Institute, 1921.

Wrigley, Julia. Class Politics and Public Schools: Chicago, 1900-1950. New Brunswick, NJ: Rutgers University Press, 1982.

Wrigley, Julia. Race, Class and Equality in Education. New Politics 1 (Winter 1988):199-200.

Wyatt-Brown, Bertram. Black Schooling during Reconstruction. In: Walter J. Fraser, Jr. and others (eds.), The Web of Southern Social Relations: Women, Family, and Education, pp. 146-65. Athens, GA: University of Georgia Press, 1985.

Young, F. W. The 30's, Donnybrook Decade in St. Louis Public School Power

MO: Nathan B. Young Historic Memorial, 1984.

Zimpher, N. L., and S. Yessayan. Recruitment and Selection of Minority
    Populations into Teaching. Metropolitan Education 5 (Fall 1987):57-
    71.

Education: Elementary and Secondary Bibliography

Cook, Katherine M. and Florence E. Reynolds (comps.) The Education of
    Native and Minority Groups: A Bibliography, 1923- 1932. Washington,
    D.C.: Dept. of Interior, Office of Education, 1933.

Newman, Richard (comp.) Afro-American Education, 1907-1922. A
    Bibliographic Index. New York: Lambeth Press, 1984.

Racism and Education: A Review of Selected Literature Relating to
    Segregation, Discrimination, and Other Aspects of Racism in
    Education. 1969. ERIC ED 034836.

Weinberg, Meyer (comp.) The Education of Poor and Minority
    Children: A World Bibliography. [3 vols.] Westport, CT:
    Greenwood, 1981, 1986.

    [See also sections 6, 10, 12, 19, 20, 22, 32, 73, and 79]

26. Education: Higher

The agitation [of the Election of 1860] was a yeomanly service to liberty. It educated the people. One such canvass makes amends for the cowardice of our scholars, and consoles us under the infliction of Harvard College.

- Wendell Phillips, *Liberator*, November 16, 1860, after election of Abraham Lincoln.

Abrahams, P. P. Black Thursday at Oshkosh [Wisconsin State University-Oshkosh, events of November 1968]. *Crisis* (November 1969).

Ackley, R. Pembroke State University [See Dial and Elisades, below]. *Indian Historian* 5 (Summer 1972).

A Group of Faculty Members At the University of Connecticut. Racism Exposed by UConn Faculty. *UAG Magazine* 1 (Summer 1972):11-26.

Aguirre, B. E., and P. Bernal. Mexican American Students at Texas A&M. *Integrateducation* 17 (September-December 1979):38-41.

Alario, C. The Gray Area Between Black and White. An Examination of Racism at UCSB. *Daily Nexus* (University of California at Santa Barbara) January 20, 1987.

Alber, H. A., and M. B. Closson. Admission Standards, the Perceived Legitimacy of Grading and Black Student protest. *Cornell Journal of Social Relations* 8 (Fall 1978):219-34.

Alexander, Amy. Student Rebels' Reunion. *San Francisco Examiner* October 8, 1988. [November 1968, San Francisco State College strike].

Allen, T. H., Jr. Mississippi Nationalism in the Desegregation Crisis of September 1962. *Canadian Review of Studies in Nationalism* 14 (Spring 1987):49-63.

Allen, W. L. Blacks in Michigan Higher Eduction. *In*: Frances S. Thomas (ed.), *The State of Black Michigan: 1987*, pp. 53-68. East Lansing, MI: Urban Affairs Programs, Michigan State University, 1987.

Allen, W. L. *Gender and Campus Race Differences in Black Student Academic Performance, Racial Attitudes and College Satisfaction*. Atlanta: Southern Education Foundation, 1986.

Allison, K. Racism, Alive and Well Within UT Greek System. *Daily Beacon* (University of Tennessee) January 7, 1987.

Alman, E. Desegregation at Rutgers University. *In*: Rhoda L. Goldstein (ed.), *Black Life and Culture in the United States*. New York: Crowell, 1971.

American Council on Education. *Minorities in Higher Education*.

Washington, D.C.: The Council, 1989.

Anderson, M. Conservatism, Cutbacks Stir Black Students [Black protests on three Illinois college campuses]. Chicago Tribune March 21, 1982.

Anderson, S. E. Black Students: Racial Consciousness and the Class Struggle, 1960-1976. Black Scholar 8 (January-February 1977):35-43.

Andres, B., and Others. The Anatomy of Racism in University Hospitals [University of Minnesota]. Minnesota Daily January 6, 1983.

Anthony, E. The Time of the Furnaces: A Case Study of Black Student Revolt [San Fernando Valley State College]. New York: Dial, 1971.

Aoki, Elizabeth. Asians Question UC Admissions Policy. California Journal (June 1988):257-61.

Applegate, Jimmie R. and Michael L. Henniger. Recruiting Minority Students: A Priority for the 90s. Thought & Action 5 (Spring 1989):53-60.

Aptheker, H. The Negro College Student in the 1920s: Years of Preparation and Protest: An Introduction. Science and Society 33 (Spring 1969).

Arce, C. H. Chicanos in Higher Education. Integrateducation 14 (May-June 1976):14-18.

Asian-American Admission at Brown University. Integrateducation 22 (January-June 1984):31-41.

Association of American Medical Colleges. Minority Students in Medical Education: Facts and Figures II. Washington, D.C.: AAMC, 1985.

Association of American Medical Colleges, Office of Minority Affairs. Minority Students in Medical Education: Facts and Figures III. Washington, D.C.: AAMC, March 1987.

Atwood, R. B., and Others. Negro Teachers in Northern Colleges and Universities in the United States. Journal of Negro Education 18 (Fall 1949).

Auerbach, Jerold S. Fighting Anti-Semitism at Wellesley. Sh'ma 15 (November 16, 1984):1-3.

Baker, R. K. Black Student, White School: The Challenge of the Total Environment [Rutgers University]. Journal of Social and Behavioral Sciences 15 (Fall 1970):53-60.

Ballard, A. B. The Education of Black Folk [C.U.N.Y.]. New York: Harper & Row, 1973.

Barlow, W. and P. Shapiro. An End to Silence: The San Francisco State Student Movement. Indianapolis: Bobbs-Merrill, 1971.

Barnes, Y. USC Students Face Up To Racism in Class. Los Angeles Times October 22, 1980.

Barol, B. and others. Why They Choose Separate Tables [Race relations on college campuses]. Newsweek on Campus (March 1983):4-13.

Barrett, R. H. Integration at Ole Miss. Chicago: Quadrangle, 1965.

Bass, J. and J. Nelson. The Orangeburg Massacre (Rev. ed.) [South Carolina State College, 1968]. Macon, GA: Mercer University Press, 1984.

Bates, A. J. Minority Law Professors: Will the Best and the Brightest Continue to Teach? Harvard Crimson December 17, 1986.

Bearak, B. Racism Haunts Ole Miss in Battle Over Rebel Flag. Los Angeles Times April 30, 1983.

Beauregard, Erving E. Ohio's First Black College Graduate, Queen City Heritage 45 (Spring 1987):19-26.

Becker, R. Black Athletes Disillusioned [Amherst College]. Amherst Student May 11, 1981.

Beeson, R. M. Desegregation and Affirmative Action in Higher Education in Oklahoma: A Historical Case Study. Doctoral dissertation, Oklahoma State University, 1986. UMO # 8701016.

Bell-Scott, P. Black Women's Higher Education: Our Legacy. SAGE: A Scholarly Journal on Black Women 1 (Spring 1984):8-11.

Bennett, D. C. Interracial Ratios and Proximity in Dormitories: Attitudes of University Students. Environment and Behavior 6 (June 1974):212-32.

Berthiaume, K. First Black Student Recalls Struggle [Mrs. Ada Lois Sipuel Fisher, University of Oklahoma Law School] [See, also, letter by George L. Cross, October 13, 1983]. Oklahoma Daily October 6, 1983.

Bindman, A. M. Participation of Negro Students in an Integrated University [University of Illinois]. Doctoral dissertation, University of Illinois, 1965.

Black and White at Northwestern University [Bargaining between demonstrating Black students and University officials]. Integrated Education 6 (May-June 1968).

Black, MacKnight. Minority Student Issues: Racial/Ethnic Data Collected by the National Center for Education Statistics Since 1969. Washington, D.C.: U.S. Dept. of Education, Office of Educational Research and Improvement, March 1989.

Blackburn, R. B., and D. Young. Faculty Quality in Black and White Public Colleges and Universities in Selected Southern States: 1954-1980.

<u>Teachers</u> <u>College</u> <u>Record</u> 86 (Summer 1985):593-614.

Black Student League of Community College of Philadelphia. Open Letter to Frank Rizzo. <u>African</u> <u>World</u> 2 (March 4, 1972):4.

Blake, J. H. The Agony and the Rage [Racism at UC Berkeley]. <u>Negro</u> <u>Digest</u> (March 1967).

Blake, J. H. Beyond Civility: Human Relations and the Academy. <u>Integrateducation</u> 20 (May-October 1982):50-56.

Bloom, J. Racism and Higher Education. <u>Independent</u> <u>Socialist</u> (April 1969).

Bok, D. C. Issues of Race at Harvard [An open letter]. <u>Harvard</u> <u>Crimson</u> February 27, 1981.

Bond, H. M. The Negro Scholar and Professional in America. <u>In</u>: John P. Davis (ed.), <u>The</u> <u>American</u> <u>Negro</u> <u>Reference</u> <u>Books</u>. Englewood Cliffs, NJ: Prentice-Hall, 1966.

Bowen, E. and others. Wrong Message from Academe [Racism in higher education]. <u>Time</u> April 6, 1987.

Bowen, J. S. <u>Black</u> <u>Student</u> <u>Militance:</u> <u>Campus</u> <u>Unrest</u> <u>among</u> <u>Black</u> <u>Students,</u> <u>1968-</u> <u>1972</u>. Doctoral dissertation, Columbia University, 1982. UMO # 8427357.

Bowles, Deborah B. <u>Factors</u> <u>Contributing</u> <u>to</u> <u>the</u> <u>Decline</u> <u>of</u> <u>Black</u> <u>Undergraduate</u> <u>Enrollment</u> <u>at</u> <u>Rutgers,</u> <u>The</u> <u>State</u> <u>University</u> <u>of</u> <u>New</u> <u>Jersey:</u> <u>1981-1985</u>. Doctoral dissertation, Temple University, 1988. UMO # 8812558.

Bowles, F. and F. A. Costa. <u>Between</u> <u>Two</u> <u>Worlds:</u> <u>A</u> <u>Profile</u> <u>of</u> <u>Negro</u> <u>Higher</u> <u>Education</u>. New York: McGraw-Hill, 1971.

Bowser, D. L. Duke and the Black Student. <u>Duke</u> <u>Chronicle</u> October 24, 1983.

Bracey, J. Confronting Bias: Toward a More Creative Scholarship. <u>Integrateducation</u> 20 (May-October 1982):62-64.

Braddock, J. H., II. Institutional Racism in Higher Eduction: The Issue of Faculty Tenure. <u>Western</u> <u>Journal</u> <u>of</u> <u>Black</u> <u>Studies</u> 2 (Winter 1978):236-43.

Brann, J. W. Students from 84 Campuses Map War on College 'Racism'. <u>Chronicle</u> <u>of</u> <u>Higher</u> <u>Education</u> December 9, 1968.

Brest, Paul. Ethnic Diversity [of Students at Stanford Law School]. <u>Stanford</u> <u>Lawyer</u> 22 (Spring 1988).

Bridges, S. Discrimination Study Met with Opposition [Discrimination within sororities and fraternities at Texas Christian University]. <u>TCU</u> <u>Daily</u> <u>Skiff</u> March 4, 1982.

Britts, M. W. Blacks on White College Campuses [Concordia College, St. Paul]. Minneapolis, MN: Challenge Productions, 1976.

Brooks, R. L. Anti-minority Mindset in the Law School Personnel Process: Towards an Understanding of Racial Mindset. Law and Inequality 5 (May 1987):1-31.

Brown, Elizabeth G. The Initial Admission of Negro Students to the University of Michigan. Michigan Quarterly Review 2 (October 1963):233-6.

Brown, P. E. Institutional Racism in the City College System in Chicago. Integrateducation 18 (June-August 1980):116-19.

Buffalo, T. Chippewa Wants to Break Barriers, Not Blend In [Macalester College]. MAC Weekly (St. Paul, MN) October 14, 1983.

Bunzel, John and Jeffrey K. D. Au. Diversity or Discrimination? Asian Americans in College. Public Interest (Spring 1987):49-63.

Burgins, S. Black Students Seek to Relieve Dorm Alienation [University of South Florida]. Tampa Oracle April 8, 1982.

Burnside, J. G. Suspicion versus Faith: Negro Criticisms of Berea College in the Nineteenth Century. Regist. Ky. Hist. Soc. 83 (Summer 1985):237-66.

Butterfield, Fox. Trustee's Remark Renews Charges of Racial Insensitivity at Wellesley. New York Times February 12, 1987.

Cain, S. Black Perspectives on the University [University of Michigan]. Ann Arbor News September 8, 1983.

Caldwell, J. How a Midwestern College Helps Black Students Combat Loneliness - and Stay [Gustavus Adolphus College, St. Peter, MN]. Boston Globe January 17, 1988.

California State Postsecondary Education Commission. The Price of Admission, 1983. An Assessment of the Impact of Student Charges on Enrollment, Student Financial Aid Needs, and Revenues in California Public Higher Education. December 1982. ERIC ED 230091.

California State Postsecondary Education Commission. Background Papers on Student Charges, Student Financial Aid, and Access to Postsecondary Education: Options for the California Community Colleges. March 1983. ERIC ED 252265.

Can Harvard Students Be Klansmen? New York Times October 24, 1923.

Carlquist-Hernandez, K. Twelve Mexican-Americans in Higher Education: Their Mobility Process. Doctoral dissertation, University of the Pacific, 1987. UMO # 8720737.

Caron, N. P. American Indians at Harvard. Harvard Crimson November 28,

1984.

Carpenter, J. N. The Illinois Union Sit-in of September 9-10, 1968, and
     Why It Happened. Master's thesis, University of Illinois, Urbana,
     1974.

Carter, L. H. How Do Black Graduate Social Work Students Benefit From a
     Course on Institutional Racism? Journal of Education for Social Work
     14 (Fall 1978):27-33.

Casey, John. At Dartmouth. The Clash of '89. New York Times Magazine
     February 26, 1989.

Casso, H. and R. Gilber (eds.) Chicanos in Higher Education.
     Albuquerque: University of New Mexico Press, 1976.

Castro, A. Higher Education in Puerto Rico, 1898-1956. Doctoral
     dissertation, Lehigh University, 1975. UMO # 7610636.

Cawthon, R., and Others. 20 Years After Meredith [Race relations at the
     University of Mississippi]. Jackson Clarion-Ledger September 26,
     1982 (supplement).

Cayton, H. R. Long Old Road [Autobiography of Black sociologist].
     Seattle: University of Washington Press, 1964.

Chamberlain, Marian K. (ed.) Women in Academe. Progress and Prospects.
     New York: Russell Sage Foundation, 1989. [Deals in part with
     minority women].

Chandler, T. On Increasing Minority Faculty. Perspectives (American
     Historical Association) 26 (January 1988):9.

Clark, K. B. Intelligence, the University, and the Society. American
     Scholar (Winter 1966-67).

Clark, M. L. and others. Dating Patterns of Black Students on White
     Southern Campuses. Journal of Multicultural Counseling and
     Development (April 1986):14.

Clark, R. Racial Awareness: The Only Way to Understand Ourselves
     [Pennsylvania State University]. Daily Collegian January 6, 1982.

Clayton, J. City Moves to Ban Student Housing Bias [Housing
     discrimination against students in Los Angeles]. Los Angeles Times
     February 18, 1982.

Clendinen, D. Citadel's Cadets Feeling Effects of a Klan-like Act. New
     York Times November 23, 1986.

Cobb, W. M. Not to the Swift: Progress and Prospects in Science and the
     Professions. Journal of Negro Education 27 (Spring 1958).

Coggs, P. R., and B. S. Johnson. Reflections on Five Continuing Education
     Programs on Race and Social Work Practice. In: George E. Carter and

James R. Parker (eds.), Urban Minority Experience, Selected Proceedings of the 4th Annual Conference on Minority Studies, pp. 41-47. La Crosse, WI: Institute for Minority Studies, University of Wisconsin-LaCrosse, 1978.

Cole, B. Appropriation Politics and Black Schools: Howard University and the U.S. Congress, 1879-1928. Journal of Negro Education 46 (1977):7-23.

Collins, Amy. Black Activist Remembers 1968 Takeover of Computer Lab. Daily Nexus October 13, 1988. [October 1968, University of California, Santa Barbara].

Committee On Race Relations. A Study of Race Relations at Harvard College. Cambridge, MA: Office of the Dean of Students, May 1980.

Cooks, H. C. The Black High School Student: Post-secondary Aspirations, Expectations, Plans, and Perceived Opportunity Options [Toledo public schools]. Doctoral dissertation, University of Toledo, 1987. UMO # 8726996.

Cooper, J. A., and D. O. Prieto. 'Entry of Black and Other Minority Students into U.S. Medical Schools: Historical Perspective and Recent Trend': Comment. New England Journal of Medicine 315 (July 1986):68 [See, below, S. Shea and M. T. Fullilove].

Cortese, A. J. The Denial of Access: Chicanos in Higher Education. Cornell Journal of Social Relations 18 (Spring 1985):28-39.

Cottle, T. J. Run to Freedom: Chicanos and Higher Education [Adams State College, CO]. Change 4 (February 1972):34-41.

Cross, C. L. A Comparison of Collegiate Retention Rates Among Black Students in Predominantly Black and White Institutions. Doctoral dissertation, American University, 1985. UMO # 8522919.

Cross, G. L. Professors, Presidents, and Politicians: Civil Rights and the University of Oklahoma, 1890-1968. Norman, OK: University of Oklahoma Press, 1981.

Curwood, S. Alienation Widespread at Many White Institutions [Second article of a series, "Blacks on Campus"]. Boston Globe May 19, 1986.

Daams, G. Summary of Segregation, Discrimination, and Open Housing [A segregationist statement by a professor of philosophy at Kent State University]. Citizen May 1965.

Da Costa, S. Minorities on Campus. Frustrations Hurt Latinos [California State University, Long Beach]. Daily Forty Niner December 7, 1981.

Daniels, A. K. and others. Academics on the Line: The Faculty Strike at San Francisco State. San Francisco: Jossey-Bass, 1970.

Daniels, Lee A. Ranks of Black Men Shrink on U.S. Campuses. New York

<u>Times</u> February 5, 1989.

Daniels, O. C. B. <u>Racism: Awareness, Tolerance</u> <u>and</u> <u>Evaluation.</u> <u>A</u>
    <u>Research</u> <u>Report</u> <u>on</u> <u>the</u> <u>Level</u> <u>of</u> <u>Interracial</u> <u>Apperception</u> <u>and</u> <u>Ideology</u>
    <u>in</u> <u>the</u> <u>Residential</u> <u>Areas</u> <u>of</u> <u>the</u> <u>University</u>. Amherst, MA: University
    of Massachusetts Press, 1974.

Davis, A. L. A Double Standard at Tennessee State. <u>Chronicle</u> <u>of</u> <u>Higher</u>
    <u>Education</u> April 10, 1985.

Davis, E. <u>Minority</u> <u>Content</u> <u>in</u> <u>Social</u> <u>Work:</u> <u>A</u> <u>Survey</u> <u>of</u> <u>Black</u> <u>Educators</u>.
    Doctoral dissertation, University of Utah, 1987. UMO # 8715888.

Davis, James Earl. <u>Differential</u> <u>Academic</u> <u>Progression</u> <u>of</u> <u>Black</u> <u>Students</u> <u>at</u>
    <u>Historically</u> <u>Black</u> <u>Public</u> <u>and</u> <u>Private</u> <u>Colleges</u> <u>and</u> <u>Universities</u>.
    Doctoral dissertation, Cornell University, 1988. UMO # 8821218.

Davis, R. L. and L. M. Poyer. For Black Faculty and Administrators, It's
    Not an Easy Life. <u>Harvard</u> <u>Crimson</u> November 25, 1974.

Day-Foley, J. Racial Parity at U-M: Black Students' Struggle Continues.
    <u>Michigan</u> <u>Chronicle</u> April 16, 1988.

Decision Resources Corporation. <u>College</u> <u>Enrollment</u> <u>Patterns</u> <u>among</u> <u>Black</u>
    <u>and</u> <u>White</u> <u>Students</u>. Washington, D. C.: U.S. Department of
    Education, 1987.

Dentler, R. A. and others. <u>University</u> <u>on</u> <u>Trial:</u> <u>The</u> <u>Case</u> <u>of</u> <u>the</u>
    <u>University</u> <u>of</u> <u>North</u> <u>Carolina</u>. Cambridge, MA: Abt, 1983.

Dial, A. and D. K. Elisades. The Lumbee Indians of North Carolina and
    Pembroke State University. <u>Indian</u> <u>Historian</u> 4 (Winter 1971):[See
    Randall Ackley, above].

Dinkelspiel, Francis. In Rift at Cornell, Racial Issues of the '60s
    Remain. <u>New</u> <u>York</u> <u>Times</u> May 4, 1989.

Dortch, Thomas W., Jr. Regents' Actions at Fort Valley State Show
    Arrogance, Contempt. <u>Atlanta</u> <u>Journal</u> October 9, 1988.

Du Bois, W. E. B. Discrimination in Northern Colleges. <u>Crisis</u> (August
    1931).

Du Bois, W. E. B. Negroes in College. <u>Nation</u> 122 (March 3, 1926).

Duncan, J. Blacks Feel Discrimination Still Exists at UK [University of
    Kentucky]. <u>Kentucky</u> <u>Kernel</u> July 8, 1982.

Edgewater, J. L. Stress and the Navajo University Students. <u>Journal</u> <u>of</u>
    <u>American</u> <u>Indian</u> <u>Education</u> 20 (May 1981):25-31.

Edley, C., Jr. Behind the Racial Squabble at Harvard Law School. <u>Boston</u>
    <u>Globe</u> August 21, 1982.

Eduarte, C. Chicano Students and the 'Daily' Boycott [University of

Minnesota]. Minnesota Daily May 5, 1981.

Edwards, H. April 1969: Confrontations at Cornell: A Case Study. In: Black Students, pp. 158-83. New York: Free Press, 1970.

Elinson, Elaine. Speak English or Else. Katipunan (August 1988). [Discrimination at UC San Francisco].

Engs, R. F., and J. B. Williams. Integration by Evasion [Princeton University]. Nation November 17, 1969.

Evans, David L. Self-Help at Its Best [The senior admissions officer at Harvard advocates self-help in Black communities]. Newsweek March 16, 1987.

Evans, G. Black Students Who Attend White Colleges Face Contradictions in their Campus Life. Chronicle of Higher Education (April 30, 1986).

Exum, W. H. Paradoxes of Protest, Black Student Activism in a White University [New York University]. Philadelphia, PA: Temple University Press, 1985.

Exum, W. H. Plus Ca Change...? Racism in Higher Education. September 1980 ERIC ED 195215.

Faitor, D. J. Black Alumni Weigh Years' Changes at Syracuse. New York Times September 26, 1983.

Falk, L. A., and N. A. Quaynor-Malm. Early Afro-American Medical Education in the United States: The Origins of Meharry Medical College in the Nineteenth Century. In: Proceedings of the XXIII Congress of the History of Medicine. London.

Feuer, L. S. The Stages in the Social History of Jewish Professors in American Colleges and Universities. American Jewish History 71 (June 1982).

Fields, C. The Hispanic Pipeline. Change 20 (May/June 1988).

Fiery Crosses Blaze on UCLA Campus. The Kourier Magazine 11 (May 1935):31.

Fishman, G. Paul Robeson's Student Days and the Fight Against Racism at Rutgers. Freedomways 9 (Summer 1969).

Fiske, E. B. Economic Realities Spur Colleges on Recruiting Hispanic Students. New York Times March 20, 1988.

Flacks, R. and M. Mankoff. The Changing Social Base of the American Student Movement. Annals of the American Association for Political and Social Science (May 1971):395.

Fleming, G. J. The Going Is Rough but They Make It [Black students in northern colleges]. Crisis 43 (August 1936).

188

Fletcher, J. D. Against the Consensus: Oberlin College and the Education of American Negroes, 1835-1865. Doctoral dissertation, American University, 1974.

Flynn, D. [Three letters on racism at the University of Colorado, Boulder]. Colorado Daily January 29, 1987.

Forbes, J. D. Racism, Scholarship and Cultural Pluralism in Higher Education. March 1977 ERIC ED 139584.

Four Years After Crisis, Fisk University Thrives. New York Times March 1, 1988.

Fox, J. R. The Development of Courses in Racism for Social Work Students. Doctoral dissertation, University of Pennsylvania, 1979. UMO # 8008668.

Franczyk, J. and V. J. Phillips. Enrollment Down, Taxes Up at Chicago City Colleges; Budget Hits $265 Million. Chicago Reporter 16 (November 1987).

Friedman, H. A. and S. Ruck. Why Not Every Man? [Edward Sparling, founder of Roosevelt University]. Integrateducation 13 (November-December 1975):33-38.

Fries, J. E. The American Indian in Higher Education: 1975-76 to 1984-85. Washington, D.C.: Center for Education Statistics, March 1987.

Frisbie, L. H. A Study of Racism and Sexism at Georgia Southwestern College. Integrateducation 18 (September-December 1980):61-64.

Fullilove, Mindy and others. Is 'Black Achievement' an Oxymoron? [Medical education] Thought and Action 4 (Fall 1988):5-20.

Fulton, K. Between the Races, the Past's Shadows [North Carolina Agricultural and Technical State University, Greensboro]. Nation May 18, 1985.

Garrell, C. S. Stung by Racial Incidents and Charges of Indifference, Berkeley Trying to Become Model Integrated University. Chronicle of Higher Education January 27, 1988.

Gelbspan, R., and J. Kaufman. Trade Unions Seen No Longer a Bastion of Racism [Employment of Black faculty in Boston area universities]. Boston Globe November 11, 1985.

Giles, N. A Black Perspective [on Blacks at Colgate University]. Colgate Scene July 1983.

Gillespie, D. A. and N. Carlson. Trends in Student Aid: 1963-1983. Washington, D.C.: College Board, December 1983.

Ginsberg, R., and M. Carter. Participants Assess the Louisiana Consent Decree [Desegregation of public higher education]. Equity & Excellence 23 (Winter 1988):75-82.

Goldberg, K. Dual Identity: Is Georgia Military College a State-Controlled or Private Institution? Education Week May 11, 1988.

Gomez, J. Racial Protests, Attacks Galvanize UMass Minorities. Boston Globe February 21, 1988.

Gomez-Quinones, J. Mexican Students Por La Raza: The Chicano Student Movement in Southern California 1967-1977. Santa Barbara, CA: Editorial La Causa, 1978.

Gonzales, P. B. A Perfect Furor of Indignation: The Racial Attitude Confrontation of 1933 [Chicanos and the University of New Mexico]. Doctoral dissertation, University of California, Berkeley, 1985. UMO # 8524964.

Goss, Kristin A. and Mei Lin Kwan-Gett. The Underside of Academic Opportunity. The Story of Harvard's Only Tenured Black Woman [Professor Eileen Southern]. Harvard Crimson May 2, 1986.

Gottschalk, M. O. The Student Power Movement on the UW-Madison Campus, 1966-1968. Doctoral dissertation, University of Wisconsin, 1987. UMO # 8713150.

Grimke, F. Colored Men as Professors in Colored Institutions. A.M.E. Church Review 2 (October 1885):142-44.

Guy-Sheftall, B. Women's Studies at Spelman College: Reminiscences from the Director. Women's Studies International Forum 9 (1986):151-55.

Haldeman-Julius, M. What the Negro Students Endure in Kansas. Haldeman-Julius Monthly 7 (January 1926).

Hamps, S. Campus Racism (letter) [Defiance College, Ohio]. Ebony 29 (June 1974):21.

Hansson, R. O. and others. The Measurement of Racism in College Students [University of Washington]. Journal of Social and Behavioral Science 20 (Summer 1974):37-48.

Hardin, C. L. Black Professional Musicians in Higher Education: A Study Based on In-Depth Interviews. Doctoral dissertation, University of Massachusetts, 1987. UMO # 8710458.

Hargrave, E. How I Feel as a Negro at a White College. Journal of Negro Education 11 (1942).

Harold, R. Exclusion. Black Students Say Vicious Circle of Inexperience and Role Shortages Block their Entrance into M.U. Theater [University of Missouri]. Columbia Missourian May 31, 1981.

Harvey, B. C. H. Problem of the Colored Student. Journal of the Association of American Medical Colleges 4 (July 1929):208-22.

Harvey, W. B. Racism on Campus: Colleges Must Take Positive Steps to

Eradicate the 'Disease'. Chronicle of Higher Education September 30, 1981.

Harwood, V., and S. Shalom. Racism and the Campus. Paper Tiger (June 1968).

Haskins, R. L. Black Administrators in Higher Education. Conditions and Perceptions. New York: Praeger, 1978.

Hassan, Thomas E. Asian-American Admissions: Debating Discrimination. College Board Review 142 (Winter 1987):42-45.

Hawkins, L. A. The 'Adams' Criteria: A Threat to Equal Access to Higher Education? [Desegregation of public higher education]. Thurgood Marshall Law Review 10 (Fall 1984):91-121.

Henderson, E., Jr. An Investigation of How Black Students in Residence Halls Perceive the Impact of Minority Aides. Black Resident Assistants and Black Caucuses in Assisting Black Students to Adjust Psychologically, Socially and Academically, at a Predominantly White University. Doctoral dissertation, Michigan State University, 1985. UMO # 8603426.

Henderson, J. Angry OU Students Feel Unwanted, Left Out [University of Oklahoma, Norman]. Tulsa Daily World December 5, 1971.

Hevesi, Dennis. Baruch's Minority Alumni Seek a Separate Group[Baruch College, CUNY]. New York Times May 7, 1989.

Hickerson, Phyllis P. The Current Status of Women and Blacks in Tennessee Higher Education Administration. Doctoral dissertation, Tennessee State University, 1986. UMO # 8809162.

Higdon, H. The Troubled Heart of Sigma Chi [Segregation in fraternities]. New York Times Magazine November 14, 1965.

Hill, J. R. A Contemporary Status Report on the Libraries of Historically Black Public Colleges and Universities. Washington, D.C.: American Association of State Colleges and Universities, 1976.

Hill, S. T. The Traditionally Black Institutions of Higher Education 1860 to 1982. Washington, D.C.: GPO, 1985.

Hine, D. C. Problems in Recruiting and Retaining Minority Graduate Students. Perspectives (American Historical Association) 26 (February 1988):20-21.

Hixson, J. and E. G. Epps. The Failure of Selection and the Problem of Prediction: Racism vs. Measurement in Higher Education. Journal of Afro-American Issues 3 (Winter 1975):117-128.

Hoffman, S. D. Black-White Differences in Returns to Higher Education: Evidence from the 1970s. Economics of Education Review 3 (1984).

Hornsby, A., Jr. (ed.) Papers of John and Lugenia Burns Hope [21 microfilm reels]. Frederick, MD: University Publications of America, 1987.

Horton, J. O. Black Education at Oberlin College: A Controversial Commitment. Journal of Negro Education 54 (Fall 1985):477-99.

Houppert, Karen. Diverse City. A Talk with City College President Bernard Harleston. Village Voice January 24, 1989.

How Thousands of Students Get Cheated in 'Innovative Education' Swindle [Malcolm X College, Chicago]. Muhammad Speaks November 5, 1971.

Hsia, J. Asian Americans in Higher Education and at Work. Hillsdale, NJ: Lawrence Erlbaum Associates, 1987.

Hughes, L. Simple Discusses Colleges and Color. Phylon (December 1949).

Hundley, K. Out from Under the Rug [Racism at Smith College]. Valley Advocate January 18, 1988.

The Hurst Report [Analysis of racist attack on Black students on campus of the University of Massachusetts, Amherst, on October 27, 1986]. Collegian (February 19, 1987):7-12.

Isgar, Tom and Susan Isgar (eds.) Racism and Higher Education. Washington, D.C.: U.S. National Student Association, 1969.

James, T. Life Begins with Freedom: The College Nisei, 1942-1945. History of Education Quarterly 25 (Spring/Summer 1985):155-74.

Jenkins, H. C. The Negro Student at the University of Iowa: A Sociological Study. Master's thesis, State University of Iowa, 1933.

Johnson, Dirk. Censoring Campus News. New York Times Education Life November 6, 1988. [Includes racial issues].

Johnson, J. Congress Acts to Ease Plight of Black Colleges. New York Times January 6, 1988.

Jones, Stephen. Racism Battle Moves Into Curriculum [Michigan State University and the University of Michigan]. Detroit Free Press April 16, 1989.

Kantrowitz, B. and others. Blacks Protest Campus Racism. Newsweek (April 6, 1987).

Karen, David. Who Gets into Harvard? Selection and Exclusion at an Elite College. Doctoral dissertation, Harvard University, 1985. UMO # 8520225.

Kelley, V. The Difficulty of Being Black at UC Berkeley. Critical Perspectives of Third World America 1 (Fall 1983):210-13.

Kenney, C. Dartmouth Halts Classes for a Day to Discuss Charges of

Sexism, Racism. Boston Globe March 9, 1979.

Kerbo, H. R. Colege Achievement among Native Americans: A Research Note. Social Forces 59 (June 1981):1275-80.

Kernek, L. Climate Still Tense for Minorities at UI [University of Illinois, Urbana]. Daily Illini December 11, 1986.

Kilson, M. L., Jr. The Black Experience at Harvard. New York Times Magazine September 2, 1973.

Kindred, D. The Black, White of It [Blacks at Brigham Young University]. Washington Post March 21, 1981.

KKK Activity on LSU Campus Reported. New Orleans Times Picayune April 24, 1974.

Klatt, M. Minority Enrollment Drops at UIC as Admissions Criteria Rise [University of Illinois at Chicago]. Chicago Reporter 15 (March 1986).

Knox, R. A. Despite Doctor Glut, Needs Unmet [Declining minority representation in medical schools]. Boston Globe October 29, 1985.

Kolbert, Elizabeth. The Scramble for Black Professors. New York Times Education Life January 8, 1989.

Kratovil, D. The Status of Blacks at Western [Michigan University]. Western Herald January 20-24, 1985.

Lang, D. D. Race Inequality and the Economic Hierarchy. Integrateducation 22 (January-June 1984):81-88.

Lang, D. D. Stratification and Professional Education within the Academic Hierarchy. Journal of Research & Development in Education 19 (Fall 1985):10-20.

Lazarus, David M. The Asian Quandary [Asian-American students at Harvard]. Harvard Crimson October 27, 1986.

Lazarus, David M. Chronicling the Black Experience at Harvard. Harvard Crimson January 7, 1987.

Lee, Felicia R. Law Students at N.Y.U. Rally Against Race Bias. New York Times March 3, 1989.

Lee, S. and L. Jones. Uplift the Race: The Construction of School Daze. New York: Simon Schuster, 1988.

Leon, D. J. Racism in the University: The Case of the Educational Opportunity Programs. September 1978. ERIC ED 160696.

Lewis, Diane E. Amid Push for Diversity, Smith [College] Struggles with Racism. Boston Globe May 4, 1989.

193

Lewis, D. N. Coping Styles by Black Female Students Attending Predominantly White Colleges. Doctoral dissertation, University of Massachusetts, 1987. UMO # 8727075.

Lindsey, R. Colleges Accused of Bias to Stem Asians' Gains [California]. New York Times January 19, 1987.

Liu, A. The Problems Blacks Meet at Iowa State. Des Moines Register May 5, 1974.

Lombardi, J. Unique Problems of the Inner City Colleges [Community colleges]. Integrated Education (May-June 1969):62-70.

Longres, J. The Impact of Racism on Social Work Education. Journal of Educaation for Social Work 8 (Winter 1974).

Loo, C. M. and G. Rolison. Alienation of Ethnic Minority Student at a Predominantly White University. Journal of Higher Education 57 (January-February 1986):58-77.

Looking Backward at KKK at University of Alabama Campus. Daily Worker February 9, 1956.

Loomis, P. A. Blacks Think Racism Affects O.D.U. Grades, Survey Finds [Old Dominion University]. Norfolk Ledger-Star August 30, 1978.

Lothian, J. Black Students React to Acts of Racial Prejudice [Purdue University]. Purdue Exponent November 5, 1982.

Lovinger, R. SMU Blacks Set Think Eyes on the Prize [Southeastern Massachusetts University]. New Bedford Standard-Times April 24, 1988.

Maldonado, C. S. 'The Longest Running Death in History': A History of Colegio Cesar Chavez, 1973-1983 [College in Mt. Angel, OR, closed in 1983]. Doctoral dissertation, University of Oregon, 1986. UMO # 8629570.

Marable, M. Neo-Racism: The White Shadow. Politics and Education 2 (Spring 1980):19-22.

Margolis, R. J. The Two Nations at Wesleyan University. New York Times Magazine (January 18, 1970).

Matthews, D. and J. Prothro. Negro Students and the Protest Movement. In: James McEvoy and Abraham Miller (eds.), Black Power and Student Rebellion. Belmont, CA: Wadsworth, 1969.

Matthews, M. D. The 1975 Student Struggle at Brown University. Monthly Review 28 (January 1977):32-49.

Mays, B. E. Coming to Chicago [Student days for Blacks at the University of Chicago during the 1920s and 1930s]. University of Chicago Magazine 71 (Spring 1979).

194

McClain, B. R. Racism in Higher Education: A Societal Reflection. Negro Educational Review 33 (January 1982):34-45.

McClendon, M. Riding on the Back of the University's Bus [Harvard University]. Harvard Crimson November 25, 1975.

McGee, D. A History of Blacks at Davidson. Davidsonian February 10, 1984.

McNichol, D. Seeds of Compromise [Racism at Rutgers University]. Passaic Herald-News January 13, 1980.

McRae, F. F. Black Males Claim Police Abuse on USC Campus. Los Angeles Sentinel January 29, 1987.

Mendoza, F. S. Increasing Minorities in Academia: The Faculty Role Model. Journal of Medical Education 61 (October 1986):850-51.

Michaeux, L. Black Students Hurt by Treatment [Fort Hays State University]. Wichita Eagle February 21, 1978 (letter).

Michigan, Senate, Committee To Investigate Campus Disorders and Student Unrest. Final Staff Report. Part I. Study Findings and Recommendations. Lansing, MI: 1970.

Middleton, E. E. Opinions of Black Persisters and Dropouts Concerning Selected Environmental Factors at Ohio University. Doctoral dissertation, Ohio University, 1987. UMO # 8715315.

Mikkelson, D. D. The Student Revolt at Berkeley in the Sixties: Impressions of a Variety of Fourteen Former Students. Doctoral dissertation, University of Southern California, 1987.

Miller, K. Education of the Negro in the North. Educational Review 62 (October 1921):232-38.

Milloy, C. Black Group Charges Racism in AU Funding Squabble [American University]. Washington Post April 21, 1979.

Mingle, J. R. Focus on Minorities: Trends in Higher Education Participation and Success. Denver, CO: Education Commission of the States and the State Higher Education Executive Officers, 1987.

Minorities at OSU: Strangers in a Strange Land [Oregon State University, Corvallis]. Portland-Oregonian December 10, 1972.

Minorities at UT [Transcript of discussion on minority students at the University of Texas]. Daily Texan April 30, 1980.

Mjoseth, J. University Combats Racism with Workshop [University of South Florida]. Tampa Oracle January 28, 1982.

Moffatt, Michael. Coming of Age in New Jersey: College and American Culture [Student life at Rutgers]. New Brunswick, NJ: Rutgers, University Press, 1989.

Moore, D. G. What Kind of Place is There for Minorities Here? Dartmouth November 4, 1982.

More on Racism [Letters on racism at the University of Pennsylvania]. Daily Pennsylvanian December 7, 1981.

Morganfield, R. Worlds Apart. Blacks and Whites on Campus [State of Michigan]. Detroit News May 1, 1988.

Morris, L. Elusive Equality: The Status of Black Americans in Higher Education. Washington, D.C.: Howard University Press, 1979.

Mosqueda, L. J., and Others. The Persistence of Institutional Racism in Higher Education: Its Roots and Remedies [University of Denver]. ERIC ED 216647.

Murphy, M. Minorities: A Place at the U? [Five articles on minorities at three public universities in Arizona]. Phoenix Gazette January 21- 25, 1985.

Myers, D. Chicano Students Victorious in Struggle at University of Minnesota. El Gallo December 1970.

Nakanishi, D. T. Asian Pacific Americans and Selective Undergraduate Admissions. Journal of College Admissions 118 (Winter 1988):17-26.

Napper, G. Blacker Than Thou: The Struggle for Campus Unity [UC Berkeley]. Grand Rapids, MI: Eerdmans, 1973.

Negri, Gloria. Distinguished Black and Asian Graduates Recall Past Problems as Harvard Students. Boston Globe September 6, 1986.

Negroes Protest Klan at Harvard. New York Times October 24, 1923.

Nettles, Michael T. with A. Robert Thoerny (ed.) Toward Black Undergraduate Student Equality in American Higher Education. Westport, CT: Greenwood, 1988.

New England Board of Higher Education. Equity and Pluralism. Boston: The Board, 1989.

New Image at Ole Miss as Students Heckle Meredith. Jackson Advocate October 7, 1982.

Newsweek on Campus Poll: Racial Issues [Some 1982-1986 comparisons, based on responses from 100 campuses]. Newsweek on Campus February 23, 1987.

Nichols, Guerdon D. Breaking the Color Barrier at the University of Arkansas. Arkansas Historical Quarterly 27 (Spring 1968).

Nieves Falcon, L. Recruitment to Higher Education in Puerto Rico, 1940- 1960. Rio Piedras, PR: Editorial Universitaria, 1965.

Novoa, J. Assignment: Racism [A workshop at University of California, Berkeley on unlearning personal racism]. Daily Californian October 7, 1983.

Nyden, P. Racism in the University [University of Pittsburgh]. Black Action Society News 1 (1976).

Oatis, B. N. Racism: How Shall We as Administrators Work for a Smooth Transition? [Higher education]. ERIC ED 157966.

Office of Minority Concerns. Sixth Annual Status Report on Minorities in Higher Education. Washington, D.C.: American Council on Education, October 1987.

Olandt, E. D. The Cooling Out Function in Higher Education: A Study of Social Stratification in a New Jersey County Community College. Doctoral dissertation, Rutgers, 1987.

Olivas, Michael A. The Dilemma of Access: Minorities in Two Year Colleges. Washington, D.C.: Howard University Press, 1979.

Olivas, Michael A. Indian, Chicano, and Puerto Rican Colleges: Status and Issues. Bilingual Review 9 (January 1982):36-58.

Olivas, Michael A. (ed.) Latino College Students. New York: Teachers College Press, 1986.

Olive, R. D., and D. Stone. Races Uneasy at U War [University of Wisconsin, Milwaukee]. Milwaukee Journal March 28, 1976.

Olson, David. Minority Enrollment and Retention Lag on State Campuses. Chicago Reporter 17 (October 1988):5-6. [Illinois].

Olson, David. Racial Tensions Still Plague Illinois Campuses. Chicago Reporter 17 (October 1988):3-5.

Olson, David. Student Enrollment at Illinois Public Universities: 1980-1987 [Data for whites, Blacks, Hispanics, and Asians]. Chicago Reporter 17 (Ocotber 1988):7.

On Being Black at Yale. Yale Alumni Magazine (May 1969).

Oppelt, Norman T. The Tribally Controlled Colleges in the 1980s: Higher Education's Best Kept Secret. American Indian Culture and Research 8 (1984):27-45.

Orfield, G. and others. The Chicago Study of Access and Choice in Higher Education. Chicago, IL: University of Chicago, Committee on Public Policy Studies, September 1984.

Orum, A. M. and A. W. Orum. The Class and Status Bases of Negro Student Protest. In: Charles M. Borjean and Norval D. Glenn (eds.), Blacks in the United States, pp. 357-69. San Francisco, CA: Chandler, 1969.

Owen, A. and W. H. Scarborough. Higher Education of the Colored Race - What Has Been Done; What Can Be Done. Proceedings & Addresses of the National Education Association, 1889 pp. 546-53.

Painter, N. Jim Crow at Harvard, 1923. New England Quarterly (December 1971).

Parent, T. Officials Cite Evidence of Discrimination at IU [Indiana University]. Indiana Daily Student December 10, 1986.

Pascarella, E. T. Racial Differences in Factors Associated with Bachelor's Degree Completion: A Nine-Year Follow-up. Research in Higher Education 23 (1985):351-73.

Payne, J. L. and others. Increasing the Graduation Dates of Minority Medical Students. Journal of Medical Education 61 (May 1986):353-58.

Pennoyer, Jacki. Students Differ on Racism Program [Illinois State University at Normal]. Daily Vidette December 6, 1988.

Perea, J. E. Ethnic Studies in Transition: A Case Study [School of Ethnic Studies, San Francisco State University, 1969-1984]. Doctoral dissertation, University of California, Berkeley, 1985. UMO # 8524858.

Perry, A. Harvard/Radcliffe Students for a Democratic Society. 1960-1972. Undergraduate thesis, Department of History, Harvard University, 1986.

Phillips, K. [Two articles about Native American students at North Dakota State Univeristy]. Spectrum May 10, 13, 1983.

Phillips, Steven C. When Words Collide [Changing the study of western culture at Stanford University]. Voice Literary Supplement (January-February 1988).

Pilgrim, D. Deception by Stratagem. Segregation in Public Higher Education. Bristol, IN: Wyndham Hall Press, 1985.

Pincus, F. Tracking in Community Colleges. Insurgent Sociologist 4 (September 1974):17-35.

Pipkin, R. M. The Effects of Social Origin in the Allocation of Law Students. Journal of Legal Education 34 (1984):385-87.

Pitts, J. P. The Politicization of Black Students: Northwestern University. Journal of Black Studies 5 (March 1975):277-319.

Pomerantz, G. Ewing Under Siege [Race-baiting of Georgetown University basketball star, Patrick Ewing]. Washington Post February 9, 1983.

Posner, J. R. Income and Occupation of Negro and White College Graduates: 1931-1966. Doctoral dissertation, Princeton University, 1979.

Pousaint, A. The Psychology of Coping with Racism. Black Collegian 4

(May-June 1974):34-35, 39.

Price, J. Minority UT Law Students Find Job Prospects Bleak. Houston Post February 7, 1982.

Price, John A. A Note on Indian Graduations from U.S. Four-Year College and Universities. Canadian Journal of Native Studies 2 (1982):181-183.

Profit, W. The Hell You Say [The politics of Afro-American studies at Harvard University]. Harvard Crimson October 8, 1974.

Pruitt, A. S. and P. D. Isaac. Discrimination in Recruitment, Admission, and Retention of Minority Graduate Students. Journal of Negro Education 54 (Fall 1985):526-536.

Pryor, W. Black Students Describe U.T. [University of Texas]. Austin American March 31, 1975.

Racism 101. [Racist incidents on college campuses]. PBS Frontline Telecast May 10, 1988.

Reeves, D. Supplements for Campus Racism. Ebony 29 (March 1974):114.

Reis, D. Minorities on Slow Tenure Track at Chicago-area Universities. Chicago Reporter 16 (May 1987):3-5.

Rezendes, M. Campus Minorities: Confronting Racism with Mature Methods. Washington Post April 27, 1988.

Richardson, R. C., Jr. and L. W. Bender. Fostering Minority Access and Achievement in Higher Education. San Francisco, CA: Jossey-Bass, 1987.

Riedel, C. Equal But Separate [Black sororities and fraternities at the University of Michigan]. Michigan Daily October 3, 1986.

Rios De Betancourt, E. The University of Puerto Rico in the Last Three Decades: An Institution of Hope, Success, and Strife. In: Josef G. Farkas (ed.), Uberlieferung und Auftrag Festschrift fur Michael de Ferdinandy. Wiesbaden: Guido Pressler, 1972.

Ripps, S. R. A Curriculum Course Designed for Lowering the Attrition Rate for the Disadvantaged Law Student. Howard Law Journal 29 (Summer 1986):457-80.

Robbins, Catherine C. University of New Mexico Marking Bitter-Sweet Centennial. New York Times May 18, 1989.

Robinson, Leslie. Against a Wall. At UNH [University of New Hampshire], Blacks Cope With Racism. Concord Monitor December 28, 1988.

Rooney, G. D. Minority Students' Involvement in Minority Student Organizations: An Exploratory Study. Journal of College Student Pesonnel 26 (September 1985):450-56.

Rose, L. B. The Secret Life of Sarah lawrence [Past quotas on enrollment of Jewish students at Sarah Lawrence College]. Commentary 75 (May 1983):52-56.

Rosenthal, S. J. Racism and Desegregation at Old Dominion University. Integrateducation 17 (January-April 1979):40-42.

Rosh, D. S. The Navajo Way: Acculturation and Native American Higher Education [College of Ganado]. Doctoral dissertation, University of Pittsburgh, 1986. UMO # 8702021.

Ross, R. S. Who's Left? [Abortive effort to organize the National Student Convention at Rutgers University, February 5-7, 1988]. Village Voice March 1, 1988.

Rothrock, Elizabeth. Joseph Carter Corbin and Negro Education in the University of Arkansas. Arkansas Historical Quarterly 30 (Winter 1971):277-314.

Rothman, M. What's It Like for a Black Man in a Lily-White World? [Southern Oregon State College, Ashland]. Siskiyou March 9, 1984.

Ruiz, J. A. The Relationship Between College Selectivity and Other Institutional Characteristics and Hispanic Participation in Senior Public Institutions in the Southwest. Doctoral dissertation, University of Washington, 1987. UMO # 8713404.

Rutledge, E. M. Students' Perceptions of Racism in Higher Education. Integrateducation 20 (May-October 1982):106-111.

Ryan, J. and C. Sackrey. Strangers in Paradise. Academics from the Working Class. Boston: South End Press, 1988.

Sampson, W. S. Desegregation and Racial Tolerance in Academia. Journal of Negro Education 55 (Spring 1986):171-84.

Sanchez, M. E. and A. M. Stevens-Arroyo (eds.) Toward a Renaissance of Puerto Rican Studies: Ethnic and Area Studies in University Education. Highland Lakes, NJ: Atlantic Research and Publications, Inc., 1987.

Sav, G. T. The Politics of Race in Higher Education: Governing Boards and Instituents. Public Choice 48 (1986).

Saxe, J. The Year of the Wounded Dove [Institutional racism at the University of Massachusetts, Amherst]. Valley Advocate October 7, 1981.

Scantlebury, J. 'How Much More?' [Overall critique of racism at Cornell University]. Cornell Daily Sun December 3, 1986.

Schiller, P. M. Biculturalism and Psychosocial Adjustment among Native American University Students. Doctoral dissertation, University of Utah, 1987. UMO # 8720632.

Schlosser, Ken. Harvard's Stocks and Apartheid's Bonds: Crashing the University's Party. Radical America 20, nos. 2-3 (1986):43-50.

Scott, R. R. The Emergence of Process Discrimination: The Columbia College (N.Y.) Experience. Afro-American New York Life and History 8 (July 1984):61-78.

Scott, W. B. Race Consciousness and the Negro Student at Indiana University. Doctoral dissertation, Indiana University, 1960.

Seamans, H. L. Policies and Practices Regarding Minority Groups in Selected Colleges and Universities. Doctoral dissertation, Stanford University, 1947.

Sessoms, V. Black Community Is Alive and Kicking Racism [University of Washington]. Daily September 30, 1981.

Shadid, Anthony. Frat 'Slave Auction' Rocks Madison Campus. Guardian (NYC) December 7, 1988. [University of Wisconsin, Madison].

Shadid, Anthony. Racism on Campus: Students Fight Back. Guardian April 5, 1989.

Shamlian, L. and K. Van Ummersen. Struggle for Ethnic Studies. California Aggie (UC Davis) April 18, 1988.

Shea, S. and M. T. Fullilove. Entry of Black and Other Minority Students into U.S. Medical Schools [Includes lengthy historical review]. New England Journal of Medicine 313 (October 1985):933-52.

Shea, S. and M. T. Fullilove. 'Entry of Black and Other Minority Students into U.S. Medical Schools': Historical Perspective and Recent Trend: Reply. New England Journal of Medicine 315 (July 1986):69.

Shenon, Philip. G.O.P. Chairman, a Sit-In Target, Quits Howard University Board [Student protest against alleged racism by Republican Party official]. New York Times March 8, 1989.

Sherman, R. B. The 'Teachings at Hampton Institute': Social Equality, Racial Integrity, and the Virginia Public Assemblage Act of 1926. Virginia Mag. Hist. Biog. 95 (July 1987):275-300.

Shevellev, J. Minorities Face Isolation [UC Davis]. California Aggie January 20, 1983.

Shipp, E. R. Bar Exam Failures a Problem For a Praised CUNY School [City University of New York Law School]. New York Times December 26, 1987.

Sievert, W. S. Black Students, White Town: Tense Taft Hunts Solutions [Taft College, CA]. Chronicle of Higher Education November 24, 1975.

Siegal, Jessica. EOP-Tions. New Paltz Offers City Students an Up State of Mind. _Village Voice_ January 24, 1989. [State University of New York at New Paltz].

Simama, J., and N. Simama. The New South: Racism and Higher Education [Atlanta Junior College]. _In:_ Marvin J. Berlowitz and Frank E. Chapman (eds.), _The United States Educational System: Marxist Approaches_, pp. 53-68. Minneapolis, MN: Marxist Educational Press, 1980.

Sims, S. Racial Issues under 'Veneer' [University of Tennessee, Knoxville]. _Daily Beacon_ November 11, 1981.

Simurda, S. J. At Smith, Questions of Racism [Smith College]. _Boston Globe_ January 17, 1988.

Sinegar, L. A. _Coping with Racial Stressors: A Case Study of Black Professors in White Academe_ [Washington, D.C. metropolitan area]. Doctoral dissertation, George Washington University, 1987. UMO # 8715642.

Smith, S. L. Is There Room for College Blacks? [Blacks in Colorado colleges and universities]. _Denver Weekly News_ September 18, 1986.

Smothers, R. Faculty at Duke Is Urged to Hire From Minorities. _New York Times_ April 16, 1988.

Sowell, Thomas. The New Racism on Campus. _Fortune_ (February 11, 1989):115-16, 118, 120.

Spaights, E. and others. Racism in Higher Education. _College Student Journal_ 19 (Spring 1985):17-22.

Staples, B. The Dwindling Black Presence on Campus. _New York Times Magazine_ April 27, 1986.

Steele, Shelby. The Recoloring of Campus Life. _Harper's Magazine_ (February 1989):47-55.

Steinberg, S. _The Academic Melting Pot: Catholics and Jews in American Higher Education_. New York: McGraw-Hill, 1974.

Stevens-Arroyo, A. M. Toward a Renaissance of Puerto Rican Studies: An Essay of Redefinition. _In:_ Maria E. Sanchez and A. M. Stevens-Arroyo (eds.), _Toward a Renaissance of Puerto Rican Studies: Ethnic and Area Studies in University Education_, pp. 123-46. Highland Lakes, NJ: Atlantic Research and Publications, Inc. 1987.

Steyer, J. and M. Calabrese. A University's Racial Problem. _Stanford Daily_ November 22, 1982.

Stivason, S. Black Students Combat Racism [Atlanta Junior College]. _Southern Struggle_ (May-June 1978).

Stone, C. Racism and Ideals at Temple [University]. _Philadelphia Daily_

News May 6, 1976.

Stone, D. Black Students Harrassed in Northfield [Carleton College, Northfield]. *Minnesota Tribune* April 25, 1976.

Strum, H. Louis Marshall and Anti-Semitism at Syracuse University. *American Jewish Archives* 35 (April 1983):1-12.

Subcommittee On Minority Education. *Review of Minority Education at Cornell University 1983*. Ithaca, NY: Board of Trustees, Committee on Academic Affairs, March 1984.

Summer, F. C. Environic Factors Which Prohibit Creative Scholarship Among Negroes. *School and Society* 22 (September 5, 1925).

Supporter. U. of M. Native Americans Demand their Treaty Rights [University of Michigan]. *News and Letters* (June 1975).

Synott, M. G. The Admissions and Assimilation of Minority Students at Harvard, Yale, and Princeton, 1900-1950. *History of Education Quarterly* 19 (Fall 1979):285-304.

Tachibanaki, T. Education, Occupation, Hierarchy and Earnings. *Economics of Education Review* 7 (1988).

Tatel, D. S. Southern Colleges-Still Segregated. *New York Times* February 10, 1988.

Taylor, Robin. Racism Exists on Catholic Campuses, Study Shows. *National Catholic Reporter* November 18, 1988.

Terrell, M. C. *A Colored Woman in a White World* [Student days at Oberlin College]. Washington, D.C.: Ramsdell, 1940.

Thoenes, Sander. Eight Days That Shook Hampshire College. *Busline. The Five College Magazine* (Fall 1988).

Thomas, G. E. *The Access and Success of Blacks and Hispanics in U.S. Graduate and Professional Education*. Washington, D.C.: National Academy Press, 1986.

Thomas, G. E. Black Students in U.S. Graduate and Professional Schools in the 1980s: A National and Institutional Assessment. *Harvard Educational Review* 57 (August 1987):261-82.

Thompson, B. A. *An Appeal for Racial Justice: The Civic Interest Progressives' Confrontation with Huntington, West Virginia and Marshall University 1963-1965*. Master's thesis, Marshall University, 1986.

Thompson, D. C. *A Black Elite: A Profile of Graduates of UNCF Colleges*. Westport, CT: Greenwood, 1986.

Thornton, K. P. Symbolism at Ole Miss and the Crisis of Southern Identity. *South Atlantic Quarterly* 86 (Summer 1987):254-68.

Tillman, N. P. The National Council of Teachers of English and Racial Discrimination. Quarterly Review of Higher Education Among Negroes 10 (October 1942):218-222.

Toyama, J. UMGSR: A Status Report [Special program to recruit graduate students, 1977-1986]. Amherst, MA: Office of Minority Graduate Student Recruitment, University of Massachusetts, October 1986.

Trillin, C. An Education in Georgia. The Integration of Charlayne Hunter and Hamilton Holmes [University of Georgia]. New York: Viking, 1964.

Turner, Jeff. [Black Students at the] University of Georgia. New York Times April 5, 1989.

Turner, Patricia. Students With Heavy Burdens [Black students attending the University of Massachusetts, Boston]. Boston Globe December 4, 1988.

U.S. Congress, 97th, 2nd session, House of Representatives, Committee On Education and Labor, Subcommittee On Post-Secondary Education. Hispanics' Access to Higher Education. Hearing. Washington, D.C.: GPO, 1983.

U.S. Congress, 99th, 1st session, House of Representatives. Staff Report on the Hispanic Access to Higher Education. Washington, D.C.: GPO, 1986.

Ullman, V. Martin R. Delany: The Beginnings of Black Nationalism [Racism at Harvard Medical School, mid-19th century]. Boston: Beacon, 1971.

Useem, M. Privilege and Domination: The Role of the Upper Class in American Higher Education. Social Science Information 14 (1975):115-45.

Vaidhyanathan, Siva. UT [University of Texas, Austin] Still Far Short of Minority Goals. Dallas News October 7, 1988.

Vassall, M. A. The 'New' Racism [letter]. Cornell Daily Sun October 29, 1982.

Veciana-Suarez, A. Blacks Shun or Quit State Universities [Florida]. Miami Herald July 18, 1983.

Wade, J. E. Black College Students' Adaptive Modes: 'Making It at Penn'. Doctoral dissertation, University of Pennsylvania, 1983. UMO # 8316102.

Wald, A. Racism at the University of Michigan. Jewish Currents (December 1987).

Walker, J. Cornell: What Black Students Wanted. Muhammad Speaks May

16, 1969.

Walker, J. Why Blacks Rebelled at Brandeis. Muhammad Speaks February
    28, 1969.

Walker, Moses. A Case Study Approach to Developing Financial Bases for
    Selected Historically Black Institutions. Doctoral dissertation,
    Iowa State University, 1987. UMO # 8805148.

Wall, Michael E. Paying the Price of a Harvard Education ["Low-income
    students are forced to face a different Harvard"]. Harvard Crimson
    December 18, 1986.

Ware, E. T. Higher Education of Negroes in the United States. Annals of
    the American Academy of Political and Social Science 49 (September
    1913).

Washington, B. T. A University Education for Negroes. Independent 68
    (March 24, 1910).

Weber, C., and M. Weber. Racial Discrimination on Catholic College
    Campuses. Ave Maria (January 15, 1966).

Weinberg, Meyer. Guarded Preserve: Black Students in Higher Education.
    In: A Chance to Learn: The History of Race and Education in the
    United States, chapter 7. New York: Cambridge University Press,
    1977.

Weinberg, Meyer. Higher Education for Other Minorities [Mexican
    Americans, American Indians, and Puerto Ricans]. In: A Chance to
    Learn: The History of Race and Education in the United States,
    chapter 8. New York: Cambridge University Press, 1977.

Weis, L. Between Two Worlds: Black Students in an Urban Community
    College. London: Routledge & Kegan Paul, 1985.

Weiss, P. and J. Cramer. Shockley's Racism Circus Comes to Yale.
    Harvard Crimson (April 1975).

Weld, E. N. Berea: A College of Equality, Community Service. Boston
    Globe February 7, 1988.

West, E. J. Black Students at Harvard: 1900-1917. Harvard Crimson
    February 9, 1972.

Wexler, N. Are Blacks Welcome? [Wake Forest University, Winston Salem,
    NC]. Winston-Salem Journal (October 7, 1979).

Wexler, N. Harvard's Indians Are Getting Ahead to Help their People.
    Harvard Crimson January 20, 1975.

Wheeler, E. L. Isaac Fisher: The Frustration of a Negro Educator at
    Branch Normal College, 1902-1911. Arkansas Historical Quarterly 41
    (Spring 1982):3-50.

White, G. Racism on Campus Concern of an 'Average' Student [Southern Methodist University]. Daily Campus December 8, 1982.

White, N. J. From Racist Jeers to a Standing Ovation [Charlayne Hunter-Gault, one of first Black students at University of Georgia]. Atlanta Journal (March 7, 1984).

Whitfield, E. L. Black Students at Cornell, Part II [First-hand account of events of April 19-20, 1969]. Muhammad Speaks May 23, 1969.

Wiener, Jon. Racial Hatred on Campus. Nation February 22, 1989.

Wilkerson, I. Campus Blacks Feel Racism's Nuances [University of Michigan]. New York Times April 17, 1988.

Wilkerson, I. Turmoil at Ohio State in Shunning of [Black] Cheerleader. New York Times January 31, 1988.

Williams, C. G. and J. E. Lyons. Black Coeds on a White Campus. Integrated Education (September-October 1972):61-64.

Williams, J. B. (ed). Desegregating America's Colleges and Universities: Title VI Regulation of Higher Education. New York: Teacher's Collge Press, 1987.

Williams, W. What's New in Marketing Black Colleges. New York Times March 13, 1988.

Willie, C. V. and R. R. Edmonds (eds.) Black Colleges in America. New York: Teacher's College Press, 1978.

Willie, C. V. and A. S. McCord. Black Students at White Colleges. New York: Praeger, 1972.

Wilson, D. Going from Black to Black and White: A Case Study of the Desegregation of Kentucky State University [1981-1986]. Doctoral dissertation, Harvard University, 1987. UMO # 8722712.

Wilson, E. M. An Historical Study of Desegregation at West Virginia State College, 1954-1973: An Application of a Theory of Mandated Academic Change. Doctoral dissertation, Kent State University, 1985. UMO # 8609189.

Woolridge, Veronica. [Black Students at the] University of Michigan. New York Times April 5, 1989.

17X, Samuel. Black Thugs Intimidate Black Teachers [Malcolm X College, Chicago]. Muhammad Speaks January 22, 1971.

Young, Eric. [Black Students at] Stanford University. New York Times April 5, 1989.

Zakhar, Arlene A. The Urban University and Native Americans in Higher Education [University of Wisconsin-Milwaukee]. Doctoral dissertation, University of Wisconsin-Milwaukee, 1987. UMO #

8811152.

Education: Higher Bibliography

Chambers, Frederick (comp.) Black Higher Education in the United States:
   A Selected Bibliography on Negro Higher Education and Historically
   Black Colleges and Universities. Westport, CT: Greenwood, 1978.

Endo, Russell (comp.) Bibliography on Asian American Studies Programs in
   Higher Education. Boulder: Colorado Institute for Social Research,
   1985.

ERIC Central (comp.) References on Traditionally Black Colleges and
   Universities in the ERIC Database. Washington, D.C.: National
   Center for Education Statistics, March 1984.

Kambule, Addis N. (comp.) Libraries in Predominantly/Historically Black
   Institutions. A Select Annotated Bibliography Education 696L.
   Amherst, MA: School of Education, University of Massachusetts,
   Spring 1987.

Newman, Richard (comp.) Afro-American Education, 1907-1922. A
   Bibliographic Index. New York: Lambeth Press, 1984.

Shrier, Irene and David E. Lavin (comps.) Open Admissions: A
   Bibliography for Research and Application. 1974. ERIC ED 090 840.

Weinberg, Meyer (comp.) The Education of Poor and Minority Children: A
   World Bibliography. [3 vols.] Westport, CT: Greenwood, 1981, 1986.

   [See also sections 1, 5, 12, 19, 29, 22, 32, 73, and 79]

207

27. Employment

*And it is only as a cultivated, industrious, and highly moral
people, that we are objected to!*

- John S. Rock, annual meeting of the Massachusetts Anti-
Slavery Society, January 27, 1860, Liberator, February 3, 1860.

American Academy of Political and Social Science. The Industrial
   Condition of the Negro in the North. Philadelphia, PA: 1906.

Bailey, K. R. A Judicious Mixture: Negroes and Immigrants in the West
   Virginia Mines, 1880-1917. West Virginia History 34 (1973):141-61.

Becker, H. J. Racial Segregation among Places of Employment. Social
   Forces 58 (March 1980):761-776.

Brimmer, A. F. Long-term Economic Growth and Black Employment
   Opportunities. Review of Black Political Economy 13 (Summer-Fall
   1984).

Bryant, P. A Long Time Coming [Fishermen and Concerned Citizens
   Association of Plaquemines Parish]. Southern Exposure 10 (May-June
   1982):83-89.

Capeci, D. J., Jr. Wartime Fair Employment Practice Committee: The
   Governor's Committee and the First FEPC in New York City, 1941-1943.
   Afro-Americans in New York Life and History 9 (July 1985):45-63.

Cogan, J. F. The Decline in Black Teenage Employment: 1950-1970.
   American Economic Review 72 (September 1982).

Committee On Youth Employment Programs. Youth Employment and Training
   Programs. Washington, D.C.: National Academy Press, 1985.

Crigler, W. R. The Employment Status of Blacks in Los Angeles: Ten Years
   After the Kerner Commission Report. Doctoral dissertation,
   University of California, Los Angeles, 1979. UMO # 7962007.

Day, R. M. The Black High School Graduate and Employment After
   Graduating: A Follow-up Study of the Labor Market Experiences of the
   1978 Black Graduates of the Columbus Public Schools. Doctoral
   dissertation, Ohio State University, 1987. UMO # 8128985.

De Jong, Gordon F. and R. W. Gardner. Asians in American Industry.
   Population Today (May 1987):6-8.

Estherby, B. J. The Occupational Progress of Mississippi Negroes, 1940-
   1960. Mississippi Quarterly 21 (Winter 1967-1968):49-62.

Fishback, P. V. Employment Conditions of Blacks in the Coal Industry,
   1900-1930. Doctoral dissertation, University of Washington, 1983.

Freeman, R. B. Changes in the Labor Market for Black Americans, 1948-1972. Brookings Papers on Economic Activity 1 (1973):67-120.

Frnka, R. L. (ed.) Mississippi Employment, 1974-1979 (seventh edition). MI: Div. of Research, College of Business and Industry, Mississippi State University, 1981.

Garfinkel, H. When Negroes March: The March on Washington Movement in the Organizational Politics for FEPC. New York: Atheneum, 1959.

Garofalo, C. Black-White Occupational Distribution in Miami During World War I. Prologue 5 (1973):98-101.

Gaston, E. A., Jr. A History of the Negro Wage Earner in Georgia, 1890-1940. Doctoral disertation, Emory University, 1957. UMO # 585143.

Gershenfeld, W. J. The Negro Labor Market in Lancaster, Pennsylvania. Doctoral dissertation, University of Pennsylvania, 1964.

Gregory, K. D. Blacks in Michigan in Private Industry in the 1980s. In: Frances S. Thomas (ed.), The State of Black Michigan: 1987, pp. 19-26. East Lansing, MI: Urban Affair Programs, Michigan State University, 1987.

Hall, E. E. The Negro Wage Earner of New Jersey. Doctoral dissertation, Rutgers Univesity, 1951.

Hill, H. The Equal Employment Opportunity Acts of 1964 and 1972: A Critical Analysis of the Legislative History and Administration of the Law. Industrial Relations Law Journal 2 (1977):1-96.

Hill, H. Twenty Years of State Fair Employment Practice Commissions: A Critical Analysis with Recommendations. Buffalo Law Review 14 (fall 1964):22-69.

Hill, R. B. (ed.) Occupational Attainment: Minorities and Women in Selected Industries, 1969 to 1979. Transaction Books, 1983.

Hill, R. B. and R. Nixon. Youth Employment in American Industry. New Brunswick, NJ: Transaction Publishers, 1984.

Hogan, L. and H. Harris. The Occupational-Industrial Structure of Black Employment in the U.S. Review of Black Political Economy 6 (1974).

Hut, M. Occupational Mobility of Black Men: 1962 to 1973. American Sociological Review 49 (June 1984):308-22.

Iden, G. The Labor Force Experience of Black Youth: A Review. Monthly Labor Review 103 (August 1980):10-16.

Kleinfeld, J. and J. A. Kruse. Native Americans in the Labor Force: Hunting for an Accurate Measure. Monthly Labor Review 105 (July 1982):47-51.

Laing, J. T. The Negro Miner in West Virginia. Doctoral dissertation,

Ohio State University, 1933.

Maldonado, E.   Contract Labor and the Origins of Puerto Rican Communities
in the United States.   International Migration Review   13 (Spring
1979):103-21.

Marshall, R. and V. L. Christian.   Employment of Blacks in the South: A
Perspective on the 1960's.   Austin: University of Texas Press, 1978.

Morse, D. W.   Pride Against Prejudice: Work in the Lives of Older Blacks
and Young Puerto Ricans.   Allenheld: Osmun, 1980.

Newman, M. J.   The Labor Market Experience of Black Youth, 1954-1978.
Monthly Labor Review   102 (October 1979):19-27.

Reed, M. E.   The FEPC, the Black Worker, and the Southern Shipyards.
South Atlantic Quarterly   74 (1975):446-67.

Rolison, G. L.   The Political Economy of the Urban Underclass: Black
Subemployment in Advanced Capitalism.   Doctoral dissertation,
University of California at Santa Cruz, 1986.   UMO # 8709125.

Scientific Manpower Commission.   Professional Women and Minorities: A
Manpower Data Resource Service.   Washington, D.C.:   The Commission,
1981.

Scott, R. J.   The Battle over the Child: Child Apprenticeship and the
Freedman's Bureau in North Carolina.   In: N. Ray Hiner and Joseph M
Howes (eds.), Growing Up in America: Children in Historical
Perspective.   Urbana, IL: University of Illinois Press, 1985.

Seeborg, I. S., and Others.   Training and Labor Market Outcomes of
Disadvantaged Blacks.   Industrial Relations   25 (Winter 1986).

Smith, A. N.   Black Employment in the Los Angeles Area, 1938-1948.
Doctoral dissertation, University of California, Los Angeles, 1978.
UMO # 7907687.

Szymanski, A.   The Growing Role of Spanish Speaking Workers in the U.S.
Economy.   Aztlan   9 (1978):177-208.

U.S. Bureau of Labor Statistics.   Linking Employment Problems to Economic
Status.   Washington, D.C.:   GPO, 1985.

Vaughn-Cooke, D.   Blacks in Labor Markets - A Historical Assessment.   Urban
League Review   7 (Summer 1983).

Worthman, P. B., and J. R. Green.   Black Workers in the New South, 1865-
1915.   In: Nathan I. Huggins and others (eds.), Key Issues in the
Afro-American Experience, Vol. 2, pp. 62-68.   Harcourt Brace, 1972.

[See also sections 13, 20, 23, 29, 38, 39, 49, 54, 75, 81, and 83]

28. Family

Slave children born in the 1840s or the 1950s grew up in a slave community made up of interrelated but well-defined immediate families. Such ties rooted them in a shared Afro-American past and helped define the identity of particular men, women, and children, allowing slave children to absorb values from parents, grandparents, other adult kin, and adult non-kin.

- Herbert G. Gutman, The Black Family in Slavery and Freedom 1750-1925, p. 87.

Allen, W. R. Black Family Research in the United States: A Review, Assessment, and Extension. Journal of Comparative Family Studies 9 (1978):167-89.

Allen, W. R. Class, Culture and Family Organization: The Effects of Class and Race on Family Structure in Urban America. Journal of Comparative Family Studies 10 (1979):301-13.

Aoyagi, K. Kinship and Friendship in Black Los Angeles, In: The Extended Family, pp. 271-353. The Hague: Mouton, 1978.

Baca Zinn, M. Minority Families in Crisis: The Public Discussion. Memphis, TN: Center for Research on Women, Memphis State University, 1987.

Baptiste, D. A. The Image of the Black Family Portrayed by Television: A Critical Comment. Marriage and Family Review 10 (April 1986):41-65.

Barnes, A. S. The Black Middle Class Family. Bristol, IN: Wyndham Hall Press, 1985.

Bass, Barbara Ann and others. The Afro-American Family: Assessment, Treatment, and Research Issues. New York: Grune and Stratton, 1982.

Bigham, D. E. The Black Family in Evansville and Vanderburgh County, Indiana: A 1900 Postscript. Indiana Magazine of History 78 (June 1982):154-69.

Billingsley, A. Black Families and White Social Science. Journal of Social Issues 26 (Summer 1970):127-42.

Billingsley, A. and M. C. Greene. Family Life among the Free Black Population in the 18th Century. Journal of Social and Behavioral Sciences 20 (Spring 1974):1-18.

Bond, H. M. Black American Scholars: A Study of Their Beginnings. Detroit: Balamp Publishing, 1972.

Bowser, B. P. Community and Economic Context of Black Families: A Critical Review of the Literature, 1909-1985. American Journal of Social Psychiatry 6 (Winter 1986):17-26.

Broadway, D. C. A Study of Middle Class Black Children and their Families: Aspirations for Children. Perceptions of Success and the Role of Culture. Doctoral dissertation, Ohio State University, 1987. UMO # 8709976.

Brooks, S. You May Plow Here: The Narrative of Sara Brooks edited by Thordis Simonsen [Black family in Alabama]. New York: Norton, 1986.

Bullock, H. A. The Texas Negro Family: The Status of Its Socioeconomic Organization. Prairie View, TX: Prairie View College Press, 1941.

Burton, O. V. In My Father's House Are Many Mansions: Family and Community in Edgefield, South Carolina. Chapel Hill, NC: University of North Carolina Press, 1985.

Children's Defense Fund. A Vision of America's Future. Washington, D.C.: The Fund, 1989.

Comer, James P. Black Fathers. In: Stanley H. Cath and others (eds.), Fathers and Their Families. Hillsdale, NJ: Lawrence Erlbaum, 1989.

Coray, Michael S. Influences on Black Family Household Organization in the West, 1850-1860. Nevada Historical Society Quarterly 31 (Spring 1988):1-31.

Dill, B. T. On Mothers' Grief: Racial Ethnic Women and the Maintenance of Families. Memphis, TN: Center for Research on Women, Memphis State University, 1986.

Dobbins, M. P., and J. Mulligan. Black Matriarchy: Transforming a Myth of Racism into a Class Model. Journal of Comparative Family Studies 11 (1980):195-217.

Du Bois, W. E. B. (ed.) The Negro American Family [Includes income and budgets]. Atlanta: Atlanta University Press, 1908.

Ebigham, D. The Black Family in Evansville and Vanderburgh County, Indiana in 1880. Indiana Magazine of History 75 (June 1979):117-146.

Edelman, M. W. Families in Peril: An Agenda for Social Change. Cambridge, MA: Harvard University Press, 1987.

Franklin, H. A Historical Note on Black Families. In: Harriette P. McAdoo (ed.), Black Families. Newbury Park, CA: Sage, 1988.

Frazier, E. Franklin. The Present Status of the Negro Family in the U.S. Journal of Negro Education 8 (July 1939).

Furstenberg, F. F., Jr. and others. Adolescent Mothers and Their Children in Later Life. Family Planning Perspectives (July-August 1987):141-51.

Furstenberg, F. F., Jr. and others. The Origins of the Female-headed

Black Family: The Impact of the Urban Experience. <u>Journal</u> <u>of</u>
<u>Interdisciplinary</u> <u>History</u> 6 (1975):211-33.

Genovese, E. D. The Slave Family. Women - A Reassessment of Matriarchy,
Emasculation, Weakness. <u>Southern</u> <u>Voices</u> 1 (August-September
1974):9-16.

Griswold Del Castillo, R. 'Only for My Family': Historical Dimensions of
Chicano Family Solidarity - The Case of San Antonio in 1860. <u>Aztlan</u>
16 (1985):145-76.

Gutman, H. G. <u>The</u> <u>Black</u> <u>Family</u> <u>in</u> <u>Slavery</u> <u>and</u> <u>Freedom,</u> <u>1750-1925</u>. New
York: 1976. [See Modell, below.]

Gutman, H. G. Mirrors of the Hard, Distorted Glass: An Examination of
Some Influential Historical Assumptions about the Afro-American
Family and the Shaping of Public Policies, 1861-1965. <u>In</u>: David
Rothman and Stanton Wheeler (eds.), <u>Social</u> <u>History</u> <u>and</u> <u>Social</u> <u>Policy</u>.
New York: Academic Press, 1981.

Gutman, H., and R. Sutch. The Slave Family: Protected Agent of
Capitalist Masters or Victim of Slave Trade? . <u>In</u>: <u>Reckoning</u> <u>With</u>
<u>Slavery</u>: <u>A</u> <u>Critical</u> <u>Study</u> <u>in</u> <u>the</u> <u>Quantitative</u> <u>History</u> <u>of</u> <u>American</u>
<u>Negro</u> <u>Slavery</u>, pp. 99-110. 1976.

Hale-Benson, J. Cultural Context for Child Care in the Black Community.
<u>In</u>: Jeffrey Lande and Sandra Scarr (eds.), <u>Caring</u> <u>for</u> <u>Children.</u>
<u>Challenge</u> <u>to</u> <u>America</u>. Hillsdale, NJ: Lawrence Erlbaum, 1989.

Handy, E. S., and M. K. Pukui. <u>The</u> <u>Polynesian</u> <u>Family</u> <u>System</u> <u>in</u> <u>Kau'u,</u>
<u>Hawaii</u>. Wellington, New Zealand: 1958.

Hardaway, R. D. Unlawful Love: A History of Arizona's Miscegenation Law.
<u>Journal</u> <u>of</u> <u>Arizona</u> <u>History</u> 27 (Winter 1986):377-90.

Harris, W. Work and Family in Black Atlanta, 1880. <u>Journal</u> <u>of</u> <u>Social</u>
<u>History</u> 9 (Spring 1976):319-30.

Haynes, Cheryl D. (ed.) <u>Risking</u> <u>the</u> <u>Future:</u> <u>Adolescent</u> <u>Sexuality,</u>
<u>Pregnancy,</u> <u>and</u> <u>Childbearing</u>. Washington, D.C.: National Academy
Press, 1987.

Heer, D. M. The Prevalence of Black-White Marriage in the United States,
1960 and 1970. <u>Journal</u> <u>of</u> <u>Marriage</u> <u>and</u> <u>the</u> <u>Family</u> 36 (May
1974):246-58.

Hill, R. B. <u>The</u> <u>Strengths</u> <u>of</u> <u>Black</u> <u>Families</u>. Washington, D.C.: National
Urban League, 1971.

Hunter, K. I. and others. Sterilization among American Indian and
Chicano Mothers. <u>International</u> <u>Quarterly</u> <u>of</u> <u>Community</u> <u>Health</u> <u>and</u>
<u>Education</u> 4 (1984):343-52.

Jewell, K. Sue. <u>Survival</u> <u>of</u> <u>the</u> <u>Black</u> <u>Family:</u> <u>The</u> <u>Institutional</u> <u>Impact</u>
<u>of</u> <u>American</u> <u>Social</u> <u>Policy</u>. New York: Praeger, 1988.

Johnson, C. and A. Sum. *Declining Earnings of Young Men: Their Relation to Poverty, Teen Pregnancy, and Family Formation*. Washington, D.C.: Children's Defense Fund, 1987.

Keir, S. S. *Middle-class Black Families in Austin, Texas: An Exploratory Analysis of Husbands and Wives*. Doctoral dissertation, University of Texas, 1987. UMO # 8717452.

Kennedy, T. R. *You Gotta Deal With It: Black Family Relations in a Southern Community*. New York: Oxford, 1980.

Kenyatta, M. I. In Defense of the Black Family: The Impact of Racism on the Family as a Support System. *Monthly Review* 34 (March 1983):12-21.

Krech, S., III. Black Family Organization in the Nineteenth Century: An Ethnological Perspective. *Journal of Interdisciplinary History* 12 (Winter 1982):429-52.

Krein, S. F. and A. H. Beller. Educational Attainment of Children from Single-Parent Families: Differences by Exposure, Gender, and Race. *Demography* 25 (May 1988).

Lacey, L. J. The White Man's Law and the American Indian Family in the Assimilation Era. *Arkansas Law Review* 40 (Fall 1986):327-79.

Ladner, J. A. *Mixed Families*. Garden City, NY: Anchor, 1977.

Lewis, J. M. and J. S. Looney. *The Long Struggle: Well-Functioning Working-class Black Families*. New York: Brunner/Mazel, 1983.

McAdoo, Harriette P. (ed.) *Black Families*. Newbury Park, CA: Sage, 1981.

McAdoo, H. P., and R. Terborg-Penn. Historical Trends and Perspectives of Afro-American Families. In: Patricia J. F. Rosof and William Zeisel (eds.), *Family History*. New York: Haworth, 1985.

McAdoo, J. L. A Black Perspective on the Father's Role in Child Development. *Marriage and Family Review* 9 (Winter 1985-86):117-33.

Modell, J. and others. A Colloquium on Herbert Gutman's 'The Black Family in Slavery and Freedom, 1750-1925. *Social Science History* 3 (January 1979):45-85.

Montiel, M. The Chicano Family: A Review of Research. *Social Work* 18 (March 1973):22-31.

Moynihan, D. P. Employment, Income, and the Ordeal of the Negro Family. *Daedalus* (Fall 1965).

Moynihan, D. P. *Family and Nation*. San Deigo, CA: Harcourt Brace Jovanovich, 1986.

Mullings, L.   Anthropological Perspectives on the Afro-American Family. *American Journal of Social Psychiatry* 6 (Winter 1986):11-16.

Nee, V. and H. Y. Wong. Asian American Socioeconomic Achievement: The Strength of the Family Bond. *Sociological Perspective* 28 (July 1985):281-306.

Norton, E. H. Restoring the Traditional Black Family. *New York Times Magazine* June 2, 1985.

Omolade, Barbara. *It's a Family Affair: The Real Lives of Black Single Mothers*. Latham, NY: Kitchen Table: Women of Color Press, 1988.

Patterson, R. P. *The Seed of Sally Good'n. A Black Family of Arkansas, 1833-1953*. Lexington: University Press of Kentucky, 1985.

Penczer, L. O. *Resources and Family Power: Portuguese Adolescents in a New England City* [Bridgeport, CT]. Doctoral dissertation, Yale University, 1986. UMO # 8701070.

Pinderhughes, E. B. Family Functioning of Afro-Americans. *Social Work* 27 (January 1982):91-96.

Porter, D. B. The Remonds of Salem, Massachusetts: A Nineteenth-Century Family Revisited. *Proceedings of the American Antiquarian Society* 95 (1985):259-95.

Rey, K. H. *The Haitian Family*. New York: 1970.

Rodgers, H. R., Jr. Youth and Poverty: An Empirical Test of the Impact of Family Demographics and Race [1959-1982]. *Youth and Society* 16 (1985):421-37.

Seck, Essie Tramel. The Impact of Unemployment on the Social Well Being of the Black Family. *Urban League Review* 10 (Summer 1986):87-97.

Smith, D. B. The Study of the Family in Early America: Trends, Problems, and Prospects. *William and Mary Quarterly* (3rd series) 39 (January 1982):3-28.

Smith, H. L. and P. Cutright. Thinking About Change in Illegitimacy Ratios, United States, 1963-1983. *Demography* 25 (May 1988).

Smits, D. D. 'Abominable Mixture': Toward the Repudiation of Anglo-Indian Intermarriage in Seventeenth-century Virginia. *Virginia Magazine of History and Biography* 95 (April 1987):157-92.

Sudarkasa, Niara. African and Afro-American Family Structure: A Comparison. *Black Scholar* 11 (November-December 1980):37-60.

Tatum, B. D. *Assimilation Blues: Black Families in a White Community* [Santa Barbara, CA]. Westport, CT: Greenwood Press, 1988.

Taylor, R. Receipt of Support from Family among Black Americans: Demographic and Familial Differences. *Journal of Marriage and the*

Family 48 (1986):67-77.

Tolnay, S. E. Black Family Formation and Tenancy in the Farm South, 1900. _American Journal of Sociology_ 90 (1984):305-25.

The Crisis of the Black Family [entire issue]. _Ebony_ (August 1986):39-162.

Trader, H. P. Welfare Policies and Black Families. _Social Work_ 24 (November 1979):548-551.

U.S. Bureau of the Census. _Fifteenth Census of the United States: 1930_, vol. 6, _Special Reports on Foreign-born White Families_. Washington, D.C.: GPO, 1933.

U.S. Department of Agriculture, Office of Governmental and Affairs. _Public People on the Farm: Black Families_. Washington, D.C.: U.S. Department of Agriculture, 1980.

U.S. Department of Labor, Office of Planning and Research. _The Negro Family. The Case for National Action_ [The Moynihan Report]. Washington, D.C.: GPO, 1965.

U.S. Immigration Commission. _Immigrants in Cities, Reports_, vol. 26 and 27 [Families]. Washington, D.C.: GPO, 1911.

Unger, Steven (ed.) _The Destruction of American Indian Families_. New York: Association on American Indian Affairs, 1977.

Valdez, Armando and others (eds.) _The State of Chicano Research on Family, Labor, and Migration_. Stanford, CA: Stanford Center for Chicano Research, 1983.

Weinberg, M. Schooling and the New Parenthood. _Journal of Negro Education_ 40 (Summer 1971):207-15.

Wells, A. S. The Parents' Place: Right in the School. _New York Times Education Life_ January 3, 1988.

Wilkinson, G. The Native American Family. _Human Services in the Rural Environment_ 3 (September 1978):8-19.

Willie, C. V. _The Family Life of Black People_. Columbus, OH: Merrill, 1970.

Wilson, W. J. and K. M. Neckerman. Poverty and Family Structure: The Widening Gap between Evidence and Public Policy Issues. _In_: Sheldon Danziger and Daniel H. Weinberg (eds.), _Fighting Povety: What Works and What Doesn't_, Cambridge, MA: Harvard University Press, 1986.

Zavella, Patricia. _Women's Work and Chicano Families: Cannery Workers of the Santa Clara Valley_. Ithaca, NY: Cornell University Press, 1987.

Family Bibliography

Allen, Walter R. (comp.) Black American Families, 1965-1984: A
     Classified, Selectively Annotated Bibliography. Westport, CT:
     Greenwood, 1986.

Davis, Lenwood G. (comp.) The Black Family in the United States: A
     Revised, Updated, Selectively Annotated Bibliography. Westport, CT:
     Greenwood, 1986.

Klotman, Phyllis R. and Wilmer H. Boatz (comps.) The Black Family and
     the Black Woman: A Bibliography. New York: Arno, 1978.

[See also section 85]

217

29. Forced Labor

Peonage infected the South like a cancer, eating away at the economic freedom of blacks, driving the poor whites to work harder in order to compete with virtual slave labor, and preserving the class structure inherited from slavery days.

- Pete Daniel, The Shadow of Slavery: Peonage in the South 1901-1969, p. 11.

Barry, R. Slavery in the South Today. Cosmopolitan 42 (March 1907):481-91.

Carleton, M. T. The Politics of the Convict Lease System in Louisiana, 1868-1901. Louisiana History 8 (Winter 1967):5-26.

Carper, N. G. Slavery Revisited: Peonage in the South. Phylon 37 (March 1976):85-99.

Cohen, W. Negro Involuntary Servitude in the South, 1865-1940: A Preliminary Analysis. Journal of Southern History 42 (1976):31-60.

Daniel, P. Up from Slavery and Down to Peonage: The Alonzo Bailey Case. Journal of American History (December 1970).

Daniel, P. The Metamorphosis of Slavery, 1865-1900. Journal of American History 66 (June 1979):88-100.

Daniel, P. The Shadow of Slavery: Peonage in the South 1901-1969. Urbana, IL: University of Illinois Press, 1972.

Daniel, P. (ed.) The Peonage Files of the U.S. Department of Justice, 1901-1945 [26 microfilm reels]. Frederick, MD: University Publications of America, 1988.

Du Bois, W. E. B. The Rural South. Publications of the American Statistical Association 13 (March 1912):80-84.

Du Bois, W. E. B. The Spawn of Slavery. The Convict-Lease System in the South. Missionary Review of the World 14 (October 1901):737-45.

Irvine, Alexander. My Life in Peonage - I. The Situation as I Found It. [First of a series] Appleton (June 1907)

Kelway, A. J. Convict Leasing System of Georgia. Outlook 90 (September 1908).

The Life Story of a Negro Peon. In: Hamilton Holt (ed.), The Life Stories of Undistinguished Americans. New York: James Pott & Co.

McDonald, F. and G. McWhiney. The South From Self-Sufficiency to Peonage: An Interpretation. American Historical Review 85 (December 1980):1095-1118.

McKelvey, B. Penal Slavery and Southern Reconstruction. <u>Journal</u> <u>of</u> <u>Negro</u> <u>History</u> (April 1935).

Novak, D. A. <u>The</u> <u>Wheel</u> <u>of</u> <u>Servitude:</u> <u>Black</u> <u>Forced</u> <u>Labor</u> <u>After</u> <u>Slavery</u>. Lexington: University of Kentucky Press, 1978.

Ransom, R. L. and R. Sutch. Debt Peonage in the Cotton South After the Civil War. <u>Journal</u> <u>of</u> <u>Economic</u> <u>History</u> 32 (September 1972):641-69.

Schmidt, B. C., Jr. Principle and Prejudice: The Supreme Court and Race in the Progressive Era. Part 2: The 'Peonage Cases'. <u>Columbia</u> <u>Law</u> <u>Review</u> 82 (May 1982):646-718.

Schwartz, M. <u>Radical</u> <u>Protest</u> <u>and</u> <u>Social</u> <u>Structure:</u> <u>The</u> <u>Southern</u> <u>Farmers'</u> <u>Alliance</u> <u>and</u> <u>Cotton</u> <u>Tenancy</u> [Debt peonage], Chapter 6. New York: 1976.

Shlomowitz, R. 'Bound' or 'Free'? Black Labor in Cotton and Sugarcane Farming, 1965-1880. <u>Journal</u> <u>of</u> <u>Southern</u> <u>History</u> 50 (November 1984):569-96.

Shelden, R. G. From Slave to Caste Society: Penal Changes in Tennessee, 1830-1915. <u>Tennessee</u> <u>Historical</u> <u>Quarterly</u> 38 (Winter 1979):462-78.

Shofner, J. H. Forced Labor in the Florida Forests, 1880-1950. <u>Journal</u> <u>of</u> <u>Forest</u> <u>History</u> 25 (January 1981):14-25.

Shofner, J. H. The Legacy of Racial Slavery: Free Enterprise and Forced Labor in Florida in the 1940s. <u>Journal</u> <u>of</u> <u>Southern</u> <u>History</u> 47 (August 1981):411-426.

Speranze, G. Forced Labor in West Virginia. <u>Outlook</u> 74 (June 13, 1903):407-10.

Stephens, L. D. A Former Slave and the Georgia Convict Lease System. <u>Negro</u> <u>History</u> <u>Bulletin</u> 39 (1976):505-7.

Taylor, A. Elizabeth. The Origins and Development of the Convict Lease System in Georgia. <u>Georgia</u> <u>Historical</u> <u>Quarterly</u> 26 (June 1942):113-28.

Van Der Zee, J. <u>Bound</u> <u>Over:</u> <u>Indentured</u> <u>Servitude</u> <u>and</u> <u>American</u> <u>Conscience</u>. New York: Simon and Schuster, 1986.

Ward, R. D. and W. W. Rogers. <u>Convicts,</u> <u>Coal,</u> <u>and</u> <u>the</u> <u>Banner</u> <u>Mine</u> <u>Tragedy</u>. University: University of Alabama Press, 1987.

Ward, R. D. and W. W. Rogers. Racial Inferiority, Convict Labor, and Modern Medicine: A Note of the Coalburg Affair. <u>Alabama</u> <u>Historical</u> <u>Quarterly</u> 44 (Fall-Winter 1982):203-10.

Wilson, W. Forced Labor in the United States. New York: AMS Press, 1971 (orig. 1933).

[See also sections 44 and 75]

30. Free Blacks

... The great characteristic of American slavery, and that which distinguishes it from all other species of oppression, is that hatred of the free colored man which makes his condition little superior to that of servitude itself.

- Thomas Paul, a black student at Dartmouth College, Liberator, February 19, 1841.

Bellamy, D. D. Free Blacks in Antebellum Missouri, 1820-1860. Missouri Historical Review 67 (1973):198-226.

Berlin, I. Slaves Without Masters. The Free Negro in the Antebellum South. New York: Pantheon, 1974.

Berlin, I. The Structure of the Free Negro Caste in the Antebellum United States. Journal of Social History 9 (1976):297-318.

Berlin, I. Time, Space, and the Evolution of Afro-American Society on British Mainland North America. American Hist. Review 85 (1980):44-78.

Bonacich, E. Abolition, the Extension of Slavery, and the Position of Free Blacks: A Study of Split Labor Markets in the United States, 1830-1863. American Journal of Sociology 81 (1975):601-28.

Breen, T. H. and S. Junes. Seventeenth-Century Virginia's Forgotten Yeomen: The Free Blacks. Virginia Cavalcade 32 (Summer 1982):10-19.

Burton, O. V. Anatomy of an Antebellum Rural Free Black Community: Social Structure and Social Interaction in Edgefield District, South Carolina, 1850-1860. Southern Studies 21 (Fall 1982):294-325.

Crew, S. Black New Jersey before the Civil War: Two Case Studies. New Jersey History 99 (Spring-Summer 1981):67-86.

Curry, L. P. The Free Black in Urban America, 1800-1850: The Shadow of the Dream. Chicago: University of Chicago Press, 1981.

Davidson, T. D. Free Blacks in Old Somerset County, 1745-1755. Maryland Hist. Magazine 80 (Summer 1985):151-56.

Day, J. and M. J. Kedro. Free Blacks in St. Louis: Antebellum Conditions, Emancipation, and the Postwar Era. Missouri Hist. Society Bulletin 30 (1974):117-35.

Della, M. R., Jr. The Problems of Negro Labor in the 1850s. Maryland Hist. Magazine 66 (1971):14-32.

Eisterhold, J. A. Savannah: Lumber Center of the South Atlantic. Georgia Hist. Quarterly 57 (1973):526-43.

Ellefson, C. A. Free Jupiter and the Rest of the World: The Problem of a Free Negro in Colonial Maryland. <u>Maryland Hist. Magazine</u> 66 (1971):1-13.

Everett, D. E. <u>Free Persons of Color in New Orleans, 1803-1865</u>. [Doctoral dissertation, Tulane University, 1952].

Fisher, J. E. The Legal Status of Free Blacks in Texas, 1836-1861. <u>Texas Law Review</u> (Summer 1977).

Fitchett, E. H. The Status of the Free Negro in Charleston, South Carolina. <u>Journal of Negro History</u> (October 1947).

Foner, L. The Free People of Color in Louisiana and St. Dominique: A Comparative Portrait of Two Three-Caste Societies. <u>Journal of Social History</u> (Gr. Brit.) 3 (1970):406-30.

Formisano, R. P. The Edge of Caste: Colored Suffrage in Michigan, 1827-1861. <u>Michigan History</u> 56 (1972):19-41.

Franklin, J. H. <u>The Free Negro in North Carolina, 1790-1860</u>. New York: Norton, 1943.

Freeman, R. C. <u>The Free Negro in New York City in the Era before the Civil War</u>. Doctoral dissertation, Columbia University, 1966.

Garvin, R. The Free Negro in Florida Before the Civil War. <u>Florida Hist. Quarterly</u> 46 (1967):1-17.

Graham, L. <u>Baltimore: The Nineteenth-Century Black Capital</u>. Washington, D.C.: University Press of America, 1982.

Hancock, H. B. The Free Negroes in Delaware in the 1830s. <u>Civil War History</u> 17 (1971):320-31.

Hanger, K. S. Free Blacks in Spanish New Orleans: The Transitional Decade, 1769-1779. [Master's thesis, University of Utah, 1985].

Hershberg, T. Free Blacks in Antebellum Philadelphia: A Study of Ex-Slaves, Freedom, and Socioeconomic Decline. <u>Journal of Social History</u> (Gr. Brit.) 5 (1971-1972):183-209.

Hodges, W. A. <u>Free Man of Color. The Autobiography of Willis Augustus Hodges</u> [Pre Civil War]. Knoxville, TN: University of Tennessee Press, 1982.

Hogan, William R. and Edwin A. Davis (eds.) <u>William Johnson's Natchez: The Antebellum Diary of a Free Negro</u>. Baton Rouge, LA: 1951.

Hopkins, L. T. The Negro Entry Book: A Document of Lancaster City's Antebellum Afro-American Community. <u>Journal of Lancaster County Hist. Society</u> 88 (1984):142-80.

Horton, James Oliver. <u>Black Bostonians: Family Life and Community</u>

Struggle in the Antebellum North. New York: Holmes & Meier, 1978.

Horton, James Oliver. Gender Conventions among Antebellum Free Blacks. Feminist Studies 12 (Spring 1986).

Jackson, L. P. Free Negro Labor and Property-Holding in Virginia, 1830-1860. New York: Atheneum, 1969.

Johnson, Michael P. and James L. Roark (eds.) No Chariot Let Down: Charleston's Free People of Color on the Eve of the Civil War. Chapel Hill, NC: University of North Carolina Press, 1984.

Johnson, W. B. Free Blacks in Antebellum Savannah: An Economic Profile. Georgia Historical Quarterly 64 (Winter 1980):418-431.

Kimmel, R. M. Free Blacks in Seventeenth-Century Maryland. Maryland Historical Magazine 71 (1976):19-25.

Lawrence-McIntyre, C. C. Free Blacks: A Troublesome and Dangerous Population in Antebellum America. Doctoral dissertation, State University of New York at Stony Brook, 1985. UMO # 8527923.

Linday, A. G. The Economic Conditions of Negroes in New York Prior to 1861. Journal of Negro History 6 (April 1921).

Littlefield, D. F., Jr. and A. Littlefield. The Beams Family: Free Blacks in Indian Territory. Journal of Negro History 60 (1976):16-35.

Litwack, L. F. The Federal Government and the Free Negro, 1790-1860. Journal of Negro History (October 1958).

Litwack, L. F. North of Slavery: The Negro in the Free States. Chicago: University of Chicago Press, 1961.

McClelland, P. D., and R. J. Zeckhauser. Demographic Dimensions of the New Republic: American Interregional Migration, Vital Statistics, and Manumissions, 1800-1860. New York: Cambridge University Press, 1982.

McRae, N. Blacks in Detroit, 1735-1833: The Search for Freedom and Community and Its Implications for Educators. Doctoral dissertation, University of Michigan, 1982. UMO # 8215046.

Miller, R. M. Georgia on Their Minds: Free Blacks and the African Colonization Movement in Georgia. Social Studies 17 (Winter 1978):349-362.

Neyland, L. The Free Negro in Florida. Negro Hist. Bulletin 29 (1965).

Oblinger, C. D. In Recognition of Their Prominence: A Case Study of the Economic and Social Backgrounds of an Ante-Bellum Negro Business and Framing Class in Lancaster County. Journal of the Lancaster County Historical Society 72 (1968):65-83.

Perdue, R. E. Black Laborers and Black Professionals in Early America, 1750-1830. New York: Vantage Press, 1975.

Perlman, D. The Free Negro in New York City. His Status and His Group Organizations, 1800-1850. Master's thesis, City College of New York, 1966.

Pingeon, F. D. Dissenting Attitudes Toward the Negro in New Jersey, 1837. New Jersey History 89 (1971):197-220.

Powell, F. L. J. A Study of the Structure of the Freed Black Family in Washington, D.C., 1850-1880. Doctoral dissertation, Catholic University of America, 1980. UMO # 8018913.

Powers, B. E., Jr. Black Charleston: A Social History 1822-1885. Doctoral dissertation, Northwestern University, 1982. UMO # 8225994.

Provine, D. The Economic Position of the Free Blacks in the District of Columbia 1800-1960. Journal of Negro History 58 (January 1973):61-72.

Rankin, D. C. The Forgotten People: Free People of Color in New Orleans, 1850-1870. Doctoral dissertation, John Hopkins University, 1976.

Rankin, D. C. The Politics of Caste: Free Colored Leadership in New Orleans during the Civil War, In: Robert R. Macdonald and others (eds.), Louisiana's Black Heritage, pp. 125-138. New Orleans: Louisiana State Museum, 1979.

Reichard, M. Black and White on the Urban Frontier: The St. Louis Community in Transition, 1800-1830 [Free Blacks and slaves]. Missouri Historical Society Bulletin 33 (1976):3-17.

Reinders, R. C. The Free Negro in the New Orleans Economy, 1850-1860. Louisiana History 6 (1965):273-85.

Richard, K. K. Unwelcome Settlers: Black and Mulatto Oregon Pioneers (Part 1). Oregon Historical Quarterly 84 (Spring 1983):29-55.

Richard, K. K. Unwelcome Settlers: Black and Mulatto Oregon Pioneers (Part II). Oregon Historical Quarterly 84 (Summer 1983):172-205.

Robinson, H. S. Some Aspects of the Free Negro Population of Washington, D.C., 1800-1862. Maryland Historical Magazine 64 (1969):43-64.

Rury, J. L. Philanthrophy, Self-Help, and Social Control: The New York Manumission Society and Free Blacks, 1785-1810. Phylon 46 (Fall 1985):231-41.

Schoen, H. The Free Negro in the Republic of Texas. Southwestern Historical Quarterly 40 (January 1937): 169-99.

Schweninger, L. The Free-Slave Phenomenon: James P. Thomas and the Black Community in Antebellum Nashville. Civil War History 22 (1976):293-307.

Schweninger, L. John H. Rapier, Sr.: A Slave and Freedman in the Ante-
    Bellum South. _Civil War History_ 20 (1974):23-34.

Senese, D. J. The Free Negro and the South Carolina Courts, 1790-1860.
    South Carolina Historical Magazine 68 (1967):140-53.

Taylor, Q. Slaves and Free Men: Blacks in the Oregon Country, 1840-1860.
    Oregon Historical Quarterly 83 (Summer 1982):153-70.

Tunnell, T. Free Negroes and the Freedmen: Black Politics in New Orleans
    during the Civil War. _Southern Studies_ 19 (Spring 1980):5-28.

Walker, J. E. K. _Free Frank: A Black Pioneer in the Antebellum Frontier_
    [Illinois and Kentucky]. Lexington, KY: University Press of
    Kentucky, 1983.

Walker, J. E. K. The Legal Status of Free Blacks in Early Kentucky, 1792-
    1825. _Filson Club History Quarterly_ 57 (October 1983):382-95.

White, Shane. 'We Dwell in Safety and Pursue Our Honest Callings': Free
    Blacks in New York City, 1783-1810. _Journal of American History_ 75
    (1988):445-70.

Wikramanayake, M. _A World in Shadow: The Free Black in Antebellum South
    Carolina_. Columbia, SC: University of South Carolina Press, 1973.

Woodson, Carter G. (ed.) _The Mind of the Negro as Reflected in Letters
    Written During the Crisis, 1800-1860_. New York: Russell, 1969
    (orig. 1926).

Woolfolk, G. R. The Free Negro and Texas, 1836-1860. _Journal of Mexican
    American History_ 3 (1973):49-75.

[See also section 34]

31. Ghetto

*If white capitalists who control trillions of dollars in this
country permit wretched whites to exist in places like
Appalachia, why does anyone think that black capitalists will
free their brothers in the ghetto?*

- Bayard Rustin, New York Times, August 26, 1973.

Adler, P. R. Watts: From Suburb to Black Ghetto. Doctoral
    dissertation, University of Southern California, 1977.

Baldwin, James. Harlem Ghetto. Commentary (February 1948).

Ballou, R. A. Even in 'Freedom's Birthplace'! The Development of
    Boston's Black Ghetto, 1900-1940 (2 vols.). Doctoral dissertation,
    University of Michigan, 1984. UMO # 8502760.

Baratz, S. S. The Unique Culture of the Ghetto. Center Magazine (July
    1969).

Bigham, J. E. Work, Residence, and the Emergence of the Black Ghetto in
    Evansville, Indiana, 1865-1900. Indiana Magazine of History 76
    (December 1980):287-318.

Blaut, J. M. Das Ghetto als Interne Neokolonie. Geographie in Ausbildung
    und Planung 5 (1976).

Blassingame, J. W. Before the Ghetto: The Making of the Black Community
    in Savannah, Georgia, 1865-1880. Journal of Social History 6
    (Summer 1973):463-88.

Browne, R. S. Cash Flow in a Ghetto Economy. Review of Black Political
    Economy (Winter/Spring 1971).

Clark, K. B. Dark Ghetto. An Analysis of the Dilemma of Social Power.
    New York: Harper & Row, 1965.

Collins, K. E. Black Los Angeles: The Maturing of the Ghetto, 1940-1950.
    Saratoga, CA: Century Twenty One, 1980.

Conant, R. R. Profits in the Ghetto. Doctoral dissertation, Columbia
    University, 1973.

Connolly, H. X. A Ghetto Grows in Brooklyn. New York: New York
    University Press, 1977.

Darden, Joe T. (ed.) The Ghetto: Readings with Interpretations.
    Port Washington, NY: Kennikat Press, 1981.

De Graaf, L. B. The City of Black Angels: Emergence of the Los Angeles
    Ghetto, 1890-1930. Pacific Historical Review 39 (1977):323-52.

Donaldson, O. F. To Keep Them in Their Place - A Socio-spatial Perspective on Race Relations in America. Doctoral dissertation, University of Washington, 1974.

Dozier, W. C. The Process by Which Public Policy Facilitated the Creation of the Black Ghetto. Master's thesis, California State University, Long Beach, 1979.

Drake, S. C. The Ghettoization of Negro Life, In: Louis A. Ferman and others (eds.), Negroes and Jobs, pp. 112-28. Ann Arbor: University of Michigan Press, 1968.

Dunbar Ortiz, R. The Reservation as a Social Enclave . Development and Socioeconomic Progress (Cairo, Egypt) 1 (January 1981):89-100.

Ensslen, Klaus. Das Ghetto in der afroamerikanischen Literatur nach 1945. In: Berndt Ostendorf (ed.), Amerikanische Getto-literatur: Zur Literatur ethnischer, marginaler und er unterdrückter Gruppen in Amerika, pp. 234-92. Darmstadt: Wissenschaftliche Buchges., 1984.

Ford, L. and E. Griffin. The Ghettoization of Paradise [San Diego]. Geographical Review 69 (April 1979):140-58.

Fusfeld, D. R. and T. Bates. The Political Economy of the Urban Ghetto. Carbondale, IL: Southern Illinois University Press, 1984.

Great Britain Foundation. Wong Ho Leun: An American Chinatown. 2 vols. 1987. The Foundation, 1236 Concord St., San Diego, CA 92106.

Hannerz, U. Research in the Black Ghetto: A Review of the Sixties. Journal of Asian and African Studies 9 (1974):139-59.

Hansberry, L. The Scars of the Ghetto. Monthly Review (February 1965).

Harris, D. J. The Black Ghetto as Colony: A Theoretical Critique and Alternative Formulation. Review of Black Political Economy (May-June 1972):505-22.

Harvey, D. Revolutionary and Counter-revolutionary Theory in Geography and the Problems of Ghetto Formation. Antipode 4 (1972).

Katzman, D. M. Before the Ghetto: Black Detroit in the Nineteenth Century. Urbana, IL: University of Illinois Press, 1973.

Kusmer, K. L. A Ghetto Takes Shape: Black Cleveland 1870-1930. Urbana, IL: University of Illinois Press, 1976.

Lacalle, J. J. From the Sun to the Ghetto: A Research Study of the Puerto Rican Youth Immigrant. Rochester NY: Liga Latino-Americana, 1969.

Lane, Winthrop D. Ambushed in the City. The Grim Side of Harlem. Survey Graphic 6 (March 1925):692-94, 713.

Lenz, Gunter H. Symbolic Space, Communal Rituals and the Surreality of the Urban Ghetto. _Callaloo_ 11 (Spring 1988).

Lyman, Stanford. Growing Up among Ghetto Dwellers. _In_: Paul C. Higgins
   and John M. Johnson (eds.), _Personal Sociology_. Westport, CT:
   Praeger, 1988.

McColl, R. W. Creating Ghettos: Manipulating Social Space in the Real
   World and the Classroom. _Journal of Geography_ 7 (November
   1972):496-502.

Ogbu, J. U. _Schooling in the Ghetto: An Ecological Perspective on
   Community and Home Influences_. January 1981. ERIC ED 252270.

Parachini, A. Chicago's Indian Ghetto, Where Hopes Slowly Die. _Chicago
   Sun-Times_ May 2, 1976.

Reynolds, Pamela. For Beleagured Ghettos, Another Blow: Store Flight.
   Boston Globe November 24, 1988. [California and elsewhere].

Rinehart, J. S. The Negro in a Congested Toledo Area. Master's thesis,
   Bowling Green State University, 1940.

Rose, H. M. _The Black Ghetto: A Spatial Behavioral Perspective_. New
   York: McGraw-Hill, 1971.

Rose, H. M., and H. McConnell. _The Geography of the Ghetto: Perceptions,
   Problems, and Alternatives_. De Kalb, IL: Northern Illinois
   University Press, 1972.

Saunders, M. S. The Ghetto: Some Perceptions of a Black Social Worker.
   Social Work 14 (1969):84-88.

Shapiro, W., and Others. The Ghetto: From Bad to Worse. _Time_ August
   24, 1987.

Spear, A. H. _Black Chicago: The Making of a Negro Ghetto, 1890-1920_.
   Chicago: University of Chicago Press, 1967.

Tabb, W. T. _The Political Economy of the Black Ghetto_. New York:
   Norton, 1970.

Taylor, T. Race and Class in the Urban Ghetto: An Interpretation. _In_:
   Rhoda Goldstein (ed.), _Black Life and Culture in the United States_,
   pp. 263-79. New York: Crowell, 1971.

Ward, D. The Emergence of Central Immigrant Ghettoes in American Cities:
   1840-1920. _Annals of the Association of American Geographers_ 58
   (1968).

Wheeler, J. O., and S. D. Brunn. An Agricultural Ghetto: Negroes in Cass
   County, Michigan, 1845-1968. _Geographical Review_ 59 (1969):310-29.

Wilson, W. J. _The Truly Disadvantaged: The Inner City, the Underclass,
   and Public Policy_. Chicago: University of Chicago Press, 1987.

Wright, C. D. Slums of Great Cities. Seventh Special Report of the U.S.
    Department of Labor. Washington, D.C.: 1894.

Ghetto Bibliography

Gaudio, R. and others (comps.) Ghetto: A Bibliography. Rochester, NY:
    St. John Fisher College Library, 1969.

Sharma, Prakash C. (comp.) Slum and Ghetto Studies: A Research
    Bibliography. Monticello, IL: Council of Planning Librarians, 1974.

[See also sections 6, 13, 15, 16, 20, 24, and 47]

32. Government and Minorities

*The handwriting is on the wall. ... Support for needy students
is either stable or slipping backwards. The day of government
commitments ensuring capable students the right to pursue
higher education is now drawing to a close.*

- Richard G. Hatcher, June 5, 1974.

Abbott, Martin. The Freedmen's Bureau in South Carolina, 1865-1872.
    Chapel Hill: University of North Carolina Press, 1967.

Atkins, T. I., and M. H. Sussman. Reaganisms, Reaganauts and the NAACP.
    Crisis 89 (January 1982):5-8.

Bee, R. L. Crosscurrents Along the Colorado: The Impact of Governmental
    Policy on the Quechan Indians. Tucson: University of Arizona Press,
    1981.

Bell, T. H. The Thirteenth Man. A Reagan Cabinet Memoir [Charge of
    racism among officials in U.S. Department of Education]. New York:
    Free Press, 1987.

Beltramo, T. J. Tax Abatement: Impact upon Public Education in a
    Selected Set of Schools in Wayne County [Michigan]. Doctoral
    dissertation, University of Michigan, 1987. UMO # 8720247.

Bentley, G. A History of the Freedmen's Bureau. New York: Octagon, 1970
    (orig. 1955).

Black, D. E. An Evaluation of Federal Contract Set-aside Goals in
    Reducing Socioeconomic Discrimination. Doctoral dissertation,
    American University, 1986. UMO # 8705000.

Bohmer, P. G. The Impact of Public Sector Employment on Racial Inequality:
    1950 to 1984. Doctoral dissertation, University of Massachusetts,
    1985. UMO # 8602614.

Brecher, C. Where Have All the Dollars Gone? Public Expenditures for
    Human Resource Development in New York City, 1961-1971. New York:
    Praeger, 1974.

Butler, R., and J. Heckman. The Government's Impact on the Labor Market
    Status. In: Leonard Hausman and others (eds.), Equal Rights and
    Industrial Relations. Madison, WI: Industrial Relations Research
    Association, 1977.

Carter, G. L. Local Police Force Size and the Severity of the 1960s Black
    Rioting. Journal of Conflict Resolution 31 (December 1987).

Chapman, A. E. The History of the Black Police Force and Court in the
    City of Miami. Doctoral dissertation, University of Miami, 1986.
    UMO # 8619500.

Colby, I. C. The Freedmen's Bureau: From Social Welfare to Segregation.
     Phylon 46 (Fall 1985):219-30.

Cole, O., Jr. Black Youth in the Program of the Civilian Conservation
     Corps for California, 1933-1942. Doctoral dissertation, University
     of North Carolina, 1986. UMO # 8711096.

Deloria, V., Jr. The Nations Within: The Past and Future of American
     Indian Sovereignty. New York: Pantheon, 1984.

Du Bois, W. E. B. [Don't scuttle W. P. A.]. Amsterdam News April 20,
     1940.

Eisinger, P. K. Black Employment in City Government, 1973-1980.
     Washington, D.C.: Joint Center for Political Studies, 1983.

Eisinger, P. K. Black Employment in Municipal Jobs: The Impact of Black
     Political Power. American Political Science Review (June 1982):380-
     392.

Ellison, W. James. Paul Robeson and the State Department. Crisis 84
     (May 1977):184-89.

Franklin, J. H., E. H. Norton and others. Black Initiative and
     Governmental Responsibility. Washington, D.C.: Joint Center for
     Poitical Studies, March 1987.

Granger, G. [Letter to Senator James Jackson of Georgia; March 23, 1802]
     [By Thomas Jefferson's postmaster general, deaaling with the
     "dangers" of equality in employing Blacks in the postal service.].
     Labor Notes 95 (January 1987):12.

Greenberg, S. B. Race and State in Capitalist Development. Comparative
     Perspectives. New Haven, CT: Yale Univesity Pres, 1980.

Greer, E. Racial Biases in the Property Tax System. Review of Radical
     Political Economy 7 (1975):22-31.

Guzda, H. P. Labor Department's First Program to Assist Black Workers
     [Division of Negro Economics, U.S. Department of Labor, 1917-1922].
     Monthly Labor Review 105 (June 1982):39-44.

Haley, Robert. Attitudes of Black Citizens in the City of East St. Louis
     Toward thier Police. Master's thesis, Western Illinois University,
     1987.

Harris, C. V. Reforms in Government Control of Negroes in Birmingham,
     Alabama, 1890-1920. Journal of Southern History 38 (November
     1972):567-600.

Kruman, M. W. Quotas for Blacks: The Public works Administration and the
     Black Construction Worker. Labor History 16 (1975):37-51.

Lang, J., and H. N. Scheiber. The Wilson Administration and the Wartime

Mobilization of Black Americans, 1917-1918. Labor History 10 (Summer 1969).

Levine, Richard R. Indian Fighters and Indian Reformers: Grant's Indian Peace Policy and the Conservative Consensus. Civil War History 31 (December 1985):329-50.

Levin, H. M. A Decade of Policy Developments in Improving Education and Training for Low-Income Populations. In: R. Haveman (ed.), Decade of Federal Antipoverty Programs. New York: Academic Press, 1977.

Lichten, E. A. Class Struggle and Fiscal Crisis: New York City and the Development of Austerity. Doctoral dissertation, City University of New York, 1981. UMO # 8203298.

Lichten, E. A. The Fiscal Crisis of New York City and the Development of Austerity. Insurgent Sociologist 9 (Fall 1979-Winter 1980):75-92.

Logan, A. Around City Hall. Stormy Weather [Racism and its reception in official quarters of New York City]. New Yorker (February 9, 1987).

Maume, D. J., Jr. Government Participation in the Local Economy and Race- and Sex-Based Earning Inequality. Social Problems 32 (February 1985).

Meier, A., and E. Rudwick. The Rise of Segregation in the Federal Bureaucracy, 1900-1930. Phylon (Summer 1967).

Mertz, P. E. New Deal Policy and Southern Rural Poverty. Baton Rouge, LA: 1978.

Murphy, T. P. Race-Base Accounting: Assigning the Costs and Benefits of a Racially Motivated Annexation. Urban Affairs Quarterly 14 (December 1978):169-194.

Neubeck, K. J. and J. L. Roach. Racism and Poverty Policies, pp. 153-164. In: Benjamin P. Bowser and Raymond G. Hunt (eds.), Impacts of Racism on White Americans. Beverly Hills, CA: Sage.

Patterson, William L. (ed.) We Charge Genocide: The Crime of Government Against the Negro People. New York: 1951.

Pear, R. Number of Blacks in Top Jobs in Administration Off Sharply. New York Times March 22, 1987.

Peebles-Wilkins, W. Reactions of Segments of the Black Community to the North Carolina Pearsall Plan, 1954-1966. Phylon 48 (June 1987):112-21.

Peroff, N. C. Menominee Drums: Tribal Termination and Restoration, 1954-1974. Norman: University of Oklahoma Press, 1982.

Persons, G. A. Reflections on Mayoral Leadership: The Impact of Changing Issues and Changing Times [Atlanta]. Phylon 46 (Fall 1985):205-18.

Rabinowitz, Howard N. The Conflict Between Blacks and the Police in the
    Urban South, 1865-1900. Historian 39 (November 1976):62-76.

Reed, M. E. Black Workers, Defense Industries, and Federal Agencies in
    Pennsylvania, 1941-1945. Labor History 27 (Summer 1986):356-84.

Russell, J. M. Politics, Municipal Services, and the Working Class in
    Atlanta, 1865 to 1890. Georgia Historical Quarterly 66 (Winter
    1982):467-91.

Schroeder, J. M. Equal Educational Opportunity: Examining Resource
    Distribution and Relative Need Characteristics of Schools Within a
    School System. Doctoral dissertation, University of North Carolina
    Chapel Hill, 1987. UMO # 8728423.

Schroeder, L. Property Tax Equalization Rates: Implications of Their Use
    in Tax Inequality Cases in the City of New York. American Journal of
    Economics and Sociology 40 (January 1981).

Skinner, H. Citizen Participation and Racism. Public Administration
    Review 32 (May-June 1972):210-211.

Stevenson, R. W. The Big Push for Pentagon Dollars [Minority suppliers of
    defense materials]. New York Times July 5, 1987.

Tabb, W. K. The Long Default: New York City and the Urban Fiscal Crisis.
    New York: Monthly Review Press, 1981.

Takagi, P. Tracing Racism in U.S. National Policies. Journal of
    Intergroup Relations 3 (September 1974):14-30.

Thornton, J. Mills, III. Fiscal Policy and the Failure of Radical
    Reconstruction in the Lower South. In: J. Morgan Kousser and James
    McPherson (eds.), Region, Race, and Reconstruction: Essays in Honor
    of C. Vann Woodward, pp. 349-94. New York: 1982.

Troyna, B. and J. Williams. Racism, Education and the State. London:
    Croom Helm, 1985.

U.S. Commission On Civil Rights, South Carolina Advisory Committee.
    Equality in Municipal Services in Mullins, South Carolina.
    Washington, D.C.: The Commission, January 1979.

Weyler, Rex. Blood of the Land: The Government and Corporate War Against
    the American Indian Movement. New York: Vintage Books, 1984.

[See also sections 1, 7, 11, 12, 17, 18, 25, 26, 29, 33, 35, 38, 44, 50,
    57, 59, 64, 71, 75, and 82]

33. Health

*... Almost 50 percent of infant deaths in the lowest
socioeconomic group are preventable.*

- U.S. Public Health Service, Infant Mortality Rates:
Socioeconomic Factors, March 1972.

Access of Hispanics to Health Care and Cuts in Services: A State-of-the-
Art Overview. American Journal of Public Health (May-June 1986).

Aday, Lu Ann and others. Health Care in the U.S.: Equitable for Whom?.
Beverly Hills, CA: Sage, 1980.

Alers, J. O. Puerto Ricans and Health: Findings from New York City. NY:
Hispanic Research Center, Fordham University, 1978.

Allen, Joyce E. and K. E. Gadson. Nutrient Consumption Patterns of Low-
Income Households. Washington, D.C.: U.S. Dept. of Agriculture,
Economic Research Service, 1983.

Anderson, Ronald and others (eds.). Equity in Health Services:
Empirical Analyses in Social Policy. Cambridge, MA: Ballinger,
1975.

Applebone, Peter. Two Nashville Hospitals Debate a Plan to Merge. New
York Times April 30, 1989. [Meharry/Hubbard Hospital and Nashville
Metropolitan General Hospital].

Arbab, D. M. and B. L. Weidner. Infectious Diseases and Field Water.
Supply and Sanitation among Migrant Farm Workers. American Journal
of Public Health 76 (1986):694-95.

Avery, K.T. The Dental Health of Children of Migrant and Seasonal
Agricultural Workers. Journal of School Health 45 (1975):24-26

Bailey, D. J. Health of Hispanics. In: The Hispanic Population of
the United States, p 89. Washington, D.C.: U.S. House of
Representatives, 1983.

Bayer, Ronald and others (eds.) In Search of Equity: Health Needs and
the Health Care System. New York: Plenum, 1983.

Beardsley, Edward H. Making Separate, Equal: Black Physicians and the
Problems of Medical Segregation in the Pre-World War II South.
Bulletin Hist. Medicine 57 (Fall 1983):382-96.

Beardsley, Edward H. A History of Neglect. Health Care for Blacks and
Mill Workers in the Twentieth-Century South. Knoxville: University
of Tennessee Press, 1988.

Black-White Differences in Health Status: Methods or Substance. Milbank
Quarterly 65 (1987):72-99 (supplement).

Blakeslee, Sandra. Race and Sex Are Found to Affect Access to Kidney Transplants. New York Times January 24, 1989.

Blendon, R. J. and others. Health Insurance for the Unemployed and Uninsured. National Journal 15 (May 28, 1983):1146-49.

Blum, Dona. The Widening Gap. The Incidence and Distribution of Infant Mortality and Low Birth Weight in the United States 1978-1982. Part II. Literature Review Washington, D.C.: Food Research and Action Center, June 5, 1984.

Blumstein, James F. Rationing Medical Resources: A Constitutional, Legal, and Policy Analysis. Texas Law Review 59 (1981). [See Rand E. Rosenblatt, below].

Bodenheimer, Thomas. Class Struggle in a Beleaguered Health System. In: Marlene Dixon and Thomas Bodenheimer (eds.), Health Care in Crisis, San Francisco, 1980.

Boone, Margaret S. Capital Crime. Black Infant Mortality in Ameria. Newbury Park, CA: Sage, 1989. [Washington, D.C.].

Bosley, A. Of Shamans and Physicians: Hmong and the U.S. Health Care System. Amherst, MA: Hampshire College, 1986.

Brennan, M. E. and R. Lancashire. Association of Childhood Mortality with Housing Status and Unemployment. Journal of Epidemiology and Community Health 32 (1978):28-33.

Brenner, Meyer Harvey. Estimating the Effects of Economic Change on National Health and Social Well-Being. Washington, D.C.: GPO, 1984.

Breslow, L. and B. Klein. Health and Race in California. American Journal of Public Health 61 (April 1971).

Brook, Robert H. and Cathleen N. Williams. Quality of Health Care for the Disadvantaged. Journal of Community Medicine 1 (Winter 1975):132-56.

Brooks, Charles H. Social, Economic, and Biologic Correlates of Infant Mortality in City Neighborhoods [Cleveland]. Journal of Health and Social Behavior 21 (March 1980):2-11.

Browman, Clifford L. The Health of Black Michigan. In: Frances S. Thomas (ed.), The State of Black Michigan: 1987, pp. 45-52. East Lansing: Urban Affairs Programs, Michigan State University, 1987.

Brown, C. Clayton. Health of Farm Children in the South, 1900-1950. Agricultural History 53 (January 1979):170-187.

Brown, J. Larry and H. F. Pizer. Living Hungry in America. NY: Macmillan, 1987.

Brozek, Josef M. and Beat Schurch (eds.) Malnutrition and Behavior:

Critical Assessment of Key Issues. New York: Van Nostrand Reinhold, 1985.

Bullough, V. L. and B. Bullough. Health Care for the Other Americans. New York: Appleton-Century-Crofts, 1982.

Callahan, Amy and Richard A. Knox. In Mass., AIDS Services for Hispanics Are Few. Boston Globe January 26, 1989.

Campbell, Gregory R. The Political Economy of Ill-Health: Changing Northern Cheyenne Health Patterns and Economic Underdevelopment, 1878-1930. Doctoral dissertation, University of Oklahoma, 1987. UMO # 8729870.

Canino, J. A. and others. The Puerto Rican Child in New York City: Stress and Mental Health. New York: Hispanic Research Center, Fordham University, 1980.

Cantazano, A. and R. J. Moser. Health Status of Refugees from Vietnam, Laos and Cambodia. Journal of the American Medical Association 247 (1982):1303-08.

Chermick, Martin. The Hawk's Nest Incident: America's Worst Industrial Disaster [Death of some 764 black workers from acute silicosis contracted while working on a tunnel in West Virginia in the 1930s]. New Haven, CT: Yale University Press, 1986.

Children's Defense Fund. The Health of America's Children: The Maternal and Child Health Data Book. Washington, D.C.: The Fund, 1987.

Chirimuuta, Richard and Rosalind. Aids, Africa and Racism. North Derby on Trent, England: Richard Chirimuuta, 1987. [Oscar Wilde Memorial Bookstore, 15 Christopher Street, New York, NY 10014].

Chirikos, Thomas N. and Gilbert Nestel. Further Evidence on the Economic Effects of Poor Health. Review of Economics and Statistics 67 (February 1985):61-69.

Chrisman, Noel J. and Arthur Kleinsman. Health Beliefs and Practices. In: Stephan Thernstrom (ed.), Harvard Encyclopedia of American Ethnic Groups, pp. 452-62 Cambridge, MA: Harvard University Press, 1980.

Christmas, June J. How Our Health System Fails Minorities. Civil Rights Digest 10 (Fall 1977):3-11.

Citizens' Commission on Hunger in New England. American Hunger Crisis, Poverty and Health in New England. Cambridge, MA: Harvard University School of Public Health, 1984.

Colburn Don. The Black-White Health Gap. Washington Post January 15, 1986.

Commonwealth of Massachusetts, Executive Office of Human Services, Department of Public Health. 1983 Massachusetts Nutrition Survey. Boston: The Department of Public Health, October 31, 1983.

236

Comptroller General of the United States. Indian Health Service Not Yet Distributing Funds Equitably Among Tribes. Washington, D.C.: General Accounting Office, 1982.

Conner, Douglas L. with John F. Marszalek. A Black Physician's Story: Bringing Hope to Mississippi Jackson: University Press of Mississippi, 1985.

Cooke, Michael A. The Health of Blacks During Reconstruction, 1862-1870. Doctoral dissertation, University of Maryland, 1983. UMO # 8402546.

Cooper, R. and others. Improved Mortality among U.S. Blacks, 1968-1978: The Role of Anti-Racist Struggle. International Journal of Health Services 11 (1981):511-22.

Cope, Nancy R. and Howard R. Hall. The Health Status of Black Women in the USA: Implications for Health Psychology and Behavioral Medicine. SAGE: A Scholarly Journal on Black Women 2 (Fall 1985):20-25.

Cornely, P. B. and Virginia M. Alexander. The Health Status of the Negro in the U.S. Journal of Negro Education 8 (July 1939).

Coye, M. J. The Health Effects of Agricultural Production: I. The Health of Agricultural Workers. Journal of Public Health Policy 6 (1985):349-70.

Crane, Stephen C. and Phyllis E. Kaye. The American Health Care System, 1986. In: Walter E. Wiest (ed.), Health Care and Its Costs. A Challenge for the Church, pp. 24-149. Latham, MD: University Press of America, 1988.

Crown, Victor. Chicago's Black Infant Mortality Rate Now First Among Nation's Big Cities. Chicago Reporter 16 (October 1987):8-9, 11. [See some statistical correction in Nov. 1987 issue].

Curtin, Philip D. African Health at Home and Abroad. Social Science History 10 (Winter 1986):369-98.

Daniels, Norman. Health Care Needs and Distributive Justice. Philosophy and Public Affairs 10 (1981).

Darity, William A. Socio-Economic Factors Influencing the Health Status of Black Americans. International Quarterly of Community Health and Education 7 (1986-1987):91-108.

Davies, J. E. and V. H. Freed. Minimizing Occupational Exposure to Pesticides: Epidemiological Overview. Residue Reviews 75 (1980):7-20.

Davis, Edith M. and others. Health Care for the Urban Poor: Directions for Policy. Totowa, NJ: Allandale, Osmun, 1982.

Davis, Karen and Cathy Schoen. Health and the War on Poverty: A Ten-Year Appraisal. Washington, D.C.: Brookings Institution, 1978.

237

Day, Barbara. Black-White Health Gap Becoming Even-Wider. _Guardian_ (NYC) May 4, 1988.

Deinard, Amos S. and T. Dunnigan. Hmong Health Care-Reflections on a Six-Year Experience. _International Migration Review_ 21 (Fall 1987):857-65.

Diangelis, A. G. and others. Dental Needs in Children of Mexican-American Migrant Workers. _Journal of School Health_ 51 (August 1981)

Division of Family Health Services. _Massachusetts Nutrition Survey_. Boston: Massachusetts Department of Public Health, October 1983.

Donabedian, Avedis and others. _Medical Care Chartbook_ (eighth edition). Ann Arbor, MI: Health Administration Press, 1986.

Douglas, Gordon K. Ethical Implications of the Revolution in Health Care Finance. _In_: Walter E. Wiest (ed.), _Health Care and Its Costs. A Challenge for the Church_, pp. 3-23. Latham, MD: University Press, of America, 1988.

Dwork, Deborah. Health Condition of Immigrant Jews on the Lower East Side of New York: 1880-1914. _Medical History_ 25 (January 1981):1-40.

Edelstein, Stuart J. _The Sickled Cell: From Myth to Molecules_. Cambridge, MA: Harvard University Press, 1986.

Edozien, J. C. and others. Medical Evaluation of the Special Supplemental Food Program for Women, Infants, and Children. _American Journal of Clinical Nutrition_ 32 (1979):677-92.

Epps, Charles H. The Black Practitioner: Challenges of the Future. _Journal of the National Medical Association_ 78 (May 1986):365-70.

Ernhart, Claire B. and others. Subclinical Lead Level and Developmental Deficit: Re-analyses of Data. _Journal of Learning Disabilities_ 18 (October 1985):475-79.

Etheridge, Elizabeth W. _The Butterfly Caste: A Social History of Pellagra in the South_. Westport, CT: Greenwood, 1972.

Expand Associates, Inc. _A National Conference on Health Policy, Planning, and Financing the Future of Health Care for Black America_. Hyattsville, MD: U.S. Dept. of Health, Education, and Welfare, National Center for Health Services Research, 1979.

Fein, Rashi. _Medical Care, Medical Costs. The Search for a Health Insurance Policy_. Cambridge, MA: Harvard University Press, 1986.

Fisher, Walter. Physicians and Slavery in the Antebellum Southern Medical Journal. _Journal of the History of Medicine and Allied Sciences_ (1968):36-49.

Fogel, Robert W. Nutrition and the Decline in Mortality since 1700: Some

Preliminary Findings. In: Stanley L. Engerman and Robert E. Gallman (eds.), Long Term Factors in American Economic Growth. Chicago, IL: University of Chicago Press, 1987.

Foster, Gaines M. The Limitations of Federal Health Care for Freedmen, 1862-1868. Journal of Southern History 48 (August 1982):348-72.

Freedberg, Louis. Young Blacks' Stress Turns into Suicide. National Catholic Reporter February 7, 1986.

Freund, D. A. Equality of Opportunity and the Demand for Medical Care by Race. Quarterly Review of Economic and Business 24 (Spring 1984).

Gamble, Vanessa N. The Negro Hospital Renaissance: The Black Hospital Movement, 1920-1940. Doctoral dissertation, University of Pennsylvania, 1987. UMO # 8714037.

Genovese, Eugene D. The Medical and Insurance Costs of Slaveholding in the Cotton Belt. Journal of Negro History 45 (1960):141-55.

Gibbs, Tyson and others. Nutrition and Slave Population: An Anthropological Examination. Medical Anthropology 4 (Spring 1980):175-262.

Ginsberg, Eli and others. From Health Dollars to Health Services: New York City, 1965-1985. Totowa, NY: Littlefield, Adams, 1986.

Gortmaker, Steven L. Medicaid and the Health Care of Children in Poverty; Some Successes and Failures. American Sociological Review 44 (1979):280-97.

Greenberg, R. S. The Impact of Prenatal Care in Different Social Groups. American Journal of Obstetrics and Gynecology 145 (1983):797-801.

Greene, S. B. and E. J. Salbert. Racial Differences in Medical Care Expenditures. Medical Care 17 (October 1979):1029-36.

Griffith, Ezra E. Blacks and American Psychiatry. Hospital and Community Psychiatry 37 (January 1986):5.

Gross, Jane. Cocaine and AIDS in New York Add to Infant Death. New York Times February 13, 1988.

Guendelman, S. Children's Health Needs in Seasonal Immigration. Journal of Public Health Policy 6 (1985):493-509.

Guerra, Fernando A. Hispanic Child Health Issues. Children Today 9 (September-October 1980):18-22.

Hanft, Ruth S. and others. Blacks and the Health Professions in the '80s: A National Crisis and a Time for Action. Atlanta, GA: Morehouse School of Medicine, June 1983.

Harsha, David and others. Densitometry and Anthropometry of Black and White Children. Human Biology 50 (1978):261-80.

Harwood, Alan. Ethnicity and Medical Care. Cambridge, MA: Harvard University Press, 1981.

Health Care for the Poor in 1986. Clearinghouse Review 20 (January 1987):1063-72.

Health Education and the Black Community. Atlanta, GA: Bureau of Health Education, Center for Disease Control, 1980.

The Health of Mexican Americans in South Texas. Austin: Lyndon B. Johnson School of Public Affairs, University of Texas, 1979.

Health of Minorities and Women Chart Book. Washington, D.C.: American Public Health Association, August 1982.

Health Professions Bureau. Minorities and Women in the Health Fields, 1984 edition. Washington, D.C.: GPO, 1984.

Health Resources Administration. Health of the Disadvantaged. Washington, D.C.: GPO, 1980.

Health Status of Minority Grooups. Integrateducation 17 (September-December 1979):50-59.

Hispanic Health Needs Committee. Hispanic Health Needs. Chicago, IL: Office of the Mayor, 1982.

Hogle, Janice and others. Ethnicity and Health: Puerto Ricans and Blacks in Hartford, Connecticut. Medical Anthropology 6 (1982):127-46.

Institute of Medicine. Health Care in a Context of Civil Rights. Washington, D.C.: National Academy Press, 1981.

Institute of Medicine, Committee on Health Care for Homeless People. Homelessness, Health and Human Needs. Washington, D.C.: National Academy Press, 1988.

Israel, Morton. Socioeconomic Correlates and Patterns of Repiratory Cancer Mortality Rates among Whites, Blacks, and Hispanics in New York City, 1979-1981. Doctoral dissertation, Columbia University, 1987. UMO # 8804217.

Jackson, Derrick Z. Blacks and Billboards: Killing Urge to Smoke and Drink. Boston Globe November 25, 1988.

Jacobs, Claude F. Strategies of Neighborhood Health - Care Among New Orleans Blacks: From Voluntary Association to Public Policy. Doctoral dissertation, Tulane University, 1980. UMO # 8109916.

Jacobsen, Richard J. Primary Care for the Urban Poor: A Case Study of Organization-Environment Relations [Hartford, CT]. Doctoral dissertation, University of Connecticut, 1987. UMO # 8728878.

James, W. H. Commentary: Black and White Birth Weights. Demography 22

(February 1985).

Johnson, E. H. and C. L. Browman. The Relationship of Anger Expression to Health Problems among Black Americans in a National Survey. _Journal of Behavioral Medicine_ 10 (1987):103-16.

Johnston, Helen L. _Health for the Nation's Harvesters: A History of the Migrant Health Program in Its Economic and Social Setting._ South Bend, IN: National Migrant Worker's Council, 1985.

Jones, Enrico E. and S. J. Korchin (eds.) _Minority Mental Health._ NY: Praeger, 1982.

Jones, James M. _Bad Blood. The Tuskegee Syphilis Experiment_ [Using Blacks in "experiment," in Macon County, Alabama]. Riverside, NJ: Free Press, 1981.

Jones, Woodrow, Jr. and Mitchell F. Rice (eds.) _Health Care Issues in Black America. Policies, Problems, and Prospects._ Westport, CT: Greenwood, 1987.

Kadin, Miriam L. _Modernization and the Social Inequality of Death in the United States, 1910-1970._ Doctoral dissertation, Brown University, 1982.

Kaltenbach, Charles. _Health Problems of the Navajo Area and Suggested Intervention._ 1975 Navajo Health Authority, Box 643, Window Rock, AZ 86515.

Kamara, J. Lawrence. The Bio-Social Paradox in the Black Community: Life Gets Longer But Not Healthier. _Omega_ 9 (1978-79):301-12.

Kendrick, Ernest A. and others. A Racial Minority: Black Americans and Mental Health Care. _American Journal of Social Psychiatry_ 3 (Spring 1983): 11-18.

Kernodle, Ruth. _Appetite and Hunger among Southern Negro Children._ Master's thesis, Alabama Polytechnic Institute, 1929.

Kerr, Peter. Rich vs. Poor: Drug Patterns Are Diverging. _New York Times_ August 30, 1987.

King, Haitung and Frances Locke. Health Effects of Migration: U.S. Chinese In and Outside of Chinatown. _International Migration Review_ 21 (Fall 1987):555-75.

Kiple, Dahila de S. _Darwin and Medical Perceptions of the Black: A Comparative Study of the United States and Brazil, 1871-1918._ Doctoral dissertation, Bowling Green State Universtiy, 1987. UMO # 8720070.

Kipple, Kenneth F. (ed.). _The African Exchange Toward a Biological History of Black People._ Durham, NC: Duke University Press, 1987.

Kipple, Kenneth F. and V. H. King. _Another Dimension to the Black_

Diaspora: Diet, Disease, and Racism. New York: Cambridge University Press, 1981.

Kipple, Kenneth F. and Virginia H. Kiple. Slave Child Mortality: Some Nutritional Answers to a Perennial Puzzle. Journal of Social History 10 (March 1977):284-309.

Knick, Stanley G. Growing Up Down Home: Health and Growth in the Lumbee Nation. Doctoral dissertation, Indiana University, 1986. UMO # 8617756. [Robeson County, NC].

Knox, Richard. Hub Infant Deaths Up 32% [Principally an increase in Black infants' deaths in Boston in 1985]. Boston Globe February 9, 1987.

Koba Associates. The Treatment Practices of Black Physicians. Hyattsville, MD: Office of Health Resources Opportunity, Health Resources Administration, 1979.

Kosa, John and Irving K. Zola. Poverty and Health: A Sociological Analysis. Cambridge, MA: Harvard University Press, 1975.

Krieger, Nancy and Mary Bassett. The Health of Black Folk: Disease, Class, and Ideology in Science. Monthly Review 38 (July-August 1986):74-85.

Kristof, Nicholas D. Health Care for Native Americans Strapped. Washington Post August 9, 1982.

Labarthe, D. and others. Health Effects of Modernization in Palau. American Journal of Epidemiology 98 (1973):161-74.

Lansdown, Richard and William Yule (eds). Lead Toxicity: History and Environmental Impact. Baltimore, MD: Johns Hopkins University Press, 1986.

Leary, Warren E. Blacks' Lifespan Falls for 2nd Consecutive Year. New York Times December 20, 1988.

Le Grand, J. Inequalities in Health: Some International Comparisons. European Economic Review 31 (February-March 1987).

Lee, Anne S. and Everett S. Lee. The Health of Slaves and the Health of Freedmen: A Savannah Study. Phylon 38 (June 1977):170-80.

Legan, Marshall S. Disease and the Freedmen in Mississippi During Reconstruction. Journal of the History of Medicine and Allied Science 28 (July 1973):257-67.

Leim, R. and P. Rayman. Health and Social Costs of Unemployment. American Psychologist (1982):116-1123.

Leinwand, Gerald. Hunger and Malnutrition in America. New York: Watts, 1985.

Littlefield, Carla and Charles L. Stout. A Survey of Colorado's Migrant

Farmworkers: Access to Health Care. <u>International</u> <u>Migration</u> <u>Review</u>
21 (Fall 1987):688-708.

Loo, Chalsa M. and Connie Youn Yu. Pulse on San Francisco's Chinatown:
Health Service Utilization and Health Status. <u>Amerasia</u> <u>Journal</u> 11
(Spring-Summer 1984):55-73.

Loslier, L. Dispantes socio-spatioles de mortalite a Porto-Rico.
<u>Canadian</u> <u>Journal</u> <u>of</u> <u>Developmental</u> <u>Studies</u> 8 (1987). [English
summary included].

Loth, Renee. When Will We Stop Poisoning Our Children? [Lead-paint
poisoning] <u>Boston</u> <u>Globe</u> <u>Magazine</u> February 21, 1988.

Louis Harris and Associates. <u>Access</u> <u>to</u> <u>Health</u> <u>Care</u> <u>Services</u> <u>in</u> <u>the</u> <u>United</u>
<u>States:</u> <u>1982</u>. New York: The Author, 1982.

McBride, David. <u>Black</u> <u>Health</u> <u>Care</u> <u>Labor</u> <u>and</u> <u>the</u> <u>Philadelphia</u> <u>Medical</u>
<u>Establishment:</u> <u>1910-1965</u>. Doctoral dissertation, Columbia
University, 1981. UMO # 8327255.

McBride, David. <u>Integrating</u> <u>the</u> <u>City</u> <u>of</u> <u>Medicine:</u> <u>Blacks</u> <u>In</u> <u>Philadephia</u>
<u>Health</u> <u>Care,</u> <u>1910-1965</u>. Philadelphia, PA: Temple University Press,
1989.

McCracken, Robert D. Growth and Nutritional Status of Migrant Farmworker
Preschool Children: Are the Programs Working? [Colorado]. <u>Farmworker</u>
<u>Journal</u> 1 (Winter 1978-79):4-20.

McIntosh, John L. and John F. Santos. Suicide Among Native Americans: A
Compilation of Findings. <u>Omega:</u> <u>Journal</u> <u>of</u> <u>Death</u> <u>and</u> <u>Dying</u> 11
(1980-1981):303-16.

McMahon, Sarah. Provisions Laid Up for the Family: Toward a History of
Diet in New England, 1650-1850. <u>Historical</u> <u>Methods</u> 14 (WInter
1981):22-30.

Malgady, Robert G. and others. Ethnocultural and Linguistical Bias in
Mental Health Evaluation of Hipanics. <u>American</u> <u>Psychologist</u> 42
(March 1987):228-34.

Margo, Robert and Richard Steckel. The Height of American Slaves: New
Evidence on Slave Nutrition and Health. <u>Social</u> <u>Science</u> <u>History</u> 6
(1982):516-38.

Markides, Kyriakos S. Mortality among Minority Populations: A Review of
Recent Patterns and Trends. <u>Public</u> <u>Health</u> <u>Reports</u> 98 (May-June
1983):252-60.

Markides, Kyriakos S. and H. P. Hazuda. Ethnicity and Infant Mortality in
Texas. <u>Social</u> <u>Biology</u> 27 (1980):261-77.

Maulsby, Maxie C., Jr. A Historical View of Blacks' Distrust of
Psychiatry, pp. 39-55 <u>in</u> Samuel M. Turner and Russell T. Jones
(eds.), <u>Behavior</u> <u>Modification</u> <u>in</u> <u>Black</u> <u>Populations</u>. NY: Plenum

Press, 1982.

Maxwell, Joan. The Prevention of Prematurity: A Strategy to Reduce Infant Mortality in the District of Columbia. November 1982. ERIC ED 224 593.

May, Philip A. Suicide Among American Indian Youth: A Look at the Issues. Children Today (July-August 1987):22-25.

Mollica Richard F. and F. Redlich. Equity and Changing Patient Characteristics, 1950-1975. Archives of General Psychiatry 37 (November 1980):1251-63.

Mollica, Richard F. and others. Equity and the Psychiatric Care of the Black Patient, 1950 to 1975. Journal of Nervous and Mental Diseases 168 (1980):279-286.

Monmaney, Terence and others. A Black Health Crisis. Newsweek July 13, 1987.

Montagu, Ashley. Sociogenic Brain Damage. American Anthropologist 74 (October 1972):1045-61.

Moses, M. Pesticides, pp. 547-71 in W. N. Rour (ed.), Environmental and Occupational Medicine. Boston, MA: Little, Brown, 1983.

National Academy of Sciences. The Future of Public Health. Washington, D.C.: National Academy Press, 1988.

National Center for Health Statistics. Health Indicators for Hispanic, Black, and White Americans: Data from the National Health Survey. Washington, D.C.: DHHS, 1984.

Navarro, Vicente. Crisis, Health and Medicine: A Social Critique. London: Tavistock, 1986.

Neighbors, Harold W. Ambulatory Medical Care among Black Americans: The Hospital Emergency Rooms. Journal of the National Medical Association 78 (April 1986):275-82.

Off to a Poor Start: Infant Health in Rural America. Washington, D.C.: Public Voice for Food and Health Policy, December 1988.

Office of Research and Improvement. Youth Indicators 1988: Trends in the Well-Being of American Youth. Washington, D.C.: U.S. Department of Education, 1988.

Omishakin, M. Ademola. Assessment of Health Needs of Black Agricultural Workers in Mid-Delta of Mississippi, U.S.A. Journal of the Royal Society of Health 103 (1983):239-41.

Omishakin, M. Ademola. The Health Needs of Black Agricultural Workers in Mid-Delta Mississippi. Phylon 43 (December 1982):344-49.

Orr, Suzanne T. and Arden Miller. Utilization of Health Services by Poor

244

Children Since Advent of Medicaid. <u>Medical Care</u> 19 (June 1981).

Outka, Gene. Social Justice and Equal Access to Health Care. <u>In</u>: Robert
    Veatch and Roy Branson (eds.), <u>Ethics and Health Policy</u>, pp. 79-88.
    Cambridge, MA: Ballinger, 1976.

Owan, Tom Choken and others (eds.). <u>Southeast Asian Mental Health:
    Treatment, Prevention, Services, Training, and Research</u>. Rockville,
    MD: National Institute of Mental Health, 1985.

Peck, R. E. and others. Nutritional Status of Southeast Asian Refugee
    Children. <u>American Journal of Public Health</u> 71 (1981):1144-48.

Pless, I. B. and R. J. Haggerty. Child Health: Research in Action, pp.
    206-35, In: <u>Children, Youth, and Families</u>, R. N. Rapoport (ed.),
    NY: Cambridge University Press, 1985.

Pope, Clayne L. Native Adult Mortality in the U.S.: 1770-1870. <u>In</u>:
    Robert W. Fogel (ed.), <u>Long-Term Changes in Nutrition and the
    Standard of Living</u>, pp. 76-85. Berne, 1986.

Porter, Veneita. Minorities and HIV Infection. <u>In</u>: <u>New England Journal
    of Public Policy</u>, (May 1988).

Postell, W. D. <u>The Health of Slaves in Southern Plantations</u>. Baton
    Rouge: Louisiana State University Press, 1951.

Powell-Griner, E. Differences in Infant Mortality among Texas Anglos,
    Hispanics, and Blacks. <u>Social Science Quarterly</u> 69 (June 1988).

Puckrein, Gary A. Climate, Health and Black Labor in the English
    Americas. <u>Journal of American Studies</u> 13 (1979):179-93.

Rabinowitz, Howard N. From Exclusion to Segregation: Health and Welfare
    Services for Southern Blacks, 1865-1890. <u>Social Service Review</u> 48
    (1974):327-54.

Ransford, H. Edward. Rare Heart Disease Worry and Health Protective
    Behavior. <u>Social Science and Medicine</u> 22 (1986):1355-62.

Raphael, Alan. Health and Social Welfare of Kentucky Black People, 1865-
    1870. <u>Societas</u> 2 (Spring 1971):143-57.

Rahbar, F. and others. Prenatal Factors Affecting Perinatal Mortality in
    Blacks. <u>Journal of the National Medical Association</u> 74 (1982):949-
    52.

Rhoades, Everett R. Barriers to Health Care: The Unique Problems Facing
    American Indians. <u>Civil Rights Digest</u> 10 (Fall 1977):25-31.

Ries, Peter W. <u>Health Characteristics According to Family and Personal
    Income, United States</u>. Washington, D.C.: GPO, 1985.

Rikard, Marlene Hunt. An Experiment in Welfare Capitalism: The Health
    Care Services of the Tennessee Coal, Iron and Railroad Company.

Journal of Economic History 45 (June 1985):467-70. [Birmingham; includes schools].

Roberts, Robert E. and Eun Sul Lee. The Health of Mexican Americans: Evidence from the Human Population Laboratory Studies. *American Journal of Public Health* 70 (April 1980):375-84.

Rosenberg, Charles E. *The Care of Strangers. The Rise of America's Health Care System*. New York: Basic Books, 1987.

Rosenblatt, Rand E. Rationing 'Normal' Health Care: The Hidden Legal Issues. *Texas Law Review* 59 (1981). [See James F. Blumstein, above].

Rousey, Dennis C. Yellow Fever and Black Policemen in Memphis: A Post-Reconstruction Anomaly. *Journal of Southern History* 51 (August 1985):357-74.

Ruiz, Pedro. The Minority Patient. *Community Mental Health Journal* 21 (Fall 1985):208-16.

Sakala, Carol. Migrant and Seasonal Farmworkers in the United States: A Review of Health Hazards, Status, and Policy. *International Migration Review* 21 (Fall 1987):659-87.

Salmon, Warren J. Monopoly Capital and the Reorganization of the Health Sector. *Review of Radical Political Economics* 9 (1977).

Savitt, Todd L. Black Health on the Plantation: Masters, Slaves, and Physicians, In: *Sickness and Health in America* (second ed.), Judith W. Leavitt and Ronald L. Numbers (eds.), Madison: University of Wisconsin Press, 1985.

Savitt, Todd L. *Medicine and Slavery: The Disease and Health Care of Blacks in Antebellum Virginia*. Urbana: University of Illinois Press, 1978.

Savitt, Todd L. Politics in Medicine: The Georgia Freedmen's Bureau and the Organization of Health Care, 1865-1866. *Civil War History* 28 (March 1982):45-64.

Savitt, Todd L. The Use of Blacks for Medical Experimentation and Demonstration in the Old South. *Journal of Southern History* 48 (August 1982):331-48.

Savitt, Todd L. and James Harvey Young (eds.) *Disease and Distinctiveness in the American South*. Knoxville: University of Tennessee Press, 1988.

Scham, Max. *Blacks and American Medical Care*. Minneapolis: University of Minnesota Press, 1974.

Secretary's Task Force on Black and Minority Health. *Report* Washington, D.C.: U.S. Department of Health and Human Services, 1985.

1940-1970. Demography 12 (1975):1-19.

Shryock, Richard H. Medical Practice in the Old South. Southern Atlantic
     Quarterly 29 (April 1930):172-82.

Slesinger, Doris P. Racial and Residential Differences in Preventive
     Medical Care for Infants in Low-Income Populations. Rural Sociology
     45 (Spring 1980):69-90.

Smith, Daniel Scott. Differential Mortality in the United States before
     1900. Journal of Interdisciplinary History 13 (Spring 1983):736-46.

Smith, G. and others. The Health Status of a Subgroup of Migrant American
     Children: The Role of a Medical Center as a Service and Educational
     Institution in the Community. Clinical Pediatrics 17 (1978):900-1003.

Sotomayor, Marta (ed.) Hispanic Mosaic: A Public Health Service
     Perspective ... 1st Annual Forum on the Status of Hispanic Health.
     Bethesda, MD: Public Health Service, Hispanic Employees
     Organization, 1984.

Southern Regional Council. Hungry Children. Atlanta, GA: ???Council,
     1967.

Spaights, Ernest and Gloria Simpson. Some Unique Causes of Black Suicide.
     Psychology: A Quarterly Journal of Human Behavior 23 (1986):1-5.

Starr, Paul. Health Care for the Poor: The Past Twenty Years. In:
     Fighting Poverty: What Works and What Doesn't, pp. 106-32.
     Cambridge, MA: Harvard University Press, 1986.

Steckel, Richard H. Birth Weights and Infant Mortality among American
     Slaves. Explorations in Economic History 23 (April 1986).

Steckel, Richard H. A Dreadful Childhood: The Excess Mortality of
     American Slaves. Social Science History 10 (Winter 1986):427-65.

Steckel, Richard H. A Peculiar Population: The Nutrition, Health, and
     Mortality of American Slaves from Childhood to Maturity. Journal of
     Economic History 46 (September 1986):721-41.

Stevens, William K. Diarrhea Kills Surprising Rate of Young. New York
     Times December 9, 1988.

Sue, Stanley and James K. Morishima. The Mental Health of Asian
     Americans. San Francisco, CA: Jossey-Bass, 1982.

Suerlick, Alan. Blacks in Medicine Face Drawbacks [Tampa, Florida].
     Tampa Tribune January 2, 1984.

Sunseri, Paul A. Racial Bias in the Diagnosis of Schizophrenia among
     Blacks. Master's thesis, California State University, Sacramento,
     1988.

Thomas, James A. and James E. Dobbins. The Color Line and Social Distance in the Genesis of Essential Hypertension. _Journal of the National Medical Association_ 78 (June 1986):532-36.

Torchia, Marion M. Tuberculosis among American Negroes; Medical Research on a Racial Disease, 1830-1950. _Jr. Hist. Medicine Allied Sci._ 32 (July 1977):252-79.

Traumer, Joan B. The Chinese as Medical Scapegoats in San Francisco, 1870-1905. _California History_ 57 (Spring 1978):70-87.

Turshen, Meredeth. The Struggle for Health. _In:_ Robert Cherry and others (eds.), _The Imperiled Economy_, Vol 2. New York: Union for Radical Political Economics, 1988.

Twining, David C. _The Politics of Health Care Reform: Health Planning for the Poor in Cleveland, 1960-1982_. Doctoral dissertation, Case Western Reserve University, 1988. UMO # 8819886.

U.S. Commission on Civil Rights. _Civil Rights Issues in Health Care Delivery_. Washington, D.C.: The Commission, 1981.

U.S. Congress, 90th, 1st session, Senate, Committee on Labor and Public Welfare, Subcommittee on Labor and Public Welfare. _Hunger and Malnutrition in America. Hearings._ Washington, D.C.: GPO, 1967.

U.S. Congress, 96th, 1st session, Senate, Select Committee on Indian Affairs. _Indian Health: Hearing_. Washington, D.C.: GPO, 1979.

U.S. Congress, 97th, 1st session, Senate, Select Committee on Indian Affairs. _Impact of Fiscal Year 1982. Budget Reductions on Indian Health Service. Hearings...._. Washington, D.C.: GPO, 1982.

U.S. Congress, 98th, 1st session, House of Representatives, Select Committee on Children, Youth, and Families. _Prevention Strategies for Healthy Babies and Healthy Children_. Washington, D.C.: GPO, 1983.

U.S. Congress, 98th, 2nd session, House of Representatives, Committee on Energy and Commerce, Subcommittee on Health and Environment. _Indian Health Care: An Overview of the Federal Government Role_. Washington, D.C.: GPO, 1984.

U.S. Congress, 98th, 2nd session, House of Representatives, Committee on Energy and Commerce, Subcommittee on Health and the Environment and the Subcommittee on Oversight and Investigations. _Infant Mortality Rate: Failure to Close the Black-White Gap. Hearing ..._ Washington, D.C.: GPO, 1984.

U.S. Congress, 98th, 2nd session, House of Representatives, Committee on Interior and Insular Affairs. _Indian Health Care Improvement Act Amendments of 1984: Hearings ..._ Washington, D.C.: GPO, 1984.

U.S. Congress, 98th, 2nd session, Senate, Committee on Appropriations, Subsommittee on Departments of Labor, Health and Human Services, Education, and Related Agencies. _Community Health Care in_

<u>Mississippi: Hearing ...</u> Washington, D.C.: GPO, 1986.

U.S. Congress, 98th, 2nd session, Senate, Committee on Finance,
Subsommitte on Health. <u>Health Care for the Economically
Disadvantaged - II: Hearings ...</u> Washington, D.C.: GPO, 1985.

U.S. Department of Health and Human Services, Public Health Service,
Health Resources Administration. <u>Health of the Disadvantages, Chart
Book II</u>. Washington, D.C.: The Department, September 1980.

U.S. Department of Health and Human Services. <u>Secretary's Task Force on
Black and Minority Health</u>, Vol. 3: <u>Hispanic Health Issues</u>.
Washington, D.C.: DHHS, 1986.

U.S. Department of Health, Education, and Welfare. <u>The Nation's Youth. A
Chart Book</u>. Children's Bureau Pub. No. 460. Washington, D.C.: GPO,
1969.

U.S. President's Commission for the Study of Ethical Problems in Medicine
and Biomedical and Behavioral Research. <u>Securing Access to Health
Care: A Report on the Ethical Implications of Differences in the
Availability of Health Services</u>. 3 vols. Washington, D.C.: March
1983.

U.S. Public Health Service. <u>Differentials in Health Characteristics by
Color. United States, July 1965-June 1967</u>. Washington, D.C.: GPO,
October 1969.

U.S. Public Health Service. <u>Minority Health Chart Book</u>. Washington,
D.C.: HEW, 1974.

Van Duesen, John M. Health/Mental Health Studies of Indochinese Refugees:
A Critical Overview. <u>Medical Anthropology</u> 6 (1982):231-52.

Ventura, Stephanie J. <u>Trends in Teenage Childbearing, United States,
1970-81: An Analytical Review of Recent Trends and Differentials in
Childbearing by Teenagers</u>. Washington, D.C.: GPO, 1984.

Vivo, Paquita (ed.) <u>Forum on the Status of Hispanic Health</u>. Rockville,
MD: Public Health Service, 1979.

Vivo, Paquita (ed.) <u>International Year of tbe Child: The United States
Hispanic Health Perspective</u>. Rockville, MD: Public Health Service,
1980.

Walter, J. P. and W. H. Leahy. Demand for Medical Services by Deprived
Urban Youth in North and South America. <u>American Economist</u> 27 (Fall
1983).

Warner, David. <u>The Health of Mexican-Americans in South Texas</u>. Austin:
University of Texas, Lyndon B. Johnson School of Public Affairs,
1979.

Wasserstrom, R. F. and R. Wiles. <u>Field Duty: U.S. Farmworkers and
Pesticide Safety</u>. Washington, D.C.: World Resource Institute, 1985.

Weisbord, Robert G. Genocide? Birth Control and the Black American.
    Westport, CT: Greenwood, 1975.

White, Ernestine H. Health and the Black Person. American Journal of
    Nursing 74 (October 1974):1839-41.

Wilk, V. A. The Occupational Health of Migrant and Seasonal Farmworkers
    in the United States. Washington, D.C.: Farworker Justice Fund,
    1986.

Wilkerson, Isabel. Infant Mortality: Frightful Odds in Inner City. New
    York Times June 26, 1987.

Zavaleta, Antonio N. Federal Assistance and Mexican American Health
    Status in Texas. Agenda 11 (January-February 1981):19-25.

Zee, Paul and others. Nutrition and Poverty Preschool Children. Journal
    of the American Medical Association 213 (1970):739-49.

Zee, Paul and others. Nutrition Improvement of Poor Urban Preschool
    Children. A 1983-1977 Comparison. Journal of the American Medical
    Association 253 (June 14, 1985):3269-72.

Zee, Paul and Marina De Leon. The Nutritional Status of Preschool
    Children in a Memphis Innercity Area. May 1979. ERIC ED 174 716.

Zelnick, Melvin. Age Patterns of Mortality of American Negroes: 1900-02
    to 1959-61. Journal of the American Statistical Association 64
    (June 1969):433-46.

Health Bibliography

Danner, Vinnie M. (comp.) A Bibliography of Published and Unpublished
    Materials on the Health Status of Blacks, Minorities, and the Poor.
    Nashville, TN: Center for Health Care Research, Meharry Medical
    College, 1972.

Davis, Lenwood G. (comp.) A History of Public Health, Health Problems,
    Facilities and Services in the Black Community: A Working
    Bibliography. [Exchange Bibliography No. 844.] Monticello, IL:
    Council of Planning Librarians, 1975.

Davis, Lenwood (comp.) A History of Selected Diseases in the Black
    Community: A Working Bibliography. Monticello, IL: Council of
    Planning Librarians, 1976.

Davis, Morris E. and Andrew Roland (comp.) The Occupational Health of
    Black Workers: A Bibliography. Monticello, IL: Vance
    Bibliographies, 1980.

Du Bois, W. E. B. (comp.) Bibliography of Negro Health and Physique. In:
    The Health and Physique of the Negro American, pp.6-13, Atlanta, GA:

250

Atlanta University Press, 1906.

Kelso, Dianne R. and Carolyn L. Attneave (comps.) Bibliography of North
    American Indian Mental Health. Westport, CT: Greenwood, 1981.

Kumabe, Kazuye T. and Yvonne Bickerton (comps.) Ethnocultural Factors in
    Social Work and Health Care: A Selected Annotated Bibliography.
    Honolulu: University of Hawaii, School of Social Work, 1982.

[See also sections 5, 6, 23, 35, and 83]

34. History

The only events in the history of this country which I think
deserve to be commemorated are the organization of the Anti-
Slavery Society and the insurrections of Nat Turner and John
Brown.

John S. Rock, Liberator, March 16, 1860.

Acuña, Rodolfo. Occupied America: A History of Chicanos (third edition).
New York: Harper and Row, 1988.

Abzug, Robert H. and Stephen E. Maizlish (eds.) New Perspectives on Race
and Slavery in America: Essays in Honor of Kenneth M. Stampp.
Lexington: University Press of Kentucky, 1986.

Adams, Terrence G. Racism in Perspective. Master's thesis, University of
Northern Iowa, 1980.

Alcock, Donald G. A Study in Continuity: Maury County, Tennessee, 1850-
1870. Doctoral dissertation, University of Southern California,
1985.

Allen, Ernest, Jr. Afro-American Identity: Reflections on the Pre-Civil
War Era. Contributions in Black Studies No. 7 (1985-1986).

Allen, Robert L. Black Awakening in Capitalist America: An Analytic
History. New York: Doubleday, 1969.

Allen, Robert L. Reluctant Reformers: Racism and Social Reform Movements
in the United States (Revised edition). Washington, D.C.: Howard
University Press, 1983.

Allen, Theodore. '... They Would Have Destroyed Me': Slavery and the
Origins of Racism. Radical America 9 (May-June 1975).

Alvarez, Rodolfo. The Psycho-historical and Socio-economic Development of
the Chicano Community in the United States. Social Science Quarterly
53 (March 1973):920-42.

Anderson, Eric. Race and Politics in North Carolina, 1872-1901: The
Black Second. Baton Rouge: Louisiana State University Press, 1981.

Anderson, James D. Secondary School History Textbooks and the Treatment
of Black History. In: Darlene Clark Hine (ed.), The State of Afro-
American History: Past, Present, and Future. Baton Rouge:
Louisiana State University Press, 1986.

Anderson, Jervis. This Was Harlem: A Cultural Portrait, 1900-1950. NY:
Farrar, 1982.

Anderson, Stuart. Race and Rapprochement: Anglo-Saxonism and Anglo-
American Relations 1895-1904. Rutherford, NJ: Fairleigh Dickinson

University, 1981.

Anthony, Arthe A. The Negro Creole Community in New Orleans, 1880-1920:
    An Oral History. Doctoral dissertation, University of California,
    Irvine, 1978. UMO # 7906396

Aptheker, Herbert. Racism and Historiography. Political Affairs May,
    1970.

Arendt, Hannah. Race Thinking Before Racism, Chapter 6 in The Origin of
    Totalitarianism. New York: 1951.

Armstead, Myra B. Y. The History of Blacks in Resort Towns: Newport,
    Rhode Island and Saratoga Springs, New York, 1870-1930.
    Doctoral dissertation, University of Chicago, 1987.

Asmus, Pamela K. The Rise and Fall of the Anglo-Saxon Myth in the United
    States, 1770-1954. Doctoral dissertation, Brown University, 1987.
    UMO # 8715447.

Axtell, James. After Columbus. Essays in the Ethnohistory of Colonial
    North America. New York: Oxford University Press, 1988.

Axtell, James. Colonial America without the Indians: Counterfactual
    Reflections. Journal of American History 73 (1987):981-86.

Axtell, James. Europeans, Indians, and the Age of Discovery in American
    History Textbooks. American Historical Review 92 (June 1987):621-
    32.

Axtell, James. Forked Tongues: Moral Judgments in Indian History.
    Perspectives: AHA Newsletter 25 (February 1987):10. 12-13.

Bacharach, Walter Z. The Development of the Race Theory From the View of
    Ideology Toward the Instrument of Political Action - From Chamberlain
    to Hitler. Tel-Aviv: Tel-Aviv University, 1973.

Bailey, Garrick A. and Roberta G. Bailey. A History of the Navajos: The
    Reservation Years. Santa Fe, NM: School of American Research Press,
    1986.

Barrett, James R. Unity and Fragmentation: Class, Race and Ethnicity on
    Chicago's South Side, 1900-1922. Journal of Social History 18
    (1984):37-56.

Barth, Gunther. Bitter Strength: A History of the Chinese in the United
    States, 1850-1870. Cambridge, MA: Harvard University Press, 1964.

Beardley, E. H. Good-Bye to Jim Crow: The Desegregation of Southern
    Hospitals, 1945-70. Bulletin of the History of Medicine 60 (Fall
    1986):367-86.

Bell, Derrick. To Make a Nation Whole [Civil rights in American history].
    New York Times Magazine September 13, 1987.

Bennett, David H. The Party of Fear. From Nativist Movements to the New Right in American History. Chapel Hill: University of North Carolina Press, 1988.

Berlin, Ira. The Revolution in Black Life. In: Alfred F. Young (ed.), The American Revolution: Explorations in the History of American Radicalism, pp. 349-82. De Kalb: Northern Illinois University Press, 1976.

Berlin, Ira and others (eds.) Freedom. A Documentary History of Emancipation, 1861-1867. Series 1, Vol. 1. New York: Cambridge University Press, 1986.

Berry, Mary F. and John W. Blassingame. Long Memory: The Black Experience in America. New York: Oxford University Press, 1982.

Betten, Neil and Raymond A. Mohl. The Evolution of Racism in an Industrial City, 1906-1940: A Case Study of Gary, Indiana. Journal of Negro History 59 (1974):51-64.

Biddiss, Michael. The Founder of Aryan Racism [Arthur de Gobineau]. Times Educational Supplement October 8, 1982.

Bigham, Darrel E. We Ask Only a Fair Trial. A History of the Black Community of Evansville, Indiana. Bloomington: Indiana University Press, 1987.

Billig, Michael. L'internationale raciste. Paris: Maspero, 1981.

Blassingame, John W. Black New Orleans, 1860-1880. Chicago: University of Chicago Press, 1973.

Bodner, John and others. Lives of their Own: Blacks, Italians, and Poles in Pittsburgh, 1900-1960. Urbana: University of Illinois Press, 1982.

Bolt, Christine. American Indian Policy and American Reform. Case Studies of the Campaign to Assimilate the American Indians. Winchester, MA: Allen & Unwin, 1987.

Bond, Horace Mann. Social and Economic Forces in Reconstruction. Journal of Negro History 23 (July 1938):290-348.

Bowen, David W. Andrew Johnson and the Negro. Knoxville: University of Tennessee Press, 1989.

Boyd, Melody V. Q. Black Population of North Hempstead, 1830-1880 [Black Manhasset]. Doctoral dissertation, State University of New York at Stony Brook, 1981. UMO # 8120710.

Bracey, John H., Jr. and others (eds.) Black Nationalism in America. Indianapolis, IN: Bobbs-Merrill, 1970.

Braden, Anne. The Southern Freedom Movement in Perspective. Monthly Review (July-August 1965):entire issue.

Bragaw, Donald H. Status of Negroes in a Southern Port City [Pensacola] in the Progressive Era. <u>Florida Hist. Quarterly</u> 51 (1973):281-302.

Brauer, Carl M. <u>John F. Kennedy and the Second Reconstruction</u>. New York: Columbia University Press, 1977.

Brock, Gene M. Mexican Opinion, American Racism, and the War of 1846. <u>Western Historical Quarterly</u> 1 (April 1970):161-74.

Buchanan, Albert R. <u>Black Americans in World War II</u>. ABC-Clio, 1977.

Cable, George W. <u>The Negro Question</u>. New York: 1888.

Calloway, Colin G. (ed.) <u>New Directions in American Indian History</u>. Norman: University of Oklahoma Press, 1988.

Camarillo, Albert. <u>Chicanos in a Changing Society: From Pueblos to American Barrios in Santa Barbara and Southern California, 1848-1930</u>. Cambridge, MA: Harvard University Press, 1979.

Camarillo, Albert. Historical Patterns in the Development of Chicano Urban Society: Southern California, 1848-1930. <u>In</u>: <u>The American West: Image and Reality</u>. Los Angeles, CA: William Andrew Clark Memorial Library, 1979.

Camejo, Peter. <u>Racism, Revolution, Reaction, 1861-1877. The Rise and Fall of Radical Reconstruction</u>. New York: Monad Press, 1976.

Campbell, Mavis. Aristotle and Black Slavery: A Study in Race Prejudice. <u>Race</u> 15 (January 1974):283-301.

Campbell, Will D. <u>Forty Acres and a Goat: A Memoir</u>. Atlanta, GA: Peachtree Publishers, 1986. [494 Armour Circle, NE, Atlanta, GA 30324].

Cardinal, Jare R. <u>Allegheny be Damned: The Seneca Nation in Crisis, 1955-1961</u>. Master's thesis, Bowling Green State University, 1987.

Carew, Jan. Columbus and the Origins of Racism in the Americas, Part 1. <u>Race and Class</u> (Spring 1988).

Carew, Jan. Columbus and the Origins of Racism in the Americas, Part 2. <u>Race and Class</u> (July-September 1988).

Carew, Jan. The Origins of Racism in the Americas. <u>Bim</u> (Christ Church, Barbados) 15 (December 1975):222-242.

Carlson, Shirley J. M. <u>The Black Community in the Rural North: Pulaski County, Illinois, 1860-1900</u>. Doctoral dissertation, Washington University, 1982. UMO # 8223770.

Carter, Dan T. From Segregation to Integration. <u>In</u>: John B. Boles and Evelyn T. Nolen (eds.), <u>Interpreting Southern History....</u>. Baton Rouge: Louisiana State University Press, 1987.

Carter, Dan T. From Segregation to Integration. In: John B. Boles and Evelyn T. Nolen (eds.), Interpreting Southern History.... Baton Rouge: Louisiana State University Press, 1987.

Carter, Thyra. Racial Elements in American History Textbooks. Historical Outlook 22 (April 1931):147-51. [6 European nationalities in 8 U.S. textbooks].

Cartwright, Joseph H. The Triumph of Jim Crow: Tennessee Race Relations in the 1880s. Knoxville: University of Tennessee Press, 1976.

Cassity, Michael J. Chains of Fear: Origins of American Race Relations. Westport, CT: Greenwood, 1983.

Caudill, Harry M. Theirs Be the Power: The Moguls of Eastern Kentucky. Urbana: University of Illinois Press, 1983.

Causey, Virginia E. Glen Allan, Mississippi: Change and Continuity in a Delta Community, 1900 to 1950. Doctoral dissertation, Emory University, 1983. UMO # 8316271.

Chinese Historical Society of America. The Life, Influence and the Role of the Chinese in the United States, 1776-1960. July 10, 1975. ERIC ED 141 422.

Chinn, Thomas W. A History of the Chinese in California. San Francisco, CA: Chinese Historical Society of America, 1969.

Christian, Marcus B. A Black History of Louisiana. Archives and Manuscript Dept., Earl K. Long Library, University of New Orleans, 1980.

Christensen, Lawrence O. Race Relations in St. Louis, 1865-1916. Missouri Historical Review 78 (January 1984):123-36.

Chu, Doris. Chinese in Massachusetts: Their Experiences and Contributions. 1988. Chinese Culture Institute, 276 Tremont St., Boston, MA 02116.

Cimprich, John. Slavery's End in Tennessee, 1861-1865. University: University of Alabama Press, 1985.

Clark, Malcolm, Jr. The Bigot Disclosed: 90 Years of Nativism. Oregon Historical Quarterly 75 (1974):109-90.

Clarke, John H. The Rise of Racism in the West. Black World 19 (1970):4-10.

Coben, Stanley. A Study in Nativism: The American Red Scare, 1919-1920. Political Science Quarterly 79 (March 1964):52-75.

Cohn, Avern. Constitutional Interpretation and Judicial Treatment of Blacks in Michigan Before 1870. Detroit College of Law Review (Winter 1986):1121-30.

Colburn, David R. Racial Change and Community Crisis: St. Augustine,
    Florida, 1877-1980. New York: Columbia University Press, 1985.

Coleman, Ronald G. A History of Blacks in Utah, 1825-1910. Doctoral
    dissertation, University of Utah, 1980. UMO # 8012508.

Conlen, Paul. The Historical Genesis and Material Basis of Racial
    Endogamy in Racist Societies [Nazi Germany, South Africa, and the
    United States]. Doctoral dissertation, University of Lund, Sweden,
    1974.

Corbett, Katharine T. and Mary E. Seematter. Black St. Louis at the Turn
    of the Century. Gateway Heritage 7 (Summer 1986):40-48.

Cortes, Carlos E. (ed.) The Chicano Heritage. [A series of 55 volumes].
    New York: 1976.

Cortes, Carlos E. (ed.) The Mexican American. [A series of 21 volumes].
    New York: 1974.

Cottrol, Robert J. The Afro-Yankees: Providence's Black Community in the
    Antebellum Era. Westport, CT: Greenwood, 1982.

Cox, Oliver C. The Nature of the Anti-Asiatic Movement of the Pacific
    Coast. Journal of Negro Education 15 (Fall 1946):603-14.

Cox, Thomas C. Blacks in Topeka, Kansas, 1865-1915: A Social History.
    Baton Rouge: Louisiana State University Press, 1982.

Crew, Spencer R. Black Life in Secondary Cities: A Comparative Analysis
    of the Black Community of Camden and Elizabeth, New Jersey, 1860-
    1920. Doctoral dissertation, Rutgers Unviersity, 1978. UMO #
    7928390.

Crow, Jeffrey J. and Flora J. Hatley (eds.) Essays on the History of
    Black Americans in North Carolina and the South. Chapel Hill:
    University of North Carolina Press, 1984.

Daniels, Roger. Asian America: Chinese and Japanese in the United States
    Since 1850. Seattle: University of Washington Press, 1988.

Daniels, Roger and Harry H. L. Kitano. Racism in Practice. In: American
    Racism: Exploration of the Nature of Prejudice, pp. 29-72. Englewood
    Cliffs, NJ: Prentice-Hall, 1970.

Daniels, Roger and Spencer C. Olin, Jr. (eds.). Racism in California: A
    Reader in the History of Oppression. New York: Macmillan, 1972.

De Graaf, Lawrence B. Recognition, Racism, and Reflections on the Writing
    of Western Black History. Pacific Historical Review 44 (February
    1975):22-51.

De Santis, Vincent P. Rutherford B. Hayes and the Removal of the Troops
    and the End of Reconstruction, in Morgan Kousser and James M.
    McPherson (eds.), Region, Race, and Reconstruction: Essays in Honor

of C. Vann Woodward. 1982.

De Vries, James E. Race and Kinship in a Midwestern Town: The Black
    Experience in Monroe, Michigan, 1900-1915. Urbana: University of
    Illinois Press, 1984.

De Witt, Howard. Anti-Filipino Movements in California: A History,
    Bibliography and Study Guide. San Francisco, CA: R and E Research
    Associates, 1976.

Degler, Carl N. Racism in the United States: An Essay Review. Journal
    of Southern History 38 (February 1972):101-108.

Dennis, Matthew J. Cultivating a Landscape of Peace: The Iroquois [17th
    century]. Doctoral dissertation, University of California, Berkeley,
    1986. UMO # 8717957.

Department of Health, Education, and Welfare (1963-1969): Official
    History and Documents [17 microfilm reels]. Frederick, MD:
    University Publications of America, 1987.

Deutsch, Sarah. No Separate Refuge, Culture, Class, and Gender on the
    Anglo-Hispanic Frontier in the American Southwest, 1880-1940 [CO &
    NM]. New York: Oxford University Press, 1987.

Dittmer, John. Black Georgia in the Progressive Era, 1900-1920. Urbana:
    University of Illinois Press, 1977.

Doyle, Don H. Nashville in the New South, 1880-1930. Knoxville:
    University of Tennessee Press, 1985.

Doyle, Don H. Nashville Since the 1920s. Knoxville: University of
    Tennessee Press, 1985.

Dressler, John. Racism: A New Analytical Tool in Recent American
    Historiography. Journal of Social and Behavioral Sciences 18 (Fall-
    Winter 1971-1972):42-49.

Drewry, Henry N. U.S. Rationalized Slavery and Produced Racism.
    University (Princeton University) Summer, 1969.

Drinnon, Richard. Facing West, The Metaphysics of Indian Hating and
    Empire-Building. Minneapolis, MN: University of Minnesota Press,
    1980.

Droker, Howard A. Seattle Race Relations during the Second World War.
    In: G. Thomas Edwards and Carlos A. Schwantes (eds.), Experiences in
    a Promised Land: Essays in Pacific Northwest History. Seattle:
    University of Washington Press, 1986.

Du Bois, W. E. B. The Black North. New York Times Nov. 17 & 24, 1901,
    p. 10, p. 11; Dec. 1, 8, & 15, 1901, p. 11, p. 20.

Du Bois, W. E. B. Black Reconstruction in America. NY: Harcourt, Brace,
    1935.

Du Bois, W. E. B. The Economics of Negro Emancipation in the United
    States. Sociological Review (Manchester) 4 (October 1911):303-13.

Du Bois, W. E. B. Social Effects of Emancipation. Survey 29 (February
    1, 1913):570-573.

Duncan, Ronald J. (ed.) The Anthropology of the People of Puerto Rico.
    San German: Interamerican University Press, 1978.

Eblin, Jack E. Growth of the Black Population in ante bellum America,
    1820-1860. Population Studies July 1972.

Eggers, Robert J. A Black History of South Dakota since Nineteen-thirty.
    Master's thesis, University of South Dakota, 1977.

Elphick, Richard A. A Comparative History of White Supremacy. (review
    article) Journal of Interdisciplinary History 13 (Winter 1983):503-
    513.

Elson, Ruth M. Guardians of Tradition: American Schoolbooks of the
    Nineteenth Century. Lincoln: University of Nebraska Press, 1964.

Engs, Robert F. Freedom's First Generation: Black Hampton, Virginia,
    1861-95. Philadelphia: University of Pennsylvania Press, 1979.

Evans, William M. From the Land of Canaan to the Land of Guinea: The
    Strange Odyssey of the 'Sons of Ham'. American Historical Review 85
    (February 1980):15-43. [See also Ephraim Isaac].

Everett, Robert Burke. Race Relations in South Carolina, 1900-1932.
    Doctoral dissertation, University of Georgia, 1969. UMO # 70-01152.

Ferris, William H. The African Abroad, or, His Evolution in Western
    Civilization, Tracing His Development Under Caucasian Milieu. 2
    vols. New Haven, CT: Tuttle, Morehouse and Taylor Press, 1983.

Fields, Barbara, J. Ideology and Race in American History. In: J.
    Morgan Kousser and James M. McPherson (eds.), Region, Race and
    Reconstruction: Essays in Honor of C. Vann Woodward, pp. 143-77.
    1982.

Fields, Barbara J. Slavery and Freedom on the Middle Ground: Maryland
    during the Nineteenth Century. New Haven, CT: Yale University
    Press, 1985.

Fields, Barbara J. The Nineteenth-Century American South: History and
    Theory. Plantation Society in the Americas. 2 (April 1983):7-28.

Fishbain, Leslie. Dress Rehearsal in Race Relations: Pre-World War I
    American Radicals and the Black Question. Afro-Americans in New York
    Life and History 6 (January 1982):7-15.

Fisher, John E. The John F. Slater Fund: A Nineteenth-Century
    Affirmative Action for Negro Education. Lanham, MD: University

Press of America, 1987.

Fitzgerald, Ruth Coder. A Different Story: A Black History of Fredericksburg, Stafford, and Spotsylvania, Virginia. Greensboro, NC: Unicorn, 1979.

Foley, Douglas E. and others. From Peones to Politicos: Ethnic Relations in a South Texas Town, 1900 to 1977. Austin: Center for Mexican American Studies, University of Texas, 1977.

Foner, Eric. Reconstruction, America's Unfinished Revolution, 1863-1877. New York: Harper & Row, 1988.

Foner, Philip S. and George E. Walker (eds.) Proceedings of the Black National and State Conventions, 1865-1900, I. Philadelphia: Temple University Press, 1985.

Foner, Philip S. and George E. Walker (eds.) Proceedings of the Black State Conventions, 1840-1865. 2 vols. Philadelphia: Temple University Press, 1979-1980.

Forbes, Jack D. The Historian and the Indian: Racial Bias in American History. The Americas (April 1963):349-62.

Foster, Herbert James. The Urban Experience of Blacks in Atlantic City, New Jersey: 1850-1915. Doctoral dissertation, Rutgers University, 1981. UMO # 8115209.

Frankel, Noralee. Jim Crow: Racism and Reaction in the New South [Exhibition at Valentine Museum, Richmond, Virginia]. Perspectives (American Historical Associatin) 27 (April 1989).

Franklin, Jimmie L. Journey Toward Hope: A History of Blacks in Oklahoma. Norman: University of Oklahoma Press, 1982.

Franklin, John Hope. Racial Equality in America. Chicago: University of Chicago Press, 1976.

Franklin, John Hope. Reconstruction After the Civil War. Chicago: University of Chicago Press, 1961.

Franklin, John Hope. Southern History: The Black-White Connection. Atlanta Historical Journal 30 (Summer 1986):7-18.

Franklin, John Hope and Alfred A. Moss, Jr. From Slavery to Freedom, A History of Negro Americans (sixth edition). New York: Knopf, 1987.

Franklin, Vincent P. The Education of Black Philadelphia: The Social and Educational History of a Minority Community, 1900-1950. Philadelphia: University of Pennsylvania Press, 1979.

Franklin, Vincent P. and James D. Anderson (eds.) New Perspectives on Black Educational History. Boston: Hall, 1978.

Frederickson, George M. The Arrogance of Race: Historical Perspectives

Fredrickson, George M. The Black Image in the White Mind: The Debate on
    Afro-American Character and Destiny, 1817-1914. Harper and Row,
    1971.

Fredrickson, George M. Towards a Social Interpretation of the Development
    of American Racism. In: Nathan I. Huggins and others (eds.), Key
    Issues in the Afro-American Experience, I. New York: 1971.

Fredrickson, George M. and Dale T. Knobel. Prejudice and Discrimination,
    History of. In: Stephan Thernstrom (ed.), Harvard Encyclopedia of
    American Ethnic Groups, pp. 829-47. Cambridge, MA: Harvard
    University Press, 1980.

Funke, Carol N. The Emergence of an Afro-American Society in Colonial
    Amelia County, Virginia. Master's thesis, Utah State University,
    1980.

Gaines, John S. Treatment of Mexican American History in High School
    Textbooks. Civil Rights Digest 5 (October 1972):35-40.

Gerard,   . The Significance of the Indian in American History.
    American Indian Culture and Research Journal 8 (1984):1-21.

Gerteis, Louis S. From Contraband to Freedman: Federal Policy Toward
    Southern Blacks, 1861-1865. Westport, CT: Greenwood, 1973.

Gibson, Arrell M. Native Americans and the Civil War. Indian Quarterly 9
    (Fall 1985):385-410.

Goggin, Jacqueline. Carter G. Woodson and the Collection of Source
    Materials for Afro-American History. American Archivist 48 (Summer
    1985):261-71.

Goings, Kenneth W. Intra-Group Differences among the Afro-Americans in
    the Rural North: Paulding County, Ohio: 1860-1900. Ethnohistory
    27 (1980):79-90.

Gomez-Quinones, Juan. Toward a Perspective on Chicano History. Aztlan 2
    (Fall 1971):1-49.

Gomez-Quinones, Juan and David Maciel. Al norte del Rio Bravo, Posado
    tejano, 1600-1930. Mexico City: Sigle XXI, 1981.

Goodrich, Linda Sharon. A Historical Survey of Cultural Racism and Its
    Subsequent Impact on the Education of Black Americans. Doctoral
    dissertation, Ohio State University, 1976. UMO # 7624651.

Goodstein, Anita S. Black History on the Nashville Frontier, 1780-1810.
    Tennessee Historical Quarterly 38 (Winter 1979):401-420.

Gopal, S. The Emergence of Modern Nationalism: Some Theoretical Problems
    in the Nineteenth and Early Twentieth Centuries. In: Sociological
    Theories: Race and Colonialism, pp. 85-91. Paris: UNESCO, 1980.

Gossett, Thomas F. Race: The History of an Idea in America. Dallas,

Theories: _Race_ _and_ _Colonialism_, pp. 85-91. Paris: UNESCO, 1980.

Gossett, Thomas F. _Race:_ _The_ _History_ _of_ _an_ _Idea_ _in_ _America_. Dallas,
Texas: 1963.

Gravely, Will B. The Dialectic of Double Consciousness in Black American
Freedom Celebrations, 1808-1868. _Journal_ _of_ _Negro_ _History_ 67
(1982).

Grenz, Suzanna M. _The_ _Black_ _Community_ _in_ _Boone_ _County,_ _Missouri,_ _1850-_
_1900_. Doctoral dissertation, University of Missouri, 1979. UMO #
8002365.

Griswold del Castillo, Richard. Tucsones and Angelenos: A Socio-Economic
Study of Two Mexican-American Barrios, 1860-1880. _Journal_ _of_ _the_
West 17 (January 1979).

Gruber, Jacob W. Racism and the Idea of Progress in the 19th Century. _In:_
Stanley Diamond (ed.),_Anthropology:_ _Ancestors_ _and_ _Heirs_. The
Hague: Mouton, 1979.

Gruber, Jacob W. The United States: Racism and Progress in the
Nineteenth Century. _In:_ Stanley Diamond (ed.), _Anthropology:_
Ancestors _and_ _Heirs_, pp. 109-122. The Hague: Mouton, 1980.

Guilbert, David C. Tacoma's Expulsion of the Chinese. _Tacoma_ _New_ _Tribune_
September 18, 1983.

Harding, Vincent. _There_ _Is_ _a_ _River:_ _The_ _Black_ _Struggle_ _for_ _Freedom_ _in_
America. New York: Harcourt Brace Jovanovich, 1981.

Harlow, Neal. _California_ _Conquered._ _The_ _Annexation_ _of_ _a_ _Mexican_
Province, _1846-1850_. Berkeley, CA: University of California Press,
1982.

Harris, Leonard. Historical Subjects and Interests: Race, Class, and
Conflict. _In:_ Mike Davis, Manning Marable and others (eds.), _The_
Year _Left_ _2:_ _An_ _American_ _Socialist_ _Yearbook_, pp. 90-105. London:
Vesco, 1987.

Harris. Robert L., Jr. _The_ _Free_ _Black_ _Response_ _to_ _American_ _Racism,_ _1790-_
_1863._ Doctoral dissertation, Northwestern University, 1974. UMO #
7428639.

Haws, Robert D. (ed.) _The_ _Age_ _of_ _Segregation:_ _Race_ _Relations_ _in_ _the_
South, _1890-1945_. University Press of Mississippi, 1978.

Hazama, Dorothy O. and Jane O. Komeyi. _Okaga_ _Sama_ _De:_ _The_ _Japanese_ _in_
Hawaii, _1885-1985_. Honolulu: Bess Press, 1986.

Heard, J. Norman. _Handbook_ _of_ _the_ _American_ _Frontier:_ _Four_ _Centuries_ _of_
Indian-White _Relationships_. Vol. I: _The_ _Southeastern_ _Woodlands_.
Metuchen, NJ: Scarecrow, 1987.

Hill, Arthur Cyrus. _The_ _History_ _of_ _the_ _Black_ _People_ _of_ _Franklin_ _County,_

Tennessee. Doctoral dissertation, University of Minnesota, 1982.
UMO # 8213990.

Hoetink, H. Slavery and Race. Historical Reflections 6 (Summer
1979):255-274.

Hoffman, Abraham. Textbooks, Mexican Americans, and Twentieth-Century
American History. Teaching History 3 (February 1978):65-72.

Holtzclaw, R. Fulton. Black Magnolias: A Brief History of the Afro-
Mississippian, 1865-1980. Shaker Heights, OH: Keeble Press, 1984.

Horsman, Reginald. Race and Manifest Destiny. The Origins of American
Racial Anglo-Saxonism. Cambridge, MA: Harvard University Press,
1981.

Howard, Victor B. Black Liberation in Kentucky: Emancipation and
Freedom, 1861-1884. Lexington: University Press of Kentucky, 1983.

Howard-Pitney, David. The Enduring Black Jeremiad: The American
Jeremiad and Black Protest Rhetoric, from Frederick Douglass to
W.E.B. Du Bois, 1841-1919. American Quarterly 38 (1986):481-92.

Howie, Don. The Origins of Racism. Negro Digest February, 1970.

Hoxie, Frederick E. (ed.) Indians in American History. Arlington
Heights, IL: Harlan Davidson, 1988.

Hubbard, Carole A. C. Roots of African-American Art: The Early Years
through the 1930s. Doctoral dissertation, Pennsylvania State
University, 1987. UMO # 8807797.

Huggins, Nathan I. Integrating Afro-American History into American
History. In: Darlene C. Hine (ed.), The State of Afro-American
History: Past, Present, and Future. Baton Rouge: Louisiana State
University Press, 1986.

Huggins, Nathan I. (ed.) Key Issues in the Afro-American Experience. [2
vols.] New York: Harcourt Brace Jovanovich, 1971.

Hurtado, Albert L. Indian Survival on the California Frontier. New
Haven, CT: Yale University Press, 1988.

Hyde, George E. Red Cloud's Folk: A History of the Oglala Sioux Indians.
Norman: University of Oklahoma Press, 1976.

Ichioka, Yuji. The Issei, The World of the First Generation Japanese
Immigrants, 1885-1924. New York: Free Press, 1988.

Isaac, Ephraim. Genesis, Judaism and the 'Sons of Ham'. Slavery and
Abolition 1 (May 1980):3-17. [See also Evans, above].

Ivanov, Robert. Blacks in United States History. Moscow: Progress
Publishers, 1985.

Jackson, Walter A. The Making of a Social Science Classic: Gunnar Myrdal's An American Dilemma. Perspectives in American History 2 (1985):221-67.

Jacobs, Donald M. William Lloyd Garrison's Liberator and Boston's Blacks, 1830-1865. New England Quarterly 44 (1971):259-77.

Japanese American Curriculum Project. Japanese American Journey: The Story of a People. San Mateo, CA: CACP Inc., 1985. [Pre-high school level].

Johnson, Charles S. Shadow of the Plantation. Chicago, IL: 1934.

Johnson, Guion G. The Ideology of White Supremacy 1876-1918. In: Fletcher M. Green (ed.), Essays in Southern History, pp. 124-56. Chapel Hill: University of North Carolina Press, 1949.

Johnson, Josie R. An Historical Review of the Role Black Parents and the Black Community Played in Providing Schooling for Black Children in the South, 1865-1954. Doctoral dissertation, University of Massachusetts, 1986. UMO # 8612051.

Johnson, Kenneth R. Slavery and Racism in Florence, Alabama, 1841-1862. Civil War History 27 (June 1981):155-71.

Jones, Yollette T. The Black Community, Politics, and Race Relations in the "Iris" City: Nashville, Tennessee, 1870-1954. Doctoral dissertation, Duke University, 1985. UMO # 8608926.

Jordan, Terry G. A Century and a Half of Ethnic Change in Texas, 1836-1986. South West Historical Quarterly 89 (April 1986):385-422.

Jordan, Winthrop D. White Over Black. The Development of American Attitudes toward the Negro, 1550-1812. Chapel Hill, NC: University of North Carolina Press, 1968.

Joyce, Frank. Racism: History and Definition. Tailorbird (2 parts), March 1969 and April 1969. [Published by Tutorial Assistance Center, U.S. National Student Assembly].

Kaplan, Sidney. Blacks in Massachusetts and the Shays' Rebellion. Contributions in Black Studies 8 (1986-1987):5-14.

Kaplan, Sidney and Emma N. Kaplan. The Black Presence in the Era of the American Revolution (Revised edition). Amherst, MA: University of Massachusetts Press, 1989.

Katz, William Loren. The Black West.

Kellogg, Peter J. Civil Rights Consciousness in the 1940s. Historian (November 1979).

Kelly, Walter J. Historical Perspectives on Racism. History Teacher 2 (1969):27-30.

Kennedy, Lawrence. *Power and Prejudice: Boston Political Conflict, 1885-1895*. Doctoral dissertation, Boston College, 1987. UMO # 8807534. [Anti-Irish prejudice].

Kharif, Wali R. Black Reaction to Segregation and Discrimination in Post-Reconstruction Florida. *Florida Historical Quarterly* 64 (October 1985):161-73.

Kharif, Wali R. *The Refinement of Racial Segregation in Florida After the Civil War*. Doctoral dissertation, Florida State University, 1983. UMO # 8404742.

Kim, Hyung-Chan (ed.) *Dictionary of Asian American History*. Westport, CT: Greenwood, 1986.

Kinshasha, Kwando M. Methodologies in African-American Historical Research: The Model and the Evolving Paradigm. *Western Journal of Black Studies* 11 (Winter 1987):185-92.

Kiple, Kenneth and Virginia Kipple. The African Connection: Slavery, Disease and Racism. *Phylon* 41 (Fall 1980):211-222.

Kirby, John B. *Black Americans in the Roosevelt Era: Liberalism and Race*. Knoxville: University of Tennessee Press, 1980.

Kirby, John B. (ed.) *New Deal Agencies and Black America*. [25 microfilm reels]. Frederick, MD: University Publications of America, 1987.

Knuth, Helen. *The Climax of American Anglo-Saxonism, 1898-1905*. Doctoral dissertation, Northwestern University, 1958.

Kolchin, Peter. Race, Class, and Poverty in the Post-Civil War South. *Reviews in American History* 7 (December 1979):515-26.

Kornweibel, Theodore, Jr. (ed.) *In Search of the Promised Land: Essays in Black Urban History*. Kennikat, 1981.

Kousser, J. Morgan and James M. McPherson (eds.) *Region, Race, and Reconstruction: Essays in Honor of C. Vann Woodward*. New York: Oxford University Press, 1982.

Ladner, Walter W. and Joyce A. Ladner. Defusing Race: Developments Since the Kerner Report. *In*: Benjamin P. Bowser and Raymond G. Hunt (eds.), *Impacts of Racism on White Americans*, pp. 51-69. Beverly Hills, CA: Sage, 1981.

Lane, Roger. *Roots of Violence in Black Philadelphia, 1860-1900*. Cambridge, MA: Harvard University Press.

Lang, Wm. L. The Nearly Forgotten Blacks on Last Chance Gulch, 1900-1912 [Helena, MT]. *Pacific Northwest Quarterly* 70 (April 1979):50-57.

Lapp, Rudolph M. *Blacks in Gold Rush California*. New Haven, CT: Yale

University Press, 1977.

Larson, Karl E. A Separate Reality: The Development of Racial Segregation in Raleigh, North Carolina, 1865-1915. Master's thesis, University of North Carolina, Greensboro, 1982.

Lazerson, Marvin (ed.) American Education in the Twentieth Century: A Documentary History. New York: Teachers College Press, 1987.

Leacock, Eleanor B. and Nancy O. Lurie (eds.) North American Indians in Historical Perspective. New York: 1971.

Levesque, George A. Interpreting Early Black Ideology: A Reappraisal of Historical Consensus. Journal of the Early Republic 1 (Fall 1981):269-87.

Levesque, George A. and Nikola A. Baumgarten. 'A Monstrous Inconsistency': Slavery, Ideology and Politics in the Age of the American Revolution. Contributions in Black Studies 8 (1986-1987):20-34.

Levine, Lawrence. Black Culture and Black Consciousness. New York: 1977.

Levy, Burton. The Racial Bureaucracy, 1941-1971: From Prejudice to Discrimination to Racism. Journal of Intergroup Relations 2 (July 1972):3-32.

Lewis, Earl. At Work and At Home: Blacks in Norfolk, Virginia, 1910-1945. Doctoral dissertation, University of Minnesota, 1984. UMO # 8503073.

Lisio, Donald J. Hoover, Blacks, and Lily-Whites. A Study of Southern Strategies. Chapel Hill: University of North Carolina Press, 1985.

Litwack, Leon F. Been in the Storm So Long: The Aftermath of Slavery. New York: Knopf, 1979.

Litwack, Leon F. Trouble in Mind: The Bicentennial and the Afro-American Experience. Journal of American History 74 (1987):315-37.

Loewenberg, Peter. Racism and Tolerance in Historical Perspective. In: Peter Orleans and William Russell Ellis, Jr. (eds.), Race, Change and Urban Setting, pp. 561-576. Beverly Hills, CA: Sage, 1971.

Logan, Rayford W. The Betrayal of the Negro. NY: Collier, 1965.

Lucas, R. Valerie. Yellow Peril in the Promised Land: The Representation of the Oriental and the Question of American Identity, vol. 1. In: Francis Barker and others (eds.), Europe and Its Others, pp. 41-57. Colchester: University of Essex, 1985.

Machado, Deirdre A. M. Cape Verdian-Americans: Their Cultural and Historical Background. Doctoral dissertation, Brown University, 1978. UMO # 7906576.

266

Maciel, David. Al norte del Rio Bravo Pasado immediato, 1930-1981. Mexico City: Siglo XXI, 1981.

Mahan, Harold E. 'We Feel to Bee a People': Historiographical Perspectives on Blacks in Emancipation and Reconstruction. Md. Historian 26 (Spring-Summer 1985):41-56.

Mahoney, Kathryn L. The Irish Community in Antebellum Richmond, 1840-1861. Master's thesis, University of Richmond, 1985.

Malpass, Elizabeth Deanne. Organized Southern Racism Since 1951. Master's thesis, University of Miami, 1963.

Mamiya, Lawrence H. and Patricia A. Kaurouma. You Never Hear About Their Struggles: Black Oral History in Poughkeepsie, New York. Afro-Am. N.Y. Life and History 4 (July 1980):55-70.

Marable, Manning. Blackwater: Historical Studies in Race, Class Consciousness and Revolution. Dayton, O: Black Praxis Press, 1981.

Martin, Calvin (ed.) The American Indian and the Problem of History. New York: Oxford University Press, 1987.

Martyn, Byron C. Racism in the United States: A History of the Anti-Miscegenation Legislation and Litigation. Doctoral dissertation, University of Southern California, 1979.

Matthew, John M. Studies in Race Relations in Georgia, 1890-1930. Doctoral dissertation, Duke University, 1970.

Matthews, Linda M. Keeping Down Jim Crow: The Railroads and the Separate Coach Bills in South Carolina. South Atlantic Quarterly 73 (1974):117-29.

McClory, Robert J. Racism in America: From Milk and Honey to Ham and Eggs. Chicago: Fides/Claretian, 1981.

McFeely, William S. Unfinished Business: The Freedmen's Bureau and Federal Action in Race Relations. In: Nathan I. Huggins and others (eds.), Key Issues in the Afro-American Experience, Vol II, pp. 5-25. New York: Harcourt Brace Jovanovich, 1971.

McKay, Claude. The Negroes in America. Port Washington, NY: Kennikat Press, 1979. [Written 1922-1923].

McKee, Delber L. The Chinese Boycott of 1905-1906 Reconsidered: The Role of Chinese Americans. Pacific Historical Quarterly 55 (May 1986):165-91.

McLemore, S. Dale. The Origins of Mexican American Subordination in Texas. Social Science Quarterly 53 (March 1973):656-70.

McMillen, Neil R. The Citizens' Council: Organized Resistance to the Second Reconstruction, 1954-64. Urbana: University of Illinois Press, 1971.

Press, 1971.

McWilliams, Carey. <u>North</u> <u>from</u> <u>Mexico:</u> <u>The</u> <u>Spanish-speaking</u> <u>People</u>.
Westport, CT: Greenwood Press, 1969 (orig. 1949).

Meier, August. <u>Negro</u> <u>Thought</u> <u>in</u> <u>America,</u> <u>1880-1915:</u> <u>Racial</u> <u>Ideologies</u> <u>in</u>
<u>the</u> <u>Age</u> <u>of</u> <u>Booker</u> <u>T.</u> <u>Washington</u>. Ann Arbor: University of Michigan
Press, 1963.

Meier, August and Elliot Rudwick. <u>Black</u> <u>History</u> <u>and</u> <u>the</u> <u>Historical</u>
<u>Profession</u>. Urbana: University of Illinois Press, 1986.

Meier, August and Elliot Rudwick. <u>From</u> <u>Plantation</u> <u>to</u> <u>Ghetto</u>. 3rd ed.
New York: Hill and Wang, 1976.

Merriam, Allen H. Racism in the Expansionist Controversy of 1898-1900.
<u>Phylon</u> 39 (December 1978):369-380.

Miller, Kelly. <u>An</u> <u>Appeal</u> <u>to</u> <u>Reason:</u> <u>An</u> <u>Open</u> <u>Letter</u> <u>to</u> <u>John</u> <u>Temple</u>
<u>Graves</u>. Washington, D.C.: Hayworth Publishing House, 1906.

Miller, Kelly. <u>As</u> <u>to</u> <u>the</u> <u>Leopard's</u> <u>Spots:</u> <u>An</u> <u>Open</u> <u>Letter</u> <u>to</u> <u>Thomas</u>
<u>Dixon,</u> <u>Jr.</u> Washington, D.C.: K. Miller, 1905.

Mindiola, Tatcho, Jr. <u>The</u> <u>Cost</u> <u>of</u> <u>Being</u> <u>Mexican</u> <u>American</u> <u>and</u> <u>Black</u> <u>in</u>
<u>Texas,</u> <u>1960-1970</u>. Doctoral dissertation, Brown University, 1978.
UMO # 7906587.

Mishler, Paul. Ourselves Alone: The Antebellum Origins of Racism Among
Boston's Irish-Americans. <u>Debate</u> <u>and</u> <u>Understanding</u> Boston:
Martin Luther King Center, Boston University, 1983.

Mohl, Raymond A. and Neil Betten. <u>Steel</u> <u>City:</u> <u>Urban</u> <u>and</u> <u>Ethnic</u> <u>Patterns</u>
<u>in</u> <u>Gary,</u> <u>Indiana,</u> <u>1906-1950</u>. New York: Holmer & Meier, 1985.

Moneyhorn, Carl H. <u>Republicans</u> <u>in</u> <u>Reconstruction</u> <u>Texas</u>. Austin:
University of Texas Press, 1980.

Montejano, David. <u>Anglos</u> <u>and</u> <u>Mexicans</u> <u>in</u> <u>the</u> <u>Making</u> <u>of</u> <u>Texas,</u> <u>1836-1986</u>.
Austin: University of Texas Press, 1987.

Morales Carrion, Arturo (ed.) <u>Puerto</u> <u>Rico,</u> <u>a</u> <u>Political</u> <u>and</u> <u>Cultural</u>
<u>History</u>. New York: Norton, 1983.

Morgan, Lynda J. <u>Emancipation</u> <u>in</u> <u>the</u> <u>Virginia</u> <u>Tobacco</u> <u>Belt,</u> <u>1850-1870</u>.
Doctoral dissertation, University of Virginia, 1986. UMO # 8801131.

Morrill, Richard L. and O. Fred Donaldson. Geographical Perspectives on
the History of Black America. <u>Economic</u> <u>Geography</u> 48 (January
1972):1-23.

Morris, Charles E. Panic and Reprisal: Reaction in North Carolina to the
Nat Turner Insurrection, 1831. <u>N.C.</u> <u>Hist.</u> <u>Review</u> 62 (January
1985):29-52.

Mullard, C. Racism in Society and Schools: History, Policy, and Practice. In: F. Rizvi (ed.), Multiculturalism as an Educational Policy, pp. 64-81. Geelong, Victoria: Deakin University Press, 1985.

Mumford, Esther H. Seattle's Black Victorians, 1852-1901. 1980. Anase Press, P.O. Box 22 565, Seattle, WA 98122.

Naison, Mark. Communists in Harlem during the Depression. Urbana: University of Illinois Press, 1983.

Nash, Gary B. Red, White, and Black: The Origins of Racism in Colonial America. In: Gary B. Nash and Richard Weiss (eds.), The Great Fear. Race in the Mind of America, pp. 1-26. New York: Holt, Rinehart and Winston, 1970.

Nash, Gary B. Red, White and Black: Peoples of Early America, 2nd edition. Englewood Cliffs, NJ: Prentice-Hall, 1982.

Nash, Gary B. and Richard Weiss (eds.) The Great Fear. Race in the Mind of America. New York: Holt, Rinehart and Winston, 1970.

Negroes in the Cities of the North. Charities 15 (October 7, 1905):1-96.

Nelson, H. Viscount. The Philadelphia NAACP: Race Versus Class Consciousness During the Thirties. Journal of Black Studies 5 (1975):255-76.

Newby, I. A. Jim Crow's Defense: Anti-Negro Thought in America, 1900-1930. Baton Rouge, LA: Louisiana State University Press, 1965.

Newby, I. A. (ed.) The Development of Segregationist Thought. Homewood, IL: Dorsey, 1968.

Nielson, David G. Black Ethos: Northern Urban Negro Life and Thought, 1890-1930. Westport, CT: Greenwood, 1977.

Noel, Donald L. A Theory of the Origin of Ethnic Stratification. Social Problems 16 (1968):157-72.

Noel, Donald L. (ed.) The Origin of American Slavery and Racism. 1972.

Officer, James E. Hispanic Arizona, 1536-1856. Tuscon: University of Arizona Press, 1987.

Osofsky, Gilbert. Harlem: The Making of a Ghetto, 1890-1930, 2nd ed. New York: Harper & Row, 1971.

Paredes, Raymond. The Origins of Anti-Mexican Sentiment in the United States. New Scholar 6 (1977):139-65. [Published at UC, La Jolla].

Patrick, Nikki. Blacks Reflect on Rich History. Pittsburg Morning Sun February 20, 1983. [History of Blacks in Pittsburg].

Patrick, Nikki. Blacks Reflect on Rich History. _Pittsburg_ _Morning_ _Sun_
February 20, 1983. [History of Blacks in Pittsburg].

Patterson, Orlando. Toward a Future that Has No Past: Reflections on the
Fate of Blacks in the Americas. _Public_ _Interest_ 27 (Spring
1972):25-62.

Paul, William G. _The_ _Shadow_ _of_ _Equality:_ _The_ _Negro_ _in_ _Balitmore,_ _1864-_
_1911_. Doctoral dissertation, University of Wisconsin, 1972.

Peal, David. The Politics of Populism: Germany and the American South in
the 1890s. _Comparative_ _Studies_ _in_ _Society_ _and_ _History_ 31 (April
1989):340-62.

Pearce, Roy Harvey. _Savagism_ _and_ _Civilization._ _A_ _Study_ _of_ _the_ _Indian_ _and_
the _Americna_ _Mind_ (second revised edition). Berkeley, CA:
University of Caifornia Press, 1988.

Perdue, Robert E. _The_ _Negro_ _in_ _Savannah,_ _1865-1900_. New York:
Exposition Press, 1973.

Peterson, Jacqueline. 'Wild' Chicago: The Formation and Destruction of a
Multiracial Community on the Midwestern Frontier, 1816-1837. _In:_
Melvin G. Holli and Peter d'A. Jones (eds.), _The_ _Ethnic_ _Frontier_ pp.
25-71. Grand Rapids, Michigan: Erdmans, 1977.

Phillips, George H. Indians in Los Angeles, 1781-1875: Economic
Integration, Social Disintegration. _Pacific_ _Historical_ _Review_ 49
(August 1980):427-51.

Pierson, William D. _Black_ _Yankees._ _The_ _Development_ _of_ _an_ _Afro-American_
Subculture _in_ _Eighteenth-Century_ _New_ _England_. Amherst, MA:
University of Massachusetts Press, 1988.

Pitre, Merline. _Through_ _Many_ _Dangers,_ _Toils,_ _and_ _Shares:_ _The_ _Black_
Leadership _of_ _Texas,_ _1870-1900_. Austin, TX: Eakin Press, 1985.

Poliakov, Leon. Racism from the Enlightenment to the Age of Imperialism.
_In:_ Robert Ross (ed.), _Racism_ _and_ _Colonialism_. The Hague: Martinus
Nijhoff, 1982.

Prudhomme, Charles and David F. Musto. Historical Perspectives on Mental
Health and Racism in the United States. _In:_ Charles V. Wilie,
Bernard M. Kramer, and Bertram S. Brown (eds.), _Racism_ _and_ _Mental_
Health, pp. 25-57. Pittsburgh, PA: University of Pittsburgh Press,
1973.

Puerto Ricans in Children's Literature and History Texts: A Ten-Year
Update. _Interracial_ _Books_ _for_ _Children_ _Bulletin_ 14 (1983):entire
issue.

Puglisi, Michael J. _The_ _Legacies_ _of_ _King_ _Philip's_ _War_ _in_ _the_
Massachusetts _Bay_ _Colony_. Doctoral dissertation, College of William
and Mary, 1987. UMO # 8717074.

Quarles, Benjamin. <u>Black Abolitionists</u>. New York: Oxford University Press, 1969.

Quarles, Benjamin. <u>Black Mosaic. Essays in Afro-American History and Historiography</u>. Amherst, MA: University of Massachusetts Press, 1988.

Rammelkauys, Julian S. The Providence Negro Community, 1820-1842. <u>Rhode Island History</u> 7 (1948):20-33.

Ransom, Roger L. and Richard Sutch. The Impact of the Civil War and Emancipation on Southern Agriculture. <u>Explorations in Economic History</u> 12 (1975):1-28.

Ransom, Roger L. and Richard Sutch. <u>One Kind of Freedom: The Economic Consequences of Emancipation</u>. New York: Cambridge University Press, 1977.

Rawick, George P. The Historical Roots of Black Liberation. <u>Radical America</u> 2 (January 1968):1-13.

Reddick, Lawrence D. Method of Combating Racially Derogatory Statements and Implications of American College Textbooks. <u>Quarterly Review of Higher Education Among Negroes</u> 3 (October 1935):207-11.

Reddick, Lawrence D. Racial Attitudes in American History Textbooks. <u>Journal of Negro History</u> 19 (July 1934):225-65.

Reed, Adolph, Jr. (ed.) <u>Race. Politics. and Culture: Critical Essays on the Radicalism of the 1960s</u>. Westport, CT: Greenwood, 1986.

Reid, Gerald F. <u>Defendants to Development: A World Systems Analysis of Elite Formation in Greenfield. Massachusetts. 1770s-1840s</u>. Doctoral dissertation, University of Massachusetts, 1987. UMO # 8805967.

Richter, Daniel K. and James H. Merrell (eds.) <u>Beyond the Covenant Chain. The Iroquois and their Neighbors. 1600-1800</u>. Syracuse, NY: Syracuse University Press, 1987.

Ridley, May A. H. <u>The Black Community of Nashville and Davidson County. 1860-1870</u>. Doctoral dissertation, University of Pittsburgh, 1982. UMO # 8317306.

Robinson, Cedric. A Critique of W.E.B. DuBois' <u>Black Reconstruction</u>. <u>Black Scholar</u> 8 (1977):44-50.

Romo, Ricardo. <u>East Los Angeles: History of a Barrio</u>. Austin: University of Texas Press, 1983.

Rose, Willie Lee. <u>Rehearsal for Reconstruction: The Port Royal Experiment</u>. New York: Oxford University Press, 1964.

Rosenstiel, Annette (ed.) <u>Red and White: Indian Views of the White Man. 1492-1982</u>. New York: Universe Books, 1983.

271

Rozett, John M. Racism and Republican Emergence in Illinois, 1848-1860:
    A Re-Evaluation of Republican Negrophobia. Civil War History 22
    (June 1976):101-15.

Ruchames, Louis. Jim Crow Railroads in Massachusetts. American Quarterly
    8 (Spring 1956):61-75.

Ruchames, Louis (ed.) Racial Thought in America. From the Puritans to
    Abraham Lincoln. Amherst, MA: University of Massachusetts Press,
    1969.

Rusco, Elmer R. Good Time Coming? Black Nevadans in the 19th Century.
    Westport, CT: Greenwood, 1975.

Saeger, James S. (ed.) Essays on Eighteenth-Century Race Relations in
    the Americas. Bethlehem, PA: Lawrence Henry Gipson Institute, 1987.

Sakihara, Mitsugu (ed.) Uchinanchu [English-language history of
    Okinawans in Hawaii]. Honolulu, HI: 1981.

Salisbury, Neal. Manitou and Providence: Indians, Europeans, and the
    Making of New England, 1500-1643. New York: 1982.

Sanders, Ronald. Lost Tribes and Promised Land: The Origins of American
    Racism. Boston: Little Brown, 1978.

Sandoval, Raymond E. Intrusion and Domination: A Study of the
    Relationship of Chicano Development to the Exercise and Distribution
    of Power in a Southwestern City, 1870-1974 [Las Cruces, NM].
    Doctoral dissertation, University of Washington, 1980. UMO #
    8026300.

Santry, Patricia. An Historical Perspective of the Factors Preventing
    Sikh Assimilation in California, 1906-1946. Master's thesis,
    California State University, Fullerton, 1981.

Saxton, Russell S. Ethnocentrism in the Historical Literature of
    Territorial New Mexico. Doctoral dissertation, University of New
    Mexico, 1980. UMO # 8025036.

Schmitz, Keith R. Milwaukee and its Black Community, 1920-1942. Master's
    thesis, University of Wisconsin, Milwaukee, 1979.

Scott,   . Segregation: A Fundamental Aspect of Southern Race
    Relations, 1800-1860. Journal of the Early Republic 4 (1984).

Scott, John Anthony. Loewen v. Turnipseed: A Landmark Case. AHA
    Newsletter (American Historical Association) 18 (October 1980).
    [Non-racist textbook on the history of Mississippi].

Sedler, Robert A. The Constitution and the Consequences of the Social
    History of Racism. Arkansas Law Review 40 (Spring 1987):677-739.

Senungetuk, Joseph. Give or Take a Century: The Story of an Eskimo
    Family. San Francisco, CA: Indian Historian Press, 1970.

Sernett, Milton C. Abolition's Axe: Beriah Green, Oneida Institute, and the Black Freedom Struggle. Syracuse, NY: Syracuse University Press, 1986.

Sernett, Milton C. First Honor: Oneida Institute's Role in the Fight against American Racism and Slavery. New York History 66 (April 1985):101-122.

Sheldon, Marianne B. Black-White Relations in Richmond, Virginia, 1782-1820. Journal of Southern History 45 (February 1979):27-44.

Sheridan, Thomas E. Los Tusconenses: The Mexican Community in Tucson, 1854-1941. Tucson: University of Arizona Press, 1986.

Shute, Gary. The Natural History of American Black-White Relations: A Question of Structural Persistence. 1971. ERIC ED 049 336.

Simar, T. Etude critique sur la formation de la doctrine des races au XVIIIe siecle et son expansion au XIXe siecle. Brussels: 1922.

Simmons, William S. Cultural Bias in the New England Puritans' Perception of Indians. William and Mary Quarterly 38 (January 1981):56-72.

Simon, Pierre-J. Ethnisme et racisme ou 'l'ecole de 1492'. Cahiers internationaux de sociologie 48 (1970):119-152.

Skinner, Byron R. The Double "V": The Impact of World War II on Black America. Doctoral dissertation, University of California, Berkeley, 1978. UMO # 7914765.

Smith, Carroll Ann. Anglo-Saxon Science: The Scientific Rationale for Immigration Restriction. Master's thesis, Columbia University, 1958.

Smith, J. Owens. Politics of Racial Inequality: A Systematic Comparative Micro-Analysis from the Colonial Period to 1770. Westport, CT: Greenwood, 1987. [13 groups].

Snowden, Frank M. Before Color Prejudice. The Ancient View of Blacks. Cambridge, MA: Harvard University Press, 1983.

Snyder, Louis L. The Idea of Racialism. Its Meaning and History. Princeton, NJ: D. Van Nostrand, 1968.

Sobel, Mechal. The World They Made Together. Black and White Values in Eighteenth-Century Virginia. Princeton, NJ: Princeton University Press, 1988.

Solomon, Benjamin and Beatrice Young. Unweaving the Threads of Racism in American History. Changing Education (Spring 1968).

SoRelle, James M. The Darker Side of "Heaven": The Black Community in Houston, Texas, 1917-1945. Doctoral dissertation, Kent State University, 1980. UMO # 8100696.

Starobin, Robert. The Negro: A Central Theme in American History. _Journal of Contemporary History_ (April 1968).

Stein, Judith. 'Of Mr. Booker T. Washington and Others': The Political Economy of Racism in the United States. _Science and Society_ 38 (Winter 1974-1975):422-463.

Stephenson, Gilbert T. The Segregation of the White and Negro Races in Cities. _South Atlantic Quarterly_ 13 (January 1904):1-18.

Stuart, Paul. _Nations Within a Nation. Historical Statistics of American Indians_. Westport, CT: Greenwood, 1987.

Swartout, Robert R., Jr. Kwantung to Big Sky: The Chinese in Montana, 1864-1900. _Montana_ 38 (Winter 1988):42-53.

Takaki, Ronald. Reflections on Racial Patterns in America: An Historical Perspective. _Ethnicity and Public Policy_ 1 (1982):1-23.

Taxel, Joel. The American Revolution in Children's Books. Issues of Racism and Classism. _Interracial Books for Children Bulletin_ 12 (1981):3-9.

Taylor, Brennen. _UNIA and American Communism in Conflict 1917-1928: An Historical Analysis in Negro Social Welfare_. Doctoral dissertation, University of Pittsburgh, 1984. UMO # 8421299.

Taylor, Joseph Earl, Sr. _The National Conferences on the Problems of the Negro and Negro Youth, 1937-1939: "A Comprehensive Program for the Full Integration into the Benefits and Responsibilities of the American Democracy"_. Doctoral dissertation, Catholic University of America, 1986. UMO # 8707368.

Ternon, Yves and Socrate Heiman. _Histoire de la medecine SS ou le mythe du racisme biologique_. Paris: Ed. d'Aujordui, 1979.

Terrell, Lloyd P. (ed.) _Black American Quotations, 1808-1978_. Atlanta: Terrell Publishing Co., 1980.

Thapar, Romila. Durkheim and Weber on Theories of Society and Race Relating to Pre-Colonial India, pp. 93-116 in _Sociological Theories: Race and Colonialism_. Paris: UNESCO, 1980.

Thornberg, Jerry. _The Development of Black Atlanta, 1865-1885_. Doctoral dissertation, University of Maryland, 1977.

Thornton, Russell. _American Indian Holocaust and Survival: A Population History Since 1492_. Norman: University of Oklahoma Press, 1987.

Thorpe, Earl E. The Day Freedom Came. _Negro History Bulletin_ 22 (1958):10-12.

Tong, Ben. The Ghetto of the Mind: Notes on the Historical Psychology of Chinese Americans. _Amerasia Journal_ 1 (1971):1-31.

Tong, Ben. The Ghetto of the Mind: Notes on the Historical Psychology of Chinese Americans. Amerasia Journal 1 (1971):1-31.

Trigger, Bruce. The Past or Power: Anthropology and the North American Indian. In: Isabel McBryde (ed.), Who Owns the Past? New York: Oxford University Press, 1985.

Tsai, Shih-shan Henry. The Chinese Experience in America. Bloomington: Indiana University Press, 1986.

Tucker, Edward. Anti-Black Attitudes in the Garrisonian Movement. Master's thesis, Queens College, 1978.

U.S. Bureau of the Census. Negroes in the United States: 1920-1932. Washington, D.C.: GPO, 1935.

U.S. Bureau of the Census. The Social and Economic Status of the Black Population: An Historical View, 1790-1978. Washington, D.C.: GPO, 1979.

Vantine, Larry L. Teaching American Indian History: An Interdisciplinary Approach. Palo Alto, CA: R & E Research Associates, 1978.

Voegelin, Erich. Die Rassenidee in de Geistesgeschichte von Ray bis Carus. Berlin: 1933.

Vogel, Virgil J. The Indian in American History. Chicago, IL: Integrated Education Associates, 1968.

Wagenheim, Kal. Puerto Rico: A Profile. New York: 1972.

Walton, Gary M. and James F. Shepherd (eds.) Market Institutions and Economic Progress in the New South, 1865-1900: The Economic Consequences of Emancipation. New York: Academic Press, 1981.

Walton, Thomas Eugene. The Negro in Richmond, 1880-1890. Master's thesis, Howard University, 1950.

Ward, David. Poverty, Ethnicity and the American City, 1840-1925. New York: Cambridge University Press, 1989.

Washington, Joseph R., Jr. Puritan Race Virtue, Vice and Values, 1620-1820. New York: Peter Lang, 1988.

Watkins, Ralph R. Black Buffalo 1920-1927. Doctoral dissertation, State University of New York at Buffalo, 1978. UMO # 7905332.

Wayne, Michael. The Reshaping of Plantation Society: The Natchez District, 1860-1880. Baton Rouge: Louisiana State University Press, 1983.

Weare, Walter B. The Idea of Progress in Afro-American Thought, 1890-1915. In: Ralph M. Aderman (ed.), The Quest for Social Justice .... Madison: University of Wisconsin Press, 1983.

Weber, David J. Foreigners in their Native Land: Historical Roots of the Mexican Americans. Albuquerque: University of New Mexico, 1973.

Weeks, Philip (ed.) The American Indian Experience. A Profile, 1524 to the Present. Arlington Heights, IL: Forum Press, 1988.

Weiss, Richard. Racism in the Era of Industrialization. In: Gary B. Nash and Richard Weiss (eds.), The Great Fear. Race in the Mind of America. New York: Holt, Rinehart and Winston, 1970.

Wells, Sharon. Forgotten Legacy: Blacks in Nineteenth Century Key West. Key West, FL: Historic Key West Preservation Board, 1982.

Weston, Rubin F. Racism in U.S. Imperialism: The Influence of Racial Assumptions on American Foreign Policy, 1893-1946. Columbia, SC: University of South Carolina Press, 1972.

Wheeler, Joanne. Together in Egypt: A Pattern of Race Relations in Cairo, Illinois, 1865-1915. In: Orville V. Burton and Robert C. McMath (eds.), Towards a New South? Studies in Post-Civil War Southern Communities. Westport, CT; Greenwood, 1982.

Wiggins, William H., Jr. O Freedom! Afro-American Emancipation Celebrations. Knoxville: University of Tennessee Press, 1987.

Williams, Juan. Eyes on the Prize: America's Civil Rights, 1954-1965. New York: Viking, 1987.

Williams, Lillian S. Afro-Americans in Buffalo, 1900-1930: A Study in Community Formation. Afro-Am. N.Y. Life and Hist. 8 (July 1984):7-35.

Williamson, Joel. The Crucible of Race: Black/White Relations in the American South Since Emancipation. New Yotk: Oxford University Press, 1984.

Willis, William. Divide and Rule: Red, White and Black in the Colonial South. Journal of Negro History 48 (July 1963):157-176.

Wilson, Raymond. Native Americans in College Textbooks. Wassaja/The Indian Historian 13 (June 1980):44-47.

Wilson, William Julius. Class Conflict and Jim Crow Segregation in the Postbellum South [1865-1900]. Pacific Sociological Review 19 (October 1976):431-46.

Wood, Forrest B. Black Scare. The Racist Response to Emancipation and Reconstruction. Berkeley, CA: University of California Press, 1968.

Wood, Peter H. 'I Did the Best I Could for My Day': The Study of Early Black History during the Second Reconstruction, 1960-1976. Wm & Mary Quarterly 35 (1978):185-225.

Woodman, Harold D. How New Was the New South? Agricultural History 58 (October 1984):529-45.

Woodman, Harold D. Sequel to Slavery: The New History Views the Postbellum South. _Journal_ _of_ _Southern_ _History_ 43 (1977):523-54.

Woodson, Carter G. _Miseducation_ _of_ _the_ _Negro_. Washington, D.C.: Associated Publishers, Inc., 1982.

Woodward, C. Vann. _American_ _Counterpoint:_ _Slavery_ _and_ _Racism_ _in_ _the_ _North-South_ _Dialogue_. Boston: Little, Brown, 1971.

Woodward, C. Vann. _Origins_ _of_ _the_ _New_ _South_, Rev. ed. Baton Rouge: Louisiana State University press, 1972.

Woodward, C. Vann. _Reunion_ _and_ _Reaction:_ _The_ _Compromise_ _of_ _1877_ _and_ _The_ _End_ _of_ _Reconstruction_. 1951.

Woodward, C. Vann. _The_ _Strange_ _Career_ _of_ _Jim_ _Crow_. 3rd rev. ed. NY: Oxford University Press, 1974.

Woodward, C. Vann. Young Jim Crow. _Nation_ July 7, 1956.

Wooster, Robert. _The_ _Military_ _and_ _United_ _States_ _Indian_ _Policy,_ _1865-1903_. New Haven, CT: Yale University Press, 1988.

Wright, Geroge C. _Life_ _Behind_ _a_ _Veil,_ _Blacks_ _in_ _Louisville,_ _Kentucky,_ _1865-1930_. Baton Rouge: Louisiana State University Press, 1985.

Wright, J. Leitch, Jr. _Creeks_ _and_ _Seminoles:_ _Destruction_ _and_ _Regeneration_ _of_ _the_ _Muscogulge_ _People_. Lincoln: University of Nebraska Press, 1987.

Wynn, Neil A. _The_ _Afro-American_ _and_ _the_ _Second_ _World_ _War_. New York: Holmes & Meier, 1976.

Wytriwal, Joseph A. _Polish-Black_ _Encounters:_ _A_ _History_ _of_ _Polish_ _and_ _Black_ _Relations_ _since_ _1619_. Detroit, MI: Endurance Press, 1982.

Yim, Sun Bin. The Social Structure of Korean Communities in California, 1903-1920. _In:_ Lucie Chang and Edna Bonacich (eds.), _Labor_ _Immigration_ _under_ _Capitalism_ pp. 515-48. Berkeley, CA: University of California Press, 1984.

York, Everett L. Ethnocentrism or Racism: Some Thoughts on the Nature of Early Indian-White Relations. _American_ _Indian_ _Quarterly_ 1 (Winter 1974-1975):281-291.

Young, Donald (ed.) The American Negro. _Annals_ _of_ _the_ _American_ _Academy_ _of_ _Political_ _and_ _Social_ _Science_ 140 (1928).

Young, Robert W. _A_ _Political_ _History_ _of_ _the_ _Navajo_ _Tribe_. Tsaile, AZ: Navajo Community College Press, 1978.

Yee, Shirley Jo-ann. _Black_ _Women_ _Abolitionists:_ _A_ _Study_ _of_ _Gender_ _and_ _Race_ _in_ _the_ _American_ _Antislavery_ _Movement,_ _1828-1860_. Doctoral dissertation, Ohio State University, 1987. UMO # 8726748.

History Bibliography

Abajian, James de T. (comp.) Blacks and Their Contributions to the American West.... Boston: Hall, 1974.

Best, Jack L. (comp.) Records of the Assistant Commissioner for the State of North Carolina Bureau of Refugees, Freedmen, and Abandoned Lands 1865-1870. Washington, D.C.: National Archives and Records Series, General Services Administration, 1973.

Blassingame, John W. and Mae G. Henderson (comps.) Antislavery Newspapers and Periodicals: An Annotated Index of Letters, 1817-1871. 3 vols. Boston: Hall, 1980-1981.

Boone, Dorothy D. A Historical Review and a Bibliography of Selected Negro Magazines, 1910-1919. Doctoral dissertation, University of Michigan, 1970.

Bouknight, L. Maine. (comp.) Records of the Assistant Commissioner for the State of Mississippi Bureau of Refugees, Freedmen, and Abandoned Lands, 1865-1869. Washington, D.C.: National Archives and Records Service, GSA, 1973.

Butterfield, L. H. and others (comps.) American Indian and White Relations to 1830, Needs and Opportunities for Study. Chapel Hill: University of North Carolina Press, 1957. [Bibliography, pp. 31-122].

Camarillo, Albert M. (ed.) Latinos in the United States: A Historical Bibliography. Santa Barbara, CA: ABC-Clio, 1986.

Du Bois, W. E. B. (comp.) A Bibliography of the Negro Artisan and the Industrial Training of Negroes. In: The Negro Artisan, pp. v-vii. Atlanta: Atlanta University Press, 1902.

Jacobs, Donald M. (comp.) Antebellum Black Newspapers: Indices to 'Freedom's Journal' (1827-1829), 'The Right of All' (1829), 'The Weekly Advocate' (1837), and the 'Colored American' (1837-1841). Westport, CT: Greenwood, 1976.

Mohr, C. L. (comp.) Southern Blacks in the Civil War, a Century of Historiography: Bibliographic Essay. Journal of Negro History 59 (April 1974):177-95.

Newman, Debra L. (comp.) Black History, A Guide to Civilian Records in the National Archives. Baltimore,MD: Smithsonian Institution Press, 1984.

Newman, Richard (comp.) Black Index: Afro-Americans in Selected Periodicals, 1907-1949. New York: Garland, 1981.

Prucha, Francis Paul. Handbook for Research in American History: A Guide to Bibliographies and Other Reference Works. Lincoln: University of

Nebraska Press, 1987.

Schor, Joel and Cecil Harvey (comps.) A List of References for the History of Black Americans in Agriculture, 1619-1974. Davis: Agricultural Historical Center, University of California, 1975.

Smith, Dwight L. (comp.) Afro-American History: A Bibliography. 2 vols. Santa Barbara, CA: ABC-CLIO, 1974, 1981.

Thompson, Edgar T. (comp.) The Plantation: A Bibliography. Washington, D.C.: Department of Cultural Affairs, Pan American Union, 1957.

[See also sections 2, 6, 14, 20, 22, 38, 44, 53, 75, and 84]

35. Housing

... The primary cause of Afro-American residential segregation is racism or racial discrimination, not racial economic inequality.

- Joe T. Darden, <u>Afro-Americans</u> <u>in</u> <u>Pittsburgh</u> (1973)

Agents Said Steering Blacks Away from Suburban Homes. <u>Springfield</u> <u>Daily</u> <u>News</u> April 6, 1981.

Akulicz de Santiago, Anne Marie. <u>Residential</u> <u>Segregation</u> <u>of</u> <u>Spanish</u> <u>Origin</u> <u>Population:</u> <u>A</u> <u>Study</u> <u>of</u> <u>Recent</u> <u>Trends</u> <u>in</u> <u>a</u> <u>Sample</u> <u>of</u> <u>U.S.</u> <u>Cities</u>. Doctoral dissertation, University of Wisconsin, 1984. UMO # 8504198.

Allen, Josephine A. V. <u>The</u> <u>Response</u> <u>of</u> <u>the</u> <u>American</u> <u>Political</u> <u>Economy</u> <u>to</u> <u>the</u> <u>Housing</u> <u>Needs</u> <u>of</u> <u>Its</u> <u>Poor,</u> <u>Its</u> <u>Black</u> <u>and</u> <u>Its</u> <u>Aged</u> <u>Citizens</u>. Doctoral dissertation, University of Michigan, 1979. UMO # 79166558. [Detroit].

Amin, Ruhul and A. G. Mariam. Racial Differences in Housing: An Analysis of Trends and Differentials, 1960-1978. <u>Urban</u> <u>Affairs</u> <u>Quarterly</u> 22 (March 1987):363-76.

Anonymous. Confessions of a Blockbuster. <u>Boston</u> <u>Metropolitan</u> <u>Real</u> <u>Estate</u> <u>Journal</u> (May 1987).

Baker, Kermit and H. James Brown. <u>Home</u> <u>Ownership</u> <u>and</u> <u>Housing</u> <u>Affordability</u> <u>in</u> <u>the</u> <u>United</u> <u>States:</u> <u>1963-1984</u>. Cambridge, MA: The Joint Center for Housing Studies of the Massachusetts Institute of Technology and Harvard University, 1985.

Barnes, William R. A National Controversy in Miniature: The District of Columbia Struggle Over Public Housing and Redevelopment, 1943-46. <u>Prologue</u> 9 (1977):91-104.

Bauman, John F. Black Slums/Black Projects: The New Deal and Negro Housing in Philadelphia. <u>Pennsylvania</u> <u>History</u> 41 (1974):311-38.

Bauman, John F. <u>Public</u> <u>Housing,</u> <u>Race,</u> <u>and</u> <u>Renewal:</u> <u>Urban</u> <u>Planning</u> <u>in</u> <u>Philadelphia,</u> <u>1920-1974</u>. Philadelphia: Temple University Press, 1987.

Bayor, Ronald H. Ethnic Residential Patterns in Atlanta, 1880-1940. <u>Georgia</u> <u>Historical</u> <u>Quarterly</u> 64 (Winter 1979):435-447.

Benign Racial Quotas in Public Housing: <u>Burney</u> v. <u>Housing</u> <u>Authority</u> <u>of</u> <u>the</u> <u>County</u> <u>of</u> <u>Beaver</u>. <u>Washington</u> <u>University</u> <u>Journal</u> <u>of</u> <u>Urban</u> <u>and</u> <u>Contemporary</u> <u>Law</u> 28 (1985):397-410.

Berry, Brian J. L. <u>The</u> <u>Open</u> <u>Housing</u> <u>Question:</u> <u>Race</u> <u>and</u> <u>Housing</u> <u>in</u> <u>Chicago,</u> <u>1966-1976</u>. Cambridge, MA: Ballinger, 1979.

Boston Urban Observatory. _Evaluation of City of Boston Fair Housing Programs_. Boston: University of Massachusetts, Boston, November 30, 1981.

Bohlen, Celestine. Yonkers and Stamford: 2 Paths, Similar Results [Racial patterns of housing in Stamford, CT]. _New York Times_ September 21, 1988.

Boucher, Norman. People Live Here, Too [Public Housing in Boston]. _Boston Globe Magazine_ March 12, 1989.

Brown, H. and J. Yinger. _Home Ownership and Housing Affordability in the U.S.: 1963-1985_. Cambridge, MA: Joint Center of Housing Studies of Harvard and MIT, August, 1986.

Buffalo Agrees to Integrate Its Public Housing. _New York Times_ May 7, 1989.

Bullard, Robert D, and Odessa L. Pierce. Black Housing Patterns in a Southern Metropolis: Competition for Housing in a Shrinking Market. _Black Scholar_ 11 (November-December 1979):60-67. [Houston].

Canellos, Peter S. A Lingering Urban Folly [The Boston Banks Urban Renewal Group and redlining of Mattapan during late 1960s and early 1970s]. _Boston Globe_ December 11, 1988.

Canellos, Peter S. Suburbs: Zoned Exclusive: After 20 Years, Anti-Snob Zoning Found Ineffective [Massachusetts]. _Boston Globe_ January 1, 1989.

Capeci, Dominic J., Jr. _Race Relations in Wartime Detroit. The Sojourner Truth Housing Controversy, 1937-1942_. Philadelphia: Temple University Press, 1984.

Chicago Urban League. _Where Blacks Live: Race and Residence in Chicago in the 1970's_. Chicago: Chicago Urban League, Spring, 1978.

Claiborne, Ron C. Institutional Reform and the Enforcement of the Fair Housing Laws. _Black Scholar_ 17 (May-June 1986):42-48.

Clouthier, Norman R. The Effect of Structural and Demographic Change on Urban Residential Segregation. _Review of Social Economy_ 42 (April 1984):32-43.

Cohen, Oscar. The Case for Benign Quotas in Housing. _Phylon_ 21 (Spring 1960):20-29.

The Color of Money. Marketing Department of Atlanta Journal Constitution, 72 Marietta Street, N.W., P.O. Box 4689, Atlanta, GA 30302. [Reprint booklet of May 1988 series of articles on mortage-lending practices in Atlanta area over 6-year period].

Comptroller General of the United States. _Substandard Indian Housing Increases Despite Federal Efforts: A Change Is Needed_. Washington,

Globe April 18, 1988. [Discrimination and desegregation in Holyoke].

Cummings, Scott (ed.) Racial Isolation in the Public Schools: The Impact of Public and Private Housing Policies. Arlington: Institute of Urban Studies, University of Texas, 1981.

Cutler, William W. III and Howard Gillette, Jr. (eds.) The Divided Metropolis: Social and Spatial Dimensions of Philadelphia, 1800-1975. Westport, CT: Greenwood Press, 1980.

Dabilis, Andrew J. Suburbs: Zoned Exclusive: Many Try to Slam Door on Subsidized Housing [Massachusetts]. Boston Globe January 2, 1989.

Dahlmann, Donald C. Housing Opportunities for Black and White Households. Special Demographic Analysis CDS-80-6. Washington, D.C.: U.S. Bureau of the Census, 1982.

Daley, Suzanne and Richard J. Meislin. New York City, the Landlord: A Decade of Housing Decay [Forty-one hundred buildings holding 37,000 families]. New York Times February 8, 1988.

Darden, Joe T. Black Residential Segregation: Impact of State Licensing Laws. Journal of Black Studies 12 (June 1982):415-26.

Darden, Joe T. The Housing Situation of Blacks in Metropolitan Areas of Michigan. In: The State of Black Michigan: 1985. East Lansing: Urban Affairs Programs, Michigan State University, 1985.

Darden, Joe T. The Residential Segregation of Hispanics in Cities and Suburbs of Michigan. East Lakes Geographer 18 (1983):25-37.

Darden, Joe T. Socioeconomic Status and Racial Residential Segregation: Blacks and Hispanics in Chicago. International Journal of Comparative Sociology 28 (January-April 1987):1-13.

Darden, Joe T. and Jane B. Haney. Measuring Adaptation: Migration Status and Residential Segregation among Anglos, Blacks, and Chicanos. East Laker Geographer 13 (June 1978):20-33.

Du Bois, W. E. B. Fair Play for the Negro. N.Y. Evening Post Nov. 25, 1910, p. 8.

Du Bois, W. E. B. The Problem of Housing the Negro. Southern Workman 30 (July 1901):390-5.

Du Bois, W. E. B. The Problem of Housing the Negro: II. The Home of the Slave. Southern Workman 30 (September 1901):486-93.

Du Bois, W. E. B. The Problem of Housing the Negro: III. The Home of the Country Freedman. Southern Workman 30 (October 1901):535-42.

Du Bois, W. E. B. The Problem of Housing the Negro: III. The Home of the Village Negro. Southern Workman 30 (November 1901):601-604.

Du Bois, W. E. B. The Problem of Housing the Negro: IV. The Southern City Negro of the Lower Class [Atlanta]. Southern Workman 30 (December 1901):688-93.

Du Bois, W. E. B. The Housing of the Negro: VI. The Southern City Negro of the Better Class. Southern Workman 3 (February 1902):65-72.

Eisinger, Peter K. The Politics of Displacement: Racial and Ethnic Transition in Three American Cities [Detroit, Boston, Atlanta]. New York: Academic Press, 1980.

Farley, J. E. P* Segregation Indices: What Can They Tell Us about Housing Segregation in 1980? Urban Studies 21 (August 1984).

Finder, Alan. Bias Remains Pervasive in Region's Housing Market [New York City and suburbs]. New York Times March 13, 1989.

First, Richard J. and others. Homelessness: Understanding the Dimensions of the Problem for Minorities. Social Work 33 (March-April 1988):120-24.

Fleming, Arthur S. The Politics of Fair Housing. Yale Law and Policy Review 6 (Spring-Summer 1988):385-92.

Flint, Barbara J. Zoning and Residential Segregation: A Social and Physical History, 1910-1940. Doctoral dissertation, University of Chicago, 1977. [Chicago].

Flournoy, Craig and George Rodrigue. Separate and Unequal. Subsidized Housing in America. Dallas Morning News February 10-17, 1985.

Foderaro, Lisa W. Neighbors Try to Secede Over Housng Plan. New York Times December 5, 1988. [Greenbergh, NY].

Fossett, J. W. and Gary Orfield. Market Failure and Federal Policy: Low Income Housing in Chicago 1970-1983. In: Gary S. Tobin (ed.), Divided Neighborhoods. Newbury Park, CA: Sage, 1987. [Housing segregation].

Freeman, Richard and Brian Hall. Permanent Homelessness in America? Pop. Res. Policy Rev. 6 (1987):3-27.

Fuerst, James S. A Decade of Racial Progress. Chicago Tribune January 4, 1982. [Trends in Chicago and suburban housing, 1970-1980].

Gold, Allan R. Boston Urges Restraint in Covering Racial Story. New York Times July 7, 1988. [Desegregation of public housing in Boston].

Goldstein, Ira. The Wrong Side of the Tracts: A Study of Residential Segregation in Philadelphia, 1930-1980. Doctoral dissertation, Temple University, 1986. UMO # 8611855.

Goldstein, Ira and Clark White. Residential Segregation and Color Stratification among Hispanics in Philadelphia: Comment on Massey and Mullan. American Journal of Sociology 91 (September 1985):391-

96.

Grable, Stephen W. The Other Side of the Tracks: Cabbagetown - A
     Working-Class Neighborhood in Transition during the Early Twentieth
     Century. Atlanta Hist. J. 26 (Summer-Fall 1982):51-66.

Granger, Lori. A South Side Horatio Alger [Dempsey Travis, Black Chicago
     realtor]. Chicago Tribune Magazine October 11, 1981.

Greenberg, Stephanie W. Neighborhood Change, Racial Transition, and Work
     Location: A Case Study of an Industrial City, Philadelphia, 1880-
     1930. Journal of Urban History 7 (May 1981):267-314.

Grigsby, J. E., III and M. L. Hruby. A Review of the Status of Black
     Renters, 1970-1980. Review of Black Political Economy 13 (Spring
     1985).

Groves, Paul A. and Edward K. Shaw. The Evolution of Black Residential
     Areas in Late Nineteenth Century Cities. Journal of Historical
     Geography 1 (April 1975):169-92.

Gup, Ted. Racism in the Raw in Suburban Chicago [Cicero and Melrose Park,
     Illinois]. Time October 17, 1988.

Hanafin, Teresa M. Realty Board Abandons Bias Checks [Greater Boston Real
     Estate Board]. Boston Glosbe October 28, 1988.

Hartman, Chester (ed.) America's Housing Crisis: What Is To Be Done?
     Boston: Routledge and Kegan Paul, 1983.

Hays, Constance L. Study Reports Racial Bias in Home Loans in New York
     [City]. New York Times December 5, 1988.

Helper, Rose. Racial Policies and Practices of Real Estate Brokers.
     Minneapolis: University of Minnesota Press, 1969.

Henwood, Doug. Subsidizing the Rich [Community Preservation Corporation,
     NYC]. Village Voice August 30, 1988.

Hirsch, Arnold R. Making the Second Ghetto: Race and Housing in Chicago,
     1940-1960. New York: Cambridge University Press, 1983.

Hirsch, Arnold R. Race and Housing: Violence and Communal Protest in
     Chicago, 1940-1960. In: Melvin G. Holli and Peter d'A. Jones (eds.),
     The Ethnic Frontier, pp. 331-368. Grand Rapids, MI: Eerdmans,
     1977.

Hopper, Kim and Jill Hamburg. The Making of America's Homeless: From
     Skid Row to New Poor, 1945-1984. New York: Community Service
     Society, 1985.

Housing Tests Revealed Bias [Louisville area]. Human Rights Report
     (October 1981). [Published by Kentucky Commission on Human Rights].

Housing the Negro in Chicago. Crisis 5 (1912):25-26.

Howe, Peter J. Former BHA Chief Says Base Was Laid for Desegregation. Boston Globe August 15, 1988. [L. Harry Spence, court-appointed receiver of the Boston Housing Authority, 1980-1984].

Hundley, Kristen. A Clash of Interests in Holyoke [Puerto Ricans and housing in Holyoke, MA]. Boston Globe Magazine October 2, 1983.

Hwang, Sean-Shong and others. The Effects of Race and Socioeconomic Status on Residential Segregation in Texas, 1970-1980. Social Forces 63 (March 1985):732-46.

Jackman, Mary R. and Robert W. Jackman. Racial Inequalities in Home Ownership. Social Forces 58 (June 1980):1221-34.

Jackson, Kenneth T. The Spatial Dimensions of Social Control: Race, Ethnicity, and Government Housing Policy in the United States, 1918-1968. In: Bruce M. Stave (ed.), Modern Industrial Cities: History, Policy, and Survival. New York: Academic Press, 1984.

Jackson, Peter. Paradoxes of Puerto Rican Segregation in New York. In: Ceri Peach and others (eds.), Ethnic Segregation in Cities, pp. 109-26. Athens: University of Georgia Press, 1981.

Joravsky, Ben. Self-Help: An Old Concept Takes On New Meaning in Poor Communities. Chicago Reporter 16 (November 1987):3-5. [LeClaire Courts public housing, Chicago].

Kaufman, Jonathan. Public Optimism, Quiet Bias in BHA Housing Assignments [Deliberate segregation in units of the Boston Housing Authority]. Boston Globe February 7, 1988.

Kellogg, John. The Formation of Black Residential Areas in Lexington, Kentucky, 1865-1887. Journal of Southern History 48 (February 1982):21-52.

Kellogg, John. Negro Urban Clusters in the Postbellum South. Geographical Review 67 (1977):310-21.

Kennedy, Duncan. The Effect of the Warranty of Habitability on Low Income Housing: Milking and Class Violence. Florida State University Law Review 15 (Fall 1987):485-519.

Kentucky Commission on Human Rights. Most Kentucky Cities Reduce Public Housing Segregation. Frankfort, KY: K.C.H.R., June 1980.

Kifner, John. Starrett City's Nightmare: End of Quotas [Brooklyn]. New York Times November 14, 1988.

King, John. In Roxbury, [Real Estate] Brokers Must Fight the Trends. Boston Globe January 22, 1989.

Krmenec, Andrew J. The Influence of Housing Market Structure on Racial Transition [Chicago]. Doctoral dissertation, Indiana University, 1983. UMO # 8401524.

Krmenec, Andrew J. The Influence of Housing Market Structure on Racial Transition [Chicago]. Doctoral dissertation, Indiana University, 1983. UMO # 8401524.

Kulieke, Marilynn J. The Effects of Residential Integration on Children's School and Neighborhood Environments, Social Interactions, and School Outcomes. Doctoral dissertation, Northwestern University, 1985. UMO # 8523552.

Kushner, James A. Apartheid in America: An Historical and Legal Analysis of Contemporary Racial Segregation in the United States. Port Washington, NY: Associated Faculty Press, 1982.

Kushner, Marc A. The Legality of Race-Conscious Access Quotas under the Fair Housing Act of 1968. Cardozo Law Review 9 (February 1988):1053-89.

Kuttner, Bob. The Culprit in Public Housing Integration. Boston Globe August 15, 1988. [Class and race].

Lake, Robert W. Changing Symptoms, Constant Causes: Recent Evolution of Fair Housing in the United States. New Community 11 (Spring 1984):206-13.

Lam, Franke K-S. Residential Segregation of Chinese and Japanese Americans in the United States Suburban Areas: 1960, 1970, and 1980. Doctoral dissertation, Purdue University, 1986. UMO # 8700920.

Lang, Marvel. Historic Settlement and Residential Segregation in Rural Neighborhoods of Japan County, Mississippi. Doctoral dissertation, Michigan State University, 1979. UMO # 8010678.

Langberg, Mark L. Residential Segregation and the Assimilation Process: The Case of Asian-Americans in 1980. Doctoral dissertation, University of Michigan, 1986. UMO # 8612563.

Langberg, Mark L. and Reynolds Farley. Residential Segregation of Asian Americans in 1980. Sociology and Social Research 70 (October 1985):71-75.

Latino Institute. Latinos in Metropolitan Chicago: A Study of Housing and Employment. Chicago: Latino Institute, 1983.

Lazin, F. A. The Failure of Federal Enforcement of Civil Rights Regulations in Public Housing, 1963-1971. Policy Sciences 42 (1973):263-273.

Lee, B. A. Racially Mixed Neighborhoods during the 1970's: Change or Stability? Social Science Quarterly 66 (June 1985).

Lee, B. A. and others. Neighborhood Revitalization and Racial Change: The Case of Washington, D.C. Demography 22 (November 1985).

Leigh, Wilhelmina A. Shelter Affordability for Blacks: Crisis or Clamor? Washington, D.C.: National Urban League, 1982.

1988).

Levine, Hillel and Lawrence Harmon. Profits and Prophets: Overcoming Civil Rights in Boston. Tikkun 3 (July/August 1988):45-48, 94-96.

Logan, John R. and Mark Schneider. Racial Segregation and Racial Change in American Suburbs, 1970-1980. American Journal of Sociology 89 (1984):874-88.

Lopez, Manuel M. Patterns of Interethnic Residential Segregation in the Urban Southwest. Social Science Quarterly 62 (March 1981):50-63.

Low-income Housing under the New Conservatism: Trickle Down or Dry Up? Santa Clara Law Review 26 (Spring 1986):461-93.

Marcotte, Paul. Discrimination to Integrate? Minorities Rejected to Maintain Racial Balance. American Bar Association Journal 73 (November 1, 1987).

Marcum, John P. and others. Residential Segregation by Race in Mississippi, 1980. Sociological Spectrum 8 (1988):117-31.

Margolis, Harry L. Public Housing in Newark: The Struggle to Survive. In: Stanley B. Winters (ed.), From Riot to Recovery: Newark After Ten Years. Washington, D.C.: 1979.

Margolis, Richard J. Homes of the Brave: A Report on Migrant Farmworker Housing 1981. ERIC ED 215-851.

Mariano, Ann. Montgomery Housing Policy Seeks to Keep Racial Balance. Washington Post November 14, 1985. [Montgomery County, MD].

Maslow-Armand, Laura. The Newark Tenant Rent Strike: Public Housing Policy and Black Municipal Governance. Patterns of Prejudice 20 (October 1986):17-30.

Massey, Douglas S. Ethnic Residential Segregation-A Theoretical Synthesis and Empirical Review. Sociology and Social Research 69 (April 1985):315-50.

Massey, Douglas S. Hispanic Residential Segregation: A Comparison of Mexicans, Cubans and Puerto Ricans. Sociology and Social Research 65 (April 1981):311-22.

Massey, Douglas S. and Nancy A. Denton. Trends in the Residential Segregation of Blacks, Hispanics, and Asians: 1970-1980. American Sociological Review 52 (December 1987):802-25.

Massey, Douglas S. and Brendan P. Mullan. Processes of Hispanic and Black Spatial Assimilation. American Journal of Sociology 89 (1984):836-73. [Southwestern, U.S.].

Massey, Douglas S. and others. The Effect of Residential Segregation on Black Social and Economic Well-Being. Social Forces 66 (September 1987):29-56. [Philadelphia, 1980].

287

Massey, Douglas S. and others. The Effect of Residential Segregation on Black Social and Economic Well-Being. Social Forces 66 (September 1987):29-56. [Philadelphia, 1980].

McChesney, Kay Y. Women Without: Homeless Mothers and their Children. Doctoral dissertation, University of Southern California, 1987.

McGlasson, Robert L. Tipping the Scales of Justice: A Race-Conscious Remedy for Neighborhood Transition. Yale Law Journal 20 (1981):377-399.

McPherson, James Alan. The Story of the Contract Buyers League [Chicago]. Atlantic Monthly (April 1972).

McTigue, Geraldine. Patterns of Residence: Housing Distribution by Color in Two Louisiana Towns, 1860-1880. Louisiana Studies 15 (1976):345-88.

Meier, August and John Bracey, editorial advisers. The Campaign against Residential Segregation, 1914-1955, part 5 of Papers of the NAACP. New Parts on Educational Equality, Voting Rights, Housing, the Scottsboro Case, and Anti-Lynching [22 microfilm reels]. Frederick, MD: University Publications of America, 1987.

Meyer, David R. Interurban Differences in Black Housing Quality. Annals of the Association of American Geographers 63 (September 1973):347-52.

Meyer, Eugene L. Realtors' Role in a Changing Neighborhood. Washington Post January 26, 1980. [Marlboro Meadows, Prince George's County].

Mieszkowski, P. and R. F. Syron. Economic Explanations for Housing Segregation. New England Economic Review November-December 1979.

Milgram, Morris. Good Neighborhood: The Challenge of Open Housing NY: Norton, 1977.

Miller, Loren. The Protest against Housing Segregation. Annals 357 (1965):73-79.

Mintz, Steven. Sources of Variability in Rates of Black Home Ownership in 1900. Phylon 44 (December 1983):312-31.

[Mount Laurel case]. Seton Hall Legislature Journal 9 (1986):569-619. [Several articles].

Muro, Mark. Colonies [Mexican-American housing in Texas]. Boston Globe July 31, 1988.

Myers-Jones, Holly. Power, Geography and Black Americans: Exploring the Implications of Black Suburbanization. Doctoral dissertation, University of Washington, 1988.

National Center for Housing Management. An Equal Opportunity Review of the Real Estate Industry. Washington, D.C.: Department of Housing

1953. Maryland Historian 26 (Spring-Summer 1985):25-39.

Orfield, Gary. Ghettoization and Its Alternatives. In: Paul E. Peterson
(ed.), The New Urban Reality, pp. 161-93. Washington, D.C.:
Brookings Institution, 1985.

Orfield, Gary. Toward a Strategy for Urban Integration: Lessons in
School and Housing Policy from Twelve Cities. New York: The Ford
Foundation, 1981.

Osofsky, Gilbert. A Decade of Urban Tragedy: How Harlem Became a Slum.
New York History 46 (1965):330-55.

Pardee, Michael J. Quotas Mean Waiting List for Minorities [Desegregation
of public housing in Worcester]. Worcester Telegram May 21, 1983.

Park, Woo-Suh. An Empirical Analysis of the Rental Housing Market, the
Burough of Manhattan, New York: Do Blacks Pay More than Whites?
Doctoral dissertation, New York University, 1979. UMO # 7918989.

Parot, Joseph. Ethnic versus Black Metropolis: The Origins of Polish-
Black Housing Tensions in Chicago. Polish-American Studies 29
(Spring, Autumn 1972).

Pearce, Diana M. Black, White, and Many Shades of Gray: Real Estate
Brokers and their Racial Practices. Doctoral dissertation,
University of Michigan, 1976. UMO # 7708009.

Phillips, Valerie J. and Hank De Zutter. [Housing] Integration in
Chicago, 1987: Changing Attitudes Slow Resegregation. Chicago
Reporter 16 (October 1987):3-5.

Power, Garrett. Apartheid Baltimore Style: The Residential Segregation
Ordinances of 1910-1913. Maryland Law Review 42 (1983):289-328.

Rabinowitz, Howard N. From Exclusion to Segregation: Southern Race
Relations, 1865-1890. Journal of American History 63 (September
1976):325-50.

Race and Mortgage Lending in New York City. New York: Medgar Evers
Center for Law and Social Justice, 1988.

Racial Steering: The Real Estate Broker and Title VIII. Yale Law Journal
85 (May 1976):808-25.

Radford, John P. Race, Residence and Ideology: Charleston, South
Carolina, in the Mid-Nineteenth Century. Journal of Historical
Geography 2 (October 1976):329-46.

Rainwater, Lee. Behind Ghetto Walls: Black Families in a Federal Slum
[Priutt-Igoe public housing project in St. Louis]. Chicago: Aldine,
1970.

Rice, Roger L. Residential Segregation by Law, 1910-1917. Journal of
Southern History 34 (May 1968):180-99.

Rimer, Sara. As Blacks in Yonkers See It, Time to Say 'You're Wrong'.
    New York Times August 11, 1988.

Robbins, Tom. Starrett City's Racial Minefield, A Verdict on Quotas
    [NYC]. Village Voice March 15, 1988.

Rolle-Kataburuki, Jo-Ann. Equity Considerations of a National Housing
    Voucher Program on Low-Income Households in Racial Submarkets.
    Doctoral dissertation, Howard University, 1984. UMO # 8425862.

Rogers, Tommy W. Racial and Geographic Differentials in Mississippi
    Housing Characteristics. Mississippi Geographer 6 (Spring 1978):19-
    31.

Roof, Wade Clark (ed.) Race and Residence in American Cities.
    Philadelphia: American Academy of Political and Social Science,
    1979.

Ropka, Gerald W. The Evolving Residential Patterns of the Mexican, Puerto
    Rican, and Cuban Population in the City of Chicago. NY: Arno, 1980.

Rose, Harold M. The Black Professional and Residential Segregation in the
    American City [Houston, Los Angeles, Milwaukee, and Philadelphia].
    In: Ceri Peach and others (eds.), Ethnic Segregation in Cities, pp.
    127-148. Athens: University of Georgia Press, 1981.

Rose, Harold M. Black Suburbanization: Access to Improved Quality of
    Life or Maintenance of Status Quo. Cambridge, MA: Ballinger, 1976.

Rose, Harold M. Spatial Development of Black Residential Subsystems.
    Economic Geography 48 (1972):43-65.

Rose-Ackerman, S. The Political Economy of a Racist Housing Market.
    Journal of Urban Economics 4 (April 1977).

Rosenthal, Robert. Homeless in Paradise: A Map of the Terrain. Doctoral
    dissertation, University of California, Santa Barbara, 1987. UMO #
    8803877.

Rossell, Christine H. Does School Desegregation Policy Stimulate
    Residential Integration? A Critique of the Research. Urban
    Education 21 (January 1987):430-20.

Rossi, Peter and others. The Coalition of the Homeless of Chicago.
    Amherst, MA: University of Massachusetts, Social and Demographic
    Research Institute, 1986.

Rural New York Farmworker Opportunities, Inc. Farm Labor Housing in New
    York State. Rochester, NY, 1985.

Salins, Peter D. A Tale of Racism in the Suburbs. New York Times July
    28, 1988. [Minority husing in affluent white suburbs].

Saltman, Juliet (ed.) Integrated Neighborhoods in Action. Washington,

28, 1988. [Minority husing in affluent white suburbs].

Saltman, Juliet (ed.) Integrated Neighborhoods in Action. Washington,
    D.C.: National Neighbors, 1978.

Sanchez Korrol, Virginia E. Settlement Patterns and Community Development
    among Puerto Ricans in New York City, 1917-1948. Doctoral
    dissertation, State University of New York at Stony Brook, 1981. UMO
    # 8119239.

Sander, Richard H. Individual Rights and Demographic Realities: The
    Problem of Fair Housing. Northwestern University Law Review 82
    (Spring 1988):874-939.

Schrag, John and Jorge Casuso. 'Open' Suburbs Fight to Avoid Racial
    'Tipping'. Chicago Reporter 14 (December 1985). [Suburbs of
    Chicago].

Schwartz, Joel. The Consolidated Tenants League of Harlem: Black Self-
    Help vs. White Liberal Intervention in Ghetto Housing, 1934-1944.
    Afro-Americans in New York Life and History 10 (January 1986):31-51.

Schwartz, Joel. Tenant Unions in New York City's Low-Rent Housing, 1933-
    1949. Journal of Urban History 12 (August 1986):414-43.

Silver, Christopher. The Changing Face of Neighborhoods in Memphis and
    Richmond, 1940-1985. In: Randall M. Miller and George E. Pozzetta
    (eds.), Shades of the Sunbelt. Westport, CT: Greenwood, 1988.

Slade, Dorothy. Evolution of Negro Areas in Atlanta. Master's thesis,
    Atlanta University, 1946.

Smothers, Ronald. Housing Segregation: New Twists and Old Results
    [N.Y.C.]. New York City April 1, 1987.

Sorenson, Annmette and others. Indexes of Racial Residential Segregation
    for 109 Cities in the United States, 1940-1970. Sociological Forces
    8 (1975):125-42.

Standing, T. G. The Problem of Rural Housing in the South. Rural
    Sociology 7 (September 1942).

Stephenson, G. T. The Segregation of the White and Negro Races in Cities.
    South Atlantic Quarterly 13 (1914):1-18.

Stokes, Geoffrey and Gary Tilzer. The Lords of Flatbush. The Economics
    of Blockbusting. Village Voice December 3, 1980. [Flatbush-East
    Flatbush].

Sullivan, James Peter. The Effects of Subsidized Housing in Black
    Families of Low-Income and Moderate Income. Doctoral dissertation,
    Wayne State University, 1973. UMO # 74-11164.

Taeuber, Karl. The Contemporary Context of Housing Discrimination. Yale
    Law and Policy Review 6 (Spring-Summer 1988):339-47.

Taeuber, Karl. Racial Residential Segregation, 28 Cities, 1970-1980.
    Madison, WI: Center for Demography and Ecology, University of
    Wisconsin, March 1983.

Taeuber, Karl and Alma. Negroes in Cities: Residential Segregation and
    Neighborhood Change. Chicago: Aldine, 1965.

Taggart, Harriet Tee and Kevin W. Smith. Redlining: An Assessment of the
    Evidence of Disinvestment in Metropolitan Boston. In: Ray C. Rist
    (ed.), Policy Studies Review Annual, Vol. 6. Beverly Hills, CA:
    Sage, 1982.

Tackeuchi, Jane S. The Housing Location Decisions and Preferences of
    Minority and Non-Minority Households in Montgomery County, Maryland:
    Implication for Residential Segregation by Race and Ethnicity.
    Doctoral dissertation, Acuerrian University, 1980. UMO # 8111205.

Thompson, Thomas L. Institutional Racism in the Housing Market: A Study
    of Growth Roles and Investment Patterns. Doctoral dissertation,
    University of Texas, 1981. UMO # 8202060.

Tobin, Gary S. (ed.) Divided Neighborhoods. Changing Pattern of Racial
    Segregation. Newbury, CA: Sage, 1987.

U.S. Commission on Civil Rights. Directing of State and Local Fair
    Housing Agencies. Washington, D.C.: The Commission, 1985.

U.S. Commission on Civil Rights, Illinois Advisory Committee. Housing,
    Chicago Style: A Consultation. Washington, D.C.: The Commission,
    1982.

U.S. Commission on Civil Rights, Indiana Advisory Committee. Fair Housing
    Enforcement in Northwest Indiana: A Report. Washington, D.C.: The
    Commission, 1983.

U.S. Commission on Civil Rights, Kentucky Advisory Committee. Fair
    Housing in Louisville: The Community Development Block Grant
    Program. Washington, D.C.: The Commission, 1983.

United States Conference of Mayors. A Status Report on Homeless Families
    in America's Cities: A 29-City Survey. The Conference, May 1987.

U.S. Congress, 96th, 2nd session, House of Representatives, Committee on
    Banking, Finance, and Urban Affairs, Subcommittee on Housing and
    Community Development. Indian and Alaskan Native Housing Programs:
    Hearings .... Washington, D.C.: GPO, 1980.

U.S. Congress, 97th, 2nd session, House of Representatives, Committee on
    Banking, Finance, and Urban Affairs, Subcommittee on Housing and
    Community Development. Homelessness in America: Hearing ....
    Washington, D.C.: GPO, 1983.

U.S. Congress, 98th, 2nd session, House of Representatives, Committee on
    Banking, Finance, and Urban Affairs, Subcommittee on Housing and

Valdez, A. Residential Patterns of Chicanos, Undocumented Mexicans, and Anglos in San Antonio (Bexar County) Texas: An Assessment of Recent Change and Social Costs. In: H. L. Browning and R. O. de la Garza (eds.), Mexican Immigrants and Mexican Americans: An Evolving Relation, pp. 120-37. Austin: University of Texas Center for Mexican-American Studies, 1986.

Vose, Clement E. Caucasians Only: The Supreme Court, the NAACP and the Restrictive Covenant Cases. Berkeley: University of California Press, 1967.

Walter, Benjamin. Ethnicity and Residential Succession: Nashville, 1850-1920. In: Blumstein and Benjamin Walter (eds.), Growing Metropolis. Nashville, TN: Vanderbilt University Press, 1975.

Warren, Elizabeth. Subsidized Housing in Chicago. 2nd edition. Chicago: Center for Urban Policy, Loyola University, October 1980.

Weatherby, Norman Lee. Racial Segregation in Dallas Public Housing: 1970-1976. Master's thesis, North Texas State University, 1978. UMO # 1312854.

White, Dana F. The Black Sides of Atlanta: A Geography of Expansion and Containment, 1870-1970. Atlanta Historical Journal 26 (Summer-Fall 1982):199-225.

Williams, Lee. Concentrated Residence: The Case of Black Toledo, 1890-1930. Phylon 43 (June 1982):167-176.

Wilson, Franklin D. Residential Consumption, Economic Opportunities, and Race. New York: Academic Press, 1979.

Winerip, Michael. How Mt. Vernon [NY] Avoided Racism: It Voted Yes [Housing]. New York Times September 30, 1988.

Winerip, Michael. Lines that Divide Towns and the Races [Racial steering in real estate market of Long island]. New York Times December 22, 1985.

Winsberg, Morton D. Ethnic Competition for Residential Space in Miami, Florida, 1970-80. American Journal of Economics and Sociology 42 (July 1983):305-14.

Winsberg, Morton D. Flight from the Ghetto: The Migration of Middle Class and Highly Educated Blacks into White Urban Neighborhoods. American Journal of Economics and Sociology 44 (October 1985):411-21.

Winsberg, Morton D. Residential Integration Among Professional Blacks in Tallahasee, Florida. May 1979. ERIC ED 205 648.

Winters, Dorothy A. The Sensitivity of Housing Quality as Related to Selected Socio-Economic Variables in Manhattan, 1950-1960, 1960-1970: An Empirical Examination. Doctoral dissertation, New York University, 1974. UMO # 74-30056.

Wood, Peter B. Racial Attitudes in Integrated and Segregated
    Neighborhoods, 1972-1986. Doctoral dissertation, Vanderbilt
    University, 1988. UMO # 8815764.

Work, Monroe N. The Negro Real Estate Owners of Chicago. Master's
    thesis, University of Chicago, 1903.

Wright, George C. The NAACP and Residential Segregation in Louisville,
    Kentucky, 1914-1917. Regis. Ky. Hist. Soc. 78 (Winter 1980):35-54.

Yinger, John M. Prejudice and Discrimination in the Urban Housing Market.
    In: Peter Mieszkowski and Malhom Straszheim (eds.), Current Issues
    in Urban Economics, pp. 430-68. Baltimore, MD: John Hopkins
    University Press, 1979.

Yu, Connie Young. A History of San Francisco Chinatown Housing. Amerasia
    Journal 8 (Spring-Summer 1981):93-109.

Zonn, Leo E. Residential Search Patterns of Black Urban Households: A
    Spatial Behavioral View [Milwaukee]. Doctoral dissertation,
    University of Wisconsin-Milwaukee, 1975.

Housing Bibliography

Boyce, Byrl N. and Sidney Turoff (comps.) Minority Groups and Housing:
    A Bibliography, 1950-1970. Morristown, NJ: General Learning Press,
    1972.

Campbell, Agnes (comp.) Negro Housing in Texas and Cities, 1927-37. NY:
    Russell Sage Foundation Library, 1937.

Davis, Lenwood G. (comp.) Housing in the Black Community: A Selected
    Bibliography of Published Works on Housing Laws, Problems, Planning
    and Covenants in the Black Community. [Exchange Bibliography No.
    925.] Monticello, IL: Council of Planning Librarians, 1975.

Momeni, Jamshid A. (comp.) Housing and Racial/Ethnic Minority Status in
    the United States: An Annotated Bibliography with a Review Essay.
    Westport, CT: Greenwood, 1987.

[See also sections 7, 16, 20, 23, 27, 28, 31, 32, 42, 44, 47, 49, 57, 60,
    64, and 83]

*First of all, I believe that in keeping with integration I feel
I am just the token black on the White House list. I want to
make it perfectly clear that Nixon was on <u>my</u> list long before I
was on Nixon's list. However, any man who would hug Sammy Davis
can't be all bad.*

- Bill Cosby, <u>Variety</u>, July 4, 1973, upon learning his name
appeared on a White House list of "enemies" of the Nixon
Administration.

Altman, Sig. <u>The Comic Image of the Jew: Explorations of a Pop Culture
Phenomenon</u>. Rutherford, NJ: Fairleigh Dickinson University Press,
1971.

Arnez, Nancy L. and Clara B. Anthony. Contemporary Negro Humor as Social
Satire. <u>Phylon</u> 29 (Winter 1968):33-46.

Barksdale, Richard K. Black America and the Mask of Comedy. <u>In</u>:
Louis D. Rubin, Jr. (ed.), <u>The Comic Imagination in American
Literature</u>, pp. 349-60. New Brunswick, NJ: Rutgers University
Press, 1973.

Barksdale, Richard K. Black Autobiography and the Comic Vision. <u>Black
American Literature Forum</u> 15 (Spring 1981):22-27.

Barrick, Mac E. Racial Riddles and the Polack Joke. <u>Keystone Folklore
Quarterly</u> 15 (Spring 1978):3-15.

Bier, Jesse. <u>The Rise and Fall of American Humor</u>. NY: Holt, Rinehart
and Winston, 1968.

Bluestein, Gene. It Only Hurts When We Laugh: Ethnic Jokes and the
International Theme. <u>Thalia</u> 4 (Spring-Summer 1981):10-13.

Boskin, Joseph. Humor and Ethnicity. <u>In</u>: <u>Humor and Social Change
in Twentieth-Century America</u>, pp. 25-60. Boston: Trustees of the
Public Library of the City of Boston, 1979.

Boskin, Joseph. Sambo, the National Jester in the Popular Culture. <u>In</u>:
Gary B. Nash and Richard Weiss (eds.), <u>The Great Fear. Race in the
Mind of America</u>, pp. 165-85. New York: Holt, 1970.

Boskin, Joseph.   . <u>In</u>: Sarah B. Cohen (ed.), <u>Jewish Wry: Essays
on Jewish American Humor</u>. Bloomington, IN: Indiana University
Press, 1987.

Boskin, Joseph. <u>Sambo: The Rise and Decline of an American Jester</u>. New
York: Oxford University Press, 1986.

Boskin, Joseph and Joseph Dorinson. Ethnic Humor: Subversion and
Survival. <u>In</u>: Arthur Power Dudden (ed.), <u>American Humor</u>. New York:

Oxford University Press, 1987.

Brooks, A. Russell. The Comic Spirit and the Negro's New Look. CLA Journal 6 (September 1963):35-43.

Cook, William W. Change the Joke and Slip the Yoke: Traditions of Afro-American Satire. Journal of Ethnic Studies 13 (Spring 1985):109-34.

Dance, Daryl C. Contemporary Militant Black Humor. Negro American Literature Forum 8 (1974):217-22.

Davidson, Chandler. Ethnic Jokes: An Introduction to Race and Nationality. Teaching Sociology 15 (July 1987):296-302.

Dorinson, Joseph. The Gold-Dust Twins of Marginal Humor: Blacks and Jews. Maledicta 8 (1984-1985):163-92.

Dresser, Norine. Metamorphosis of the Humor of the Black Man. New York Folklore Quarterly 26 (September 1970):216-28.

Du Bois, W. E. B. The Humor of Negroes. Mark Twain Quarterly 5 (Fall-Winter 1942-43):12.

Dundes, Alan. Study of Ethnic Slurs: The Jew and the Polack in the United States. Journal of American Folklore 84 (1971):186-203.

Dundes, Alan (ed.) Mother Wit from the Laughing Barrel: Readings in the Interpretation of Afro-American Folklore. Englewood, NJ: Prentice-Hall, 1973.

Foster, Frances S. Charles Wright: Black Black Humorist. CLA Journal 15 (September 1971):44-53.

Foxx, Redd and Norma Miller. Redd Foxx Encyclopedia of Black Humor. Pasadena, CA: Ward Ritchie, 1977.

Gadfield, Nicholas J. and others. Dynamics of Humor in Ethnic Group Relations. Ethnicity 6 (December 1979):373-382.

Glanz, Rudolf. The Jew in Early American Wit and Graphic Humor. New York: Ktav Publishing House, 1973.

Hughes, Langston. Best of Simple. New York: Hill and Wang, 1961.

Hughes, Langston. Jokes Negroes Tell on Themselves. Negro Digest 9 (June 1951):21-25.

Hughes, Langston (ed.) Book of Negro Humor. New York: Dodd, Mead, 1966.

Jackson, Blyden. The Harlem Renaissance. In: Louis D. Rubin, Jr. (ed.), The Comic Imagination in American Literature pp. 295-303. New Brunswick, NJ: Rutgers University Press, 1973.

Joyner, Charles. The Trickster and the Fool: Folktales and Identity among Southern Plantation Slaves. Plantation Society 2 (December

1986):149-56.

Klumpp, James F. and Thomas A. Hollihan. Debunking the Resignation of
Earl Butz: Sacrificing an Official Racist. Quarterly Journal of
Speech 65 (February 1979):1-11.

McDowell, Edwin. Ethnic Jokebooks Flourish But Are Criticized. New York
Times July 30, 1983.

Middleton, Russell and John Moland. Humor in Negro and White Subcultures:
A Study of Jokes among University Students. American Sociological
Review 24 (1959):61-69.

Nichols, Charles H. Comic Modes in Black America (A Ramble through Afro-
American Humor). In: Sarah B. Cohen (ed.), Comic Relief.
Humor in Contemporary American Literature, pp. 105-26. Urbana:
University of Illinois Press, 1978.

Not All of It Was Noble---or Funny. American School Board Journal 163
(August 1976):13-14. [Self-critical review of racism in this journal
in past years].

Pen an' Wit: The Newsletter of African American Cartoonists. 1 (Fall
1987). [Association of African-American Cartoonists, c/a Corum, 2116
Suitland Terrace, S.E., Washington, D.C. 20020].

Peterson, John H., Jr. Black-White Joking Relationships among Newly-
Integrated Faculty. Integrateducation 13 (January-February
1975):33-37.

Rafky, David M. Wit and Racial Conflict among Colleagues. Integrated
Education (January-February 1972):39-43.

Rebolledo, Tey Diana. Walking the Thin Line: Humor in Chicano
Literature. In: Maria Herrera-Skobek (ed.), Beyond
Stereotypes, pp. 91-107. Binghamton, NY: Bilingual, 1985.

Salwak, Dale. A Checklist of American Humor Relating to Economic
Depression. Studies in American Humor. 3 (Summer-Fall 1984):253-66.

Sarris, Andrew. All About Eddie [Murphy]. Village Voice February 16,
1988.

Schuyler, George S. Black No More: Being an Account of the Strange and
Wonderful Workings of Science in the Land of the Free, A.D. 1933-
1940. New York: Maculay Co., 1931.

Shapiro, Laura. When Is a Joke Not a Joke? Newsweek May 23, 1988, p.
79. [Campus jokes about Jewish-American Princess and hostility
toward Jews].

Sheppard, Alice. From Kate Sanborn to Feminist Psychology: The Social
Context of Women's Humor, 1885-1985. Psychology of Women Quarterly
10 (June 1986):155-69.

Sheffey, Ruthe. Wit and Irony in Militant Black Poetry. <u>Black</u> <u>World</u> 22 (June 1973):14-21.

Simmons, Donald C. Anti-Italian-American Riddles in New England. <u>Journal of American Folklore</u> 79 (July-September 1966):475-78.

Simmons, Donald C. Protest Humor! Folklorist Re-action to Prejudice. <u>American Journal of Psychiatry</u> 120 (December 1963):567-70.

Solotaroff, Ivan. Tears of a Clown [Charlie Barnett]. <u>Village Voice</u> January 17, 1989.

Spence, Bruce. Charlie Hill Interview. Oneida's Stand-Up Comic. <u>Abwekon</u> Nos. 2-3 (September 1985):55-56, 117.

Sterling, Philip. <u>Laughing on the Outside: The Intelligent White Reader's Guide to Negro Tales and Humor</u>. New York: Grossett and Dunlap, 1965.

Teague, Bob. Charlie Doesn't Even Know His Daily Racism Is a Sick Joke. <u>New York Times Magazine</u> September 15, 1968.

Toll, Robert C. <u>Blacking Up. The Minstrel Show in Nineteenth-Century America</u>. NY: Oxford, 1974.

Walker, Nancy A. <u>A Very Serious Thing. Women's Humor and American Culture</u>. Minneapolis: University of Minnesota Press, 1988.

Walker, Nancy and Zita Dresner (eds.) <u>Redressing the Balance. American Women's Literary Humor from Colonial Times to the 1980s</u>. Jackson: University Press of Mississippi, 1988.

Waters, Harry F. with Michael Reese. Arsenio Hall's Late Arrival. <u>Newsweek</u> April 10, 1989.

Watkins, Mel. <u>On the Real Side</u>. [Book on Afro-American humor scheduled to be published in 1989].

Wohl, Alexander. Borscht Belt Humor Hits Broadway. Yea or Oy Veh? <u>Moment</u> 13 (July-August 1988):36-43.

[See also sections 6, 46, 77]

37. I.Q. and Race

*It should ... be the aim of every Negro student to ... better
equip himself as an active agent against the insidious
propaganda which ... seeks to demonstrate that the Negro is
intellectually and physically incapable of assuming the
dignities, rights and duties which devolve upon him as a member
of modern society.*

> - Horace Mann Bond, "Intelligence Tests and Propaganda,"
> Crisis, June 1924.

Allen, Garland E. Genetics, Eugenics, and Class Struggle. Genetics 79
   (June 1975):29-45.

Ashton, Geoffrey C. Blood Polymorphisms and Cognitive Abilities.
   Behavior Genetics 16 (September 1986):517-29.

Bardis, Panos D. Jensenism and Interracial Peace: A Multidisciplinary
   Essay on Intercultural Synthesis. International Journal of World
   Peace 4 (January-March 1987):77-104.

Block, N. Q. and Gerald Dworkin (eds.) The IQ Controversy: Critical
   Readings NY: Pantheon, 1975.

Boas, Franz. Fallacies of Racial Inferiority. Current History (February
   1927).

Bodmer, W. F. and L. L. Cavalli-Sforza. Intelligence and Race.
   Scientific American 223 (October 1970):19-29.

Bond, Horace Mann. Intelligence Tests and Propaganda. Crisis 28 (June
   1924):61-64.

Bond, Horace Mann. What the Army 'Intelligence Tests' Measure.
   Opportunity (July 1924).

Bond, Lloyd. The IQ Controvery and Academic Performance. In: Samuel M.
   Turner and Russell T. Jones (eds.), Behavior Modification in Black
   Populations, pp. 95-120. New York: Plenum Press, 1982.

Canady, H.G. The American Caste System and the Question of Negro
   Intelligence. Journal of Educational Psychology 33 (1942):161-72.

Carmines, Edward G. and Donald J. Baxter. Race, Intelligence and
   Political Efficacy among School Children. Adolescence 21 (Summer
   1986):443-47.

Cartwright, Walter J. and Thomas R. Burtis. Race and Intelligence:
   Changing Opinions in Social Science. Social Science Quarterly 49
   (December 1968).

Chase, Allan. The Legacy of Malthus: The Social Costs of the New

Scientific Racism. New York: Knopf, 1977.

Chapman, Paul D. _Schools as Sorters. Lewis M. Terman. Applied Psychology and the Intelligence Testing Movement. 1890-1930_. New York: New York University Press, 1989.

Colman, Andrew M. 'Scientific' Racism and the Evidence on Race and Intelligence. _Race_ 14 (October 1972):137-153.

Cowley, Geoffrey. A Confederacy of Dunces. Are the Best and the Brightest Making Too Few Babies. _Newsweek_ May 22, 1989. [See, below, Herrnstein].

Davey, A. G. Teachers, Race, and Intelligence. _Race_ 15 (October 1973):195-211.

Delgado and others. Can Science be Inopportune? Constitutional Validity of Governmental Restrictions on Race - IQ Research. _UCLA Law Review_ 31 (1983):128-44, 225.

Dobzhansky, Theodosius. Race Equality. _In_: R. H. Osborne (ed.), _The Biological and Social Meaning of Race_. San Francisco, CA: Freeman, 1971.

Dreeben, Robert and Adam Gamoran. Race, Instruction, and Learning. _American Sociological Review_ 51 (October 1986):660-69.

Du Bois, W. E. B. Race Intelligence. _Crisis_ 20 (July 1920):118-19.

Epps, Edgar G. Race, Intelligence, and Learning: Some Consequences of the Misuse of Test Results. _Phylon_ 34 (June 1973):153-59.

Fancher, Raymond E. _The Intelligence Men: Makers of the IQ Controversy_. New York: Norton, 1985.

Franklin, Vincent P. Black Social Scientists and the Mental Testing Movement, 1920-1940. _In_: Reginald L. Jones (ed.), _Black Psychology_. New York: Harper and Row, 1980.

Garnett, Henry E. 'Facts' and 'Interpretation' Regarding Race Differences. _Science_ 101 (1945):404-405.

Goldsby, Richard A. _Race and Races_. 2nd ed. NY: Macmillan, 1977.

Goleman, Daniel. An Emerging Theory on Black's I.Q. Scores. _New York Times Education Life_ April 10, 1988.

Harwood, Jonathan. The Race and Intelligence Controversy: A Sociological Approach, I: Professional Factors; II: External Factors. _Social Studies of Science_ 6 (Autumn 1976), 7 (February 1977).

Herrnstein, Richard J. I.Q. _Atlantic_ 228 (September 1971):43-64.

Herrnstein, Richard J. IQ and Falling Birth Rates. _Atlantic_ (May 1989). [See, above, Cowley].

300

Hirsch, Jerry. Behavior-Genetic Analysis and Its Biosocial Consequences. Seminars in Psychiatry 2 (February 1970):89-105.

Hirsch, Jerry. To 'Unfrock the Charlatans'. Race Relations Abstracts 6 (May 1981):1-65.

Humphrey, Lloyd G. Race Differences and the Spearman Hypothesis. Intelligence 9 (July-September 1985):275-83. [In re: Jensen; see Jensen, below].

Ioannides, Y. M. Heritability of Ability, Intergenerational Transfers and the Distribution of Wealth. International Economic Review 27 (October 1986).

Jencks, Christopher. Genes and Crime. New York Review of Books February 12, 1987.

Jenkins, Martin D. The Mental Ability of the American Negro. Journal of Negro Education 8 (July 1939).

Jensen, Arthur R. How Much Can We Boost I.Q. and Scholastic Achievement? Harvard Educational Review (Winter 1969).

Jensen, Arthur R. Humphrey's Attenuated Test of Spearman's Hypothesis. Intelligence 9 (July-September 1985):285-89. [See Humphrey, above].

Jensen, Arthur R. IQs and Genes. Time December 15, 1986. [Letter].

Jerrison, Harry J. Evolution of the Brain and Intelligence. Current Anthropology 16 (September 1975):403-26. [Symposium on Jensen's work].

Johnson, Charles S. Mental Measurement of Negro Groups. Opportunity 1 (February 1923):21-25.

Johnson, Charles S. and Horace Mann Bond. The Investigation of Racial Differences Prior to 1910. Journal of Negro Education 3 (July 1934):328-39.

Jordan, Winthrop D. A Sense of Success: Heredity, Intelligence, and Race in American History and Culture. In: Peggy R. Sanday (ed.), Anthropology and the Public Interest. New York: Academic Press, 1976.

Jorgensen, Carl C. Racism in Mental Testing: The Use of I.Q. Tests to Mislabel Black Children. In: Albert A. Harrison (ed.), Explorations in Psychology, pp. 194-215. Monterey, CA: Brooks/Cole, 1974.

Kamin, Leon J. The Science and Politics of I.Q.. New York: Wiley, 1974.

King, Larry L. The Traveling Carnival of Racism [Debate at Princeton University between William B. Schockley and Ashley Montagu on racial factors in intelligence]. New Times 1 (December 1973):36-40.

301

Kleinfeld, J. S.   Intellectual Strengths in Culturally Different Groups:
An Eskimo Illustration. Review of Educational Research 43 (Summer
1973):341-59.

Lawler, James. IQ, Heritability, and Racism. NY: International
Publishers, 1978.

Lewontin, Richard C. Race and Intelligence. Bulletin of the Atomic
Scientists 26 (1970):2-8.

Mayo, Marion J. The Mental Capacity of the American Negro. New York:
Science Press, 1913. [Review: Journal of Phil. Psych. and Sci.
Methods, Sept. 24, 1914, vol. 11, 557-8].

Mercer, Jane R. Ethnic Differences in IQ Scores: What Do They Mean? (A
Response to Lloyd Dunn). Hispanic Journal of Behavioral Sciences 10
(September 1988):199-218.

Modgil, Sohan and Celie Modgil (eds.) Arthur Jensen: Consensus and
Controversy. Falmer Press, 1986.

Montagu, Ashley (ed.) Race and IQ. New York: Oxford, 1975.

Morris, Frank L. The Jensen Hypothesis: Was It the White Perspective or
White Racism? Journal of Black Studies 2 (March 1972):371-386.

Paul, Diane. Eugenics and the Left. Journal of the History of Ideas 45
(October-December 1984):567-90.

Rury, John L. Race, Region, and Education: An Analysis of Black and
White Scores on the 1917 Army Alpha Intelligence Test. Journal of
Negro Education 57 (Winter 1988):51-65.

Sacks, Karen. The New Rassenscience. The Racism of the Jensens and
Schockleys. Jewish Currents 32 (February 1978):4-12.

Scarr, S. and R. A. Weinberg. The Nature-Nurture Problem Revisited: The
Minnesota Adoption Studies. In: Irving E. Sigel and Gene Brody
(eds.), Methods of Family Research, Vol. 1. Hillsdale, NJ:
Erlbaum, 1989.

Schlesinger, K. Behavioral Genetics and the Nature-Nurture Question. In:
A. Kimble and K. Schlesinger (eds.), Topics in the History of
Psychology, II. Hillsdale, NJ: Lawrence Elbaum Associates, 1985.

Sowell, Thomas. New Light on Black I.Q. New York Times Magazine March
27, 1977.

Spencer, M. B. and others (eds.) Beginnings: The Social and Affective
Development of Black Children. Hillsdale, NJ: Lawrence Elbaum
Associates, 1985.

Spitz, Herman H. (ed.) The Raising of Intelligence: A Selected History
of Attempts to Raise Retarded Intelligence. Hillsdale, NJ: Lawrence

Erlbaum Associates, 1986.

Spring, Joel H. Psychologists and the War: The Meaning of Intelligence in the Alpha and Beta Tests. *History of Education Quarterly* 12 (1972):3-15.

Tobias, Phillip V. Brain-size, Grey Matter and Race - Fact or Fiction? *American Journal of Physical Anthropology* 32 (1970):3-25.

Valentine, Charles A. and Bettylou Valentine. Brain Damage and the Intellectual Defense of Inequality. *Current Anthropology* 16 (March 1975):117-150.

Weinberg, Meyer. Race and Intelligence in America, pp. 54-93 *in The Search for Quality Integrated Education*. Westport, CT: Greenwood Press, 1983.

Williams, Robert L. On Black Intelligence. *Journal of Black Studies* 4 (September 1973):29-39.

Work, Monroe N. The Negro Brain. *In*: W.E.B. Du Bois (ed.), *The Health and Physique of the Negro American*, pp. 25-27. Atlanta: Atlanta University Press, 1906.

Yergin, Peter. "I'm Not a Racist. I'm a Raceologist" [Interview with William Schockley]. *Times Higher Education Supplement* May 1974.

Zenderland, Leila C. *Henry Herbert Goddard and the Origins of American Intelligence Testing*. Doctoral dissertation, University of Pennsylvania, 1986. UMO # 8624043.

[See also sections 25, 26, 73, 77, and 79]

38. Immigration

The Filipinos came to the United States with a feeling of belonging, due to their long occupation by U.S. forces and expected to be treated as equals. ... [Yet,] the statement claiming that Filipinos were culturally unassimilable was made as vehemently concerning the Filipino as it was made concerning the Japanese and Chinese.

- Violet Rabaya, "Filipino Immigration: the Creation of a New Social Problem," 1971.

Abrams, Bruce A. A Mutual Cry: White Opposition to the Japanese Exclusion Movement, 1911-1924. Doctoral dissertation, City University of New York, 1987. UMO # 8801676.

Albuquerque, Klaus de and Jerome L. McElroy. West Indian Migration to the United States Virgin Islands: Demographic Impacts and Socioeconomic Consequences. International Migration Review 16 (Spring 1982):61-101.

Alegado, Dean T. Profile: U.S. Filipino in the 80s. Katipunan 1 (September-October 1987):19-20.

Allen, Zita. Kick 'Em Out and You Might Die. Village Voice July 12, 1988. [Filipino nurses in the U.S.].

Almirol, Edwin B. Exclusion and Acceptance of Filipinosin America. Asian Profile (Hong Kong) 13 (1985):395-408.

Asher, Robert. Union Nativism and the Immigrant Response. Labor History 23 (Summer 1982):325-41.

Beckford, George. Persistent Poverty [Caribbean area]. London: Oxford University Press, 1972.

Bodner, John E. The Impact of the 'New Immigration' on the Black Worker: Steelton, Pennsylvania, 1880-1920. Labor History 17 (1976):214-29.

Bounett, A. W. Institutional Adaptation of West Indian Immigrants to America: An Analysis of Rotating Credit Associations. Washington, D.C.: University Press of America, 1981.

Bryce-Laporte, Roy S. and Delores M. Mortimer. Caribbean Immigration to the United States. Washington, D.C.: Research Institute on Immigration and Ethnic Studies, 1983.

Bukowczyk, John J. Polish Culture and Immigrant Working Class Formation, 1880-1914. Polish American Studies 41 (Autumn 1984):23-44.

Cardenas, Gilberto. U.S. Immigration Policy Toward Mexico: An Historical Perspective. Chicano Law Review 2 (Summer 1975):66-91.

Cardoso, Lawrence A. *Mexican Emigration to the United States, 1897-1931*. Tucson: University of Arizona Press, 1980.

Carrasquilla, A. L. and E. E. Saudis. *Schooling, Job Opportunities, and Ethnic Mobility among Caribbean Youth in the United States*. NY: Fordham University. [Conference in 1982 sponsored by Aspira].

Center for Migration Studies. *In Defense of the Alien*. 6 vols. Staten Island, NY: The Center, 1984.

Chandrasekhar, S. (ed.) *From India to America: A Brief History of Immigration; Problems of Discrimination; Admission and Assimilation*. Population Review, 1984.

Chierici, Rose-Marie C. *Demele: "Making It," Migration and Adaptation among Haitian Boat People in the United States* [Entered U.S., 1978-1982]. Doctoral dissertation, University of Rochester, 1986. UMO # 8615275.

City of New York, Office of Immigrant Affairs. *Caribbean Immigrants in New York City, a Demographic Summary*. NY: The Office, 1985.

Cloud, P. and D. W. Galenson. Chinese Immigration and Contract Labor in the Late Nineteenth Century. *Explorations in Economic History* 24 (January 1987).

Compton, Daniel. Asylum for Persecuted Social Groups: A Closed Door Left Slightly Ajar. *Washington Law Review* 62 (October 1987):913-39.

Coolidge, Mary R. *Chinese Immigration*. 1909.

Craig, Susan (ed.) *Contemporary Caribbean: A Sociological Reader*. 2 vols. Maracas, Trinidad and Tobago: College Press, 1981.

Crewdson, John M. Thousands of Aliens Held in Virtual Slavery in U.S. *New York Times* October 19, 1980.

Curran, J. *Xenophobia and Immigration, 1820-1930*. Twayne, 1975.

Daniels, Roger. Change in Immigration Law and Nativism since 1924. *American Jewish History* 76 (December 1986):159-80.

De Freitas, G. Hispanic Immigration and Labor Market Segmentation. *Industrial Relations* 27 (Spring 1988).

Deng, Shusheng. Chinese Americans. A Review of Their Past and Present. *Beijing Review* July 4, 1988.

Dominquez, Virginia. *From Neighbor to Stranger: The Dilemmas of Caribbean Peoples in the United States*. New Haven, CT: 1975.

Dunbar, Barrington. *Factors in Cultural Backgrounds on the British West Indian Negro and the American Southern Negro that Conditioned their Adjustment in Harlem*. Master's thesis, Columbia University, 1936.

Edelstein, Eleanor R. From Immigrant to Ethnic: A Study of Portuguese-
    Americans in Bristol, Rhode Island. Doctoral dissertation, American
    University, 1986. UMO # 8701293.

Ehrlich, Richard (ed.) Immigrants in Industrial America, 1850-1920.
    Charlottesville: University of Virginia Press, 1977.

Fawcett, James T. and Benjamin V. Carino (eds.) Pacific Bridges: The
    New Immigration from Asia and the Pacific Islands. New York: Center
    for Migration Studies, 1987.

Fawcett, James T. and others. Asia-Pacific Immigration to the United
    States. Honolulu: East-West Population Institute, 1985.

First, Joan M. and others. New Voices. Immigrant Students in U.S. Public
    Schools. Boston: National Coalition of Advocates for Students,
    1988.

Foner, Nancy. Race and Color: Jamaican Migrants in London and New York
    City. International Migration Review 19 (Winter 1985):708-27.

Foner, Nancy. West Indians in New York City and London: A Comparative
    Analysis. International Migration Review 13 (Summer 1979):284-297.

Foner, Nancy (ed.) New Immigrants in New York [1960s-1980s in New York
    City]. New York: Columbia University Press, 1987.

Fouron, G. E. The Black Immigrant Dilemma in the U.S.: The Haitian
    Experience. Journal of Caribbean Studies 3, 242-65.

Fragomen, Austin T., Jr. and Lydia F. Tomasi (eds.) In Defense of the
    Alien. 4 vols. 1979. ERIC ED 222 592-222 595.

Garcia, Mario T. Desert Immigrants: The Mexicans of El Paso, 1880-1920.
    New Haven, CT: Yale University Press, 1981.

Gonzalez, Nancie L. Garifuna Settlement in New York: A New Frontier.
    International Migration Review 13 (Summer 1979):255-263. [Black
    Caribs].

Gonzalez, Nancie L. Peasant's Progress: Dominicans in New York.
    Caribbean Studies 10 (October 1970):154-171.

Gordon, Monica H. West Indian Immigrants and the United States Education
    Process. August 1979. ERIC ED 197 005.

Gutierrez, David G. Ethnicity, Ideology, and Political Development:
    Mexican Immigration as a Political Issue in the Chicano Community,
    1910-1977. Doctoral dissertation, Stanford University, 1988. UMO #
    8808364.

Guttmacher, S. Immigrant Workers: Health, Law, and Public Housing
    Policy. Journal of Health Politics, Policy and Law 9 (1984):505-14.

Halter, Marilyn B. Cape Verdian-American Immigration and Patterns of

Settlement, 1860-1940 [Southeastern Massachusetts]. Doctoral
dissertation, Boston University, 1986. UMO # 8616128.

Haskins, Jim. The Statue of Liberty: An All-American Vision. American
Visions 1 (July-August 1986):12-19. [Black immigrants].

Hellwig, David J. Black Reactions to Chinese Immigration and the Anti-
Chinese Movement: 1850-1910. Amerasia Journal 6 (1979):25-44.

Hellwig, David J. Patterns of Black Nativism, 1830-1930. American
Studies 23 (Spring 1982):85-98.

Hendricks, Glenn (ed.) The Hmong in Transition. Staten Island, NYC:
Center for Migration Studies, 1985. [Proceedings of a 1983
conference].

Hershberg, Theodore. Blacks in Philadelphia: 1850-1980. Immigrants,
Opportunities, and Racism. In: The State of Black Philadelphia
1981, pp. 4-29. Philadelphia: Urban League of Philadelphia, 1981.

Hershberg, Theodore and others. A Tale of Three Cities: Blacks and
Immigrants in Philadelphia: 1850-1880, 1930, and 1970. Annals of
the American Academy of Political and Social Science 441 (January
1979):55-81.

Hoerder, Dirk (ed.) "Struggle a Hard Battle": Essays on Working-Class
Immigrants. De Kalb, IL: Northern Illinois University Press, 1986.

Hogan, Lawrence. Afro-American History as Immigration History: The
Anguillans of Perth Amboy. Social Studies 78 (September-October
1987):210-12.

Holleran, Thomas R. Racism and Restriction: American Immigration to
1924. Master's thesis, Central Connecticut State University, 1987.

Ichioka, Yuh. 'Attorney for the Defense': Yamato Ichihashi and Japanese
Immigration. Pacific Historical Review 55 (May 1986):192-225.

Immigration and American Public Policy. Annals of the American Academy of
Political and Social Science (September 1986):9-217.

Immigration: Special Studies. 1969-1982 and 1982-1985 [16 microfilm
reels]. Frederick, MD: University Publications of America, 1987.

Inoki, T. Japanese Emigration to Hawaii and North America in 1890s.
Osaka Economic Papers 34 (December 1984). [In Japanese, with
English summary].

Ishi, Tomoji K. International Linkage and National Class Conflict: The
Migration of Korean Nurses to the United States. Amerasia Journal
14 (1988):23-50.

Ishi, Tomoji K. The Political Economy of International Migration: Indian
Physicians to the United States. South Asia Bulletin 2 (Spring
1982).

Kasinitz, Philip. West Indian Diaspora: Race, Ethnicity and Politics in New York City. Doctoral dissertation, New York University, 1987. UMO # 8801547.

Kaspi, Andre. L'Immigrant voila L'ennemi: Le Nativism aux Etas-Unis entre 1880 et 1914. Etudes Anglaises: Grand Bretagne, Etas Unis 40 (January-March 1987):28-38.

Koo, H. and E. Yu. Korean Immigration to the United States: Its Demographic Pattern and Social Implications for Both Societies. Honolulu: East-West Population Institute, 1981.

Laguerre, Michel S. American Odyssey: Haitians in New York City. Ithaca, NY: Cornell University System, 1984.

Laguerre, Michel S. Haitian Americans. In: Alan Harwood (ed.), Ethnicity and Medical Care, pp. 172-210. Cambridge, MA: Harvard University Press, 1981.

Lai, H. M. and others. Island: Poetry and History of Chinese Immigrants on Angel Island, 1910-1940. San Francisco, CA: 1980.

Lane, A. T. Solidarity or Survival? American Labor and European Immigrants, 1830-1924. Westport, CT: Greenwood, 1987.

Lee, Letha A. International Migration and Refugee Problems: Conflict between Black Americans and Southeast Asian Refugees. Journal of Intergroup Relations 14 (Winter 1987):38-50.

Lewis, Gordon K. Main Currents in Caribbean Thought. The Historical Evolution of Caribbean Society in Its Ideological Aspects, 1492-1900. Baltimore, MD: Johns Hopkins University Press, 1983.

Lieberson, Stanley. A Piece of the Pie: Blacks and White Immigrants Since 1880. Berkeley, CA: University of California Press, 1981.

Loescher, Gil and John A. Scanlan. Calculated Kindness: Refugees and America's Half-Open Door, 1945 to the Present. New York: Free Press, 1986.

Massey, Douglas S. and Kathleen M. Schnabel. Recent Trends in Hispanic Immigration to the United States. International Migration Review 17 (Summer 1983):212-44.

Massey, Douglas S. and others. Return to Aztlan: The Social Processes of International Migration from Western Mexico. Berkeley, CA: University of California Press, 1987.

McAdoo, William. The Settler State: Immigration Policy and the Rise of Institutional Racism in Nineteenth-Century Michigan. 2 vols. Doctoral dissertation, University of Michigan, 1983. UMO # 8324245.

McCarthy, Kevin F. and R. Burciago Valdez. Current and Future Effects of Mexican Immigration in California. Santa Monica, CA: Rand Corp.,

May 1986.

McLaughlin, Megan E. West Indian Immigrants: Their Social Networks and Ethnic Identification [Brooklyn]. Doctoral dissertation, Columbia University, 1981. UMO # 8125341.

Miller, J. The Plight of Haitian Refugees. New York: Praeger, 1984.

Miller, Stuart C. The Unwelcome Immigrant, The American Image of the Chinese, 1785-1882. Berkeley, CA: University of California Press, 1969.

Millette, Robert E. Social Stratification among First Generation Grenadians in Brooklyn: A Look at Adaptations to Deal with the New Society. Doctoral dissertation, New School for Social Research, 1982. UMO # 8303578.

Mink, Gwendolyn. Old Labor and New Immigrants in American Political Development: Union, Party, and State, 1875-1920. Ithaca, NY: Cornell University Press, 1986.

Morawska, Ewa. Labor Migrations of Poles in the Atlantic World Economy, 1880-1914. Comparative Studies in Society and History 31 (April 1989):237-72.

Moriyama, Alan T. Imigaisha, Japanese Emigration Companies and Hawaii, 1894-1908. Honolulu: University of Hawaii Press, 1985.

Muller, Thomas and Thomas J. Espenshade. The Fourth Wave: California's Newest Immigrants [Mexican immigration into California]. Washington, D.C.: Urban Institute, 1985.

Naff, Alixa. Becoming American: The Early Arab Immigrant Experience. Carbondale: Southern Illinois University Press, 1985.

Nigem, Elias T. Arab Americans: Migration, Socioeconomic and Demographic Characteristics. International Migration Review 20 (Fall 1986):629-49.

Palmer, R. W. A Decade of West Indian Migration to the United States, 1962-1972. Social and Economic Studies 23 (1974):571-87.

Pascual-Moran, Vanessa. The Shadow of Public Opinion and Various Interlocking Issues on U.S. Immigration Policy: 1965-1982. Doctoral dissertation, Columbia University, 1987. UMO # 8809402.

Pavalko, R. M. Racism and the New Immigration: A Reinterpretation of the Assimilation of White Ethnics in American Society. Sociology and Social Research 65 (October 1980):56-77.

Payne, A. J. and P. K. Button (eds.) Dependency Under Challenge: The Political Economy of the Commonwealth Caribbean. Dover, NH: Manchester University Press, 1984.

Petras, Elizabeth M. Jamaican Labor Migration, White Capital and Black

Labor. 1850-1930. Boulder, CO: Westview Press, 1987.

Pido, Antonio. The Philipinos in America: Macro/Micro Dimensions of Immigration and Integration. Staten Island, NY: Center for Migration Studies, 1986.

Reid, Ira De A. The Negro Immigrant ... 1899-1937. New York: Columbia University Press, 1939.

Reynolds, C. W. and R. K. McCleery. The Political Economy of Immigration Law: Impact of Simpson-Rodino on the United States and Mexico. Journal of Economic Perspective 2 (Summer 1988).

Romo, Ricardo. Responses to Mexican Immigration, 1910-1930. Aztlan 6 (Summer 1975):173-94.

Rubin, Jay. Black Nativism: The European Immigrant in Negro Thought, 1830-1860. Phylon 39 (Fall 1978):193-202.

Saveth, Edward. The Immigrant in American Textbooks, Good Stocks and Lesser Breeds. Commentary (May 1949).

Shankman, Arnold M. Ambivalent Friends: Afro-Americans View the Immigrant. Westport, CT: Greenwood, 1982.

Shepperson, Wilbur. Emigration and Disenchantment [Immigrants who failed to r U.S.]. Norman: University of Oklahoma Press, 1965.

Shorris, Earl. Raids, Racism and I.N.S. [U.S. Immigration and Naturalization Service]. Nation May 8, 1989.

Shughart, W. F. and others. The Political Economy of Immigration Restriction. Yale Journal on Regulation 4 (Fall 1986).

Silverman, Andrew. An Historical and Legal Prospective of Mexican Migration. Arizona Journal of International and Comparative Law (1988):138-51.

Simon, Rita J. Immigration and American Attitudes. Public Opinion (July-August 1987):47-50.

Smith, J. Owens. The Politics of Income and Education Differences between Black and West Indians. Journal of Ethnic Studies 13 (Fall 1985):17-30.

Smith, Raymond T. Race and Class in the Post-Emancipation Caribbean. In: Robert Ross (ed.), Racism and Colonialism. The Hague: Martinus Nijhoff, 1982.

Stepick, Alex. Haitians Released from Krome [Detention Center]: Their Prospects for Adaptation and Integration in South Florida. March 2, 1984. ERIC ED 246 155.

Stinner, William F. and others (eds.) Return Migration and Remittances: Developing a Caribbean Perspective. Washington, D.C.: Research

Institute on Immigration and Ethnic Studies, Smithsonian Institution, 1982.

Sutton, Constance R. and Elsa M. Chaney. Caribbean Life in New York City: Sociocultural Dimensions. Staten Island, NY: Center for Migration Studies, 1987.

Toney, Joyce R. The Development of a Culture of Migration among a Caribbean People: St. Vincent and New York, 1836-1979. Doctoral dissertation, Columbia University, 1986. UMO # 8623623.

Thanh Van Tran. Ethnic Community Supports and Psychological Well-Being of Vietnamese Refugees. International Migration Review 21 (Fall 1987):833-44.

Thomas, Bert J. Historical Functions of Caribbean-American Benevolent/Progressive Associations. Afro-Americans in New York Life and History 12 (July 1988):45-58.

Thompson, James. The Black as Ironic Immigrant: Self-Perception in the Early Republic. Arbeiten aus Anglistick und Americkenistik 12 (1987):57-70.

Ueda, Reed. West Indians. In: Stephan Thernstrom (ed.), Harvard Encyclopedia of American Ethnic Groups, pp. 1020-27. Cambridge, MA: Harvard University Press, 1980.

U.S. Commission on Civil Rights. Civil Rights Issues of Euro-Ethnic Americans in the United States: Opportunities and Challenges. Washington, D.C.: The Commission, 1980.

Wakatsuki, Yasuo. Japanese Emigration to the United States 1866-1924. A Mongraph. In: Donald Fleming (ed.), Perspectives in American History. 12 (1979).

Walter, John C. West Indian Immigrants: Those Arrogant Bastards. Contributions in Black Studies No. 5 (1981-1982).

Widen, Alan. Immigration, the Public School, and the 20th Century American Ethos. Lanham, MD: University Press of America, 1985.

Zolberg, Aristide R. The Roots of American Refugee Policy [Touches on Jewish immigration, 1890s-1930s]. Social Research (Winter 1988):649-78.

Immigration Bibliography

Brana-Shute, R. (ed.) A Bibliography of Caribbean Migration and Caribbean Immigrant Communities. Gainesville: University of Florida Libraries, 1983.

Burciaga Valdez, R. and others (comps.) An Annotated Bibliography of Sources on Mexican Immigration. Santa Monica, CA: RAND, March 1987.

Center for Afroamerican and African Studies, The University of Michigan
   (comp.) Black Immigration and Ethnicity in the United States: An
   Annotated Bibliography. Westport, CT: Greenwood, 1985.

Cordasco, Francesco (comp.) The New American Immigration: Evolving
   Pattern of Legal and Illegal Emigration: A Bibliography of Selected
   References. New York: Garland, 1987.

Hoglund, A. William (comp.) Immigrants and their Children in the United
   States. A Bibliography of Doctoral Dissertations, 1885-1982. New
   York: Garland.

Jerabek, Esther (comp.) Czechs and Slovaks in North America. New York:
   1977.

Saito, Shiro (comp.) Filipinos Overseas: A Bibliography. New York:
   1977.

[See also sections 11, 15, 20, 23, 32, 34, 40, 41, 44, 48, 52, 60, and 77]

312

39. Industry, Employment by

*He is a hotel-waiter, a vendor of peanuts and cakes, or a mere
beast of burden.*

   - <u>Liberator</u>, September 21, 1860, on black employment,
perhaps especially in Boston.

Anderson, Bernard E. <u>Negro Employment in Public Utilities:</u> <u>Study of
Racial Policies in the Electric Power, Gas, and Telephone Industries</u>.
Philadelphia: University of Pennsylvania Press, 1970.

Anderson, Bernard E. <u>The Negro in the Public Utility Industries</u>.
Philadelphia: University of Pennsylvania Press, 1970.

Anthony, Carl. <u>Blacks in Construction</u>. Berkeley, CA: University of
California, 1977.

Armstrong, Thomas F. The Transformation of Work: Turpentine Workers in
Coastal Georgia, 1865-1901. <u>Labor History</u> 25 (Fall 1984):518-32.

Barnum, Darold T. <u>The Negro in the Bituminous Coal Mining Industry</u>.
Philadelphia: University of Pennsylvania Press, 1970.

Bergman, Barbara R. and Jerolyn R. Lyle. The Occupational Standing of
Negroes by Areas and Industries. <u>Journal of Human Resources</u> 6 (Fall
1971):411-433.

Bishir, Catherine W. Black Builders in Antebellum North Carolina. <u>North
Carolina History Review</u> 61 (October 1984):423-61.

Bloom, Gordon F. and F. Marion Fletcher. <u>The Negro in the Supermarket
Industry</u>. Philadelphia: University of Pennsylvania Press, 1972.

Bloom, Gordon F. and others. <u>Negro Employment in Retail Trade:</u> <u>A Study
of Racial Policies in the Department Store, Drugstore, and
Supermarket Industries</u>. Philadelphia: University of Pennsylvania
Press, 1972.

Campbell, Robert A. <u>An Added Objection:</u> <u>The Use of Blacks in the Coal
Mines of Washington, 1880-1896</u>. Master's thesis, University of
British Columbia, 1978.

Campbell, Robert A. Blacks and the Coal Mines of Western Washington,
1888-1896. <u>Pac. N. W. Q.</u> 73 (October 1982):146-55.

Dickerson, Dennis C. <u>Out of the Crucible:</u> <u>Black Steelworkers in Western
Pennsylvania, 1875-1980</u>. Albany: State University of New York
Press, 1986.

Farr, James B. <u>Black Odyssey:</u> <u>The Seafaring Traditions of Afro-
Americans</u>. Doctoral dissertation, University of California, Santa
Barbara, 1982. UMO # 8310195.

313

Fickle, James E. Management Looks At the Labor Problem: The Southern Pine Industry During World War I and the Postwar Era. _Journal of Southern History_ 40 (1974):61-76.

Fishback, Price. _Employment Conditions of Blacks in the Coal Industry, 1900-1930_. Doctoral dissertation, University of Washington, 1983.

Fletcher, F. Marion. _The Negro in the Drug Manufacturing Industry_. Philadelphia: University of Pennsylvania Press, 1970.

Fletcher, F. Marion. _The Negro in the Drugstore Industry_. Philadelphia: University of Pennsylvania Press, 1971.

Fletcher, F. Marion. _The Negro in the Insurance Industry_. Philadelphia: University of Pennsylvania Press, 1970.

Fogel, Walter A. _The Negro in the Meat Industry_. Philadelphia: University of Pennsylvania Press, 1970.

Frederickson, Mary. Four Decades of Change: Black Workers in Southern Textiles, 1941-1981. _Radical America_ 16 (November-December 1982):27-44.

Fulmer, William E. _The Negro in the Furniture Industry_. Philadelphia: University of Pennsylvania Press, 1973.

Goins, John B. _The American Colored Waiter_. New York: Hotel Monthly, 1902.

Gutman, Herbert G. Reconstruction in the Hocking Valley Coal Mines in 1873 and 1874. _Labor History_ 3 (Fall 1962):243-64.

Harris, Abram. The Negro in the Coal Mining Industry. _Opportunity_ (February 1926):45-8.

Herbst, Alina. _The Negro in the Slaughtering and Meat-Packing Industry in Chicago_. New York: Arno, 1970 (orig. 1932).

Hill, Herbert. Employment Manpower Training and the Black Worker. _Journal of Negro Education_ 38 (Summer 1969):204-17.

Howard, John C. _The Negro in the Lumber Industry_. Philadelphia: University of Pennsylvania Press, 1970.

Huntley, Horace. _Iron Coal Miners and Mine Mill in Alabama: 1933-1952_. Doctoral dissertation, University of Pittsburgh, 1977.

Irons, Edward D. and Gilbert Moore. _Black Managers: The Case of the Banking Industry_. New York: Praeger, 1985.

James, Samuel D. K. _The Impact of Cybernation Technology on Black Automotive Workers in the U.S._ Ann Arbor, MI: UMI Research Press, 1985.

314

Jeffress, Philip W. The Negro in the Urban Transit Industry.
     Philadelphia: University of Pennsylvanina, 1970.

Kilar, Jeremy W. Black Pioneers in the Michigan Lumber Industry. Journal
     of Forest History 24 (July 1980):142-149.

King, Carl B. and Howard W. Risher, Jr. The Negro in the Petroleum
     Industry. Philadelphia: University of Pennsylvania Press, 1969.

Koziana, Edward C. and Karen S. Koziana. The Negro in the Hotel Industry.
     Philadelphia: University of Pennsylvania Press, 1968.

Leone, Richard D. The Negro in the Trucking Industry. Philadelphia:
     University of Pennsylvania Press, 1970.

Lewis, Ronald L. Job Control and Race Relations in Coal Fields, 1870-
     1920. Journal of Ethnic Studies 12 (Winter 1985):35-64.

The Negro in Industry. [Bulletin No. 66.] New York: Russell Sage
     Foundation Library, 1924.

Northrup, Herbert R. The Negro in the Aerospace Industry. Philadelphia:
     Unversity of Pennsylvania Press, 1968.

Northrup, Herbert R. The Negro in the Automobile Industry. Philadelphia:
     University of Pennsylvania Press, 1968.

Northrup, Herbert R. The Negro in the Paper Industry. Philadelphia:
     University of Pennsylvania Press, 1969.

Northrup, Herbert R. The Negro in the Tobacco Industry. Philadelphia:
     University of Pennsylvania Press, 1970.

Northrup, Herbert R. and Alan B. Batchelder. The Negro in the Rubber Tire
     Industry. Philadelphia: University of Pennsylvania Press, 1969.

Northrup, Herbert R. and others. Negro Employment in Basic Industry: A
     Study of Racial Policies in Six Industries. Philadelphia:
     University of Pennsylvania Press, 1970.

Northrup, Herbert R. and others. Negro Employment in Land and Air
     Transport: A Study of Racial Policies in the Railroad, Airlines,
     Trucking, and Urban Transit Industries. Philadelphia: University of
     Pennsylvania Press, 1971.

Northrup, Herbert R. and others. Negro Employment in Southern Industry:
     A Study of Racial Policies in the Paper, Lumber, Tobacco, Coal
     Mining, and Textile Industries. Philadelphia: University of
     Pennsylvania Press, 1971.

Northrup, Herbert R. and others. The Negro in the Air Transport Industry.
     Philadelphia: University of Pennsylvania Press, 1971.

Olson, James S. Organized Black Leadership and Industrialization: The
     Racial Response, 1936-1945 [C.I.0]. Labor History 10 (1969):475-86.

315

Ozanne, Robert. The Negro in the Farm Equipment and Construction Machinery Industry. Philadelphia: University of Pennsylvania Press, 1972.

Peake, Charles F. Negro Occupation-Employment Participation in American Industry: Historical Perspective, Improvements during the 1960s, and Recent Plateauing. American Journal of Economics and Sociology 34 (1975):67-86.

Perry, Charles R. The Negro in the Department Store Industry. Philadelphia: University of Pennsylvania Press, 1971.

Peterson, Joyce S. Black Automobile Workers in Detroit, 1910-1931. Journal of Negro History 44 (1979):177-190.

Porter, Kenneth W. Negro Labor in the Western Cattle Industry, 1866-1900. Labor History 10 (1969):346-74.

Purcell, Theodore V. and Gerald F. Cavanaugh. Blacks in the Industrial World [Electrical manufacturing industry]. New York: Free Press, 1972.

Purcell, Theodore V. and Daniel Mulvey. The Negro in the Electrical Manufacturing Industry. Philadelphia: University of Pennsylvania Press, 1973.

Quay, William H., Jr. The Negro in the Chemical Industry. Philadelphia: University of Pennsylvania Press, 1969.

Risher, Howard W., Jr. The Negro in the Railroad Industry. Philadelphia: University of Pennsylvania Press, 1971.

Rodgriguez, Clara E. Economic Survival in New York City. In: Rodriguez and others (eds.), The Puerto Rican Struggle, pp. 31-46. New York: Puerto Rican Migration Research Consortium, 1980.

Rowan, Richard L. The Negro in the Steel Industry. Philadelphia: University of Pennsylvania Press, 1968.

Rowan, Richard L. The Negro in the Textile Industry. Philadelphia: University of Pennsylvania Press, 1970.

Rubin, Lester. The Negro in the Shipbuilding Industry. Philadelphia: University of Pennsylvania Press, 1970.

Rubin, Lester and William S. Swift. The Negro in Longshore Industry. Philadelphia: University of Pennsylvania Press, 1973.

Simmons, Charles and others. Negro Coal Miners in West Virginia. Midwest Journal 6 (Spring 1954):60-69.

Stuart, Reginald. Businesses Said to Have Barred New Plants in Largely Black Communities [Alabama]. New York Times February 15, 1983.

Swift, William S. The Negro in the Offshore Maritime Industry.
    Philadelphia: University of Pennsylvania Press, 1973.

Walker, Joseph E. A Comparison of Negro and White Labor in Charcoal Iron
    Community [Black County, PA]. Labor History 10 (1969):487-97.

Walker, Joseph E. Negro Labor in the Charcoal Iron Industry of
    Southeastern Pennsylvania. Pennsylvania Magazine of History and
    Biography 92 (1969):466-87.

Wells, Dave and Jim Stodder. A Short History of New Orleans Dockworkers.
    Radical America 10 (1976):43-69.

Wrong, Elaine G. The Negro in the Apparel Industry. Philadelphia:
    University of Pennsylvania Press, 1973.

Yu, Winifred. Asian-Americans Charge Prejudice Slows Climb to Management
    Ranks. Wall Street Journal September 11, 1985.

317

40. KKK

*I was born poor - and colored - and almost all the prettiest
roses I have seen have been in rich people's yards, not in mine.
That is why I cannot write exclusively about roses and
moonlight - for sometimes in the moonlight my brothers see a
fiery cross and a circle of Klansmen's hoods. Sometimes in the
moonlight a dark body swings from a lynching tree, but for his
funeral there are no roses.*

- Langston Hughes, "My Adventures as a Social Poet," 1947.

Abbey, Sue W. The Ku Klux Klan in Arizona, 1921-1925. Journal of
    Arizona History 14 (Spring 1973):10-30.

Alexander, Charles C. Crusade for Conformity: The Ku Klux Klan in
    Texas, 1920-1930. Houston: Texas Gulf Coast Historical Association,
    1962.

Alexander, Charles C. Defeat, Decline, Disintegration: The Ku Klux Klan
    in Arkansas, 1924 and After. Arkansas Historical Quarterly 22
    (Winter 1963):311-31.

Alexander, Charles C. Kleagles and Cash: The Ku Klux Klan as a Business
    Organization, 1915-1930. Business History Review 39 (1965):348-367.

Alexander, Charles C. The Ku Klux Klan Comes to Arkansas, 1921-1922.
    Arkansas Historical Quarterly 22 (Spring 1963):8-23.

Alexander, Charles C. The Ku Klux Klan in the Southwest. Lexington:
    University of Kentucky Press, 1965.

Alexander, Charles C. White Robes in Politics: The Ku Klux Klan in
    Arkansas, 1922-1924. Arkansas Historical Quarterly 22 (Fall
    1963):195-214.

Baiamonte, John V., Jr. Spirit of Vengeance: Nativism and Louisiana
    Justice, 1921-1924. Baton Rouge: Louisiana State University Press,
    1986. [Ku Klux Klan in Tangipahoa Parish].

Blee, Kathleen. Women in the 1920s Ku Klux Klan Movement. Feminist
    Studies 15 (1989).

Calbreath, Dean. Kovering the Klan: How the Press Gets Tricked into
    Boosting the KKK. Columbia Journalism Review (March-April 1981).

Chalmers, David M. Hooded Americanism. The History of the Ku Klux Klan
    (second edition). New York: Franklin Watts, 1980.

Chalmers, David M. The Ku Klux Klan in Politics in the 1920s.
    Mississippi Quarterly 18 (Fall 1965):234-47.

Chalmers, David M. The Ku Klux Klan in the Sunshine State: The 1920s.

Florida Historical Quarterly 42 (January 1964).

Clark, Malcolm, Jr. The Bigot Disclosed: 90 Years of Nativism. Oregon Historical Quarterly 75 (June 1974):109-90. [Major attention to KKK in Oregon].

Cocoltchos, Christopher N. The Invisible Government and the Viable Community: The Ku Klux Klan in Orange County, California During the 1920's. Doctoral dissertation, University of California, Los Angeles, 1979. UMO # 7913716.

Connor, R. D. W. Ku Klux Klan and Its Operations in North Carolina. North Carolina University Magazine 30 (April 1900):224-34.

Cowett, Mark. Birmingham's Rabbi: Morris Newfield and Alabama, 1895-1940. University: University of Alabama Press, 1986. [Touches on KKK in 1920's].

Craig, John M. and T. H. Silver. 'Tolerance of the Intolerant': J.A.C. Chandler and the Ku Klux Klan at William and Mary. South Atlantic Quarterly 84 (Spring 1985):213-22.

Craven, Charles. Robeson County Indian Uprising against the KKK. South Atlantic Quarterly 57 (Fall 1958):433-42.

Croft, Laurie J. The Women of the Ku Klux Klan in Oklahoma. Master's thesis. University of Oklahoma, 1985.

Ellis, C. P. Why I Quit the Klan [Interview by Studs Terkel]. Southern Exposure 8 (Summer 1980):95-100.

Five Klansmen Jailed for School Bomb Plot. Raleigh News and Observer February 17, 1958.

Flynn, Charles L. The Ancient Pedigree of Violent Repression: Georgia's Klan as a Folk Movement. In: Walter J. Fraser and Winfred B. Moore, Jr. (eds.), The Southern Enigma: Essays on Race, Class, and Folk Culture. Westport, CT: Greewood, 1983.

Foley, Albert S. The KKK in Mobile, Alabama. America 95 (December 8, 1956):298-299.

Gerlach, Larry R. Blazing Crosses in Zion: The Ku Klux Klan in Utah. Logan: Utah State University Press, 1982.

Goldberg, Robert Alan. Hooded Empire: The Ku Klux Klan in Colorado, 1921-32. Urbana: University of Illinois Press, 1981.

Greene, Johung. In Alabama the Klan's Legacy Recedes Into Impotence. Los Angeles Times August 19, 1979.

Hall, Kermit L. Political Power and Constitutional Legitimacy: The South Carolina Ku Klux Klan Trials, 1871-1872. Emory Law Journal 33 (Autumn 1984):921-52.

Hall, Kermit L. and Lou Falkner Williams. Constitutional Tradition amid
    Social Change: Hugh Lennox and the Ku Klux Klan in South Carolina.
    Maryland Historian 16 (Fall-Winter 1985):43-58.

Hallberg, Carl V. 'For God, Country, and Home': The Ku Klux Klan in
    Pekin, 1923-1925. Journal of the Illinois State Historical Society
    77 (Summer 1984):82-93.

Harvard in Grip of the Ku Klux Klan. California Eagle January 27, 1923.

Hilewitz, Yehuda. The Ku Klux Klan and the Jews. Master's thesis,
    Yeshiva University, 1972.

Hirshson, Paul. Is Ku Klux Klan Suffering From Loss of Support? Boston
    Globe July 3, 1983. [In Connecticut].

Hoshall, Lee David. Under the Banner of Hatred [About Edward Fields,
    leader of KKK in Georgia]. Baltimore Jewish Times November 26,
    1982.

Hux, Roger K. The Ku Klux Klan and Collective Violence in Horry County,
    1922-1925. South Carolina Historical Magazine 85 (July 1984):211-
    19.

Hux, Roger K. The Ku Klux Klan in Macon, 1919-1925. Georgia Historical
    Quarterly 62 (Summer 1978):155-68.

Jackson, Kenneth T. The Ku Klux Klan in the City, 1915-1930. NY:
    Oxford, 1967.

Jenkins, Philip. The Ku Klux Klan in Pennsylvania, 1920-1940. Western
    Pennsylvania Historical Society 69 (April 1986):120-37.

Jenkins, William D. The Ku Klux Klan in Youngstown, Ohio: Moral Reform
    in the Twenties. Historian 41 (November 1978):76-93.

Johnson, Guy B. A Sociological Interpretation of the New Ku Klux Klan
    Movement. Journal of Social Forces 1 (May 1923):440-45.

Johnson, James Weldon. What Do They Require? New York Age December
    30, 1922. [K.K.K.].

Kallal, Edward W., Jr. St. Augustine and the Ku Klux Klan: 1963 and
    1964. Bachelor's thesis, History Department, University of Florida,
    1976.

Kaplan, David A. Is the Klan Entitled to Public Access [TV]? New York
    Times July 31, 1988.

Keil, Thomas J. Capital, Labor, and the Klan: A Case Study [Wilkes-
    Barre, Luzerne County, Pennsylvania]. Phylon 46 (December
    1985):341-52.

King, Wayne. The Violent Rebirth of the Klan. New York Times Magazine
    December 7, 1980.

320

Kornbluth, Jesse. The Woman Who Beat the Klan [Ms. Beulah Mae MacDonald, Mobile, Alabama]. New York Times Magazine November 1987.

Ku Klux Klan in Hawaii. New York Times October 19, 1922.

Ku Klux Klan in South Dakota. Grand Forks Herald January-February 1923.

Lay, Shawn. War, Revolution, and the Ku Klux Klan: A Study of Intolerance in a Border City [El Paso, Texas]. El Paso: Texas Western Press, University of Texas at El Paso, 1985.

Loucks, Emerson H. The Ku Klux Klan in Pennsylvania. New York: Telegraph Press, 1936.

Maine and the Klan. New York Times September 10, 1924.

Mark of the Beast. Southern Exposure 8 (Summer 1980).

Martin, Guy. Ain't Nothing You Can Do But Join the Klan. Esquire (March 1980):27-38.

Marx, Andrew and Tom Tuthill. Mississippi Organizers. Southern Exposure 8 (Summer 1980):73-76. [Anti-KKK movement].

Mecklin, John M. The Ku Klux Klan: A Study of the American Mind. NY: Harcourt Brace, 1924.

Meltzer, Milton. The Truth About the Ku Klux Klan. New York: Watts, 1982. [Juvenile literature].

Miller, Robert M. The Ku Klux Klan. In: John Braeman and others (eds.), Change and Continuity in Twentieth-Century America: The 1920s, pp. 215-55. Columbus, Ohio State University Press, 1968.

Moore, Leonard J. White Protestant Nationalism in the 1920s: The Ku Klux Klan in Indiana. Doctoral dissertation, University of California, Los Angeles, 1985. UMO # 8606470.

Moseley, Clement C. Invisible Empire: A History of the Ku Klux Klan in Twentieth Century Georgia, 1915-1965. Doctoral dissertation, University of Georgia, 1968. UMO # 69-03473.

Moseley, Clement C. The Political Influence of the Ku Klux Klan in Georgia, 1915-1925. Georgia Historical Quarterly 57 (Summer 1973):235-55.

Newly Resurgent Ku Klux Klan Exploits Racial Tensions in American Schools. NEA Reporter 20 (June 1981):8-9.

Oakley, Andy. '88: An Undercover News Reporter's Expose of American Nazis and the Ku Klux Klan. P.O. Publishing Co., 1987.

Olsen, Otto H. The Ku Klux Klan: A Study in Reconstruction Politics and Propaganda. North Carolina Historical Review 39 (Summer 1962):340-

62.

Perkins, Duane. The Ku Klux Klan in Lyon County in the 1920s. Master's thesis, Emporia State University, 1981. [Kansas].

Racine, Philip N. The Ku Klux Klan, Anti-Catholicism, and Atlanta's Board of Education, 1916-1927. Georgia Historical Quarterly 57 (Spring 1973):63-75.

Raines, Edgar F., Jr. The Ku Klux Klan in Illinois, 1867-1875. Illinois Historical Journal 78 (Spring 1985):17-44.

Rambow, Charles. The Ku Klux Klan in the 1920s: A Concentration on the Black Hills. South Dakota History 4 (Winter 1973):63-81.

Rawls, Wendell, Jr. Civil Rights Advocates Upset at Rise in Klan-Style Harassment. New York Times August 20, 1981.

Rice, Arnold B. The Ku Klux Klan in American Politics. Washington, D.C.: Public Affairs Press, 1962.

Rich, Evelyn. Ku Klux Klan Ideology, 1954-1988. 2 vols. Doctoral dissertation, Boston University, 1988. UMO # 8814385.

Ridgeway, James and others. Conduct Unbecoming a Racist [Former Klansman David Duke in Louisiana]. Village Voice March 7, 1989.

Scharlott, Bradford W. The Hoosier Newsmen and the Hooded Order: Indiana Press Reaction to the Ku Klux Klan in the 1920s. August 1979. ERIC ED 173 821.

Schuyler, Michael W. The Ku Klux Klan in Nebraska, 1920-1930. Nebraska History 66 (Fall 1985):234-56.

Simkins, Francis B. The Ku Klux Klan in Southe Carolina, 1868-1871. Journal of Negro History 12 (October 1927).

Sims, Patsy. The Klan.

Snell, William R. Fiery Crosses in the Roaring Twenties: Activities of the Revised Klan in Alabama, 1915-1930. Alabama Review 23 (October 1970):256-76.

Stagg, J. C. A. THe Problem of Klan Violence: The South Carolina Up-Country, 1868-1871. Journal of American Studies 8 (December 1974):303-18.

Stolz, James. The KKK [in Connecticut]. Sunday News Magazine March 7, 1982. [New York Daily News].

Suall, Irwin J. The Ku Klux Klan Malady Lingers On. Perspective 12 (Fall 1980-Winter 1981):11-15.

Swallow, Craig F. The Ku Klux Klan in Nevada during the 1930s. Master's thesis, University of Nevada, 1978.

Swallow, Craig F. The Ku Klux Klan in Nevada during the 1920s. Nevada Historical Society Quarterly 24 (Fall 1981):203-20.

Swinney, Everette. Suppressing the Ku Klux Klan: The Enforcement of the Reconstruction Amendments, 1870-1877. New York: Garland, 1986.

Thompson, Jenny. My Life in the Klan. New York: Putnam, 1982.

Tourgee, Albin W. A Fool's Errand, by One of the Fools. New York: Fords, Howard, and Hulbert, 1902.

Toy, Eckard V. The Ku Klux Klan in Oregon. In: G. Thomas Edwards and Carlos A. Schwantes (eds.), Experiences in a Promised Land: Essays in Pacific Northwest History. Seattle: University of Washington Press, 1986.

Trelease, Allen W. White Terror. The Ku Klux Klan Conspiracy and Southern Reconstruction. New York: Harper and Row, 1971.

Trusty, Lance. All Talk and No 'Kash': Valparaiso University and the Ku Klux Klan. Indiana Magazine of History 82 (March 1986):1-36.

Turner, John and others. The Ku Klux Klan. A History of Racism and Violence. Montgomery: Klanwatch, The Southern Poverty Law Center, 1981.

University of Oklahoma and the Ku Klux Klan. School and Family 16 (October 7, 1922):412-13.

Wade, Wyn C. The Fiery Cross: The Ku Klux Klan in America. New York: Simon and Schuster, 1986.

Wieck, Agnes. Ku Kluxing in the Miner's Country. New Republic 38 (March 26, 1924):122-4.

Wilhaus, Oliver. Klan Runs Students from State. Raleigh News and Observer June 20, 1964. [N.C.].

Yaffe, Richard. The Grand Dragon Runs for Congress. Present Tense (Summer 1981):25-30. [Tom Metzger. Grand Dragon, California KKK].

KKK Bibliography

Davis, Lenwood G. and Janet L. Sims-Wood (comps.) The Ku Klux Klan: A Bibliography. Westport, CT: Greenwood, 1984.

Fisher, William H. (comp.) The Invisible Empire: A Bibliography of the Ku Klux Klan. Metuchen, NJ: Scarecrow Press, 1980.

Meyer, H. H. B. (comp.) Select List of References on Ku Klux Klan. <u>In</u>:
    Betty K. Gubert (comp.), <u>Early</u> <u>Black</u> <u>Bibliographies,</u> <u>1863-1918</u>, pp.
    253-60. New York: Garland, 1982.

[See also sections 4, 12, 14, 20, 32, 34, 38, 44, 47, 69, 78, and 82]

41. Labor

There has already been a strong public opinion manufactured in the country which looks upon the training of the Negroes in the South as cheap, contented labor to be used in emergency and for keeping white union labor from extravagant demands as a feasible and workable program. It is, in fact, one of the most dangerous programs ever thought out and is responsible for much of the lynching, unrest, and unhappiness in the South.

- W. E. B. Du Bois, "Negro Education" (1918).

Adedji, Moses. Crossing the Colorline: Three Decades of the United Packinghouse Workers of America's Crusade Against Racism in the Trans-Mississippi West, 1936-1968. Doctoral dissertation, North Texas State University, 1978.

Alegado, Dean T. Fighters in Paradise: Filipino Labor in Hawaii in 1920-1940. Katipunan (August 1988):21-22.

Allen, Ernest, Jr. The League of Revolutionary Black Workers: An Assessment. In: James Green (ed.), Worker's Struggles, Past and Present. Philadelphia: Temple University Press, 1983.

Andrew, Mildred G. "The Men and Mills.": A History of the Southern Textile Industry. Macon, GA: Macon University Press, 1987.

Arnesen, Eric. Waterfront Workers of New Orleans: Race, Class and Politics, 1863-1923. Doctoral dissertation, Yale University, 1986. UMO # 8728101.

Aronowitz, Stanley. Too Narrow a Focus. New Politics 1 (Summer 1987):31-35. [See, below, H. Hill, 1987].

Bailey, Kenneth R. A Judicious Mixture: Negroes and Immigrants in the West Virginia Mines, 1880-1917. In: William H. Turner and Edward J. Cabbell (eds.), Blacks in Appalachia. Lexington: University of Kentucky Press, 1985.

Bailey, Robert E. The 1968 Memphis Sanitation Strike. Master's thesis, Memphis State University, 1974.

Baron, Harold. The Demand for Black Labor: Historical Notes on the Political Economy of Racism. Radical America 2 (March-April 1971).

Baron, Harold. Racial Domination in Advanced Capitalism: A Theory of Nationalism and Divisions in the Labor Market. In: Richard Edwards and others (eds.), Labor Market Segmentation. Lexington, MA: Heath, 1975.

Barrett, James R. Work and Community in the Jungle. Chicago's Packinghouse Workers, 1894-1922. Urbana: University of Illinois Press, 1987.

Beecher, John. The Share Croppers' Union in Alabama. Social Forces 13 (1934):124-32.

Beechert, Edward D. The History of Work and the Words of the Worker. International Journal of Oral History 8 (June 1987):112-21. [Hawaii].

Beifuss, Joan T. At the River I Stand: The 1968 Strike, and Martin Luther King. Memphis: B and B Books, 1985.

Bennetts, David P. Black and White Workers: New Orleans, 1880-1900. Doctoral dissertation, University of Illinois, 1972.

Berglund, Abraham and others. Labor in the Industrial South. Charlottesville: University of Virginia Press, 1930.

Berlin, Ira and others (eds.) The Terrain of Freedom: The Struggle over the Meaning of Free Labor in the U.S. South. History Workshop 22 (Autumn 1986):108-30.

Black, Paul V. The Knights of Labor and the South, 1873-1893. Southern Quarterly 1 (1963):201-12.

Bloch, Herman D. Craft Unions and the Negro in Historical Perspective. Journal of Negro History 43 (1958):10-33. [1866-1945].

Bloch, Herman D. The Employment Status of the New York Negro in Retrospect. Phylon 20 (1959):327-344.

Bloch, Herman D. Labor and the Negro 1866-1910. Journal of Negro History 50 (1965):163-84.

Bloch, Herman D. and Carol M. Banks. The National Labor Union and Black Workers. Journal of Ethnic Studies 1 (1973):13-21.

Bobinska, Celina and Anrej Pilch (eds.) Employment-Seeking Emigrations of Poles World Wide in the 19th and 20th Centuries. Cracow, Poland, 1975.

Bonacich, Edna. Advanced Capitalism and Black/White Relations in the United States: A Split Labor Market Interpretation. American Sociological Review 41 (1976):34-51.

Bonacich, Edna. Asian Labor in the Development of California and Hawaii, In: Lucie Cheng and Edna Bonacich (eds.), Labor Immigration Under Capitalism, pp. 130-85. Berkeley, CA: University of California Press, 1984.

Born, Kate. Memphis Negro Workingmen and the NAACP. West Tennessee Historical Society Papers 28 (1974):90-107.

Brazeal, Brailsford R. The Brotherhood of Sleeping Car Porters: Its Origin and Development. 1946.

Briggs, Vernon M., Jr. and others. The Chicano Worker. Austin: University of Texas Press, 1977.

Brody, David. Hill Discounts Larger Context. New Politics 1 (Summer 1987):38-41. [See, below, H. Hill, 1987].

Brody, David. Labor. In: Stephan Thernstrom (ed.), Harvard Encyclopedia of American Ethnic Groups, pp. 609-18. Cambridge, MA: Harvard University Press, 1980.

Brooks, George Q. Racism and the Drift Toward Oligarchy. New Politics 1 (Summer 1987):27-29. [See, below, H. Hill, 1987].

Brown, Myland R. The IWW and the Negro Worker. Doctoral dissertation, Ball State University, 1968.

Calvert, Robert A. (ed.) The Freedmen and Agricultural Prosperity [Texas]. Southwestern Historical Quarterly 76 (1973):461-71.

Campbell, Duane. Bert Corona: Labor Radical. Socialist Review 19 (January-March 1989):41-55. [Humberto Corono and the Latino Labor Movement].

Cantor, Milton (ed.) Black Labor in America. Westport, CT: Negro Universities Press, 1970.

Cattan, P. The Growing Presence of Hispanics in the U.S. Work Force. Montly Labor Review 111 (August 1988).

Cayton, Horace R. and George S. Mitchell. Black Workers and the New Unions. 1939.

Chacon, Ramon. The 1933 San Joaquin Valley Cotton Strike: Strikebreaking Activities in California Agriculture. In: Mario Barrera and others (eds.), Work, Family, Sex Roles, Language. Berkeley, CA: Tonatiuh-Quinto Sol, 1980.

Chinese Labor Committee. History of Chinese Working People In America. San Francisco, CA: United Front Press, 1974.

Chiswick, B. R. The Labor Market Status of Hispanic Men. Journal of American Ethnic History 7 (Fall 1987):30-58.

Chiu, Ping. Chinese Labor in California, 1850-1880: An Economic Study. Madison, 1963.

Cloud, Patricia and David W. Galenson. Chinese Immigration and Contract Labor in the Late Nineteenth Century. Explorations in Economic History 24 (January 1987):22-42.

Cohen, William. Black Immobility and Free Labor: The Freedmen's Bureau and the Relocation of Black Labor, 1865-1868. Civil War History 30 (September 1984):221-34.

Collins, Thomas W. An Analysis of the Memphis Garbage Strike of 1968.

Public Affairs Forum 3 (April 1974):1-6.

Cook, Bernard A. and James R. Watson. _Lousiana Labor from Slavery to "Right-to-Work"_. Lanham, MD: University Press of America, 1985.

Corbin, David A. Class over Caste: Interracial Solidarity in the Company Town. _In_: William H. Turner and Edward J. Cabbell (eds.), _Blacks in Appalachia_. Lexington: University of Kentucky Press, 1985.

Cornford, Daniel A. _Workers and Dissent in the Redwood Empire_. Philadelphia: Temple University Press, 1987.

Critchlow, Donald T. Communist Unions and Racism: A Comparative Study of the Responses of United Electrial Radio and Machine Workers and the National Maritime Union to the Black Question During World War II. _Labor History_ 17 (Spring 1976):230-44.

Davis, Ronald L. F. _Good and Faithful Labor: From Slavery to Sharecropping in the Natchez District, 1860-1890_. Westport, CT: Greenwood, 1982.

De Witt, Howard A. _Violence in the Fields: California Filipino Farm Labor Unionization during the Great Depression_. Saratoga, CA: Century Twenty One, 1980.

Dickerson, Dennis C. _Black Steelworkers in Western Pennsylvania, 1915-1950_. Doctoral dissertation, Washington University, 1978. UMO # 7911485.

Dickerson, Dennis C. _Out of the Crucible: Black Steelworkers in Western Pennsylvania_. Albany: State University of New York Press, 1986.

Dickerson, Dennis C., Joseph Boskin, and Stanford M. Lyman. Further Response[s] to Herbert Hill. _New Politics_ 1 (Winter 1988):220-22.

Du Bois, W. E. B. Black and White Workers. _Crisis_ 35 (March 1928):96-8. [In "Postscript"].

Du Bois, W. E. B. The Black Man and Labor. _Crisis_ 31 (December 1925):59-62. [In "Opinion"].

Du Bois, W. E. B. The Black Man and the Unions. _Crisis_ 15 (March 1918). [In editorial section].

Du Bois, W. E. B. The Black Worker. _In_: William H. Turner and Edward J. Cabbell (eds.), _Blacks in Appalachia_. Lexington: University of Kentucky Press, 1985.

Du Bois, W. E. B. [Blacks in unions]. _Chicago Defender_ November 22, 1947.

Du Bois, W. E. B. L'Ouvrier negre en Amerique. _Revue Economique Internationale_ (Belgium) 4 (November 1906):298-348.

Du Bois, W. E. B. [On Harry Bridges]. _Amsterdam News_ June 13, 1942.

Du Bois, W. E. B. "Postscript." _Crisis_ 39 (March 1932):93-94, 101. [Miner's strikes].

Du Bois, W. E. B. "Postscript." _Crisis_ 40 (February 1933):44-46. [Sharecroppers at Camp Hill, Alabama].

Du Bois, W. E. B. The Pullman Porter. _New York Times_ 8 (March 16, 1914):5.

Du Bois, W. E. B. The World Last Month. _Crisis_ 13 (November 1916). [Rights of Blacks to be in unions].

Du Bois, W. E. B. and Augustus G. Dill. _The Negro American Artisan_. Atlanta: Atlanta University Press, 1912.

Du Pont, Patricia and others. Black Migrant Farmworkers in New York State: Exploitable Labor. _Afro-Americans in New York Life and History_ 12 (January 1988):7-26.

Dubovsky, Melvyn. _"Big Bill" Haywood_. New York: St. Martin's Press, 1987.

Dubovsky, Melvyn. _We Shall Be All. A History of the Industrial Workers of the World_ (second edition). Urbana: University of Illinois Press, 1987.

Dunbar, T. and L. Kravitz. _Hand Traveling: Migrant Farm Workers in America_. Cambridge, MA: Ballinger, 1976.

Dutcher, Dean. _The Negro in Modern Industrial Society_ [1910-1920]. Lancaster, PA: Author, 1930.

Eckert, Edward K. Contract Labor in Florida during Reconstruction. _Florida Historical Quarterly_ 47 (1968):34-50.

Edwards, Laura. _The Illusion of Freedom: Wage Labor and Tenancy in Granville County, North Carolina, 1865-1900_. Master's thesis, University of North Carolina, Chapel Hill, 1986.

Falcon-Rodriguez, Luis M. _Puerto Ricans on the Mainland: An Analysis of Labor Market Standing. 1970-1980_. Doctoral dissertation, Cornell University, 1987. UMO # 8715601.

Fink, Leon. 'Irrespective of Party, Color or Social Standing': The Knights of Labor and Opposition Politics in Richmond, Virginia. _Labor History_ 19 (Summer 1978):325-49.

Flaherty, Stacy A. Boycott in Butte: Organized Labor and the Chinese Community, 1896-1897. _Montana_ 37 (Winter 1987):34-47.

Foner, Philip S. The IWW and the Black Worker. _Journal of Negro History_ 55 (1970):45-64.

Foner, Philip S. A Labor Voice for Black Equality: The Boston Daily Evening Voice, 1864-1867. Science and Society 38 (Fall 1974):304-25.

Foner, Philip S. Organized Labor and the Black Worker, 1619-1973. New York: Praeger, 1974.

Foner, Philip S. and Ronald L. Lewis (eds.) The Black Worker: A Documentary History from Colonial Times to the Present. 8 vols. Philadelphia: Temple University Press, 1978-1984.

Finney, John D., Jr. A Study of Negro Labor During and After World War I. Doctoral dissertation, Georgetown University, 1967.

Frederickson, Mary. Four Decades of Change: Black Workers in Southern Textiles, 1941-1981. Radical America 16 (November-December 1982):27-44.

Freeman, Richard B. Changes in the Labor Market for Black Americans, 1948-72. Brookings Papers on Economic Activity. 1 (1973):67-120.

Fujito, Kuniko. Black Workers' Struggles in Detroit's Auto Industry, 1935-1975. Master's thesis, Michigan State University, 1977.

Fujito, Kuniko. Black Worker's Struggles in Detroit's Auto Industry, 1935-1975. Saratoga, CA: Century Twenty One, 1980.

Fusfield, Daniel R. Capitalist Exploitation and Black Labor: An Extended Conceptual Framework. Review of Black Political Economy 10 (1980).

Galarza, Ernesto. Farm Workers and Agri-business in California, 1947-1960. Notre Dame, IN: University of Notre Dame Press, 1977.

Gambino, Ferrucio. W.E.B. Du Bois and the Proletariat in Black Reconstruction. In: Dirk Hoerder (ed.), American Labor and Immigration History 1877-1920s: Recent European Research, pp. 43-60. Urbana: University of Illinois Press, 1983.

Gamboa, Erasmo. Braceros in the Pacific Northwest: Laborers on the Domestic Front, 1942-1947. Pacific Historical Review 56 (August 1987):378-98.

Garcia, Mario T. Racial Dualism in the El Paso Labor Market, 1880-1920. Aztlan 6 (Summer 1975):197-218.

Geschwender, James A. Class, Race and Worker Insurgency: The League of Revolutionary Black Workers. New York: 1977.

Glaberman, Martin. Black Workers and the Labor Movement. New Politics 1 (Winter 1988).

Glaberman, Martin. Class Is a Missing Element. New Politics 1 (Summer 1987):58-61. [See, below, H. Hill, 1987].

Göbel, T. Becoming American: Ethnic Workers and the Rise of the CIO.

Labor History 29 (Spring 1988).

Goldfarb, R. A. Migrant Farm Workers: A Caste of Despair. Ames: Iowa State University Press, 1981.

Gomez-Quinones, Juan and David Maciel. Historia del trabajor Mexicana en Los Estados Unidos. Mexico, D.F.: Siglio Veintiuno y UNAM, 1981.

Gomez-Quinones, Juan and David Maciel. The Origins and Development of the Mexican Working Class in the United States: Laborers and Artisans North of the Rio Bravo, 1600-1900. In: Elsa C. Frost and others (eds.), El Trabajo y Los Trabajadores en la Historia de Mexico. Tucson: University of Arizona Press, 1979.

Gottlieb, Peter. Black Miners and the 1925-28 Bituminous Coal Strike: The Colored Committee of Non-Union Miners, Montour Mine No. 1, Pittsburgh Coal Company. Labor History 28 (Spring 1987):233-37.

Gould, William B. Black Workers in White Unions: Job Discrimination in the United States. Ithaca, NY: Cornell University Press, 1977.

Gould, William B. Black Workers Inside the House of Labor. Annals of the American Academy of Political and Social Science. 407 (1973):78-90.

Graham, Glennon. From Slavery to Serfdom: Rural Black Agriculturalists in South Carolina, 1865-1900. Doctoral dissertation, Northwestern University, 1982. UMO # 8225925,

Green, Earl, Jr. Labor in the South: A Case Study of Memphis, the 1968 Sanitation Strike and Its Effects on an Urban Community. Doctoral dissertation, New York University, 1980.

Green, Jim. The Brotherhood. Southern Exposure 4 (1976):21-9. [Brotherhood of Timber Workers].

Green, Shirley Mae. Anchorage, Alaska: The Myth of Racial Equality. A Study of the Experiences of Anchorages Black Workers. Doctoral dissertation, The Union for Experimenting Colleges and Universities, 1987. UMO # 8806728.

Greene, Lorenzo J. Negro Sharecroppers. Negro History Bulletin 31 (1968):17-19. [Bootheel, MO, 1939].

Greene, Lorenzo J. and Carter G. Woodson. The Negro Wage Earner [ca. 1890-1930]. Washington, D.C.: Association for the Study of Negro Life and History, 1930.

Greene, Victor R. The Slav Community on Strike: Immigrant Labor in Pennsylvania Anthracite. Notre Dame, IN: University of Notre Dame Press, 1968.

Griffin, Keith H. The Failure of an Interracial Southern Rhetoric: The Southern Tenant Farmers Union in North Carolina. October 1982. ERIC ED 222 964. [William Thomas Brown, organizer of STFU in N.C.].

Grob, Gerald. Organized Labor and the Negro Worker, 1865-1900. Labor History 1 (Spring 1960):164-76.

Gross, James A. Historians and the Literature of the Negro Worker. Labor History 10 (1969):536-46.

Grossman, James (ed.) Black Workers in the Era of the Great Migration, 1916-1929 [25 microfilm reels]. Frederick, MD: University Publications of America, 1987.

Guinier, Ewart. Impact of Unionization on Blacks [NYC, 1933-1970]. Proceedings of the Academy of Political Science 30 (1970):173-81.

Gunderson, Morley. Male-Female Wage Differentials and Policy Responses. Journal of Economic Literature 27 (March 1989):46-72.

Hammett, Hugh B. Labor and Race: The Georgia Railroad Strike of 1909. Labor History 16 (1975):470-84.

Harris, Abram L. Negro Labor's Quarrel with White Workingmen. Current History 24 (1926):903-08.

Harris, Donald J. Capitalist Exploitation and Black Labor: Some Conceptual Issues. Review of Black Political Economy 8 (1978).

Harris, William H. The Harder We Run. Black Workers Since the Civil War. New York: Oxford University Press, 1981.

Harris, William H. Keeping the Faith: A. Philip Randolph, Milton P. Webster, and the Brotherhood of Sleeping Car Porters, 1925-37. Urbana: University of Illinois Press, 1977.

Helmbold, L. R. Downward Occupational Mobility during the Great Depression: Urban Black and White Working Class Women. Labor History 29 (Spring 1988).

Hicks, Helena S. The Black Apprentice in Maryland Courts Records from 1661 to 1865. Doctoral dissertation, University of Maryland, 1988. UMO # 8818404.

Higgs, R. Racial Wage Differences in Agriculture: Evidence from North Carolina in 1887. Agricultural History 52 (1978):308-311.

Hill, Arnold T. The Dilemma of the Negro Workmen: Shall He or Shall He Not Join the Union? Opportunity 4 (1926):39-41.

Hill, Herbert. The AFL-CIO and the Black Worker: Twenty-Five Years after the Merger. Journal of Intergroup Relations 10 (Spring 1982):5-78.

Hill, Herbert. Black Labor and the American Legal System: Race, Work, and the Law. Madison: University of Wisconsin Press, 1985, reprint.

Hill, Herbert. Herbert Hill Replies [to His Critics]. New Politics 1 (Summer 1987):61-71.

Hill, Herbert. Mythmaking as Labor History: Herbert Gutman and the United Mineworkers of America. International Journal of Politics, Culture and Society 2 (January 1989).

Hill, Herbert. Race and Ethnicity in Organized Labor: The Historical Sources of Resistance to Affirmative Action. Journal of Intergroup Relations 12 (1984):5-49.

Hill, Herbert. Race, Ethnicity and Organized Labor: The Opposition to Affirmative Action. New Politics 1 (Winter 1987).

Hill, Herbert. The Racial Practices of Organized Labor - The Age of Gompers and After. In: A. Ross and H. Hill (eds.), Employment, Race and Poverty. New York: Harcourt Brace and World, 1967.

Hill, Herbert. The Racial Practices of Organized Labor: The Contemporary Record. In: J. Jacobson (ed.), The Negro and the American Labor Movement. Garden City, NJ: Anchor, 1968.

Hill, Herbert. Racism and Organized Labor. New School Bulletin 28 (February 8, 1971).

Hill, Herbert. Racism within Organized Labor: A Report of Five Years of the AFL-CIO, 1955-1960. Journal of Negro Education 30 (Spring 1961):109-18.

Hine, William B. Black Organized Labor in Reconstructed Charleston. Labor History 25 (Fall 1984):504-17.

A History of Rhode Island Working People. Rhode Island Labor History Society, reprint. [c/o Paul Buhle, 363 Morris Ave., Providence, RI 02906].

Holzer, Harry J. Unions and Labor Market Status of White and Minority Youth. Industrial and Labor Relations Review 35 (April 1982):392-405.

Hoyman, M. M. and L. Stallworth. Participation in Local Unions: A Comparison of Black and White Members. Industrial and Labor Relations Review 40 (April 1987).

Huggins, Nathan I. Herbert Gutman and Afro-American History. Labor History 29 (Summer).

Hughes, C. Alvin. Let Us Do Our Part: The New York City Based Negro Labor Victory Committee, 1941-1945. Afro-Am. New York Life and Hist. 10 (January 1986):19-29.

Humphrey, George D. The Failure of the Mississippi Freedmen's Bureau in Black Labor Relations, 1865-1867. Journal of Mississippi History 45 (February 1983):23-37.

Industrial Relations and Labor Conditions: Economic Condition of the Negro in West Virginia. Monthly Labor Review 18 (1922):713-14.

Jacobson, Julius (ed.) The Negro and the Labor Movement. Garden City, NY: 1968.

Janiewski, Dolores. Subversive Sisterhood: Black Women and Unions in the Tobacco Industry. Memphis, TN: Center for Research on Women, Memphis State University, 1984.

Jaynes, Gerald D. Branches Without Roots: Genesis of the Black Working Class in the American South, 1862-1882. New York: Oxford University Press, 1986.

Jenkins, J. Craig. The Politics of Insurgency: The Farm Worker Movement in the 1960s. New York: Columbia University Press, 1985.

Jimenez, Andres E. Political Domination in the Labor Market: Racial Division in the Arizona Copper Industry. Berkeley, CA: Institute for the Study of Social Change, 1977.

Jimenez, Andres E. The Political Formation of a Mexican Working Class in the Arizona Copper Industry, 1870-1917. Review 4 (Winter 1981):535-70.

Johnson, Charles S. Shadow of the Plantation. 1934. [Macon County, Ala.].

Johnson, Christopher H. Maurice Sugar. Law, Labor, and the Left in Detroit, 1912-1950. Detroit: Wayne State University Press, 1987.

Johnson, Merrill L. Postwar Industrial Development in the Southeast and the Pioneer Role of Labor-Intensive Industry. Economic Geography 61 (January 1985):46-65.

Kann, Kenneth. The Knights of Labor and the Southern Black Worker. Labor History 18 (1977):49-70.

Kaye, Herb. Fighting to Preserve a Fair Apprentice Plan in Chicago. People's Daily World December 24, 1986. [Discrimination against minorities at Washburne Trade School].

Keil, Hartmut and John B. Jentz (eds.) German Workers in Chicago. A Documentary History of Working-Class Culture from 1850 to World War I. Urbana: University of Illinois Press, 1987.

Keiser, John H. Black Strikebreakers and Racism in Illinois, 1865-1900. Journal of the Illinois State Historical Society 65 (Autumn 1972).

Kessler, Sidney. The Negro in Labor Studies. Midwest Journal 16 (Summer 1954):16-35.

Kessler, Sidney. Organization of Negroes in the Knights of Labor. Journal of Negro History 37 (1952):248-76.

Kester, Howard. Revolt among the Sharecroppers. 1936. [Southern Tenant Farmers Union].

Kleinfeld, Judith and John A. Kruse. Native Americans in the Labor Force: Hunting for an Accurate Measure. Monthly Labor Review 105 (July 1982):47-51.

Kremm, Thomas W. and Diane Neal. Clandestine Black Labor Societies and White Fear: Hiram F. Hoover and the 'Cooperative Workers of America' in the South. Labor History 19 (Spring 1978):226-37.

Kress, Sylvia H. Will the Freedmen Work? White Alabamians Adjust to Free Black Labor. Alabama Historical Quarterly 36 (1974):151-63.

Kwong, Peter. Chinatown, NY: Labor and Politics, 1930-1950. New York: Monthly Review Press, 1979.

Laing, James T. The Negro Miner in West Virginia. In: William H. Turner and Edward J. Cabbell (eds.), Blacks in Appalachia. Lexington: University of Kentucky Press, 1985.

Lamar, Howard. From Bondage to Contract: Ethnic Labor in the American West, 1600-1890. In: Stephen Hahn and Jonathan Prude (eds.), The Countryside in the Age of Capitalist Transformation: Essays in the Social History of Rural America. Chapel Hil;, NC: University of North Carolina Press, 1985.

Leigh, Duane E. Occupational Advancement in the Late 1960s: An Indirect Test of the Dual Labor Market Hypothesis. Journal of Human Resources 11 (Spring 1976):155-71.

Leonard, J. S. The Effect of Unions on the Employment of Blacks, Hispanics, and Women. Industrial and Labor Relations Review 39 (October 1985).

Leung, Peter C. Y. and L. Eve Armentrout. Chinese Farming Activities in the Sacramento-San Joaquin Delta: 1910-1941. Amerasia Journal 14 (1988):1-18.

Lewis, Ronald L. Black Coal Miners in America. Race, Class, and Community Conflict, 1780-1980. Lexington: University Press of Kentucky, 1987.

Lewis, Ronald L. The Black Presence in the Paint-Cabin Creek Strike 1912-1913. West Virginia History 46 (1985-1986):59-71.

Lewis, Ronald L. Race and the United Mine Workers' Union in Tennessee: Selected Letters of William R. Riley, 1892-1895. In William H. Turner and Edward J. Cabbell (eds.), Blacks in Appalachia. Lexington: University of Kentucky Press, 1985.

Lichtenstein, Nelson. Labor's War at Home. The CIO in World War II. New York: Cambridge University Press, 1982.

Lichtenstein, Nelson. An Unbalanced Rendering. New Politics 1 (Summer 1987):53-55. [See, above, H. Hill, 1987].

Logan, Frenise A. Factors Influencing the Efficiency of Negro Farm Laborers in Post-Reconstruction North Carolina. Agricultural History 33 (1959):185-9.

MacKay, Kathryn L. Warrior into Welden: A History of Federal Employment Programs for American Indians, 1878-1972. Doctoral dissertation, University of Utah, 1987. UMO # 8807974.

Manning, Seaton W. Negro Trade Unionists in Boston. Social Forces 27 (1938):256-66.

Marable, Manning. The Crisis of the Black Working Class, pp. 23-51 in How Capitalism Underdeveloped Black America. Boston: South End Press, 1983.

Marcus, Irwin M. Benjamin Fletcher: Black Labor Leader. Negro History Bulletin 35 (1972):138-40. [IWW, Philadelphia, 1900-1925].

Marcus, Irwin M. The Southern Negro and the Knights of Labor. Negro History Bulletin 30 (1967):5-7.

Marks, Bayly E. Skilled Blacks in Antebellum St. Mary's County, Maryland. Journal of Southern History 53 (November 1987):537-64.

Marable, Manning. The Crisis of the Black Working Class: An Economic and Historical Analysis. Science and Society 46 (Summer 1982).

Marshall, Ray. Black Workers and Their Unions. Dissent 19 (1972):295-302.

Marshall, Ray. The Negro and Organized labor. 1965.

Marshall, Ray. The Negro Worker. New York: Random House, 1967.

Marshall, Ray. Some Reflections on Labor History. Southwestern Historical Quarterly 75 (1971):137-57. [Texas].

Marshall, Ray. Unions and the Black Community. In: David Brody (ed.), The American Labor Movement. Lanham, MD: University Press of America, 1985.

Marshall, Ray and Arvil V. Adams. The Memphis Public Employees Strike [in 1968]. In: W. Ellison Chalmers and Gerald W. Cormick (eds.), Racial Conflict and Negogiations, pp. 71-107. Ann Arbor: Institute of Labor and Industrial Relations, University of Michigan, 1971.

Martinez, Camilo A., Jr. The Mexican and Mexican-American Laborers in the Lower Rio Grande Valley of Texas, 1870-1930. Doctoral dissertation, Texas A & M University, 1987. UMO # 8808798.

Mason, Jack K. and Donald L. Gurimary. Pilipinos and Unionization of the Alaskan Canned Salmon Industry. Amerasia Journal 8 (Fall/Winter 1981):1-30.

Matison, Sumner E. The Labor Movement and the Negro during

Reconstruction. Journal of Negro History 33 (October 1948):426-68.

Matthews, John M. The Georgia Race Strike of 1909. Journal of Southern History 40 (1974):613-30.

McElvaine, Robert S. Claude Ramsay, Organized Labor, and the Civil Rights Movement in Mississippi, 1959-1966. In: Merl E. Reed and others (eds.), Southern Workers and Their Unions, 1880-1975, pp. 110-142. Westport, CT: Greenwood, 1981.

McGahey, Richard. Minorities and the Labor Market. Washington, D.C., 1985.

McHugh, Cathy L. Mill Family. The Labor System in the Southern Cotton Textile Industry. New York: Oxford University Press, 1988.

McKinney, Ernest R. The Negro's Road to Freedom. Labor Age September 1932.

McLaurin, Melton A. The Knights of Labor in the South. Westport, CT: Greenwood, 1978.

McLaurin, Melton A. The Racial Policies of the Knights of Labor and the Organization of Southern Black Workers. Labor History 17 (Fall 1976):568-85.

McLeod, Jonathan W. Black and White Workers: Atlanta during Reconstruction. Doctoral dissertation, University of California, Los Angeles, 1987. UMO # 8719950. [Racism and class conflict].

McMath, Robert C., Jr. Southern White Farmers and the Organization of Black Farm Workers: A North Carolina Document. Labor History 18 (1977):115-19.

Medford, Edna G. The Transition from Slavery to Freedom in a Diversified Economy: Virginia's Lower Peninsula, 1860-1900. Doctoral dissertation, University of Maryland, 1987. UMO # 8808584.

Meier, August and Elliott Rudwick. Black Detroit and the Rise of the UAW. New York: Oxford University Press, 1979.

Messner, William F. Freedmen and the Ideology of Free Labor: Louisiana, 1862-1865. Lafayette: University of Southern Louisiana, 1978.

Millner, Reginald. Conversations with the "Ole Man": The Life and Times of a Black Appalachian Coal Miner. In: Wm. H. Turner and Edward J. Cabbell (eds.), Blacks in Appalachia. Lexington: University of Kentucky Press, 1985.

Minard, Ralph. Race Relations in the Pocahontas Coal Fields. Journal of Social Forces 8 (1952):37. [W. Va.].

Miner, Claudia. The 1886 Convention of the Knights of Labor. Phylon 44 (June 1983):147-59. [Blacks in the Knights of Labor].

Mitchell, Brian C. The Paddy Camps: The Irish of Lowell, 1821-1861. Urbana, IL: University of Illinois Press, 1988.

Mitchell, Harry Leland. Roll the Union On. Chicago: Charles Kerr Company, 1987. [Helped found the Southern Tenant Farmers' Union in 1917].

Montejano, David. Race, Labor Repression, and Capitalist Agriculture: Notes from South Texas, 1920-1930. Berkeley, CA: Institute for the Study of Social Change, 1977.

Moore, Gilbert W. Poverty, Class Consciousness, and Racial Conflict: The Social Basis of Trade Union Politics in the UAW-CIO, 1937-1955. Doctoral dissertation, Princeton University, 1978.

Moore, Howard. Black Labor: Slavery to Fair Hiring. Black Scholar 4 (1973):22-31.

Morawska, Ewa. For Bread With Butter: Life-Worlds of East Central Europeans in Johnstown, Pennsylvania, 1890-1940. New York: Cambridge University Press, 1985.

Morgan, Glen. Class Theory and the Structural Location of Black Workers. Insurgent Sociologist 10 (1981):21-34.

Morgan, Philip D. Work and Culture: The Work System and the World of Lowcounty Blacks, 1700 to 1880. William and Mary Quarterly 3rd series, 39 (October 1982):563-99.

Muraskin, William. The Harlem Boycott of 1934: Black Nationalism and the Rise of Labor Union Consciousness. Labor History 13 (1972):361-73.

Murayama, Y. Contractors, Collusion and Competition: Japanese Immigrant Railroad Laborers in the Pacific Northwest, 1898-1911. Explorations in Economic History. 21 (July 1984).

The Negro and the American Labor Movement: Some Selected Chapters. Labor History 10 (Summer 1969):entire issue.

Nelli, Humbert S. The Italian Padrone System in the United States. Labor History 5 (1964):153-67.

Newman, Mark J. Black Labor in the 1960s: The Negro American Labor Council. Bachelor's thesis, Princeton University, 1976.

Noble, Kenneth B. Cutting Labor Costs With a Battle-Axe. New York Times January 5, 1986. [All-Black union at Trojan Luggage Co., Memphis, TN].

Northrup, Herbert R. The Negro and the United Mine Workers of America. Southern Economic Journal 9 (1943).

Northrup, Herbert R. Organized Labor and the Negro. New York: Kraus, 1976 (orig. 1944).

Nyden, Linda. Black Miners in Western Pennsylvania, 1925-1931: The
     National Miners Union and the United Mine Workers of America.
     Science and Society 41 (1977):69-101.

Officer, James E. Yaqui Forty Niners in Hispanic Arizona: Interethnic
     Relations on the Sonoran Frontier. Journal of Arizona History 28
     (Summer 1987):101-34.

Olson, James. Race, Class, and Progress: Black Leadership and Industrial
     Unionism, 1936-1945. In: Milton Cantor (ed.), Black Labor in
     America. Westport, CT: Negro Universities Press, 1970.

Perdue, Robert E. Black Laborers and Black Professionals in Early
     America, 1750-1830. New York: Vantage Press, 1975.

Perlo, Victor. The Negro in Southern Agriculture. New York:
     International Publishers, 1953.

Potts, Mark. Minority Gains Being Eroded by Decline in Apprenticeships.
     Chicago Tribune January 25, 1982.

Puette, Bill. The Hilo Massacre: Hawaii's Bloody Monday August 1st 1938.
     Honolulu: Center for Labor Education and Research, University of
     Hawaii, 1988.

Rachleff, Peter J. Black Labor in the South. Richmond, Virginia, 1865-
     1890. Philadelphia: Temple University Press, 1984.

Rachleff, Peter J. Black, White, and Gray: The Rise and Decline of
     Working Class Activity in Richmond, Va., 1865-1890. Master's thesis,
     University of Pittsburgh, 1976.

Rauber, Paul. One City's Hispanics Win All-important Right to Win. In
     These Times April 26,. 1989. [Watsonville, CA].

Rediker, Marcus. Between the Devil and the Deep Blue Sea. Merchant
     Seamen, Pirates, and the Anglo-American Maritime World, 1700-1750.
     New York: Cambridge University Press, 1987.

Reid, Ira D. A. (ed.) Negro Membership in American Labor Unions. New
     York: Negro Universities Press, 1969 (orig. 1930).

Reidy, Joseph P. Aaron A. Bradley: Voice of Black Labor in the Georgia
     Lowcountry. In: Howard N. Rabinowitz (ed.), Southern Black
     Leaders of the Reconstruction Era, pp. 281-308. Urbana: University
     of Illinois Press, 1982.

Reinecke, John E. Feigned Necessity: Hawaii's Attempt to Obtain Chinese
     Contract Labor, 1921-1923. 1979.

Richardson, Herbert N. Black Workers and their Responses to Work Through
     the Songs they Sang. Doctoral dissertation, Rutgers University,
     1987. UMO # 8727327.

Richardson, Joe M. The Freedmen's Bureau and Negro Labor in Florida.

Florida Historical Quarterly 39 (1960):176-84.

Robbins, Lynn A. Navajo Workers and Labor Unions. Southwest Economy and Society 3 (Spring 1978):4-23.

Roediger, Dave. Three Problems in Hill's Major Contribution. New Politics 1 (Summer 1987):46-48. [See, above, H. Hill, 1987].

Rogers, William W. Negro Knights of Labor in Arkansas: A Case Study of the 'Miscellaneous' Strike. Labor History 10 (1969):498-505.

Rose, Margaret E. Women in the United Farm Workers: A Study of Chicano and Mexicana Participation in a Labor Union, 1950-1980. Doctoral dissertation, University of California, Los Angeles, 1988. UMO # 8822299.

Ross, M. H. Labor and the South. Nation July 7, 1956.

Rudolph, Frederick. Chinamen in Yankeedom: Anti-Unionism in Massachusetts in 1870. American Hisorical Review 53 (October 1947):1-29.

Ruiz, Vicki L. Cannery Women, Cannery Lives: Mexican Women, Unionization, and the California Food Processing Industry, 1930-1950. Albuquerque: University of New Mexico Press, 1987.

Salinger, Sharon V. "To Serve Well and Faithfully." Labor and Indentured Servants in Pennsylvania, 1682-1800. New York: Cambridge University Press, 1987.

Salvatore, Nick. Workers, Racism and History: A Response. New Politics 1 (Summer 1987):22-26. [See, above, H. Hill, 1987].

Saville, Julie. A Measure of Freedom: From Slave to Wage Laborer in South Carolina, 1860-1868. Doctoral dissertation, Yale University, 1986. UMO # 872894.

Saxton, Alexander. The Indispensable Enemy. Labor and the Anti-Chinese Movement in California. Berkeley, CA: University of California Press, 1971.

Saxton, Alexander. Race and the House of Labor. In: Gary B. Nash and Richard Weiss (eds.), The Great Fear: Race in the Mind of America. New Yrk: 1970.

Schwartz, Harvey. A Union Combats Racism: The ILWU's Japanese-American 'Stockton Incident' of 1945. Southern California Quarterly 62 (Summer 1980):161-76.

Schwarzchild, Steven S. American History Marked by Racism. New Politics 1 (Summer 1987):56-58. [See, above, H. Hill, 1987].

Schweninger, Loren. James Rapier and the Negro Labor Movement, 1869-1872. Alabama Review 28 (1975):185-201.

Schweninger, Loren. James Rapier and the Negro Labor Movement, 1869-1872. _Alabama Review_ 28 (1975):185-201.

Schweider, Dorothy and others. _Buxton, Work and Racial Equality in a Coal-Mining Community_. Ames: Iowa State University Press, 1987.

Scruggs, Otey M. _The History of Mexican Agricultural Labor in the United States, 1942-1954_. New York: Garland, 1987.

Shlomowitz, Ralph. 'Bound' or 'Free'? Black Labor in Cotton and Sugarcane Farming, 1865-1880. _Journal of Southern History_ 50 (November 1984).

Shlomowitz, Ralph. Planter Combinations and Black Labour in the American South, 1865-1880. _Slavery and Abolition_ 9 (May 1988):72-84.

Shofner, Jerrell H. The Labor of Jacksonville: A Negro Union and White Strikebreakers. _Florida Historical Quarterly_ 50 (1972):272-82.

Shofner, Jerrell H. Militant Negro Laborers in Reconstruction Florida. _Journal of Southern History_ 39 (1973):397-408. [Agricultural and non-agricultural].

Shofner, Jerrell H. The Pensacola Workingman's Association: A Militant Negro Labor Union During Reconstruction. _Labor History_ 13 (1972):55-9.

Smallwood, James. Perpetuation of Caste: Black Agricultural Workers in Reconstruction Texas. _Mid-America_ 61 (January 1979):2-24.

Sowell, David. Racial Patterns of Labor in Postbellum Florida: Gainesville, 1870-1900. _Florida Historical Quarterly_ 63 (April 1985):434-44.

Spero, Sterling and Abram Harris. _The Black Worker_. Port Washington, NY: Kennikat Press, 1966 (orig. 1933).

Stanback, Howard J. _Racism, Black Labor, and the Giant Corporation_. Doctoral dissertation, University of Massachusetts, 1980. UMO # 8101399.

Stokes, Allen H., Jr. _Black and White Labor and the Development of the Southern Textile Industry, 1800-1920_. Doctoral dissertation, University of South Carolina, 1977.

Straw, Richard A. The Collapse of Biracial Unionism: The Alabama Coal Strike of 1908. _In:_ Wm. H. Turner and Edward J. Cabbell (eds.), _Black in Appalachia_. Lexington: University of Kentucky Press, 1985.

Strickland, Arvarh E. The Plight of the People in the Sharecropping Demonstration in Southeast Missouri. _Missouri Historical Review_ 81 (July 1987):403-16.

Surface, G. T. Negro Mine Laborers: Central Appalachian Coal Field. _Annals of the American Academy of Political Science_ 33 (March

1909):116-17.

Swan, James H. Racism in Labor Markets. 2 vols. Doctoral dissertation, Northwestern University, 1981. UMO # 8125020.

Taft, Philip. Organizing Dixie: Alabama Workers in the Industrial Era. Ed. by Gary Fink. Westport, CT: Greenwood, 1981.

Takaki, Ronald. The Making of a Multiethnic Working Class in Hawaii. Critical Perspectives of Third World America. 1 (1983):151-63.

Tate, Merze. Decadence of the Hawaiian Nation and Proposals to Import a Negro Labor Force. Journal of Negro History 47 (1963):248-63.

Taylor, Paul S. Mexican Labor in the United States. 2 vols. Berkeley, CA: University of California Press, 1930-1932.

Thomas, Norman. The Negro. In: Human Exploitation in the United States, pp. 258-83. New York: Stokes, 1934.

Torres, Andrés J. Human Capital, Labor Segmentation and Inter-Minority Relative Status: Black and Puerto Rican Labor in New York City, 1960-1980. Doctoral dissertation, New School for Social Research, 1988. UMO # 8817304.

Tripp, Anne H. The I.W.W. and the Paterson Silk Strike of 1913. Urbana: University of Illinois Press, 1987.

Trotter, Joe William, Jr. Black Milwaukee: The Making of an Industrial Proletariat, 1915-45. Urbana: University of Illinois Press, 1985.

Trotter, Joe William, Jr. The Making of an Industrial Proletariat: Black Milwaukee, 1915-1945. Doctoral dissertation, University of Minnesota, 1980. UMO # 8109519.

Turner, William H. Blacks in Appalachian America: Reflections on Biracial Education and Unionism. Phylon 44 (September 1983):198-208.

United Mine Workers Journal. January 15, 1919, p. 5. [Black vs. white miners, companies].

U.S. Commission on Civil Rights, North Carolina Advisory Committee. Where Mules Outrate Men. Migrant and Seasonal Farmworkers in North Carolina. Washington, D.C.: The Commission, 1979.

U.S. Commission on Civil Rights, Virginia Advisory Committee. Migrant Farm Workers on Virginia's Eastern Shore. Washington, D.C.: The Commission, November 1983.

Valdez, Armando and others (eds.) The State of Chicano Research on Family, Labor, and Migration. Stanford, CA: Stanford Center for Chicano Research, 1983.

Vance, Rupert B. When Southern Labor Comes of Age. Monthly Labor Review

91 (1968):1-4.

Vittoz, Stanley. New Deal Labor Policy and the American Industrial Economy. Chapel Hill: University of North Carolina Press, 1987.

Waltzer, Kenneth. The Need to Explore Distinctions. New Politics 1 (Summer 1987):41-46. [See, above, H. Hill, 1987].

Ward, Robert D. and William Rodgers. Labor Revolt in Alabama. Tuscaloosa, Alabama, 1965. [White vs. Black miners and coal employers].

Weaver, Robert C. Negro Labor: A National Problem. 1946.

Weems, Robert E., Jr. Black Working Class, 1915-1925. Milwaukee Hist. 6 (Winter 1983):107-14.

Weir, Stan. Looking Beyond Union Bureaucracy. New Politics 1 (Summer 1987):48-52. [See, above, H. Hill, 1987].

Wesley, Charles H. Negro Labor in the United States, 1850-1925. New York: Vanguard, 1927.

Wilber, George L. and others. Minorities in the Labor Market. Vol. I: Spanish Americans and Indians in the Labor Market. Lexington, KY: Social Welfare Research Institute, University of Kentucky, 1975.

Williamson, Handy and Noel A. D. Thompson. An Economic Study of the Alabama Black Belt. Institute, AL: Tuskegee Institute, 1975.

Williamson, John. The Trade Unions and the Negro Workers. Political Affairs (November 1947).

Wilson, Joseph. Cold Steel: The Political Economy of Black Labor and Reform in the United States. Doctoral dissertation, Columbia University, 1980.

Winn, Frank. Labor Tackles the Race Question. Antioch Review 3 (Fall 1943).

Wollenberg, Charles. Working on El Traque: The Pacific Elective Strike of 1933. In: Norris Hundley (ed.), The Chicano, pp. 96-107. Santa Barbara, CA: Clio Books, 1975.

Wolters, Raymond. Closed Shop and White Shop: The Negro Response to Collective Bargaining, 1933-35. In: Milton Cantor (ed.), Black Labor in America. Westport, CT: Negro Universities Press, 1970.

Wolters, Raymond. Section 7A and the Black Worker. Labor History 10 (1969):459-74.

Womack, Richard G. Civil Rights and the AFL-CIO. New Politics 1 (Summer 1987):29-30. [See, above, H. Hill, 1987].

Woodson, Carter G. The Rural Negro. 1930.

Work, Monroe N. The South's Labor Problem. South Atlantic Quarterly 19 (January 1920):1-8.

Worthman, Paul B. A Black Worker and the Bricklayers and Masons' Union. Journal of Negro History 54 (1969):398-404.

Worthman, Paul B. Black Workers and Labor Unions in Birmingham, Alabama, 1897-1904. Labor History 10 (1969):375-407.

Worthman, Paul B. and James R. Green. Black Workers in the New South, 1865-1915. In: Nathan J. Huggins and others (eds.), Key Issues in Afro-American Experience, pp. 47-69. New York: Harcourt Brace Jovanovich, 1971.

Wright, Charles H. Robeson: Labor's Forgotten Champion. Detroit, MI: 1975.

Wright, Gavin. Postbellum Southern Labor Markets. In: Peter Kilby (ed.), Quantity and Quiddity: Essays in U.S. Economic History. Middletown, CT: Wesleyan University Press, 1987.

Wright, R. R. Negro in Times of Industrial Unrest. Charities 15 (October 7, 1905):69-73. [Strikebreaking].

Wyche, Billy H. Southern Industrialists View Organized Labor in the New Deal Years, 1933-1941. Southern Studies 19 (Summer 1980):157-71.

Wynne, Lewis N. The Role of Freedmen in the Post Bellum Cotton Economy of Georgia. Phylon 42 (Winter 1981):309-321.

Yellowitz, Irwin. Black Militancy and Organized Labor: An Historical Parallel. Midwest Quarterly 13 (1972):169-83.

Yoneda, Karl. Asian Pacific Workers and the U.S. Labor Movement. NST: Nature, Society, and Thought 1 (1988).

Zamora, Emilio. Mexican Labor Activity is South Texas, 1900-1920. Doctoral dissertation, University of Texas, 1983. UMO # 8319707.

Labor Bibliography

Bibliography on Negro Labor. Washington, D.C.: U.S. Bureau of Labor Statistics, 1937.

Du Bois, W. E. B. and Augustus G. Dill (comps.) A Select Bibliography of the Negro American Artisan. In: The Negro American Artisan, pp. 9-12. Atlanta: Atlanta University Press, 1912.

King, William M. (comp.) Black Labor in the Cities: A Selected Bibliography. [Exchange Bibliography No. 548.] Monticello, IL: Council of Planning Libraries, 1974.

Kirkley, A. Roy, Jr. (comp.) Labor Unions and the Black Experience: A
    Selected Bibliography. New Brunswick, NJ: Labor and Education
    Library, Rutgers University, 1972.

Miles, Dione (comp.) Something in Common - An IWW Bibliography.
    Detroit: Wayne State University, 1986.

Neufeld, Maurice F. and others (comps.) American Working Class History:
    A Representative Bibliography. New York: Bowker, 1983.

Newman, Debra L. (comp.) Selected Documents Pertaining to Black Workers
    Among the Records of the Department of Labor and Its Component
    Bureaus, 1902-1969. Washington, D.C.: National Archives and Records
    Service, General Services Administration, 1977.

Oxley, Lawrence A. (comp.) Bibliography on Negro Labor. Washington,
    D.C.: U.S. Bureau of Labor Statistics, 1937. Also, supplement,
    1938.

Wilson, Joseph (comp.) Black Labor in America, 1865-1983: A Selected
    Annotated Bibliography. Westport, CT: Greenwood, 1986.

42. Land

[After the end of slavery] our next work will be ... to do all in our power to succor and elevate the liberated bondmen; to see that they have all desirable means of education - that they are fully protected on the soil where they belong - in all their rights and interests - that they are fairly paid for their labor, and allowed to possess land and become freeholders, like others who are of a different complexion.

- William Lloyd Garrison, *Liberator*, February 6, 1863.

Baldwin, Sidney. *Poverty and Politics: The Rise and Decline of the Farm Security Administration*. Chapel Hill: University of North Carolina Press, 1968.

Barsh, Russel L. Indian Land Claims Policy in the United States. *North Dakota Law Review* 58 (1982):1081.

Bleser, Carol K. R. *The Promised Land: A History of the South Carolina Land Commission, 1869-1890*. Columbia, SC: 1969.

Chinen, J. *The Great Mahele, Hawaii's Land Division of 1948*. 1958.

Clift, Eleanor. Black Land Loss: 6,000,000 Acres and Fading Fast. *Southern Exposure* 2 (1974):108-11.

Clow, Richard L. Cattlemen and Tribal Rights: The Standing Rock Leasing Conflict of 1902. *North Dakota History* 54 (Spring 1987):23-30.

Cox, LaWanda. The Province of Land for the Freedman. *Mississippi Valley Historical Review* 45 (December 1958):413-39.

Du Bois, W. E. B. [Black farmers in the South]. *Pittsburgh Courier* November 28, 1936.

Du Bois, W. E. B. *The Negro Farmer*. U.S. Bureau of the Census. *Bulletin* 8 (1904):69-98.

Du Bois, W. E. B. *The Negro Farmer*. *Special Reports: Supplementary Analysis and Derivative Tables*, pp. 511-579. U.S. Twelfth Census. Washington, D.C.: GPO, 1906.

Du Bois, W. E. B. *The Negro Landholder of Georgia*. U.S. Department of Labor, *Bulletin* 6 (July 1901):647-777.

Du Bois, W. E. B. Real Estate in New York. *Crisis* 8 (July 1914). [Harlem].

Du Bois, W. E. B. The World and Us. *Crisis* 23 (February 1922):151-5. [Blacks and land in U.S.].

Endrich, Louise and Michael Dorris. Who Owns the Land? *New York Times*

Magazine September 9, 1988. [White Earth Indian Reservation, Minnesota].

Fierce, Milfred C. Black Struggle for Land During Reconstruction. Black Scholar 5 (1974):13-18.

Gottlieb, Manuel. The Land Question in Georgia during Reconstruction. Science and Society 3 (Summer 1939):356-88.

Hewitt, Ronald S. The Afro-American Struggle to Acquire Land during Reconstruction Period and the Effects of Their Failure: A Case Study of South Carolina 1865-1900. Master's thesis, Cornell University, 1986.

Higgs, Robert. Race, Tenure, and Resource Allocation in Southern Agriculture. Journal of Economic History 33 (1973):149-69.

Highsmith, William E. Louisiana Landholding during War and Reconstruction. Louisiana Historical Quarterly 38 (1955):39-54.

Hoffnagle, Warren. The Southern Homestead Act: Its Origins and Operation. Historian 32 (1970):612-29.

Holley, Donald. The Negro in the New Deal Resettlement Program. Agricultural History 45 (1971):179-93. [See criticism, pp. 195-200].

Horowitz, Robert F. Land to the Freedmen: A Vision of Reconstruction. Ohio History 86 (1977):187-99.

Ichioka, Yuyi. Japanese Immigrant Response to the 1920 California Alien Land Law. Agricultural History 58 (April 1984):157-78.

Iverson, Peter. Knowing the Land, Leaving the Land: Navajos, Hopis, and Relocation in the American West. Montana 38 (Winter 1988):67-70.

Jacobs, Wilbur R. Dispossessing the American Indian: Indians and Whites on the Colonial Frontier. New York: Scribner's, 1972.

Janiewski, Dolores E. Sisterhood Denied: Race, Gender and Class in a New South Community [Durham, NC]. Philadelphia, PA: Temple University Press, 1985.

Lam, Maivan. The Imposition of Anglo-American Laws of Land Tenure on Hawaiians. Journal of Legal Pluralism 22 (1985).

Limeburner, Wayne T. The Dominance of a White View of History or and Indian View of History in Court Cases Involving Lands of the Six Nations of the Iroquois League of New York, 1919-1982. Master's thesis, Central Connecticut State University, 1985.

Magdol, Edward. A Right to Land: Essays on the Freedmen's Community. Westport, CT: Greenwood, 1977.

Marable, Manning. The Politics of Black Land Tenure, 1877-1915.

Agricultural History 53 (January 1979):142-152.

McGee, Leo and Robert Boone. Black Rural Land Decline in the South [1910-1974]. Black Scholar 8 (1977):8-11.

McGee, Leo and Robert Boone. The Black Rural Landowner - Endangered Species, Political, and Economic Implications. Westport, CT: Greenwood, 1979.

McGuire, Mary J. Getting their Hands on the Land: Black Farmers in St. Helena Parish, 1861-1900. Master's thesis, University of South Carolina, 1982.

O'Connell, Mary M. The 1920 Anti-Alien Land Initiative: Perspectives in the San Diego Press. Master's thesis, San Diego State University, 1977.

Oubre, Claude F. Forty Acres and a Mule: The Freedmen's Bureau and Black Land Ownership. Baton Rouge: Louisiana State University Press, 1978.

Oubre, Claude F. 'Forty Acres and a Mule': Lousiana History 17 (1976):143-57.

Pope, Christie F. Southern Homesteads for Negroes. Agricultural History 44 (1970):201-12.

Range, Willard. The Land and the Landless: Georgia Agriculture, 1920-1940. In: Harry N. Scheiber (ed.), United States Economic History: Selected Readings. New York: 1964.

Riddleberger, Patrick W. George W. Julian: Abolitionist Land Reformer. Agricultural History 29 (1955):108-15.

Ross, Steven J. Freed Soil, Freed Labor, Freed Men: John Eaton and the Davis Bend Experiment. Journal of Southern History 44 (May 1978):213-32.

Salamon, Lester M. Land and Minority Enterprise: The Crisis and the Opportunity. Washington, D.C.: GPO, 1973.

Salamon, Lester M. The Time Dimension in Policy Evaluation: The Case of the New Deal Land-Reform Experiments. Public Policy 27 (Spring 1979):129-83.

Smith, Burton M. Politics and the Crow Indian Land Cessions. Montana 36 (Autumn 1986):24-37.

Sutton, Imre (ed.) Irredeemable America: The Indians' Estate and Land Claims. Albuquerque: University of New Mexico Press, 1985.

U.S. Commission on Civil Rights. The Decline of Black Farming in America. Washington, D.C.: The Commission, 1982.

Vecsey, Christopher and William A Starna. Iroquois Land Claims Syracuse,

348

New York: Syracuse University Press, 1988.

Washburn, Wilcomb E.   Red Man's Land/White Man's Law: A Study of the Past
     and Present Status of the American Indian.   New York: Scribner's,
     1971.

Washington, Booker T.   Land-hunger in the Black Belt.   Lippincott   77
     (June 1906):757-64.

Work, Monroe N.   Racial Factors and Economic Forces in Land Tenure in the
     South, 1860-1930.   Social Forces   15 (December 1936):205-15.

Wright, J. Leitch, Jr.   The Only Land They Knew: The Tragic Story of the
     American Indians in the Old South.   New York: Free Press, 1981.

43. Language

In the 1960s I would have been talking ... [with] white linguists about black language. Now we have the possibility of black and white linguists jointly bringing their experience to bear upon the problems [of Black English]. ... The Ann Arbor trial marks a turning point ... The trial was the initiative of black people. ... The only permanent advance in the condition of life in any field occurs when people take their own affairs into their own hands. I believe that this is true of the study of Black English as it is true everywhere.

William Labov, "Objectivity and Commitment in Linguistic Science: The Case of the Black English Trial in Ann Arbor, " Language in Society, 11 (August 1980).

Allen, I. L. The Language of Ethnic Conflict: Social Organization and Lexical Culture [Over 1,000 terms of abuse of 53 ethnic groups in the U.S.]. New York: Columbia University Press, 1983.

Axtell, James. Forked Tongues: Moral Judgments in Indian History. Perspectives: AHA Newsletter 25 (February 1987):10, 12-13.

Baldwin, Elizabeth F. Linguistics and Ideology in the "English-Only" Movement. Doctoral dissertation, University of Minnesota, 1988. UMO # 8815265.

Baugh, John. Black Street Speech: Its History, Structure, and Survival. Austin: University of Texas Press, 1983.

Baugh, John. Language and Race: Some Implications for Linguistic Science. In: Frederick Newmeyer (ed.), Linguistics: The Cambridge Survey. Forthcoming.

Billig, Michael and others. Prejudice and Tolerance. In: Ideological Dilemmas. A Social Psychology of Everyday Thinking. Newbury Park, CA: Sage, 1988.

Bosmajian, Haig A. The Language of White Racism. College English 31 (December 1969).

Buck, Elizabeth. English in the Linguistic Transformation of Hawaii: Literacy, Languages and Discourse. World Englishes 5 (Winter 1986):141-52.

Burgest, David R. Language, Culture and White Supremacy. Doctoral dissertation, Syracuse University, 1974. UMO # 76-7886.

Busby, Delia. 'And What Do You Do When They Call You Nigger.' Integrateduction 15 (January-February 1977).

Chicano Rhetoric. Western Journal of Speech Communication. (Summer 1980).

Cole, Johnnetta B. Culture: Negro, Black, and Nigger. Black Scholar (June 1970).

Derrida, Jacques. Racism's Last Words. Critical Inquiry 12 (Autumn 1985).

Dillard, Joey Lee. Black English: Its History and Usage in the United States. New York: Random House, 1972.

Dillard, Joey Lee. Lexicon of Black English. New York: Seabury Press, 1977.

Epstein, Erwin H. Linguistics Orientation and Changing Values in Puerto Rico. International Journal of Comparative Sociology 9 (1968):61-76.

Fernandez, R. R. and W. Velez. Race, Color, and Language in the Changing Public Schools. In: Lionel Maldonado and Joan Moore (eds.), Urban Ethnicity in the United States. Newbury Park, CA: Sage, 1985.

Fernandez, Robert M. and Francois Nielsen. Bilingualism and Hispanic Scholastic Achievement: Some Baseline Results. Social Science Research 15 (March 1986):43-70.

Fishman, Joshua A. Language Maintenance. In: Stephan Thernstrom (ed.), Harvard Encyclopedia of American Ethnic Groups, pp. 629-38. Cambridge, MA: Harvard University Press, 1980.

Forrest, Leon. Move to Paint Black Dialects as Language Has Bantustan Odor. Muhammad Speaks August 7, 1970.

Garcia, John F. Is It the Language Barrier? Integrated Education (February-March 1967).

Garner, T. and D. L. Rubin. Middle Class Blacks' Perceptions of Dialect and Style Shifting: The Case of Southern Attorneys. Journal of Language and Social Psychology 5 (1986):33-48.

Gonzalez, Rafael J. Pachuco: The Birth of a Creole Language. Arizona Quarterly 23 (1967):343-56.

Greenfield, Thomas A. Race and Passive Voice at Monticello. Integrateducation 15 (March-April 1977).

Habuta, Kenji. Degree of Bilingualism and Cognitive Ability in Mainland Puerto Rican Children. Child Development 58 (October 1987):1372-88.

Hall, Linda. In Black and White. Times Higher Education Supplement November 12, 1982. [The non-racist history of the word "black"].

Hansen, Kristine. Rhetoric and Epistemology in Texts from the Social Sciences: An Analysis of Three Disciplines' Discourse about Modern American Blacks. Doctoral dissertation, University of Texas, 1987. UMO # 8728566.

Hawthorne, Lucia. The Public Address of Black America. In: Jack L. Daniel (ed.), Black Communication. New York: Speech Communication Association, 1974.

Heath, Shirley and Charles A. Ferguson (eds.) Language in the U.S.A. Cambridge, MA: 1979.

Hernandez, Orlando J. This Uncanny, Tricky Business: Translation and Ideology in Puerto Rican Literature. In: Asela Rodriguez de Laguna (ed.), Images and Identities. The Puerto Rican in Two World Contexts, pp. 181-86. New Brunswick, NJ: Transaction Books, 1987.

Hoaglund, Edward. 'WASP' Stings. It Isn't Amusing [Criticism of use of WASP, White Anglo-Saxon Protestant]. New York Times September 16, 1988.

James, Alan. 'Black;" An Inquiry into the Perjorative Association of an English Word. New Community 9 (Spring-Summer 1981):19-30.

Jordan, June. Nobody Mean More to Me Than You and the Future Life of Willie Jordan. Harvard Educational Review 58 (August 1988):363-74.

Joyce, Joyce A. Semantic Development of the Word 'Black': A History from Indo-European to the Present. Journal of Black Studies 11 (March 1981):307-12.

Labov, William. Objectivity and Commitment in Linguistic Science: The Case of the Black English Trial in Ann Arbor. Language in Society 11 (1982):165-201.

Language Minority Voting Rights and the English Language Amendment. Hastings Constitutional Legal Questions 14 (Spring 1987):657-81.

Leeds-Hurwitz, Wendy. The Committee on Research on Native American Language [1927-1937]. Proc. Am. Phil. Soc. 129 (June 1985):129-6

Leibowitz, Arnold H. The Imposition of English as the Language of Instruction in American Schools. Revista de Derecho Puertoriqueño (October-December 1970):175-244.

Lemaire, Herve-B. Franco-American Efforts on Behalf of the French Language in New England. In: Joshua Fishman (ed.), Language Loyalty in the United States. The Hague, 1966.

Logue, Cal M. Rhetorical Ridicule of Reconstruction Blacks. Quarterly Journal of Speech 62 (December 1976):400-09.

Medicine, Bea. "Speaking Indian": Parameters of Language Use Among American Indians. March 1981. ERIC ED 209 052.

Moore, Robert B. Racism in the English Language. A Lesson Plan and Study Essay, 1976. Racism and Sexism Resource Center for Educators, 1841 Broadway, New York, NY 10023.

Morris, Richard J. Contemporary Native American Discourse: A Case Study [Speeches at Wounded Knee]. In: James P. Danky and others (eds.), Native American Pressin Wisconsin and the Nation, pp. 167-82. Madison: University of Wisconsin Library School, 1982.

Mukherjee, Tuku. ESL: An Imported New Empire? Journal of Moral Education 15 (January 1986):43-49.

Nelson, John S. and others (eds.) The Rhetoric of the Human Sciences: Language and Rhetoric in Scholarship and Public Affairs. Madison: University of Wisconsin Press, 1987.

Ney, James W. Elitism, Racism and Some Contemporary Views of English Spelling, 1974. ERIC ED 097 731.

Pap, Leo. Portugese-American Speech. New York: 1949.

Penalosa, Fernando. Chicano Sociolinguistics Rowley, MA: Newbury House, 1980.

Penalosa, Fernando. Sociolinguistic Theory and the Chicano Community. Aztlan 6 (Spring 1975):1-11.

Purnell, Rosentene B. Teaching Them to Curse: Racial Bias in Language, Pedagogy and Practices. Phylon 43 (Fall 1982):231-241.

Rasky, Susan F. What's In a Name? For Indians, Cultural Survival [White Mountain Apaches, eastern Arizona]. New York Times August 4, 1988.

Ridgway, Jack. Social Factors and Language Development: An Exploration of the Bernstein-Labov Controversy. CORE: Collected Original Resources 1 (June 1977):1415-1511.

Ruether, Rosemary R. We Need Better Words than Black and White. National Catholic Reporter September 16, 1988.

Safire, William. People of Color. New York Times Magazine November 20, 1988.

Scott, Patricia Bell. The English Language and Black Womanhood: A Low Blow at Self-esteem. Journal of Afro-American Issues 2 (Summer 1974):218-25.

Smith, Nancy J. and others. Making the Literate Environment Equitable. Reading Teacher 40 (January 1987):400-07.

Smitherman, Geneva. Language and Liberation. Journal of Negro Education 52 (Winter 1983):15-23.

Smitherman-Donaldson, Geneva and Teun A. van Dijle (eds.) Discourse and Discrimination. Detroit: Wayne State University Press, 1988.

Sniezek, Janet A. and Christine H. Jazwinski. Gender Bias in English: In Search of Fair Language. Journal of Applied Social Psychology 16 (1986):642-62.

Sommerfield, Linda L. *An Historical Descriptive Study of the Circumstances that Led to the Elimination of German from the Cleveland Schools: 1860-1918*. Doctoral dissertation, Kent State University, 1986. UMO # 8705821.

Svensson, Frances. Language as Ideology: The American Indian Case. *American Indian Culture and Research Journal* 1 (1975):29-35.

Underwood, Charles F. *The Indian Witness: Narrative Style in Courtroom Testimony*. Doctoral dissertation, University of California, Berkeley, 1986. UMO # 8624970.

van Dijk, Teun A. *Communication Racism. Ethnic Prejudice in Thought and Talk*. Sage, 1987.

Wallinger, Michael J. *Dispersal of the Japanese Americans: Rhetorical Strategies of the War Relocation Authority, 1942-1945*. Doctoral dissertation, University of Oregon, 1975.

Wideman, John. Fame and Dialect: The Evolution of the Black Voice in American Literature. *American Poetry Review* 5 (September-October 1976):34-37.

Wittlin, Curt J. Synchronic Etymologies of Ethnonyms as Cause of Traditional Belief in Monstrous Races. *In*: Hector Hammerly and Isabel Sawyer (eds.), *Second Language Teaching*, 1975. ERIC ED 138 042.

Wolfson, N. and J. Manes (eds.) *Language of Inequality*. Berlin: Mouton, 1985.

Wolfram, W. Black English and Mathematics? The Latest Flap. *National Black Association for Speech, Language and Hearing Newsletter*. 1 (1987):1-2.

Language Bibliography

Brasch, Ila W. and Walter M. Brasch. (comps.) *A Comprehensive Annotated Bibliography of American Black English*. Baton Rouge: Louisiana State University Press, 1974.

Hite, Roger (comp.) Racial Rhetoric: A Bibliography. *In*: James E. Roever (ed.), *Proceedings: Speech Association of America Summer Conference V*, pp. 88-124. New York: Speech Association of America, 1969.

Williams, Frederick and Rita C. Naremore (comps.) *Language and Poverty: An Annotated Bibliography*. Madison: University of Wisconsin, Institute for Research on Poverty, 1967.

> *Oh, for a Supreme Court ... which shall be as true to the claims of humanity as the Supreme Court formerly was to the demands of slavery!*

> \- Frederick Douglass, __Life__ __and__ __Times__ __of__ __Frederick__ __Douglass__, p. 550 (1892). The U.S. Supreme Court had in 1883 invalidated the Civil Rights Act of 1875.

All Rise Please [Asian American Judge]. __Rice__ (February 1988):34-45.

Allen, Milton B. A Black Prosecutor's Perspective on Justice, pp. 110-29 __in__ Gilbert Ware (ed.), __From__ __the__ __Black__ __Bar.__ __Voices__ __for__ __Equal__ __Justice__. New York: Putnam's, 1976.

Allocating the Burden of Proof after a Finding of Unitariness in School Desegregation Litigation. __Harvard__ __Law__ __Review__ 100 (January 1987):653-71.

Anderson, Charles W., Jr. The South's Challenge to the Negro Lawyer. __National__ __Bar__ __Journal__ 3 (March 1945):39-41.

Applebone, Peter. Indian Hostage Case Brings Up Questions about Rural Justice [Tuscarora Indians in Robeson County, NC]. __New__ __York__ __Times__ February 8, 1988.

__Attica:__ __The__ __Official__ __Report__ __of__ __the__ __New__ __York__ __State__ __Special__ __Commission__ __on__ __Attica__. New York: Bantam Books, 1972.

Auerbach, Jerold S. __Unequal__ __Justice:__ __Lawyers__ __and__ __Social__ __Change__ __in__ __Modern__ __America__. New York: Oxford, 1976.

Balbus, Isaac D. __The__ __Dialectics__ __of__ __Legal__ __Repression.__ __Black__ __Rebels__ __before__ __the__ __American__ __Criminal__ __Courts__. New York: Basic Books, 1973.

Ball, Milner S. Constitution, Court, Indian Tribes. __American__ __Bar__ __Foundation__ __Research__ __Journal__ (Winter 1987).

Baltimore, Roderick R. and Robert F. Williams. The State Consitutional Roots of the Separate but Equal Doctrine: __Roberts__ v.__City__ __of__ __Boston__. __Rutgers__ __Law__ __Journal__ 17 (Spring-Summer 1986):537-52.

Barsh, Russell L. Indigenous North America and Contemporary Law. __Oregon__ __Law__ __Review__ 62 (1984):83-125.

Bell, Derrick A., Jr. Black Faith in a Racist Land. __Journal__ __of__ __Public__ __Law__ 20 (1971).

Bell, Derrick A., Jr. __Race,__ __Racism,__ __and__ __American__ __Law__. Boston: Little, Brown.

Bell, Derrick A., Jr. The Racial Imperative in American Law, pp. 26-28 __in__

Robert Haws (ed.), The Age of Segregation: Race Relations in the South, 1890-1954. Jackson: University Press of Mississippi, 1978.

Bell, Derrick A., Jr. Racism in American Courts. California Law Review 62 (1973).

Benedict, Michael Les. Racism and Equality in America. Reviews in American History 6 (March 1978):18-20.

Berman, Howard R. The Concept of Aboriginal Rights in the Early Legal History of the U.S. Buffalo Law Review 27 (Fall 1978):637-68.

Berry, Mary F. Black Resistance/White Law: A History of Constitutional Racism in America. New York: Appleton-Century-Crofts, 1971.

Berry, Mary F. Military Necessity and Civil Rights Policy. Port Washington, NY: Kennikat Press, 1977.

Bloomfield, Maxwell. From Deference to Confrontation: The Early Black Lawyers of Galveston, Texas, 1895-1920. In: Gerard W. Gawalt (ed.), The New High Priests: Lawyers in Post-Civil War America. Westport, CT: Greenwood, 1984.

Blumrosen, Alfred W. The Legacy of Griggs: Social Progress and Subjective Judgements. Chicago-Kent Law Review 63 (Winter 1987):1-42.

Bodenhamer, David J. and James W. Ely, Jr. (eds.) Ambivalent Legacy: A Legal History of the South. Jackson: University Press of Mississippi, 1984.

Bogen, D. S. The Transformation of the Fourteenth Amendment: Reflections from the Admission of Maryland's First Black Lawyers. Maryland Law Review 44 (1985):939-1046.

Braden, Anne. The Constitution and the Civil Rights Movement: The First Amendment and the Fourteenth. In: Jules Lobel (ed.), A Less Than Perfect Union, pp. 174-89. New York: Monthly Review Press, 1988.

Brennan, William J., Jr. The Equality Principle: A Foundation of American Law. U.C. Davis Law Review 20 (Summer 1987):673-78.

Burnham, Margaret. Reflections on the Civil Rights Movement and the First Amendment. In: Jules Lobel (ed.), A Less Than Perfect Union, pp. 335-45. New York: Monthly Review Press, 1988.

Burns, Haywood. The Activism is Not Affirmative in Herman Schwartz (ed.), The Burger Years: Rights and Wrongs in the Supreme Court, 1969-1986. New York: Viking, 1987.

Burns, Haywood. Black People and the Tyranny of Law. Annals of the American Academy of Political and Social Science 407(May 1973).

Burns, Haywood. Can A Black Man Get a Fair Trial in This Country? New York Times Magazine (July 12, 1970).

Burns, Haywood. From Brown to Bakke and Back: Race, Law, and Social Change in America. Daedalus 110 (Spring 1981):219-231.

Burns, Haywood. Political Uses of the Law. Howard Law Journal 17 (1973).

Burns, Haywood. Racism and American Law in Robert Lefcourt (ed.), Law Against the People: Essays to Demystify Law, Order and the Courts. New York: Vintage, 1971.

Burns, Haywood. The Role of the Black Bar in Black People's Struggle for Social Justice. In: Christine P. Clark (ed.), Minority Opportunities in Law for Blacks, Puerto Ricans and Chicanos. New York: Law Journal Press, 1974.

Canby, William C., Jr. The Status of Indian Tribes in American Law Today. Washington Law Review 62 (January 1987):1-22.

Canellos, Peter S. Class, Wealth Seen as Advantages in Court. Boston Globe September 24, 1988.

Carrott, M. Browning. Prejudice Goes to Court: The Japanese and the Supreme Court in the 1920s. California History 62 (Summer 1982):122-38.

Carter, Dan T. Scottsboro: A Tragedy of the American South. Revised edition. Baton Rouge: Louisiana State University Press, 1979.

Carter, Dan T. (editorial advisor). Papers of the NAACP. Part 6: The Scottsboro Case, 1931-1950 [24 microfilm reels.] Frederick, MD: University Publications of America, 1987.

Carter, Robert L. Reexamining Brown Twenty-five Years Later: Looking Backward into the Future. Harvard Civil Rights Law Review 14 (Fall 1979):615-34.

Carter, S. L. When Victims Happen to Be Black. Yale Law Journal 97 (December 1987).

Char, Tin-yuke. Legal Restrictions on Chinese in English-speaking Countries of the Pacific - I. Chinese Social and Political Science Review 16 (1932):472-513.

Chesler, Mark and others. Social Science in Court: Mobilizing Experts in the School Desegregation Cases. Madison: University of Wisconsin Press, 1988.

Chuman, Frank F. The Bamboo People: The Law and Japanese Americans. Del Mar, CA: 1976.

Colker, Ruth. Anti-subordination Above All: Sex, Race, and Equal Protection. New York University Law Review 61 (December 1986):1003-66.

Cottrol, Robert J. Law, Politics and Race in Urban America: Towards a New Synthesis. Rutgers Law Journal 17 (Spring-Summer 1986):483-536.

Cover, Robert. Justice Accused. Antislavery and the Judicial Process. New Haven, CT: Yale University Press,

Cresswell, Stephen. Enforcing the Enforcement Acts: The Department of Justice in Northern Mississippi, 1870-1890. Journal of Southern History 53 (August 1987):421-40.

Crockett, George W., Jr. Racism in the Courts. In: Gilbert Ware (ed.), From the Black Bar. Voices for Equal Justice, pp. 104-109. New York: Putnam's, 1976.

Crockett, George W., Jr. Racism in the Law. Muhammad Speaks November 1969.

Crockett, George W., Jr. The Role of the Black Judge. Journal of Public Law 20 (1971):397-400.

Deloria, Vine, Jr. Beyond the Pale: American Indians and the Constitution. In: Jules Lobel (ed.), A Less Than Perfect Union, pp. 249-67. New York: Monthly Review Press, 1988.

Deloria, Vine, Jr. and Clifford M. Lytle. American Indians, American Justice. University of Texas Press, 1983.

Division of Legal Information and Community Service. It's Not the Distance, "It's the Niggers". Comments on the Controversy Over School Busing, May 1972. NAACP Legal Defense and Educational Fund, 10 Columbus Circle, New York, NY 10019.

Dominiquez, V. R. White by Definition: Social Classification in Creole Louisiana. 1986.

Dong, Nelson G. The Chinese and the Anti-Chinese Movement: The Judicial Response in California, 1850-1886. Seminar paper, Yale Law School, 1974.

Elman, Philip. Response (to Randall Kennedy). Harvard Law Review 100 (June 1987):1949-57. [See Randall Kennedy, below].

Elman, Philip and Norman Silber. The Solicitor General's Office, Frankfurter, and Civil Rights Legislation. Harvard Law Review 100 (February 1987):817-52.

Entin, Jonathan L. Sweatt v. Painter, The End of Segregation, and the Transformation of Law. Review of Litigation 5 (Winter 1986):3-71.

Fede, Andrew. Legal Protection for Slave Buyers in the U.S. South: A Caveat Concerning Caveat Emptor. American Journal of Legal History 31 (October 1987):332-58.

Fehrenbacher, Don E. The Dred Scott Case: Its Significance in American Law and Politics.

Finkelman, Paul. The Law of Freedom and Bondage: A Casebook. New York: Oceana, 1986.

Finkelman, Paul. The Law of Slavery and Freedom in California, 1848-1860. California Western Law Review (1981).

Finkelman, Paul. Prelude to the Fourteenth Amendment: Black Legal Rights in the Antebellum North. Rutgers Law Journal 17 (Spring-Summer 1986):415-82.

Finkelman, Paul. Prigg v. Pennsylvania and Northern State Courts: Antislavery Use of a Pro-Slavery Decision. Civil War History (March 1979).

Finkelman, Paul. Slavery and the Constitutional Convention: Making a Covenant with Death. In: Richard Beeman and others (eds.), Beyond Confederation: Origins of the Constitution and American National Identity. Chapel Hill, NC: University of North Carolina Press, 1987.

Finkelman, Paul. Slavery, Race and the American Legal System, 1700-1872. New York: Garland, 1987. [16 volume series reproducing 180 pamphlets].

Fiss, Owen. Why the State? [Role of the state in constitutional law]. Harvard Law Review 100 (February 1987):781-94.

Foner, Eric. Rights and the Constitution of Black Life during the Civil War and Reconstruction. Journal of American History 74 (1987):863-83.

Fresia, Jerry. Toward An American Revolution. Exposing the Constitution and Other Illusions. Boston: South End Press, 1988.

Fritz, Christian G. A Nineteenth Century 'Habeas Corpus Mill': The Chinese Before the Federal Courts in California. American Journal of Legal History 32 (October 1988):347-72.

Freyer, Tony. The Little Rock Crisis: A Constitutional Interpretation. Westport, CT: Greenwood, 1984.

Fukuda, Moritoshi. Legal Problems of Japanese-Americans. Tokyo: Keio, 1986.

Galanter, Marc. Why the 'Haves' Come Out Ahead: Speculations on the Limits of Legal Change. Law and Society Review (Fall 1974).

Galloway, Russell. The Rich and the Poor in Supreme Court History, 1790-1982. Greenbrae, CA: Partigm Press, 1983.

Gara, Larry. The Fugitive Slave Law: A Double Paradox. Civil War History (September 1964).

Genovese, Eugene and Elizabeth Fox-Genovese. Slavery, Economic

Development and the Law: The Dilemma of the Southern Political
Economists, 1800-1860 [Paternalism]. Washington and Lee Law Review
41 (1984):1-30.

Gill, Robert L. The Afro-American before the Warren Court: 1953-1969.
Journal of Social and Behavioral Science 19 (Summer-Fall 1972):21-
34.

Ginger, Ann Fagan. Combating Racism in U.S. Law Schools. Lawyers Guild
Practitioner 31 (1974).

Ginger, Ann Fagan. The Use of the Law Against Racism in the United
States. Review of Contemporary Law 2 (1976):43-47.

Ginger, Ann Fagan and Eugene M. Tobin. The National Lawyers Guild: From
Roosevelt to Reagan. Philadelphia: Temple University Press, 1987.

Goldstein, Robert J. An American Gulag? Summary Arrest and Detention of
Political Dissidents in the United States. Columbia Human Rights Law
Review 10 (1978):541-73.

Grabiner, Gene. The Bakke Decision: Its Unconstitutionality and the
Intensification of White Supremacy in Higher Education. In: Paul
Zarembka (ed.), Research in Political Economy, Volume 3, pp. 27-81.
Greenwich, CT: JAI Press, 1980.

Grant, J. A. C. Testimonial Exclusion Because of Race: A Chapter in the
History of Intolerance in California. U.C.L.A. Law Review (1970).

Greenberg, Jack. Race Relations and American Law. New York: Columbia
University Press, 1959.

Greenberg, Jack (ed.) Blacks and the Law. Annals of the American
Academy of Political and Social Science (May 1973):entire issue.

Griffith, Ezra E. and Elwin J. Griffith. Racism, Psychological Injury,
and Compensatory Damages. Hospital and Community Psychiatry 37
(January 1986):71-75.

Haar, Charles M. and Daniel W. Fessler. The Wrong Side of the Tracks. A
Revolutionary Rediscovery of the Common Law Tradition of Fairness in
the Struggle Against Inequality [Shaw, MS]. New York: Simon and
Schuster, 1986.

Haines, Andrew W. The Critical Legal Studies Movement and Racism: Useful
Analytics and Guides for Social Action or an Irrelevant Modern Legal
Sceptisim and Solopsism? William Mitchell Law Review 13 (Fall
1987):685-736.

Hall, Gwendolyn M. The Myth of Benevolent Spanish Slave Law. Negro
Digest (February 1970).

Harding, Vincent. Wrestling with the Dawn: The Afro-American Freedom
Movement and the Changing Constitution. Journal of American History
74 (1987):718-39.

Hastie, William H. Observations of the Judicial Process. In: Gilbert
    Ware (ed.), From the Black Bar. Voices for Equal Justice, pp. 172-
    83. New York: Putnam's, 1976.

Hastie, William H. Toward an Equalitarian Legal Order: 1930-1950.
    Annals 407 (May 1973):18-31.

The William H. Hastie Papers [107 microfilm reels]. Frederick, MD:
    University Publications of America, 1987. [First black federal
    judge].

Helis, Thomas W. Of Generals and Jurists: The Judicial System of New
    Orleans under Union Occupation, May 1862-April 1865. Louisiana
    History 29 (Spring 1988):143-62.

Higginbotham, A. Leon, Jr. Double Stanards for Black Judges. In:
    Gilbert Ware (ed.), From the Black Bar. Voices for Equal Justice,
    pp. 61-72. New York: Putnam's, 1976. [From: Commonwealth of Pa.
    et al. v. Local Union No. 542, Int'l Union of Operating Engineers
    et al., 388 F. Supp. 155 (1974)].

Higginbotham, A. Leon, Jr. In the Matter of Color: Race and the American
    Legal Process. Vol. I.: The Colonial Period. New York: Oxford
    University Press, 1978.

Higginbotham, A. Leon, Jr. Racism and the Early American Legal Process,
    1619-1896. Annals 407 (May 1973):1-17.

Hill, Herbert. Black Labor and the American Legal System: Race, Work and
    the Law, Vol 1. Washington, D.C.: Bureau of National Affairs, 1977.

Hinds, Lennox S. Illusions of Justice: Human Rights Violations in the
    United States. University of Iowa Press, 1978.

Hindus, Michael S. Black Justice under White Law: Criminal Prosecutions
    of Blacks in Antebellum South Carolina. Journal of American History
    (December 1976).

History of the Department of Justice (1963-1969) [6 microfilm reels].
    Frederick, MD: University Publications of America, 1986.

Horton, James O. Weevils in the Wheat: Free Blacks and the Constitution,
    1787-1860. This Constitution 8 (Fall 1985):4-41.

Horwitz, Morton J. The Jurisprudence of Brown and the Dilemmas of
    Liberalism. In: Michael V. Namorato (ed.), Have We Overcome? Race
    Relations Since "Brown", pp. 173-87. Jackson: University Press of
    Mississippi, 1979.

Houston, Charles. Educational Inequalities Must Go! Crisis 42 (October
    1935).

Howard, Joseph C. Administration of Rape Cases in the City of Baltimore
    and the State of Maryland. In: Gilbert Ware (ed.), From the Black

Bar. Voices for Equal Justice, pp. 130-44. New York: Putnam's, 1976.

Howard, Victor B. The Black Testimony Controversy in Kentucky, 1866-1872. Journal of Negro History 58 (April 1973):140-65.

Howington, Arthur F. According to the Law: The Treatment of Slaves and Free Blacks in the State and Local Courts of Tennessee. New York: Garland, 1986.

Howington, Arthur F. 'Not in the Condition of a Horse or an Ox': Ford v. Ford, the Law of Testamentary Manumission and the Tennessee Courts' Recognition of Slave Humanity. Tenessee Historical Quarterly (Fall 1975).

Hurd, John C. Topics of Jurisprudence Connected with the Condition of Freedom and Bondage. New York, 1856.

Hyatt, Bernard F. A Legal Legacy for Statehood: The Development of the Territorial Judicial System in Dakota Territory, 1861-1889. 2 vols. Doctoral dissertation, Texas Tech University, 1987. UMO # 8713598.

Irons, Peter. The Courage of their Convictions. Sixteen Americans Who Fought Their Way to the Supreme Court. New York: Free Press, 1988.

Jackson, Derrick Z. To Be Black in Boston. Boston Globe September 23, 1988.

Janisch, Hudson N. The Chinese, the Courts and the Constitution: A Study of the Legal Issues Raised by Chinese Immigration to the United States, 1850-1902. Doctoral dissertation, University of Chicago, 1971.

Jones, Augustus J. Law, Bureaucracy and Politics: The Implementation of Title VI of the Civil Rights Act of 1964. University Press of America, 1982.

Jones, Mark E. Racism in Special Courts. In: Gilbert Ware (ed.), From the Black Bar. Voices for Equal Justice, pp. 53-60. New York: Putnam's, 1976.

Kaminaga, Yuriko. Social Change through Legal Means: A Case Study of the Japanese American Legal Movement. Doctoral dissertation, University of San Diego, 1987.

Katz, Jonathan. Resistance at Christiana [Black resistance to Fugitive Slave Law]. New York: 1974.

Kawashima, Yasu. Legal Origins of the Indian Reservation to Colonial Massachusetts. American Journal of Legal History 13 (1969):42-56.

Keith, Damon J. Should Color Blindness and Representativeness Be a Part of American Justice? Howard Law Journal 26 (Winter 1983):1-7.

Kennedy, Randall L. Race and the Fourteenth Amendment: The Power of

Interpretational Choice. In: Jules Lobel (ed.), A Less Than Perfect Union, pp. 273-302. New York: Monthly Review Press, 1988.

Kennedy, Randall L. Race Relations and the Tradition of Celebration: The Case of Professor Schmidt. Columbia Law Review 86 (December 1986):1622-61.

Kennedy, Randall L. A Reply to Philip Elman. Harvard Law Review 100 (June 1987):1938-48. [See Philip Elman, above].

Kickingbird, Kirke. American Indian Foundations of the Constitution. American Indian Journal 9 (Fall 1987):4.

Kim, Chin and Bok-Lim Kim. Asian Immigrants in American Law: A Look at the Past and the Challenge Which Remains. American University Law Review 26 (1977).

Kly, Yussef N. International Law and the Black Minority in the U.S. Atlanta: Clarity, 1986. [3277 Rosewell Rd., Atlanta, GA 30305].

Kmiec, Douglas W. Exclusionary Zoning and Purposeful Race Segregation in Housing: Two Wrongs Deserving Separate Remedies. Land Use and Environment Law Review 18 (1987):229-58.

Konvitz, Milton R. The Alien and the Asiatic in American Law. 1946.

Kretzmer, David. Freedom of Speech and Racism. Cardozo Law Review 8 (February 1987):445-513.

Kurland, Philip B. and Gerhard Casper (eds.) Landmark Briefs and Arguments of the Supreme Court of the United States: Constitutional Law [1793-1985]. [167 volumes.] Frederick, MD: University Publications of America, 1987.

Lacewell, Linda A. and Paul A. Shelowitz. Beyond a Black and White Reading of Sections 1981 and 1982: Shifting the Focus from Racial Status to Racist Acts. University of Miami Law Review 41 (March 1987):823-54.

Lawson, Steven F. and others. Groveland: Florida's Little Scottsboro. Florida Historical Quarterly 65 (July 1986):1-26.

Levy, Leonard W. and others (eds.) Encyclopedia of the American Constitution. 4 vols. New York: Macmillan, 1986.

Lott, J. R., Jr. Should the Wealthy Be Able to Buy Justice? Journal of Political Economy 95 (December 1987).

Lindberg, James. William Howard Taft and His Posture toward Black America. Master's thesis, Alabama State University, 1985.

London, Joyce I. Black Jurists/Black Juveniles. In: Gilbert Ware (ed.), From the Black Bar. Voices for Equal Justice, pp. 165-71. New York: Putnam's, 1976.

Lundsgaarde, H. P. Racial and Ethnic Classifications: An Appraisal of the Role of Anthropology in the Lawmaking Process. Houston Law Review 10 (1973):641-654.

MacMillan, Michael E. Unwanted Allies: Koreans as Enemy Aliens in World War II. Hawaiian Journal of History 19 (1985):179-203.

Machnacki, David. Skin Color Doesn't Reason: Closing the Door on the Discriminatory Use of Peremptory Challenges. University of Detroit Law School 64 (Fall 1986):171-200.

Mandel, J. Hispanics in the Criminal Justice System: The 'Nonexistent' Problem. Agenda 9 (May-June 1979):16-20.

Mangum, Charles, Jr. The Legal Status of the Negro. Chapel Hill, NC: University of North Carolina Press, 1940.

Marshall, Thurgood. Group Action in the Pursuit of Justice. In: Norman Dorsen (ed.), The Evolving Constitution: Essays on the Bill of Rights and the U.S. Supreme Court. Middletown, CT: Wesleyan University Press, 1987.

Marshall, Thurgood. The Legal Attack to Secure Civil Rights. In: Francis L. Broderick and August Meier (eds.), Negro Protest through the Twentieth Century. Indianapolis: Bobbs-Merrill, 1965. [Address given in 1944].

Marshall, Thurgood. Those the Constitution Left Out. Judges Journal 26 (Summer 1987).

Martin, Charles H. The Angelo Herndon Case and Southern Justice. Baton Rouge: Louisiana State University Press, 1976.

Martin, Charles H. The International Labor Defense and Black America. Labor History 26 (Spring 1985):165-94.

Matsuda, Mari J. Law and Culture in the District Court of Honolulu, 1844-1845: A Case Study of the Rise of Legal Conciousness. American Journal of Legal History 32 (January 1988):16-41.

McBride, David. Mid-Atlantic State Courts and the Struggle with the Separate but Equal Doctrine: 1880-1939. Rutgers Law Journal 17 (Spring-Summer 1986):569-89.

McCree, Wade H., Jr. Completing Emancipation: A Commencement Address. Integrateducation 15 (September-October 1977).

McGoveney, Dudley O. The Anti-Japanese Land Laws of California and Ten Other States. California Law Review 35 (March 1947):7-60.

McNeil, Genna Rae. Groundwork: Charles Hamilton Houston and the Struggle for Civil Rights. Philadelphia: University of Pennsylvania Press, 1983.

Meier, August and John Bracey, editorial advisers. The Scottsboro Case,

1931-1950, part 6 Papers of the NAACP. New Parts on Educational Equality, Voting Rights, Housing, the Scottsboro Case, and Anti-Lynching [24 microfilm reels]. Frederick, MD: University Publications of America, 1987.

Miller, Loren. The Petitioners: The Story of the Supreme Court of the United States and the Negro. New York: Pantheon, 1966.

Ming, W. Robert. Disabilities Affecting Negroes as to Carrier Accommodations, Property and Judicial Proceedings. Journal of Negro Education 8 (July 1939).

Minority Critique of the Critical Legal Studies Movement. Harvard Civil Rights - Civil Liberties Law Review 22 (Spring 1987):297-447.

Modey, Yao F. Black Justice under White Law: Criminal Prosecutions of Blacks in Antebellum North Carolina. Master's thesis, Wake Forest University, 1978.

Mooney, Ralph J. Matthew Deady and the Federal Judicial Response to Racism in the Early West. Oregon Historical Review 63 (1984).

Moore, Howard, Jr. Racism as Justice. Black Law Journal 3 (Spring 1973):54-66.

Moreland, Lois B. White Racism and the Law. Columbus, OH: Merrill, 1971.

Morris, Thomas D. 'As If the Injury was Effected by the Natural Elements of Air or Fire': Slave Wrongs and the Liability of Masters. Law and Society Review 16 (1981-82):569-99.

Morrison, Kenneth. The Bias of Colonial Law: English Paranoia and the Abenaki Arena of King Phillip's War, 1675-1678. New England Quarterly 53 (September 1980):363-87.

Motley, Constance Baker. Race Discrimination Cases: The Legacy of Justice Lewis F. Powell. Suffolk University Law Review 21 (Winter 1987):971-87.

Naidu, Arjuna. The Right to Be Free from Slavery, Servitude and Forced Labour. Cooperative International Law Journal of South Africa 20 (March 1987):108-13.

Nash, A. E. Keir. A More Equitable Past? Southern Supreme Courts and the Protection of the American Negro. North Carolina Law Review (1970).

Nash, A. E. Keir. Reason of Slavery: Understanding the Judicial Role in the Peculiar Institution. Vanderbilt Law Review 32 (January 1979):7-218.

A New York Panel Hears Charge of Racial Bias in Judicial System. New York Times July 3, 1988.

Newby, I. A. Challenge to the Court: Social Scientists and the Defense of Segregation, 1954-1966 (second edition). Baton Rouge: Louisiana State University Press, 1969.

Nieman, Donald G. To Set the Law in Motion: The Freedmen's Bureau and the Legal Rights of Blacks, 1865-1868. Millwood, NY: KTO Press, 1979.

Norgen, Gill and Serena Nanda. American Cultural Pluralism and Law. New York: Praeger, 1988.

Oakes, James. A Failure of Vision: The Collapse of the Freedman's Bureau Courts. Civil War History 25 (March 1979):66-76.

Olsen, Otto H. Reflections on the Plessy v. Ferguson Decision of 1896, In: Edward F. Haas (ed.), Louisiana's Legal Heritage, pp. 163-87. Pensacola: 1983.

Papers of the International Labor Defense [22 microfilm reels]. Frederick, MD: University Publications of America, 1987.

Paterson, Basil A. Blacks and the Justice System. In Gilbert Ware (ed.), From the Black Bar. Voices for Equal Justice, pp. 184-190. New York: Putnam's, 1976.

Pedersen, Donald B. Agricultural Labor Law in the 1980s. Alabama Law Review 38 (Spring 1987):663-99.

Price, Edward J., Jr. Let the Law Be Just: The Quest for Racial Equality in Pennsylvania, 1780-1915. Doctoral dissertation, Pennsylvania State University, 1973. UMO # 74-16068.

Price, Monroe E. and Robert N. Clinton. Law and the American Indian: Readings, Notes, and Cases (second edition). Charlottesville, VA: 1983.

Racism in the Law: A Symposium. Guild Practitioner 27 (Fall 1968):169.

Rangel, Jorge C. and Carlos M. Alcala. De Jure Segregation of Chicanos in Texas Schools. Harvard Civil Rights and Civil Liberties Review 7 (1972).

Rhode, Deborah L. Gender and Jurisprudence: An Agenda for Research. University of Cincinnati Law Review 56 (Fall 1987):521-34.

Roberts, Sam. Race and Justice: Realm of Reality and Perception. New York Times September 8, 1988. [About Franklin Williams and the Judicial Commission on Minorities, New York State].

Ruznow, Lawrence A. Fairness and Justice in the Navajo Nation and Apache County. (letter) Navajo Times June 16, 1984.

Samson, Gloria G. Toward a New Social Order - the American Fund for Public Service: Clearinghouse for Radicalism in the 1920s. Doctoral dissertation, University of Rochester, 1987. UMO # 8803326.

Santiago Santiago, Isaura. A Community's Struggle for Equal Educational
     Opportunity: Aspira v. Board of Education. Princeton, NJ: Office
     for Minority Education, Educational Testing Service, 1978.

Schafer, Judith K. 'Guaranteed Against the Vices and Maladies Prescribed
     by Law': Consumer Protection, the Law of Slave Sales, and the
     Supreme Court in Antebellum Louisiana. American Journal of Legal
     History 31 (October 1987):306-21.

Schmidt, Benno C., Jr. Principle and Prejudice: The Supreme Court and
     Race in the Progressive Era. Part 1: Heyday of Jim Crow. Columbia
     Law Review 82 (April 1982):444-524.

Schwartz, Bernard. Swann's Way: The School Busing Case and the Supreme
     Court. New York: Oxford University Press, 1986. [Charlotte].

Schwartz, Herman. Packing the Courts. The Conservative Campaign to
     Rewrite the Constitution. New York: Scribner's, 1988.

Sedler, Robert A. Beyond Bakke: The Constitution and Redressing the
     Social History of Racism. Harvard Civil Rights -- Civil Liberties
     Law Review 14 (Spring 1979):133-171.

Segal, Geraldine R. Blacks in the Law: Philadelphia and the Nation.
     Philadelphia: University of Pennsylvania Press, 1982.

Shofner, Jerrell H. Custom, Law, and History: The Enduring Influence of
     Florida's 'Black Code'. Florida Historical Quarterly (January
     1977).

Simpson, Janice C. White Justice, Black Defendants. Time August 8,
     1988.

Smith, Michael D. Race versus Robe: The Dilemma of Black Judges. Port
     Washington, NY: Associated Faculty Press, 1983.

Soifer, Avian. The Paradox of Paternalism and Laissez Faire
     Constitutionalism: United States Supreme Court, 1888-1921. Law and
     History Review 5 (Spring 1987):249-79.

Spence, Gerry. With Justice for None. Destroying an American Myth. New
     York: Times Books, 1989.

Stephan, Cookie W. and Walter G. Stephan. Habla Ingles? The Effects of
     Language Translation on Simulated Juror Decisions. Journal of
     Applied Social Psychology 16 (1986):577-89.

Stephenson, George. Race Distinctions in American Law. New York:
     Russell and Russell, 1969 (orig. 1910).

Stewart, John E. Appearance and Punishment: The Attraction-Leniency
     Effect in the Courtroom. Journal of Social Psychology 125 (June
     1985):373-78.

Sydnor, Charles S. The Southerner and the Laws. Journal of Southern

<u>History</u>   6 (February 1940):3-24.

Taylor, William L. <u>Hanging Together.</u> <u>Equality</u> <u>in</u> <u>an</u> <u>Urban</u> <u>Nation</u>. New York: Simon and Schuster, 1971.

Terez, Dennis G. Protecting the Remedy of Unitary Schools. <u>Case</u> <u>Western</u> <u>Reserve</u> <u>Law</u> <u>Review</u> 37 (Fall 1986):41-71.

Tombs, Jacqueline. <u>Law</u> <u>and</u> <u>Slavery</u> <u>in</u> <u>North</u> <u>America:</u> <u>The</u> <u>Development</u> <u>of</u> <u>a</u> <u>Legal</u> <u>Category</u>. Doctoral dissertation, University of Edinburgh, 1982.

Turner, Billy M. and others. Race and Peremptory Challenges during voir dire: Do Prosecution and Defense Agree? <u>Journal</u> <u>of</u> <u>Criminal</u> <u>Justice</u> 14 (1986):61-69.

Tushnet, Mark. The American Law of Slavery, 1810-1860: A Study in the Persistence of Legal Autonomy. <u>Law</u> <u>and</u> <u>Society</u> <u>Review</u> (Fall 1975).

Tushnet, Mark. <u>The</u> <u>American</u> <u>Law</u> <u>of</u> <u>Slavery,</u> <u>1810-1860:</u> <u>Consideration</u> <u>of</u> <u>Humanity</u> <u>and</u> <u>Interest</u>. 1981.

Tushnet, Mark. The Constitution from a Progressive Point of View. <u>In</u> Jules Lobel (ed.), <u>A</u> <u>Less</u> <u>Than</u> <u>Perfect</u> <u>Union</u>, pp. 40-55. New York: Monthly Review Press, 1988.

Tushnet, Mark. An Essay on Rights. <u>Texas</u> <u>Law</u> <u>Review</u> 62 (1984).

Tushnet, Mark. The Politics of Equality in Constitutional Law: The Equal Protection Clause, Dr. Du Bois, and Charles Hamilton Houston. <u>Journal</u> <u>of</u> <u>American</u> <u>History</u> 74 (December 1987):884-903.

Tushnet, Mark. <u>Red,</u> <u>White,</u> <u>and</u> <u>Blue:</u> <u>Critical</u> <u>Analysis</u> <u>of</u> <u>Constitutional</u> <u>Law</u>. Cambridge, MA: Harvard University Press, 1988.

U.S. House of Representatives, Committee on Government Operations. Failure and Fraud in Civil Rights Enforcement by the Department of Education. <u>Equity</u> <u>and</u> <u>Excellence</u> 23 (published Winter 1988):47-66.

Vishneski, John S., III. What the Court Decided in <u>Dred</u> <u>Scott</u> v. <u>Sundford</u>. <u>American</u> <u>Journal</u> <u>of</u> <u>Legal</u> <u>History</u> 32 (October 1988):373-90.

Walton, Eugene. Will the Supreme Court Revert to Racism? <u>Black</u> <u>World</u> 21 (October 1972):46-48.

Walton, Hanes, Jr. <u>When</u> <u>the</u> <u>Marching</u> <u>Stopped:</u> <u>The</u> <u>Politics</u> <u>of</u> <u>Civil</u> <u>Rights</u> <u>Regulatory</u> <u>Agencies</u>. Albany: State University of New York Press, 1988.

Washburn, Wilcomb E. <u>Red</u> <u>Man's</u> <u>Land</u> <u>-</u> <u>White</u> <u>Man's</u> <u>Law:</u> <u>A</u> <u>Study</u> <u>of</u> <u>the</u> <u>Past</u> <u>and</u> <u>Present</u> <u>Status</u> <u>of</u> <u>the</u> <u>American</u> <u>Indian</u>. New York: Scribner's, 1971.

Washington, Booker T. Law and Order and the Negro. <u>Outlook</u> November 6,

1909.

Weinberg, Meyer. *Race and Place: A Legal History of the Neighborhood School*. Washington, D.C.: GPO, 1968.

Weisberg, D. Kelly (ed.) *Women and the Law: A Social Historical Perspective*. Cambridge, MA: Schenkman, 1982.

Westwood, Howard C. Getting Justice for the Freedmen. *Howard Law Journal* (1971).

Whalen, Charles W. and Barbara Whalen. *The Longest Debate. A Legislative History of the 1964 Civil Rights Act*. New York: New American Library, 1988.

Wheeler, Stanton and others. Do the 'Haves' Come Out Ahead? Winning and Losing in the Supreme Court. *Law and Society Review* 3 (1987):403-48.

White, Vibert L. *Developing a "School" of Civil Rights Lawyers: From the New Deal to the New Frontier*. Doctoral dissertation, Ohio State University, 1988. UMO # 8820369.

Wiecek, William W. Slavery and Abolition before the United States Supreme Court, 1820-1860. *Journal of American History* (June 1978).

Wiecek, William W. The Statutory Law of Slavery and Race in the Thirteen Mainland Colonies of British North America. *William and Mary Quarterly* (Spring 1977).

Wilbanks, William. The Myth of a Racist Juvenile Justice System. *Prosecutor, Journal of the National District Attorneys Association* 22 (Summer 1988):5-8.

Wilkinson, Charles P. *American Indians, Time, and the Law. Native Societies in a Modern Constitutional Democracy*. New Haven, CT: Yale University Press, 1987.

Willard, Eric. Federal Practice: Clarifying the Desegregation Process. *Oklahoma Law Review* 39 (Fall 1986):519-39.

Wilhelm, Sidney. A Sociological Perspective of Racism and the Supreme Court. *The Catholic Lawyer* 16 (Spring 1970).

Wilhelm, Sidney. Black Man, Red Man, and White America: The Constitutional Approach to Genocide. *Catalyst* (Spring 1969).

Williams, G. Scott. Unitary School Systems and Underlying Vestiges of State-Imposed Segregation. *Columbia Law Review* 87 (May 1987):794-816.

Williams, Patricia J. Alchemical Notes: Reconstructing Ideals from Deconstructed Rights. *In:* Jules Lobel (ed.), *A Less Than Perfect Union*, pp. 56-70. New York: Monthly Review Press, 1988.

Williams, Patricia J. Spirit-Murdering the Messenger: The Discourse of
    Finger-Pointing as the Law's Response to Racism. University of Miami
    Law Review 42 (September 1987):127-57.

Williams, Robert A., Jr. The Algebra of Federal Indian Law: The Hard
    Trial of Decolonizing and Americanizing the White Man's Indian
    Jurisprudence. Wisconsin Law Review (March-April 1986):219-99.

Williams, R. A., Jr. Taking Rights Aggressively: The Perils and Promise
    of Critical Legal Theory for Peoples of Color. Law and Inequality 5
    (May 1987):103-34.

Wilson, Theodore B. The Black Codes of the South. University:
    University of Alabama Press, 1965.

Woodward, C. Vann. The Strange Career of Jim Crow (second edition). New
    York: Oxford, 1965.

Worthy, Barbara A. The Travail and Triumph of a Southern Black Civil
    Rights Lawyer: The Legal Career of Alexander Pierre Tureaud, 1899-
    1971. Doctoral dissertation, Tulane University, 1984. UMO #
    8420730.

Wright, Bruce. Black Robes, White Justice. Lyle Stuart, 1987.

Wright, Bruce. A View from the Bench. In: Gilbert Ware (ed.), From the
    Black Bar. Voices for Equal Justice, pp. 85-103. New York:
    Putnam's, 1976.

Wright, J. Skelly. The Courts Have Failed the Poor. New York Times
    Magazine. March 9, 1969.

Wunder, John R. The Chinese and the Courts in the Pacific Northwest:
    Justice Denied? Pacific Historical Review 52 (May 1983):191-211.

Wunder, John R. The Courts and the Chinese in Frontier Idaho. Idaho
    Yesterday 25 (Spring 1981):23-32.

Wunder, John R. Law and Chinese in Frontier Montana. In: Robert R.
    Swartout, Jr. (ed.), Montana Vistas: Selected Historical Essays.
    Washington, D.C.: University Press of America, 1981.

Yarbrough, Tinsley E. A Passion for Justice. J. Waties Waring and Civil
    Rights. New York: Oxford University Press, 1987.

Zimroth, Peter L. Perversions of Justice: The Prosecution and Acquittal
    of the Panther 21. New York: Viking, 1974.

Law Bibliography

Finkleman, Paul (comp.) Slavery in the Courtroom: An Annotated
    Bibliography of American Cases. Washington, D.C.: GPO, 1985.

Hall, Kermit L. (comp.) A <u>Comprehensive</u> <u>Bibliography</u> <u>of</u> <u>American</u>
<u>Constitutional</u> <u>and</u> <u>Legal</u> <u>History.</u> <u>1896-1979</u>. 5 vols. Millwood, NY:
Kraus International Publications, 1983.

45. Libraries

I am taxed for the Carnegie Public Library of Atlanta, where I cannot enter to draw my own books.

- W. E. B. Du Bois, "Politics and Industry" (1909).

Ayala, J. L. (ed.) Chicano Library Service. California Librarian 34 (January 1973):4-7.

Berman, Sanford. Racism and Library Science. Library Journal February 1969.

Books, Libraries, and Racism. Race Today 5 (October-November 1973).

Dickeman, Mildred. Racism in the Library: A Model from the Public Schools. School Library Journal February 1973.

Dumont, Rosemary R. The Education of Black Librarians: An Historical Perspective. Journal of Education for Library and Information Science 24 (Spring 1986):223-49

Dunlap, A. Library Services to Mexican-Americans. Idaho Librarian 23 (January 1971):3-7.

Hall, Patricia A. 'Yassuh! I's the Reference Librarian.' American Libraries (November 1988):900-901.

Haro, Robert P. How Mexican-Americans View Libraries. Libraries and the Spanish-speaking. Wilson Library Bulletin 44 (1970):736-42.

Josey, E. J. Black Aspirations, White Racism, and Libraries. Wilson Library Bulletin September 1969.

Josey, E. J. and Ann Allen Shockley (comps.) Handbook of Black Librarianship. Littleton, CO: Libraries Unlimited, 1977.

McAllister, Jane. Library Service to the Colored Race. Mississippi Library News 17 (September 1953):112-19.

Shields, Gerald R. and George Sheppard. American Indians: Search for Fort Hall's Library Service [Pocatello, Idaho]. American Libraries 1 (October 1970):856-60.

Tate, Binnie. LAPL Racism Workshop Reaction to SLJ Feature. Library Journal 96 (May 1971):1753+.

Yeh, Thomas Y-R. and Eugene T. Frosio. The Treatment of the American Indian in the Library of Congress E-F Schedule. Library Resources and Techinical Services 15 (Spring 1971):122-31.

46. Literature

*Why was it that the [Harlem] Renaissance of literature, which
began among Negroes ten years ago, has never taken real and
lasting root? It was because it was a transplanted and exotic
thing. It was a literature written for the benefit of white
people and at the behest of white readers, and started out
privately from the white point of view. It never had a real
Negro constituency, and it did not grow out of the inmost heart
and frank experience of Negroes; on such an artificial basis no
real literature can grow.*

- W. E. B. Du Bois, "The Negro College," 1933.

Aaron, Daniel. The 'Inky Case': Miscegenation in the White American
Literary Imagination. Social Science Information 22 (1983):169-90.

Abderabou, A. A. The Human Dimension in Multicultural Relations: A
Critical Study of Twain's Huckleberry Finn. Journal of English 14
(September 1986):1-5.

Abramson, Doris. The Great White Way: Critics and the First Black
Playwrights on Broadway. Educational Theatre Journal 28 (March
1976).

Algarin, Miguel. Nuyorican Literature. Melus 8 (Summer 1981).

Algarin, Miguel and Miguel Pinero (eds.) Nuyorican Poetry New York:
Morrow, 1975.

Alurista. Cultural Nationalism and Chicano Literature, 1965-75. In:
Renate von Bardeleben and others (eds.), Mission in Conflict: Essays
on U.S.-Mexican Relations and Chicano Culture, pp. 41-52. Tübingen:
Narr, 1986.

Babin, Maria T. and Stan Steiner (eds.) Borinquen: An Anthology of
Puerto Rican Literature New York: Random House, 1975.

Bacon, Betty. How Much Truth Do We Tell the Children? The Politics of
Children's Literature. Minneapolis, MN: MEP Publications, 1988.

Baglin, Roger F. The Mainland Experience in Selected Puerto Rican
Literary Works. Doctoral dissertation, State University of New York
at Buffalo, 1971.

Banks, Marva O. An Analysis of Nineteenth Century Black Responses to
Uncle Tom's Cabin as Recorded in Selected Antebellum Black
Newspapers: 1852-1855. Doctoral dissertation, Rensselaer
Polytechnic Institute, 1986. UMO # 8619963.

Baraka, Amiri. Afro-American Literature and Class Struggle. Black
American Literature Forum 14 (1980):5-14.

373

Baraka, Amiri. Black Theater in the Sixties. In: Joe Weixlmann and
    Chester J. Fontenot (eds.), Belief vs. Theory in Black American
    Literary Criticism, pp. 225-37. Greenwood, FL: Penkevill, 1986.

Barnett, Louise K. The Ignoble Savage: American Literary Racism, 1790-
    1890. Westport, CT: Greenwood, 1975.

Bartlett, Mary D. (ed.)   The New Native American Novel: Works in
    Progress. Abuquerque: University of New Mexico Press, 1986.

Bell, Bernard W. The Afro-American Novel and Its Tradition. Amherst, MA:
    University of Massachusetts Press, 1987.

Berger, Joseph. U.S. Literature: Canon Under Siege. New York Times
    January 6, 1988.

Berkman, Brenda. The Vanishing Race: Conflicting Images of the American
    Indian in Children's Literature, 1880-1930. North Dakota Quarterly
    44 (Spring 1976):31-40.

Blatt, Gloria T. The Mexican-American in Children's Literature.
    Elementary English 45 (April 1968):446-57.

Bouleware, Marcus H. The Oratory of Negro Leaders 1900-1968. Westport,
    CT: Negro Universities Press, 1969.

Brown, Carl R. V. Cultural Democracy and Cultural Variability in Chicano
    Literature. English Education 8 (Winter 1977):83-89.

Brown, Kenneth J. The Lean Years: The Afro-American Novelist during the
    Depression (1929-1941). Doctoral dissertation, University of Iowa,
    1987. UMO # 8721383.

Brown, Sterling A. A Century of Negro Portraiture in American Literature.
    Massachusetts Review (Winter 1966):73-96.

Brown, Sterling A. The Negro Author and His Publisher. Quarterly Review
    of Higher Education among Negroes. 9 (July 1941):140-46.

Brown, Sterling A. The Negro in American Fiction. Washington, D.C.:
    Associates in Negro Folk Education, 1937.

Brown-Guillory, Elizabeth. Their Place on Stage: Black Women Playwrights
    in America. Westport, CT: Greenwood, 1988.

Bus, Heiner. The Presence of Native Americans in Chicano Literature.
    Revista Chicano-Riquena 13 (1985):148-62.

Butcher, P. (ed.) The Ethnic Image in Modern American Literature, 1900-
    1950. 2 vols. Washington, D.C.: Howard University Press, 1984.

Castro, Michael. Interpreting the Indian: Twentieth-Century Poets and
    the Native American. Albuquerque: University of New Mexico Press,
    1983.

Chambers, Bradford. Book Publishing: A Racist Club? Publishers Weekly
    February 1971.

Chametzky, Jules. Main Currents in American Jewish Literature from the
    1880s to the 1950s (and Beyond). Ethnic Groups 4 (1982):85-101.

Chan, J. and others. Aiieeeee! An Anthology of Asian-American Writers.
    Washington, D.C.: Howard University Press, 1974.

Charles, James P. A Content Analysis of American Indian Literature as
    Presented in North Carolina High School Textbooks. Doctoral
    dissertation, University of North Carolina, 1986. UMO # 8618328.

Charles, James P. For the Sake of a Fad: The Misrepresentation of
    American Indians and their Literature in High School Anthologies.
    Journal of Ethnic Studies 15 (Summer 1987):131-40.

Chilcoat, George W. The History Student and the American Slave
    Experience: The Dime Novel as Method. Western Journal of Black
    Studies 11 (Winter 1987):193-97.

Chrisman, Robert. Blacks, Racism and Bourgeois Culture. College English
    38 (April 1977).

Chrisman, Robert. Blacks, Racism and Bourgeois Culture. Black Scholar 7
    (January-February 1976):2-10.

Churchill, Ward. Literature and Colonization of the American Indian.
    Journal of Ethnic Studies 10 (Fall 1982):37-56.

Clayton, Hazel (ed.) On Being Black: Stories and Poems by Minnesota
    Authors. Robbinsdale, MN: Guide Press, 1981.

Cobb, Nina K. Alienation and Expatriation: Afro-American Writers in
    Paris after World War II. Doctoral dissertation, City University of
    New York, 1975, 1975. UMO # 7518708.

Colon, Jesus. A Puerto Rican in New York. New York: International,
    1982.

Cooke, Gwendolyn J. How Students Feel About Black Literature. Negro
    American Literature Forum. 8 (Winter 1974):293-95.

Cooley, John R. Savages and Naturals: Black Portraits by White Writers
    in Modern American Literature. East Brunswick, NJ: University of
    Delaware Press, 1982.

Daniel, Walter C. Black Journals of the United States. Westport, CT:
    Greenwood, 1982.

Dasenbrock, Reed W. Intelligibility and Meaningfulness in Multicultural
    Literature in English. PMLA 102 (January 1987):10-19.

Davis, Thadious M. (ed.) Black Writers on Adventures of Huckleberry Finn
    One Hundred Years Later. Mark Twain Journal 22 (Fall 1984):entire

375

issue.

Dearborn, Mary V. _Pocahantas' Daughters: Gender and Ethnicity in American Culture_. New York: Oxford University Press, 1986. [Native American, black and immigrant women writers of fiction in 19th and early 20th centuries].

Diaz-Ortiz, Elia Mar. _The Use of Chicano Literature in University and College Spanish-language Courses in the Southwestern United States_. Doctoral dissertation, University of Texas, 1987. UMO # 8717397.

Diedrich, Maria. _Kommunismus in afroamerikanischen Roman. Das Verhältnis afroamerikanischer Schriftsteller zur kommunistichen Partei der USA zwischen den Weltkriegen_. Stuttgart: Metzler, 1979.

Egan, Michael E. _Huckleberry Finn: Race, Class and Society_. London: Sussex University Press, 1977.

Escott, Paul D. _Slavery Remembered: A Record of Twentieth-Century Slave Narratives_. Chapel Hill, NC: University of North Carolina Press, 1979.

Evangelista, Susan. Filipinos in America: Literature as History. _Phillipine Studies_ 36 (1988):36-53.

Evere, Lawrence J. Native Americans Oral Literature in the College English Classroom: An Omaha Example. _College English_ 36 (February 1975):649-62.

Fanning, Charles (ed.) _The Exiles of Erin. Nineteenth-Century Irish-Americans Fiction_. Notre Dame, IN: University of Notre Dame Press, 1988.

Field, Claire. Defense Mechanisms Employed by the Faulkner White Racist and their Effect on the Faulkner Negro. _Research in the Teaching of English_ 4 (Spring 1970):20-36.

Fernandez Olmos, Margarite. Survival, Growth, and Change in the Prose Fiction of Contemporary Puerto Rican Women Writers. In: Asela Rodriguez de Laguna (ed.), _Images and Indentities. The Puerto Rican in Two World Contexts_, pp. 76-88. New Brunswick, NJ: Transaction Books, 1987.

Fisher, Dexter and Robert B. Stepto (eds.) _Afro-American Literature: The Reconstruction of Instruction_. New York: Modern Language Association of America, 1979.

Ford, Nick Aaron. The English Department and the Challenge of Racism. _Integrated Education_ (July-August 1969):24-30.

Frank, Zelma A. L. _The Portrayal of Black Americans in Pictures and Content in the Caldecott Award Books and Honor Books from 1938-1978_. Doctoral dissertation, University of Missouri, 1979. UMO # 8002358.

Frank Chin: An Interview with Robert Murray Davis. _Amerasia Journal_ 14

(1988):81-95. [Chin is playwright].

Frisbie, Charlotte J. (ed.) Southwestern Indian Ritual Drama. Albuquerque: University of New Mexico Press, 1980.

Frye, Charles A. and others. How to Think Black: A Symposium on Toni Cade Bambara's The Salt Eaters. Contributions in Black Studies 6 (1983-1984).

Galloway, Margaret G. Indian Princess or Indian Squaw: The Stereotype Lives On. Master's thesis, Texas Woman's University, 1986.

Gates, Henry Louis, Jr. Authority (White) Power and the (Black) Critic: It's All Greek to Me. Cultural Critique 7 (Fall 1987):19-47.

Gayle, Addison. The Black Aesthetic. Black World 24 (December 1974):31-43.

Gerard, Jeremy. David Hwang, Riding on the Hyphen. New York Times Magazine March 13, 1988. [Chinese-American playwright].

Gibson, Donald B. Is There a Black Literary Tradition? New York University Education Quarterly 2 (1971):12-16.

Gibson, Donald B. The Politics of Literary Expression: A Study of Major Black Writers. Westport, CT: Greenwood, 1981.

Gong, Ted. Approaching Cultural Change through Literature: From Chinese to Chinese American. Amerasia Journal 7 (Spring 1980):73-86.

Gordils, Janice. Puerto Rican Studies and Romance Languages: Language and Literature in Puerto Rican Studies. In: Maria E. Sanchez and Antonio M. Stevens-Arroyo (eds.), Toward an Renaissance of Puerto Rican Studies: Ethnic and Area Studies in University Education, pp. 63-71. Highland Lakes, NJ: Atlantic Research and Publications, Inc., 1987.

Graham, Maryemma (ed.) Complete Poems of Frances E.W. Harper. New York: Oxford University Press, 1988 reprint.

Graham, Thomas. Harriet Beecher Stowe and the Question of Race. New England Quarterly 46 (December 1973).

Grose, Burl D. "Here Come the Indians": An Historical Study of the Representatives of the Native American upon the North American Stage, 1808-1969. Doctoral dissertation, University of Missouri, 1979. UMO # 8002367.

Gross, Seymour L. and John E. Hardy (eds.) Images of the Negro in American Literature. Chicago: University of Chicago Press, 1966.

Guiness, Gerald. Images in Contemporary Puerto Rican Literature. In: Asela Rodgriguez de Laguna (ed.), Images and Identities. The Puerto Rican in Two World Contexts. New Brunswick, NJ: Transaction Books, 1987.

377

Asela Rodrgriguez de Laguna (ed.), Images and Identities. The Puerto Rican in Two World Contexts. New Brunswick, NJ: Transaction Books, 1987.

Gwin, Minrose. Black and White Women of the Old South: The Peculiar Sisterhood in American Literature. Knoxville: University of Tennessee Press, 1985.

Harap, Louis. Creative Awakening: The Jewish Presence in Twentieth-Century American Literature, 1900-1940's. Westport, CT: Greenwood, 1987.

Harap, Louis. Dramatic Encounters: The Jewish Presence in Twentieth-Century American Drama, Poetry, and Humor and the Black-Jewish Literary Relationship. Westport, CT: Greenwood, 1987.

Harap, Louis. In the Mainstream: The Jewish Presence in Twentieth-Century American Literature, 1950s-1980s. Westport, CT: Greenwood, 1987.

Harper, Frances E. W. Iola Leroy, or Shadows Uplifted. New York: Oxford University Press, 1988 (orig. 1982). [Novel written by black author].

Harris, Trudier. From Mammies to Militants. Domestics in Black American Literature. Philadelphia: Temple University Press, 1982.

Haslam, Gerald W. Literature of the People: Native American Voices. CLA Journal 15 (December 1971):153-70.

Haslam, Gerald W. Por La Causa! Mexican-American Literature. College English 31 (April 1970):695-700.

Hawkins, Hunt. The Issue of Racism in [Joseph Conrad's] Heart of Darkness. Conradiana 14 (1982):163-171.

Hill, Errol. Shakespeare in Sable: A History of Black Shakespearean Actors. Amherst, MA: University of Massachusetts Press, 1984.

Hogan, Linda. The 19th Century Native Americans Poets. Wassaja/The Indian Historian. 13 (November 1980):24-29.

Hopkins, Pauline E. Contending Forces. A Romance Illustrative of Negro Life North and South. New York: Oxford University Press, 1988, orig. 1900. [Written by black author].

Hopkins, Pauline E. The Magazine Novels of Pauline Hopkins. New York: Oxford University Press, 1988 (orig. 1900). [Written by black author].

Horno-Delgado, Asuncion and others (eds.) Breaking Boundaries. Latina Writing and Critical Readings. Amherst, MA: University of Massachusetts Press, 1989.

Hull, Gloria T. Color, Sex, and Poetry. Three Women Writers of the

Hull, Gloria T. Notes on a Marxist Interpretation of Black American Literature. Black American Literature Forum 12 (Winter 1978):148-53.

Hull, Gloria T. (ed.) The Works of Alice Dunbar-Nelson. 3 vols. New York: Oxford University Press, 1988 reprint.

Hymes, Dell H. "In Vain I Tried to Tell You": Essays in Native American Ethnopoetics. Philadelphia: University of Pennsylvania Press, 1981.

Jackson, Shirley M. Afro-Hispanic Literature: A Valuable Cultural Resource. Foreign Language Annals 11 (September 1978):421-25.

Jahner, Elaine (ed.) American Indians Today: Their Thought, Their Literature, Their Art. Book Forum 5 (1981):entire issue.

Jamison, Angelene. Crisis of the Black Journal. Western Journal of Black Studies 6 (Spring 1982):50-54.

Jimenez, Francisco (ed.) The Identification and Analysis of Chicano Literature. New York: Bilingual Press, 1979.

Johnson, A. E. (Mrs.). Clarence and Corinne; or God's Way. New York: Oxford University Press, 1988, orig. 1890. [Novel written by black author].

Johnson, A. E. (Mrs.). The Hazeley Family. New York: Oxford University Press, 1988 (orig. 1894). [Novel written by black author].

Johnson, Abby A. and Ronald M. Johson. Propaganda and Aesthetics: The Literary Politics of Afro-American Magazines in the Twentieth Century. Amherst, MA: University of Massachusetts Press, 1979.

Johnson, Charles. Being and Race. Black Writing since 1970. Bloomington: Indiana University Press, 1988.

Johnson, James Weldon. Negro Authors and White Publishers. Crisis 36 (July 1929).

Jones, Leroi. The Myth of 'Negro Literature'. In: Charles T. Davis and Daniel Walden (eds.), On Being Black: Writings by Afro-Americans from Frederick Douglass to the Present. Westport, CT: Greenwood, 1970.

Jones, Lisa. Civilization's Discontent. Professor Hazel Carby on Canons, Curricula, and Change. Village Voice January 24, 1989.

Kanellos, Nicolas. Toward a History of Hispanic Literature in the United States. In: Asela Rodriguez de Laguna (ed.), Images and Identities. The Puerto Rican in Two World Contexts, pp. 236-45. New Brunswick, NJ: Transaction Books, 1987.

Katz, Jane B. (ed.) I Am the Fire of Time. New York: Dutton, 1978. [Writing by Native American women].

Katz, Jane B. (ed.) I Am the Fire of Time. New York: Dutton, 1978. [Writing by Native American women].

Keller, Gary D. and Francisco Jimenez (eds.) Hispanics in the United States: An Anthology of Creative Literature. Bilingual Review 6 (May-December 1979):1-165.

Kelley-Hawkins, Emma Dunham. Four Girls at Cottage City. New York: Oxford University Press, 1988 (orig. 1898). [Novel written by black author].

Kelley-Hawkins, Emma Dunham. Megda New York: Oxford University Press, 1988 (orig. 1891). [Novel written by black author].

Kellner, Bruce. 'Refined Racism': White Patronage in the Harlem Renaissance. In: Victor A. Kramer (ed.), The Harlem Renaissance Reexamined, pp. 93-106. New York: AMS, 1987.

Kelly, Ernece B. (ed.) Searching for America. Urbana, IL: National Council of Teachers of English, 1972. [Report of the Task Force on Racism and Bias in the Teaching of English and Textbook Review Committee].

Kessner, Carole. More Devils Than Hell Can Hold: Anti-Semitism in American Literature. In: Herbert Hirsch and Jack D. Spiro (eds.), Persistent Prejudice: Perspectives on Anti-Semitism. Fairfax, VA: George Mason University Press, 1988.

Kiah, Rosalie and Elaine P. Witty. The Portrayal of the Black Mother in Fiction for Children and Adolescents. Child and Youth Services 7 (Spring 1985):81-91.

Kilson, Martin. The Black Aesthetic. Black World 24 (December 1974):30, 44-48.

Kim, Elaine H. Asian-American Literature, an Introduction to the Writings and their Social Context. Philadelphia: Temple University Press, 1982.

Kim, Elaine H. Defining Asian American Realities Through Literature. Cultural Critique 6 (Spring 1987).

Kingston, Maxine Hong. China Man New York: Knopf, 1980. [Novel].

Kroeber, Karl (ed.) Traditional Literatures of the American Indian: Texts and Interpretations. Lincoln: University of Nebraska Press, 1981.

Krupat, Arnold. The Indian Autobiography: Origins, Type, and Function. American Literature 53 (March 1981):22-42.

Krupat, Arnold. Native Americans Literature and the Canon. Critical Inquiry 10 (September 1983):145-71.

Larson, Charles R. American Indian Fiction. Albuquerque: University of New Mexico Press, 1979.

Lauter, Paul. Race and Gender in the Shaping of the American Literary Canon: A Case Study from the Twenties. Feminist Studies 9 (Fall 1983):435-63.

Leong, Russell. Toshio Mori: An Interview. Amerasia Journal 7 (Spring 1980):89-108.

Lester, Julius. The Black Writer. Contribution in Black Studies 5 (1981-1982).

Levine, Lawrence W. Black Culture and Black Conciousness. New York: Oxford, 1977.

Lin, Mao-chu. Identity and Chinese-American Experience: A Study of Chinatown American Literature Since World War II. Doctoral dissertation, University of Minnesota, 1987. UMO # 8727423.

Lincoln, Kenneth. Native American Renaissance. Berkeley, CA: University of California Press, 1983.

Lopez, Adalberto. Puerto Ricans and the Literature of Puerto Rico. Journal of Ethnic Studies 1 (Summer 1973):56-65.

Lucero-White, Lea Aurora. Literary Folklore of the Hispanic Southwest. San Antonio, TX: Naylor, 1953.

Marquez, Antonie. A Discordant Image: The Mexican in American Literature. Minority Voice 5 (Spring-Fall 1981):41-52.

McDade, Georgia L. From Hopeful to Hopeless: A Study of the Novels of Jessie Redmon Fauset. Doctoral dissertation, University of Washington, 1987. UMO # 8802296.

McGhee, Patricia O. South Pacific Revisted: Were We Carefully Taught or Reinforced? Journal of Ethnic Studies 15 (Winter 1987):125-30.

McKay, Nellie. Reflections on Black Woman Writers: Revising the Literary Canon. In: Christe Farnham (ed.), The Impact of Feminist Research in the Academy, pp. 174-89. Bloomington, IN: Indiana University Press, 1987.

Melosh, Barbara. Historical Memory in Fiction: The Civil Rights Movement in Three Novels. Radical History Review 40 (Winter 1988):64-76.

Marshment, Margaret. Racist Ideology and Popular Fiction. Race and Class 19 (Spring 1978):331-344.

Matilla, Alfredo. Poesia Puertorriquena en Nueva York. Revista del Instituto de Estudios Puertorriqueños 1 (1971).

Miller, Jeanne-Marie A. More Than a Servant in the House: Black Female

Characters in American Drama, A Sketch. Theatre News 10 (April 1978):6-7.

Miller, John C. Cross Currents in Hispanic U.S. Contemporary Drama. In: Asela Rodriguez de Laguna (ed.), Images and Identities. The Puerto Rican in Two World Contexts, pp. 246-53. New Brunswick, NJ: Transaction Books, 1987.

Miller, R. Baxter (ed.) Black American Literature and Humanism. Lexington, KY: University Press of Kentucky, 1981.

Mirikitani, Janice. Shedding Silence. Berkeley, CA: Celestial Arts, 1987.

Mirikitani, Janice (ed.) Ayumi: The Japanese American Anthology. San Francisco, CA: Japanese American Anthology Committee, 1979.

Mohr, Eugene V. The Nuyorican Experience: Literature of the Puerto Rican Minority. Westport, CT: Greenwood, 1982.

Momaday, N. Scott. The Native Voice. In: Columbia Literary History of the United States. New York: Columbia University Press, 1988.

Moraberger, Robert E. Segregated Surveys: American Literature. Negro American Literature Forum. 4 (March 1970):3-8.

Morrison, Toni. The Pain of Being Black. Time [Interview]. May 22, 1989.

Moses, Wilson J. The Lost World of the Negro, 1895-1919: Black Literary and Intellectual Life before the 'Renaissance'. Black American Literature Forum 21 (Spring-Summer 1987):61-84.

Moyer, Dorothy C. The Growth and Development of Children's Books about Mexico and Mexican Americans. Doctoral dissertation, Lehigh University, 1974. UMO # 7421432.

Nelson, Alice Dunbar. Negro Literature for Negro People. Southern Workman 51 (February 1922):59.

Nesteby, James R. The Tarzan Series of Edgar Rice Burroughs: Lost Races and Racism in American Popular Culture. Doctoral dissertation, Bowling Green State University, 1978. UMO # 79-01450.

Nichols, Harold J. The Prejudice against Native-American Drama from 1778-1830. Quarterly Journal of Speech 60 (October 1974):279-88.

Nielsen, Aldon L. Reading Race. White American Poets and the Racial Discourse in the Twentieth Century. Athens: University of Georgia Press, 1989.

Onunwa, Paschal U. Eugene O'Neill: The Evolution of Racial Justice and Brotherhood in Five Plays. Doctoral dissertation, Fordham University, 1988. UMO # 8809478.

Ortego, Felipe and David Conde (eds.) The Chicano Literary World - 1974. The National Symposium in Chicano Literature and Critical Analysis. March 1975. ERIC ED 101 924.

Ortiz, Simon J. (ed.) Earth Power Coming: Short Fiction in Native American Literature. Tsailo, AZ: Navajo Community College Press, 1983.

Pace, Charles. Theatre in Black. In: Geneva Gay and Willie L. Baber (eds.), Expressively Black: The Cultural Basis of Ethnic Identity. Westport, CT: Greenwood, 1987.

Palmer, Polly. Factors Influencing the Offering of Minority Literature in Colorado High Schools, 1971-1983. Doctoral dissertation, University of Colorado, 1984. UMO # 8422635.

Paredes, Raymond A. Early Mexican-American Literature. In: Max Westbrook (ed.), A Literary History of the American West pp. 1079-1100. Fortworh, TX: Texas Christain University Press, 1987.

Paredes, Raymond A. The Evolution of Chicano Literature. In: Houston A. Baker, Jr. (ed.), Three American Literature ..., pp. 33-79. New York: Modern Language Association of America, 1982.

Paredes, R. A. The Image of the Mexican in American Literature. Doctoral dissertation, University of Texas, 1973. UMO # 7326059.

Parker, Bettye J. Black Literature Teachers: Torch-Bearers of European Myths? Black World 25 (December 1975):61-65.

Peterson, Bernard L., Jr. Contemporary Black American Playwrights and Their Plays. A Biographical Directory and Dramatic Index. Westport, CT: Greenwood, 1988.

Peyer, Bernd C. The Importance of Native American Authors. American Indian Culture and Research Journal 5 (1981):1-12.

Pitts, Ethel L. The American Negro Theatre: 1940-1949. Doctoral dissertation, University of Missouri, 1975. UMO # 767538.

Quintero Alfaro, Angel G. Image and Identity: Puerto Rican Literature in the School Curriculum. In: Asela Rodriguez de Laguna (ed.), Image and Identities. The Puerto Rican in Two World Contexts, pp. 199-210. New Brunswick, NJ: Transaction Books, 1987.

'Race,' Writing, and Difference. Critical Inquiry 12 (Autumn 1985):entire issue.

Ramsdell, Daniel B. Asia Askew: U.S. Best-Sellers on Asia, 1931-1980. Bulletin of Concerned Asian Scholars 15 (October-December 1983):3-25.

Redding, J. Saunders. The Black Arts Movement: A Modest Dissent. Crisis 84 (February 1977):50-52.

Redding, J. Saunders. To Make a Poet Black. Chapel Hill, NC: University of North Carolina Press, 1939.

Reed, Ishmael. Writin' Is Fightin'. New York: Atheneum, 1988.

Rios, Francisco A. The Mexican Fact, Fiction, and Folklore. El Grito (Summer 1969).

Roberts, Margaret O. Writing to Liberate: Selected Black Women Novelists from 1859 to 1982. Doctoral dissertation, University of Maryland, 1987. UMO # 8808596.

Robinson, Cecil. With the Ease of Strangers: The Mexican in American Literature. Tuscon: University of Arizona Press, 1963.

Robinson, Forrest G. In Bad Faith: The Dynamics of Deception in Mark Twain's America. Cambridge, MA: Harvard University Press, 1986. [Racism in literature].

Robles, Al and others (eds.) Liwanag: Literature and Graphic Expression by Filipinos in America. San Francisco, CA: Liwanag Publications, 1975.

Romano-V., Octavio I. and H. Rios C. (eds.) El Espejo/The Mirror: Selected Chicano Literature. Berkeley, CA: Quinto SOl Publications, 1969.

Rushing, Andrea B. Images of Black Women in Afro-American Poetry. Black World 24 (September 1975):18-30.

Sanchez, Marta E. Contemporary Chicana Poetry: A Critical Approach to an Emerging Literature. Berkeley, CA: University of California Press, 1985.

Sanders, Leslie C. The Development of Black Theater in America: From Shadows to Selves. Baton Rouge: Louisiana State University Press, 1988.

Sekora, John. Black Message/White Envelope: Genre, Authenticity, and Authority in the Antebellum Slave Narrative. Callaloo 10 (Summer 1987).

Sekora, John (ed.) The Art of the Slave Narrative: Original Essays in Criticism and Theory. Macomb: Western Illinois University, 1982.

Sherman, Joan R. Invisible Poets: Afro-Americans of the Nineteenth Century. Urbana: University of Illinois Press, 1974.

Sherman, Joan R. (ed.) Collected Black Women's Poetry. 4 vols. New York: Oxford University Press, 1988 reprint.

Shields, John C. (ed.) The Collected Works of Phillis Wheatley. New York: Oxford University Press, 1988 reprint.

Shields, John C. (ed.) The Collected Works of Phillis Wheatley. New
    York: Oxford University Press, 1988 reprint.

Shipp, E. R. Their Muse Is Malcolm X. New York Times December 4, 1988.

Shuler, Antonio C. and others (eds.) Chicano Literature: Text and
    Context. Englewood Cliffs, NJ: Prentice-Hall, 1972.

Sims, Rudine. Strong Black Girls: A Ten-Year-Old Responds to Fiction
    about Afro-Americans. Journal of Research and Development in
    Education 16 (1983):21-28.

Simson, Renate. The Unsung Past: Afro-American Women Writers of 19th
    Century. November 1979. ERIC ED 182 764.

Smith, Susan. The Asian-American Roots of 'Hito Hata.' Los Angeles Times
    December 26, 1980. [The East-West Players, Los Angeles].

Sollors, Werner. Literature and Ethnicity. In: Stephan Thernstrom
    (ed.), Harvard Encyclopedia of American Ethnic Groups, pp. 647-65.
    Cambridge, MA: Harvard University Press, 1980.

Sommers, Joseph and Tomes Ybarra-Frausto (eds.) Modern Chicano Writers:
    A Collection of Critical Essays. Englewood, NJ: Prentice-Hall,
    1979.

Stanford, Barbara D. and K. Amin. Black Literature for High School
    Students. Urbana, IL: National Council of Teachers of English,
    1978.

Stanford, Barbara D. and Jean Procope-Martin. Black Literature - A 'Fad'
    of the Sixties? Interracial Books for Children Bulletin. 10
    (1979):10-13.

Stensland, Anna Lee. Indian Writers and Indian Lives. Integrateducation
    12 (November-December 1974):3-7.

Stoddard, Ellwyn R. and others. Borderlands Sourcebook: A Guide to the
    Literature of Northern Mexico and the American Southwest. Norman:
    University of Oklahoma Press, 1983.

Sullivan, Sherry. Indians in American Fiction, 1820-1850: An
    Ethnohistorical Perspective. CLIO: A Journal of Literature,
    History, and the Philosophy of History 15 (Spring 1986):239-57.

Tachibana, Judy M. Outwitting the Whites: One Image of the Chinese in
    California Fiction and Poetry, 1849-1924. Southern California
    Quarterly 61 (Winter 1979):379-89.

Telemaque, Eleanor W. It's Crazy to Stay Chinese in Minnesota.
    Nashville, TN: Thomas Nelson, 1978. [Novel].

Talking of Black Art, Theatre, Revolution, and Nationhood. Black Theatre
    5 (1971):18-31.

Turner, Darwin T. Introductory Remarks about the Black Literary Tradition in the United States of America. Black American Literature Forum 12 (Winter 1978):140-47.

Turner, Faythe. Puerto Rican Writers on the Mainland, the Neoricans. Doctoral dissertation, University of Massachusetts, 1978. UMO # 79-03855.

Valdez, Luis and Stan Steiner (ed.) Aztlan: An Anthology of Mexican American Literature. New York: Knopf, 1972.

Velie, Alan R. (ed.) American Indian Literature: An Anthology. Norman: University of Oklahoma Press, 1979.

Walker, Margaret. The Humanistic Tradition of Afro-American Literature. American Libraries 1 (October 1970):849-54.

Warren, Kenneth W. Race and the Agenda of American Literary Realism. Doctoral dissertation, Stanford University, 1988. UMO # 8808443.

Washington, Earl M. Black Interpretation, Black American Literature, and Grey Audiences. Communication Education 30 (July 1981):209-16.

Watkins, Mel. Hard Times for Black Writers. New York Times Book Review February 22, 1981.

Watson, Betty and William Smith. Freeing the Spirit: Black Revolutionary Literature of the Sixties. Social Epistemology 1 (April-June 1987):131-40.

Watson, Carole M. Prologue: The Novels of Black American Women, 1891-1965. Westport, CT: Greenwood, 1985.

Weber, Brown. Our Multi-ethnic Origins and American Literary Studies. Melus 2 (March 1975):5-19.

Werner, Craig. James Baldwin: Politics and the Gospel Impulse. New Politics 2 (Winter 1989):106-24.

Wideman, John. The Black Writer and the Magic of the Word. New York Times Book Review January 24, 1988.

Wiget, Andrew. Native American Literature. Boston: Twayne, 1985.

Williams, Mance. Black Theatre in the 1960s and 1970s: A Historical-Critical Analysis of the Movement. Westport, CT: Greenwood, 1985.

Woll, Allen. Black Musical Theatre. From Coontown to Dreamgirls. Baton Rouge: Louisiana State University Press, 1988.

Wong, Nelli and others (eds.) Unbound Feet: A Collection of Chinese American Writers. San Francisco, CA: Isthmus Press, 1981.

Yarborough, Richard. The Crisis in Afro-American Letters. College English 43 (December 1981):773-78.

Zyla, Wolodymyr T. and W. M. Aycock (eds.) *Ethnic Literatures since 1776: The Many Voices of America*. Lubbock, TX: Texas Tech University, 1978.

Literature Bibliography

Arata, Esther S. and Nicholas J. Rotoli (comps.) *Black American Playwrights, 1800 to the Present: A Bibliography*. Metuchen, NJ: Scarecrow Press, 1976.

Arata, Esther S. and others (comps.) *More Black American Playwrights: A Bibliography*. Metuchen, NJ: Scarecrow Press, 1978.

Blount, Marcellus (comp.) Studies in Afro-American Literature: An Annual Annotated Bibliography, 1983. *Callaloo* 7 (Fall 1984):104-39.

Chapman, Dorothy (comp.) *Index to Black Poetry*. Boston: Hall, 1974.

Cheung, King-bok and Stan Yogi (comps.) *Asian American Literature: An Annotated Bibliography*. New York: Modern Language Association, 1988.

Clark, Edward (comp.) *Black Writers in New England: A Bibliography with Biographical Notes, of Books by and about Afro-American Writers Associated with New England in the Collection of Afro-American Literature, Suffolk University, Museum of Afro-American History, Boston African American National Historic Site*. Boston: National Park Service, U.S. Department of the Interior, 1985.

Colonnese, Tom and Louis Owens (comps.) *Native American Novelists: An Annotated Critical Bibliography*. New York: Garland, 1984.

Hatch, James V. (comp.) A White Folk's Guide to 200 Years of Black and White Drama. *Drama Review* 16 (December 1972):5-24.

Hatch, James V. and Omanii Abdullah (comps.) *Black Playwrights, 1823-1977: An Annotated Bibliography*. New York: Bowker, 1977.

Inge, M. Thomas and others (comps.) *Black American Writers: Bibliographic Essays*. 2 vols. New York: St. Martin's Press, 1978.

Kallenbach, Jessamine S. (comp.) *Index to Black American Literary Anthologies* Boston: Hall, 1979.

Keyssar-Franke, Helene (comp.) Afro-American Drama and Its Criticism, 1960-1972: An Annotated Check List with Appendices. *New York Public Library Bulletin*. 78 (Spring 1975):276-364.

Lomeli, Francisco A. and D. W. Urioste. (comps.) *Chicano Perspectives in Literature: A Critical and Annotated Bibliography*. Albuquerque, NM: Pajarto Publications, 1976.

Peavy, Charles D. (comp.) *Afro-American Literature and Culture Since*

<u>World</u> <u>War</u> <u>II:</u> <u>A</u> <u>Guide</u> <u>to</u> <u>Informative</u> <u>Sources</u>. Detroit, MI: Gale, 1979.

Ralph, George (comp.) <u>The</u> <u>American</u> <u>Theatre,</u> <u>the</u> <u>Negro,</u> <u>and</u> <u>the</u> <u>Freedom</u> <u>Movement:</u> <u>A</u> <u>Bibliography</u>. Chicago, IL: City Missionary Society, 1964.

Rowell, Charles H. and Kimberly Chanbers (comps.) Studies in Afro-American Literature: An Annotated Bibliography, 1985. <u>Callaloo</u> 9 (Fall 1986):583-622.

Rowell, Charles H. and William Lyne (comps.) Studies in Afro-American Literature: An Annotated Bibliography. <u>Callaloo</u> 8 (Fall 1985):630-60.

Ruoff, A. Lawrence B. (comp.) American Indian Literatures: Introduction and Bibliography. <u>American</u> <u>Studies</u> <u>International</u> 24 (October 1986):2-52.

Rush, Theresa G. and others (comps.) <u>Black</u> <u>American</u> <u>Writers</u> <u>Past</u> <u>and</u> <u>Present:</u> <u>A</u> <u>Biographical</u> <u>and</u> <u>Bibliographical</u> <u>Dictionary</u>. Metuchen, NJ: Scarecrow Press, 1975.

47. Localities

If ... [Atlanta] is a City Too Busy to Hate, I hope I'm not
around when they get some time.

- Juanita Odessa Abernathy, New Yorker, March 17, 1973.

Alabama

Barton, O. and others. Race in Alabama. Birmingham News August 19-26,
   1979. [Series of articles].

Broder, David S. In a Birmingham Vault. Washington Post January 19,
   1986. [Blacks in Birmingham].

Corley, Robert G. In Search of Racial Harmony: Birmingham Business
   Leaders and Desegregation, 1950-1963. In: Elizabeth Jacoway and
   David R. Cotburn (eds.), Southern Businessmen and Desegregation, pp.
   170-90. Baton Rouge: Louisiana State University Press, 1982.

Davis, Thulani. Whose Black Power? Village Voice September 2, 1986.
   [Black politics in Alabama].

Edginton, John. Alabama Story. New Society (November 28, 1986). [Race
   relations in Montgomery since 1955].

Fly, Jerry W. and George R. Reinhart. Racial Segregation During the
   1970s: The Case of Birmingham. Social Forces 58 (June 1980):1255-
   1262.

Holmes, Jack D. L. The Role of Blacks in Spanish Alabama: The Mobile
   Districts, 1780-1813. Alabama Historical Quarterly 37 (1975):5-18.

Jaynes, Gregory. A Stubborn Company Town Wins Delay in Its Death
   Sentence. New York Times December 25, 1981. [Praco].

Kaufman, Jonathan. In Alabama Town, Blacks and Whites Still Go Separate
   Ways. Boston Globe March 6, 1985. [Selma].

Kolchin, Peter. First Freedom: The Response of Alabama's Blacks to
   Emancipation and Reconstruction. Westport, CT: Greenwood, 1972.

McKiven, Henry M., Jr. The Household Composition of Working Class
   Families in the Birmingham District, 1900. Southern Historian 6
   (Spring 1985):40-52.

Milloy, Courtland. Montgomery, Alabama, 30 Years After Start. Washington
   Post January 20, 1986. [Blacks in Montgomery].

Norrell, Robert J., II. Reaping the Whirlwind: Change and Conflict in
   Macon County, Alabama, 1941-1972. Doctoral dissertation, University
   of Virginia, 1983. UMO # 8419901.

Rogers, Willbraim W. and Robert D. Ward. August Reckoning: Jack Turner and Racism in Post-Civil War Alabama. Baton Rouge: Louisiana State University Press, 1973.

U.S. Commission on Civil Rights. Fifteen Years Ago ... Rural Alabama Revisited. Washington, D.C.: The Commission, December 1983.

Alaska

Flanders, Nicholas E. Passage: Socioeconomic Change and Cultural Continuity in an Alaskan Community. Doctoral dissertation, Columbia University, 1983. UMO # 8604620. [Chevak, Yukon-Kuskowkim Delta].

Arizona

Izakowitz, Pam. Being Black in a Very White Town. Mesa Tribune May 22, 1983.

Weisman, Alan. Up in Arms in Arizona. New York Times Magazine November 1, 1987. [The campaign to recall Gov. Evan Mecham; aspects of the governor's racism].

Arkansas

Graves, John William. Town and Country: Race Relations and Urban Development in Arkansas 1865-1905. Doctoral dissertation, University of Virginia, 1978. 448 p. UMO # 7903542.

Richards, Eugene. Few Comforts or Surprises: The Arkansas Delta. Cambridge, MA: MIT Press,

California

Broussard, Albert S. The New Racial Frontier: San Francisco's Black Community, 1900-1940. Doctoral dissertation, Duke University, 1977. UMO # 78-10793.

Broussard, Albert S. Strange Territory, Familiar Leadership: The Impact of World War II on San Francisco's Black Community. California History 65 (March 1986):18-25, 71-73.

Carlton, Robert L. Blacks in San Diego County 1850-1900. Master's thesis, San Diego State University, 1977.

Carlton, Robert L. Blacks in San Diego County: A Social Profile, 1850-1880. Journal of San Diego History 21 (1975):7-20.

Cortez, Gregoria P. The Filipinos in California: With Focus on Vallejo from 1927 to the Present. Master's thesis, Sonoma State University, 1978.

Daniels, Douglas H. Pioneer Urbanites: A Social and Cultural History of Black San Francisco. Philadelphia: Temple University Press, 1979.

Gaines-Carter, Patrice and Jay Mathews. Washington Post January 21,

Gaines-Carter, Patrice and Jay Mathews. <u>Washington</u> <u>Post</u> January 21, 1986. [Black life in Pasadena].

Gamber, Wendy E. <u>The</u> <u>Myth</u> <u>of</u> <u>Western</u> <u>Opportunity:</u> <u>Social</u> <u>Structure</u> <u>in</u> <u>Sacramento, California, 1860-1880</u>. Master's thesis, University of California, Davis, 1985.

Gillenbirk, Jeff and James Motlow. <u>Bitter</u> <u>Melon:</u> <u>Stories</u> <u>from</u> <u>the</u> <u>Last</u> <u>Rural</u> <u>Chinese</u> <u>Town</u> <u>in</u> <u>America</u>. Seattle: University of Washington Press, 1987. [Locke, CA].

Kinder, Donald R. and David O. Sears. <u>Symbolic</u> <u>Racism</u> <u>versus</u> <u>Racial</u> <u>Threats</u> <u>to</u> <u>"The</u> <u>Good</u> <u>Life"</u>. 1978. ERIC ED 189 219. [Suburban Los Angeles].

Lapp, Rudolph M. <u>Afro-Americans</u> <u>in</u> <u>California</u>. San Francisco, CA: Boyd and Fraser Pub. Co., 1979.

Lewthwaite, Gordon and others. From Polynesia to California: Samoan Migration and its Sequel. <u>Journal</u> <u>of</u> <u>Pacific</u> <u>History</u> 8 (1973):133-57.

Madyun, Gail and Larry Malon. Black Pioneers in San Diego: 1880-1920. <u>Journal</u> <u>of</u> <u>San</u> <u>Diego</u> <u>History</u> 27 (Spring 1981):91-114.

Matsumoto, Valerie J. <u>The</u> <u>Cortez</u> <u>Colony:</u> <u>Family, Farm</u> <u>and</u> <u>Community</u> <u>among</u> <u>Japanese</u> <u>Americans, 1919-1982</u>. Doctoral dissertation, Stanford University, 1986. UMO # 8608184. [San Joaquin Valley, CA].

Reed, Karen L. <u>The</u> <u>Chinese</u> <u>in</u> <u>Tehama</u> <u>County, 1860-1890</u>. Chico, CA: Association for Northern California Records and Research, 1984.

Tapia, Lola A. <u>Urban</u> <u>Indians</u> <u>in</u> <u>Orange</u> <u>County</u>. Master's thesis, California State University, Fullerton, 1977.

Won, Ji Moon. <u>The</u> <u>Koreans</u> <u>in</u> <u>Los</u> <u>Angeles</u>. Master's thesis, Brigham Young University, 1978.

Colorado

Cooper, Kenneth J. Denver: Skilled Blacks Thrive. <u>Boston</u> <u>Globe</u> July 14, 1981.

Knudson, Thomas J. Denver Is Becoming a Beacon of Black Opportunity. <u>New</u> <u>York</u> <u>Times</u> August 5, 1987.

Smith, Phyllis. City's History Shows Record of Discrimination Against Blacks. <u>Colorado</u> <u>Daily</u> (University of Colorado) September 30, 1982. [Boulder].

The Tarnished Dream/Black Denver 1968-88. <u>Rocky</u> <u>Mountain</u> <u>News</u> May 22-27, 1988. [Series of articles].

Connecticut

New Haven, CT: New Haven Civic Federation, 1913.

McCarthy, Peggy. Conn. Town Rejects Racist Label. Boston Globe January 31, 1988. [State Human Rights and Opportunities Commisssion reports Rocky Hill, a Hartford suburb, is a racist community].

Madden, Richard L. Panel Cites Racism in a Connecticut Town. New York Times January 16, 1988. [Rocky Hill].

Miller, William Lee. Analysis of the 'White Blacklash'. New York Times Magazine August 23, 1964. [Deals, in part, with New Haven, CT].

District of Columbia

Alexander, Bill. Black Art Galleries Turning Financial Corner. Washington Post October 15, 1981. [Washington, D.C. metropolitan area].

Borchert, James. Alley Life in Washington: Family, Community, Religion, and Folklife in the City, 1850-1970. Urbana: University of Illinois Press, 1980.

Cherkasky, Mara. Slices of the Pie: Black and White Dupont Circle from the 1920s to the 1950s. Master's thesis, George Washington University, 1985.

Gale, Dennis E. Washington, D.C.: Inner-City Revitalization and Minority Suburbanization. Philadelphia: Temple University Press, 1987.

Gamarekin, Barbara. Black Race Capital: An Equal Opportunity City? New York Times July 21, 1982.

Granat, D. and others. Blacks and Whites in Washington: How Separate? How Equal? Washingtonian 22 (1986):152-82.

Horton, Lois E. and James O. Horton. Race, Occupation, and Literacy in Reconstruction Washington, D.C. In: Orville V. Burton and Robert C. McMath (eds.), Towards a New South? Studies in Post-Civil War Southern Communitites. Westport, CT: Greenwood, 1982.

Hughes, Langston. Our Wonderful Society: Washington. Opportunity 5 (1927):226-27.

Ingle, Edward. The Negro in the District of Columbia. Baltimore, MD: Johns Hopkins Press, 1893.

Noble, Ken. The Black and White Washington. New York Times March 21, 1984.

Szegedy-Maszak, Marianne. D.C., the Other Washington. New York Times Magazine November 20, 1988.

Terrell, Mary Church. What It Means to Be Colored in the Capital in the United States. Independent January 24, 1907.

United States. _Independent_ January 24, 1907.

Williams, Lena. A Neighborhood Divided. _New York Times_ November 24, 1986. [Conflict in Anacostia between blacks and Asian-American merchants].

Florida

Colburn, David R. The Saint Augustine Business Community: Desegregation, 1963-1964. _In:_ Elizabeth Jacoway and David R. Colburn (eds.), _Southern Businessmen and Desegregation_, pp. 211-35. Baton Rouge: Louisiana State University Press, 1982.

Crouch, Stanley. The Failure of Tantrum Politics. _Village Voice_ August 27, 1980. [Blacks in Miami].

Department of Human Resources. _Profile of Social and Economic Conditions in Low-Income Areas in Dade County, Florida_. Miami, FL: Metropolitan Dade County, 1980.

Dunn, Marvin. The Cities' Black Poor: America's Angry Untouchables. _Los Angeles Times_ August 24, 1980. [Liberty City, Miami].

Evans, Arthur S. Pearl City: The Formation of a Black Community in the New South. _Phylon_ 48 (June 1987):152-64. [Boca Raton].

Fair, T. Willard. The State of Black Dade County - It Isn't Good. _Miami Herald_ January 11, 1981. [President, Urban League of Greater Miami].

Fair, T. Willard. State of the Black Community: Poverty, Racism Still Prevalent. _Miami Herald_ April 6, 1980.

Hirsley, Michael. Hispanics Overwhelm Blacks in Miami Labor Fight. _Chicago Tribune_ January 18, 1983.

Middleton, DeWight R. The Organization of Ethnicity in Tampa. _Ethnic Groups_ 3 (1981):281-305.

Richardson, Barbara A. _A History of Blacks in Jacksonville, Florida, 1860-1895: A Socio-Economic and Political Study_. Doctoral dissertation, Carnegie-Mellon University, 1975.

Schmalz, Jeffrey. Miami Tensions Simmering 3 Months After Violence. _New York Times_ April 10, 1989.

Thompson, Charles S. The Growth of Colored Miami. _Crisis_ 49 (March 1942).

Thompson, Sylvia A. _Community Leadership in Greater Miami, Florida: What Role for Blacks and Cuban-Americans?_ Doctoral dissertation, Southern Illinois University, 1985. UMO # 8526741.

Whitman, D. The Class Conflict Behind the Miami Riot. _USA Today_ 109 (November 1980).

the Cuban and Black Economies in Miami. American Journal of Sociology 88 (July 1982):135-60.

Georgia

Bayor, Ronald H. A City Too Busy to Hate: Atlanta's Business Community and Civil Rights. In: Harold I. Sharlin (ed.), Business and Its Environment: Essays for Thomas C. Cochran. Westport, CT: Greenwood, 1983.

Deskins, D. R. Race as an Element in the Intra-City Regionalization of Atlanta's Population. Southeastern Geographer 3 (1971):90-100.

Du Bois, W. E. B. Georgia: Invisible Empire State. In: Ernest Gruening (ed.), These United States, Vol. 2, pp. 322-345. New York: Boni and Liveright, 1924.

Du Bois, W. E. B. The Negro As He Really Is. World's Work 2 (June 1901):848-66. [GA county].

Ifill, Given and David Maraniss. In Atlanta, Struggling With Success. Washington Post January 20, 1986. [Blacks in Atlanta].

McDonald, Laughlin. Jim Crow is Alive and Well in the Old 'New South'. Bridge: A Review of Cross Cultural Affairs 3 (February 1978):14-15, 30-31. [Moulton].

Matthews, John M. Black Newspapermen and the Black Community in Georgia, 1890-1930. Georgia Historical Quarterly 68 (Fall 1984):356-81.

Schmidt, William E. Racial Roadblock Seen in Atlanta Transit System. New York Times July 22, 1987.

Smith, David M. Inequality in an American City: Atlanta, Georgia, 1960-1970. London: Department of Geography, Queen Mary College, University of London, January 1981.

Stone, Clarence N. Economic Growth and Neighborhood Discontent: System Bias in the Urban Renewal Program of Atlanta. Chapel Hill, NC: University of North Carolina Press, 1976.

Work, Monroe N. The Negroes of Warsaw, Georgia. Southern Workman 37 (January 1908):29-40.

Hawaii

Kirkpatrick, J. Ethnic Antagonism and Innovation in Hawaii. In: Jerry Boucher and others (eds.), Ethnic Conflict. International Perspectives. Newbury Park, CA: Sage, 1987.

Nomura, Gail M. The Debate Over the Role of Nisei in Prewar Hawaii: The New American Conference, 1927-1941. Journal of Ethnic Studies 15 (Spring 1987):95-115.

Illinois

Compton, James. Chicago Is Failing Its Blacks. _Chicago_ _Tribune_ February
    20, 1984.

Dorsey, James W. Blacks in North Chicago. Master's thesis, Roosevelt
    University, 1977.

Dorsey, James W. _Up_ _South:_ _Blacks_ _in_ _Chicago's_ _Suburbs,_ _1719-1983_.
    Bristol, IN: Wyndam Hall Press, 1986.

Edsall, Thomas B. Black vs. White in Chicago. _New_ _York_ _Review_ _of_ _Books_
    April 3, 1989.

Grimshaw, William. _Black_ _Politics_ _in_ _Chicago:_ _The_ _Quest_ _for_ _Leadership,_
    _1939-1979_. Chicago: Center for Urban Policy, Loyola University,
    1980.

Hutchison, Earl R., Jr. _Black_ _Suburbanization:_ _A_ _History_ _of_ _Social_
    Change _in_ _a_ _Working_ _Class_ _Suburb_. Doctoral dissertation, University
    of Chicago, 1984. [Harvey, Ill.]

Jackson, Verne. Several Summers. _Chicago_ July 1979. [Ada Street and
    62nd St. black neighborhood, with emphasis on economic differences].

Squires, Gregory D. and others. _Chicago:_ _Race,_ _Class,_ _and_ _the_ _Response_
    _to_ _Urban_ _Decline_. Philadelphia: Temple University Press, 1987.

Wojnusz, Helen K. Racial Hostility Among Blacks in Chicago. _Journal_ _of_
    Black _Studies_ 10 (September 1979):40-59.

Wright, R. R. The Negro in Chicago. _Charities_ 15 (October 7, 1905):69-
    73.

Indiana

Boland, Ronald T. _The_ _War_ _on_ _Poverty_ _in_ _Fort_ _Wayne,_ _1965_ _to_ _1975_ _-_ _A_ _Case_
    Study. Doctoral dissertation, University of Kansas, 1981. UMO #
    8218740.

Galen, Joan. USX Pulls the Plug. _People's_ _Daily_ _World_ September 18,
    1986. [The steel corporation's political and legal power in Gary].

Muhammed, Lawrence. Hatcher's Gary: Decline of an Urban Dynasty. _In_
    These _Times_ May 7, 1986.

Iowa

Dykstra, Robert R. The Issue Squarely Met: Toward an Explanation of
    Iowan's Racial Attitudes, 1865-1868. _Annals_ _of_ _Iowa_ 47 (Summer
    1984):430-50.

Hall, Barbara and others. Discrimination: Does It Exist Here? _Oklahoma_
    Herald July 6-14, 1982. [Series of articles on Oklahoma and Mahaska

Newmeyer, Robert. May Harmony Prevail: The Early History of Black
    Waterloo. _Palimpsest_ 61 (May-June 1980):80-91.

Kentucky

Howard, Victor B. _Black Liberation in Kentucky: Emancipation and
    Freedom, 1862-1884_. Lexington, KY: 1983.

Wright, George C. _Blacks in Louisville, Kentucky, 1890-1930_. Doctoral
    dissertation, Duke University, 1977.

Louisiana

Lee and Associates. _The Economic Profile of Blacks in New Orleans_. New
    Orleans, LA: Lee and Associates, November 7, 1983.

MacDonald, Robert R. and others (eds.) _Louisiana's Black Heritage_. New
    Orleans: Louisiana State Museum, 1979.

Maguire, Robert E. _Hustling to Survive: Social and Economic Change in a
    South Louisiana Black Creole Community_. Doctoral dissertation,
    McGill University, 1987.

McMillen, Neil R. The [White] Citizen's Council in New Orleans:
    Organized Resitance to Social Change in a Deep South City. _In_:
    Robert Fisher and Peter Romanofzky (eds.), _Community Organization for
    Urban Social Change: A Historical Perspective_. Westport, CT:
    Greenwood, 1981.

Maryland

Hamlin, Walter R. _Rural Black Kinship: A Study of the Black Community of
    Calvert County, Maryland_. Doctoral dissertation, University of
    Rochester, 1980. UMO # 811361.

Justice, Sandra. _Black Perspectives on the Eastern Shore: 1640-1860_.
    Master's thesis, Virginia State University, 1982.

McDaniel, George W. _Hearth and Home: Preserving a People's Culture_.
    Philadelphia: Temple University Press, 1982. [Black life in
    southern Maryland].

Rollo, Vera A. Foster. _The Black Experience in Maryland_. Lanham, MD:
    Maryland Historical Press, 1980.

Massachusetts

Clark, Edward. Boston Black and White: The Voice of Fiction. _Black
    American Literature Forum_ 19 (Summer 1985):83-89. [Blacks in
    Boston].

Cormier, Agnes T. and others. _The Effect of Racism on the Puerto Rican in
    Boston_. Master's thesis, Boston University, 1977.

Cowen, Peter. Black Professionals and Boston's Image. Boston Globe June 20, 1982.

Del Guidice, Marguerite and others. Racism in Boston. Boston Globe December 14, 1980.

Graham, Renee and Ellen J. Bartlett. Shadow of Racism Mars the Good Life. Many Boston Blacks Feel Like Outsiders. Boston Globe March 27, 1988.

Kaufman, Jonathan. Leaders Get Low Performance Rating. Boston Globe June 14, 1988. [Boston's Black community].

Kenny, Charles. The Politics of Turmoil. Boston Globe Magazine April 19, 1987. [The harsh realities of life for Boston's Black people].

Ruchames, Louis. Race, Marriage, and Abolition in Massachusetts. Journal of Negro History (July 1955).

Thernstrom, Stephan. The Other Bostonians. Cambridge, MA, 1973. [Chapter on blacks, 1880-1970].

Thomas, Jack. Blue-Collar Barrier. Boston Globe January 4, 1988. [About Ken Hudson and attitudes toward blacks in Boston].

Michigan

Darden, Joe T. and others. Detroit: Race and Uneven Development. Philadelphia: Temple University Press, 1987.

DeVries, James E. Home Grown: The Black Experience in the City of Monroe, Michigan, 1900-1915. Doctoral dissertation, Ball State University, 1978. UMO # 7908442.

Fine, Sidney. Violence in the Model City: The Cavanagh Administration, Race Relations, and the Detroit Riot of 1967. Ann Arbor, University of Michigan Press, 1989.

Hill, Richard Child. At the Crossroads: The Political Economy of Postwar Detroit. Urbanism Past and Present 6 (Summer 1978):1-21.

Holli, Melvin G. (ed.) Detroit. New York: New Viewpoints, 1976.

Mc Gehee, Scott and Susan Watson. Blacks in Detroit. Detroit: Detroit Free Press, December 1980. [Reprint of articles that appeared in the Detroit Free Press between November 30 and December 12, 1980].

Sinclair, Robert and Bryan Thompson. Detroit: An Analysis of Social Change. Cambridge, MA: Ballinger, 1977.

Thomas, Frances S. (ed.) The State of Black Michigan: 1987. East Lansing, MI: Urban Affairs Programs, Michigan State University, 1987.

Wilson, Benjamin C. The Rural Black Heritage between Chicago and Detroit,

Change. Cambridge, MA: Ballinger, 1977.

Thomas, Frances S. (ed.) The State of Black Michigan: 1987. East
Lansing, MI: Urban Affairs Programs, Michigan State University,
1987.

Wilson, Benjamin C. The Rural Black Heritage between Chicago and Detroit,
1850-1929. Kalamazoo, MI: New Issues Press, Western Michigan
University, 1985.

Minnesota

Harpole, Patricia C. (ed.) The Black Community in Territorial St.
Anthony: A Memoir [Emily O. Goodridge Grey]. Minnesota History 49
(Summer 1984):42-55.

Turbeville, Gus. The Negro Population in Duluth, Minnesota, 1950.
Sociology and Social Research 36 (1952):231-238.

Mississippi

Bailey, R. Black-White Relations in Mississippi. In: Jerry Boucher and
others (eds.), Ethnic Conflict. International Perspectives. Newbury
Park, CA: Sage, 1987.

Farrell, John A. In Miss. Delta, Dream Is Still Deferred. Boston Globe
August 3, 1988. [Greenwood].

Harris, Art. In Town of Boycott, White Folks No Longer Cut in Line.
Washington Post July 3, 1982. [Port Gibson].

Heard, Alex. Of Time, Reform, and the River. Education Week September
25, 1985. [Greenville].

Piore, Michael J. Negro Workers in the Mississippi Delta. Monthly Labor
Review 91 (1968):23-5.

Powdermaker, Hortense. After Freedom: A Cultural Study in the Deep
South. New York: Atheneum, 1968 (orig. 1939). [Indianola, MS,
1932-1934].

Smith, Mary J. A Study of Race and Community in the New South:
Washington, County, Mississippi, 1920-1940. Master's thesis,
Louisiana State University, 1987.

Missouri

Chu-Luu. The Vietnamese Refugees in Kansas City. Master's thesis,
University of Missouri, Kansas City, 1982.

Coplon, Jeffrey R. and others. Being Black in Kansas City. Kansas City
Times July 28-30, 1980.

Crossland, W. A. Industrial Conditions Among Negroes in St. Louis. St.
Louis, MO: Washington University Press, 1914.

U.S. Commission on Civil Rights, Missouri Advisory Committee. <u>Race Relations</u> <u>in</u> <u>Cooper</u> <u>County, MO.</u> - <u>1978</u>. Washington, D.C.: The Commission, 1979.

U.S. Commission on Civil Rights, Missouri Advisory Committee. <u>Race Relations</u> <u>in</u> <u>the</u> <u>"Kingdom"</u> <u>of</u> <u>Calloway</u>. Washington, D.C.: The Commission, 1979. [Fulton].

Nevada

Patrick, Elizabeth N. Notes and Documents: The Black Experience in Southern Nevada. <u>Nevada</u> <u>Historical</u> <u>Soc.</u> <u>Quarterly</u> 22 (Summer 1979):128-140.

New Hampshire

Doane, Ashley W. <u>The</u> <u>Franco-Americans</u> <u>of</u> <u>New</u> <u>Hampshire:</u> <u>A</u> <u>Case</u> <u>Study</u> <u>of</u> <u>Ethnicity</u> <u>and</u> <u>Social</u> <u>Stratification</u>. Master's thesis, University of New Hampshire, 1983.

New Jersey

Garsson, Robert M. The Black Minority [in Asbury Park, New Jersey]. <u>Asbury</u> <u>Park</u> <u>Press</u> June 29, 1980+. [Series of articles].

Willcox, Isobel. Hackensack Is Recalled as Hostile Racist Town. <u>New</u> <u>York</u> <u>Times</u> July 15, 1973.

New York

Byrne, Thomas. The Negro in Elmira. <u>Chemnung</u> <u>Historical</u> <u>Journal</u> (September 1968):1751.

Clarke, John H. (ed.) <u>Harlem:</u> <u>A</u> <u>Community</u> <u>in</u> <u>Transition</u>. New York: Citadel, 1964.

Denowitz, Ronald M. Racial Successions in New York City, 1960-70. <u>Social</u> <u>Forces</u> 59 (December 1980):440-455.

Feron, James. Why Yonkers? The Long Path to an Integration Order. <u>New</u> <u>York</u> <u>Times</u> January 19, 1988.

Freedman, Samuel. New York Race Tension is Rising Despite Gains. <u>New</u> <u>York</u> <u>Times</u> March 29, 1987. [1st of a series of 5 articles].

Glazer, Nathan and Daniel P. Moynihan. <u>Beyond</u> <u>the</u> <u>Melting</u> <u>Pot:</u> <u>The</u> <u>Negroes, Puerto</u> <u>Ricans, Jews, Italians, and</u> <u>Irish</u> <u>of</u> <u>New</u> <u>York</u> <u>City</u>. 2nd ed. Cambridge, MA: MIT Press, 1970.

Handlin, Oscar. <u>Newcomers:</u> <u>Negroes</u> <u>and</u> <u>Puerto</u> <u>Ricans</u> <u>in</u> <u>a</u> <u>Changing</u> <u>Metropolis</u>. Cambridge, MA: Harvard University Press, 1959.

Ovington, Mary W. <u>Half-a-Man:</u> <u>The</u> <u>Status</u> <u>of</u> <u>the</u> <u>Negro</u> <u>in</u> <u>New</u> <u>York</u>. New York: Longmans, Green, 1911.

Handlin, Oscar. Newcomers: Negroes and Puerto Ricans in a Changing Metropolis. Cambridge, MA: Harvard University Press, 1959.

Ovington, Mary W. Half-a-Man: The Status of the Negro in New York. New York: Longmans, Green, 1911.

Perlman, Robyn. A Case Study: The Korean-Americans of Flushing. Master's thesis, Queens College, 1982.

Rimer, Sara. Yonkers Anguish: Black and White in 2 Worlds. New York Times December 22, 1987.

Task Force on the New York State Dropout Problem. Dropping Out of School in New York State: The Invisible People of Color. New York: African American Institute of the State University of New York, 1986.

White Supremacy is Gravely Menaced by Long Island Negroes. The Kourier Magazine 9 (August 1933):19.

Williams, Lillian S. The Development of a Black Community: Buffalo, New York, 1900-1940. Doctoral dissertation, State University of New York at Buffalo, 1979. UMO # 7921904.

North Carolina

Alexander, Roberta S. North Carolina Faces the Freedmen: Race Relations During Presidential Reconstruction, 1865-67. Durham, NC: 1985.

Chafe, William H. Civilities and Civil Rights: Greensboro, North Carolina, and the Black Struggle for Equality. New York: Oxford University Press, 1980.

Craige, Ernst T. A. The Education of the Boat People: Background, Adaptations and Aspirations of North Carolina's Haitian Farmworkers. Doctoral dissertation, North Carolina State University at Raleigh, 1986. UMO # 8624105.

Gaillard, Frye and others. Becoming Truly Free: 300 Years of Black History in the Carolinas. Charlotte, NC: Charlotte Observer, 1985.

Haley, John H. Charles N. Hunter and Race Relations in North Carolina. Chapel Hill, NC: University of North Carolina Press, 1987. [Former slave].

Schmidt, William E. Jim Crow Is Gone, but White Resistance Remains. New York Times April 6, 1985. [Greensboro].

West, Harry L. The Race War in North Carolina. Forum 26 (January 1899):578-99.

White, Walter F. The Shambles of North Carolina. Crisis 33 (1926):72-75.

Ohio

Brown, Mary Ann. Vanished Black Rural Communities in Western Ohio. In: Camille Wells (ed.), Perspectives in Vernacular Architecture, Vol I. Columbia: University of Missouri Press, 1987.

Dayton Desegregation: A 10-Year Report Card. Dayton Daily News and Journal Herald September 7-12, 1986 (series of articles; also available as single reprint).

Gilbert, G. and others. The State of Black Columbus. Columbus, OH: Columbus Urban League, 1980.

Pusateri, Paul J. The Cleveland Puerto Rican Community. Master's thesis, Case Western Reserve University, 1988.

Ross, Steven J. Workers on the Edge. Work, Leisure, and Politics in Industrializing Cincinnati, 1788-1890. New York: Columbia University Press,

Urban League of Greater Cincinnati. State of Black Cincinnati. September 1980. ERIC ED 228 347.

Wilkerson, Isabel. A City Finds Its Racist Image Is Hard to Shed. New York Times October 30, 1988. [Parma].

Oklahoma

Muzny, Charles C. The Vietnamese in Oklahoma City: A Study of Ethnic Change. Doctoral dissertation, University of Oklahoma, 1985. UMO # 8601149.

Oregon

Little, William A. Blacks in Oregon. A Statistical and Historical Report. Portland: Black Studies Center and the Center for Population Research and Census, Portland State University, 1978.

Williams, Linda. The Black Influence. Oregonian November 15-16, 1982. [Series of articles on the black community of Portland].

Pennsylvania

Du Bois, W. E. B. The Philadelphia Negro: A Social Study. Boston: Ginn, 1899.

Hershberg, Theodore and Henry Williams. Mulattoes and Blacks: Intra-Group Color Differences and Social Stratification in Nineteenth-Century Philadelphia. In: Theodore Hershberg (ed.), Philadelphia: Work, Space, Family and Group Experience in the Nineteenth Century. New York: Oxford University Press, 1981.

Hopkins, Leroy T. Black Eldorado on the Susquehanna: The Emergence of Black Columbia, 1726-1861. Journal of the Lancaster County Historical Society 89 (1985):110-32.

Stevens, William K. Neighbors Rebuff Philadelphia Koreans. New York Times August 3, 1986.

Rhode Island

Cottrol, Robert J. Black Providence 1800-1860: A Community's Formation. Doctoral dissertation, Yale University, 1978. UMO # 8121402.

South Carolina

Burton, Orville. The Rise and Fall of Afro-American Town Life: Town and Country in Reconstruction Edgefield, South Carolina. In: Orville V. Burton and Robert C. McMath (eds.), Towards a New South? Studies in Post-Civil War Southern Communities. Westport, CT: Greenwood, 1982.

Fields, Mamie Garvin with Karen Fields. Lemon Swamp and Other Places. A Carolina Memoir. New York: Free Press, 1983.

Sulton, James, Jr. Things Have Changed in Edgefield County. Jackson Advocate March 21, 1985.

Thomas, June Manning. Blacks on the South Carolina Sea Islands: Planning for Tourist and Land Development. Doctoral dissertation, University of Michigan, 1977.

Voigt, Gilbert P. A South Carolina Negro Paradise. Negro History Bulletin 22 (1958):7-9. [Beaufort County, early reconstruction].

White, Walter F. The Shambles of South Carolina. Crisis 33 (December 1926):72-75.

Texas

Barrineau, Mary. Blacks in Dallas: The Racism is Subtle. Dallas Times Herald January 13, 1982.

Campbell, Randolph B. A Southern Community in Crisis: Harrison County, Texas, 1850-1880. Austin: Texas State Historical Association, 1983. [Black-majority county].

Feagin, Joe R. Free Enterprise City. Houston in Political and Economic Perspective. New Brunswick, NJ: Rutgers University Press, 1988.

Garnett, William E. Immediate and Pressing Race Problems of Texas. Proceedings of the Southeastern Political and Social Science Association (1925):31-48.

Goldberg, Robert A. Racial Change of the Southern Periphery: The Case of San Antonio, 1960-1965. Journal of Southern History 49 (August 1983):349-74.

Hemmila, Herbert W. The Adjustment and Assimilation of Cambodian Refugees in Texas Doctoral dissertation, East Texas State University, 1984. UMO # 8503156.

Integrateducation 15 (September-October 1977).

Schutze, Jim. The Accommodation: The Politics of Race in an American
     City. Dallas, TX: Taylor Pub. Co., 1986. [Dallas].

Vermont

Dalton, Terence A. Racism in Vermont. Boston Globe March 15, 1988.

Vermont's Few Blacks Finding Special Problems. New York Times August 23,
     1987. [Associated Press story].

Virginia

Craig, John M. Community Cooperation in Ruthville, Virginia 1900-1930.
     Phylon 48 (June 1987):132-40.

Dent, Edward E. Race Relations in Hopewell, Virginia, 1635 to 1932.
     Master's thesis, Virginia State University, Petersburg, 1988.

Du Bois, W. E. B. The Negroes of Farmville, Virginia: A Social Study.
     U.S. Labor Dept, Bulletin, 3 (January 1898):1-38.

Tyler-McGraw, Marie and Gregg D. Kimball. In Bondage and Freedom:
     Antebellum Black Life in Richmond, Virginia, 1790-1860. Chapel Hill,
     NC: University of North Carolina Press, 1988.

White, Ronald D. A Black Reporter in Virginia: The Old South Never Died.
     Washington Post September 21, 1980.

Washington

Wilson, Margaret E. An Ethnohistorical Study of the Dominant Community
     Reaction to the Chinese and Japanese Immigrant Communities in
     Bellingham, WA. Master's thesis, Western Washington University,
     1981.

Wisconsin

McNealy, R. L. and M. R. Kinlow. Milwaukee Today: A Racial Gap Study.
     Milwaukee, WI: Milwaukee Urban League, 1987.

Wyoming

Guenther, Todd R. At Home on the Range: Black Settlement in Rural
     Wyoming, 1850-1905. Master's thesis, University of Wyoming, 1988.

48. Mass Media

We wish to plead our own cause. ...

   - Freedom's Journal, March 16, 1827; introductory issue
of the first black newspaper in the U.S.

Ajami, Joseph G. The Arabic Press in the United States since 1892: A
  Socio-historical Study. Doctoral dissertation, Ohio University,
  1987. UMO # 8719358.

Alford, Terry. 'Attention White People!': The Underground Press in
  Mississippi, 1962-1968. Journal of Mississippi History 49 (May
  1987):139-51.

Alter, Jonathan and others. No Room at the Top. Newsweek December 1,
  1986. [Management jobs for minorities in mass media].

Arab Image in the Western Mass Media. London: Morris International, 1979.

Archer, Leonard C. Black Images in the American Theatre: NAACP Protest
  Campaigns - Stage, Screen, Radio and Television. New York: Pageant-
  Poseidon, Ltd., 1973.

Astroff, R. Communication and Contemporary Colonialism: Broadcast
  Television in Puerto Rico. In: H. E. Hinds, Jr. and C. M. Tatum
  (eds.), Studies in Latin American Popular Culture, Vol. 6, pp. 11-26.
  Tucscon: Department of Spanish and Portuguese, University of Arizona,
  1987.

Auletta, G. S. and J. C. Hammerback. A Relational Model for Interracial
  Interactions on Television. Western Journal of Speech Communication
  49 (Fall 1985):301-21.

Barnett, Marguerite R. and Doris Wilkinson. Image of Blacks in American
  Popular Culture: 1865-1955. New York: Holmes and Meier, 1955.

Beecher, Jules. The Course of Exclusion, 1882-1924: San Francisco
  Newspaper Coverage of the Chinese and Japanese in the United States.
  Doctoral dissertation, University of California, Berkeley, 1986. UMO
  # 8624704.

Blackwell, Ed. Challenging the Establishment: A Black Reporter Looks at
  the Press. Communication: Journalism Education Today 8 (February
  1974):10-11.

Bogle, Donald. Toms, Coons, Mulattoes, Mammies and Bucks: An
  Interpretive History of Blacks in America Films. New York: Viking,
  1973.

Broh, C. Anthony. A House of a Different Color: Television's Treatment
  of Jesse Jackson's 1984 Presidential Campaign. Washington, D.C.:

Joint Center for Political Studies, 1987.

Brasch, Walter M. Black English and the Mass Media. Amherst, MA:
    University of Massachusetts Press, 1981.

Broussard, Vanessa. Afro-American Images in Advertising 1880-1920.
    Master's thesis, George Washington University, 1986.

Bullock, Penelope L. The Negro Periodical Press in the United States,
    1838-1909. Baton Rouge: Lousiana State University Press, 1981.

Campbell, Georgette M. Extant Collection of Early Black Newspapers: A
    Research Guide to the Black Press, 1880-1915, with an Index to the
    Boston 'Guardian', 1902-1904. Troy, NY: Whitston, 1981.

Cham, Mbye B. and Claire Andrade Watkins (eds.) Black Frames: Critical
    Perspectives on Independent Black Cinema. Cambridge, MA: MIT Press,
    1988.

Chin, Daryl. Writings an Unexpurgated History of Asian American Film.
    CinVue 3 (June 1988):5-6.

Cohen, P. and C. Gardner. It Ain't Half Racist, Mum: Fighting Racism in
    the Media. London: Comedia/CARM, 1982.

Coley, Geraldine J. Black News in the Leading San Diego Daily Newspapers.
    Doctoral dissertation, United States International University, 1976.
    UMO # 7909530.

Comstock, George and Robin E. Cobbey. Television and the Children of
    Ethnic Minorities. August 1978. ERIC ED 168 002.

Cose, Ellis. Rape in the News: Mainly About Whites. New York Times May
    7, 1989.

Covert, Catherine L. and John D. Stevens (eds.) Mass Media between the
    Wars: Perceptions of Cultural Tension, 1918-1941. Syracuse, NY:
    Syracuse University Press, 1984.

Cracking the Color Code: Minorities in Media. Media and Values 38 (Fall
    1986):entire issue.

Cripps, Thomas R. The Death of Rastus: Negroes in American Films Since
    1945. Phylon 28 (Fall 1967):267-75.

Cripps, Thomas R. Slow Fade to Black: The Negro in American Films, 1900-
    1942. New York: Oxford University Press, 1977.

Daniel, Walter C. Black Journals of the United States. Westport, CT:
    Greenwood, 1982.

Davis, Ralph. The Negro Newspaper in Chicago. Master's thesis,
    University of Chicago, 1939.

Demeter, John. Winter in America. Notes on the Media and Race. Radical

America   20 (September-October 1986):63-71.

Duke, Lois L. _Cultural Redemption of News: Racial Issues in South Carolina, 1954-1984_. Doctoral dissertation, University of South Carolina, 1986. UMO # 862668.

Ely, Melvin P. _Amos 'N' Andy: Lineage, Life, and Legacy_. Doctoral dissertation, Princeton University, 1985. UMO # 8526826. [621 pp.].

Emerson, Frank E. _The Community News Service: A Structural-Functional Analysis and Evaluation_. Doctoral dissertation, New York University, 1981. UMO # 8210913. [Reporting black and Puerto Rican news in New York City].

Ethnic Diversity: Challenging the Media. _Media and Values_ 43 (Spring 1988):entire issue.

Eure, Dexter D., Sr. Newspapers and their Relationship to the Black Agenda. _Trotter Institute Review_ 1 (Summer 1987):16-19.

Fife, Marilyn D. Black Image in American TV: The First Two Decades. _Black Scholar_ (November 1974):7-15.

Finkle, Lee. _Forum for Protest: The Black Press During World War II_. Fairleigh Dickinson University Press, 1975.

Fultz, Guy M. _"Agitate then, Brother": Education in the Black Monthly Periodical Press, 1900-1930_. Doctoral dissertation, Howard University, 1987. UMO # 8722683.

Gabler, Neal. _An Empire of Their Own. How the Jews Invented Hollywood_. New York: Crown, 1988.

Gaines, Jane. White Privilege and Looking Relations: Race and Gender in Feminist Film Theory. _Cultural Critique_ 4 (Fall 1986).

Gallagher, Brian. Racist Ideology and Black Abnormality in _The Birth of a Nation_. _Phylon_ 43 (March 1982):68-76.

Gandy, O. H., Jr. and P. Metabane. Television and Social Perceptions among African Americans and Hispanics. In: Molefi Kete Asante and William B. Gudyburst (eds.); _Handbook of International and Intercultural Communication_ Newbury Park, CA: Sage, 1989.

Gelbspan, Ross. Study: Media in Boston Reinforce Racism by News Coverage Decisions. _Boston Globe_ January 28, 1987.

Go, Rance and Godart H. Wong. Bad Times on Gold Mountain. _Bridge_ 3 (June 1974):22-27. [Critical analysis of a broadcast documentary on Chinese American life].

Gray, H. Television and the New Black Man: Black Male Images in Prime-Time Situation Comedy. _Media, Culture and Society_ 9 (April 1986):223-42.

Greenberg, Bradley S. and Gerhard J. Hanneman. Racial Attitudes and the Impact of TV Blacks. _Educational Broadcasting Review_ 4 (April 1970):27-34.

Greenberg, Bradley S. and others. _Mexican Americans and the Mass Media._ Norwood, NJ: Ablex, 1983.

Gresson, Aaron D. _The Dialectics of Betrayal: Sacrifice, Violation, and Oppressed._ Norwood, NJ: Ablex, 1981. [Afro-Americans and mass media].

Gutierrez, Felix. _Through Anglo Eyes: Chicanos as Portrayed in the News Media._ August 1978. ERIC ED 159 693.

Harkey, Ira. Over and Under the Editor's Desk [How the Pascagoula Chronicle-Star and Moss Point Advertiser Handles the Negro in the News]. _Chronicle Star_ (Mississippi) June 23, 1950.

Harrington, Richard. Race Lines on the Radio: What Color is Pop? _Washington Post_ February 7, 1982.

Harris, Jay T. (ed.) _Minority Employment in Daily Newspapers._ Evanston, IL: School of Journalism, Northwestern University, 1978.

Heiser, David W. _Asian-American Journalism: A Brief Historical Analysis._ Master's thesis, University of Texas, 1981.

Hellwig, David J. The Afro-American Press and Woodrow Wilson's Mexican Policy, 1913-1917. _Phylon_ 48 (Winter 1987):distributed late 1988.

Hicks, Gay. _Black-owned Radio Stations (1945-1978)._ Master's thesis, University of Missouri, 1978.

Himmelstein, Hal. _Television Myth and the American Mind._ New York: Praeger, 1984.

Hogan, Lawrence D. _A Black National News Service: The Associated Negro Press and Claude Barnett, 1919-1945._ Fairleigh Dickinson University Press, 1983.

Hogan, Lawrence D. _A Black National News Service: Claude Barnett, the Associated Negro Press, and Afro-American Newspapers, 1919-1945._ Doctoral dissertation, Indiana University, 1978. UMO # 7906700.

Holly, Ellen. The Role of Media in the Programming of an Underclass. _Black Scholar_ 10 (January-February 1979):31-37.

Hwang, David. Are Movies Ready for Real Orientals? _New York Times_ August 11, 1985.

Inscol, John C. _The Clansman_ on Stage and Screen: North Carolina Reacts [_Birth of a Nation_]. _North Carolina Historical Magazine_ 64 (Spring 1987):139-61.

Jackson, Anthony (ed.) _Black Families and the Medium of Television._ Ann

Arbor, MI: Bush Program in Child Development and Social Policy, University of Michigan, 1982.

Johnson, Charles S. The Rise of the Negro Magazine. _Journal of Negro History_ 13 (January 1928):7-21.

Johnson, Fern L. and R. Buttny. White Listeners' Responses to 'Sounding Black': The Effects of Message Content on Judgements about Language. _Communication Monographs_ 49 (1982):33-49.

Johnson, Kirk A. Black and White in Boston. _Columbia Journalism Review_ (May/June 1987). [Differential treatment of Blacks and whites in Black and white media in Boston].

Johnson, Kirk A. _Media Images of Boston's Black Community_. Boston: William Monroe Trotter Institute, University of Massachusetts, Boston, January 28, 1987.

Jones, Alex S. Black Papers: Businesses with a Mission. _New York Times_ August 17, 1987. [N.Y.C.].

Jones, Patricia. Some Declaration of Independents. Black Filmakers Reclaim Their Roots. _Village Voice_ August 27, 1980.

Joyce, Donald F. _Gatekeepers of Black Culture: Black-Owned Book Publishing in the United States, 1817-1981_. Westport, CT: Greenwood, 1983.

Kaku, Michio. Racism in the Comics. _Bridge_ 3 (February 1974):25-29. [Anti-Asian racism].

Kalmanir, Karen A. A Strange Animal: The FCC and Broadcast EEO. _Communications and the Law_ 6 (April 1984):25-46.

Keller, Gary (ed.) _Chicano Cinema: Research, Reviews, and Resources_. Binghampton, NY: Bilingual, 1985.

Kennedy, Lisa. Review of "The Glaring Light: TV Coverage of Civil Rights in the Peabody Collection," American Museum of the Moving Image, New York City. _Village Voice_ April 18, 1989.

King, Wayne. Fact vs. Fiction in Mississippi. _New York Times_ December 4, 1988. [The film _Mississippi Burning_, about the murder of three civil rights workers James Chaney, Michael Schwerner, and Andrew Goodman].

Kinley-Cooper, Kimberly. _Transition in Print: A Southern Town's Newspaper Coverage of Black Events Surrounding Desegregation_. Master's thesis, University of South Carolina, 1987.

Klassen, T. C. and O. V. Johnson. Sharpening of the _Blade_: Black Consciousness in Kansas, 1892-97. _Journalism Quarterly_ 63 (Summer 1986):298-304. [Parsons, KS].

Kneebone, John T. _Southern Liberal Journalists and the Issue of Race,_

1920-1944. Chapel Hill, NC: University of North Carolina Press, 1985.

Koppes, Clayton R. and Gregory D. Black. Blacks, Loyalty, and Motion-Picture Propaganda in World War II. Journal of American History 73 (September 1986):383-406.

Kreiling, Albert. The Rise of Black Consumer Magazines: The Case of the "Half-Century". August 1980. ERIC ED 189 632. [Published in Chicago, 1916-1925].

Lamar, O. Sylvia. Black Women in Television, 1981: Their Role and Scope in Florida's Network Affiliate Stations. Master's thesis, University of Florida, 1981.

Leab, Daniel J. From Sambo to Superspade: The Black Experience in Motion Pictures. Boston: Houghton Mifflin, 1975.

Leab, Daniel J. The Gamut from A to B: The Image of the Black in Pre-1915 Movies. Political Science Quarterly 88 (March 1973):53-70.

Lee, Spike. The Instigator. Life 11 (Spring 1988):100.

Lewis, Freda D. The Jackson Advocate: The Rise and Eclipse of a Leading Black Newspaper in Mississippi, 1939-1964. Master's thesis, Iowa State University, 1985.

Liebert, Robert M. Effects of Television on Children and Adolescents. Journal of Development and Behavioral Pediatrics 7 (February 1986):43-48.

Lowry, Dennis T. Racial and Religious Bias on Radio Call-in Programs. A Philadelphia Study. Philadelphia: American Jewish Committee, June 1981.

MacDonald, J. Fred. Blacks and White TV: Afro-Americans in Television Since 1948. Chicago: Nelson-Hall, 1983.

Martin, Michael T. The Afro-American Image in Film and Television: The Legitimization of the Racial Divisions in the American Social Order. Presence Africaine 124 (1982):144-67.

Martindale, C. The White Press and Black America. Westport, CT: Greenwood.

Martinez, Thomas M. Advertising and Racism: The Case of the Mexican-American. El Grito (Summer 1969).

Martinez, Thomas M. and Jose Peralez. Chicanos and the Motion Picture. La Raza 1 (1971).

Mattelart, Armand and Seth Siegelaube (eds.) Communication and Class Struggle. Vol I: Capitalism and Imperialism. New York: International General, 1979.

McCallum, Joseph P. The Rhetoric of Ethnic Journalism: The
    Filipino-American Press and Its Washington, D.C. Audience. Doctoral
    dissertation, Catholic University of America, 1987. UMO # 8717098.

McFarland, Donna A. Black Ownership of Commercial Television Stations in
    the Continental United States: A Historical, Critical and Legal
    Analysis. Master's thesis, University of Kansas, 1979.

Media Network and Center for Third World Organizing. Images of Color: A
    Guide to Media from and for Asian, Black, Latino and Native American
    Communitites. Oakland, CA: Center for Third World Organizing, 1987.

Meier, August and Elliott Rudwick, editorial advisers. The Claude A.
    Barnett Papers: The Associated Negro Press [198 microfilm reels].
    Frederick, MD: University Publications of America, 1987.

Merritt, B. D. Jesse Jackson and Television: Black Image Presentation
    and Affect in the 1984 Democratic Campaign Debates. Journal of Black
    Studies 16 (June 1986):347-67.

Miller, Loren. Uncle Tom in Hollywood. Crisis 41 (November 1934):329,
    336.

Miller, Sally M. (ed.) The Ethnic Press in the United States: A
    Historical Perspective and Handbook. Westport, CT: Greenwood, 1986.

Moreland, Pamela. Black Magazines: Publishing Field's 'Invisible' Giant
    Flexes Its Muscles. Los Angeles Times October 4, 1981.

Morrow, Frank S., Jr. The U.S. Power Structure and the Mass Media.
    Doctoral dissertation, University of Texas, 1984. UMO # 8728688.

Murrill, Bridgette B. Media Portrayal of Minorities: The Jesse Jackson
    Campaign of 1984. Master's thesis, University of North Carolina,
    Chapel Hill, 1987.

Native North American Americans and the Media. Anthropologia 25
    (1983):entire issue.

Neufield, Amos. Bomb in Gilead. A Look at Costa-Gavras' Betrayed.
    Jewish Frontier 55 (November-December 1988):23-26. [Film about
    racism and antisemitism in U.S.].

Newman, Mark A. Entrepreneurs of Profit and Pride: From Black-Appeal to
    Radio Soul. Doctoral dissertation, University of California, Los
    Angeles, 1986. UMO # 8712310. [1929-1960].

Obatala, J. K. Blacks on TV: A Replay of Amos 'n' Andy? Los Angeles
    Times November 26, 1974.

O'Sullivan, Theresa H. A Content Analysis of Black Characters in
    Advertisements in Home Fashion Magazines, 1962-1982. Master's
    thesis, California State University, Chico, 1983.

Patterson, Pat. Race and the Media in the 1980's. In: James D.

Williams (ed.), The State of Black America 1982, pp. 239-63. New York: National Urban League, January 14, 1982.

Payne, Les. Black Reporters, White Press - and the [Jesse] Jackson Campaign. Columbia Journalism Review (July-August 1984).

Poindexter, Paula M. and Carolyn A. Stroman. Blacks and Television: A Review of the Research Literature. Journal of Broadcasting 25 (Spring 1981):103-22.

Pollard, Kevin D. Eddie Murphy Sends Oscar a Message. Boston Globe April 16, 1988. [Blacks in the movies].

Rainville, Raymond E. and Edward McCormick. Extent of Covert Racial Prejudice in Pro-Football Announcers' Speech. Journalism Quarterly (Spring 1977):20-26.

Reid, Mark A. Black-Oriented Film (1961-1977): Form, Black Culture, Ideological Content. Doctoral dissertation, University of Iowa, 1988. UMO # 8815127.

Roberts, C. The Presentation of Blacks in Television Newscasts. Journalism Quarterly 52 (1975).

Rubin, Bernard (ed.) Small Voices and Great Trumpets: Minorities and the Media. New York: Praeger, 1980.

Ruggles, Robert M. Wanted: Minorities in the Newsroom. School Press Review 55 (December 1979):2-7.

Saxton, Alexander. Problems of Class and Race in the Origins of Mass Circulation Press. American Quarterly 36 (1984):211-35.

Schuyler, George S. Freedom of the Press in Mississippi. Crisis 43 (October 1936).

Seko, Alan K. The Japanese Evacuation Issue of 1942: A Content Analysis of the Editorial Pages of Nine California Newspapers. Master's thesis, University of Utah, 1979.

Selman-Earnest, Cora. Black Owned Radio and Television Stations in the United States from 1950-1982: A Descriptive Study. Doctoral dissertation, Wayne State University, 1985. UMO # 8605043.

Shankman, Arnold. The Image of Mexico and the Mexican-American in the Black Press, 1890-1935. Journal of Ethnic Studies 3 (Summer 1975):43-56.

Shankman, Arnold. The Image of the Italian in the Afro-American Press 1886-1936. Italian Americana 4 (Fall/Winter 1978):30-49.

Shipp, E. R. Black Journalists Gather for 20 Years' Reflection. New York Times August 31, 1988.

Simon, Rita J. Public Opinion and the Immigrant: Mass Media Coverage,

<u>1880-1980</u>. Lexington, MA: Lexington Books, 1985.

Snead, James A. Images of Blacks in Black Independent Films: A Brief
    Survey. <u>In</u>: Mbye B. Cham and Claire Andrade-Watkins (ed.),
    <u>Blackframes. Critical Perspectives on Black Independent Cinema</u>, pp.
    16-25. Cambridge, MA: MIT Press, 1988.

Sterritt, David. Minorities in the Media. <u>Christian Science Monitor</u> May
    9-10, 1983.

Stevens, John D. <u>"Color" in the Comic Strips: Racial Steriotyping Trends
    in Black and in White Newspapers</u>, 1976. ERIC ED 157 081.

Stroman, C. A. The Socialization of Influence of Television on Black
    Children. <u>Journal of Black Studies</u> 15 (September 1984):79-100.

Suggs, Henry L. <u>P.B. Young, Newspapermean: Race, Politics, and
    Journalism in the New South, 1910-62</u>. Charlottesville: University
    Press of Virginia, 1988.

Suggs, Henry L. (ed.) <u>The Black Press in the South, 1865-1979</u>.
    Westport, CT: Greenwood, 1983.

Sylvie, George. <u>Black Journalists in the Newsroom: A Study of
    Educational and Career Patterns</u>. Master's thesis, University of
    Missouri, 1978.

Torras, Luis R. Distortions in Celluloid: Hispanics and Film. <u>Agenda</u>
    11 (May-June 1981):37-40.

Turner, Patricia A. Reel Blacks. <u>Trotter Institute Review</u> 1 (Summer
    1987):19-21. [Analysis of two films, <u>Gremlins</u> (1984) and <u>Little Shop
    of Horrors</u> (1986)].

Twitchin, John (ed.) <u>The Black and White Media Show: Handbook for the
    Study of Racism and Television</u>. Stoke-on-Trent: Trentham Books,
    1988. [Britain].

Tyler, Bruce M. Racist Art and Politics at the Turn of the Century.
    <u>Journal of Ethnic Studies</u> 15 (Winter 1988):85-103. ["Birth of a
    Nation" film].

Wallace, Michele. She's Gotta Have It. School Daze. <u>Nation</u> June 4,
    1988.

Wang, Caroline. White 'Asians' Back in Movies. <u>Asian Week</u> July 5, 1986.

Warner, Malcolm-Jamal with Daniel Paisner. Cosby, Racism and Me. <u>TV
    Guide</u> 36 (September 24, 1988):4-7.

Washburn, Patrick S. <u>A Question of Sedition. The Federal Government's
    Investigation of the Black Press During World War II</u>. New York:
    Oxford University Press, 1986.

Waters, Beth A. <u>A Historical Examination of Black Women in Broadcast News,</u>

1964 to the Present. Master's thesis, University of South Carolina, 1987.

Weigel, Russell H. and Paul W. Howes. Race Relations on Children's Television. Journal of Psychology 111 (May 1982):109-12.

Weigel, Russell H. and others. Race Relations on Prime Time Television. Journal of Personality and Social Psychology 39 (November 1980).

Weyr, Thomas. Minorities in Publishing. Publishers Weekly October 17, 1980.

Wilson, Clint C., II and Felix Gutierrez. Minorities and Media. Diversity and the End of Mass Communication. Beverly Hills, CA: Sage, 1985.

Wimmer, Kurt A. Deregulation and the Market Failure in Minority Programming: The Socioeconomic Dimensions of Broadcast Reform. Master's thesis, Syracuse University, 1987.

Wimmer, Kurt A. Deregulation and Market Failure in Minority Programming: The Socioeconomic Dimensions of Broadcast Reform. COMM-ENT 8 (Spring-Summer 1986):329-480.

Winston, Michael R. Racial Consciousness and the Evolution of Mass Communications in the United States. Daedalus (Fall 1982):171-82.

Won-Doornink, Nyong Jin. Television Viewing and Acculturalization of Korean Immigrants. Amerasia 14 (1988):79-92.

Wong, Eugene F. On Visual Media Racism: Asians in the American Motion Pictures. Doctoral dissertation, University of Denver, 1978. UMO # 7823800. [1930-1975].

Wong, Eugene F. On Visual Media Racism: Asians in the American Motion Pictures. New York: Arno Press, 1978.

Wong, William. Asians and the San Francisco Media. Bridge 5 (Winter 1977):34-36.

Zogby, James. Jewish Souls Arab Bones. Propaganda Review 2 (Summer 1988):15-20. [Anti-Arab bias of American media].

Mass Media Bibliography

Bataille, Gretchen M. and Charles L. P. Silet (comps.) Images of American Indians on Film: An Annotated Bibliography. New York: Garland, 1985.

Culpepper, Betty M. (comp.) Portrayal of Blacks in the Media: A Selected Bibliography. Washington, D.C.: Moorland-Spingarn Research Center, Howard University, January 1982.

413

Hill, George H. and Sylvia Saverson Hill (comps.) Blacks on Television:
     A Selectively Annotated Bibliography Metuchen, NJ: Scarecrow Press,
     1985.

Hyatt, Marshall (comp.) The Afro-American Cinematic Experience.
     Wilmington, DE: Scholarly Resources, 1983.

La Brie, Henry G. (comp.) A Survey of Black Newspapers (third edition).
     Kennebunkport, ME: Mercer House, 1980.

Martindale, Carolyn (comp.) The White Press and Black America.
     Westport, CT: Greenwood, 1986.

Powers, Anne (comp.) Blacks in American Movies: A Selected
     Bibliography. Metuchen, NJ: Scarecrow Press, 1974.

Snorgrass, J. William and Gloria Woody (comps.) Blacks and Media: A
     Selected Annotated Bibliography, 1962-1982. Gainesville, FL:
     University Presses of Florida, 1987.

Woll, A. L. and R. M. Miller (comps.) Ethnic and Racial Images in
     American Film and Television: Historical Essays and Bibliography.
     New York: Garland, 1987.

[See also sections 10, 20, 36, 43, 46, 60, and 77]

49. Migration

The South, with all its race prejudice, would rather fight than lose its great black laboring force.

    - W. E. B. Du Bois, "The Negro Race in the United States of America," (1911).

Athearn, Robert G. In Search of Canaan: Black Migration to Kansas, 1879-80. University Press of Kansas, 1978.

Barr, Alwyn. Black Migration into Southwestern Cities, 1865-1900. In: Gary W. Gallagher (ed.), Essays on Southern History: Written in Honor of Barnes F. Lathrop. Austin: General Libraries, University of Texas, 1980.

Bontemps, Arna and Jack Conroy. Anyplace But Here. New York: Hill and Wang, 1966.

Brown, Frederick J. The Northward Movement of the Colored Population. A Statistical Study. Baltimore, MD, 1897.

Brown, Phil. Negro Labor Moves Northward. Opportunity 1 (May 1923):5-6.

Brunn, Stanley D. Where Have All the Mississippians Gone? Mississippi Geographer 5 (Spring 1977):5-10. [1960-1970].

Carlson, Shirley J. Black Migration to Pulaski County, Illinois, 1860-1900. Illinois Historical Journal 80 (Spring 1987):37-46.

Crew, S. R. The Great Migration of Afro-Americans, 1915-40. Monthly Labor Review 110 (March 1987).

Davis, P. O. Negro Exodus and Southern Agriculture. American Review of Reviews 68 (October 1923):401-7.

Dillingham, Harry C. and D. F. Sly. The Mechanical Cotton Picker, Negro Migration and the Integration Movement. Human Organization 25 (1966):344-51.

Donald, Henderson. The Negro Migration of 1916-1918. Journal of Negro History 6 (October 1921):383-498.

Du Bois, W. E. B. The Migration of Negroes. Crisis 14 (June 1917):63-66.

Du Bois, W. E. B. [U.S. Dept. of Labor tries to dissuade Blacks from going North]. Crisis 15 (April 1918).

Espada, Frank. Puerto Rican Diaspora Documentary Project. Left Curve No. 12.

Farley, Reynolds. The Urbanization of Negroes in the United States.

Journal *of* *Social* *History* (Spring 1968).

Fligstein, Neil. *Going* *North:* *Migration* *of* *Blacks* *and* *Whites* *from* *the* *South,* *1900-1950*. New York: Academic Press, 1981.

Fligstein, Neil. The Transformation of Southern Agriculture and the Migration of Blacks and White, 1930-1940. *International* *Migration* *Review* 17 (Summer 1983):268-90.

Gill, Flora. *Economics* *and* *the* *Black* *Exodus*. New York: Garland, 1979. [1910-1970].

Gill, Flora. *The* *Economics* *of* *the* *Black* *Exodus*. Doctoral dissertation, Stanford University, 1974.

Gist, F. W. Migratory Habits of the Negro Worker Under Past and Present Conditions. *Manufacturers* *Record* (March 13, 1924): 77-9.

Gottlieb, Peter. *Making* *Their* *Own* *Way.* *Southern* *Blacks'* *Migration* *to* *Pittsburgh,* *1916-30*. Urbana: University of Illinois Press, 1987.

Grant, Robert B. *Black* *Man* *Comes* *to* *the* *City:* *A* *Documentary* *Account* *from* *the* *Great* *Migration* *to* *the* *Great* *Depression,* *1915-1930*. Chicago, IL: Nelson-Hall, 1975.

Grossman, James R. Blowing the Trumpet: The *Chicago* *Defender* and Black Migration during World War II. *Illinois* *Historical* *Journal* 78 (Summer 1985):82-96.

Grossman, James R. (ed.) *Black* *Sources* *in* *the* *Era* *of* *the* *Great* *Migration,* *1916-1929*. Frederick, MD: University Publications of America [Federal government materials].

Hamilton, Roy L. *Expectations* *and* *Realities* *of* *a* *Migrant* *Group:* *Black* *Migration* *from* *the* *South* *to* *Milwaukee*. Master's thesis, University of Wisconsin, Milwaukee, 1982.

Harris, Abram. Negro Migration to the North. *Current* *History* 20 (September 1924):921-5.

Hawkins, Hower C. Trends in Black Migration from 1863-1960. *Phylon* 34 (June 1973):140-52.

Haynes, George. Negro Migration. *Opportunity* (October 1924):303-6.

Henri, Florette. *Black* *Migration:* *Movement* *North,* *1900-1920*. Garden City, NJ: Anchor Press, 1975.

Higgs, Robert. The Boll Weevil, the Cotton Economy, and Black Migration, 1910-1930. *Agricultural* *History* 50 (1976):335-50.

History Task Force, Centro. *Labor* *Migration* *under* *Capitalism:* *The* *Puerto* *Rican* *Experience*. New York: Monthly Review Press, 1979.

Johnson, Charles S. How Much Is the Migration a Flight from Persecution.

Opportunity 1 (1923):272-74.

Johnson, Charles S. How Much Is the Migration a Flight from Persecution?
In: August Meier and Elliot Rudwick (eds.), The Black Community in
Modern America, II. New York, 1969.

Johnson, Daniel M. and Rex R. Campbell. Black Migration in America: A
Social Demographic History. Durham, NC: Duke University Press,
1981.

Johnson, Guy. Negro Migration and Its Consequences. Social Forces 2
(March 1924):404-8.

Jones, Marcus E. Black Migration in the United State with Emphasis on
Selected Central Cities. San Francisco, CA: R and E Research
Asociates, 1980. [1950s-1970s].

Kasl, Stanislav V. and Lisa Berkman. Health Consequences of Migration.
Annual Review of Public Health 4 (1983):69-90.

Katznelson, Ira. Black Men, White Cities: Race, Politics and Migration
in the United States, 1900-1930, and Britain, 1948-1968. New York:
Oxford University Press, 1973.

Kellog, John. Negro Urban Clusters in the Post-Bellum South.
Geographical Review 67 (1977):310-21.

Kirby, Jack T. The Southern Exodus, 1910-1960: A Primer for Historians.
Journal of Southern History 49 (November 1983):585-600.

Kulikoff, Allan. Uprooted Peoples: Black Migrants in the Age of the
American Revolution, 1790-1820. In: Ira Berlin and Ronald
Hoffman (eds.), Slavery and Freedom in the Age of the American
Revolution, pp. 143-71. Charlottesville, Va., 1983.

Laing, James. Negro Migration to the Mining Fields of West Virginia.
Proceedings of the West Virginia Academy of Science 10 (1936).

Maldonado-Denis, Manuel (Translated by Roberto S. Crespi). The
Emigration Dialectic: Puerto Rico and the U.S.A. New York:
International Publishers, 1980.

Marks, Carole. Farewell - We're Good and Gone. The Great Black
Migration. Bloomington: Indiana University Press, 1989.

Marullo, Sam. The Migration of Blacks to the North 1911-1918. Journal of
Black Studies 15 (1985):291-306.

McDougall, Gerald S. and Harold Bunce. Race, Moving Status, and Urban
Services in Central Cities. Social Science Research 15 (March
1986):82-96.

McHugh, K. E. Determinants of Black Interstate Migration, 1965-1970 and
1975-80. Annals of Regional Science 22 (March 1988).

Mier, R. and R. P. Giloth. Spatial Change and Social Justice in Chicago In: Robert A. Beauregard (ed.), Economic Reconstructing and Political Response. Newbury Park, CA: Sage, 1988.

Mohr, Eugene V. Intellectuals and Emigrants: Puerto Rican Dilemma. R. Interam. 12 (Winter 1982-83):521-33.

Morales, Julio, Jr. Puerto Rican Poverty and the Migration to Elsewhere: Waltham, Massachusetts: A Case Study. Doctoral dissertation, Brandeis University, 1979. UMO # 8012759.

Morales, Julio, Jr. Puerto Rican Poverty and Migration: We Just Had to Try Elsewhere. New York: Praeger, 1986.

O'Hare, William P. Blacks on the Move: A Decade of Demographic Change. Washington, D.C.: Joint Center for Political Studies, 1982.

Painter, Nell Irvin. Exodusters: Black Migration to Kansas after Reconstruction. New York: Knopf, 1977.

Painter, Nell Irvin. Millenarian Aspects of the Exodus to Kansas of 1879. Journal of Social History 9 (Spring 1976):331-38.

Pleck, Elizabeth H. Black Migration and Poverty. Boston 1865-1900. New York: Academic Press, 1979.

Schwendenmann, Glenn. The 'Exodusters' on the Missouri. Kansas Historical Quarterly 29 (1963):25-40.

Shofner, Jerrell H. Florida and the Black Migration. Florida Historical Quarterly 57 (January 1979):267-288.

Smith, T. Lynn. The Redistribution of the Negro Population of the United States, 1910-1960. Journal of Negro History 51 (July 1966):155-73.

Valdez, Armando and others (eds.) The State of Chicano Research on Family, Labor, and Migration. Stanford, CA: Stanford Center for Chicano Research, 1983.

Vickery, William. The Economics of the Negro Migration. 1900-1960. Doctoral dissertation, University of Chicago, 1969.

Wilkie, Jane R. The Black Urban Population of the Pre-Civil War South. Phylon 37 (September 1976):250-62.

Wilkie, Jane R. The United States Population by Race and Urban-Rural Residence 1790-1860: Reference Tables. Demography 13 (February 1976):139-48.

Wilkie, Jane R. Urbanization and De-urbanization of the Black Population before the Civil War. Demography 13 (August 1976).

Williams, Nudie E. Black Newspapers and the Exodusters of 1879. Kansas History 8 (Winter 1985-86):217-25.

Woodson, Carter G. A Century of Negro Migration. Washington, D.C.:
    Association for the Study of Negro Life and History, 1918.

Migration Bibliography

Ross, Frank A. and Louise V. Kennedy (comps.) A Bibliography of Negro
    Migration. New York: Columbia University Press, 1934.

[See also sections 7, 15, 27, 34, and 47]

50. Military

The colored troops are leading in the Mexican foray. ... So in America, in Europe, and in Africa, black men are fighting for the liberties of white men and pulling their chestnuts out of the fire. One of these bright mornings black men are going to learn how to fight for themselves.

- W. E. B. Du Bois, "To the Rescue, " 1916.

Anderson, Clinton E. Historical Profile of Adult Basic Education Programs in the United States Army. Doctoral dissertation, Columbia University, 1986. UMO # 8611659.

Austerman, Wayne R. Black Regulars: The 41st Infantry in Texas, 1867-1869. Master's thesis, Lousiana State University, 1977.

Basso, Ralph. Nationalism, Nativism, and the Black Soldier: Daniel Ullman, A Biography of a Man Living in a Period of Transition, 1810-1892. Doctoral dissertation, St. John's University, 1986. UMO # 8613747.

Belli, Robert E. Racism: Problem for the Officer. Maxwell Air Force Base, AL: Air War College, Air University, April 1973.

Berlin, Ira and others (eds.) Freedom: A Documentary History of Emancipation, 1861-1867. Series II: The Black Military Experience. New York: Cambridge University Press, 1983.

Berryman, Sue E. Who Serves? The Persistent Myth of the Underclass Army. Boulder, CO: Westview Press, 1986.

Biggs, Bradley. The Triple Nickles: America's First All-Black Paratroop Unit. Archon, 1986.

Billington, Monroe. Black Soldiers at Fort Selden, New Mexico, 1866-1891. New Mexico Historical Review 62 (January 1987):65-80.

Binkin, Martin and Jan Eitelberg. Blacks and the Military. Washington, D.C.: Brookings Institution Press, 1982.

Bogart, Leo (ed.) Social Research and the Desegregation of the US Army. Chicago: Markham, 1969.

Butler, John Sibley. Inequality in the Military: An Examination of Promotion Time for Black and White Enlisted Men. American Sociological Review 41 (1976):807-818.

Carlisle, David K. Black Veterans: Justice Overdue. New York Times November 11, 1988.

Caro, Manuel. A Chicano in Vietnam. Newsweek October 17, 1988.

Carroll, John M. (ed.) The Black Military Experience in the American
    West. New York: Liveright, 1974.

Cooper, David I., Jr. Race in the Military: The Tarnished Sword.
    Retired Officer, February 1971.

Culver, Thomas. Race at German Bases. Civil Liberties (A.C.L.U.)
    January 1972.

Dalfiume, Richard M. Desegregation of the U.S. Armed Forces. Fighting on
    Two Fronts, 1939-1953. Columbia: University of Missouri Press,
    1971.

Du Bois, W. E. B. An Essay Toward a History of the Black Man in the Great
    War. Crisis 18 (June 1919):63-87. [World War I].

Du Bois, W. E. B. [Universal military service means universal
    segregation]. Chicago Defender April 24, 1948.

Duus, Masayo U. Unlikely Liberators: The Men of the 100th and 442nd.
    [Translated by Peter Duus]. Honolulu: University of Hawaii Press,
    1987. [100th Infantry Battalion and 442d Regimented Combat Team].

Erving, Lee. It Can Happen Here. Family, Supplement of Army Times,
    August 1971. [Racial conflict at Travis Air Force Base, May 22-24,
    1971].

Fletcher, Marvin E. America's First Black General: Benjamin O. Davis,
    Sr., 1880-1970. Lawrence, KS: University Press of Kansas, 1989.

Fletcher, Marvin E. The Black Soldier and Officer in the United States
    Army, 1891-1917. Columbia: University of Missouri Press, 1974.

Flipper, Henry O. The Colored Cadet at West Point. New York: Homer, Lee
    and Co., 1878.

Foner, Jack D. Blacks and the Military in American History: A New
    Perspective. New York: Praeger, 1974.

Fowler, Arlen L. The Black Infantry in the West, 1869-1891. Westport,
    CT: Greenwood, 1971.

Franco, Jere. Loyal and Heroic Service: The Navajos and World War II.
    Journal of Arizona History 27 (Winter 1986):391-406.

Garrant, Richard L. Racial Minority Understanding and Awareness
    Educational Programs in the Ft. G.G. Meade, Maryland Community.
    Doctoral dissertation, George Washington University, 1986. UMO #
    8607172.

Gatewood, Willard B., Jr. Alabama's Negro Soldier Experiment, 1898-1899.
    Journal of Negro History 57 (1972):333-51.

Gatewood, Willard B., Jr. Alonzo Clifton Mc Clennan: Black Midshipman
    from South Carolina, 1873-1874. South Carolina Historical Magazine

89 (January 1988):24-39.

Gatewood, Willard B., Jr. Black Americans and the White Man's Burden 1898-1903. Urbana: University of Illinois Press, 1975.

Gatewood, Willard B., Jr. John Hanks Alexander of Arkansas: Second Black Graduate of West Point. Arkansas Historical Quarterly 41 (Summer 1982):103-28.

Gatewood, Willard B., Jr. "Smoked Yankees" and the Struggle for Empire: Letters from Negro Soldiers, 1898-1902. Urbana: University of Illinois Press, 1971.

General Accounting Office. A Need to Address Illiteracy Problems in the Military Services. 1977. ERIC ED 164 893.

Gill, Gerald R. Afro-American Opposition to the United States' Wars of the Twentieth Century: Dissent, Discontent and Disinterest. Doctoral dissertation, Howard University, 1985. UMO # 8627903.

Gillis, Katherine A. The Performance of the Black Union Soldier in Mississippi. Master's thesis, Mississippi University for Women, 1978.

Gould, William Stuart. Racial Conflict in the U.S. Army. Race 15 (July 1973):1-24.

Gropman, Alan L. The Air Force Integrates: 1945-1964. Washington, D.C.: Office of Air Force History, 1978.

Halloran, Richard. The All-Volunteer Force is More Popular Than Ever. New York Times October 16, 1988.

Halloran, Richard. Blacks and Women Find Roads for Advancement through Life in Military. New York Times August 26, 1986.

Halloran, Richard. Navy is Studying Bias in Promotions. New York Times July 24, 1988.

Halloran, Richard. The Pride of the Military Has Become Its People. New York Times May 16, 1985.

Halloran, Richard. Wide Bias Against Minorities Found in Navy. New York Times December 20, 1988.

Halloran, Richard. Women, Blacks, Spouses Transforming the Military. New York Times August 25, 1986.

Halter, S. F. An Examination of the Quality and Future Military Enlisted Personnel: A Thesis. Monterey, CA: Naval Postgraduate School, December 1979.

Hargrove, Hondon B. Buffalo Soldiers in Italy: Black Americans in World War II. Jefferson, NC: McFarland, 1985.

Hastie, William H. On Clipped Wings: The Story of Jim Crow in the Army
    Air Corps. New York: NAACP, 1943.

Hayles, Robert and Ronald Perry. Racial Equality in the American Naval
    Justice System. Ethnic and Racial Studies 4 (1981).

Higginson, Thomas W. Army Life in a Black Regiment. Boston: Beacon,
    1962. [Civil War].

Hines, Charles A. Military Job Performance Evaluation Patterns in
    Intraracial and Interracial Dyads: Quantitative and Narrative
    Aspects. Doctoral dissertation, John Hopkins University, 1983. UMO
    # 8403095.

Hope, Richard O. Racial Strife in the U.S. Military: Toward the
    Elimination of Discrimination. New York: Praeger, 1979.

Johnson, Charles. The Army, the Negro, and the Civilian Conservation
    Corps: 1933-1942. Military Affairs 36 (1972):82-8.

Johnson, Hayden C. The Fighting 99th Air Squadron, 1941-45. New York:
    Vantage Press, 1987.

Johnson, Jesse J. (ed.) Black Women in the Armed Forces, 1942-1974.
    Hampton, VA: Johnson, 1975.

Keller, Ella T. Black Families in the Military System. Doctoral
    dissertation, Mississippi State University, 1980. UMO # 8021115.

King, Larry L. We've Been Ordered to Make this Thing Work [Desegregation
    of U.S. Army, 1948]. Parade Magazine February 19, 1984.

Lane, Ann J. The Brownsville Affair: National Crisis and Black Reaction.
    Port Washington, NY: Kennikat Press, 1971.

Langley, Harold D. The Negro in the Navy and Merchant Service, 1798-1860.
    Journal of Negro History 52 (October 1967):273-286.

Langley, Harold D. Social Reform in the United States Navy, 1798-1862.
    Urbana, IL: University of Illinois Press, 1967.

Lawrence, Ken. Thirty Years of Selective Service Racism, 1971. National
    Black Draft Counselors, 711 North Dearborn St., Chicago, IL 60605.

Leckie, William H. The Buffalo Soldiers: A Narrative of the Negro
    Cavalry in the West. Norman, OK: University of Oklahoma Press,
    1967.

Lee, Ulysses. United States Army in World War II. The Employment of
    Negro Troops. Washington, D.C.: GPO, 1966.

Linn, Brian M. The U.S. Army and Counterinsurgency in the Phillippine
    War, 1899-1902. Chapel Hill, NC: University of North Carolina
    Press, 1989.

Little, Arthur W. From Harlem to the Rhine. New York: Covici Friede, 1936.

MacGregor, Morris J. Integration of the Armed Forces, 1940-1965. Washington, D.C.: GPO, 1981.

MacGregor, Morris J. and Bernard C. Nalty (eds.) Blacks in the United States Armed Forces: Basic Documents. 13 vols. Scholarly Resources, 1977.

Maness, Lonnie E. The Fort Pillow Massacre: Fact or Fiction. Tennessee Historical Quarterly 45 (Winter 1986):287-315.

Marks, George P. III. The Black Press Views American Imperialism. 1971.

Massaquoi, Hans J. A Battle the Army Can't Afford to Lose. Ebony 29 (February 1974):116-124. [Racism in U.S. Army in Germany].

May, Robert E. Invisible Men: Blacks and the U.S. Army in the Mexican War. Historian 49 (August 1987):463-77.

McGlone, John D. A. Monuments and Memorials to Black Military History, 1775-1891. Doctoral dissertation, Middle Tennessee State University, 1985. UMO # 8603505.

McGuire, Phillip. Black Civilian Aides and the Problems of Racism and Segregation in the United States Armed Forces: 1940-1950. Doctoral dissertation, Howard University, 1975.

McGuire, Phillip. He Too Spoke for Democracy. Judge Hastie, World War II, and Black Soldier. Westport, CT: Greenwood, 1988.

McGuire, Phillip. Judge Hastie, World War II, and Army Racism. Journal of Negro History 62 (October 1977):351-362.

McGuire, Phillip. Taps for a Jim Crow Army: Letters from Black Soldiers in World War II. Santa Barbara, CA: ABC-CLIO, 1983.

McPherson, James M. The Negro's Civil War: How American Negroes Felt and Acted During the War for the Union. Urbana: University of Illinois Press, 1965.

Minoin, John A. Negro Soldiers in the Confederate Army. Crisis 77 (1970):230-2.

Moore, Brenda L. Effects of the All-Voluntary Force on Civilian Status Attainment of Black Men and Women. Doctoral dissertation, University of Chicago, 1987.

Moskos, Charles C., Jr. Racial Integration in the Armed Forces. American Journal of Sociology 72 (1966).

Motley, Mary P. (ed.). The Invisible Soldier: The Experience of the Black Soldier, World War II. Detroit, MI: Wayne State University Press, 1975.

Miller, Robert. Blacks in America's Wars. The Shift in Attitudes from the Revolutionary War to Vietnam. New York: Monad Pres, 1974.

Murray, Paul Thom, Jr. Blacks and the Draft: An Analysis of Institutional Racism, 1917-1971. Doctoral dissertation, Florida State University, 1972. UMO # 72-31420.

Nalty, Bernard C. Strength for the Fight. A History of Black Americans in the Military. New York: Free Press, 1986.

Nalty, Bernard C. and Morris J. MacGregor (eds.) Blacks in the Military: Essential Documents. Wilmington, DE: Scholarly Resources Inc., 1982.

Nordlie, Peter G., C. G. Friedman and G. R. Marbury. Race Relations in the Army: Policies, Problems, Programs. McLean, VA: Human Sciences Research, 1972.

Office of the Deputy Assistant Secretary of Defense for Equal Opportunity and Safety Policy, Department of Defense. Black Americans in Defense for Our Nation. Washington, D.C.: GPO, 1985.

Office of the Deputy Assistant Secretary of Defense for Equal Opportunity and Safety Policy. Hispanics in America's Defense. Washington, D.C.: Department of Defense, 1982.

Quarles, Benjamin. The Negro in the American Revolution. Chapel Hill, NC: University of North Carolina Press, 1961.

Racism in the Military: A New System for Rewards and Punishment. Congressional Record 118, Part 2 (October 14, 1972):E 8674-E 8688. [Congressional Black Caucus Report].

Redkey, Edwin S. Black Chaplains in the Union Army. Civil War History 33 (December 1987):331-50.

Rastani, Raymond. The Immigrant Soldier in the Frontier Army: 1865-1895. Master's thesis, University of New Hampshire, 1979.

Reynolds, David. The Churchill Government and the Black American Troops in Britain during World War II. Trans. Royal Historical Society 35 (1985):113-34.

Russell, Francis. Liberty to Slaves: Black Loyalists in the American Revolution. Timeline 4 (April-May 1987):3-15.

Schnexider, Alvin J. The Development of Racial Solidarity in the Armed Forces. Journal of Black Studies (June 1975):415-435.

Schnexider, Alvin J. Representation in the American Military and Its Implications for Public Policy. In: Winston A. Van Horne (ed.), Ethnicity and War. Milwaukee, WI: American Ethnic Studies Coordinating Committee, Urban Corridor Consortium, University of Wisconsin System, 1984.

Shibutani, Tamotsu. The Derelicts of Company K: A Sociological Study of Demoralization. Berkeley, CA: University of California Press, 1978. [Japanese-American army unit].

Smith, Frances W. Black Militia in Savannah, Georgia 1872-1905. Master's thesis, Georgia Southwestern College, 1981.

Smith, Graham. When Jim Crow Met John Bull. London: J.B. Tauris, 1987. [History of black GIs in Britain during World War II].

Steele, M. F. Condemnation of the Color Line in the Army. North American December 21, 1906.

Ware, Gilbert. Spider Webs and Racism in the Armed Forces. Urban League News (April, 1973).

Werrell, Kenneth P. Mutiny at Army Air Force Station 569: Bamber Bridge, England, June 1943. Aerospace Historian 22 (1975):202-9.

Westwood, Howard C. The Cause and Consequence of a Union Black Soldier's Mutiny and Execution. Civil War History 31 (September 1985):222-36.

Westwood, Howard C. Generals David Hunter and Rufus Saxton and Black Soldiers. South Carolina Hist. Magazine 86 (July 1985):165-81.

White, William B. The Military and the Melting Pot: The American Army and Minority Groups, 1865-1924. Doctoral dissertation, University of Wisconsin, 1968.

Military Bibliography

Cameron, Colin and Judith Blackstone (comps.) Minorities in the Armed Forces: A Selected, Occasionally Annotated Bibliography. Madison: Institute for Research on Poverty, University of Wisconsin, 1970.

Davis, Lenwood G. and George Hill (comps.) Blacks in the American Armed Forces, 1776-1983: A Bibliography. Westport, CT: Greenwood, 1985.

Slonaker, John (comp.) The U.S. Army and the Negro. Carlisle Barracks, PA: U.S. Army Military Research Collection, 1971. Also, supplement, 1972.

51. **Minorities**

*No slaves or children of slaves shall be taught to read or
write, in or at any school or academy in the [Choctaw] Nation.*

- The Choctaw Council, <u>Liberator</u>, September 22, 1854.

Abel, Annie H. <u>The American Indian as Slaveholder and Secessionist</u>. ...
    Vol 1 of <u>The Slaveholding Indians</u>. Cleveland, OH: Clark, 1915.
    Also, vol. 3.

Bailey, Kenneth R. A Judicious Mixture: Negroes and Immigrants in the
    West Virginia Mines, 1880-1917. <u>West Virginia History</u> 34 (1973).

Billington, Monroe. Black Slavery in Indian Territory: The Ex-Slave
    Narratives. <u>Chronicles of Oklahoma</u> 60 (Spring 1982):56-65.

Bowman, La Barbara. The Koreans: Corner Store Revolution. <u>Washington
    Post</u> May 28, 1979.

Churchill, Ward. [Critical Discussion of June Jordan's <u>On Call:
    Political Essays</u>]. <u>Journal of Ethnic Studies</u> 15 (Winter 1987):139-
    42.

Dale, Edward E. The Cherokees in the Confederacy. <u>Journal of Southern
    History</u> 13 (May 1947):159-85.

Deloria, Vine, Jr. Minorities and the Social Contract. <u>Georgia Law
    Review</u> 20 (Summer 1986):917-33.

Doran, Michael. Negro Slaves of the Five Civilized Tribes. <u>Annals of the
    Association of American Geographers</u> 68 (September 1978):335-50.

Douglas, Carlyle C. Korean Merchants Are Target of Black Anger. <u>New York
    Times</u> January 19, 1985. [N.Y.C.].

Ellison, Mary. Black Perceptions and Red Images: Indian and Black
    Literacy Links. <u>Phylon</u> 44 (Spring 1983):44-55.

Eng, Peter and Edward D. Sargent. A Troubled American Dream. <u>Washington
    Post</u> September 17, 1981. [Conflict between Korean shop-owners and
    blacks in Washington, D.C.].

Forbes, Jack D. <u>Black Africans and Native Americans: Color, Race and
    Caste in the Evolution of Red and Black People</u>. New York:
    Blackwell, 1988.

Forbes, Jack D. The Evolution of the Term Mulatto: A Chapter in Black-
    Native American Relations. <u>Journal of Ethnic Studies</u> 10 (Summer
    1982):45-66.

Forbes, Jack D. Mulattoes and People of Color in Anglo-North America:
    Implications for Black-Indian Relations. <u>Journal of Ethnic Studies</u>

12 (Summer 1984):17-61.

Forbes, Jack D. Mustees, Half-Breeds, and Zambos in Anglo North America: Aspects of Black-Indian Relations. American Indian Quarterly 7 (1983):57-83.

Fortune, T. Thomas. Good Niggers and Good Indians. Independent 51 (June 1899):1689-90.

Foster, Lawrence. Negro-Indian Relationships in the Southwest. New York: AMS Press, 1978.

Halliburton, Janet. Black Slavery in the Creek Nation. Chronicles of Oklahoma 56 (Fall 1978):298-314.

Halliburton, R., Jr. Black Slave Control in the Cherokee Nation. Journal of Ethnic Studies 3 (1975):23-35.

Halliburton, R., Jr. Origin of Black Slavery Among the Cherokees. Chronicles of Oklahoma 52 (Winter 1974-1975):483-96.

Halliburton, R., Jr. Red Over Black: Black Slavery Among the Cherokee Indians. Westport, CT: Greenwood, 1977.

Hellwig, David J. Afro-American Reactions to the Japanese and the Anti-Japanese Movement, 1906-1924. Phylon 38 (March 1977):93-104.

Hemley, David D. and T. Ozawa. Intra-racial and Minority Inter-racial Discrimination. Journal of Economics and Business 25 (Spring-Summer 1973).

Hornblower, Margot. Cultures Clash. Liberty (March-April 1988):24-26. [Hispanics and Hasidic Jews in Williamsburg, Brooklyn].

Hudson, Charles M. (ed.) Red, White, and Black: Symposium on Indians in the Old South. Athens, GA: University of Georgia Press, 1971.

Jeltz, Wyatt F. The Relations of Negroes and Choctaw and Chickasaw Indians. Journal of Negro History 33 (January 1948):24-37.

Jones, Rhett S. Black and Native American Relations before 1800. Western Journal of Black Studies 1 (September 1977):151-63.

Katz, William Loren. Blacks-Indians Alliance Has Deep Roots. New York Times March 2, 1988 (letter).

Kwong, Peter and Joann Lum. From Soul to Seoul. Village Voice July 12, 1988. [Koreans on 125th St., NYC].

Lazare, Daniel. New York's Latest Race Rift Pits Blacks Against Koreans. In These Times October 5, 1988.

Littlefield, Daniel F., Jr. Africans and Creeks: From the Colonial Period to the Civil War. Westport, CT: Greenwood, 1979. [Blacks as slaves of Creek Indians].

Littlefield, Daniel F., Jr. Africans and Seminoles: From Removal to
    Emancipation. Westport, CT: Greenwood, 1977.

Littlefield, Daniel F., Jr. The Cherokee Freedmen: From Emancipation to
    American Citizenship. Westport, CT: Greenwood, 1978.

Littlefield, Daniel F., Jr. The Chickasaw Freedmen: A People Without a
    Country. Westport, CT: Greenwood, 1980.

Mahon, John K. History of the Second Seminole War, 1835-1842.
    Gainesville, Fl: University of Florida Press, 1967. [Blacks in the
    war].

McAlexander, Hubert H. The Saga of a Mixed-Blood Chickasaw Dynasty.
    Journal of Mississippi History 49 (November 1987):288-300.

McLouglin, William G. Cherokees and Missionaries, 1789-1839. New Haven,
    CT: Yale University Press, 1984.

McLouglin, William G. Red Indians, Black Slavery, and White Racism:
    America's Slaveholding Indians. American Quarterly 26 (October
    1974):367-85.

Merrell, James H. The Racial Education of the Catawba Indians. Journal
    of Southern History 50 (August 1984):363-84. [Native Americans and
    Blacks].

Murray, Paul T. Who Is an Indian? Who Is a Negro? Virginia Indians in
    the World War II Draft. Virginia Magazine Hist. Biog. 95 (April
    1987):255-31.

Nash, Gary. Red, White and Black: Peoples of Early America. 2nd
    edition. Englewood Cliffs, NJ: Prentice-Hall, 1982.

Parry, Ellwood. The Image of the Indian and the Black Man in American
    Art, 1590-1900. New York: Braziller, 1974.

Perdue, Theda. Cherokee Planters, Black Slaves, and African Colonization.
    Chronicles of Ioklahoma 60 (Fall 1982):322-31.

Perdue, Theda. Slavery and the Evolution of Cherokee Society, 1540-1866.
    Knoxville, TN: University of Tennessee Press, 1979.

Porter, Kenneth W. The Negro on the American Frontier. New York: Arno,
    1976 (orig. 1971).

Reynolds, Pamela. Miami Blacks Say Racism by Hispanics Fueled Rioting.
    Boston Globe January 22, 1989.

Salholz, Eloise and others. A Conflict of the Have-nots. Newsweek
    December 12, 1988. [Hispanics and Blacks].

Schmalz, Jeffrey. Miami's New Ethnic Conflict: Haitians vs. American
    Blacks. New York Times February 19, 1989.

Searcy, Martha C.   The Introduction of African Slavery into the Creek
    Indian Nation.   Georgia Historical Quarterly 66 (Spring 1982):21-32.

Smith, C. Calvin.   The Oppressed Oppressors: Negro Slavery Among the
    Choctaw Indians of Oklahoma.   Red River Valley Hist. Review 2
    (1975):240-54.

Smith, J. Owens.   The Politics of Racial Inequality: A Systematic
    Comparative Macro-Analysis from the Colonial Period to 1970.
    Westport, CT: Greenwood, 1987.

Steele, C. Hoy.   Bonds between Indians and Other Racial Groups in an Urban
    Setting.   In: Rhoda J. Blumberg and Wendell J. Roye (eds.),
    Interracial Bonds.   Bayside, NY: General Hall, Inc., 1979.

Stubbs, Caroline L.   Slavery and the Creeks: Indians and Negro Slavery
    among the Creek Indians.   In: Ian W. Brown (ed.), Essays on the
    Ethnohistory of the North American Indian, vol. 3, pp. 133-50.   1984.

Usner, Daniel H., Jr.   American Indians on the Cotton Frontier: Changing
    Economic Relations with Citizens and Slaves in the Mississippi
    Territory.   Journal of American History 72 (September 1985):297-317.

Watts, Jill M.   'We Do Not Live For Ourselves Only':   Seminole Black
    Perceptions and the Second Seminole War.   UCLA Hist. Journal 7
    (1986):5-28.

Willis, William S.   Anthropology and Negroes on the Southern Colonial
    Frontier.   In: James C. Curtis and Lewis L. Gould (eds.), The Black
    Experience in America.   Austin: 1970.

Willis, William S.   Divide and Rule: Red, White, and Black in the
    Southeast.   Journal of Negro History 48 (July 1963):157-76.

Wright, J. Leitch, Jr.   A Note on the First Seminole War as Seen by the
    Indians, Negroes, and Their British Advisers.   Journal of Southern
    History 34 (November 1968):565-75.

Wright, J. Leitch, Jr.   Creeks and Seminoles. The Destruction and
    Regeneration of the Muscogulge People.   Lincoln: University of
    Nebraska Press, 1987.

Wrone, David R.   The Cherokee Act of Emancipation.   Journal of Ethnic
    Studies 1 (1973):87-90.

[See also sections 4, 8, 11, 24, 32, 34, 38, 41, 44, 52, 58, and 77]

52. Multiculturalism

This country has no value, except as the home of all races.
That is the idea underlying all our history.

- Wendell Phillips, Liberator, July 10, 1863.

Berlowitz, Marvin J. Multicultural Education: Fallacies and Alternatives.
    In: Marvin J. Berlowitz and Ronald S. Edari (eds.), Racism and the
    Denial of Human Rights: Beyond Ethnicity. Minneapolis, MN: MEP
    Publications, 1984.

Katz, Judy A. Multicultural Education: Games Educators Play.
    Integrateducation 18 (January-August 1980):101-104.

Leander, Terry. Multicultural Education and the Notion of Rights.
    Multicultural Teaching 1 (1983):36-40.

Lynch, James. Human Rights, Racism and the Multicultural Curriculum.
    Educational Review 37 (1985):141-152.

Lyseight-Jones, Pauline. More Equal. Times Educational Supplement
    December 3, 1982. [Multicultural education and racism].

Macias, J. The Hidden Curriculum of Papago Teachers: American Indian
    Strategies for Mitigating Cultural Discontinuity in Early Schooling.
    In: George Spindler and Louise Spindler (eds.), Interpretive
    Ethnography of Education at Home and Abroad. Hillsdale, NJ:
    Lawrence Erlbaum Associates, 1987.

Payne, Charles. Multicultural Education and Racism in American Schools.
    Theory Into Practice 23 (1984):124-131.

Pearl, Arthur. Can the Cause be the Cure. Journal of Teacher Education
    20 (1969):427-434. [Racism and teacher-training].

Rizvi, F. (ed.). Multiculturalism as an Educational Policy Geelong,
    Victoria: Deakin University Press, 1985.

Roe, Michael. Multiculturalism, Racism and the Classroom. Toronto:
    Canadian Education Association, 1982.

Sleeter, Christine E. and Carl A. Grant. An Analysis of Multicultural
    Education in the United States. Harvard Education Review 57
    (November 1987):421-43.

Thernstrom, Stephan and others (eds.) Harvard Encyclopedia of American
    Ethnic Groups. Cambridge, MA: Harvard University Press, 1986.

Multiculturalism Bibliography

Buttlar, Lois (comp.) Multicultural Education: A Guide to Reference
     Sources. Ethnic Forum 7 (1987):77-96.

53. Nationalism

Mr. Petit ... explained that he had never been able to induce teachers and scholars to sing any of the patriotic tunes; they said that it wasn't a free country for black people, and they could not call it a "happy land."

- Southern public figures visit New York's colored school on Mulberry Street but few children agree to sing in honoring them; Liberator, November 19, 1858.

Alston, Jaquelyn G. Comparative Nationalism: Definitions, Interpretations, and the Black American and British West African Experience to 1947 (second edition). Washington, D.C.: Historical Dimensions Press, 1985.

Aptheker, Herbert. Consciousness of Negro Nationality: An Historical Survey. Political Affairs 28 (June 1949):88-95.

Aptheker, Herbert. Consciousness of Negro Nationality in 1900. In: Toward Negro Freedom. New York: New Century, 1956.

Baraka, Amiri. Black Literature and the Afro-American Nation: The Urban Voice. In: Michael C. Jaye and others (eds.), Literature and the Urban Experience: Essays on the City and Literature, pp. 139-59. New Brunswick, NJ: Rutgers University Press, 1981.

Bell, Howard H. The Negro Emigration Movement, 1849-1854. A Phase of Negro Nationalism. Phylon 9 (Summer 1959):132-42.

Bolden, Darwin W. Economic Nationalism: The Case of the Afro-American. Afro-American Studies 1 (1970):97-101.

Bracey, John. [On Black Nationalism]. In: Bracey and others (eds.), Black Nationalism in America, pp. lvi-lvx. Indianapolis, IN: Bobbs-Merrill, 1970.

Bracey, John and others (eds.). Black Nationalism in America. Indianapolis, IN: Bobbs-Merrill, 1970.

Brown, Thomas M. Irish-American Nationalism, 1870-1890. Philadelphia: Lippincott, 1966.

Carlisle, Rodney P. The Roots of Black Nationalism. Kennikat, 1975.

Carrion, Juan Manuel. The Origins of Puerto Rican Nationalism: Precocity and Limitations of the Nineteenth-Century Movement. In: Francis O. Ramirez (ed.), Rethinking the Nineteenth Century: Contradictions and Movements. Westport, CT: Greenwood, 1988.

Clark, John Henrik. The New Afro-American Nationalism. Freedomways 1 (Fall 1961):285-95.

Clark, Kenneth B. Black Power and Basic Power: An Examination of the
     Futility of Black Nationalism, and a Program for Negro and Jewish
     Relationships. Congress Bi-Weekly 35 (January 8, 1968):6-10.

Cleage, Albert B., Jr. Fear is Gone. Liberator (November 1967). [A
     Black nationalist statement].

Cronon, Edmund D. Black Moses: The Story of Marcus Garvey and the
     Universal Negro Improvement Association (second edition). Madison:
     University of Wisconsin Press, 1969.

Cruse, Harold. Revolutionary Nationalism and the Afro-American. Studies
     on the Left 2 (1972).

Draper, Theodore. The Rediscovery of Black Nationalism. New York:
     Viking, 1970.

Du Bois, W. E. B. A Negro Nation Within the Nation. Current History 42
     (June 1935):265-70.

Du Bois, W. E. B. One Hundred Years in the Struggle for Negro Freedom.
     Freedom January 1953. [Blacks not a nation].

Du Bois, W. E. B. [We are a nation within a nation]. Amsterdam News
     April 10, 1943.

Essien-Udom, E. U. Black Nationalism: A Search for an Identity in
     America. Chicago: University of Chicago Press, 1962.

Franklin, Vincent P. Black Self-Determination. A Cultural History of the
     Faith of the Fathers. Westport, CT: Lawrence Hill and Co., 1986.

Genovese, Eugene D. The Legacy of Slavery and the Roots of Black
     Nationalism. Studies on the Left 6 (November-December 1966):3-65.
     [Comments and reply].

Green, Louis C. Economics of a Separatist State: U.S. Blacks in Five
     Southern States. Doctoral dissertation, University of California at
     Berkeley, 1975.

Green, Louis C. Some Economic Considerations for a Black Separatist State
     in the United States. Review of Black Political Economy 8 (Spring
     1978):229-53.

Hall, Raymond L. Black Separatism in the United States. University Press
     of New England, 1978.

Hutchings, Phil. What Program for Black Liberation Movement? Guardian
     June 1974. [Conference on Racism and Imperialism, Howard University,
     May 23-24, 1974].

Jensen, Richard J. and John C. Hammerback. Radical Nationalism among
     Chicanos: The Rhetorics of Jose Angel Gutierrez. Western Journal of
     Speech Communication 5 (Summer 1980):191-202.

434

Lawson, Ellen. Sarah Woodson Early: Nineteenth Century Black Nationalist
     'Sister'. Umoja 5 (Summer 1981):15-26.

Marable, Manning. The Third Reconstruction: Black Nationalism and Race
     in a Revolutionary America. Social Text 2 (1981):3-27.

Meier, August. The Emergence of Negro Nationalism. Master's thesis,
     Columbia University, 1949.

Meier, August. The Emergence of Negro Nationalism (A Study in
     Ideologies). Midwest Journal 4 (Winter 1951-52):96-104; 4 (Summer
     1952):95-111.

Miller, Floyd J. The Search for a Black Nationality. Black Colonization
     and Emigration, 1787-1863. Urbana: University of Illinois Press,
     1975.

Moses, Wilson J. The Golden Age of Black Nationalism, 1850-1925. Hamden,
     CT: Archon Books, 1978.

Meier, August. Emergence of Negro Nationalism: A Study in Ideologies.
     (2 parts) Midwest Journal (Winter, 1951-1952), (Summer 1952).

Mkalimoto, Ernest. Theoretical Remarks on Afro-American Cultural
     Nationalism. Journal of Ethnic Studies 2 (Summer 1974):1-10.

Neuberger, Benjamin. W. E. B. Du Bois on Black Nationalism and Zionism.
     Jewish Journal of Sociology 28 (December 1986):139-44.

Ortiz, Simon J. Towards a National Indian Literature: Cultural
     Authenticity in Nationalism. MELUS 8 (Summer 1981):7-12.

Ramirez-Barbot, Jaime. A History of Puerto Rican Radical Nationalism,
     1920-1965. Doctoral dissertation, Ohio State University, 1973. UMO
     # 7326892.

Redkey, Edwin. Black Exodus, Black Nationalism and Back-to-Africa
     Movements, 1890-1910. New Haven, CT: Yale University Press, 1969.

Stuckey, Sterling. The Ideological Origins of Black Nationalism. Boston:
     1972.

Stuckey, Sterling. Slave Culture: Nationalist Theory and the Foundation
     of Black America. New York: Oxford University Press, 1987.

Vaca, Nick C. The Black Power. El Grito (Fall 1968). [Critique of
     some features of black nationalism].

Walters, Ronald. African-American Nationalism. Black World 22 (October
     1973):9-27.

Wilson, William J. Revolutionary Nationalism 'versus' Cultural
     Nationalism: Dimensions of the Black Power Movement. Sociological
     Focus 3 (Spring 1970):43-51.

Wright, Louis Edward, Jr. The Political Thought of Elijah Muhammad:
Innovation and Continuity in Western Tradition. Doctoral
dissertation, Howard University, 1987. UMO # 8807170.

Nationalism Bibliography

Herod, Agustina and Charles C. Herod (comps.) Afro-American Nationalism:
An Annotated Bibliography of Militant Separatist and Nationalist
Literature. New York: Garland, 1986.

Herod, Charles C. (comp.) Afro-American Nationalism. Canadian Review of
Studies of Nationalism 14 (1987):1-35.

Jenkins, Betty L. and Susan Phillips (comps.) The Black Separatism
Controversy: An Annotated Bibliography. Westport, CT: Greenwood,
1976.

Kaiser, Ernest (comp.) Recent Literature on Black liberation Struggles
and the Ghetto Crisis (A Bibliographic Survey). Science and Society
33 (Spring 1969):168-96.

54. Occupations

*Aspiring Mexican-Americans have become a nation of "Assistant
Americans" ... Assistant Principals, Assistant Superintendents
... Assistant Parish Priests, Assistant Groundsmen, Assistant
Foremen, Assistants to the Chancellor, Assistant to the Editor,
Assistant to the Assistant, Assistants ad infinitum.*

> - Arthur D. Martinez, <u>Southwest</u> <u>Economy</u> <u>and</u> <u>Society</u>, Winter
> 1977.

Berkman, Dave. Minorities in Public Broadcasting. <u>Journal</u> <u>of</u>
   <u>Communication</u> 30 (Summer 1980):179-188.

Berryman, Sue E. Integrating the Sciences. <u>New</u> <u>Perspectives</u> 17 (Winter
   1985):16-22.

Berryman, Sue E. <u>Who</u> <u>Will</u> <u>Do</u> <u>Science?</u> <u>Trends,</u> <u>and</u> <u>their</u> <u>Causes,</u> <u>in</u>
   <u>Minority</u> <u>and</u> <u>Female</u> <u>Representation</u> <u>among</u> <u>Holders</u> <u>of</u> <u>Advanced</u> <u>Degrees</u>
   <u>in</u> <u>Science</u> <u>and</u> <u>Mathematics</u>. New York: The Rockefeller Foundation,
   November 1983.

Black Journalists Report Progress in Hiring and a Lag in Promotion. <u>New</u>
   <u>York</u> <u>Times</u> August 27, 1988.

Blackwell, James. <u>Mainstreaming</u> <u>Outsiders:</u> <u>Production</u> <u>of</u> <u>Black</u>
   <u>Professionals</u>. Bayside, NY: General Hall, Inc., 1981.

Blackwell, James and others (eds.) The Status of Racial and Ethnic
   Minorities in Sociology. <u>Footnotes</u> (August 1977), special
   supplement.

Brenson, Michael. Black Artists: A Place in the Sun. <u>New</u> <u>York</u> <u>Times</u>
   March 12, 1989.

Broches, Paul. Social Content in Teaching and Design: An Interview with
   Max Blood. <u>Journal</u> <u>of</u> <u>Architectural</u> <u>Education</u> 35 (Fall 1981):51-56.
   [Blacks in architecture].

Campbell, Bebe Moore. Black Executives and Corporate Stress. <u>New</u> <u>York</u>
   <u>Times</u> <u>Magazine</u> December 12, 1982.

Carnegie, Mary E. <u>The</u> <u>Path</u> <u>We</u> <u>Tread:</u> <u>Blacks</u> <u>in</u> <u>Nursing,</u> <u>1854-1984</u>.
   Philadelphia: Lippincott, 1986.

Cash, Rosalind. Working: The Black Actress in the Twentieth Century.
   <u>Contributions</u> <u>in</u> <u>Black</u> <u>Studies</u> 8 (1986-1987):67-76. [Edited by Irma
   McClaurin-Allen].

Cherry, Robert. Racial Thought and the Early Economics Professor in the
   USA. <u>Review</u> <u>of</u> <u>Social</u> <u>Economy</u> 34 (1976):147-62.

Coar, Valencia H. (ed.) <u>A</u> <u>Century</u> <u>of</u> <u>Black</u> <u>Photographers,</u> <u>1840-1960</u>.

Providence, RI: Museum of Art, Rhode Island School of Design, 1983.

Conyers. James E. Black American Doctorates in Sociology: A Follow-Up Study of their Social and Educational Origins. _Phylon_ 47 (Winter 1987):303-17.

Copeland, Elaine J. _Black Women and Power: Perspectives from Black Women Administrators_. 1979. ERIC ED 178 628.

Cunningham, Bill. _Blacks in the Performing Arts_. Hamden, CT: Archon Books, 1980.

Davila, Linda E. The Underrepresentation of Hispanic Attorneys in Corporate Law-Firms. _Stanford Law Review_ 39 (July 1987):1403-52.

Davis, George. _Black Life in Corporate America: Swimming in the Mainstream_. Garden City, NY: Anchor, 1982.

Dewberry, Jonathan. _Black Actors Unite: The Negro Actors Guild of America, 1937-1982_. Doctoral dissertation, New York University, 1988. UMO # 8812625.

Durham, Philip and Everett L. Jones. _The Negro Cowboys_. Lincoln: University of Neberaska Press, 1965.

Erickson, Mary E. Speaking Their Minds: Black [Law] Grads Talk of Challenge and Success, Burdens and Rewards. _Stanford Lawyer_ 2 (Spring 1988).

Fossum, Donna. Law Professors: A Profile of the Teaching Branch of the Legal Profession. _American Bar Foundation Research Journal_ (Summer 1980):501-554.

Freedman, Samuel G. Leaving His Imprint on Broadway. _New York Times Magazine_ November 22, 1987. [Lloyd Richards, director].

Gaines, Victor Pryor. _Career Counseling as Experienced by Practicing Black Opthamologists_. 1977. ERIC ED 185 200.

Gittell, Marilyn. _Increasing the Participation of Women and Minorities in Educational Research and Development_. September 1980. ERIC ED 212 694

Goodwin, Stefan. _Afro-American Anthropologists as Scientists: A Moment in Time_. 1981. ERIC ED 251 040.

Green, Alexis. Tomorrow's Technical Talent. _Change_ 11 (October 1979):16-18. [Minorities in engineering].

Gussow, Mel. Blacks on Stage: The Progress is Deceptive. _New York Times_ August 3, 1986.

Hall, Eleanor R. and Phyllis Post-Kammer. Black Mathematics and Science Majors: Why So Few? _Career Development Quarterly_ 35 (March

1987):206-19.

Hangt, Ruth S., Linda E. Fishman and Wendy J. Evans. Blacks and the Health Profession: A National Crisis, Exerpted from Blacks and the Health Professions in the 80s: A National Crisis and A Time for Action, prepared for the Association of Minority Health Professions School, Integrateducation 22 (January-June 1984):61-72.

Harmetz, Aljean. Minority Film Actors: Few, but Better Roles. New York Times April 13, 1985.

Harmon, William and Mark A. Quinones. Training Minorities for Health Careers: A Five Year Follow-Up Study. Journal of Allied Health 8 (August 1979):153-159.

Harrison, Ira E. Black Anthropologists in the Southern Region. Anthropology and Education Quarterly 10 (Winter 1979):267-275.

Hartigan, Patti. An Actor Breaks Barriers on Stage [Wiley Moore, black actor]. Boston Globe January 12, 1989.

Haynes, M. Alfred. Problems Facing the Negro in Medicine Today. Journal of the American Medical Association 209 (August 18, 1969).

Humphrey, Sheila M. Women and Minorities in Science: Strategies for Increasing Participation. Boulder, CO: Westview, 1982.

Jackson, Irene V. (ed.) More Than Dancing: Essays on Afro-American Music and Musicians. Westport, CT: Greenwood, 1985.

Jackson, Jaqueline J. Black Female Sociologists. In: James E. Blackwell and Morris Janowitz (eds.), Black Sociologists: Historical and Contemporary Perspectives. Chicago: University of Chicago Press, 1974.

Johnson, Charles D. Black Musicians in Music City, USA [Nashville]. Doctoral dissertation, University of Tennessee, 1985. UMO # 8524127.

Jones, Patricia. Some Declaration of Independents. Black Filmmakers Reclaim Their Roots. Village Voice August, 27, 1980.

Kaufman, Jonathan. Minority Count Off in Law Firms. Boston Globe January 18, 1985. [Blacks and Hispanics in Boston law firms].

Kenschaft, Patricia C. Black Women in Mathematics in the United States. American Mathematical Weekly 88 (October 1981):592-604.

Key, Richard Charles. A Critical Analysis of Racism and Socialization in the Sociological Enterprise: The Sociology of Black Sociologists. Doctoral dissertation, University of Missouri, 1975. UMO # 76-7513.

Kidd, Foster (ed.) Profile of the Negro in American Dentistry. Washington, D.C.: Howard University Press, 1979.

Kiernan, Laura A. Survey Found Only 12 Blacks as Partners in Nation's 50

Biggest Firms. Washington Post July 16, 1979. [Law firms].

Leonard, William T. Masquerade in Black. Metuchen, NJ: Scarecrow Press, 1986. [Blacks in the performing arts].

Lewis, Charles H. The Future of Blacks in the Recreation Profession. April 14, 1980. ERIC ED 189 062.

London, Michael. Minorities in Telecommunications: A Black Appraisal. Los Angeles Times May 13, 1982.

Newell, Virginia K. and others (eds.) Black Mathematicians and Their Work. Ardmore, PA: Dorrance, 1980.

Maran, Paul. The Motion Picture Industry and Institutional Racism. Doctoral dissertation, University of Southern California, 1984.

Marshall, William. [Interview about Blacks on stage and screen]. People's Daily World November 6, 1986.

Melnick, Vijaya L. and Franklin D. Hamilton. Participation of Blacks in the Basic Sciences: An Assessment. In: Gail E. Thomas (ed.), Black Students in Higher Education, pp. 282-293. Westport, CT: Greenwood, 1981.

Melnick, V. L. and F. D. Hamilton (eds.) Minorities in Science: The Challenge for Change in Biomedicine. New York: Plenum Press, 1977.

Miller, Helen S. and Ernest D. Mason (eds.). Contemporary Minority Leaders in Nursing: Afro-American, Hispanic, Native American Perspectives. Kansas City, MO: American Nurses Association, 1983.

Minority Education for Environmental and Natural Resource Professions: Higher Education. 1981. Human Environment Center, 1302 18th St., N.W., Washington, D.C. 20036.

Molnar, Hedi. Accounting for Blacks. New York Times Magazine June 8, 1986. [Blacks employed in the accounting field].

Monroe, Sylvester and Carolyn Friday. Blacks and the Wall St. Purge. Newsweek February 1, 1988. [Black employment on Wall Street].

Nelson, F. Howard. Black Computer Workers: Closing the Gap in High Technology Employment. Journal of Negro Education 54 (Fall 1985):548-57.

Nelson, Robert. The Changing Structure of Opportunity: Recruitment and Careers in Large Law Firms. American Bar Foundation Research Journal 1 (1983).

Pace, Eric. Blacks in the Arts: Evaluating Recent Success. New York Times June 14, 1987.

Pearson, Willie, Jr. Black Scientists, White Society, and Colorless Science: A Study of Universalism in American Science. Port

Washington, NY: Associated Faculty Press, 1985.

Pearson, Willie, Jr. One in a Hundred: A Study of Black American Science
    Doctorates. Doctoral dissertation, Southern Illinois University,
    1981. UMO # 8122658.

Phinazee, Annette L. (ed.) The Black Librarian in the Southeast:
    Reminiscences, Activities, Challenges. 1983. North Carolina
    Central University Alumni Association, Box 197975, Durham, NC 27707.

Preston, Michael B. and Maurice Woodard. The Rise and Decline of Black
    Political Scientists in the Profession. Political Science 17 (Fall
    1984):787-92.

Putney, Martha S. Black Sailors: Afro-American Merchant Seamen and
    Whalemen Prior to the Civil War. Westport, CT: Greenwood, 1987.

Rivas, Maggie. The Problems of Black Lawyers. Boston Globe February 18,
    1982. [Boston].

Roberts, Fletcher. Minorities Seek Access to Cable [TV]. Boston Globe
    February 22, 1982.

Russo, Nancy F. and others. Women and Minorities in Psychology. American
    Psychologist 36 (November 1981):1315-1363.

Savitt, Todd L. Entering a White Profession: Black Physicians in the New
    South, 1880-1920. Bull. Hist. Medicine 61 (Winter 1987):507-40.

Schleiter, Mary Kay. Occupation and Social Groups: Blacks in Internal
    Medicine. Doctoral dissertation, University of Chicago, 1982.

Schonberg, Harold C. A Bravo for Opera's Black Voices. New York Times
    Magazine January 17, 1982.

Sertina, Ivan Van (ed.) Blacks in Science: Ancient and Modern. New
    Brunswick, NJ: Transaction Books, 1983.

Sinclair, Benito A. Reflections on My Profession by a Black Civil
    Engineer. Engineering Issues 99 (July 1973):357-360.

Slater, Jack. Where Are the Blacks in Ballet? Los Angeles Times June 8,
    1980.

Stewart, Roma. Subtle Prejudice Still Undermines Black Attorneys. Legal
    Times of Washington February 1983.

Stokes, Geoffrey. The 'News' New York's Racist Newspaper. Village Voice
    April 28, 1987. [Black journalists on the New York Daily News].

Smith, Elsie J. Career Development of Minorities in Nontraditional
    Fields. Journal of Non-White Concerns in Personnel and Guidance 8
    (April 1980):141-156. [Science and engineering].

Smith, Ralph. Great Expectations and Dubious Results: A Pessimistic

441

Prognosis for the Black Lawyer. <u>Black Law Journal</u> 7 (1980).

Temin, Christine. Why So Few Blacks in Ballet? <u>Boston Globe</u> June 21, 1981.

Tesser, Neil. Chicago's Two Major Dailies at Standstill on Minority Hiring; Net Gain of One. <u>Chicago Reporter</u> 16 (May 1987):1, 6-7, 11

Trayes, Edward J. Black Journalists in U.S. Metropolitan Daily Newspapers: A Follow-Up Study. <u>Journalism Quarterly</u> 56 (Winter 1979):711-714.

Vetter, Betty M. and Eleanor L. Babco. <u>Professional Women and Minorities: A Manpower Data Resource Service</u> (fifth edition). Washington, D.C.: Scientific Manpower Commission, August 1984.

Wells, Alan. Black Artists in American Popular Music, 1955-1985. <u>Phylon</u> 48 (Winter 1987):309-16.

Wilkerson, Isabel. Blacks Left Out of Movie Boom. <u>Boston Globe</u> August 29, 1982. [Reprinted from <u>Washington Post</u>].

Wilkinson, D. A Profile: Minorities in Sociology and Other Behavioral Sciences. <u>Footnotes</u> 6 (1978):6-7.

Williams, Luther S. Educational Opportunities for Blacks in the Sciences, 1955-1980: An Assessment of the Impact of the 1954 Supreme Court Decision. <u>Negro Educational Review</u> 32 (January 1981):101-105.

Willie, Charles V. The Recruitment and Retention of Minority Health Professionals. <u>Alabama Journal of Medical Sciences</u> (July 1982).

Wilson, Clint C., II. Desegregating the Newsroom. <u>Change</u> 11 (October 1979):20-23. [Overcoming discrimination in journalism].

Writers Guild Contends Producers Practice Bias. <u>New York Times</u> June 24, 1987.

Yost, Barbara. Minorities in Medicine. <u>Phoenix Gazette</u> Novmeber 15, 1983.

Occupational Bibliography

Bauchum, Rosalind G. and James W. A. Bauchum, III (comps.) <u>The Black Architect</u>. Monticello, IL: Vance Bibliographies, 1982.

Tischler, Alice (comp.) <u>Fifteen Black American Composers: A Bibliography of Their Works</u>. Detroit: Information Coordinators, 1981.

Weintraub, Irwin (comp.) <u>Black Agriculturalists in the U.S. (1865-1973): An Annotated Bibliography</u>. University Park, PA: Office of the Dean, Pennsylvania State University Libraries, 1976.

Wheat, C. (comp.) Selected Bibliography: Minority Group Participation in the Legal Profession. <u>University</u> <u>of</u> <u>Toledo</u> <u>Law</u> <u>Review</u> (Spring 1970):935-81.

[See also sections 5, 7, 18, 20, 23, 27, 29, 39, 41, 48, 50, 73, 75, and 81]

55. Oppression

We [Mexican Americans] are very much an oppressed,
discriminated-against group in this country ... and Texas is our
Mississippi.

- Vilma Martinez, <u>Washington</u> <u>Post</u>, March 28, 1978.

Almaguer, Tomas. Historical Notes on Chicano Oppression: The Dialectics
of Racial and Class Domination in North America. <u>Aztlan</u> 5 (Spring
and Fall 1972):27-56.

Collier, Betty. Economics, Psychology, and Racism: An Analysis of
Oppression. <u>Journal</u> <u>of</u> <u>Black</u> <u>Psychology</u> 3 (February 1977):50-60.

Franklin, Woodman. Chicano Politics: Oppression as a Cultural
Phenomenon. <u>Bilingual</u> <u>Review</u> 2 (September-December 1975):321-30.

Hodge, John L. <u>Cultural</u> <u>Bases</u> <u>of</u> <u>Racism</u> <u>and</u> <u>Group</u> <u>Oppression</u>. Berkeley,
CA: Two Riders Press, 1975.

Hopps, June G. Oppression Based on Color. <u>Social</u> <u>Work</u> 27 (January
1982):3-5.

Kutenplon, Deborah and others. <u>Overcoming</u> <u>Oppression</u> <u>Within</u> <u>Groups</u>.
Amherst, MA: Student Center for Educational Research and Advocacy,
University of Massachusetts, 1987.

Mhone, Guy C. Structural Oppression and the Persistence of Black Poverty.
<u>Journal</u> <u>of</u> <u>Afro-American</u> <u>Issues</u> 3 (Summer-Fall 1976):395-419.

Turner, Jonathan H. and Royce Singleton, Jr. A Theory of Ethnic
Oppression: Toward a Reintegration of Cultural and Structural
Concepts in Ethnic Relations Theory. <u>Social</u> <u>Forces</u> 56 (June
1978):1001-1018.

Turner, Jonathan H. and others. <u>Oppression:</u> <u>A</u> <u>Socio-History</u> <u>of</u> <u>Black-</u>
<u>White</u> <u>Relations</u> <u>in</u> <u>America</u>. Chicago, IL: Nelson-Hall, 1984.

William, R. Towards a Pedagogy of Oppressed Youth. <u>Convergence</u> 4
(1972).

Wolf, Charlotte. Legitimation of Oppression: Response and Reflexivity.
<u>Symbolic</u> <u>Interaction</u> 9 (Fall 1986):217-34.

[See also sections 4, 8, 12, 13, 14, 17, 20, 24, 29, 32, 40, 44, 59, 78,
and 82]

56. Philosophy

Abject as our condition has been, our whole lives prove us superior to the influences that have been brought upon to crush us.

- John S. Rock, Liberator, February 14, 1862.

Bracken, Harry M. Philosophy and Racism. Philosophia 8 (1978):241-260.

Bruening, William H. Racism: A Philosophical Analysis of a Concept. Journal of Black Studies 5 (September 1974):3-17.

Dover, Cedric. The Racial Philosophy of Jehuda Halevi. Phylon 13

Duffield, Mark. New Racism ... New Realism. Radical Philosophy (Summer 1984).

Frye, Charles. The Role of Philosophy in Black Studies. Contributions in Black Studies 4 (1980-1981).

Harris, Leonard (ed.) The Philosophy of Alain Locke: Harlem Renaissance and Beyond. Philadelphia, PA: Temple University Press, 1988.

McLachlan, Hugh V. Hume and the 'New Racism': A Comment. New Community 11 (Spring 1984):309-311.

Meade, Homer L., II. A Pragmatist: William Edward Burghardt Du Bois. Master's thesis, University of Massachusetts, Amherst, 1980.

Okolo, C. B. Racism--A Philosophic Probe. New York: Exposition Press, 1974.

Popkin, Richard H. The Philosophical Basis of Eighteenth Century Racism. In: Harold E. Pagliaro (ed.), Racism in the Eighteenth Century. Cleveland, OH: Press of Case Western Reserve University, 1973.

Varet, G. Racisme et philosophie. Essai sur une limite de la pensee. Paris: Denoel-Gontheir, 1973.

Washington, Johnny. Alain Locke and Philosophy: A Quest for Cultural Pluralism. Westport, CT: Greenwood, 1986.

57. Planning

*The Board of Trade and the real estate board, with its
representatives from twenty-five banks, insurance and title
companies, and building and loan associations, had already
defined their policy of tightening racial segregation and
controlling the city's pattern of growth by every financial and
political means at their command.*

> - Constance McL. Green, The Secret City. A History of Race
> Relations in the Nation's Capital, p. 272. Reference is to the
> year 1945 in Washington D.C.

Baron, Harold M. (ed.) The Racial Aspects of Urban Planning. Chicago,
    IL: Chicago Urban League, 1968.

Clay, Philip L. and Robert M. Hollister (eds.) Neighborhood Policy and
    Planning. Lexington, MA: Lexington Books, 1983.

Du Bois, W. E. B. Social Planning for the Negro, Past and Present.
    Journal of Negro Education 5 (Janaury 1936):110-25.

Keller, Suzanne. Social Class in Physical Planning. International Social
    Science Journal 18 (1966).

Silver, Christopher. Twentieth-Century Richmond: Planning, Politics, and
    Race. Knoxville, TN: University of Tennessee Press, 1984.

Stafford, Walter and Joyce Ladner. Comprehensive Planning and Racism.
    Journal of the American Institute of Planners March 1969.

Stone, Clarence N. Economic Growth and Neighborhood Discontent: System
    Bias in the Urban Renewal Program of Atlanta. Chapel Hill, NC:
    University of North Carolina Press, 1976.

[See also sections 1, 7, 13, 16, 20, 23, 32, 33, 35, 41, 42, 44, 49, 59,
    and 71]

58. Pluralism

*... Very often the parents and children [in San Francisco] don't
communicate because when the children get into school they ...
[are] taught to suppress their Chinese language speaking
ability. In fact, the teacher tends to frown upon their Chinese
... laugh at them for their Chinese accent and to try to
indoctrinate them that the English language is the language.*

- L. Ling-Chi Wang, Roots (1971)

Abramson, Harold J. Assimilation and Pluralism. In: Stephan Thernstrom
    (ed.), Harvard Encyclopedia of American Ethnic Groups, pp. 150-160.
    Cambridge, MA: Harvard University Press, 1980.

Cervantes, Fred A. Chicanos Within the Political Economy: Some Questions
    Concerning Pluralist Ideology Representation and the Economy. Aztlan
    7 (Fall 1976):337-45.

Churchill, Ward. The Seamy Side of English Only. Zeta Magazine 1 (July-
    August 1988):21-23.

Clausen, Edwin G. and Jack Bermingham (eds.) Pluralism, Racism, and
    Public Policy: The Search for Equality. Boston: Hall, 1981.

Cox, Oliver C. The Question of Pluralism. Race 12 (April 1971):385-400.

Cross, Malcom. On Conflict, Race Relations, and the Theory of the Plural
    Society. Race 12 (April 1971):477-494.

Cruse, Harold. Plural but Equal: A Critical Study of Blacks and
    Minorities and the American Plural Society. New York: Morrow, 1986.

Dahl, Robert A. Pluralist Democracy in the United States. Chicago, IL:
    Rand McNally, 1967.

Erie, Steven P. The Development of Class and Ethnic Politics in San
    Francisco, 1870-1910: A Critique of the Pluralist Interpretation.
    Doctoral dissertation, University of California, Los Angeles, 1975.

Jiobu, Robert M. Ethnicity and Assimilation: Blacks, Chinese, Filipinos,
    Koreans, Japanese, Mexicans, Vietnamese, and Whites. Albany: State
    University of New York Press, 1988.

Kallen, Horace M. Cultural Pluralism and the American Idea: An Essay in
    Social Philosophy. Philadelphia, PA, 1956.

Klassen, Frank H. and Donna M. Gollnick (eds.) Pluralism and the
    American Teacher: Isssues and Case Studies. Washington, D.C.:
    American Asociation of Colleges for Teacher Education, 1977.

Korman, Gerd. Ethnic Democracy and Its Ambiguities. American Jewish
    History 75 (June 1986).

Kuper, Leo. The Theory of the Plural Society, Race and Conquest. In Sociological Theories: Race and Colonialism, pp. 239-266. Paris: UNESCO, 1980.

Laumann, Edward O. Bonds of Pluralism: The Form and Substance of Urban Social Networks. New York, 1973. [Detroit].

Manners, Robert A. Pluralism and the American Indian. America Indigena 22 (1962):25-38.

Matthews, Fred H. Cultural Pluralism in Context: External History, Philosophic Premise, and Theories of Ethnicity in Modern America. Journal of Ethnic Studies 12 (Summer 1984):63-79.

Matthews, Fred H. The Revolt Against Americanism: Cultural Pluralism as an Ideology of Liberation. Canadian Review of American Studies 1 (Spring 1970):4-31.

Metzger, L. Paul. American Sociology and Black Assimilation: Conflicting Perspectives. American Journal of Sociology 76 (January 1971):627=-47.

Newman, William M. American Pluralism: A Study of Minority Groups and Social Theory. New York: Harper and Row, 1973.

Novak, Michael. Pluralism: A Humanistic Perspective. In: Stephan Thernstrom (ed.), Harvard Encyclopedia of American Minority Groups, pp. 772-81. Cambridge, MA: Harvard University Press, 1980.

Ono, Shino'Ya. The Limits of Bourgeois Pluralism. Studies on the Left (Summer 1965).

Pareles, Jon. Eurocentrism? We Aren't the Word. New York Times April 23, 1989.

Phinney, Jean S. and Mary Jane Rotheram (eds.) Children's Ethnic Socialization: Pluralism and Development. Beverly Hills, CA: Sage, 1986.

Pinderhughes, Dianne M. Race and Ethnicity in Chicago Politics: A Reexamination of Pluralist Theory. Urbana: University of Illinois Press, 1987.

Powell, James H. The Concept of Cultural Pluralism in American Social Thought, 1915-1965. Doctoral dissertation, University of Notre Dame, 1971.

Seda Bonilla, Eduardo. Cultural Pluralism and the Education of Puerto Rican Youths. Phi Delta Kappan 53 (January 1972):294-96.

Triandis, Harry C. The Future of Pluralism. Journal of Social Issues 32, No. 4(1976):179-208.

Wacker, R. Fred. Ethnicity, Pluralism, and Race: Race Relations Theory in America before Myrdal. Westport, CT: Greenwood, 1983.

Walzer, Michael. Pluralism: A Political Perspective. In: Stephan Thernstrom (ed.), Harvard Encyclopedia of American Ethnic Groups, pp. 781-87. Cambridge, MA: Harvard University Press, 1980.

Washington, Johnny. Alain Locke and Philosophy: A Quest for Cultural Pluralism. Westport, CT: Greenwood, 1986.

Young, Pai. Cultural Pluralism and American Education. Korean Christian Journal 2 (1977):100-25.

Zung, Olivier. Genese du pluralisme americain. An: Ec., Soc. Civil. 42 (March-April 1987):429-44.

Pluralism Bibliography

Inglehart, Babette F. and Anthony R. Mangione (comps.) The Image of Pluralism in American Literature: An Annotated Bibliography on the American Experience of European Ethnic Groups. New York, 1974.

59. Politics and Racism

*Saint Francis of Assisi is said to have prayed: "God grant me
the serenity to accept the things I cannot change, the courage
to change the things I can, and the wisdom to know the
difference." But at times it may be better for the Omnipotent
One to give men the wit and the will to continue to plan
purposefully and to struggle as best they know how to change
things that seem immutable.*

- William H. Hastie, <u>Annals</u>, May 1973

Adams, Howard. Red Powerlessness: Bureaumetric Authoritarianism on
    Indian Reservations. <u>Cornell Journal of Social Relations</u> 18 (Fall
    1984):28-40.

Akin, Edward N. When a Minority Becomes the Majority: Blacks in
    Jacksonville Politics, 1887-1907. <u>Florida Historical Quarterly</u> 53
    (October 1974):123-45.

Alkimat, Abdul. Chicago: Black Power Politics and the Crisis of the
    Black Middle Class. <u>Black Scholar</u> 19 (March-April 1988):45-54.

Alkimat, Abdul and Doug Gills. Black Power vs. Racism: Harold
    Washington Becomes Mayor. <u>In</u>: Rod Bush (ed.), <u>The New Black Vote</u>.
    San Francisco, CA: Synthesis Publications, 1984.

Applebone, Peter. Dallas Taking Stock of Its Divisions. <u>New York Times</u>
    February 1, 1988.

Ball, Joanne. Blacks, Proud of Electoral Gains, Still Feeling Held Back
    by Prejudice. <u>Boston Globe</u> April 25, 1988. [Second of two
    articles].

Banks, Manley E. <u>Consociational Democracy: The Outcome of Racial
    Political Polarization in Atlanta, Georgia, 1973-1986</u>. Doctoral
    dissertation, University of Texas, 1987. UMO # 8728515.

Baraka, Amiri. Black Power 20 Years Later. <u>New York Newsday</u> August 17,
    1986.

Barker, Lucius J. <u>Our Time Has Come. A Delegate's Diary of Jesse
    Jackson's 1984 Presidential Campaign</u>. Urbana: University of
    Illinois Press, 1988.

Barker, Lucius J. (ed.) <u>Jesse Jackson and the 1984 Presidential
    Campaign</u>. Urbana: University of Illinois Press, 1987.

Barker, Lucius J. and Jesse J. McCorry. <u>Black Americans and the Political
    System</u>. Cambridge, MA, 1980.

Baron, Harold and others. Black Powerlessness in Chicago. <u>In</u>: Edward S.
    Greenberg and others (eds.), <u>Black Politics: The Inevitability of</u>

Conflict, pp. 105-15. New York: Holt, Rinehart and Winston, 1971.

Beatty, Bess. A Revolution Gone Backward: The Black Response to National Politics, 1876-1896. Westport, CT: Greenwood Press, 1987.

Ben-Tovim, Gideon and others. The Local Politics of Race. London: Macmillan, 1986. [Britain].

Berlet, Chip. Fiction, and the New Alliance Party. Radical America 21 (September-October 1987):7-15. [Printed November 1988].

Bernd, Joseph L. White Supremacy and the Disfranchisement of Blacks in Georgia, 1946. Georgia Historical Quarterly 66 (Winter 1982):492-513.

Berry, Mary Frances. Increasing Women's Influence in Government and Politics: The Inclusion of Women of Color. Proteus 3 (Fall 1986):1-5.

Black Americans and Public Policy. Washington, D.C.: National Urban League, 1988.

Bond, Julian. Feudal Politics and Black Serfdom. Afro-American Studies 1 (October 1970):147-59.

Bond, Julian. The Roots of Racism and War. Black Scholar (November 1970):20-24.

Branham, Charles R. Black Chicago: Accomodationist Politics Before the Great Migration. In: Melvin G. Holli and Peter d'A. Jones (eds.), The Ethnic Frontier, pp. 211-262. Grand Rapids, MI: Eerdmans, 1977.

Brantley, Daniel. Blacks and Louisiana Constitutional Development 1890-Present: A Study in Southern Political Thought and Race Relations. Phylon 48 (March 1987):51-61'.

Brischetto, Robert R. and others. The Mexican American Electorate: An Explanation of Their Opinions and Behavior. San Antonio, TX: Southwest Voter Registration Education Project, Hispanic Population Studies Program of the Center for Mexican American Studies, University of Texas, 1984.

Brown, Tommie F. The Struggle to Control Black Leadership: A Study in Community Power. Doctoral dissertation, Columbia University, 1984. UMO # 8623490. [Chattanooga].

Browning, Rufus P. Protest Is Not Enough: The Struggle of Blacks and Hispanics in Urban Politics. Berkeley: University of California Press, 1984.

Bunche, Ralph J. The Political Status of the Negro in the Age of FDR. Chicago, 1973.

Bush, Rod. Racism and the Rise of the Right. In: Marlene Dixon and others (eds.), World Capitalist Crisis and the Rise of the Right, pp.

40-47. San Francisco, CA: Synthesis Publications, 1982.

Button, J. The Outcomes of Black Protest and Violence. In: Ted R. Gurr (ed.), Violence in America, vol. 2 (third edition). Newbury Park, CA: Sage, 1989.

Cavanagh, Thomas E. Inside Black America: The Message of the Black Vote in the 1984 Elections. Washington, D.C.: Joint Center for Political Studies, 1985.

Cavanagh, Thomas E. Working Paper: Black Voter Participation in the United States: A Review of the Literature. Washington, D.C.: Joint Center for Political Studies, 1983.

Cavanagh, Thomas E. (ed.) Race and Political Strategy: A/JCPS Roundtable. Washington, D.C.: Joint Center for Political Studies, 1983.

Cavanagh, Thomas E. and Lorn S. Foster. Jesse Jackson's Campaign: The Primaries and Caucuses. Washington, D.C.: Joint Center for Political Studies, 1984.

Chang, Edward. Korean Community Politics in Los Angeles: The Impact of the Kwanju Uprising. Amerasia Journal 14 (1988):51-67. [1980].

Chavis, Benjamin F., Jr. Keysville Blacks Reach for Power. Guardian December 30, 1987. [Georgia].

Citizens' Commission on Civil Rights. Barriers to Registration and Voting: An Agenda for Reform. Wahington, D.C.: National Center for Policy Alternatives, 1988.

Clemente, Frank (ed.) Keep Hope Alive. Jesse Jackson's 1988 Presidential Campaign. Boston: South End Press, 1988.

Colby, David C. Black Power, White Resistance, and Public Policy: Political Power and Poverty Grants in Mississippi. Journal of Politics 47 (May 1985):579-95.

Coles, Robert. The Political Life of Children. Boston, MA: Houghton Mifflin, 1987.

Collins, Sheila D. The Rainbow Challenge. The Jackson Campaign and the Future of U.S. Politics. New York: Monthly Review Press, 1986.

Conway, M. Margaret. The White Backlash Re-Examined: Wallace and the 1964 Primaries. Social Science Quarterly 49 (December 1968).

Curry, Richard O. (ed.) Radicalism. Racism, and Party Realignment: The Border States During Reconstruction. Baltimore, 1969.

Dates, Jannette L. and Oscar Gandy, Jr. The Jackson Presidential Campaign: Setting the Public Agenda. November 1984. ERIC ED 251 882.

Dialogue: Jesse Jackson, the Rainbow and the Movements. Against the Currents 3 (July-August 1988):5-22. [Series of articles].

Dionne, E. J., Jr. Black Residents of New York [City] See a Campaign Tinged with Racism. New York Times April 18, 1988. [Presidential primary election campaign].

Dionne, E. J., Jr. 'Solid South' Again, but Republican. New York Times November 13, 1988.

Dittmer, John. The Politics of the Mississippi Movement, 1954-1964. In: Charles W. Eagles (ed.), The Civil Rights Movement in America. Jackson: University Press of Mississippi, 1986.

Doyle, Judith K. Maury Maverick and Racial Politics in San Antonio, Texas, 1938-1941. Journal of Southern History 53 (May 1987):194-224.

Drinan, Robert F. Subtle But Disturbing Racism Marred Election. National Catholic Reporter November 18, 1988. [Presidential election, 1988].

Edsall, Thomas B. Black vs. White in Chicago. New York Review of Books April 13, 1989.

Edsall, Thomas B. The New Politics of Inequality. New York: Norton, 1984.

Effort to Restore Government in a Georgia Town is Blocked. New York Times December 31, 1987. [Keysville].

Elliot, Jeffrey M. (ed.) Black Voices in American Politics. San Diego, CA: Harcourt Brace Jovanovich, 1986.

Ervin, Alexander M. The Emergence of Native Alaskan Political Capacity, 1959-1971. Musk-Ox 19 (1976):3-14.

Escott, Paul D. Many Excellent People: Power and Privilege in North Carolina, 1850-1900. Chapel Hill, NC: University of North Carolina Press, 1985.

Evans, Eola A. Activity of Black Women in the Woman Suffrage Movement 1900-1920. Master's thesis, Lamar University, 1987.

Faw, Bob and Nancy Skelton. Thunder in America. Austin, TX: Texas Monthly, 1986. [On the 1984 presidential campaign of Jesse Jackson].

Field, Phyllis F. The Politics of Race in New York: The Struggle for Black Suffrage. Ithaca, NY: Cornell University Press, 1982.

Fishel, Leslie H., Jr. Northern Prejudice and Negro Suffrage, 1865-1870. Journal of Negro History 39 (January 1954):8-26.

Foner, Eric. Black Reconstruction Leaders at the Grass Roots. In: Leon Litwack and August Meier (eds.), Black Leaders of the Nineteenth

Century. Urbana: University of Illinois Press, 1988.

Foster, E. C. A Time of Challenge: Afro-Mississippi Political
     Developments Since 1965. _Journal of Negro History_ 68 (Spring
     1983):185-200.

Frisby, Michael K. Black Clergy Play Key Role In Tuesday Vote. _Boston
     Globe_ March 6, 1988. [Southern campaign for Jesse Jackson].

Gaither, Gerald. _Blacks and the Populist Revolt: Ballots and Bigotry in
     the "New South"_. University: University of Alabama Press, 1977.

Gonzalez Diaz, Emilio. Luchas politicas y democracio en Puerto Rico,
     1968-1985. _R. Mex. Sociol._ 48 (July-September 1986):89-102.

Green, David G. _The New Conservatism: The Counter-Revolution in
     Political. Economic and Social Thought_. New York: St. Martin's
     Press, 1987. [Great Britain and the U.S.A.].

Greer, Edward. _Big Steel: Black Politics and Corporate Power in Gary,
     Indiana_. New York: Monthly Review Press, 1979.

Grimke, Archibald H. _The Ballotless Victim of One-Party Government_.
     Washington, D.C.: American Negro Academy, 1912.

Grimke, Archibald H. and others. _The Negro and the Election Franchise_.
     Washington, D.C., 1905.

Grimshaw, William J. _Black Politics in Chicago: The Quest for
     Leadership. 1939-1979_. Chicago, IL: Center for Urban Policy, Loyola
     University, 1980.

Grimshaw, William J. _The Daley Legacy: A Declining Politics of Party,
     Race. and Public Unions_. Evanston, IL: Center for Urban Affairs,
     Northwestern University, 1980.

Gutman, Herbert G. Black Coal Miners and the Greenback-Labor Party in
     Redeemer, Alabama: 1878-1879. _Labor History_ 10 (1969):506-35.

Guzman, Ralph C. The Function of Anglo-American Racism in the Political
     Development of Chicanos. _California Historical Quarterly_ 50
     (1971):321-37.

Hamilton, Charles V. The Phenomenon of the Jesse Jackson Candidacy and
     the 1984 Presidential Election. _In_: James Williams (ed.), _The State
     of Black America_. New York: National Urban League, 1985.

Hanks, Lawrence J. _Black Political Empowerment in the Black Belt South:
     The Quest for Black Political Power in Three Black Belt Georgia
     Counties_. Doctoral dissertation, Howard University, 1984. UMO #
     8419350. [Hancock, Peach, and Clay counties].

Henriques, J. Social Psychology and the Politics of Racism. _In_: J.
     Henriques (ed.), _Changing the Subject_, pp. 60-9. London: Methuen,
     1984.

454

Hill, Richard C. Race, Class and the State: The Metropolitan Enclave System in the United States. Insurgent Sociologist 10 (Fall 1980):45-67.

Hiller, Amy M. The Disfranchisement of Delaware Negroes in the Late Nineteenth Century. Delaware History 13 (October 1968):124-54.

Hine, Darlene C. Black Victory: The Rise and Fall of the White Primary in Texas. Millwood, NY: KTO Press, 1979.

Holloway, Harry. Negro Political Strategy: Coalition or Independent Power Politics? Social Science Quarterly 49 (December 1968).

Horwitz, Gerry. Benjamin Davis, Jr. and the American Communist Party: A Study in Race and Politics. UCLA Historical Journal 1 (1983):92-107.

Hunter, Floyd. The Power Structure of the Black Community, pp. 66-84 in Community Power Succession. Atlanta's Policy-Makers Revisited. Chapel Hill, NC: University of North Carolina Press, 1980.

Hunter, Robert N., Jr. Racial Gerrymandering and the Voting Rights in North Carolina. Campbell Law Review 9 (Spring 1987):255-91.

Jackson, Jesse L. Straight from the Heart. Ed. by Roger D. Hatch and Frank E. Watkins. Philadelphia: Fortress Press, 1987.

James, C. L. R. Black Power, pp. 221-36 in Spheres of Existence. Westport, CT: Lawrence Hill and Co., 1980. [Orig. August 1967].

Jennings, James. Puerto Rican Politics in New York City. Washington, D.C.: University Press of America, 1977.

Jennings, James and Mel King (eds.) From Access to Power: Black Politics in Boston. Cambridge, MA: Schenkman, 1986.

Jennings, James and Monte Rivera (eds.) Puerto-Rican Politics in Urban America. Westport, CT: Greenwood, 1984.

Johnson, Christopher. Maurice Sugar: Law, Labor and the Left in Detroit, 1912-1950. Detroit, MI: Wayne State University Press, 1988.

Johnson, Dirk. For Chicago, Racial Politics Is Becoming a Tradition. New York Times October 16, 1988.

Johnson, Dirk. Racial Politics. Chicago's Raw Nerve. New York Times Magazine February 19, 1989.

Johnson, Terry. To Stop the Madness. African-American Summit Hears Many Voices. Village Voice May 9, 1989. [African-American Summit, New Orleans, April 1989].

Jones, Mack H. Black Political Empowerment in Atlanta: Myth and Reality. Annals 439 (1978):90-117.

Jordan, June. The Rainbow Next Time. *Village Voice* November 29, 1988. [Jesse Jackson's candidacy for President].

Kantowicz, Edward R. Politics. *In*: Stephan Thernstrom (ed.), *Harvard Encyclopedia of American Ethnic Groups*, pp. 803-13. Cambridge, MA: Harvard University Press, 1980.

Kaufman, Jonathan. Ballot Box Is New Frontier of Civil Rights. *Boston Globe* April 24, 1988. [First of two articles].

Kennicott, Patrick C. Black Persuaders in the Antislavery Movement. *Journal of Black Studies* 1 (September 1970):5-20.

Kopkind, Andrew. Creating a Democratic Majority [Jesse Jackson]. *Nation* December 26, 1988.

Kopkind, Andrew. The Jackson Movement. *New Left Review* 172 (November-December 1988):83-91.

Kousser, J. Morgan. *The Shaping of Southern Politics: Suffrage Restriction and the Establishment of the One-Party South, 1880-1910*. New Haven, CT: Yale University Press, 1974.

Kurtz, D. M. Who Runs Louisiana? *In*: G. William Domhoff and Thomas R. Dye (eds.), *Power Elites and Organization*. Newbury Park, CA: Sage, 1986.

Ladner, Joyce. What 'Black Power' Means to Negroes in Mississippi. *Trans-Action* 5 (November 1967):7-15.

Lapidus, Steven L. Eradicating Racial Discrimination in Voter Registration: Rights and Remedies under the Voting Rights Act Amendments of 1982. *Fordham Law Review* 52 (October 1983):93-132.

Lawson, Steven F. *Black Ballots: Voting Rights in the South, 1944-1969*. New York: Columbia University Press, 1976.

Lawson, Steven F. *In Pursuit of Power. Southern Blacks and Electoral Politics, 1965-1982*. New York: Columbia University Press, 1985.

Love, John L. *The Disfranchisement of the Negro*. Washington, D.C.: American Negro Academy, 1899.

Marable, Manning. *Black American Politics: From the Washington Marches to Jesse Jackson*. New York: Verso, 1985.

Marable, Manning. Black Brahmins: The Underdevelopment of Black Political Leadership. *In*: *How Capitalism Underdeveloped Black America*, pp. 169-94. Boston: South End Press, 1983.

Marable, Manning. *Blackwater: Historical Studies in Race, Class Conciousness and Revolution*. Dayton, OH: Black Praxis Press, 1981.

Marable, Manning. Jackson and the Rise of the Rainbow Coalition. *New*

Left _Review_ 149 (January-February 1985):3-44.

Marine, Gene. _The_ _Black_ _Panthers_. New York: Signet, 1969.

McAdam, D. and K. Moore. The Politics of Black Insurgency: 1930-1975.
_In_: Ted R. Gurr (ed.), _Violence_ _in_ _America_, Vol. 2 (third edition).
Newbury Park, CA: Sage 1989.

McKay, Robert B. Race, Politics and the Run-Off Primary. _Brooklyn_ _Law_
Review 53 (Summer 1987):499-514. [NYC].

McMillen, Neil R. Black Enfranchisement in Mississippi: Federal
Enforcement and Black Protest in the 1960s. _Journal_ _of_ _Southern_
History 43 (August 1977):351-72.

Meier, August and John Bracey, editorial advisers. The Voting Rights
Campaign, 1916-1950, part 4 of _Papers_ _of_ _the_ _NAACP._ _New_ _Parts_ _on_
Educational _Equality,_ _Voting_ _Rights,_ _Housing,_ _the_ _Scottsboro_ _Case,_
and _Anti-Lynching_ [13 microflims reels.] Frederick, MD:
University Publications of America, 1987.

Misnik, Joanna (ed.) _Jesse_ _Jackson,_ _the_ _Rainbow_ _and_ _the_ _Democratic_
Party _-_ _New_ _Politics_ _or_ _Old?_ Solidarity, 7012 Michigan Avenue,
Detroit, MI 48210.

Mohl, Raymond A. Ethnic Politics in Miami, 1960-1986. _In_: Randall M.
Miller and George E. Pozzetta (eds), _Shades_ _of_ _the_ _Sunbelt_.
Westport, CT: Greenwood, 1988.

Moneyhon, Carl H. Black Politics in Arkansas during the Gilded Age,
1876-1900. _Arkansas_ _Historical_ _Quarterly_ 44 (Autumn 1985):222-45.

Monroy, Douglas G. Like Swallows at the Old Mission: Mexicans and Racial
Politics of Growth in Los Angeles in the Interwar Period. _Western_
Historical _Quarterly_ 14 (1983):435-58.

Moreland, Lawrence W. and others (eds.) _Blacks_ _in_ _Southern_ _Politics_.
New York: Praeger, 1987.

Moore, Douglas E. _The_ _Buying_ _and_ _Selling_ _of_ _the_ _D.C._ _City_ _Council_.
Washington, D.C.: The Author, 1978.

Moreland, Lawrence W. and others (eds.). _Blacks_ _in_ _Southern_ _Politics_.
New York: Praeger, 1987.

Muwakkil, Salim. Black America's Apathy about Social Movements. _In_ _These_
Times April 26, 1989.

Muwakkil, Salim. Black Community Caught in Ideological Whirlpool. _In_
These _Times_ October 19, 1988.

Muwakkil, Salim. The Black Electorate: Ignored by the GOP and Treated
'Like Pariahs' by Democrats. _In_ _These_ _Times_ November 23, 1988.

Nakanishi, Don T. Asian American Politics: An Agenda for Research.

Amerasia Journal 12, No. 2 (1985-86):1-27.

Nowak, Jeremy. *Social Space, Politics Process, and Community Identity in a Multi-Racial Philadelphia Neighborhood*. Doctoral dissertation, New School for Social Research, 1987. UMO # 8711443. [Puerto Rican-black neighborhood].

Omi, Michael A. *We Shall Overturn: Race and the Contemporary Right*. Doctoral dissertation, University of California, Santa Cruz, 1987. UMO # 8810865.

Oreskes, Michael. In Racial Politics, Democrats Losing More than Elections. *New York Times* November 20, 1988.

Oreskes, Michael. New Generation of Blacks Drawn Less to Democrats. *New York Times* October 27, 1988.

Parenti, Michael. *Democracy for the Few* (fourth edition). New York: St. Martin's Press, 1983.

Perry, Huey L. The Socioeconomic Impact of Black Political Empowerment in a Rural Southern Locality. *Rural Sociology* 45 (Summer 1980):207-22. [Greene County, Alabama].

Phillips, Kathryn. Putting Minority Women in Office. *In These Times* March 16, 1988.

Pierce, Paulette. The Roots of the Rainbow Coalition. *Black Scholar* 19 (March-April 1988):2-16.

Poinsett, Alex. Unity without Uniformity. *Ebony* 27 (June 1972):45-54. [National Black Political Convention, Gary, IN].

Piven, Frances Fox and Richard A. Cloward. *Why Americans Don't Vote*. New York: Pantheon, 1988.

Preston, Michael B. Black Politics in the Post-Daley Era. *In*: Samuel K. Gove and Louis H. Masotti (eds.), *After Daley. Chicago Politics in Transition*, pp. 88-117. Urbana: University of Illinois Press, 1982.

Preston, Michael B. and others (eds.) *The New Black Politics: The Search for Political Power*. New York: Longman, 1982.

Price, Catherine M. *Chiefs, headmen, and Warriors: Oglala Politics, 1851-1889*. Doctoral dissertation, Purdue University, 1987. UMO # 8807661.

Procope, John. The New Political Power Among Blacks. *Journal of the Institute for Socioeconomic Studies* (Spring 1978).

Rankin, David C. The Politics of Caste: Free Colored Leadership in New Orleans During the Civil War. *In*: Robert R. MacDonald and others (eds.), *Louisiana's Black Heritage*. New Orleans: 1979.

Rashid Farokhi, Nasrolah. *The Influence of Nongovernmental Business, and*

Interest Group Organization on Urban Politics and Policy Making: A
Case Study of the Leadership Role and Influence of the Atlanta
Chamber of Commerce, 1960-1978. Doctoral dissertation, Atlanta
University, 1979. UMO # 8008643.

Record, Wilson. The Negro and the Communist party. Chapel Hill, NC:
University of North Carolina Press, 1951.

Reed, Adolph, Jr. The Jesse Jackson Phenomenon: The Crisis of Purpose in
Afro-American Politics. New Haven, CT: Yale University Press, 1986.

Reed, Adolph, Jr. Narcissistic Politics in Atlanta. Telos 48 (Summer
1981):98-105.

Reed, Adolph, Jr. (ed.) Race, Politics, and Culture: Critical Essays on
the Radicalism of the 1960s. Westport, CT: Greenwood, 1986.

Reed, Christopher R. A Study of Black Politics and Protest in Depression-
Decade Chicago: 1930-1939. Doctoral dissertation, Kent State
University, 1982. UMO # 8216951.

Robles, Jennifer Juarez. Hispanic Women in Politics Break New Ground.
Chicago Reporter 17 (April 1988):6-7, 11.

Rogers, William W. The Negro Alliance in Alabama. Journal of Negro
History 45 (1960):38-44.

Sagrera, Martin. Racismo y Politica en Puerto Rico. Rio Piedres:
Editorial Edil, 1973.

Sandary, R. Jean Genet and the Black Panther Party. Journal of Black
Studies. 16 (March 1986):269-82.

Sanders, Hank. Defending Voting Rights in the Alabama Black Belt. Black
Scholar 17 (May-June 1986):25-34.

Santillan, Richard A. The Chicano Community and the Redistricting of the
Los Angeles City Council, 1971-1973. Chicano Law Review 6
(1983):122-45.

Santillan, Richard A. The Politics of Cultural Nationalism: El Partido
de la Raza Unida in Southern California: 1969-1978. Doctoral
dissertation, Claremont Graduate School, 1978. UMO # 7911545.

Saunders, Robert. Southern Populists and the Negro, 1893-1895. Journal
of Negro History 54 (July 1969):140-61.

Schmidt, Benno C., Jr. Principle and Prejudice: The Supreme Court and
Race in the Progressive Era. Part 3: Black Disfranchisement from
the KKK to the Grandfather Clause. Columbia Law Review 82 (June
1982):835-905.

Schwartz, Michael. Radical Protest and Social Structure. The Southern
Farmers' Alliance and Cotton Tenancy, 1880-1890. Chicago, IL:
University of Chicago Press, 1988.

Seidel, Gill. The Concept of Culture, 'Race' and 'Nation'. In: R.
    Levitas (ed.), The Ideology of the New Right. Oxford: Blackwell,
    1986.

Sidanius, Jim. Race and Ideology in America: An Exploratory Study.
    Reports from the Department of Psychology, University of Stockholm.
    624 (October 1984).

Serrette, Dennis L. Inside the New Alliance Party. Radical America 21
    (September-October 1987):17-21. [Printed November 1988].

Sifry, Micah L. Jesse and the Jews: Palestine and the Struggle for the
    Democratic Party. Middle East Report 155 (November-December
    1989):4-10.

Simpson, William. The Primary Runoff: Racism's Reprieve? North Carolina
    Law Review 65 (January 1987):359-99.

Skaggs, William H. The Southern Oligarchy: An Appeal in Behalf of the
    Silent Masses of Our Country Against the Despotic Rule of the Few.
    New York: Devin-Adair, 1924.

Skelton, George. 15 Years After [Watts] Riot: Blacks Still Pessimistic.
    Los Angeles Times August 1, 1980.

Sklar, Holly. Jackson Campaign: California to Atlanta. Zeta Magazine 1
    (July-August 1988):50-54.

Smothers, Ronald. Vote Puts Small-Town Blacks on Top. New York Times
    January 6, 1988. [Keysville, GA].

Smothers, Ronald. Why the Higher Rings of Power Elude Black Politicians.
    New York Times February 26, 1989.

Snorgrass, J. W. The Baltimore Afro-American and the Election Campaign of
    FDR. American Journalism 1 (1984):35-50.

Sosna, Morton. The South in the Saddle: Racial Politics during the
    Wilson Years. Wisconsin Magazine of History 54 (Autumn 1970):30-49.

Spitzberg, Irving J., Jr. Racial Politics in Little Rock, 1954-1964. New
    York: Garland, 1986.

Stanley, Harold W. Voter Mobilization and the Politics of Race: The
    South and Universal Suffrage, 1952-1984. New York: Praeger, 1987.

Sudheendran, Kesavan. Community Power Structure in Atlanta: A Study in
    Decision Making, 1920-1939. Doctoral dissertation, Georgia State
    University, 1983. UMO # 8324418.

Sullivan, Brenda A. African-American Political Empowerment in the
    Realignment Era: A Case Study of the North Carolina General
    Assembly. Doctoral dissertation, Atlanta University, 1988. UMO #
    8817603.

Tillman, Joseph M. A Faustian Example of Betrayal: The Ramsey County
    Citizens Committee for Economic Opportunity. Doctoral dissertation,
    University of Minnesota, 1984. [St. Paul, 1965-1970].

Tourgee, Albion W. Shall White Minorities Rule? Forum 7 (April
    1889):143-56.

Travis, Dempsey J. An Autobiography of Black Politics. Chicago, IL:
    Urban Research Institute, 1986.

Walter, John C. The Harlem Fox: J. Raymond Jones and Tammany, 1920-1970.
    Albany: State University of New York Press, 1988.

Walters, Ronald W. The American Crisis of Credibility and the 1988 Jesse
    Jackson Campaign. Black Scholar 19 (March-April 1988):31-44.

Walton, Hanes, Jr. Invisible Politics: Black Political Behavior.
    Albany: State University of New York Pres, 1985.

Walton, Hanes, Jr. The Recent Literature on Black Politics. PS 18 (Fall
    1985):769-80.

Weeks, Stephen B. The History of Negro Suffrage in the South. Political
    Science Quarterly 9 (1894):671-703.

Weinraub, Bernard. [Jesse] Jackson Looks Back at Insults Endured. New
    York Times May 10, 1988.

Weiss, Nancy J. Farewell to the Party of Lincoln: Black Politics in the
    Age of FDR. Princeton, NJ: Princeton University Press, 1983.

Werner, Craig. James Baldwin: Politics and the Gospel Impulses. New
    Politics 1 (Winter 1988):106-24.

Wesley, Charles H. Negro Suffrage in the Period of Constitution-Making,
    1787-1865. Journal of Negro History (April 1947).

West, Cornel. Reconstructing the American Left: The Challenge of Jesse
    Jackson. Social Text 11 (Winter 1984-1985).

Wills, Gary. New Votuhs. New York Review of Books August 18, 1988.

Wilmoth, Stanley C. The Development of Blackfeet Politics and Multiethnic
    Categories: 1934-84. Doctoral dissertation, University of
    California, Riverside, 1987. UMO # 8714708.

Wiseman, John B. Racism in Democratic Politics, 1904-1912. Mid-America
    51 (January 1969):38-58.

Young, T. R. Class Warfare in the 80s and 90s: Reaganomics and Social
    Justice. Wisconsin Sociologist 25 (1988):68-75.

Politics and Racism Bibliography

Snowden, George (comp.) Negro Political Behavior: A Bibliography.
    Bloomington: Indiana University, Dept. of Government, 1941.

Stevenson, Rosemary (comp.) Black Politics in the U.S.: A Survey of
    Recent Literature. Black Scholar 19 (March-April 1988):58-=61.

Walton, Hanes, Jr. (comp.) The Study and Analysis of Black Politics: A
    Bibliography. Metuchen, NJ: Scarecrow Press, 1973.

[See also sections 3, 4, 12, 14, 17, 20, 24, 32, 34, 38, 40, 44, 51, 55,
    60, 64, 69, 76, 78, and 82]

60. Public Opinion

*We do not consider it necessary to inform the Legislature of
Ohio, that their laws oppress us. They know that already. They
made them on purpose to oppress us. ... But ... the people
[here] are better than their laws; and we are permitted to live
in some degree of quiet and safety. ... We have been treated in
a kind and friendly manner.*

    - Representatives of black community in Carthagenia, Mercer
County, Ohio, *Liberator*, August 4, 1843.

Apostle, Richard A. and others. The Anatomy of Racial Attitudes.
    Berkeley: University of California Press, 1983. [San Francisco
    area].

Banks, Sandy. Legacy of Rights Era: Cynicism. Los Angeles Times August
    23, 1982. [Poll of black Angelenos, ages 30-44].

Bowser, Benjamin P. Race Relations in the 1980s: The Case of the United
    States. Journal of Black Studies 15 (1985):307-324.

Brink, William and Louis Harris. Black and White. New York: Simon and
    Schuster, 1967.

Campbell, Angus. White Attitudes Toward Black People. Ann Arbor, MI:
    Institute for Social Research, University of Michigan, 1971.

Campbell, Angus and Howard Schuman. Racial Attitudes in Fifteen American
    Cities, Supplemental Studies for the National Advisory Commission on
    Civil Disorders. Survey Research Center, Institute for Social
    Research, University of Michigan, June 1968.

Colasanto, Diane. Black Attitudes in The Kerner Commission: Twenty Years
    Later. Public Opinion (January-February 1988):41-54.

Condran, John. Changes in White Attitudes Toward Blacks: 1963-1977.
    Public Opinion Quarterly 43 (Winter 1979):463-76.

Denton, Herbert H. and Barry Sussman. [Series of three articles on
    Washington Post-ABC News Poll on race relations in the United
    States]. Washington Post March 24-26, 1981.

Farley, Reynolds and others. A Note on Changes in Black Racial Attitudes
    in Detroit: 1968-1976. Social Indicators Research 6 (October
    1979):439-43.

Fein, Helen. Toleration of Genocide. Patterns of Prejudice 7
    (September-October 1973):22-28. [Attitudes in U.S., 1933-1945].

Ferguson, Thomas and Joel Rogers. The Myth of America's Turn to the
    Right. Atlantic Monthly (May 1986):43-53.

Fernandez, R. Cohort Replacement and Racial Attitude Change, 1956-1976-7. Honors thesis, Harvard University, 1978.

Friedrich, Otto. Racism on the Rise. Time (February 2, 1987). [Includes results of national public opinion poll].

Giles, Micheal W. and Arthur Evans. The Power Approach to Intergroup Hostility. Journal of Conflict Resolution 30 (September 1986):469-86.

Greeley, Andrew M. and Paul B. Sheatsley. Attitudes Toward Racial Integration. Scientific American 225 (December 1971):13-19.

Hardee, Betty B. and Valerie Batts. Has Racism Declined in America? Journal of Conflict Resolution 25 (December 1981):563-579.

Hatchett, Shirley Jean. Black Racial Attitude Change in Detroit, 1968-1976. Doctoral dissertation, University of Michigan, 1982. UMO # 8215007.

Jackman, Mary R. and Marie Crane. 'Some of My Best Friends are Black': Interracial Friendship and Whites' Racial Attitudes. Public Opinion Quarterly (Winter 1986):459-486.

Kluegel, James R. and Eliot R. Smith. Opportunity for Blacks, pp. 179-213 in Beliefs About Inequality. Americans' Views of What Is and What Ought To Be. New York: Aldine de Gruyter, 1986.

Kluegel, James R. and Eliot R. Smith. Whites' Beliefs about Blacks' Opportunity. American Sociological Review 47 (August 1982):518-532.

Louis Harris and Associates, Inc. A Study of Attitudes Toward Racial and Religious Minorities and Toward Women. Prepared for the National Conference of Christians and Jews. Study No. 52829-B. November 1978.

Large Majorities Willing to Vote for Women, Jew, or Black for President. Gallup Report (July 1987):16-20.

Lee, Patrick. Asians Feel the Perils of Racism. Los Angeles Times July 17, 1981. [Asian-Pacific American Round Table (A-PART), Los Angeles].

Lindsey, Robert. Asian-Americans See Growing Bias. New York Times September 10, 1983.

Marx, Gary T. Protest and Prejudice. New York: Harper and Row, 1967. Second edition, 1969.

Market Facts, Inc., Public Affairs Division. A National Survey of Black Americans. Los Angeles, CA: Simon Wiesenthal Center, 1985.

Meislin, Richard J. New Yorkers Say Race Relations Have Worsened in the Last Years. New York Times January 19, 1988. [Public opinion poll].

Merriman, William R., Jr. The Changing American Dilemma: Liberalism and
    Race, Public Opinion and Public Policy. Doctoral dissertation,
    Indiana University, 1986. UMO # 8617785. [1956-1981].

Noel, Joseph R. White Anti-Black Prejudice in the United States.
    International Journal of Group Tensions 1 (January 1971):59-76.

Paige, Jeffery M. Changing Patterns of Anti-White Attitudes Among Blacks.
    Journal of Social Issues 26 (Fall 1970):69-86.

Petrocik, John R. and Frederick T. Steeper. The Political Landscape in
    1988. Public Opinion (September-October 1987):41-44.

Schuman, Howard and others. Racial Attitudes in America, Trends and
    Interpretations. Cambridge, MA: Harvard University Press, 1985.
    [1940s-1980s].

Simmons, Arthur, Jr. Charlie and His Polls. Liberator June 1969.

Smith, A. Wade. Cohorts, Education, and the Evolution of Tolerance.
    Social Science Research 14 (1985):205-225.

Smith, A. Wade. Racial Tolerance as a Function of Group Positions.
    American Sociological Review 46 (October 1981):558-573.

Smith, A. Wade. White Attitudes Toward School Desegregation, 1954-1980:
    An Update on Continuing Trends. Pacific Sociological Review 25
    (1982):3-25.

Smith, E. R. and J. R. Kluegel. Beliefs and Attitudes about Women's
    Opportunity: Comparing with Beliefs about Blacks and a General
    Perspective. Social Psychological Quarterly 46 (1984):81-94.

Smith, Tom W. and Paul B. Sheatsley. American Attitudes toward Race
    Relations. Public Opinion 7 (October-November 1984):14-15, 50-53.

The State of Intolerance in America. Public Opinion (July-August
    1987):21-30. [Survey data, 1948-1987, on Blacks, Mexican-Americans,
    Filipino-Americans, Chinese Americans, Jewish-Americans, Italian
    Americans, and Catholics and Protestants].

Sussman, Barry. What Americans Really Think: And Why Our Politicians Pay
    No Attention. New York: Pantheon, 1988.

Tuch, Steven A. Urbanism, Region, and Tolerance Revisited: The Case of
    Racial Prejudice. American Sociological Review (August 1987):504-10.

Weinberg, Meyer. The Minority Community and Its Schools. In: The Search
    for Quality Integrated Education, pp. 231-69. Westport, CT:
    Greenwood, 1983. [Public opinion polls of minorities, mainly Blacks,
    on school desegregation].

What We Believe. Life 11 (Spring 1988):69-70. [Public opinion poll on
    integration].

White and Negro Attitudes Towards Race Related Issues and Activities. A
    CBS News Public Opinion Survey. Research Park, Princeton, NJ:
    Opinion Research Corporation, July 1968.

Whitfield, Ruth H. Public Opinion and the Chinese Question in San
    Francisco, 1900-1947. Master's thesis, University of California,
    Berkeley, 1947.

Wright, James D. and others. Survey Research. In: Stephan Thernstrom
    (ed.), Harvard Encyclopedia of American Ethnic Groups, pp. 954-71.
    Cambridge, MA: Harvard University Press, 1980.

Zinsmeister, Karl. Asians: Prejudice from Top to Bottom. Public Opinion
    (July-August 1987).

Public Opinion Bibliography

Obudho, Constance E. (comp.) Black-White Racial Attitudes: An Annotated
    Bibliography. Westport, CT: Greenwood Press, 1976.

[See also sections 33, 34, 35, 36, 43, 48, 58, 71, 77, and 84]

61. Racism, Defining

It is not because we are black, that our race is enslaved. It is that domineering spirit that would enslave every man if it had the power.

- Mr. Cole, a colored citizen of Boston, Liberator, February 23, 1838.

Aberger, Peter. Leopold and the Issue of Reverse Racism. Phylon 41 (Fall 1980):276-283.

Allen, W. G. The American Prejudice Against Color. London, 1853.

Banton, Michael. Race As A Social Category. Race July 1966.

Banton, Michael. What Do We Mean by Racism? New Society April 10, 1969.

Barker, Martin. Racism: The New Inheritors. Radical Philosophy 21 (1979).

Bell, C. C. Racism, Narcissism and Integrity. Journal of the National Medical Association 70 (1978):89-92.

Bennett, Lerone, Jr. Was Abe Lincoln a White Supremacist? Ebony 23 (February 1968):35-38.

Berreman, Gerald D. Race, Caste, and Other Invidious Distinctions in Social Stratification. Race 13 (April 1972):385-414.

Betances, Samuel. The Prejudice of Having No Prejudice in Puerto Rico. [2 parts]. The Rican (Winter 1972):41-54, (Spring 1973):22-37.

Blanco, T. Prejudicio racial en Puerto Rico. San Juan, PR: Biblioteca de autores Puertoriquenos, 1942.

Boas, Franz. The Real Race Problem From the Point of View of Anthropology. New York: NAACP, 1910.

Bresnahan, James F. White Racism. America March, 1969.

Brown, K. Turning a Blind Eye: Racial Oppression and the Unintended Consequences of White 'Non-racism.' Sociological Review 33 (1985):670-90.

Carter, George F. Innovation, Diffusion, and Racism. Anthropological Journal of Canada 19 (1981):10-12.

Cashmore, E. Ellis. Dictionary of Race and Ethnic Relations. London: Routledge and Kegan Paul, 1984.

Cowlishaw. Gillian. Race for Exclusion. Australian and New Zealand Journal of Sociology 22 (March 1986):3-24.

467

Dovidio, John F. The Subtlety of White Racism: Three Studies
    Investigating the Dimensions of Prejudice. Doctoral dissertation,
    University of Delaware, 1977. UMO # 7722187.

Egerton, John. Racism Differs in Puerto Rico. Race Relations Reporter 2
    (July 6, 1971):6-7.

Field, Geoffrey G. Nordic Racism. Journal of the History of Ideas 38
    (July-September 1977):523-540.

Glasser, Ira. Racism is Alive and Well and Living in Disguise.
    Christianity and Crisis 41 (March 30, 1981):67-74.

Fleischaker, David. Racism - Or Cultural Bias? Newsweek July 25, 1988.

Guillaumin, Colette. Characteres specifiques de l'ideologie raciste.
    Cahiers Internationaux de Sociologie 53 (1972):247-274.

Guillaumin, Colette. The Idea of Race and Its Elevation to Autonomous,
    Scientific and Legal Status. In: Sociological Theories and
    Colonialism, pp. 37-67. Paris: UNESCO, 1980.

Hardee, Betty B. and Valerie Batts. Has Racism Declined in America?
    Journal of Conflict Resolution 25 (December 1981):563-79.

Hooks, Bell. Overcoming White Supremacy. Zeta Magazine 1 (January
    1988):24-27.

Jones, James M. The Concept of Racism and Its Changing Reality. In:
    Benjamin P. Bowser and Raymond G. Hurt (eds.), Impacts of Racism on
    White Americans, pp. 27-49. Beverly Hills, CA: Sage, 1981.

Joyce, Frank. What Is Racism? Paper Tiger June, 1968.

Killian, Lewis M. The Perils of 'Race' and 'Racism' as Variables. New
    Community 9 (1981-1982):378-388.

Kinder, Donald R. The Contusive American Dilemma: White Resistance to
    Racial Change 40 Years after Myrdal. Journal of Social Issues 42
    (Summer 1986):151-71. [See, below, Sniderman and Tetlock].

Kushnick, Louis. Parameters of British and North American Racism. Race
    and Class 23 (Autumn 1981-Winter 1982):187-206.

Locke, Alain. Concept of Race as Applied to Social Culture. Howard
    Review 1 (June 1924):290-299.

Marable, Manning. Beyond the Race-Class Dilemma. Nation April 11, 1981.

McConahay, John and others. Has Racism Declined: It Depends Upon Who's
    Asking and What Is Asked. Durham, NC: Institute of Policy Science
    and Public Affairs, Duke University, 1980.

McConahay, John B. and Joseph C. Hough, Jr. Value Roots of Symbolic

Racism. Durham, NC: Institute of Policy Sciences, Duke University, October 1975.

McConahay, John B. and Others. Has Racism Declined in America? It Depends on Who Is Asking and What Is Asked. _Journal of Conflict Resolution_ 25 (1981):563-579.

Memmi, Albert. Racism Today. _UNESCO Courier_ 11 (November 1983):11-13.

Millner, S. M. The New South - The New Racism. _Revue Francaise d'Etudes Americaines_ 23 (February 1985):99-114.

Morgan, Glenn. The Analysis of Race: Conceptual Problems and Policy Implications. _New Community_ 12 (Summer 1985):285-294.

Moyer, Charles R. Concerning the Cant of 'White Racism.' _Dissent_ January-February, 1969.

Moynihan, Daniel P. The New Racialism. _Atlantic_ August, 1968.

Nyerere, Julius K. Under Racism, Man Either Becomes Less Than a Man, or He Must Fight. _Objective: Justice_ 3 (January-March 1972):26-27.

O'Callaghan, Marion G. Introductory Notes, pp. 1-36 in _Sociological Theories: Race and Colonialism_. Paris: UNESCO, 1980.

O'Callaghan, Marion G. and C. Guillaumin. Race et race ... la mode 'naturelle' en sciences humaines. _L'Homme et la societe_ 31-32 (1974):195-210.

Rex, John. Racism [letter]. _New Society_ 1969. [Comment on Banton, What Do We Mean by 'Racism?'].

Robeson, Paul. Thoughts on the Colour Bar. In: Philip S. Jones (ed.), _Paul Robeson Speaks. Writings, Speeches, Interviews 1918-1974_, pp. 82-85. New York: Brunner/Mazel, 1978. [Written in 1931].

St. Pierre, Brian (ed.) _The Devil's Advocate: An Ambrose Bierce Reader_. Chronicle Books, 1987.

Sniderman, Paul M. and Philip E. Tetlock. Reflections on American Racism. _Journal of Social Issues_ 42 (Summer 1986):173-87. [See above, Kinder].

Sniderman, Paul M. and Philip E. Tetlock. Symbolic Racism: Problems of Motive Attribution in Political Analysis. _Journal of Social Issues_ 42 (Summer 1986):129-50.

Tajfel, Henri. Racism (letter). _New Society_ May 29, 1969. [Reply to Banton, _New Society_, April 10, 1969].

Taylor, Jerome. Proposal for a Taxonomy of Racialism. _Bulletin of the Menninger Clinic_ 35 (November 1971):421-428.

Taylor, M. C. Fraternal Deprivation and Competitive Racism: A Second

Look. <u>Sociology</u> <u>and</u> <u>Social</u> <u>Research</u> 65 (October 1980):37-55.

Thalberg, Irving. Visceral Racism. <u>Monist</u> 56 (January 1972).

Wald, Alan. The 'New Racism' in the United States. <u>International</u>
    <u>Viewpoint</u> (Montreuil, France) April 4, 1988.

Weigel, Russell H. and Paul W. Howes. Conceptions of Racial Prejudice:
    Symbolic Racism Reconsidered. <u>Journal</u> <u>of</u> <u>Social</u> <u>Issues</u> 41 (Fall
    1985):117-38.

White, J. and J. S. Frideres. Race, Prejudice and Racism: A Distinction.
    <u>Canadian</u> <u>Review</u> <u>of</u> <u>Sociology</u> <u>and</u> <u>Anthropology</u> 14 (February 1977)

Wideman, John Edgar. The Divisible Man. <u>Life</u> 11 (Spring 1988):116.

Wilcox, Preston. Humanness In a Racist Society. <u>Black</u> <u>Caucus</u> 3 (Fall
    1970):50-59.

Wright, W. D. The Faces of Racism. <u>Western</u> <u>Journal</u> <u>of</u> <u>Black</u> <u>Studies</u> 11
    (Winter 1987):168-76.

62. Racism, Exporting

... In the Darwinian and imperialist ambience of the last third of the nineteenth century, racism blossomed forth in a garland of malodorous forms. Imperialism not only nourished, but indeed required theories of western European racial superiority.

- George W. Stocking, Jr., American Social Scientists and Race Theory: 1890-1915 (1960).

Ahari, Mohammed E. (ed.) Ethnic Groups and U.S. Foreign Policy. Westport, CT: Greenwood, 1987.

Aptheker, Herbert. U.S. Imperialism and Racism: A History. Political Affairs 52 (July 1973):75-85.

Black Americans and the Shaping of U.S. Foreign Policy. Washington, D.C.: Joint Center for Political Studies, 1980.

Chapman, Gregory D. Taking Up the White Man's Burden: Tennesseans in the Phillipine Insurrection, 1899. Tennessee Historical Quarterly 47 (Spring 1988):27-40.

Conway, Lydia. The Lost People. New Society April 29, 1988. [Native communities in Alaska].

Du Bois, W. E. B. Education. Crisis 40 (October 1931):350. [Touches on Canal Zone].

Evenson, Debra. Competing Views of Human Rights: The U.S. Constitution from an International Perspective. In: Jules Lobel (ed.), A Less Than Perfect Union, pp. 379-86. New York: Monthly Review Press, 1988.

Hayashi, Wayne. Decolonization Within and Without. Hawaii Pono Journal 1 (April 1971):2-5.

Hornblower, Margot. Puerto Rico. The Underside of Paradise. Washington Post June 21-23, 1981. [Three articles].

Howell, Bing P. The Anatomy of Discrimination in the Canal Zone vis-a-vis United States Policy from 1940-1977. Doctoral dissertation, University of California, Los Angeles, 1979. UMO # 8002486. [Panama].

Kairys, David. Exporting Freedom of Speech In: Jules Lobel (ed), A Less Than Perfect Union, pp. 387-95. New York: Monthly Review Press, 1988.

Paz, B. Sadith. The Status of West Indian Immigrants in Panama from 1850-1941. Master's thesis, University of Massachusetts, 1978.

Quintero-Viera, A. G. Notes on Puerto Rican National Development: Class and Nation in a Colonial Context. Marxist Perspectives 3 (Spring 1980).

Rodriguez, Clara E. and others (eds.) The Puerto Rican Struggle. New York: Puerto Rican Migration Research Constortium, 1980.

Smith, Graham. When Jim Crow Met John Bull. Black American Soldiers in World War II Britain. New York: St. Martin's Press, 1988.

Sundiata, J. K. Black Scandal, America and the Liberian Labor Crisis, 1929-1936. Philadelphia, PA: Institute for the Study of Human Issues, 1980.

Thompson, Winfred L. The Introduction of American Law in the Philippines and Porto Rico, 1898-1905. Doctoral dissertation, University of Chicago, 1987. [Mainly, Philippines].

Trask, Haunani-Kay. Hawaiians, American Colonization, and the Quest for Independence. Social Process in Hawaii. 31 (1984-1985):101-36.

Weston, Rubin F. Racism in U.S. Imperialism: The Influence of Racial Assumptions on American Foreign Policy, 1893-1946. Columbia, S.C.: University of South Carolina Press, 1972.

Whalen, Jeffrey B. and others. Does the Law of Human Rights Guide - or Rationalize - U. S. Foreign policy. American Society of International Law Proceedings. (April 1985):18-34.

White, Philip V. Race Against Time: The Role of Racism in U.S. Foreign Relations. In: Benjamin P. Bowser and Raymond G. Hunt (eds.), Impacts of Racism on White Americans, pp. 177-189. Beverly Hills, CA: Sage, 1981.

Wrage, Stephen D. Human Rights and the American National Myth. Doctoral dissertation, Johns Hopkins University, 1987. UMO # 8716671.

63. Racism in Other Countries

*Racism, understood as a developed theoretical justification for
a system of discrimination and ethnic exploitation, is a
distinctly European contribution to world civilization.*

- Eugene E. Genovese, In Red and Black, 1972

Adams, Howard. Prison of Grass: Canada from the Native Point of View.
    Toronto: New Press, 1975.

Addleston, David F. and Susan Sherer. Race in Viet Nam. Civil Liberties
    February, 1973.

Arens, Richard (ed.). Genocide in Paraguay. Philadelphia, PA: Temple
    University Press, 1976. [Campaign to eliminate the Aché Indians].

Babu, Yuko. A Study of Minority-Majority Relations: The Ainu and the
    Japanese in Hokkaido. Japan Interpreter 13 (Summer 1980):60-92.

Bagley, Christopher. Racialism and Pluralism: A Dimensional Analysis of
    Forty-Eight Countries. Race 13 (January 1972):347-354.

The Baha'is of Iran. London: Minority Rights Group, 1982.

Banac, Ivo. The National Question in Yugoslavia. Ithaca, NY: Cornell
    University Press, 1985.

Barker, Anthony J. The African Link: British Attitudes to the Negro in
    the Era of the Atlantic Slave Trade, 1550-1807. Totowa, NJ: Cass,
    1978.

Bartels, Dennis. Ethnicity, Ideology, and Class Struggle in Guyanese
    Society. Anthropologica (Ottawa) 22 (1981):45-60.

Bell, Colin (ed.) Race, Class and Rebellion in the South Pacific.
    London: George Allen and Unwin, 1979.

Ben-Tovim, Gideon and John Gabriel. The Politics of Race in Britain,
    1962 to 1979: A Review of the Major Trends and of the Recent
    Literature. Sage Race Relations Abstracts 4 (November 1979):1-56.

Berger, Thomas R. Fragile Freedoms: Human Rights and Dissent in Canada.
    Toronto: Clarke, Irwin, 1982.

Bernard, W. S. Racism, a Worldwide Factor Opposing Migrant Adjustment and
    How to Combat it. The Hague: Research Group for European Migration
    Problems, 1978.

Blakely, Allison. Russia and the Negro: Blacks in Russian History and
    Thought. Washington, D.C.: Howard University Press, 1986.

Bock, Gisela. Racism and Sexism in Nazi Germany: Motherhood, Compulsory

Sterilization, and the State. *Signs* 8 (Spring 1983):400-421.

Bose, Nemai S. *Racism, Struggle for Equality, and Indian Nationalism*. Calcutta: Firma KLM, 1981.

Bourgois, Philippe. Class, Ethnicity, and the State among the Miskitu Amerindians of Northeastern Nicaragua. *Latin American Perspectives* 2 (Spring 1981):22-39.

Brennan, Martin. Class, Politics and Race in Modern Malaysia. *Journal of Contemporary Asia* 12 (1982):188-215.

Broome, Richard. *Aboriginal Australians: Black Response to White Dominance, 1788-1980*. Boston: Allen and Unwin, 1982.

Burg, Steven L. Ethnic Conflict and the Federalization of Socialist Yugoslavia: The Serbo-Croat Conflict. *Publius* 7 (Fall 1977):119-43.

Cadzow, John F. and others (eds.) *Transylvania: The Roots of Ethnic Conflict*. Kent, OH: Kent State University Press, 1983. [Rumania].

Cannon, Terry and Johnnetta Cole. *Free and Equal. The End of Racial Discrimination in Cuba*. New York: Venceremos Brigade, 1978.

Carmack, Robert M. Spanish-Indian Relations in Highland Guatemala, 1800-1944 in M. MacLeod and R. Wasserstrom (eds.), *Spaniards and Indians in Southeastern Mesoamerica*. Lincoln: University of Nebraska Press, 1983.

Cashmore, Ernest Ellis. *The Logic of Racism*. Boston: Allen and Unwin, 1986. [England].

Centre for Contemporary Cultural Studies (eds.) *The Empire Strikes Back: Race and Racism in 70s Britain*. London: Hutchinson, 1983.

Chaliard, Gerard and Yves Ternon. *The Armenians, from Genocide to Resistance*. Translated by Tony Berrett. London: Zed Press, 1983. [Turkey].

Clark, Robert P. *The Basque Insurgents: ETA, 1952-1980*. Madison: University of Wisconsin Press, 1984. [Spain].

Cohen, J. Colonialism and Racism in Algeria. In: Anthony H. Richmond (ed.), *Readings in Racial and Ethnic Relations*. Oxford: Pergamon Press, 1972.

Cohen, William B. *The French Encounter with Africans: White Response to Blacks, 1530-1880*. Bloomington: Indiana University Press, 1980. [See Th. Mpuyi-Buatu, below].

Constantino, Renato. *Neocolonial Identity and Counterconsciousness: Essays on Cultural Decolonization*. White Plains, NY: M.E. Sharpe, 1979. [Phillipines].

Cooper, Mark N. Racialism and Pluralism as Dimensions of Nations: A Further Investigation. Race 15 (January 1974):370-381.

Corbett, Anne. Racism Surfaces in France. New Society November 3, 1983.

Cotler, Julio. The Mechanisms of Internal Domination and Social Change in Peru. In: Irving L. Horowitz (ed.), Masses in Latin America. New York: Oxford University Press, 1970.

Cox, Oliver C. Color Prejudice, A World Problem. The Aryan Path (Bombay) (June 1947).

Dam, Nikolaos van. The Struggle for Power in Syria: Sectarianism, Regionalism, and Tribalism in Politics, 1961-1978. New York: St. Martin's Press, 1979.

Daniels, Roger. Chinese and Japanese in North America: The Canadian and American Experiences Compared. Canadian Review Studies 17 (Summer 1986):173-87.

Daninos, Guy. Le Racisme colonial a travers la litterature congolaise. Mois Afrique 16 (April-May 1981):120-26.

Dean, Elizabeth and others. History in Black and White: An Analysis of South African School History Textbooks. New York: UNIPUB, 1983.

Dennis, Philip A. The Anti-Chinese Campaigns in Sonora, Mexico. Ethnohistory 26 (Winter 1979):65-80.

Dew, Edward. The Difficult Flowering of Surinam: Ethnicity and Politics in a Plural Society. The Hague: Martinus Niyhoff, 1978.

Fevre, Ralph. Cheap Labour and Racial Discrimination. Aldershot: Gower, 1984. [Asian migrants in British textile industry since 1945].

Forbes, Andrew D. W. Thailand's Muslim Minorities: Assimilation, Secession or Coexistence? Asian Survey 22 (November 1982):1056-73.

Franklin, A. E. Black and White Australians - An Interracial History 1788-1975. Melbourne: Heinemann Educational, 1976.

Gershoni, Y. Black Colonialism: The Americo-Liberian Scramble for the Hinterland. Boulder, CO: Westview, 1984.

Ghareeb, Edmund A. The Kurdish Question in Iraq. Syracuse, NY: Syracuse University press, 1981.

Ghassemlou, A. R. Kurdistan in Iran. In: Gerard Chaliard (ed.), People Without a Country. The Kurds and Kurdistan, pp. 107-34. [Translated by Michael Pallis.] London: Zed, 1980.

Gilman, Sander I. On Blackness without Blacks: Essays on the Image of the Black in Germany. Boston: Hall, 1982.

Gilbroy, Paul. You Can't Fool the Youths ... Race and Class Formation in the 1980s. <u>Race</u> <u>and</u> <u>Class</u> 23 (Autumn 1981-Winter 1982):207-22. [Britain].

Goldberg, M. Class, Race and Ideology in Ghana. <u>Social</u> <u>Dynamics</u> 6 (1980):53-56.

Gordon, Paul. <u>White</u> <u>Law:</u> <u>Racism</u> <u>in</u> <u>the</u> <u>Police,</u> <u>Courts,</u> <u>and</u> <u>Prisons</u>. London: Pluto Press, 1983. [Britain].

Gowing, Peter G. <u>Muslim</u> <u>Filipinos:</u> <u>Heritage</u> <u>and</u> <u>Horizon</u>. Quezon City: New Day, 1979.

Griffith, Albert R. Cuba from a Black Perspective. <u>Crisis</u> 87 (May 1980):181-83.

Gutman, Nelly. The Reaction against Immigrants in France. <u>Research</u> <u>Report</u> (Institute of Jewish Affairs) 13 (November 1984).

Haddock, Mike. 20th Century Austrian Minority Problems. <u>Kansas</u> <u>Geographer</u> 14 (1979):5-12.

Hancock, Ian F. Gypsies in Germany: The Fate of Romany. <u>Michigan</u> <u>Germanic</u> <u>Studies</u> 6 (Fall 1980):247-64.

Hasenbalg, Carlos A. and Suellen Huntington. Brazilian Racial Democracy: Reality or Myth? <u>Humboldt</u> <u>Journal</u> <u>of</u> <u>Social</u> <u>Relations</u> 10 (Fall-Winter 1982-83):129-42.

Hellman, Ellen and Henry Lever (eds.) <u>Race</u> <u>Relations</u> <u>in</u> <u>South</u> <u>Africa</u> <u>1929-1979</u>. New York: St. Martin's Press, 1980.

Higman, Charles. <u>The</u> <u>Maoris</u>. New York: Cambridge University Press, 1981.

Holzner, Lutz. The Myth of Turkish Ghettos: A Geographic Case Study of West German Responses towards a Foreign Minority. <u>Journal</u> <u>of</u> <u>Ethnic</u> <u>Studies</u> 9 (Winter 1982):65-85.

Horrell, Muriel. <u>Race</u> <u>Relations</u> <u>as</u> <u>Regulated</u> <u>by</u> <u>Law</u> <u>in</u> <u>South</u> <u>Africa</u>. Johannesburg: South African Institute of Race Relations, 1982.

Howard, Michale C. (ed.) <u>Aboriginal</u> <u>Power</u> <u>in</u> <u>Australian</u> <u>Society</u>. Honolulu: University of Hawaii Press, 1982.

Inter-American Commission on Human Rights. <u>Report</u> <u>on</u> <u>the</u> <u>Situation</u> <u>of</u> <u>Human</u> <u>Rights</u> <u>of</u> <u>a</u> <u>Segment</u> <u>of</u> <u>the</u> <u>Nicaraguan</u> <u>Population</u> <u>of</u> <u>Miskito</u> <u>Origin</u>. Washington, D.C.: Organization of American States, 1984.

Irving, R. E. M. <u>The</u> <u>Flemings</u> <u>and</u> <u>Walloons</u> <u>of</u> <u>Belgium</u>. London: Minority Rights Group, 1980.

Jacob, James E., IV. Ethnic Conflict in Contemporary France. <u>Contemporary</u> <u>French</u> <u>Civilization</u> 5 (Fall 1980):23-42.

Jahreskog, B. <u>The</u> <u>Sami</u> <u>National</u> <u>Minority</u> <u>in</u> <u>Sweden</u>. [Translated by A.

Nordin and L. Schenk.] Atlantic Highlands, NJ: Humanities Press, 1981.

James, C. L. R. An Accumulation of Blunders. New Society December 3, 1981. [Commentary on the Scarman Report; discusses racism in Britain].

Janics, Kolman. Czechoslovakia Policy and the Hungarian Minority, 1945-1948. [Translated by Stephen Barsody]. New York: Social Science Monographs, 1982.

Jiryis, Sabri. The Arabs in Israel, 1973-79. Journal of Palestine Studies 8 (Summer 1979):31-56.

Kapo, Remi. A Savage Culture: Racism - a Black British View. London: Quartet Books, 1981.

Kendal. Kurdistan in Turkey. In: Gerard Chaliard (ed.), People Without a Country. The Kurds and Kurdistan, pp. 47-106. [Translated by Michael Pallis]. London: Zed Press, 1980.

Kolack, Shirley. Ethnic Minorities in the Soviet Union: The Unfinished Revolution. Journal of Ethnic Studies 13 (Summer 1985):125-32.

Krisjjanson, Lowell G. Estratificacion socio-racial y economica de Costa Rica: 1700-1850. San Jose: Editorial Universidad Estatal a Distancia, 1978.

Kushnick, Louis V. Parameters of British and North American Racism. Race and Class 23 (Autumn 1981-Winter 1982):187-206.

Lee, Changaoo and George De Vos. Koreans in Japan: Ethnic Conflict and Accomodation. Berkeley: University of California Press, 1982.

Lippmann, Lorna. Generations of Resistance: The Aboriginal Struggle for Justice. Melbourne, 1981. [Australia].

Lloyd, Cathie. What is the French CP Up to? Race and Class 22 (Spring 1981):403-07. [Racism in the French Communist Party].

Lustick, Ian. Arabs in the Jewish State. Israel's Control of a National Minority. Austin: University of Texas Press, 1980.

Mar'i, Sami K. The Future of Palestinian Arab Education in Israel. Journal of Palestine Studies 14 (Winter 1985):52-73.

Maybury-Lewis, David and James Howe. The Indian Peoples of Paraguay: Their Plight and their Prospects. Cultural Survival Quarterly (October 1980).

Mayer, Kurt. Ethnic Tensions in Switzerland: The Jura Conflict. In: Charles R. Foster (ed.), Nations Without a State, pp. 189-208. New York: Praeger, 1980.

Mayerson, Philip. Anti-Black Sentiment in the Vitae Patrum. Harvard

Theological Review 71 (1978):304-11. [Egyptian monastic communities 3rd-5th centuries].

Miles, Robert and Annit Phizacklea (eds.) Racism and Political Action in Britain. Boston: Routledge and Kegan Paul, 1979.

Milza, Pierre. Le Racisme anti-italien en France. La'tuerie d'Aigues Mortes. L'Histoire 10 (March 1979):23-31.

Mörner, Magnus. The Andean Past: Land, Societies, and Conflicts. New York: Columbia University Press, 1984. [Bolivia].

Mpuyi-Buatu, Th. William B. Cohen et le racism francais anti-noir. Peuples Noirs. Peuples Afric. 5 (May-June 1982):71-112. [See William B. Cohen, above].

Muller-Wille, Ludger. The Sami Parliament in Finland: A Model for Ethnic Minority Management? Etudes Inuit Studies 3 (1979):63-72.

Nahamd Sitton, Salomon. Mexican Colonialism? Society 19 (November-December 1981):51-58. [Education of Indians].

Nahaylo, Bohdan and C. J. Peters. The Ukrainians and Georgians. London: Minority Rights Group, 1981. [USSR].

Nazdan, Mustafa. The Kurds in Syria. In: Gerard Chaliard (ed.), People Without a Country. The Kurds and Kurdistan, pp. 211-19. [Translated by Michael Pallis]. London: Zed Books, 1980.

Niani. Black Consciousness vs. Racism in Brazil. Black Scholar 11 (January 1980):59-70.

Nicholls, David. From Dessalines to Duvalier: Race, Colour, and National Independence in Haiti. New York: Cambridge University Press, 1980.

Nkomo, Mokubong O. Student Culture and Activism in Black South African Universities. The Roots of Resistance. Westport, CT: Greenwood, 1984.

Norway: Sami Rights and the Alta-Kautokeino Case. International Work Group for Indigenous Affairs Newsletter 27 (1981):63-76. [Lapps in Norway].

Okpu, U. Ethnic Minority Problems in Nigerian Politics 1960-1965. Uppola: Scandanavian Institute of African Studies, 1977.

Olszewski, Marian. The Policy of Exterminating Polish Intellectuals during the Nazi Occupation. Polish W. Affairs 21 (1980):121-28.

Osborne, Robert D. Religious Discrimination and Disadvantage in the Northern Ireland Labour Market. Int. Jr. Social Econ. 7 (1980):206-33.

Osoba, Segun. The Nigerian Power Elite, 1952-65. In: P. Gutkind and P. Waterman (eds.), African Social Studies: A Radical Reader. London: Heinemann, 1977.

Pao Min Chang. The Sino-Vietnamese Conflict over the Ethnic Chinese. China Quarterly 90 (1982). [Vietnam].

Paraf, P. Le racisme dans le monde (third edition). Paris: Payot, 1969.

Patai, Daphne. Race and Politics in Two Brazilian Utopias. Luso-Brazilian Review 19 (1982):67-81.

Patel, H. H. Race, Class, and Citizenship in Uganda: The Indian Minority, 1900-72. Berkeley, CA: University of California Press, 1977.

Pauley, Bruce F. Hitler and the Forgotten Nazis: A History of Austrian National Socialism. Chapel Hill, NC: University of North Carolina Press, 1981.

Pi-Sunyer, Oriol. Dimensions of Catalan Nationalism. In: Charles R. Foster (ed.), Nations Without a State, pp. 101-15. New York: Praeger, 1980. [Spain].

Piyadasa, L. Sri Lanka: The Holocaust and After. London: Marram Books, 1984.

Ponnambalam, Satchi. Sri Lanka: The National Question and the Tamil Liberation Struggle. London: Zed Books, 1983.

Poole, P. A. The Vietnamese in Thailand: A Historical Perspective. Ithaca, NY: Cornell University Press, 1970.

Poulin, Richard. La politique de sinisation des nationalites minoritaires en Republique Populaire de Chine. Pluriel 25 (1981):65-78.

Pristinger, Flavia. Ethnic Conflict and Modernization in the South Tyrol. In: Charles R. Foster (ed.), Nations Without a State, pp. 153-88. New York: Praeger, 1980. [Italy].

Racialism in Sweden. Patterns of Prejudice 14 (July 1980):31-34.

Racism and the Struggle Against It in the Contemporary World. Moscow: Nauka for "Social Sciences Today" Editorial Board, USSR Academy of Sciences, 1982.

Radical Racists' International. Patterns of Prejudice 10 (September-October 1976):18-21.

Roth, Stephen J. The Second World Conference on Racism. Research Report (Institute of Jewish Affairs), No. 17 (September 1983).

Samoff, Joel. Pluralism and Conflict in Africa: Ethnicity, Institutions and Class in Tanzania. Civilisations 32 (1982):and 33 (1983).

Sanborn, Anne F. and G. W. de Czege (eds.) Transylvania and the Hungarian-Rumanian Problem: A Symposium. Astor, FL: Danubian Press, 1979. [Rumania].

Schmid, Carl. Majority-Minority Relations in a Multicultural Society: The Case of Switzerland. Doctoral dissertation, McMaster University, 1979.

Schubert, Grace. To Be Black is Offensive: Racist Attitudes in San Lorenzo. In: Norman E. Whitten, Jr. (ed.), Cultural Transportations and Ethnicity in Modern Ecuador, pp. 563-85. Urbana, IL: University of Illinois Press, 1981.

Searle, Chris. Beyond the Skin: How Mozambique is Defeating Racism. London: Liberation, 1979.

Shipler, David. Arab and Jew: Wounded Spirits in a Promised Land. New York: Times Books, 1986.

Singer, Daniel. France, Racism and the Left. Nation September 18, 1985.

Singh, K. S. (ed.) Tribal Movements in India, Vol. 1. New Delhi: Manoham, 1983.

Sivanandan, Ambelavenar. Race and Resistance: The IRR Story, 1974. Race Today Publications 1974, 184 King's Cross Rd., London W.C.1, 01-8370041 England. [In re: Institute of Race Relations].

Skidmore, Thomas E. Race and Class in Brazil: Historical Perspectives. Luso-Braz. Review 20 (Summer 1983):104-18.

Smith, Richard Chase. The Dialectics of Discrimination in Peru: Native Communities and the Myth of the Vast Amazonian Emptiness. Cultural Survival Quarterly (October 1982).

Sunahara, Ann G. The Politics of Racism: The Uprooting of Japanese Canadians during the Second World War. Toronto: Lorimer, 1981.

The Untouchables of India. London: Minority Rights Group, 1982.

van Amersfoort, J. M. M. Immigration and the Formation of Minority Groups. The Dutch Experience 1945-1975. New York: Cambridge University Press, 1982.

Voll, John O. and Sarah P. Voll. The Sudan: Unity and Diversity in a Multicultural State. Boulder, CO: Westview Press, 1985.

Wan, Hashim. Race Relations in Malaysia. Heinemann Asian, 1983.

Washbrook, D. A. Ethnicity and Racialism in Colonial Indian Society in Robert Ross (ed.), Racism and Colonialism The Hague: Martinus Nyhoff, 1982.

Wirsing, Robert. The Baluchis and Pathans. London: Minority Rights Group, 1981. [Pakistan].

Wojatsek, Charles. From Trianon to the First Vienna Arbitral Award. The Hungarian Minority in the First Czechoslavak Republic, 1918-1939.

480

Institute of Comparitive Civilizations, c/o M.M. Kolbe Editions, P.O. Box 2058, Station J-C, Sherbrook, Quebec, Canada J1 J 341.

Wolfers, Michael. Race and Class in Sudan. Race and Class 23 (Summer 1981):65-79.

Yoshino, J. Roger and B. Murakoshi. The Invisible Visible Minority: Japan's Burakumin. Osaka: Buraku Kaiho Kenyus Kenkyusho, 1977.

Ziegler, Suzanne. Diagnosis and Treatment of a Community Illness: Primary Prevention of Racism in Ethnically Heterogenous Communities. August 26, 1981. ERIC ED 210 414. [Toronto].

Racism in Other Countries Bibliography

Minority Rights Group, London, England. A large series of short reports on racism and allied subjects in many countries of the world.

64. Racism, Institutional

... It is impossible to eliminate prejudice through education unless the institutions through which people relate are also reconstructed so they reinforce the teaching.

- Dan W. Dodson, March 5, 1972

Allen, Sheila. The Institutionalization of Racism. *Race* 15 (July 1973):99-106.

Anderson, K. The Idea of Chinatown: The Power of Place and Institutional Practice in the Making of a Racial Category. *Annals of the Association of American Geographers* 77 (December 1987):580-98.

Baratz, Joan C. and others. *Who Is Going to Medical School? A Look at the 1984-85 Underrepresented Minority Medical School Applicant Pool.* Princeton, NJ: Educational Testing Service, October 1985.

Barbarin, Oscar A. and Renee Gilbert. Institutional Racism Scale: Assessing Self and Organizational Attributes. *In:* Oscar A. Barbarin and other (eds.), *Institutional Racism and Community Competence*, pp. 147-171. Washington, D.C.: GPO, 1981.

Baron, Harold. Web of Urban Racism. Appendix to *Institutional Racism in America.* Edited by Kenneth Prewitt and Louis Knowles. Englewood Cliffs, NJ: Prentice-Hall, 1969.

Benokratis, Nijole and Joe Feagin. Institutional Racism: A Perspective in Search of Clarity and Research. *In:* Charles V. Willie (ed.), *Black/Brown/White Relations.* New Brunswick, NJ: Transaction, 1977.

Berlowitz, Marvin J. Institutional Racism and School Staffing in an Urban Area. *Journal of Negro Education* 43 (Winter 1974):25-29.

Bowser, Benjamin P. *Institutional Racism: Toward a Critical Reassessment of American Institutions.* September 1, 1979. ERIC ED 179 645.

Brophy, Michael C. and others. *Advocacy and Institutional Racism,* September 1976. ERIC ED 141 649.

Bullock, Charles S., III and Harrell R. Rodgers, Jr. Institutional Racism: Prerequisites, Freezing, and Mapping. *Phylon* 37 (September 1976):212-223.

Butler, John S. *Unsanctioned Institutional Racism in the U.S. Army.* Doctoral dissertation, Northwestern University, 1974.

Chan, Adrian and others. *Advocate Counseling and Institutional Racism,* 1978. ERIC ED 162 005.

Chin, Jean Lau. Institutional Racism and Mental Health: An Asian-American Perspective. *In:* Oscar A. Barbarin and others (eds.),

Institutional Racism and Community Competence, p 445. Washington, D.C.: GPO, 1982.

Dodson, Dan W. Institutionalized Racism in Social Welfare Agencies. In: The Social Welfare Forum 1970, pp. 88-89. New York: Columbia University Press, 1970.

Dodson, Dan W. Perspectives on Institutional Racism. In: Arnold H. Grossman (ed.), New Challenge to Social Agency Leadership, 1979. Groupwork Today, Inc., P.O. Box 258, South Plainfield, NJ 07080.

Drinnon, Richard. Keeper of Concentration Camps. Dillon S. Myer and American Racism. Berkeley, CA: University of California Press, 1987.

Eidson, Bettye. Institutional Racism: Minority Group Manpower Policies of Major Urban Employers. Doctoral dissertation, Johns Hopkins University, 1971.

Fiman, Byron G. The Difference Indicator: Quantitative Index of Institutional Racism. In: Oscar A. Barbarin and others (eds.), Institutional Racism and Community Competence, pp. 179-192. Washington, D.C.: GPO, 1982.

Friedman, R. Institutional Racism: How to Discriminate Without Really Trying. In: Thomas F. Pettigrew (ed), Racial Discrimination in the United States, pp. 384-407. New York: Harper and Row, 1975.

Gamoran, Adam. The Institutionalization of Educational Stratification. August 1984. ERIC ED 253 849.

Gilbert, Neil and Harry Specht. Institutional Racism. Urban and Social Change Review 6 (February 1972):2-6.

Glott, Charles S. and George D. King. Institutional Racism and White Racists: A Socio-Psychological View of Race and Educational Development. In: G. H. Verma and Christopher Bagley (eds.), Race and Education Across Cultures. Stamford, CT: Greylock Publishers, 1975.

Goodman, James (ed.) Dynamics of Racism in Social Work Practice. Washington, D.C.: National Association of Social Workers, 1973.

Haas, Michael. Filipinos in Hawaii and Institutional Racism. Phillippine Sociological Review 32 (January-December 1984):41-53.

Hurley, Daniel J. and others. An Empirical Study of Racism in Community Functioning. In: Oscar A. Barbarin and others (eds.), Institutional Racism and Community Competence, pp. 134-145. Washington, D.C.: GPO, 1982.

Institutional Racism Awareness Seminar. Evanston, IL: National School Boards Association, 1973.

Institutional Racism in the Military. Congressional Record 118 (March

1972):E1902-E1910.

Johnson, Charles S. The Present Status of Race Relations. Journal of
    Negro Education 8 (July 1939).

Jones, Delmos J. Not in My Community: The Neighborhood Movement and
    Institutional Racism. Social Policy 10 (September-October 1979):44-
    46.

Jones, Terry. Institutional Racism in the United States. Social Work 19
    (March 1974):218-225.

Klitgaard, R. E. Institutional Racism: An Analytic Approach. J. Peace
    Res. 1 (1972):41-49.

Knowles, Louis and Kenneth Prewitt (eds.) Institutional Racism in
    America. Englewood Cliffs, NJ: Prentice-Hall, 1969.

Lee, Patrick. Asians Feel the Perils of Racism. Los Angeles Times July
    17, 1981. [Asian-Pacific American Round Table (A-PART), Los
    Angeles].

Leon, David Jess. Institutional Racism and the Educational Opportunity
    Program: A Study of Organizational Change and Strategies for Reform,
    1979. ERIC ED 179 170.

Lewis, Hylan. Race, the Policy, and the Professions. Education for
    Social Work 5 (1969):19-30.

Lopez, Richard E. and Donald Cheek. The Prevention of Institutional
    Racism: Training Counseling Psychologists as Agents for Change.
    Counseling Psychologist 7 (1977):64-68.

Marginalization. Corvalis, OR: Western Rural Development Center, Oregon
    State University, 1974.

Mason, David. After Scarman: A Note on the Concept of 'Institutional
    Racism.' New Community 10 (Summer 1982):38-45.

Massey, Grace C., Mona V. Scott and Sanford M. Dornbusch. Racism Without
    Racists: Institutional Racism in Urban Schools. Black Scholar 7
    (November 1975):2-11.

McAdoo, William. The Settler State: Immigration Policy and the Rise of
    Institutional Racism in Nineteenth Century Michigan. 2 vols.
    Doctoral dissertation, University of Michigan, 1983. UMO # 8324245.

Peirson, Gwynne Walker. An Introductory Study of Institutional Racism in
    Police Law Enforcement. Doctoral dissertation, University of
    California, Berkeley, 1977. UMO # 78-12452. [Oakland, California].

Piliawsky, Monte. Racial Equality in the United States: From
    Institutionalized Racism to 'Respectable' Racism. Phylon 45 (June
    1984):135-143.

484

Racism in the YMCA. Southern Courier, July 1968.

Sabshin, Melvin, Herman Diesenhaus and Raymond Wilkerson. Dimensions of Institutional Racism in Psychiatry. American Journal of Psychiatry 127 (December 1970):787-793.

Sanders, Charles. Black Professionals' Perceptions of Institutional Racism in Health and Welfare Organizations. Fair Lawn, NJ: R.E. Burdick, 1974.

Sanders, Charles. A Typology of Racism in Bureaucratic Systems. In: National Association of Black Social Workers, Diversity: Cohesion or Chaos-Mobilization for Survival, pp. 252-268. Proceedings of the Fourth Annual Conference of N.A.B.S.W. Nashville, TN: Fisk University, 1973.

Sawyer, Jack and David J. Senn. Institutional Racism and the American Psychological Association. Journal of Social Issues 29 (1973):67-79.

Thalberg, Irving. Justification of Institutional Racism. Philosophical Forum 3 (Winter 1971-1972).

Scott, Beverly D. Institutional Racism: A Behavioral Measure. Doctoral dissertation, Stanford University, 1974. UMO # 74-27109.

Shaw, Van B. The Concept of Institutional Racism. Journal of Intergroup Relations 5 (November 1976):3-12.

Spears, Arthur K. Institutionalized Racism and the Education of Blacks. Anthropology and Education Quarterly 9 (Summer 1978):127-136.

Washington Task Force on African Affairs. A Black Paper. Institutional Racism in African Studies and U.S.-African Relations. 1969. The Washington Task Force on African Affairs, P.O. Box 13033, Washington, D.C. 20009.

Williams, Jenny. Redefining Institutional Racism. Ethnic and Racial Studies 8 (1985).

Williams, Leon F. Indices of Institutional Racism: A Survey of Non-Discriminatory Practices and Educational Quality in Baccalaureate Programs of Social Work. Doctoral dissertation, Brandeis University, 1981. UMO # 8124664.

65. Racism, Psychology of

Why ... do you attempt to degrade me on account of my color - and refuse to put me on my good conduct and behavior?

- Henry Scott, a black man from Worcester, Mass., *Liberator*, December 14, 1838.

Adam, Barry. Social Psychology of Inferiorized Peoples. Doctoral dissertation, University of Toronto, 1978.

Ahearn, Wilbert H. Assimilationist Racism: The Case of the 'Friends of the Indian'. Journal of Ethnic Studies 4 (Summer 1976):23-32.

Allen, Ben P. Implications of Social Reaction Research for Racism. Psychological Reports 29 (December 1971):883-891.

American Journal of Psychiatry 127 (1970):787-814. [Special section on racism].

Ashmore, Richard D. and Frances K. Del Boca. Psychological Approaches to Understanding Intergroup Conflict. In: Phyllis A. Katz (ed), Towards the Elimination of Racism, pp. 73-123. New York: Pergamon, 1976.

Baldwin, Joseph A. Theory and Research Concerning the Notion of Black Self-Hatred: A Review and Reinterpretation. Journal of Black Psychology 5 (February 1979):51-77.

Banton, Michael. Pluralistic Ignorance as a Factor in Racial Attitudes. New Community 13 (Spring-Summer 1986):18-26.

Bell, C. C. Racism, Narcissism and Integrity. Journal of the National Medical Association 70 (1978):89-92.

Billig, Michael. Ideology and Social Psychology. Oxford: Blackwell, 1982.

Billig, Michael. The Origins of Race Psychology -- I. Patterns of Prejudice 16 (July 1982):3-16.

Billig, Michael. The Origins of Race Psychology -- II. Patterns of Prejudice 17 (January 1983):25-31.

Boas, Franz. Race Problems in America. Science May 28, 1909.

Bogle, Kathryn H. 'An American Negro Speaks of Color.' Oregon Historical Quarterly 89 (Spring 1988):70-91.

Bowser, Benjamin P. Racism and Mental Health: An Exploration of the Racist's Illness and the Victim's Health. In: Oscar A. Barbarin and others (eds.), Institutional Racism and Community Competence, pp. 107-113. Washington, D.C.: GPO, 1982.

Bowser, Benjamin P. and Raymond G. Hunt (eds.) The Impact of Racism on White Americans. Beverly Hills, CA: Sage, 1981.

Butts, Hugh F. Psychoanalysis and Unconscious Racism. Journal of Contemporary Psychotherapy 3 (Spring 1971):67-81.

Butts, Hugh F. Psychoanalyis, the Black Community and Mental Health. Contemporary Psychoanalysis 7 (Spring 1971):147-152.

Butts, Hugh F. White Racism: Its Origin, Institution, and the Implication for Professional Practice in Mental Health. International Journal of Psychiatry 8 (1969):914-944.

Clark, Kenneth B. and Mamie Phipps. What Do Blacks Think of Themselves? Ebony 36 (November 1980).

Collier, Betty J. Economics, Psychology, and Racism: A Model of Oppression. Journal of Black Psychology 3 (January 1978).

Comer, James P. White Racism: Its Root, Form, and Function. American Journal of Psychiatry 126 (December 1969):802-06.

Dala, Farhad. The Racism of Jung. Race and Class (Winter 1988).

Delany, Lloyd T. Racism and Strategy for Change. Psychology Today August 1968.

Derman-Sparks, Louise. Children, Race and Racism: How Race Awareness Develops. Interracial Books for Children Bulletin 11, nos. 3-4 (1980).

Edwards, Daniel W. Blacks versus Whites: When Is Race a Relevant Variable? Journal of Personality and Social Psychology 29 (Janaury 1974):39-49.

Ehrlich, Howard J. The Social Psychology of Prejudice: A Systematic Theoretical Review and Propositional Inventory of the American Social Psychological Study of Prejudice. New York: Wiley, 1973.

Ellis, S. W. The Psychology of American Race Prejudice. Journal of Race Development 5 (1914-1915):297-315.

Flynn, James R. The Racist and His Need for Evidence. In: Race, IQ and Jensen, pp. 1-24. London: Routledge and Kegan Paul, 1980.

Goodman, Paul. Reflections on Racism, Spite, Guilt, and Violence. New York Review of Books May 1968.

Hauer, Stuart T. and E. Kasendorf. Black and White Identity Formation (second edition). Malabar, FL: R.E. Krieger, 1983.

Jones, Reginald L. Racism, Mental Health, and the Schools. In: Charles V. Willie, Bernard M. Kramer and Bertram S. Brown (eds.), Racism and Mental Health, pp. 319-352. Pittsburgh, PA: University of

Pittsburgh Press, 1973.

Kline, Hayes K. An Exploration of Racism in Ego Ideal Formation. Smith College Studies in Social Work 40 (June 1970):211-235.

Kovel, Joel. White Racism. New York: 1984.

Lawrence, Charles R., III. The Id, the Ego, and Equal Protection: Reckoning with Unconscious Racism. Stanford Law Review 39 (January 1987):317-88.

Levine, Barry B. Salpicar and the Specter of Self-Hate among Puerto Ricans: On the Testimonial Literature of Modernization and Ethnicity. In: Asela Rodgriguez de Laguna (ed.), Images and Identities. The Puerto Rican in Two World Contexts, pp. 89-95. New Brunswick, NJ: Transaction Books, 1987.

Mazon, Mauricio. The Zoot-Suit Riots: The Psychology of Symbolic Annihilation. Austin: University of Texas Press, 1984.

McCarthy, John D. and William L. Yancey. Uncle Tom and Mr. Charlie: Metaphysical Pathos in the Study of Racism and Personal Disorganization. American Journal of Sociology 76 (January 1971):648-672.

Miller, Herbert A. Some Psychological Considerations on the Race Problem. Bibliotheca Sacra (April 1906).

Morales, Armando. The Collective Preconscious and Racism. Social Casework (May 1971):285-93.

Murray, Joan and Paul R. Abramson (eds.) Bias in Psychotherapy. New York: Praeger, 1983.

Pettigrew, Thomas F. The Mental Health Impact. In: Benjamin P. Bowser and Raymond G. Hunt (eds.), Impacts of Racism on White Americans, pp. 97-118. Beverly Hills, CA: Sage, 1981.

Pinderhughes, Charles A. The American Racial Dilemma: A Social Psychiatric Formulation. American Journal of Social Psychiatry 6 (Spring 1986):107-113.

Poussaint, Alvin F. A Black Psychiatrist Examines Racism. Science for the People 14 (March-April 1982):21-24.

Profit, Wesley E. Blacks in Homogeneous and Heterogeneous Racial Groups: The Effects of Racism and the Mundane Extreme Environment. Doctoral dissertation, Harvard University, 1977. UMO # 77-23423.

Shannon, Barbara E. The Impact on Personality Development. Social Casework 54 (November 1973):519-525.

Thomas, Alexander and Samuel Sillen. Racism and Psychiatry. New York: Brunner/Mazel, 1972.

Tong, Ben R. The Ghetto of the Mind: Notes on the Historical Psychology of Chinese America. _Amerasia Journal_ 1 (November 1971):1-31.

Vander Zanden, James W. The Ideology of White Supremacy. _Journal of the History of Ideas_ 20 (1959):385-402.

Whitaker, Ben. Minority Conflicts in Present-Day Societies: A Sociopsychological Analysis. _In_: George Sweeney (ed.), _Selected Proceedings of the 3rd Annual Conference on Minority Studies, April, 1975_, pp. 5-10. La Crosse, WI: Institute for Minority Studies, University of Wisconsin, La Crosse, 1976.

Willie, Charles V., Bernard M. Kramer and Bertram S. Brown (eds.) _Racism and Mental Health: Essays_. Pittsburgh, PA: Univerity of Pittsburgh Press, 1972.

Wilson, R. Psychology and the Black Community. _Newsletter of the Michigan Black Psychologists_ (December 1969).

Wright, Bobby. The Psychopathic Radical Personality. _Black Books Bulletin_ 2 (February 1974):24-32.

66. Racism, Scholarly

*We said we'd like the National Institute of Mental Health to set
up an institute or task force to study racism or white
supremacy. They didn't say they wouldn't set up such a task
force or institute. They said we will set up an institute to
study minority groups. In other words, "we won't study
ourselves, but we will study you."*

  - Frances Cress Welsing, Washington Post, September 9,
    1973.

Aldrich, Mark. Progressive Economists and Scientific Racism: Walter
    Willcox and Black Americans, 1895-1910. Phylon 40 (Spring 1979):1-
    14.

Barber, Lucius J. Dialogue on a New Dilemma. Society 24 (January-
    February 1987):29-37. [The Study on the Status of Black Americans].

Barsh, Russel L. Are Anthropologists Hazardous to Indians' Health?
    Journal of Ethnic Studies 15 (Winter 1988):1-38.

Bean, Robert Bennett. The Negro Brain. Century Magazine (September
    1906):778-784.

Bell, Michael J. The Relation of Mentality to Race: William Wells Newell
    and the Celtic Hypothesis. Journal of American Folklore 92
    (1979):25-43.

Black, Isabella. Race and Unreason: Anti-Negro Opinion in Professional
    and Scientific Literature Since 1954. Phylon Spring, 1965.

Black Psychiatrists: How Racism is Reflected in Referrals. Frontier of
    Clinical Psychiatry (Roche Report) July, 1969.

Boller, Paul F., Jr. American Thought in Transition: The Impact of
    Evolutionary Naturalism, 1865-1900. Chicago, 1969. ["Scientific"
    racism].

Cerroni-Long, E. L. Benign Neglect? Anthropology and the Study of Blacks
    in the United States. Journal of Black Studies 17 (June 1987):438-
    59.

Chachere, Bernadette and others. Causes for Action. Society 24
    (January-February 1987):22-28. [The Study on the Status of Black
    Americans].

Chase, Allan. The Legacy of Malthus. The Social Cost of the New
    Scientific Racism. New York: Knopf, 1977.

Davidson, Douglas. Black Culture and Liberal Sociology. Berkeley Journal
    of Sociology 14 (1969).

Duchene, Marlys. GIANT LAW, GIANT EDUCATION, and ANT: A Story About Racism and Native Americans. Harvard Educational Review 58 (August 1988):354-62.

Drake, St. Clair. Reflections on Anthropology and the Black Experience. Anthropology and Education Quarterly 9 (Summer 1978):85-109.

Duster, Troy. Purpose and Bias. Society 24 (January-February 1987):8-12. [The Study on the Status of Black Americans].

Ethnic Minorities: Resistance to Being Researched. Professional Psychology 3 (1972):11-17.

Faris, J. C., A. S. Kroch and P. Newcomer. On the Continuing Revival of Scientific Racism. Newsletter of the American Anthropological Association 13 (1972):10-11.

Gaertner, Samuel L. and John F. Davidio. Racism among the Well-Intentioned. In: Edwin G. Clausen and Jack Bermingham (eds.), Pluralism, Racism, and Public Policy: The Search for Equality. Boston: Hall, 1981.

Guthrie, R. V. Even the Rat Was White: A Historical View of Psychology. New York: Harper and Row, 1976.

Haller, John S., Jr. Outcasts from Evolution: Scientific Attitudes of Racial Inferiority, 1859-1900. Urbana: University of Illinois Press, 1971.

Henry, Jeanette. A Rebuttal to the Five Anthropologists on the Issue of the Wampum Return. Indian Historian 3 (1970):15-17.

Horsman, Reginald. Scientific Racism and the American Indian in the Mid-Nineteenth Century. American Quarterly 27 (May 1975).

Jaynes, Gerald D. and Robin M. Williams, Jr. Challenges and Opportunities. Society 24 (January-February 1987):3-7; see also pp. 37-78. [The Study on the Status of Black Americans].

Karcher, Carolyn L. Melville's 'The Gees': A Forgotten Satire on Scientific Racism. American Quarterly 27 (October 1975):421-442.

Kroch, Anthony. Racist Ideology in Recent Social Science. The UAG Magazine 2 (Winter 1973):5-14.

Ladner, Joyce A. (ed.) The Death of White Sociology. New York: Random House, 1973.

Ledvinka, James. The Intrusion of Race: Black Responses to the White Observer. Social Science Quarterly 52 (March 1972):907-20.

Lewis, Daine. Anthropology and Colonialism. Current Anthropology 14 (December 1973):581-602.

Lofgren, Charles A. The Intellectual Environment: Racist Thought in the

Late Nineteenth Century. In: The Plessy Case. A Legal-Historical Interpretation, Chapter 5. New York: Oxford University Press, 1987.

Lyons, A. P. The Question of Race in Anthropology from the Time of Johann Friederich Blumenbach to that of Franz Boas, with Particular Reference to the Period 1830-90 (Approximately). Doctoral dissertation, Oxford University, 1974.

Mechalin, John M. Democracy and Race Friction. New York: Macmillan, 1914.

Miller, Maurice Lim. Whom Should Academic Researchers Serve? Amerasia Journal 12, no. 2 (1985-86):95-99.

Montalto, Nicholas. The Intellectual Education Movement, 1924-1941: The Growth of Tolerance as a Form of Intolerance. In: Bernard J. Weiss (ed.), American Education and the European Immigrant: 1840-1940, pp. 142-60. Urbana: University of Illinois Press, 1982.

Newby, I. A. Jim Crow's Defense: Anti-Negro Thought in America, 1900-1930. Baton Rouge: Louisiana State University Press, 1965.

Novick, Peter. That Noble Dream: The "Objectivity Question" and the American Historical Profession. New York: Cambridge University Press, 1988.

Padilla, A. M. Psychological Research and the Mexican American. In: M. M. Margold (ed.), La Causa Chicana: The Movement for Justice. New York: Family Service Association of America, 1972.

Richards, P. The Ideology of European Dominance. Western Journal of Black Studies 3 (1979):244-50.

Roucek, Joseph. Roots of Racism of American Social Scientists. Indian Sociological Bulletin April, 1969.

Schuman, Howard. Sociological Racism. Transaction 7 (1969):44-48.

Seyd, T. 'Scientific' Racism Again. Marxism Today 17 (January 1973).

Stanfield, John H. Philanthropy and Jim Crow in American Social Science. Westport, CT: Greenwood Press, 1985.

Stanfield, John H. Race Relations Research and Black Americans Between the Two World Wars. Journal of Ethnic Studies 11 (Fall 1983):61-93.

Stanton, William. The Leopard's Spots: Scientific Attitudes Toward Race in America, 1815-59. Chicago: 1960.

Stocking, George W., Jr. Race, Culture, and Evolution. New York: 1968.

Theilman, Samuel B. Psychiatry and Social Values: The American Psychiatric Association and Immigration Restriction, 1880-1930. Psychiatry 48 (November 1985):299-310.

Turner, James and W. Eric Perkins. Towards A Critique of Social Science. _Black Scholar_ 7 (April 1976):2-11.

Trumpbour, Jack (ed.) _How Harvard Rules_. Boston: South End Press, 1989.

Vaca, Nick C. The Mexican-American in the Social Sciences, 1912-1970. [2 parts] _El Grito_ 3 (1970):3-24; 4 (1970):17-51.

Wiener, Jon. Bringing Nazi Sympathizers to the U.S. _Nation_ March 6, 1989. [Talcott Parsons and others].

Williams, Robert L. The Death of White Research in the Black Community. _Journal of Non-White Concerns in Personnel and Guidance_ 2 (April 1974):116-32.

Williams, Thelma L. _The Social Sciences: Are They Reinforcing Racism in Professional Nursing Education and Practice?_ Doctoral dissertation, Temple University, 1987. UMO # 8711427.

Williams, William S., Jr. Skeletons in the Anthropological Closet [Racism among anthropologists]. _In_: Dell Hymes (ed.), _Reinventing Anthropology_, pp. 121-152. New York: Vintage.

Willie, Charles V. Appearances and Sensitivities. _Society_ 24 (January-February 1987):19-22. [The Study on the Status of Black Americans].

67. Racism, Testing for

The Government that makes all its mistakes on one side must have a constitutional bias in that direction.

- Wendell Phillips, <u>Liberator</u>, February 13, 1863

Alley-Claiborne, Joyce G. and Jerome Taylor. The Realistic Incidents Inventory: Measuring Awareness of Racialism. <u>In</u>: Oscar A. Barbarin and others (eds.), <u>Institutional Racism and Community Competence</u>, pp. 172-178. Washington, D.C.: GPO, 1981.

Bromley, Stephanie and others. <u>Black and White Racism: An Unobtrusive Experimental Assessment</u>, April 1977. ERIC ED 151 626.

Harmon, Rosemary. <u>The Measurement of Racism and Sexism Through the Select-a Face Inventory</u>. Doctoral dissertation, University of Virginia, 1977. UMO # 79-01138.

Hiett, Robert L. and others. <u>The Racial Attitudes and Perceptions Survey (RAPS)</u>. Alexandria, VA: U.S. Army Research Institute for Behavioral and Social Sciences, 1978.

Hilliard, Asa G., III and others. <u>Behavioral Criteria in Research and the Study of Racism</u>. 3 parts, January 1979-February 1981. ERIC ED 220 471 - 220 473.

Williams, Leon F. Measuring Racism: An Example from Education. <u>Social Work</u> 27 (January 1982):111-115.

68. Racism, Theory of

Blackness is the crime of crimes. ... Why is it a crime?
Because it threatens white supremacy.

-W. E. B. Du Bois, "Triumph," 1911

Alexander, Peter. Racism, Resistance and Revolution. London: Bookmarks, 1987.

Allen, Robert L. Racism and the Black Nation Thesis. Socialist Revolution 6 (January-March 1976):145-150.

Allen, Robert L. Rap Brown Raps: Racism and Revolution. Guardian June 1968.

Baca Zinn, Maxine. Sociological Theory in Emergent Chicano Perspectives. Pacific Sociological Review 24 (April 1982):255-72.

Banton, Michael. Ethnic Groups and the Theory of Rational Choice. In: Sociological Theories: Race and Colonialism, pp. 475-499. Paris: UNESCO, 1980.

Barker, Martin. The New Racism: Conservatives and the Ideology of the Tribe. Frederick, MD: Aletheia Books, 1982.

Barkham, Elazar. From Race to Ethnicity: Changing Concepts of Race in England and the United States between the Two World Wars. Doctoral dissertation, Brandeis University, 1988. UMO # 8811114.

Baron, Harold. Racism Transformed: The Implications of the 1960s. Review of Radical Political Economics 17 (1985):10-33.

Beechey, V. The Ideology of Racism. Doctoral dissertation, University of Oxford, 1978.

Berlowitz, Marvin J. and Ronald S. Edari (eds.) Racism and the Denial of Human Rights: Beyond Ethnicity. Minneapolis, MN: Marxist Educational Press, 1984.

Blumer, Herbert. The Future of the Color Line. In: John C. McKinney and Edgar T. Thompson (eds.), The South in Continuity and Change. Durham, NC: Duke University Press, 1965.

Blumer, Herbert and Troy Duster. Theories of Race and Social Action. In: Sociological Theories: Race and Colonialism, pp. 211-238. Paris: UNESCO, 1980.

Boas, Franz. Fallacies of Racial Inequality. Current History 25 (1927):676-82.

Bonacich, Edna. Sociology of Race Relations in the United States. In: Edgar F. Borgatta and Karen S. Cook (eds.), The Future of Sociology.

Newbury Park, CA: Sage, 1988.

Boyd, D. A. C. The Historical Materialist Symbolist Theory of Race
Discrimination. Social and Economic Studies 36 (June 1987).

Brown, Roy. Racism: The Worst Tool of Cruelty. Integrated Education
(May-June 1972):3-10.

Carruthers, Iva Elayne Johnson Wells. Black Power and Integration: A
Reformulation of the Theory of Race Relations. Doctoral
dissertation, Northwestern University, 1972. UMO # 72-32400.

Castro, Rudolph and others. The Problem of Racism: An Attitudinal Study
of the Spanish Surname. Master's thesis, University of Denver, 1972.

Chesler, Mark S. Contemporary Sociological Theories of Racism. In:
Phyllis A. Katz (ed.), Towards the Elimination of Racism, pp. 21-71.
New York: Pergamon, 1976.

Clark, Cedric C. On Racism and Racist Systems. Negro Digest August
1969.

Clark, Kenneth B. A Challenge. Southern Exposure 7 (Summer 1979):136-
137.

Clark, Kenneth B. Any Kind of Racism Is a Constriction of the Mind
[Interview]. This Week June 1969.

Clark, Kenneth B. As Old as Human Cruelty. New York Times Book Review
September 1968.

Comarmond, Patrice de and Claude Duchet. Racisme et Societe. Paris:
N.p., 1969.

Comer, James P. White Racism: Its Roots, Form, and Function. American
Journal of Psychiatry 120 (1969):802-806.

Daniels, Roger and Harry H. L. Kitano. American Racism: Exploration of
the Nature of Prejudice. Englewood Cliffs, NJ: Prentice-Hall, 1970.

Douglass, Frederick. The Color Line. North American Review 132 (1881).

Dovidio, John F. and Samuel L. (eds.) Prejudice, Discrimination, and
Racism. Orlando, FL: Academic Press, 1986.

Dreyfus, Joel. The New Racism. Black Enterprise 8 (January 1978):41-44,
54.

Drimmer, Melvin. Thoughts on the Persistence of American Racism. Afro-
American Studies 1 (April 1971):309-313.

Feagin, Joe R. and C. B. Feagin. Discrimination American Style.
Englewood Cliffs, NJ: Prentice-Hall, 1978.

Fenton, C. Stephen. Race, Class and Politics in the Work of Emile

496

Englewood Cliffs, NJ: Prentice-Hall, 1978.

Fenton, C. Stephen. Race, Class and Politics in the Work of Emile
    Durkheim. In: Sociological Theories: Race and Colonialism, pp.
    143-181. Paris: UNESCO, 1980.

Frazier, E. Franklin. The Pathology of Race Prejudice. Forum 77
    (1927):856-62.

Frederickson, George. The Arrogance of Race: Perspectives in the History
    of Slavery and White Supremacy. Middleton, CT: Wesleyan University
    Press, 1988.

Gabriel, John G. The Concepts of Race and Racism: An Analysis of
    Classical and Contemporary Theories of Race. Doctoral dissertation,
    University of Liverpool, 1977.

Gabriel, John G. and G. Ben-Tovim. The Conceptualization of Race
    Relations in Sociological Theory. Ethnic and Racial Studies 3
    (1980).

Gabriel, John G. and G. Ben-Tovim. Marxism and the Concept of Racism.
    Economy and Society 7 (May 1978):118-154.

Gay, Geneva. Racism in America: Imperatives for Teaching Ethnic Studies.
    In: James A. Banks (ed.), Teaching Ethnic Studies: Concepts and
    Strategies. Washington, D.C.: National Council for the School
    Studies, 1973.

Gayle, Addison, Jr. Black Power or Black Fascism? Liberator, May, 1968.

George, Hermon, Jr. American Race Relations Theory: A Review of Four
    Models. Lanham, MD: University Press of America, 1984.

Geschwender, James A. Racial Stratification in America. Dubuque, IA:
    Brown, 1978.

Gloor, Pierre-Andre. A propos de la xenophobie et du racisme.
    L'Anthropologie 84 (1980):583-601. [English summary].

Goldschmid, Marcel L. (ed.) Black Americans and White Racism: Theory
    and Research. New York: Holt, Rinehart and Winston, 1970.

Grubbs, Donald H. and Clifford E. Landers. Racism: From Irrational
    Anachronism to Functional Social Condition. Review of Black
    Political Economy 6 (Fall 1975).

Guillaumin, Colette. L'ideologie racist, genese et langage actuel. The
    Hague: Mouton, 1972.

Guillaumin, Colette. Race et Nature: systeme de marques, idee de groupe
    naturel et rapports sociaux. Pluriel Debat 11 (1977):39-56.

Guillauin, Colette and Leon Poliakov. Max Weber et les theories
    bioraciales due XXe siecle. Cahiers Internationaux de Sociologie

56, pp. 115-126.

Hilliard, Asa G., III and others. Behavioral Criteria in Research and the Study of Racism. [3 parts]. January 1979-February 1981. ERIC ED 220 471- 220 473.

Isaacs, Charles. Racism, Reaction, and Repression. Edcentric 36 (October 1975):4-8, 33-34.

Jackman, Mary R. and Michael J. Muha. Education and Intergroup Attitudes: Moral Enlightenment Superficial, Democratic Commitment, Ideological Refinement. American Sociological Review 49 (December 1984):751- 769.

Jackson, Monica L. Competitive and Symbolic Racism as Status Politics. Master's thesis, University of Oklahoma, 1987.

Jones, James M. The Concept of Racism and its Changing Reality. In: Benjamin P. Bowser, and Raymond G. Hunt (eds.), Impacts of Racism on White Americans, pp. 27-49. Beverly Hills, CA: Sage, 1981.

Jones, James M. Prejudice and Racism. Reading, MA: Addison-Wesley, 1972.

Kimmel, Michael S. A Prejudice against Prejudice. Psychology Today 20 (December 1986):46-48, 50-52. [About Thomas F. Pettigrew].

Le Vine, Robert A. and Donald T. Campbell. Ethnocentrism: Theories of Conflict, Ethnic Attitudes and Group Behavior. New York: Wiley, 1972.

Lecourt, Dominique. On Marxism as a Critique of Sociological Theories. In: Sociological Theories: Race and Colonialism, pp. 267-285. Paris: UNESCO, 1980.

Lefait, P. Science and Racism. Paris: UNESCO, 1982.

Lieberman, Leonard and Lary T. Reynolds. The Debate Over Race Revisited: An Empirical Investigation. Phylon 39 (December 1978):333-343.

Locke, Alain. Reason and Race. Phylon 8 (1947):17-27.

Lowy, Richard F. and David V. Baker. Transcendence, Critical Theory and Emancipation: Reconceptualizing the Framework for a Chicano Sociology. Journal of Ethnic Studies 15 (Winter 1988):57-83.

Malcolm X. The End of White World Supremacy. Four Speeches. New York: Monthly Review Press, 1971.

Martin W. On the Social Mechanism of White Supremacy. Pacific Sociological Review 15 (1972):203-224.

Maynor, Waltz. Racism and Indian Policies in North Carolina. In: George E. Carter and James R. Parker (eds.), Selected Proceedings of the 4th Annual Conference on Minority Studies. La Crosse, WI: Institute for

Minority Studies, University of Wisconsin, La Crosse, 1978.

McConahay, John B. and Joseph C. Hough, Jr. Symbolic Racism. Journal of Social Issues 32 (1976):23-45.

McConahay, John B. and others. Has Racism Declined in America? It Depends on Who is Asking and What is Asked. Journal of Conflict Resolution 25 (1981):563-579.

Miles, Robert. Marxism versus the Sociology of Race Relations? Ethnic and Racial Studies 76 (1984).

Miller, Kelly. The Harvest of Race Prejudice. Survey Graphic 6 (March 1925):682-83, 711-12.

Miller, Kelly. Race Prejudice, Innate or Acquired. Journal of Applied Sociology 11 (1927):516-24.

Mirande. Alfredo. Sociology of Chicanos or Chicano Sociology? A Critical Assessment of Emergent Paradigms. Pacific Sociological Review 25 (October 1982):495-508.

Mitchell, Roxanne and Frank Weiss. A House Divided: Labor and White Supremacy. New York: United Labor Press, 1981.

Moore, Carlos. Were Marx and Engels White Racists? Berkeley Journal of Sociology 19 (1974-1975).

Moore, Carlos. Were Marx and Engels White Racists? The Proletaryan Outlook of Marx and Engels., 1973. Black People's Information Centre, 301 Portobello Rd., London, W.10, England.

Muhammmad, W. D. The Dravidian Roots of Aryan White Supremacy and Diabolic Consciousness. Muhammad Speaks, August, 1975.

Mullard, Chris. Race, Power and Resistance. London: Routledge and Kegan Paul, 1985.

Munford, Clarence J. The Function of Racism in Contemporary America. In: Production Relations, Class and Black Liberation, pp. 89-114. Amsterdam: Gruner, 1978.

Munford, Clarence J. Ideology, Racist Mystification and America. Revolutionary World: An International Journal of Philosophy (Amsterdam) 17-18 (1976):57-85.

Nash, Manning. Race and Ideology of Race. Current Anthropology, June, 1962.

Ochillo, Yvonne. The Race-consciousness of Alain Locke. Phylon 47 (Fall 1986):173-81.

Omi, Michael and Howard Winant. Racial Formation in the United States: From the 1960s to the 1980s. New York: Routledge and Kegan Paul, 1986.

Omi, Michael and Howard Winant. Racial Theory in the Post-War United States: A Review and Critique. _Sage Race Relations Abstracts_ 12 (May 1987).

Orans, M. Race and Class Conflict in Crosscultural Perspective. _Urban Affairs Annual Reviews_ 5 (1971):1-68.

Pettigrew, Thomas F. _Racially Separate or Together?_ New York: McGraw-Hill, 1971.

Phelps, Edwin. The Statistical Theory of Racism and Sexism. _American Economic Review_ (September 1972).

Pierre-Charles, Gerard. Racialism and Sociological Theories. _In: Sociological Theories: Race and Colonialism_, pp. 69-83. Paris: UNESCO, 1980.

Platt, Steve. Are Dolphins Racist? _New Society_ April 1, 1988. [In re: genetic determination of racism].

Poliakov, Leon (ed.) _Ni Juif ni Grec: Entretiens sur le racisme._ New York: Mouton, 1978.

Poliakov, Leon and others. _Le Racisme._ Paris: Seghers, 1976.

Prager, Jeffrey. White Racial Privilege and Social Change: An Examination of Theories of Racism. _Berkeley Journal of Sociology_ 17 (1972):117-150.

Racism: An American Ideology. _Akwesane Notes_ 9 (Autumn 1977):6-7.

Rex, John. _Race and Ethnicity._ Philadelphia, PA: Open University Press, 1986.

Rex, John. _Race Relations in Sociological Theory._ London: Weidenfeld and Nicolson, 1970.

Rex, John. The Theory of Race Relations - A Weberian Approach. _In: Sociological Theories: Race and Colonialism_, pp. 117-142. Paris: UNESCO, 1980.

Rex, John and David Mason (eds.) _Theories of Race and Ethnic Relations._ New York: Cambridge University Press, 1986.

Reynolds, Vernon and others (eds.) _The Sociology of Ethnocentrism: Evolutionary Dimensions of Xenophobia, Discrimination, Racism, and Nationalism._ Athens, GA: University of Georgia Press, 1987.

Rodgers, B. _Race: No Peace without Justice._ Geneva: World Council of Churches, 1980.

Rodgers, Harrell R., Jr. (ed.) _Racism and Racial Inequality: The Policy Alternatives._ San Francisco, CA: Freeman, 1975.

Saxton, Alexander. Historical Explanations of Racial Inequality. <u>Marxist</u> <u>Perspectives</u> 2 (Summer 1979):145-168.

Schuman, William. Sociological Racism. <u>Trans-action</u> (December 1969).

Schwartz, Barry N. and Robert Disch (eds.). <u>White</u> <u>Racism:</u> <u>Its</u> <u>History,</u> <u>Pathology</u> <u>and</u> <u>Practice</u>. New York: Dell, 1970.

Scott, James F. White-Racism: Explanation or Anathema? <u>Journal</u> <u>of</u> <u>Social</u> <u>and</u> <u>Behavioral</u> <u>Sciences</u> 18 (Fall-Winter, 1971-1972):27-34.

See, K. O'Sullivan and W. J. Wilson. Race and Ethnicity. <u>In</u>: Neil J. Smelser (ed.), <u>Handbook</u> <u>of</u> <u>Sociology</u>. Newbury Park, CA: Sage, 1988.

Silverman, I. Race, Race Differences, and Race Relations: Perspectives from Psychology and Sociobiology. <u>In</u>: Charles B. Crawford and others (eds.), <u>Sociobiology</u> <u>and</u> <u>Psychology</u>. Hillsdale, NJ: Lawrence Erlbaum Associates, 1987.

Simon, Yves R. Secret Source of the Success of the Racist Ideology. <u>In</u>: <u>Community</u> <u>of</u> <u>the</u> <u>Free</u>. New York: Holt, 1948.

Singleton, Royce, Jr. and Jonathan H. Turner. Racism: White Oppression of Blacks in America. <u>In</u>: D. H. Zimmerman, D. L. Wieder, and S. Zimmerman (eds.), <u>Understanding</u> <u>Social</u> <u>Problems</u>, pp. 130-160. New York: Praeger, 1976.

Sivanandan, Ambelavenar. Race, Class and Power: An Outline for Study. <u>Race</u> 14 (April 1973):383-391.

Southern, David W. <u>Gunnar</u> <u>Myrdal</u> <u>and</u> <u>Black-White</u> <u>Relations.</u> <u>The</u> <u>Use</u> <u>and</u> <u>Abuse</u> <u>of</u> <u>An</u> <u>American</u> <u>Dilemma,</u> <u>1944-1969</u>. Baton Rouge: Louisiana State University Press, 1987.

Spiegel, Marjorie. <u>The</u> <u>Dreaded</u> <u>Companion:</u> <u>Race</u> <u>and</u> <u>Animal</u> <u>Slavery</u>. Santa Cruz, CA: New Society, 1988.

Stanfield, John H. Theoretical and Ideological Barriers to the Study of Race-making. <u>Research</u> <u>in</u> <u>Race</u> <u>and</u> <u>Etnhic</u> <u>Relations</u> 4 (1985):161-81.

Strauss, Sylvia. Gender, Class, and Race in Utopia. <u>In</u>: Daphne Patai (ed.), <u>Looking</u> <u>Backward,</u> <u>1988-1888</u>. Amherst, MA: University of Massachusetts Press, 1989.

Takaki, Ronald (ed.) <u>From</u> <u>Different</u> <u>Shores.</u> <u>Perspectives</u> <u>on</u> <u>Race</u> <u>and</u> <u>Ethnicity</u> <u>in</u> <u>America</u>. New York: Oxford University Press, 1987.

Taylor, Howard F. Quantitative Racism: A Partial Documentation. <u>Journal</u> <u>of</u> <u>Afro-American</u> <u>Issues</u> 3 (Winter 1975):19-42.

Taylor, M. C. Fraternal Deprivation and Competitive Racism: A Second Look. <u>Sociology</u> <u>and</u> <u>Social</u> <u>Research</u> 65 (October 1980):37-55.

Tillman, James A., Jr. Why America Needs Racism. [2 parts]. <u>Liberator</u>, June, July, 1968.

Van Den Berghe, Pierre L. Race and Racism. A Comparative Perspective. New York: Wiley, 1967.

West, Cornel. Marxist Theory and the Specificity of Afro-American Oppression. In: Cary Nelson and Lawrence Grossberg (eds.), Marxism and the Interpretation of Culture. Urbana: University of Illinois Press, 1988.

Wilkerson, Cathy. The False Privilege [White racism]. New Left Notes October, 1968.

Willhelm, Sidney M. Equality in America's Racist Ideology. In: Joyce Ladner (ed.), The Death of White Sociology. New York: Random House, 1973.

Willie, Charles V. Oreo: A Perspective on Race and Marginal Men and Women. Wakefield, MA: Parameter Press, 1975.

Wilson, C. E. Black Power and the Myth of Black Racism. Liberation September, 1966.

Wilson, William J. Power, Racism, and Privilege. Race Relations in Theoretical and Sociohistorical Perspective. New York: Macmillan, 1973.

Wobogo, V. Diop's Two Cradle Theory and the Origin of White Racism. Black Books Bulletin 4 (Winter 1976):20-29.

Wolpe, Harold. Class Concepts, Class Struggle and Racism. In: John Rex and D. Mason (eds.), Theories of Race and Ethnic Relations, pp. 110-30. New York: Cambridge University Press, 1986.

Zubaida, Sami (eds.) Race and Racialism. New York: Barnes and Noble, 1970.

Theory of Racism Bibliography

Center for Minority Group Mental Health Programs (comps.) Bibliography on Racism. Rockville, MD: U.S. National Institute of Mental Health, 1972.

Wade, Jacqueline (comp.) American Racism Bibliography. Philadelphia, PA: University of Pennsylvania, School of Social Work, 1981.

69. Racist Groups

Back of the writhing, yelling, cruel-eyed demons who break,
destroy, maim, and lynch and burn at the stake is a knot, large
or small, of normal human beings and these human beings at heart
are desperately afraid of something. Of what? Of many things
but usually of losing their jobs, of being declassed, degraded
or actually disgraced; of losing their hopes, their savings,
their plans for their children; of the actual pangs of hunger;
of dirt, of crime. And of all this, most ubiquitous in modern
society is that fear of unemployment.

> - W. E. B. Du Bois, "The Shape of Fear," North American
> Review (June 1926).

Amann, Peter H. Vigilante Fascism: The Black Legion as an American
Hybrid. Comparative Studies in Society and History 25 (July
1983):490-524.

Anti-Defamation League. The Growing Menace of America's Neo-Nazi
Skinheads. New York: Anti-Defamation League, 1988.

Beaver, Gene Marvin. The Beliefs of the Citizens' Councils: A Study in
Segregationist Thought. Master's Thesis, California State College at
Fullerton, 1968. UMO # M-1669.

Bilbo, Theodore G. Take Your Choice: Separation or Mongrelization
[Racist book]. Poplarville, MS: Dream House Publishing Co., 1947.

Bishop, Katherine. Judge Blocks Neo-Nazi 'Woodstock' in California. New
York Times March 4, 1989.

Bishop, Katherine. Neo-Nazi Activity Is Arising Among U.S. Youth. New
York Times June 13, 1988.

Canfield, James L. A Case of Third Party Activism: The George Wallace
Campaign Worker and the American Independent Party. Lanham, MD:
University Press of America, 1984.

Clark, Susan C. America's Nazis: The German American Bund. Doctoral
dissertation, Texas A & M University, 1987. UMO # 8802067.

DeSilver, Drew. Hate Can't Be Imprisoned. In These Times (May 13,
1987):2. [Racist-antisemitic groups in U.S.].

Dudley, J. Wayne. 'Hate' Organizations of the 1940's: The Columbians,
Inc. Phylon 42 (September 1981):262-74.

Fink, Leonard. Growing Menace [of Teenage Skinhead Groups]. Detroit
Jewish News (February 17, 1989):24-26.

Flynn, Kevin and Gary Gerhardt. The Silent Brotherhood. Inside America's
Racist Underground. New York: Free Press, 1989.

Galloway, Paul. Survivalists Get Set for Armageddon. Los Angeles Times, December 19, 1980. [Freedom Festival of the Christian-Patriots Defense League].

Hate Groups in America. A Record of Bigotry and Violence. New York: Anti-Defamation League of B'nai B'rith, October 1982.

Higham, Charles. American Swastika. Garden City, NY: Doubleday, 1985.

Jeansome, Glen. Gerald L.K. Smith, Minister of Hate. New Haven: Yale University Press, 1988.

Jordan, Robert A. Spreading Hatred [Neo-Nazi Skinheads in U.S.]. Boston Globe November 26, 1988.

King, Wayne. Link Seen Among Heavily Armed Rightist Groups. New York Times June 11, 1983.

King, Wayne. Violent Racism Attracts New Breed: Skinheads. New York Times January 1, 1989.

Lipset, Seymour M. and Earl Rabb. The Politics of Unreason: Right-Wing Extension in America, 1790-1970. New York: Harper and Row, 1970.

McCuen, Garry E. (ed.). The Racist Reader: Analyzing Primacy Source Readings by American Race Supremacists. Anoka, MN: Greenhaven Press, 1974.

Mintz, Frank P. The Liberty Lobby and the American Right: Race, Conspiracy, and Culture. Westport, CT: Greenwood, 1985.

Newman, Edwin S. (ed.) The Hate Reader. Dobbs Ferry, NY: Oceana Press, 1964.

Pelz, Mary E. The Aryan Brotherhood of Texas: An Analysis of Right-Wing Extremism in the Texas Prisons. Doctoral dissertation, Sam Houston State University, 1988. UMO # 8814623.

U.S. Commission on Civil Rights, Georgia Advisory Committee. Perceptions of Hate Group Activity in Georgia. Washington, D.C.: The Commission, 1983.

U.S. Commission on Civil Rights, Michigan State Advisory Committee. Hate Groups in Michigan: A Sham or a Shame: A Report. Washington, D.C.: The Commission, 1982.

Vaughn, Doug. Terror on the Right. In These Times March 13, 1985. ["Aryan Nations," an anti-semitic and racist group].

Zeskind, Leonard. The "Christian Identity" Movement. A Theological Justification for Racist and Anti-Semitic Violence. Division of Church and Society of the National Council of Churches of Christ in the USA, 1986.

[See also sections 3, 4, 8, 14, 32, 40, 44, 82, and 84]

70. Racist Thoughtways

For two or more centuries ... [the United States] has marched
proudly in the van of human hatred. She makes bonfires of human
flesh and laughs at them hideously. She makes the insulting of
millions more than a matter of dislike - it becomes a great
religion, a world war cry: Up white, down black. ...

   - W. E. B. Du Bois, "Of the Culture of White Folk," 1917

Aptheker, Herbert. Racism, Imperialism and Peace. Minneapolis, MN:
   M.E.P., 1987.

Burns, Emmett C. NASA [National Aeronautics and Space Administration] and
   Blacks: Triumph in Tokenism. Jackson Advocate December 30, 1982.

Cottrol, Robert J. Liberalism and Paternalism: Ideology, Economic
   Interest and the Business Law of Slavery. American Journal of Legal
   History 31 (October 1987):359-73.

Friedman, Lawrence J. The Search for Docility: Racial Thought in the
   White South, 1861-1917. Phylon 31 (Fall 1970):313-23.

Gallay, Alan. The Origins of Slaveholders' Paternalism: George
   Whitefield, the Bryan Family, and the Great Awakening in the South.
   Journal of Southern History 53 (August 1987):369-94.

Hoffman, Charles and Tess Hoffmann. The Limits of Paternalism: Driver-
   Master Relations on a Bryan County Plantation. Georgia Historical
   Quarterly 67 (Fall 1983):321-35.

Home-Brewed Racism: Targeting of Arab-Americans. Rikka 12 (1987):23-24.

Johnson, Guion G. Southern Paternalism toward Negroes After Emancipation.
   Journal of Southern History 28 (1957):483-509.

Kleinig, John. Paternalism. Totowa, NJ: Rowman and Allanheld, 1983.

Krebs, Sylvia H. Life without 'My Folks': Letters to Former Slaves.
   Atlanta Historical Journal 29 (Summer 1985):47-50.

Nickerson, Steve. Paternalism and Its Mates. Race Relations Reporter 6
   (January-February 1974):22-28. [B.I.A.].

Parker, James R. Paternalism and Racism: Senator John C. Spooner and
   American Minorities, 1897-1907. Wisconsin Magazine of History 57
   (Spring 1974):195-200.

Phillips, William M, Jr. and Rhoda L. Blumberg. Tokenism and
   Organizational Change. Integrateducation 20 (January-April
   1982):34-49.

Phillips, William M., Jr. and Rhoda L. Blumberg. Tokenism and

Organizational Change: Theoretical Examination of an Aspect of Race Relations in Educational Context, 1982. ERIC ED 213 815.

Sepulveda, Ciro H. Social Life and Nativism in La Colonia del Harbor. In: James B. Lane and Edward J. Escobar (eds.), Forging a Community: The Latino Experience in Northwest Indiana, 1919-1975. Bloomington, IN: Indiana University Press, 1987.

Siegel, Fred. The Paternalist Thesis: Virginia as a Test Case. Civil War History 25 (September 1979):246-61.

[See also sections 4, 15, 17, 20, 37, 43, 46, 48, 55, 65, 77, and 80]

71. <u>Recreation</u>

*The Negroes of Memphis are taxed for public parks where they
cannot sit down.*

    - W. E. B. Du Bois, "Politics and Industry," (1969)

Brune, Tom. Park District Spends U.S. Poverty Funds in Wealthy Areas.
<u>Chicago</u> <u>Reporter</u> 9 (April 1980).

Fuerst, James S. Parks as Catalytic Agents for Racial Change.
<u>Integrateducation</u> 19 (May-December 1981):61-63. [Chicago].

Koehler, David H. and Margaret T. Wrightson. Inequality in the Delivery
of Urban Services: A Reconsideration of the Chicago Parks. <u>Journal</u>
<u>of</u> <u>Politics</u> 49 (February 1987):80-99.

Scott, Emmett. Leisure Time and the Colored Citizen. <u>Playground</u> 18
(January 1925):593-96.

Stamps, Spurgeon M. and M. B. Stamps. Race, Class and Leisure Activities
of Urban Residents. <u>Journal</u> <u>of</u> <u>Leisure</u> <u>Research</u> 17 (1985):40-56.

Thomas, Jo. On City's Playgrounds, Boy Joy and Danger [Disparities among
New York City playgrounds]. <u>New</u> <u>York</u> <u>Times</u> August 11, 1986.

Trumpbour, Jack. Leisure Under Late Capitalism. <u>Zeta</u> <u>Magazine</u> 1 (July-
August 1988):64-66.

Yarbrough, Roy E. <u>Perceptions</u> <u>of</u> <u>Three</u> <u>Black</u> <u>Leaders</u> <u>of</u> <u>the</u> <u>National</u>
<u>Intramural-Recreational</u> <u>Sports</u> <u>Association:</u> <u>The</u> <u>Formative</u> <u>Years,</u>
<u>1950-1975</u>. Doctoral dissertation, University of North Carolina at
Greensboro, 1986. UMO # 8710681.

72. Religion

The pride [that led to creation of black churches] was really a growing feeling of strength and a conviction that black identity, self-sufficiency, self-determination, and the search for freedom and equality in a recalcitrant white world could best be nourished in the early years of the republic through independent black action.

-Gary B. Nash, Forging Freedom. The Formation of Philadelphia's Black Community 1720-1840, p. 133

Alho, Olli. The Religion of the Slaves: A Study of the Religious Tradition and Behavior of the Plantation Slaves in the United States, 1830-1865. Helsinki, Finland: Suomalainen Tiedeakatemia, Academia Scieniarum Fennica, 1976.

Abonyi, Malvina H. The Role of Ethnic Church Schools in the History of Education in the United States: The Detroit Experience, 1850-1920. Doctoral dissertation, Wayne State University, 1987. UMO # 8714526. [Bilingual ethnic schools].

Alberts, William E. Religion and Racism in Boston: Piety Preferred Over a Prophecy. Christianity and Crisis (August 15, 1983):305-09.

Alexander, George W. Racism and the Chaplaincy. Military Chaplains' Review 2 (August 1973):45-51.

Are the New Fundamentalist Schools Racist Havens or Moral Alternatives? Phi Delta Kappan 61 (June 1980):724-725.

Austin, Allan D. African Muslims in Antebellum America: A Sourcebook. New York: Garland, 1984.

Baer, Hans A. Black Mainstream Churches: Emancipatory or Accommodative Responses or Racism and Social Stratification in American Society? Review of Religious Research (December 1988).

Baer, Hans A. The Black Spiritual Movement: A Religious Response to Racism. Knoxville, TN: University of Tennessee Press, 1984.

Bailey, David T. Shadow on the Church: Southwestern Evangelical Religion and the Issue of Slavery, 1783-1860. Ithaca, NY: Cornell University Press, 1985.

Bailey, Kenneth K. The Post-Civil War Racial Separations in Southern Protestantism: Another Look. Church History 47 (December 1977):453-73.

Barsh, Russel L. The Illusion of Religious Freedom for Indigenous Americans [Native Americans]. Oregon Law Review 65 (Fall 1986):363-412.

Bastone, William. The Priest [Father Louis Gigante, NYC] and the Mob.
     Village Voice March 7, 1989.

Bechler, Le Roy. The Black Mennonite Church in North America, 1886-1986.
     Scottdale, PA: Herald Press, 1986.

Bellah, Robert N. and Frederick E. Greenspahn (eds.). Uncivil Religion
     Crossroad, 1988. [Conflicts of Catholics and Protestants and
     Christians with non-Christians in the United States].

van der Bent, Ans J. (ed.) World Council of Churches' Statements and
     Actions on Racism, 1948-1979. Geneva, Switzerland: Programme to
     Combat Racism, World Council of Churches, 1980.

Boles, John B. (ed.) Master and Slaves in the House of the Lord - Race
     and Religion in the American South, 1740-1870. Lexington, KY:
     University Press of Kentucky, 1988.

Boles, John B. Slaves in Biracial Protestant Churches. In: Samuel S.
     Hill (ed.), Varieties of Southern Religious Experience. Baton Rouge:
     Louisiana State University Press, 1988.

Bowen, Trevor. Divine White Right: A Study of Race Segregation and
     Interracial Cooperation in Religious Organizations and Institutions
     in the United States. New York: Harper and Co., 1934.

Bringhurst, Newell G. Saints, Slaves, and Blacks: The Changing Place of
     Black People within Mormonism. Westport, CT: Greenwood, 1981.

Cadena, Gilbert R. Chicanos and the Catholic Church: Liberation Theology
     as a Form of Empowerment. Doctoral dissertation, University of
     California, Riverside, 1987. UMO # 8729402.

Camposer, James M. Anti-Catholic Prejudice in Early New England: The
     Dailey-Halligan Murder Trial. Historical Journal of Western
     Massachusetts 6 (Spring 1978):5-17. [Northampton].

Clark, Dennis. Color and Catholic Classrooms. Integrated Education
     (June 1963).

Creel, Margaret W. "A Peculiar People." Slave Religion and Community
     Culture Among the Gullah. New York: New York University Press,
     1987.

Crouch, Archie. Racial-Ethnic Ministry Politics - An Historical Overview.
     United Presbyterian Church Mission 57 (Fall 1979):272-312.

Cunningham, Floyd T. Wandering in the Wilderness: Black Baptist Thought
     after Emancipation. American Baptist Quarterly 4 (September
     1985):268-81.

Davies, Alan. Infected Christianity: A Study of Modern Racism.
     Montreal: McGill-Queen's University Press, 1988.

Davison, D. Ralph, Jr. James Hardy Dillard: A Christian Education in the

Segregated South. *Historical* *Magazine* *of* *the* *Protestant* *Episcopal* *Church* 55 (June 1986):113-26.

Demallie, Raymond J. and Douglas R. Parks (eds.) *Sioux* *Indian* *Religion:* *Tradition* *and* *Innovation*. Norman: University of Oklahoma Press, 1987.

Diggs, Margaret A. *Catholic* *Negro* *Education* *in* *the* *United* *States*. Houston, TX: Standard Printing and Lithograph Co., 1936.

Dittmer, John. The Education of Henry McNeal Turner. *In:* Leon Litwack and August Meier (eds.), *Black* *Leaders* *of* *the* *Nineteenth* *Century*. Urbana, IL: University of Illinois Press, 1988.

Dowd, Gregory E. *Paths* *of* *Resistance:* *American* *Indian* *Religion* *and* *the* *Quest* *for* *Unity,* *1745-1815*. [2 vols.] Doctoral dissertation, Princeton University, 1986. UMO # 8629429.

Drewitt, Donald A. *Ransom* *on* *Race* *and* *Racism:* *The* *Racial* *and* *Social* *Thought* *of* *Reverdy* *Cassius* *Ransom* *-* *Preacher,* *Editor* *and* *Bishop* *in* *the* *African* *Methodist* *Episcopal* *Church,* *1861-1959*. Doctoral dissertation, Drew University, 1988. UMO # 8817626.

Du Bois, W. E. B. The Religion of the American Negro. *New* *World* 9 (December 1900):614-25.

Edwards, Herbert O., Jr. *Christian* *Ethics* *and* *Racism*. Doctoral dissertation, Brown University, 1974.

Fichter, Joseph H. American Religion and the Negro. *Daedalus* (Fall 1965).

Fitts, Leroy. *A* *History* *of* *Black* *Baptists*. Nashville, TN: Broadman Press, 1985.

Flinn, Patricia. I Teach in a Racist School. *America* September 26, 1970. [Catholic high school in Midwest].

Franklin, James L. Chance, Challenge for Black Catholics. *Boston* *Globe* February 5, 1988.

Fullinwider, Robert K. and Claudia Mills (eds.) *The* *Moral* *Foundations* *of* *Civil* *Rights*. Totowa, NJ: Rowman and Littlefield, 1987.

Garvin, Richard and Carol Garvin. What Has God Done for Black People. *Liberator* (October 1968).

George, Carol V. R. *Segregated* *Sabbaths,* *Richard* *Allen* *and* *the* *Rise* *of* *Independent* *Black* *Churches,* *1760-1840*. New York: Oxford, 1973.

Guarneri, Carl and David Alvarez (eds.) *Religion* *and* *Society* *in* *the* *American* *West:* *Historical* *Essays*. Lanham, MD: University Press of America, 1987. [Includes Blacks, Mexican Americans, Filipino Americans, Indians, and Jews].

Harding, Vincent. Out of the Cauldron of Struggle: Black Religion and the Search for a New America. Soundings 61 (Fall 1978):339-54.

Harding, Vincent. The Religion of Black Power. In: Donald R. Cutler (ed.), The Religious Situation: 1968, pp. 3-38. Boston: Beacon Press, 1968.

Haynes, Leonard L., Jr. The Negro Community within American Protestantism, 1619-1844. Boston: Christophers, 1953.

Heckel, Roger. The Struggle Against Racism. Some Contributions of the Church. Vatican City: Iustitia Et Pax, 1979.

Hopkins, Jerry B. Billy Graham and the Race Problem, 1949-1969. Doctoral dissertation, University of Kentucky, 1986. UMO # 870526.

Howard, John. The Making of a Black Muslim. In: E. F. Dickie-Clark (ed.), Social Process in Minority Dominant Relations, pp. 127-290. New York: Free Press, 1968.

Hultkrantz, Abe. The Religions of the American Indians. [Translated by Monica Setterwall]. Berkeley, CA: University of California Press, 1979.

Isaac, Ephraim. Genesis, Judaism, and the 'Sons of Ham.' Slavery and Abolition 1 (May 1980):3-17.

Johnson, Otis Samuel. The Social Welfare Role of the Black Church. Doctoral dissertation, Brandeis University, 1980. UMO # 8024554. [Boston, Mass. and Savannah, Ga.].

Johnston, Robert L. Church on Racism? 'Disinterest Deafening.' National Catholic Reporter September, 1975.

Jones, William. Is God a White Racist? Garden City, NY: Doubleday, 1973.

Juarez, Jose R. La Igelsia Catolica y el Chicano en Sud Texas, 1836-1911. Aztlan 4 (February 1973):217-55.

Kelsey, George D. Racism and the Christian Understanding of Man. New York: Scribner's, 1965.

Labbé, Delores E. Jim Crow Comes to Church: The Establishment of Segregated Catholic Parishes in South Louisiana (second ed.) Lafayette, LA: University of Southwestern Louisiana, 1971.

Lapsansky, Emma. Since They Got Those Separate Churches: Afroamericans and Racism in Jacksonian Philadelphia. American Quarterly 22 (1980).

Lecky, Robert B. and H. Elliot Wright (eds.) Black Manifesto: Religion, Racism, and Reparations. New York: Sheed and Ward, 1969.

Lesick, Lawrence T. The Lane Rebels: Evangelicalism and Antislavery in Antebellum America. Metuchen, NH: Scarecrow Press, 1980. [Lane Theological Seminary, Cincinnati].

Lincoln, C. Eric. The Black Heritage in Religion in the South. In: Charles R. Wilson (ed.), Religion in the South. Jackson, MS: University Press of Mississippi, 1985.

Lincoln, C. Eric. The Black Church in the Context of American Religion. In: Samuel S. Hill (ed.), Varieties of Southern Religious Experience. Baton Rouge: Louisiana State University Press, 1988.

Lincoln, C. Eric. Race, Religion and the Continuing American Dilemma. New York: Hill and Wang, 1984.

Lomax, Louis E. When the Word Is Given: A Report on Elijah Muhammad, Malcolm X, and the Black Muslim World. Westport, CT: Greenwood, 1979 (orig. 1964).

Lucas, Isidro. The Browning of America. The Hispanic Revolution in the American Cburch. Chicago, IL: Fiede/Claretian, 1981.

Maddex, Jack P., Jr. Proslavery Millenialism: Social Eschatology in Antebellum Southern Calvinism. American Quarterly 31 (Spring 1979):46-62.

Mamiya, Lawrence H. From the Black Muslim to Bilabian: The Evolution of a Movement. Journal for the Scientific Study of Religion 21 (1982):138-52.

Manis, Andrew M. Southern Civil Religions in Conflict. Black and White Baptists and Civil Rights, 1947-1957. Athens, GA: University of Georgia Press, 1987.

Marable, Manning. The Ambiguous Politics of the Black Church. In: How Capitalism Underdeveloped Black America, pp. 195-214. Boston: South End Press, 1983.

Marsh, Clifton E. From Black Muslims to Muslims: The Transition from Separation to Islam, 1930-1980. Metuchen, NJ: Scarecrow Pres, 1984.

Mathews, Donald G. Religion in the Old South. Chicago, IL: University of Chicago Press, 1977.

McClain, William B. Black People in the Methodist Church: Whither Thou Goest? Cambridge, MA: Schenkman, 1984.

McDonnell, Thomas J. and Alfred V. Puccini. Text of Pastoral Letter. Boston Globe June 20, 1988. [Two Catholic priests in South Boston explain why they have not endorsed a plan to desegregate public housing in that area].

Miller, Randell M. The Failed Mission: The Catholic Church and Black Catholics in the Old South. In: Edward Magdol and Jon L. Wakelyn (eds.), The Southern Common People: Studies in Nineteenth- Century

Social History, pp. 37-54. Westport, CT: Greenwood, 1980.

Miller, Richard R. Slavery and Catholicism. Durham, NC: North State
     Publishers, 1957.

Misch, Edward J. The Catholic Church and the Negro, 1865-1884.
     Integrateducation 12 (November-December 1974):36-40.

Mitchell, Ella P. Oral Tradition: Legacy of Faith for the Black Church.
     Religious Education 81 (Winter 1986):93-112.

Murray, Peter C. Christ and Caste in Conflict: Creating a Racially
     Inclusive Methodist Church. Doctoral dissertation, Indiana
     University, 1985. UMO # 8527025. [Role of civil rights movement].

O'Brien, John T. Factory, Church, and Community: Blacks in Antebellum
     Richmond. Journal of Southern History 44 (November 1978):509-36.

Ochs, Stephen J. Deferred Mission: The Josephites and the Struggle for
     Black Catholic Priests, 1871-1960. 3 vols. Doctoral dissertation,
     University of Maryland, 1985. UMO # 8614263.

One Faith, One Lord, One Baptism. The Hopes and Experiences of the Black
     Community in the Archbishop of New York, Vol. 1. New York:
     Archdiocese of New York, 1988.

Osborne, William A. The Segregated Church, Herder and Herder, 1967.

Paris, Arthur E. Black Pentacostalism: Southern Religion in an Urban
     World [Boston]. Amherst, MA: University of Massachusetts Press,
     1982.

Pillsbury, Peter W. Some Thoughts on White Supremacy and the Church.
     August, 1968. [People Against Racism, 2631 Woodward Avenue, Detroit,
     MI 48201].

Ponce, Frank. The Enculturation of Hispanics in the Catholic Church.
     Agenda 10 (November-December 1980):11-15.

Pridgen, Joseph W. United Methodist Churches and Racism in Blacksburg,
     South Carolina. Doctoral dissertation, Drew University, 1984. UMO #
     8500729.

Prucha, Francis P. The Churches and the Indian Schools, 1886-1912.
     Lincoln: University of Nebraska Press, 1979.

Purifoy, Lewis M. The Southern Methodist Church and the Proslavery
     Argument. Journal of Southern History 32 (August 1966):325-41.

Raboteau, Albert J. Richard Allen and the African Church Movement. In:
     Leon Litwack and August Meier (eds.), Black Leaders of the Nineteenth
     Century. Urbana, IL: University of Illinois Press, 1988.

Raboteau, Albert J. Slave Autonomy and Religion. Journal of Religious
     Thought 38 (Fall-Winter 1982):51-64.

Raboteau, Albert J. <u>Slave Religion:</u> The <u>"Invisible Institution" in the Antebellum South</u>. New York: Oxford, 1978.

Race Relations and Religious Education. <u>Religious Education</u> (January-February 1964).

Randolph, A. Philip and Chandler Owen. The Failure of the Negro Church. <u>Messenger</u> 2 (October 1919).

Rector, Theresa A. Black Nuns as Educators. <u>Journal of Negro Education</u>. 51 (Summer 1982):238-53.

Reimers, David M. <u>White Protestantism and the Negro</u>. New York: Oxford, 1965.

Rice, Madeline H. <u>American Catholic Opinion in the Slavery Controversy</u>. New York: Columbia University Press, 1944.

Richardson, Joe M. <u>Christian Reconstruction:</u> The <u>American Missionary Association and Southern Blacks, 1861-1890</u>. Athens, GA: University of Georgia Press, 1986.

Rosenberg, Bruce A. <u>The Art of the American Negro Folk Preacher</u>. New York, 1970.

Sandos, James A. Junipero Serra's Canonization and the Historical Record. <u>American Historical Review</u> 93 (December 1988):1253-69.

Sawyer, Mary. Black Ecumenical Movements: Proponents of Social Change. <u>Review of Religious Research</u> (December 1988).

Scott, James A. Racism, the Church, and Educational Strategies. <u>Foundations</u> 17 (July-September 1974):268-280.

Sernett, Milton C. <u>Black Religion and American Evangelicalism:</u> White <u>Protestants, Plantation Missions, and the Flowering of Negro Christianity, 1787-1865</u>. Metuchen, NJ: Scarecrow Press, 1975.

Smith, Edward D. <u>Climbing Jacob's Ladder:</u> The <u>Rise of Black Churches in Eastern American Cities, 1740-1877</u>. Washington, D.C.: Smithsonian Institution, 1988.

Smith, H. Shelton. <u>In His Image, But ... Racism in Southern Religion, 1780-1910</u>. Durham, NC: Duke University Press, 1972.

Smith, Timothy L. Religion and Ethnicity in America. <u>American Historical Review</u> 83 (December 1978):1115-85.

Smith, Timothy L. Slavery and Theology: The Emergence of Black Christian Consciouness in Nineteenth-Century America. <u>Church History</u> 41 (December 1972):497-512.

Sobel, Mechal. <u>Trabelin' On:</u> The <u>Slave Journey to an Afro-Baptist Faith</u>. Westport, CT: Greenwood, 1979.

Stark, Rodney. Correcting Church Membership Rates: 1971 and 1980. Review of Religious Research 29 (September 1987):69-77.

Stevens Arroyo, A. M. (ed.) Prophets Denied Honor: An Anthology on the Hispano Church of the United States. Maryknoll, NY: Orbis Books, 1980.

Stringfellow, William. My People Is The Enemy. New York: Holt, Rinehart, and Winston, 1964.

Stuart, Paul. The Christian Church and Indian Community Life. Journal of Ethnic Studies 9 (Fall 1981):47-55.

Swift, David E. Black Presbyterian Attacks on Racism: Samuel Cornish, Theodore Wright, and Their Contemporaries. In: David W. Wills and Richard Newman (eds.), Black Apostles at Home and Abroad: Afro-Americans and the Christian Mission from the Revolution to Reconstruction, pp. 43-84. Boston, 1982.

Talbot, Steve. Desecration and American Indian Religious Freedom. Journal of Ethnic Studies 12 (Winter 1985):1-18.

Taylor, Robert J. Correlates of Religious Non-Involvement Among Black Americans. Review of Religious Research (December 1988).

Taylor, Robert J. Structural Determinants of Religious Participation Among Black Americans. Review of Religious Research (December 1988).

U.S. Congress, 95th, 2nd session, Senate, Select Committee on Indian Affairs. American Indian Religious Freedom. Hearings .... Washington, D.C.: GPO, 1978.

Walker, Clarence E. A Rock in a Weary Land: The African Methodist Episcopal Church during the Civil War and Reconstruction. Baton Rouge: Louisiana State University Press, 1982.

Walker, Wyatt T. The Contemporary Black Church. In: Harold A. Carter and others (eds.), The Black Church Look at the Bicentennial, pp. 43-74. Elgin, IL: Progressive National Baptist Publishing House, 1976.

Wheeler, Edward L. Uplifting the Race: The Black Minister in the New South, 1865-1902. Lanham, MD: University Press of America, 1986.

Williams, Gilbert A. The A.M.E. Christian Recorder: A Forum for the Social Ideas of Black Americans, 1854-1902. Doctoral dissertation, University of Illinois, 1979. UMO # 8004305.

Wilmore, Gayraud. Black Religion and Black Radicalism: An Interpretation of the Religious History of Afro-American People (second edition). Maryknoll, NY: Orbis Books, 1983.

Wilmore, Gayraud (ed.) African American Religious Studies. An Interdisciplinary Anthology. Durham, NC: Duke University Press,

1989.

Wilson, Basil and Charles Green. The Black Church and the Struggle for Community Empowerment in New York City. Afro-Americans in New York City Life and History 12 (January 1988):51-79.

Windsor, Pat. LCWR Tackles Racism in Communities, Society. National Catholic Reporter September 9, 1988. [Leadership Conference of Women Religious].

Woodson, Carter G. The History of the Negro Church. Washington, D.C.: Associated Publishers, 1921.

Religion Bibliography

Burr, Nelson and others (comps.) The Negro Church, vol. 4, pp. 348-81; Negro Religious Literature, vol. 4, pp. 938-43. A Critical Bibliography of Religion in America. Princeton, NJ: Princeton University Press, 1961.

Evans, James H., Jr. Black Theology: A Critical Assessment and Annotated Bibliography. Westport, CT: Greenwood, 1987.

Ferm, D. W. (comp.) Contemporary Black Theology: A Historical Sketch. Choice 16 (February 1980):1539-50.

Haddad, Yvonne Y. (comp.) Muslims in America: A Select Bibliography. Muslim World 76 (April 1986):93-122.

Richardson, Marilyn (comp.) Black Women and Religion: A Bibliography. Boston, MA: Hall, 1980.

Thompson, Edgar T. (comp.) Race and Religion: A Descriptive Bibliography Compiled with Special Reference to the Relations between Whites and Negroes in the United States. Chapel Hill, NC: University of North Carolina Press, 1949.

Tinney, James S. (comp.) Black Pentacostalism: An Annotated Bibliography. Spirit: A Journal of Issues Incident to Pentacostalism. 3 (1979).

Truesdell, Marilyn P. (comp.) Black Women and Religion: A Bibliography. Cambridge, MA: Harvard Divinity School, 1975. [Addendum, 1976].

Williams, Ethel L. and Clifton L. Brown (comps.) The Howard University Bibliography of African and Afro-American Religious Studies (with Locations in American Libraries). Wilmington, DE: Scholarly Resources, 1977.

73. Science

We have had little chance in engineering, in physics, in chemistry, in the whole great field of modern technology, chiefly because no matter what our gifts were, no chance was given to us to prepare and no career promised after preparation.

- W. E. B. Du Bois, "A Graduate School," 1929

Beardsley, Edward H. The American Scientist as Social Activist. Franz Boas, Burt G. Wilder, and the Cause of Racial Justice, 1900-1915. Isis 64 (March 1973):50-66.

Blacks in Technology: Beyond the Bicentennial. Baltimore, MD: National Technical Association, 1978.

Brown, Janet W. Native American Contributions to Science, Engineering, and Medicine. Science 189 (July 1975):38-40.

Cox, Uri. Goose Father. Human Behavior 3 (March 1974):17-22. [Includes discussion of early racist writings by Nobel Laureate Karl Lorenz].

Du Bois, W. E. B. The Negro Scientist. American Scholar 8 (1939).

Fong, M. and L. O. Johnson. The Eugenics Movement: Some Insight into the Institutionalization of Racism. Issues in Criminology 9 (1974):89-115.

Gilman, Stuart C. Degeneracy and Race in the Nineteenth Century: The Impact of Clinical Medicine. Journal of Ethnic Studies 10 (Winter 1983):27-50.

Glass, Bentley. Geneticists Embattled: Their Stand Against Rampant Eugenics and Racism in America During the 1920s and 1930s. Proc. Am. Phil. Society 130 (March 1986):130-154.

Gonzalez, Ciriaco and Paul Diehl. Chicanos and the Sciences. Agenda (Summer 1976).

Hines, Linda O. White Mythology and Black Duality: George W. Carver's Response to Racism and the Radical Left. Journal of Negro History 62 (April 1977):134-46.

Kremer, Gary R. (ed.) George Washington Carver: In His Own Words. Columbia: University of Missouri Press, 1987. [Extracts from letters].

Lefait, P. Science and Racism. Paris: UNESCO, 1982.

Mackintosh, B. George Washington Carver: The Making of a Myth. Journal of Southern History (November 1976):507-528.

Manning, Kenneth R. Black Apollo of Science: The Life of Ernest Everett

<u>Just</u>. New York: Oxford University Press, 1983.

Marcus, Lawrence R. and Franklin O. Smith. Black Faculty and Survival Systems [Discrimination against Black scientists in academe before World War II]. <u>Integrateducation</u> 17 (May-August 1979):31-36.

McMurry, Linda. <u>George Washington Carver: Scientist and Symbol</u>. New York: Oxford University Press, 1981.

Metress, James. The Scientific Misuse of the Biological Concept of Race. <u>Social Studies</u> 66 (May-June 1975):114-116.

Ogilvie, Marilyn B. <u>Women in Science: Antiquity through the Nineteenth Century: A Bibliographical Dictionary with Annotated Bibliography</u>. Cambridge, MA: MIT Press, 1986.

Pearson, Willie, Jr. <u>Black Scientists, White Society, and Colorless Science: A Study of Universalism in American Science</u>. Associated Faculty Press, 1985.

Pearson, Willie, Jr. The Roles of Colleges and Universities in Increasing Black Representation in the Scientific Professions. <u>In</u>: Michael T. Nettles (ed.), <u>Toward Black Undergraduate Student Equality in American Higher Education</u>. Westport, CT: Greenwood, 1988.

Pearson, Willie, Jr. The Social Origins of Black American Doctorates in the Sciences. <u>Sociological Spectrum</u> 2 (April-June 1982):13-29.

Pearson, Willie, Jr. and H. Kenneth Bechtel (eds.) <u>Blacks, Science, and American Education</u>. New Brunswick, NJ: Rutgers University Press, 1989.

Rose, Steven, John Hambley and Jeff Haywood. Science, Racism, and Ideology. <u>Socialist Register</u> 1973.

Selden, Steven. Eugenics and Curriculum: 1860-1929. <u>Educational Forum</u> 43 (November 1978):67-82.

Stepan, Nancy. <u>The Idea of Race in Science: Great Britain, 1800-1960</u>. Hamden, CT: Archon Books, 1982.

Turner, Henrie M. and others. <u>Factors Influencing Persistence/Achievement in the Sciences and Health Professions by Black High School and College Women</u>. Atlanta: Center for Research on Women in Science, Morris Brown College, 1983.

Young, Herman A. and Barbara H. Young. Science and Black Studies. <u>Journal of Negro Education</u> 46 (Fall 1977):373-79.

74. Sexism

Until the women's movement became vocal it never occurred to me that I was discriminated against as a woman. But since I've always been black, that has occurred to me all my life.

- Mary F. Berry, quoted in Ruth Fischer, "Black, Female - and Qualified, " Change, December-January, 1974-1975.

Almquist, Elizabeth M. Minorities, Gender and Work. Lexington, MA: Lexington Books, 1979.

American Library Association. Resolution on Racism and Sexism Awareness. Integrateducation 15 (January-February 1977).

Avakian, Arlene Voski. Women's Studies and Racism. New England Journal of Black Studies (1981):31-36.

Baca Zinn, Maxine. Chicano Men and Masculinity. Journal of Ethnic Studies 10 (Summer 1982):29-44.

Balkin, Joseph. Why Policemen Don't Like Policewomen. Journal of Police Science and Administration 16 (March 1988):29-38.

Brenner, O. C. and Joseph Towkiewicz. Race Differences in Attitudes of American Business School Graduates toward the Role of Women. Journal of Social Psychology 126 (April 1986):251-53.

Brittan, Arthur and Mary Maynard. Sexism, Racism, and Oppression. New York: Basil Blackwell, 1984.

Chapman, Thomas Howard. Simulation Game Effects on Attitudes Regarding Racism and Sexism. Doctoral dissertation, University of Maryland, 1974. UMO # 75-17882.

Davis, Angela Y. Racism and Contemporary Literature on Rape. Freedomways 16 (1976):25-33.

Elshtain, Jean B. The Feminist Movement and the Question of Equality. Polity 8 (Summer 1975):452-477.

Estéves, Sandra M. The Feminist Viewpoint in the Poetry of Puerto Rican Women in the United States. In: Asela Rodriguez de Laguna (ed.), Images and Identities. The Puerto Rican in Two World Contexts, pp. 171-77. New Brunswick, NJ: Transaction Books, 1987.

Ferguson, Ann. Women as a Revolutionary Class in the U.S. In: P. Walker (ed.), Between Labor and Capital. Boston: South End Press, 1979.

Fernandez, John P. Racism and Sexism in Corporate Life: Changing Values in American Business. Lexington, MA: Lexington Books, 1982.

Fernandez de Cintron, Celia and M. Rivera Quintero. Bases de la Sociedad

Sexista en Puerto Rico. Revista/Review Interamericana 4 (Summer 1974):239-45.

Frank, Francine W. and Paula A. Treichler. Language, Gender, and Professional Writing. New York: Modern Language Association, 1989. [Part 2: "Guidelines for Nonsexist Usage"].

Freeman, James A. Donald Duck: How Children (Mainly Boys) Viewed their Parents (Mainly Fathers), 1941-1960. Children's Literature 6 (1977):150-164.

Grant, Carl A. and Christine E. Sleeter. Race, Class, and Gender and Abandoned Dreams. Teachers College Record (Fall 1988).

Green, Raya. Diary of a Native American Feminist. Ms. Michigan (August 1982).

Harris, Barbara and JoAnn K. McNamara (eds.) Women and the Structure of Society: Selected Research from the Fifth Berkshire Conference on the History of Women. Durham, NC: Duke University Press, 1984.

Hernton, Calvin C. Sex and Racism in America. Garden City, NY: Doubleday, 1965.

Holden, Constance. Proposed New Psychiatric Diagnoses Raise Charges of Gender Bias. Science 231 (January 1986):327-28.

Hooks, Bell. Black Women and Feminism. Zeta Magazine 1 (July-August 1988):39-42.

Intons-Peterson, Margaret J. Gender Concepts of Swedish and American Youth. Hillsdale, NJ: Lawrence Erlbaum Associates, 1988.

King, Deborah K. Multiple Jeopardy, Multiple Consciousness: The Context of Black Feminist Ideology. Signs 14 (Autumn 1988):42-72.

Lakes Matya, M. and M. Collins. Minority Women: Conquering Both Sexism and Racism. In: Jane B. Kahle (ed.), Women in Science. Philadelphia, PA: Falmer Press, 1985.

Lennox, Sara. Der Versuch, man Selbst zu Sein: Christa Wolf und der Feminismus. In: Wolfgang Paulsen (ed.), Die Frau als Heldin und Autorin, pp. 217-222. Bern: Francke Verlag, 1979.

Lewis, Diane K. A Response to Inequality: Black Women, Racism, and Sexism. Signs 3 (Winter 1977):339-61.

Lueptow, Lloyd B. Conceptions of Femininity and Masculinity: 1974-1983. Psychological Reports 57 (December 1985):859-62.

McClain, Shirla and Norma L. Spencer. Racism and Sexism in America: The Black Woman's Dilemma. 1978. ERIC ED 159 272.

McDougald, Elsie J. The Double Talk: The Struggle of Negro Women for Sex and Race Emancipation. Survey Graphic 6 (March 1925).

McHugh, Maureen C. and others. Issues to Consider in Conducting Nonsexist
    Psychological Research: A Guide for Researchers. American
    Psychologist 41 (August 1986):879-90.

Meeks, Catherine. The Mule of the World: An Exploration of Sexist
    Oppression with Zora Neale Hurston and Alice Walker. Doctoral
    Dissertation, Emory University, 1987. UMO # 8716127.

Miller, A. H. and others. The Politicization of Gender Identification.
    In: Kathleen B. Jones and Anna G. Jonasdottir (eds.), The Political
    Interests of Gender. Developing Theory and Research with a Feminist
    Face. Newbury Park, CA: Sage, 1988.

Nieto, Consuelo. The Chicano and the Woman's Rights Movement: A
    Perspective. Civil Rights Digest (September 1974):36-42.

Ortiz, Larry. The Feminist Movement: Its Effects Upon Minorities. Mano
    a Mano 5 (October 1976):1-4.

Papke, Mary and others. Women Respond to Racism. Telos 50 (Winter 1981-
    1982):180-187. [Third (1981) National Annual Conference of National
    Women's Studies Conference].

Parker, Seymour and Hilda Parker. The Myth of Male Superiority. American
    Anthropologist 81 (1979):289-309.

Pico, Isabel. Machismo y educacion en Puerto Rico. Comision para el
    Mejoramiento de los derechos de la Mujer, 1979.

Powers, Pauline S. Group Process within the American Psychiatric
    Association on the Issue of the Equal Rights Amendment. American
    Journal of Social Psychiatry 3 (Fall 1983):33-36.

Russell, Denise. Psychiatric Diagnosis and the Oppression of Women.
    International Journal of Social Psychiatry 31 (Winter 1985):298-305.

Sachs, Albie and Joan Hoff Wilson. Sexism and the Law: A Study of Male
    Beliefs and Legal Bias in Britain and the United States. Oxford,
    1978.

Schniedewind, Nancy. Confronting Racism and Sexism: A Practical Handbook
    for Educators. New Paltz, NY: Commonground Press, 1977.

Sedlacek, William E. and others. Racism and Sexism: A Comparison and
    Contrast. 1974. ERIC ED 098 133.

Sexism and Racism in Popular Basal Readers 1964-1976, 1976. Racism and
    Sexism Resource Center for Educators, 1841 Broadway, New York, NY
    10023.

Sizemore, Barbara A. Sexism and the Black Male. Black Scholar 4 (March-
    April 1973):2-11.

Smith, Althea and Abigail J. Stewart. Approaches to Studying Racism and

Sexism in Black Women's Lives. <u>Journal of Social Issues</u> 39 (1983):1-15.

Stember, Charles Herbert. <u>Racial Sexism. The Emotional Barrier to an Integrated Society</u>. New York: Elsevier, 1976.

Stepan, Nancy L. Race and Gender: The Role of Analogy in Science. <u>Isis</u> 77 (June 1986):261-77.

Stetson, Erlene. Black Feminism in Indiana, 1893-1933. <u>Phylon</u> 44 (December 1983):292-98.

Syron, Lisa. <u>Discarded Minds. How Gender, Race and Class Biases Prevent Young Women from Obtaining an Adequate Math and Science Education in New York City Public Schools</u>. New York: The Full Access and Rights to Education Coalition and the Center for Public Advocacy Research, February 1987.

Taxel, Joel. Justice and Cultural Conflict: Racism, Sexism, and Instructional Materials. <u>Interchange</u> 9 (1978-1979):56-84.

Walking, Philip H. and Chris Brannigan. Anti-sexist/anti-racist Education: A Possible Dilemma. <u>Journal of Moral Education</u> 15 (January 1986):16-25.

Watkins, Mel. Sexism, Racism and Black Women Writers. <u>New York Times Book Review</u> June 15, 1985.

Weaver, Jerry L. and Sharon D. Garrett. Sexism and Racism in the American Health Industry: A Comparative Analysis. <u>International Journal of Health Services</u> 8 (1978):677-703.

Witt, Shirley H. Native Women Today. Sexism and the Indian Woman. <u>Civil Rights Digest</u> 6 (Spring 1974):29-35.

Wolff, Robert P. There's Nobody Here But Us Persons: The Denial of the Human Condition in the Liberal Tradition. <u>In</u>: Carol C. Gould and Marx W. Wartofsky (eds.), <u>Women and Philosophy</u>, pp. 128-144. New York: Putnam's, 1976.

Wong, Linda. The Esther Lau Trial: A Case Study of Oppression and Sexism. <u>Amerasia Journal</u> 3 (Summer 1975):16-27.

75. Slavery

*The present industrial development of America is built on the
blood and brawn of unpaid Negro toil in the 17th, 18th and 19th
centuries.*

- W. E. B. Du Bois, Boston Post, February 12, 1904

Albert, Jonathan L. The Origin of Slavery in the United States - The
Maryland Precedent. American Journal of Legal History (July 1970).

Anderson, Ralph V. and Robert E. Gallman. Slaves as Fixed Capital: Slave
Labor and Southern Economic Development. Journal of American History
44 (1977):24-46.

Anstey, Roger T. Capitalism and Slavery: A Critique. Economic
Historical Review 21 (1968):307-20.

Aufhauser, R. Keith. Slavery and Technological Change. Journal of
Economic History 34 (1974):36-50.

Bailey, Ronald W. The Slave Trade and the Development of Capitalism in
the United States: A Critical Reappraisal of Theory and Method in
Afro-American Studies. Doctoral dissertation, Stanford University,
1980. UMO # 8011603.

Bancroft, Frederic. Slave Trading in the Old South. Baltimore, MD:
J.H. Furst Co., 1931.

Bean, R. N. and R. P. Thomas. The Adaptation of Slave Labor in British
America. In: Henry A. Gemery and Jan S. Hogendorm (eds.), The
Uncommon Market: Essays in the Economic History of the Atlantic
Slave Trade, pp. 377-98. New York: 1979.

Bellomy, Donald C. Black Life in Eighteenth-Century Charleston. In:
Bernard Bailyn and others (eds.), Perspectives in American History.
New series, I (1984).

Berlin, Ira and Ronald Hoffman (eds.) Slavery and Freedom in the Age of
the American Revolution. Charlottesville, VA: University Press of
Virginia, 1982.

Berlin, Ira and others (eds.) The Destruction of Slavery. New York:
Cambridge University Press, 1986.

Blassingame, John W. The Slave Community: Plantation Life in the
Antebellum South (second edition). New York: Oxford University
Press, 1979.

Blassingame, John W. (ed.) Slave Testimony: Two Centuries of Letters,
Speeches, Interviews, and Autobiographies. Baton Rouge: Louisiana
State University Press, 1977.

Boles, John B. Black Southerners, 1619-1869. Lexington: University of Kentucky Press, 1983.

Bradford, S. Sydney. The Negro Ironworker in Ante Bellum Virginia. Journal of Southern History 25 (1959):194-206.

Breeden, James O. Advice Among Masters: The Ideal in Slave Management in the Old South. Westport, CT: Greenwood, 1980.

Breen, T. H. A Changing Labor Force and Race Relations in Virginia 1660-1710. Journal of Social History (Great Britain) 7 (1973):3-25.

Breen, T. H. and Stephen Innes. "Myne Owne Ground": Race and Freedom on Virginia's Eastern Shore, 1640-1676. New York: Oxford University Press, 1980.

Brown, Barbara W. Black Roots in Southeastern Connecticut, 1650-1900. Detroit, MI: Gale, 1980.

Campbell, Randolph B. Slave Hiring in Texas. American Historical Review 93 (February 1988):107-14.

Cohn, Raymond L. Deaths of Slaves in the Middle Passage. Journal of Economic History 45 (September 1985):685-92.

Cohn, Raymond L. and R. A. Jensen. The Determinants of Slave Mortality Rates on the Middle Passage. Explorations in Economic History 19 (1982):269-82.

Cohn, Raymond L. and R. A. Jensen. Mortality in the Atlantic Slave Trade. Journal of Interdisciplinary History 12 (1982):317-29.

Conrad, Alfred H. and others. Slavery as an Obstacle to Economic Growth in the United States: A Panel Discussion. Journal of Economic History 27 (1967):518-60. [Symposium].

Coughtry, Jay. The Notorious Triangle: Rhode Island and the African Slave Trade, 1700-1807. Philadelphia, PA: Temple University Press, 1981.

Craven, Wesley F. White, Red, and Black: The Seventeenth-Century Virginia. Charlottesville, VA: 1971.

Curet, Jose. From Slave to Liberto: A Study on Slavery and Its Abolition in Puerto Rico, 1840-1880. Doctoral dissertation, Columbia University, 1980. UMO # 8016913.

Curtin, Philip D. The Atlantic Slave Trade: A Census. Madison, WI: 1969.

Darity, William A., Jr. A General Equilibrium Model of the Eighteenth Century Atlantic Slave Trade: A Least-Likely Test for the Caribbean School. Research in Economic History 7 (1982).

Darity, William A., Jr. Mercantilism, Slavery and the Industrial

Revolution. In: Paul Zarembka (ed.), Research in Political Economy, Volume 5, pp. 1-21. Greenwich, CT: JAI Press, 1982.

Darity, William A., Jr. The Numbers Game and the Profitability of the British Trade in Slaves. Journal of Economic History 45 (September 1985):693-703.

Davis, Charles T. and Henry Louis Gates, Jr. The Slave's Narrative: Texts and Contexts. New York: Oxford University Press, 1984.

Dew, Charles B. Black Ironworkers and the Slave Insurrection Panic of 1856. Journal of Southern History 41 (1975):321-38.

Dew, Charles B. David Ross and the Oxford Iron Works: A Study of Industrial Slavery in the Early Nineteenth Century. William and Mary Quarterly 31 (1974):189-224.

Dew, Charles B. Disciplining Slave Ironworkers in the Antebellum South: Coercion, Concilation and Accomodation. American Historical Review 79 (1974):383-418.

Dibble, Ernest F. Slave Rentals to the Military: Pensacola and the Gulf Coast. Civil War History 23 (1977):101-13.

Domar, Evsey D. The Cause of Slavery or Serfdom: A Hypothesis. Journal of Economic History 30 (1970):18-32.

Drago, Edmund L. How Sherman's March Through Georgia Affected the Slaves. Georgia Historical Quarterly 57 (1973):361-75.

Du Bois, W. E. B. The Suppression of the African Slave Trade to the United States of America, 1638-1870. New York: Longman, Green, 1896. [1954 edition contains "Apologia," pp. 327-29].

Edmondson, Locksley. Trans-Atlantic Slavery and the Internationalization of Race. Caribbean Quarterly 22 (June-September 1976):5-25.

Ekberg, Carl J. Black Slaves in the Illinois Country, 1721-1765. Proc. Fr. Colonial Hist. Soc. (1985, publ. 1987):265-78.

Elkins, Stanley M. and Eric Mc Kitrick. Institutions and the Law of Slavery in Capitalist and Non-Capitalist Cultures. American Quarterly (Summer 1957).

Engerman, Stanley L. The Effects of Slavery upon the Southern Economy: A Review of the Recent Debate. Explorations in Entrepreneurial History 4 (Winter 1967):71-97.

Engerman, Stanley L. The Realities of Slavery: A Review of Recent Evidence. International Journal of Comparative Sociology 20 (1979):46-66.

Engerman, Stanley L. The Slave Trade and British Capital Formation in the Eighteenth Century: A Comment on the Williams Thesis. Business History Review 46 (1972):430-43.

Engerman, Stanley L. Slavery and Emancipation in Comparative Perspective: A Look at Some Recent Debates. _Journal of Economic History_ 46 (June 1986):317-39.

Engerman, Stanley L. Some Considerations Relating to Property Rights in Man. _Journal of Economic History_ 33 (1973):43-65.

Engerman, Stanley L. Some Economic and Demographic Comparisons of Slavery in the United States and the British West Indies. _Economic History Review_ 29 (1976):258-75.

Engerman, Stanley L. and E. D. Genovese (eds.) _Race and Slavery in the Western Hemisphere: Quantitative Studies_. Princeton, 1975.

Escott, Paul D. _Slavery Remembered: A Record of Twentieth Century Slave Narratives_. Chapel Hill, NC: University of North Carolina Press, 1979.

Fede, Andrew. Legitimized Violent Slave Abuse in the American South, 1619-1865: A Case Study of Law and Social Change in Six Southern States. _American Journal of Legal History_ 29 (April 1985):93-150.

Fields, Barbara J. _Slavery and Freedom on the Middle Ground: Maryland During the Nineteenth Century_. New Haven, CT: Yale University Press, 1985.

Finkelman, Paul. _The Law of Freedom and Bondage: A Casebook_. New York: Oceana Publications, 1985.

Finkelman, Paul. The Nationalization of Slavery: A Counter Factual Approach to the 1860s. _Louisiana Studies_ 14 (1975):213-40.

Fischbaum, Marvin and Julius Rubin. Slavery and the Economic Development of the American South. _Explorations in Entrepreneurial History_ 6 (1968):116-27.

Fleisig, Heywood. Slavery, the Supply of Agricultural Labor, and the Industrialization of the South. _Journal of Economic History_ 36 (1976):572-97.

Fleming, Dan B. A Review of Slave Life in Fourteen United States History Textbooks. _Journal of Negro Education_ 56 (Fall 1987):550-56.

Fogel, Robert W. and Stanley L. Engerman. _Time on the Cross_, 2 vols. Boston: Little, Brown, 1974.

Foshee, Andrew W. Slave Hiring in Rural Louisiana. _Louisiana History_ 26 (Winter 1985):63-73.

Franklin, John Hope. _From Slavery to Freedom_ (fifth edition). New York: Knopf, 1980.

Freehling, William W. The Founding Fathers and Slavery. _American Historical Review_ (February 1972).

Frey, Sylvia. Between Slavery and Freedom: Virginia Blacks in the American Revolution. Journal of Southern History 49 (1983):375-98.

Galenson, David W. Traders, Planters, and Slaves. Market Behavior in Early English America. New York: Cambridge University Press, 1986.

Galenson, David W. White Servitude and the Growth of Black Slavery in Colonial America. Journal of Economic History 61 (1981):39-47.

Gallman, Robert E. Slavery and Southern Economic Growth. Southern Economic Journal 45 (1979):1007-22.

Genovese, Eugene D. The Political Economy of Slavery 1966.

Genovese, Eugene D. Roll, Jordan, Roll: The World the Slaves Made. New York: Random House, 1974.

Genovese, Eugene D. The Significance of the Slave Plantation for Southern Economic Development. Journal of Southern History 28 (1962):422-37.

Genovese, Eugene D. and Elizabeth Fox-Genovese. The Slave Economies in Political Perspective. Journal of American History 66 (June 1979):7-23.

Genovese, Eugene D. and Elizabeth Fox-Genovese. Slavery, Economic Development, and the Law: The Dilemma of the Southern Economists, 1800-1860. Washington and Lee Law Review (1984).

Gilmore, Al-Tony (ed.) Revisiting Blassingame's "The Slave Community": The Scholars Respond. Westport, CT: Greenwood, 1978.

Glasrud, Bruce A. and Alan M. Smith (eds.) Race Relations in British North America, 1607-1783. Chicago: Nelson-Hall, 1982.

Goodfriend, Joyce D. Burghers and Blacks: The Evolution of a Slave Society at New Amsterdam. New York History 59 (1978):125-44.

Gratus, J. The Great White Lie: Slavery, Emancipation, and Changing Racial Attitudes. New York: 1973.

Gray, Ralph and Betty Wood. The Transition from Indentured to Involuntary Servitude in Colonial Georgia. Explorations in Economic History 13 (1976):353-70.

Greene, Jack P. 'Slavery - or Independence': Some Reflections on the Relationships among Liberty, Black Bondage, and Equality in Revolutionary South Carolina. South Carolina Historical Magazine (July 1979).

Greene, Lorenzo. The Negro in Colonial New England. New York: Atheneum, 1968.

Gutman, Herbert G. The Black Family in Slavery and Freedom, 1750-1925. New York: Pantheon, 1976.

Gutman, Herbert G. *Slavery and the Numbers Game: A Critique of Time on the Cross*. Urbana, IL: University of Illinois Press, 1975.

Halliburton, R., Jr. Free Black Owners of Slaves: A Reappraisal of the Woodson Thesis. *South Carolina Historical Magazine* 76 (1975):129-42.

Harper, Celil, Jr. Slavery Without Cotton: Hunt County, Texas, 1846-1864. *S.W. Hist. Q.* 88 (April 1985):387-405.

Harris, J. William. *Plain Folk and Gentry in a Slave Society: White Liberty and Black Slavery in Augusta's Hinterland*. Middleton, CT: Wesleyan University Press, 1985.

Henry, H. M. *Police Control of the Slave in South Carolina*. New York, 1914, repr. 1968.

Higgins, W. Robert. The Geographical Origins of Negro Slaves in Colonial South Carolina. *South Atlantic Quarterly* 70 (1971):34-47.

Higginson, Thomas W. *Black Rebellion*. New York: 1969.

Hoetink, H. Slavery and Race. *Historical Reflections* 6 (Summer 1979):255-274. [Includes comments].

Huggins, Nathan I. *Black Odyssey: The Afro-American Ordeal in Slavery*. New York: Pantheon, 1977.

Hunter, Lloyd A. Slavery in St. Louis 1804-1860. *Missouri Historical Society Bulletin* 30 (1974):233-65.

Inikori, J. E. Market Structure and Profits: A Further Rejoinder. *Journal of Economic History* 45 (September 1985):708-11.

Inikori, J. E. Measuring the Atlantic Slave Trade: An Assessment of Curtin and Anstey. *Journal of African History* 17 (1976):197-223.

Jacobs, Harriet A. *Incidents in the Life of a Slave Girl, Written by Herself*. [Edited by Jean Fagan Yellin]. Cambridge, MA: Harvard University Press, 1987.

James, C. L. R. The Atlantic Slave Trade and Slavery: Some Interpretations of their Significance in the Development of the United States and the Western World. *Amistad 1* (1970):119-64.

Johnson, Kenneth R. Slavery and Racism in Florence, Alabama, 1841-1862. *Civil War History* 27 (June 1981):155-171.

Jones, Rhett S. Structural Differentiation and the Status of Blacks in British Colonial America, 1630-1775. *Journal of Human Relations* 19 (1971):322-46.

Jordan, Winthrop D. *White Over Black: American Attitudes toward the Negro, 1550-1812*. Chapel Hill, NC: University of North Carolina

Press, 1968.

Joyner, Charles. Down by the Riverside: A South Carolina Slave
    Community. Champaign, IL: University of Illinois Press, 1984. [All
    Saints Parish].

Katzman, David. Black Slavery in Michigan. Midcontinent Am. Studies
    Journal 11 (1970):56-66.

Kilson, Marion De B. Towards Freedom: An Analysis of Slave Revolts in
    the United States. Phylon 25 (Summer 1964):175-87.

Kiple, Kenneth F. The Caribbean Slave: A Biological History. New York:
    Cambridge University Press, 1984.

Koger, Larry. Black Slaveowners: Free Black Slave Masters in South
    Carolina, 1790-1860. Jefferson, NC: McFarland, 1985.

Kruger, Vivienne L. Born to Run: The Slave Family in Early New York,
    1626-1827. Doctoral dissertation, Columbia University, 1985. UMO #
    8523186.

Kulikoff, Allan. Tobacco and Slaves: The Development of Southern
    Cultures in the Chesapeake, 1680-1800. Chapel Hill, NC: University
    of North Carolina Press, 1986.

Lack, Paul D. An Urban Slave Community: Little Rock, 1831-1862.
    Arkansas Historical Quarterly 41 (Autumn 1982):258-87.

Lander, E. M. Slave Labor in South Carolina Cotton Mills. Journal of
    Negro History 38 (April 1953):161-73.

Lewis, Ronald L. Coal, Iron, and Slaves: Industrial Slavery in Maryland
    and Virginia, 1715-1865. Westport, CT: Greenwood, 1979.

Lewis, Ronald L. Slavery on Chesapeake Iron Plantations before the
    American Revolution. Journal of Negro History 59 (1974):242-54.

Lewis, Ronald L. The Use and Extent of Slave Labor in the Chespeake Iron
    Industry: The Colonial Era. Labor History 17 (1976):388-405.

Lovejoy, Paul E. The Volume of the Atlantic Slave Trade: A Synthesis.
    Journal of African History 23 (1982):473-501.

Lythgoe, Dennis L. Negro Slavery in Utah. Utah Historical Quarterly 39
    (1971):40-54.

Main, Gloria L. Tobacco Colony: Life in Early Maryland, 1650-1720.
    Princeton, 1982.

Mathias, Frank F. John Randolph's Freedmen: The Thwarting of a Will.
    Journal of Southern History 39 (1973):263-72. [383 slaves].

McGowan, James T. Planters Without Slaves: Origins of New World Labor
    Systems. Southern Studies 16 (1977):5-26. [Louisiana, 1790-1820].

McManus, Edgar J. Black Bondage in the North. Syracuse, NY: Sryacuse University Press, 1973.

McManus, Edgar J. A History of Negro Slavery in New York. 1966.

Menard, Russell R. From Servants to Slaves: The Transformation of the Chesapeake Labor System. Southern Studies 16 (1977):355-390.

Miller, Joseph C. Mortality in the Atlantic Slave Trade: Statistical Evidence on Causality. Journal of Interdisciplinary History 11 (1981):385-423. See 13 (1982):331-6 for comment on Cohn and Jensen, above.

Miller, Randall M. and John David Smith (eds.) Dictionary of Afro-American Slavery. Westport, CT: Greenwood, 1988.

Mohr, Clarence L. On the Threshold of Freedom: Masters and Slaves in Civil War Georgia. Athens, GA: University of Georgia Press, 1986.

Moore, John H. Simon Gray, Riverman: A Slave Who Was Almost Free. Mississipppi Valley Historical Review 49 (1962):471-84.

Morgan, Edmund S. American Slavery, American Freedom: The Ordeal of Colonial America. New York, 1975.

Morgan, Philip D. The Ownership of Property by Slaves in the Mid-Nineteenth-Century Low Country. Journal of Southern History 49 (August 1983):399-420.

Morgan, Philip D. Work and Culture: The Task System and the World of Lowcountry Blacks, 1700-1880. William and Mary Quarterly 39 (October 1982):563-599.

Morgan, Philip D. and Georgia D. Terry. Slavery in Microcosm: A Conspiracy Scare in Colonial South Carolina. Southern Studies 21 (Summer 1982):121-45.

Morrow, Nancy V. The Problem of Slavery in the Polemic Literature of the American Enlightenment. Early American Literature 20 (Winter 1985-1986):236-55.

Moss, Richard S. Slavery on Long Island: Its Rise and Decline during the Seventeenth through Nineteenth Centuries. Doctoral dissertation, St. John's University, 1985. UMO # 8602014.

Myers, John. The Writing of History of the Rise and Fall of the Slave Power in America. Civil War History 31 (June 1985):144-62.

Nash, Gary B. Slaves and Slaveowners in Colonial Philadelphia. William and Mary Quarterly 30 (1973):223-56.

Norde, Gerald S. From Genesis to Phoenix: The Breeding of Slaves during the Domestic Slave Era, 1807-1863, and Its Consequences. Doctoral dissertation, University of Delaware, 1985. UMO # 8609057.

Nordstrom, Carl. Slavery in a New York County: Rockland County, 1686-1827. _Afro-Americans in New York Life and History_ 1 (1977):145-66.

Note. Sexual Control in the Slaveholding South: The Implementation of a Racial Caste System. _Harvard Women's Law Journal_ 7 (1984).

Oakes, James. _The Ruling Race: A History of American Slaveholders_. New York: Knopf, 1982.

O'Brien, Mary L. Slavery in Louisville during the Antebellum Period: 1820-1860. Master's thesis, University of Louisville, 1979.

1,500 Slave Descendants at Carolina 'Reunion.' _New York Times_ August 31, 1986.

Otto, John Solomon. _Cannon's Point Plantation, 1794-1860: Living Conditions and Status Patterns in the Old South_. New York: Academic Press, 1984.

Owens, Harry P. (ed.) _Perspectives and Irony in American Slavery_ (second edition). Jackson: University Press of Mississippi, 1976.

Owens, Leslie H. _This Species of Property: Slave Life and Culture in the Old South_. New York: Oxford University Press, 1976.

Palmer, Paul C. Servant Into Slave: The Evolution of the Legal Status of the Negro Laborer in Colonial Virginia. _South Atlantic Quarterly_ 65 (Summer 1966):355-70.

Parker, Freddie Lee. _Runaway Slaves in North Carolina, 1775 to 1835_. Doctoral dissertation, University of North Carolina, 1987. UMO # 8722334.

Passell, Peter and Gavin Wright. The Effects of Pre-Civil War Territorial Expansion on the Price of Slaves. _Journal of Political Economy_ 80 (1972):1188-1202.

Pease, Jane H. and William H. Pease. _They Who Would Be Free: The Blacks' Search for Freedom, 1830-1861_. New York: Atheneum, 1974.

Peniston, Gregory S. The Slave Builder-Artisan. _Western Journal of Black Studies_ 2 (Winter 1978):284-95.

Perdue, Charles L., Jr. and others (eds.). _Weevils in the Wheat, Interviews with Virginia Ex-slaves_. Bloomington, IN: Indiana University Press, 1980.

Pieterse, Jan Nederveen. Slavery and the Triangle of Emancipation. _Race and Class_ 30 (October-December 1988):1-21.

Polsky, Milton. The American Slave Narrative: Exciting Resource Material for the Classroom. _Negro Educational Review_ 26 (January 1975):22-36.

Port, Edward M. Kentucky Law Concerning Emancipation or Freedom of
    Slaves. Filson Culb Hist. Q. 59 (July 1985):344-67.

Preyer, Norris W. The Historian, the Slave, and the Antebellum Textile
    Industry. Journal of Negro History 46 (1961):67-82.

Rawick, George (ed.) The American Slave. [41 vols]. Westport, CT:
    Greenwood, 1972-1979.

Robinson, Donald L. Slavery in the Structure of American Politics, 1765-
    1820. New York: Norton, 1979.

Roediger, David R. And Die in Dixie: Funerals, Death, and Heaven in the
    Slave Community, 1700-1865. Massachusetts Review 22 (Spring
    1981):163-83.

Russell, Francis. Liberty to Slaves: Black Loyalists in the American
    Revolution. Timeline 4 (April-May 1987):3-15.

Savitt, Todd L. Slave Life Insurance in Virginia and North Carolina.
    Journal of Southern History 43 (1977):583-600.

Scarano, Francisco A. Sugar and Slavery in Puerto Rico: The Plantation
    Economy of Ponce, 1800-1850. Madison: University of Wisconsin
    Press, 1984.

Scarpino, Philip V. Slavery in Callaway County, Missouri: 1845-1855
    [Commercial and subsistence farming]. Missouri Historical Review 71
    (1976):22-43.

Schnittman, Suzanne S. Slavery in Virginia's Urban Tobacco Industry -
    1840-1860. Doctoral dissertation, University of Rochester, 1987.
    UMO # 8709511.

Schwarz, Philip J. Emancipators, Protectors, and Anomalies: Free Black
    Slaveowners in Virginia. Va. Mag. Hist. Biog. 95 (July 1987):317-
    38.

Sekora, John. Black Message/White Envelope: Genre, Authenticity, and
    Authority in the Antebellum Slave Narrative. Callaloo 10 (Summer
    1987):482-515.

Sekora, John and Darwin T. Turner (eds.) The Art of the Slave Narrative:
    Original Essays in Criticism and Theory. Western Illinois University
    Press, 1982.

Shafer, Robert S. White Persons Held to Racial Slavery in Antebellum
    Arkansas. Arkansas Historical Quarterly 44 (Summer 1985):134-55.

Smith, John D. The Unveiling of Slave Folk Culture, 1865-1920. Journal
    of Folklore Research 21 (April 1984):47-62.

Smith, Julia F. Slavery and Rice Culture in Low Country Georgia, 1750-
    1860. Knoxville, TN: University of Tennessee Press, 1985.

Smith, Julia F. Slavetrading in Antebellum Florida. Florida Historical
    Quarterly 50 (1972):252-61.

Solow, Barbara L. Caribbean Slavery and British Growth: The Eric
    Williams Hypothesis. Journal of Development Economics 17 (1985):99-
    115.

Solow, Barbara L. and Stanley L. Engerman (eds.) British Capitalism and
    Caribbean Slavery. The Legacy of Eric Williams. New York:
    Cambridge University Press, 1987.

Stampp, Kenneth M. The Peculiar Institution: Slavery in the Ante-Bellum
    South. New York: Knopf, 1956.

Stampp, Kenneth M. (general editor). Records of Ante-Bellum Southern
    Plantations from the Revolution through the Civil War [257
    microfilm reels in 6 series]. Frederick, MD: University
    Publications of America, 1987.

Starling, Marion W. The Slave Narrative: Its Place in American History.
    Boston: Hall, 1981.

Starobin, Robert S. The Economics of Industrial Slavery in the Old South.
    Business History Review 44 (Summer 1970):131-74.

Starobin, Robert S. Industrial Slavery in the Old South. New York:
    Oxford University Press, 1970.

Statom, Thomas R., Jr. Negro Slavery in Eighteenth-Century Georgia.
    Doctoral dissertation, University of Alabama, 1982. UMO # 8314051.

Stealey, John E., III. The Responsibilities and Liabilities of the Bailee
    of Slave Labor in Virginia. American Journal of Legal History 12
    (1968):336-53.

Steckel, Richard H. The Economics of U.S. Slave and Southern White
    Fertility. New York, 1985.

Steckel, Richard H. and Richard A. Jensen. New Evidence on the Causes of
    Slave and Crew Mortality in the Atlantic Slave Trade. Journal of
    Economic History 46 (March 1986):57-77.

Strickland, John S. Across Space and Time: Conversion, Commmunity and
    Cultural Change among South Carolina Slaves. Doctoral dissertation,
    University of North Carolina, 1985. UMO # 8527327.

Sutch, Richard. The Breeding of Slaves for Sale and the Westward
    Expansion of Slavery, 1850-1860. In: Stanley L. Engerman and E. D.
    Genovese (eds.), Race and Slavery in the Western Hemisphere:
    Quantitative Studies, pp. 173-210. Princeton, 1975.

Sweig, Donald M. The Importation of African Slaves to the Potomac River,
    1732-1772. William and Mary Quarterly 42 (October 1985):507-24.

Taylor, Joe G. Slavery in Lousiana during the Civil War. Lousiana Hist.

534

8 (1967):27-33.

Thomas, Robert P. and R. N. Brown. The Fishers of Men: The Profits of the Slave Trade. Journal of Economic History 34 (1974):885-914.

Thornton, J. Mills, III. Politics and Power in a Slave Society: Alabama, 1800-1860. Baton Rouge: Louisiana State University Press, 1978.

Tise, Larry E. Proslavery. A History of the Defense of Slavery in America. 1700-1840. Athens, GA: University of Georgia Press, 1987.

Tully, Alan. Patterns of Slaveholding in Colonial Pennsylvania: Chester and Lancaster Counties, 1729-1758. Journal of Social History 6 (1973):284-305.

Turner, Edward R. The Negro in Pennsylvania. Slavery - Servitude - Freedom. 1639-1861. Washington, D.C.: 1911.

Tushnet, Mark V. The American Law of Slavery. 1810-1860. Considerations of Humanity and Interest. Princeton, NJ: Princeton University Press, 1981.

Van De Burg, William C. The Slave Drivers: Black Agricultural Labor Supervisors in the Antebellum South. New York: Oxford University Press, 1988.

Van Horne, John C. (ed.) Religious Philanthropy and Colonial Slavery: The American Correspondence of the Associates of Dr. Bray. 1717-1777. Urbana, IL: University of Illinois Press, 1986.

Vedder, Richard K. The Slave Exploitation (Expropriation) Rate. Explorations in Economic History 12 (1975):453-7.

Wade, Richard C. Slavery in the Cities: The South 1820-1860. New York: Oxford University Press, 1967.

Wallerstein, Immanuel. American Slavery and the Capitalist World Economy. American Journal of Sociology 81 (March 1976).

Wax, Darold D. The Demand for Slave Labor in Colonial Pennsylvania. Pennsylvania History 34 (1967):331-45.

Wax, Darold D. Preferences for Slaves in Colonial America. Journal of Negro History 58 (1973):371-401.

Webber, Thomas L. Deep Like the Rivers: Education in the Slave Quarter Community. 1831-1865. New York: Norton, 1978.

Weir, Robert M. Colonial South Carolina: A History. Millwood, NY: KTO Press, 1983.

Westbury, Susan. Slaves of Colonial Virginia: Where They Came From. William and Mary Quarterly 42 (April 1985):228-37.

White, Deborah G. Ain't I a Woman? Female Slaves in the Antebellum

South. Doctoral dissertation, University of Illinois, Chicago, 1979. UMO # 7923030.

White, Deborah G. Ar'n't I a Woman? Female Slaves in the Plantation South. New York: Norton, 1985.

Wiecek, William M. The Statutory Law of Slavery and Race in the Thirteen Mainland Colonies of British America. William and Mary Quarterly 34 (1977):258-80.

Williams, Eric. Capitalism and Slavery. New York: Russell and Russell, 1961 repr.

Williams-Myers, A. J. The African Presence in the Hudson River Valley: The Defining of Relationships Between the Masters and the Slaves. Afro-Americans in New York Life and History 12 (January 1988):81-88.

Wood, Betty. Some Aspects of Female Resistance to Chattel Slavery in Low Country Georgia, 1763-1815. Hist. Journal 30 (September 1987):603-22.

Wood, Peter H. Black Majority: Negroes in Colonial South Carolina from 1670 through the Stono Rebellion. New York: Knopf, 1974.

Woodson, Carter G. Free Negro Owners of Slaves in the United States in 1830. Journal of Negro History 9 (January 1924).

Wright, Gavin. Slavery and the Cotton Boom. Explorations in Economic History 12 (1975):439-51.

Wyatt-Brown, Bertram. The Mask of Obedience: Male Slave Psychology in the Old South. American Historical Review 93 (December 1988):1228-52.

Young, Tommy R., III. The United States Army and the Institution of Slavery in Louisiana, 1803-1815. Part I. Louisiana Studies 13 (1974):201-22.

Slavery Bibliography

Barnard, Henry (comp.) Slavery, Part I: A Bibliography of the Microfilm Collection. Sanford, NC: Microfilming Corp. of America, 1980.

Jacobs, Donald M. and Steven Fershleiser (comps.) Index to the 'American Slave'. Westport, CT: Greenwood, 1981.

Miller, Joseph C. (comp.) Slavery: A Comparative Teaching Bibliography. Waltham, MA: Crossroads Press, 1977.

Olson, James S. (comp.) Slave Life in America: A Historiography and Selected Bibliography. Lanham, MD: University Press of America, 1983.

Smith, John David (comp.) Black Slavery in the Americas: An
    Interdisciplinary Bibliography. 1865-1980. [2 vols]. Westport, CT:
    Greenwood, 1982.

76. Socialism and Racism

No recent convention of [U.S.] Socialists has dared to face fairly the Negro problem and make a straightforward declaration that they regard Negroes as men in the same sense that other persons are.

-W. E. B. Du Bois, "Socialism and the Negro Problem," 1913

Bell, Leland. Radicalism and Race: The IWW and the Black Worker. Journal of Human Relations 19 (1971):48-56.

Drake, Willie A. From Reform to Communism: The Intellectual Development of W.E.B. Du Bois. Doctoral dissertation, Cornell University, 1985. UMO # 8525681.

Du Bois, W. E. B. A Field for Socialists. New Review 1 (January 11, 1913):54-7.

Du Bois, W. E. B. The Negro and Socialism. In: Helen Alfred (ed.), Toward a Socialist America, pp. 179-191. New York: Peace Publications, 1958.

Du Bois, W. E. B. The Problem of Problems. Intercollegiate Socialists 6 (December 1917-January 1918):5-9.

Du Bois, W. E. B. Socialism and the Negro Problem. New Review 1 (February 1, 1913):138-41.

Du Bois, W. E. B. Socialism Is Too Narrow for Negroes. Socialist Call January 21, 1912.

Fairclough, Adam. Was Martin Luther King a Marxist? History Workshop 15 (Spring 1983):117-25.

Foner, Philip S. American Socialism and Black Americans: From the Age of Jackson to World War II. Westport, CT: Greenwood, 1978.

Foner, Philip S. (ed.) Black Protest and Socialism. New York: Capricorn, 1975.

Harris, Abram L. The Negro and Economic Radicalism. Modern Quarterly 2 (1924-25):198-208.

Harrison, Hubert. Socialism and the Negro. International Socialist Review 13 (July 1912):65-68.

Kelley, R. D. G. 'Comrades, Praise Gawd for Lenin and Them': Ideology and Culture among Black Communists in Alabama, 1930-1935. Science and Society 52 (Spring 1988).

Kelley, R. D. G. Hammer n' Hoe: Black Radicalism and the Communist Party in Alabama, 1929-1941. Doctoral dissertation, University of

California, Los Angeles, 1987. UMO # 8803688.

Kim, Sam Gon. Black Americans' Commitment to Communism: A Case Study
    Based on Fiction and Autobiographies by Black Americans. Doctoral
    dissertation, University of Kansas, 1986. UMO # 8711234. [Centers
    on Richard Wright].

Marable, Manning. A. Philip Randolph and the Foundations of Black
    American Socialism. Radical America 14 (March-April 1980):7-32.

Meredith, H. L. Agrarian Socialism and the Negro in Oklahoma, 1900-1918.
    Labor History 11 (1970):277-86.

Moore, R. L. Flawed Fraternity - American Socialist Response to the
    Negro, 1901-1912. Historian 32 (November 1969):1-18.

Mumford, Clarence J. Production Relations, Class and Black Liberation: A
    Marxist Perspective on Afro-American Studies. Atlantic Highlands,
    NJ: Humanities Press, 1979.

Naison, Mark D. Communism and Black Nationalism in the Depression: The
    Case of Harlem. Journal of Ethnic Studies 2 (1974):24-36.

Painter, Nell and Hosea Hudson. Hosea Hudson: A Negro Communist in the
    Deep South. Radical America 11 (1977):7-23.

Pease, William H. and Jane H. Pease. Black Utopia: Negro Communal
    Experiments in America. Madison: State Historical Society of
    Wisconsin, 1963.

Pulley, Andrew. How I Became a Socialist. New York: Pathfinder Press,

Randolph, A. Philip. The Negro and Economic Radicalism. Opportunity 4
    (1926):61-64.

Record, Wilson. The Negro and the Communist Party. Westport, CT:
    Greenwood, 1980 (orig. 1971).

Reed, Adolph, Jr. Scientific Socialism: Notes on the New Afro-American
    Magic Marxism. Endarch 1 (Fall 1974):21-39.

Robinson, Cedric J. Black Marxism. The Making of the Black Radical
    Tradition. London: Zed Press, 1983.

Rony, Vera. Sorrow Song in Black and White [Socialists and southern farm
    labor in 1930s]. New South 22 (1967):2-39.

Scales, Junius I. and Richard Nickson. Cause at Heart. A Former
    Communist Member. Athens, GA: University of Georgia Press, 1987.

Solomon, Mark I. Red and Black: Communism and Afro-Americans, 1929-1935.
    New York: Garland, 1987.

West, Cornel. Left Strategies: A View from Afro-America. Socialist
    Review 86 (1985):41-49.

West, Cornel. <u>Toward a Socialist Theory of Racism</u>. New York: Democratic Socialists of America, 1986.

Winter, J. M. The Webbs and the Non-White World: A Case of Socialist Racialism. <u>Journal of Contemporary History</u> 9 (January 1974).

77. Stereotypes

Colored folk, like all folk, love to see themselves in pictures;
but they are afraid to see the types which the white world has
caricatured.
                                    - W.E.B. DuBois, "In Black," 1920.

Abrahams, Roger D. Positively Black. Englewood, NJ: Prentice-Hall, 1970.

Abu-Laban, Sharon M. Stereotypes of Middle East People: An Analysis of
    Church School Curricula. In: Baha Abu Laban and Faith T. Zeodey
    (eds.), Arabs in America: Myth and Realities, pp. 149-69. Wilmette,
    IL: Medina University Press International, 1975.

Adler, Jerry and Frank S. Washington. Cookie Jars of Oppression [Racist
    artifacts]. Newsweek, May 16, 1988.

Agard, Nadema. Art as a Medium of Countering Race Stereotypes. Interracial
    Books for Children Bulletin, 11, No. 8 (1980):3-5.

Agogino, George. A Study of the Stereotypes of the American Indian.
    Master's thesis, University of New Mexico, 1950.

Aljeaid, Manour O. Perceptions of American College Students about Arabs:
    The Role of Mass Media and Personal Contact in the Formation of
    Stereotypes. Doctoral dissertation, Western Michigan University,
    1986. UMO #8625606.

American Indian Historical Society. Common Misconceptions About American
    Indians. San Francisco, CA: Indian Historical Press, 1968.

Appel, John and Selma Appel. The Distorted Image: Stereotype and Caricature
    in American Popular Graphics 1850-1922 [filmstrip]. New York:
    Anti-Defamation League.

Baldwin, James. The Nigger We Invent. Integrated Education (March-April
    1969).

Barker, Jade. I Was a Token in the Left. Zeta Magazine 1 (July-August
    1988):43-45.

Barnett, Louise K. The Ignoble Savage: American Literary Racism,
    1790-1890. Westport, CT: Greenwood, 1975.

Bean, Lowell J. The Language of Stereotype Distortion Inaccuracy. Indian
    Historian (Fall 1969).

Becker, Helen. Selling the Stereotype: Sexist, Ageist, Typecasting in
    Network Television Advertising in 1986. Master's thesis, University of
    Central Florida, 1987.

Bicha, Karel D. Hunkies: Stereotyping the Slavic Immigrants, 1890-1920. *Journal of American Ethnic History* 2 (Fall 1982):16-38.

Bischoff, Peter and Peter Nocon. The Image of the Irish in Nineteenth-Century American Popular Culture, III. In: Wolfgang Zach and Heinz Kosok (eds.), *Literary Interrelations*, 2 vols., pp. 61-75. Tübingen: Narr, 1987.

Bodenhausen, Galen V. and Meryl Lichtenstein. Social Stereotypes and Information Processing Strategies: The Impact of Task Complexity. *Journal of Personality and Social Psychology* 52 (May 1987):871-80.

Brabant, Sarah and Linda Mooney. Sex Role Stereotyping in the Sunday Comics: Ten Years Later. *Sex Roles* 14 (February 1986):141-48.

Brizee, Robert L. *The Stereotyping of the Indian in the New Mexico Press*. Master's thesis, University of New Mexico, 1954.

Brown, Sterling A. Negro Character as Seen by White Authors. *Journal of Negro Education* (April 1933):179-203.

Brown, Sterling A. Negro Character as Seen by White Authors. *Callaloo* 5 (February-May 1982):55-89.

Caldwell, Dan. The Negroidization of the Chinese Stereotype in California. *Southern California Quarterly* (June 1971):123-31.

Campbell, Paul Vance. *The Classroom Modification of Children's Gender Stereotyping of Careers*. Doctoral dissertation, Utah State University, 1986. UMO # 8719470.

Casas, J. Manuel and others. Stereotyping the Stereotyper: A Mexican American Perspective. *Journal of Cross-Cultural Psychology* 18 (1987):45-57.

Cauthen, Nelson R. and others. Stereotypes: A Review of the Literature, 1926-1968 [Ethnic group stereotypes]. *Journal of Social Psychology* 84 (June 1971):103-125.

Chan, Raymond K. *Chinatown Family* in Review. *Yellow Journal* 2 (Spring 1988):40-48.

Chin, Frank. From the Chinaman 'Year of the Dragon' to the Fake 'Year of the Dragon'. *Quilt* 5 (1986):58-71.

Chin, Frank and Jeffrey Paul Chan. Racist Love. In: Richard Kostelanetz (ed.), *Seeing Through Shuck*. New York: Ballantine, 1972.

Churchill, Ward. Film Stereotyping of Native Americans. *Book Forum* 5 (1981):370-75.

Clark, M. L. Social Stereotypes and Self-Concept in Black and White College Students. *Journal of Social Psychology* 125 (December 1985):753-60.

Collins, Sheila D. Arab Americans: Beyond the Stereotype. In: Sheila D. Collins (ed.), The Rainbow Challenge. The Jackson Campaign and the Future of American Politics, pp. 202-205. New York: Monthly Review Press, 1986.

Council on Interracial Books for Children. Stereotypes, Distortions, and Omissions in United States History Textbooks. New York: The Council, 1977.

Cunningham, George E. Derogatory Image of the Negro and Negro History. Negro History Bulletin (March 1965).

Deane, Paul C. The Persistence of Uncle Tom: An Examination of the Image of the Negro in Children's Fiction Series. Journal of Negro Education (Spring 1968).

Deaux, Kay and May E. Kite. Gender Stereotypes: Some Thoughts for the Cognitive Organization of Gender-related Information. Academic Psychology Bulletin 7 (Summer 1985):123-44.

Deloria, Vine, Jr. The American Indian Image in North America, pp. 49-54 in The Pretend Indians. Ames, IA: Iowa State University Press, 1980.

Devine, P. G. Automatic and Controlled Processes in Prejudice: The Role of Stereotypes and Personal Beliefs. In: Anthony R. Pratkanis and others (eds.), Attitude Structure and Function. Hillsdale, NJ: Lawrence Erlbaum Associates, 1988.

Dill, Robert L. Portraits in Red and Black: Racial Stereotypes in Oklahoma Newspapers 1900-1925. Master's thesis, Texas Christian University, 1979.

Donovan, Kathleen. Good Old Pat: An Irish-American Stereotype in Decline. Eire-Ireland 14 (1980):6-14.

Dovidio, John F. and others. Racial Stereotypes: The Contents of their Cognitive Representations. Journal of Experimental Social Psychology 22 (January 1986):22-37.

Elfenbein, Anna S. Women on the Color Line: Evolving Stereotypes and the Writings of George Washington Cable, Grace King, Kate Chopin. Charlottesville, VI: University Press of Virginia, 1988.

Estrada, Jorge A. The Depiction of Hispanic People in the California State-adopted Sixth-grade Reading Texts in 1982. Doctoral dissertation, University of San Francisco, 1987. UMO # 8802587.

Farquhar, Judith and May L. Doi. Bruce Lee vs. Fu Manchu: Kung Fu Films and Asian American Stereotypes in America. Bridge 6 (Fall 1978):23-40.

Fernandez, Enrique. La Boomba [Stereotypes of Hispanics in American films]. Village Voice January 5, 1988.

Fessler, Loren W. (ed.) *Chinese in America: Stereotyped Past, Changing Present*. New York: Vantage Press, 1983.

Fiske, Susan T. On the Road: Comment on the Cognitive Stereotyping Literature on Pettigiew and Martin. *Journal of Social Issues* 43 (1987):113-18.

Flake, Floyd H. Michel's Amos 'n' Andy Slur [Congressman Robert Michel]. *New York Times* November 21, 1988.

Frederickson, George M. *The Black Image in the White Mind: The Debate on Afro-American Character and Destiny, 1817-1914*. New York: 1971.

Freundlich, Joyce Y. Images of the Puerto Rican in Young Adult Books: Fact or Fancy. *NABE: The Journal for the National Association for Bilingual Education* 5 (Winter 1980-81):69-80.

Friar, Ralph and Natasha Friar. *The Only Good Indian: The Hollywood Gospel*. New York: Drama Books, 1973.

Friedman, Lawrence J. *The White Savage: Racial Fantasies in the Postbellum South*. Englewood Cliffs, NJ: Prentice-Hall, 1971.

Garcia, Jesus. From Bloody Savages to Heroic Chiefs. *American Indian Education* 17 (January 1978):15-19.

Gates, Henry L., Jr. The Trope of a New Negro and the Reconstruction of the Image of the Black. *Representations* 24 (Fall 1988).

Ghareeb, Edmund. *Split Vision: The Portrayal of Arabs in the American Media*. Washington, D.C.: American-Arab Affairs Council, 1983.

Gibbs, P. J. *Black Collectibles Sold in America*. Paducah, KY: Collector Books, 1987.

Gilliam, Dorothy. Cultural Icons: Aunt Jemima, Pickaninnies, Smiling Rastus. *Washington Post* July 7, 1980. [Collection of anti-black memorabilia].

Gilman, Sander L. *Difference and Pathology: Stereotypes of Sexuality, Race, and Madness*. Ithaca, NY: Cornell University Press, 1985.

Goldstein, Richard. The [Charlie] Chan Syndrome. *Village Voice* May 5, 1980.

Gould, Ketayun H. Asian and Pacific Islanders: Myth and Reality. *Social Work* 33 (March-April 1988):142-47.

Greenwald, John and Kumiko Makihara. Prejudice and Black Sambo [Anti-black stereotypes in Japan]. *Time* August 15, 1988.

Harari, Herbert and John W. McDavid. Name Stereotypes and Teachers' Expectations. *Journal of Educational Psychology* 65 (October 1973):222-25.

Haru, Sumi. What's Wrong with Charlie Chan? *Pacific Citizen* January 2, 1981.

Heller, Steven. Racist Ephemera: The Melting Pot Reconsidered. *American Book Collector* 3 (January-February 1982):14-21.

Helmreich, William B. *The Things They Say Behind Your Back. Stereotypes and the Myths Behind Them*. New Brunswick, NJ: Transaction Publishers, 1984.

Hentoff, Nat. The Boy With a Confederate Flag on His Back. *Village Voice* July 5, 1988. [North Garner Middle School, near Raleigh, NC].

Herrera-Sobek, Maria (ed.) *Beyond Stereotypes: The Critical Analysis of Chicano Literature*. Binghampton, NY: Bilingual, 1985.

Hevesi, Dennis. 7 Rail Officers Suspended in Taping Case [Race-baiting by New York City private railroad police]. *New York Times* August 4, 1988.

Hirschfelder, Arlene B. *American Indian Stereotypes in the World of Children: A Reader and Bibliography*. Metuchen, NJ: Scarecrow Press, 1982.

Honour, Hugh. *The Image of the Black in Western Art*. Vol. 4: Two Parts: Part 1. *Slaves and Liberators*, Part 2. *Black Models and White Myths*. Cambridge, MA: Harvard University Press. 1989.

Hooten, Richard J. *Race, Skin Color, and Dress as Related to the American Indian Stereotypes*. Doctoral dissertation, Utah State University, 1972.

Huerta, Jorge A. From Stereotypes to Archetypes: Chicano Theaters' Reflection of the Mexicano in the United States. *In*: Renate von Bardeleben and others (eds.), *Missions in Conflict: Essays on U.S.-Mexican Relations and Chicano Culture*, pp. 75-84. Tübingen: Narr, 1986.

Jackson, Derrick Z. Calling the Plays in Black and White [Racial stereotyping in national sports broadcasting]. *Boston Globe* January 22, 1989.

Jacoby, Tamar and Lynda Wright. When Cops Act on a Hunch. *Newsweek* October 10, 1988.

Johnson, Kirk A. Media Images and Racial Stereotyping. *Trotter Institute Review* 1 (Summer 1987):4-9.

Jussium, Lee and others. The Nature of Stereotypes: A Comparison and Integration of Three Theories. *Journal of Personality and Social Psychology* 52 (March 1987):536-46.

Keen, Sam. *Faces of the Enemy: Reflections of the Hostile Imagination*. San Francisco, CA: Harper and Row, 1986.

Kiah, Rosalie B. and Elaine P. Witty. The Portrayal of the Black Mother in Fiction for Children and Adolescents. Child and Youth Services 7 (1985):81-91.

King, Mae C. The Politics of Sexual Stereotypes. Black Scholar 4 (March-April 1973):12-23.

Klagabrun, Francine. 'The Goldbergs' - Stereotypes Loved by Americans. New York Times August 8, 1988. [TV show, late 1940s and early 1950s].

Kleinfeld, Judith. Positive Stereotyping: The Cultural Relativist in the Classroom. Northian 12 (Spring 1976):20-25.

Knobel, Dale T. Hans and the Historian: Ethnic Stereotypes and American Popular Culture, 1820-1860. Journal of German-American Studies 15 (December 1980):65-74.

Knobel, Dale T. Paddy and the Republic: Ethnicity and Nationality in Antebellum America [Stereotypes of Irish in mid-19th century USA]. Middleton, CT: Wesleyan University Press, 1986.

Landrine, Hope. Race and Class Stereotypes of Women. Sex Roles 13 (July 1985):65-75.

Lemons, J. Stanley. Black Stereotypes as Reflected in Popular Culture, 1880-1920. American Quarterly (Spring 1977):102-16.

Leung, Yin Ling. The Model Minority Myth: Asian Americans Confront Growing Backlash. Minority Trendsletter 1 (September/October 1987):6-7.

Lewis, Marvin A. The Puerto Rican in Popular U.S. Literature: A Culturalist Perspective. In: Asela Rodriguez de Laguna (ed.), Images and Identities. The Puerto Rican in Two World Contexts, pp. 65-75. New Brunswick, NJ: Transaction Books, 1987.

Limón, José E. Stereotyping and Chicano Resistance: An Historical Dimension. Aztlan 4 (Fall 1973):25-70.

Lieberson, Stanley. Stereotypes: Their Consequences for Race and Ethnic Interaction. Research in Race and Ethnic Relations 4 (1985):113-37.

Linneman, William R. Immigrant Stereotypes: 1880-1900. Journal of American Humor 1 (April 1974):28-39.

Long, Richard A. Those Magnolia Myths. Nation July 7, 1956.

Lubbers, Klaus. Text as Pretext: Stereotyping the North American Indian. In: Dieter Meindl and Friedrich W. Horlacher (eds.), Mythos und Aufklärung in der amerikanischen Literatur, pp. 129-42. Erlangen: Universitätsbund Erlangen-Nürnberg, 1985.

Lusky, Louis. The Stereotype: Hard Core of Racism. Buffalo Law Review 13 (1964):450-61.

Macaruso, Victor. Cowboys and Indians: The Image of the Indian in American Literature. <u>American Indian Culture and Research Journal</u> 8 (1984):13-21.

Madsen, Jane M. and Rebecca Robbins. Native Americans Visual and Verbal Images in the Caldecott and Newbery Award Books. <u>Minority Voices</u> 5 (Spring-Fall 1981):17-40.

Matz, Duane A. <u>Images of Indians in American Popular Culture Since 1865</u>. Doctoral dissertation, Illinois State University, 1988. UMO # 8818716.

Maykovich, Minako K. Changes in Racial Stereotypes. <u>Human Relations</u> 24 (October 1971):371-85. [Japanese Americans].

McLaurin, Melton. Images of Negroes in Deep South Public School State History Texts. <u>Phylon</u> 32 (Fall 1971):237-46.

McPherson, James M. How U.S. Histories Falsified Slave Life. <u>University</u> (Princeton University) (Summer 1967).

McPherson, James M. The 'Saga' of Slavery: Setting the Textbook Straight. <u>Changing Education</u> (Winter 1967).

Melzer, Richard. New Mexico in Caricature: Images of the Territory on the Eve of Statehood. <u>New Mexico Historical Review</u> 62 (October 1987):335-60.

Meyer, Doris L. Early Mexican-American Responses to Negative Stereotyping. <u>New Mexico History Review</u> 53 (January 1978):75-92.

Meyers, Anat E. <u>The Gypsy as Child Stealer: Stereotype in American Folklore</u>. Master's thesis, University of California, Berkeley, 1987.

Minrath, Marilyn. Breaking the Race Barrier: The White Therapist in Interracial Psychotherapy. <u>Journal of Psychosocial Nursing and Mental Health Services</u> 23 (August 1985):19-24.

Morris, Joann S. Indian Portrayal in Teaching Materials. <u>In</u>: Jack D. Forbes and others (eds.), <u>Multicultural Education and the American Indian</u>, pp. 83-92. Los Angeles: American Indian Studies Center, University of California, 1979.

Mowere, Mary. <u>Sex-Role Stereotyping and Sexism: Implications for Attorney - Female Client Relationships</u>. Master's thesis, University of Central Florida, 1986.

Neira, Christian. Building 860. <u>Harvard Educational Review</u> 58 (August 1988):337-42.

Nolen, Claude H. <u>The Negro's Image in the South: The Anatomy of White Supremacy</u>. Lexington, KY: University of Kentucky Press, 1967.

Obidinski, Eugene. Polish American Social Standing, Status and

Stereotypes. <u>Polish</u> <u>Review</u> 21 (1976):79-102.

Ogawa, Dennis M. <u>From</u> <u>Japs</u> <u>to</u> <u>Japanese:</u> <u>The</u> <u>Evolution</u> <u>of</u> <u>Japanese-</u>
<u>Americans</u> <u>Stereotypes</u>. Berkeley, CA: McCutchan, 1971.

Orfalea, Gregory. Literary Devolution: The Arab in the Post-World II
Novel in English. <u>Journal</u> <u>of</u> <u>Palestine</u> <u>Studies</u> 17 (Winter
1988):109-28.

Osajima, Keith. Asian Americans as the Model Minority: An Analysis of
the Popular Press Image in the 1960s and 1980s. <u>In</u>: Gary Okihuro and
others (eds.), <u>Reflections</u> <u>on</u> <u>Shattered</u> <u>Windows:</u> <u>Promises</u> <u>and</u>
<u>Prospects</u> <u>for</u> <u>Asian</u> <u>American</u> <u>Studies</u>. Pullman, WA: Washington State
University Press, 1988.

Otis, Morgan. Textbooks and the People Known as American Indians. <u>Indian</u>
<u>Historian</u> 5 (Fall 1972):40-50.

Padilla, Eligio R. and Kevin E. O'Grady. Sexuality among Mexican
Americans: A Case of Sexual Stereotyping. <u>Journal</u> <u>of</u> <u>Personality</u>
<u>and</u> <u>Social</u> <u>Psychology</u> 52 (January 1987):5-10.

Palomares, Geraldine D. <u>The</u> <u>Effects</u> <u>of</u> <u>Stereotyping</u> <u>on</u> <u>the</u> <u>Self-Concept</u>
<u>of</u> <u>Mexican</u> <u>Americans</u>. 1970. ERIC ED 056 806.

Pang, Valerie Ooka. Ethnic Prejudice: Still Alive and Hurtful. <u>Harvard</u>
<u>Educational</u> <u>Review</u> 58 (August 1988):375-79.

Parker, Paula. Assorted Images of Racism [Mary Kimbrough's collection of
racist artifacts]. <u>Los</u> <u>Angeles</u> <u>Times</u> August 8, 1979.

Pearce, Roy Harvey. <u>Savagism</u> <u>and</u> <u>Civilization.</u> <u>A</u> <u>Study</u> <u>of</u> <u>the</u> <u>Indian</u> <u>and</u>
<u>the</u> <u>American</u> <u>Mind</u>. Berkeley, CA: University of California Press,
1988 (orig. 1953).

Peterson, Thomas V. <u>Ham</u> <u>and</u> <u>Japheth:</u> <u>The</u> <u>Mythic</u> <u>World</u> <u>of</u> <u>Whites</u> <u>in</u> <u>the</u>
<u>Antebellum</u> <u>South</u>. Metuchen, NJ: Scarecrow Press, 1978.

Petroni, Frank A. 'Uncle Toms': White Stereotypes in the Black Movement.
<u>Human</u> <u>Organization</u> 29 (Winter 1970):260-66.

Pines, Jim. The Study of Racial Images: A Structural Approach. <u>Screen</u>
<u>Education</u> 23 (Summer 1977):24-32.

Quindlen, Anna. Life in the 30's [Development of ethnic stereotypes in
New York City, especially those regarding Italian- and Irish-
Americans]. <u>New</u> <u>York</u> <u>Times</u> December 30, 1987.

Radzialowski, Thaddeus. The Competition for Jobs and Racial Stereotypes:
Poles and Blacks in Chicago. <u>Polish</u> <u>American</u> <u>Studies</u> 33 (Autumn
1976):5-18.

Real, W. (ed.) <u>Racism</u> <u>in</u> <u>America.</u> <u>Role</u> <u>Behavior</u> <u>and</u> <u>Stereotyping</u> <u>as</u>
<u>Obstacles</u> <u>to</u> <u>Black</u> <u>Identity</u>. Paderborn, West Germany: Schoningh,
1977.

Rice, David G. and Richard A. Sternbach. The New York Jewish Student
    Syndrome: Stereotype and Facts. Personnel and Guidance Journal
    (January 1969).

Riggs, Marlon (director). Ethnic Notions. San Francisco, CA: California
    Newsreel, 1987. [Film on history of anti-Black stereotypes in USA].

Robison, Joleen A. History of the Aunt Jemima Trademark Figure from 1889-
    1926. Master's thesis, University of Kansas, Lawrence, 1986.

Roebuck, Julian B. and M. L. Hickson. The Southern Redneck: A
    Phenomenological Class Study. New York: Praeger, 1982.

Rosenberg, Neil Vandraegen. Stereotype and Tradition: White Folklore
    about Blacks (Volumes 1 and 2). Doctoral dissertation, Indiana
    University, 1970.

Salvador-Burris, Juanita. Changing Asian-American Stereotypes. Bridge 6
    (Spring 1978):29-35.

Schulte, Steven C. Indians and Politicians: The Origins of a 'Western'
    Attitude toward Native Americans in Wyoming 1868-1906. Annals of
    Wyoming 56 (Spring 1984):2-11.

Shaheen, Jack. The TV Arab. Bowling Green, OH: The Popular Press,
    Bowling Green State University, 1987.

Siu, Paul C. P. The Chinese Laundryman. A Study of Social Isolation.
    Edited by John Kuo Wei Tchen. New York: New York University Press,
    1988.

Slater, Jack. Oops, Their Stereotypes Are Showing [Anti Asian-American
    stereotypes in films]. Los Angeles Times February 22, 1981.

Smith, Jesse Carney (ed.) Images of Blacks in American Culture.
    Westport, CT: Greenwood, 1988.

Spochs, Luther W. Sambo and the Heathen Chinese: Californians' Racial
    Stereotypes in the Late 1870s. Pacific Historical Review 42 (May
    1973).

Stedman, Raymond W. Shadows of the Indian: Stereotypes in American
    Culture. Norman, OK: University of Oklahoma Press, 1982.

Strom, Robert D. The Mythology of Racism. International Education 1
    (Spring 1972):37-45.

Sue, Stanley and Harry H. L. Kitano. Stereotypes as a Measure of Success.
    Journal of Social Issues 29 (1973):83-98.

Suleiman, Michael W. The Arabs in the Mind of America. Brattleboro, VT:
    Amana Books, 1988.

Sundquist, Asebrit. Pocahantes and Co.: The Fictional American Indian

Woman in Nineteenth-Century Literature: A Study of Method. Atlantic Highlands, NJ: Humanties, 1987.

Sybrandy, Unchalee. Characteristics of Southeast Asians Presented in Children's Realistic Fiction Published in the United States between 1960 and 1980. Doctoral dissertation, Temple University, 1987. UMO # 8803846.

Talbot, Steve. The Myth of Indian Economic and Political Incompetence: The San Carlos Case. Southwest Economy and Society 3 (Spring 1977):3-46.

Tenkate, Herman F. C. The Indian in Literature [Stereotypes]. Indian Historian 3 (Summer 1970):12-32.

Terry, Janice J. Mistaken Identity: Arab Stereotypes in Popular Writing. Washington, D.C.: American-Arab Affairs Council, 1985.

Trecker, Janice L. Sex Stereotyping in the Secondary School Curriculum. Phi Delta Kappan 50 (1973).

U.S. Commission on Civil Rights. Civil Rights Issues of Asian and Pacific Americans: Myths and Realities. Washington, D.C.: The Commission, 1980.

Vaughn, Alden T. From White Man to Redskin: Changing Anglo-American Perceptions of the American Indian. American Historical Review 87 (October 1982):917-53.

Walvin, J. Black Caricature: The Roots of Racialism. In: C. Hurland (ed.), "Race" in Britain. London: 1982.

Weidman, Bette S. and Nancy Black. White on Red: Images of the American Indian. Port Washington, NY: Kennikat Press, 1976.

Wells, Elmer E. Destroying a Racial Myth. Social Studies 69 (September-October 1978):204-206. ["Racial" body odors].

Wiener, Jonathan M. The 'Black Beast Rapist': White Racial Attitudes in the Postwar South. Reviews in American History 13 (June 1985).

Williams, F. and others. Ethnic Stereotyping and Judgements of Children's Speech. Speech Monographs 63 (1971):264-71.

Williams, David P., III. The Contribution of Selectively Focused Print Coverage to the Negative Stereotyping of a Challenging Group. Doctoral dissertation, Arizona State University, 1987. UMO # 8722039. [Black Panther Party].

Williams, Lena. Black Memorabilia: The Pride and the Pain. New York Times December 8, 1988.

Work, Monroe N. An Anthropological Study of Negro Types. National Baptist Union Review (November 19, 1910).

Wyatt, Gail E. Identifying Stereotypes of Afro-American Sexuality and Their Impact upon Sexual Behavior. In: Barbara Ann Bass and others (eds.), The Afro-American Family, pp. 333-46. New York: Grune and Stratton, 1982.

Young, Donna and others. Reducing Stereotypic Attitudes: A Prerequisite to Educational Equity. March 1982. ERIC ED 218 382.

Young, Robert L. Perceptions of Crime, Racial Attitudes, and Firearms Ownership. Social Forces 64 (December 1985):473-86.

Zeligs, Rose. Children's Concepts and Stereotypes of Norwegian, Jew, Scotch, Canadian, Swedish, and American Indian. Journal of Educational Research 45 (September 1951):349-60.

Zinkhan, G. M. and others. Changes in Stereotypes: Blacks and Whites in Magazine Advertisements [1983 and 1984]. Journalism Quarterly 63 (Autumn 1986).

[See also sections 3, 4, 10, 15, 36, 37, 40, 59, 70, and 80]

78. Surveillance

To Intelligence Officers -
1. A man by name of Dubois [i.e., W.E.B. Du Bois], with
visitor's pass, reported on his way to visit this Division. His
presence of station of any unit will be immediately reported in
secret enclosure to Asst. Chief of Staff, G-2, these
headquarters. Likewise prompt report will be made to G-2 of all
his moves and actions while at station of any unit. ...

F.P. Schoonmaker, Major, General Staff, January 1, 1919.

-Herbert Aptheker (ed.), The Correspondence of W.E.B. Du
Bois, Vol. I, p. 232. Du Bois was studying the treatment of
black troops in France.

Amnesty International. Proposal for a Commission of Inquiry into the
Effect of Domestic Intelligence Activities on Criminal Trials in the
United States of America. London: Amnesty International, 1981.

Bastone, William and others. The Hustler. How Al Sharpton Conned the
Movement, the Media, and the Government [NYC]. Village Voice
February 2, 1988.

Bergman, Lowell and David Weir. Revolution on Ice: How the Black
Panthers Lost the FBI's War of Dirty Tricks. Rolling Stone
(September 9, 1976):41-49

Blackstock, Nelson. Cointelpro: The FBI's Secret War on Political
Freedom. New York: Vintage, 1975.

Blum, Richard H. (ed.) Surveillance and Espionage in a Free Society.
New York: Praeger, 1972.

Boas, Franz. Scientists as Spies. Nation 109 (1919):797.

Branch, Taylor. Parting the Waters: America in the King Years, 1954-
1963. New York: Simon and Schuster, 1988.

Brown, Julia. I Testify: My Years as an FBI Undercover Agent. Belmont,
MA: Western Islands, 1966.

Burns, Haywood. The Federal Government and Civil Rights. In: Leon
Friedman (ed.), Southern Justice, pp. 228-54. New York: Random
House, 1965.

Cagin, Seth and Philip Dray. We Are Not Afraid: The Story of Goodman,
Schwerner, and Chaney and the Civil Rights Campaign in Mississippi.
New York: Macmillan, 1988.

Chen, Serena. A Look Back at the Chinese Confession Program [1950s].
East West 21 (April 1987).

Churchill, Ward. Due Process Be Damned [The U.S. government versus the Portland Four, Native American leaders]. Zeta Magazine 1 (January 1988):77-83.

Churchill, Ward and James Vander Wall. Agents of Repression. The FBI's Secret War against the Black Panther Party and AIM. Boston: South End Press, 1988.

Churchill, Ward and James Vander Wall. Cointelpro Papers. Documents from the FBI's Secret Wars Against Dissent in the United States. Boston: South End Press, 1989.

Churchill, Ward and James Vander Wall. We Will Remember. FBI Operations on Pine Ridge, 1972-1976. Boston: South End Press, 1987.

Citizens Research and Investigation Committee and Louis E. Tackwood [Former agent of the Los Angeles Police Department]. The Glass House Tapes. New York: Avon Books, 1973.

Cook, Fred J. The FBI Nobody Knows. New York: Macmillan, 1964.

Cowan, Paul and others. State Secrets: Police Surveillance in America. New York: Holt, Rinehart and Winston, 1974.

Crewdson, John. Seeing RED: An FBI 'Commie Hunter' Rebels at Illegal Tactics. Chicago Tribune Magazine March 2, 1985.

Curry, Richard O. Freedom at Risk: Secrecy, Censorship, and Repression in the 1980s. Philadelphia, PA: Temple University Press, 1988.

Davidson, Osha. The [Federal] Bureau [of Investigation] Goes to San Juan. Nation November 7, 1988.

Day, Barbara. Victims of 'Black Desk' Surveillance Sue N.Y. Police. Guardian (NYC) August 3, 1988.

Dewing, Rolland (ed.) The FBI Files on the American Indian Movement and Wounded Knee [26 microfilm reels]. Frederick, MD: University Publications of America, 1987.

Donner, Frank J. The Age of Surveillance. New York, 1981.

Elliff, John T. Aspects of Federal Civil Rights Enforcement: The Justice Department and the FBI, 1939-1964. Perspectives in American History 5 (1971):605-73.

F.B.I. Accused of Intimidation By Bureau Agents' Attorneys. New York Times August 27, 1988. [Lawsuit by 311 Hispanic FBI agents].

FBI Dropped Plan to Block Du Bois Memorial. Springfield Morning Union (Mass.) December 3, 1976.

FBI Files on the Reverend Jesse Jackson. [1 roll of microfilm]. Wilmington, DE: Scholarly Resources, 1988. [1967-1984].

Farber, M. A. Rights Figure Reported To Be a U.S. Informant. New York Times January 21, 1988.

Farmer, James. Lay Bare the Heart. An Autobiography of the Civil Rights Movement. New York: Arbor House, 1985.

Garrow, David J. Bearing the Cross: Martin Luther King, Jr., and the Southern Christian Leadership Conference. New York: Morrow, 1986.

Garrow, David J. The FBI and Martin Luther King, Jr. New York: Norton, 1981.

Garrow, David J. (ed.) The Martin Luther King, Jr. FBI File [16 microfilm reels]. Frederick, MD: University Publications of America, 1987.

Garrow, David J. (ed.) The Martin Luther King, Jr. FBI File, Part II: The King-Levison File [9 microfilm reels]. Frederick, MD: University Publications of America, 1987.

Gelbspan, Ross. FBI Altered Lie Test Result, Papers Show. Boston Globe December 29, 1988.

Gelbspan, Ross. FBI Misled Congress on Its Latin Inquiry. Boston Globe January 2, 1989.

Gilfoyle, Timothy J. The Moral Origins of Political Surveillance: The Preventive Society in New York City, 1867-1918. American Quarterly 38 (Fall 1986):637-52.

Glick, Brian. War At Home. Covert Action Against U.S. Activists and What We Can Do About It. Boston: South End Press, 1989.

Goodman, Ernest. The NLG, the FBI, and the Civil Rights Movement: 1964 - A Year of Decision. Guild Practitioner 38 (Winter 1981):1-17.

Gutierrez, Jose Angel. Chicanos and Mexicans Under Surveillance: 1940-1980. Renato Rosaldo Lecture Series Monograph 2 (Spring 1986):29-58.

Halperin, Morton. The FBI and the Civil Rights Movement. First Principles 4 (September 1978).

Halperin, Morton and others. The Lawless State: The Crimes of the U.S. Intelligence Agencies. New York: Penguin, 1976.

Hill, Robert A. 'The Foremost Radical Among His Race' Marcus Garvey and the Black Scare, 1918-1921. Prologue 16 (Winter 1984):214-31.

Hinds, Lennox S. Illusions of Justice: Human Rights Violations in the United States. University of Iowa Press, 1978.

Horne, Gerald. Communist Front? The Civil Rights Congress, 1946-1956. Rutherford, NJ: Fairleigh Dickinson University Press, 1988.

Hughes, C. Alvin. We Demand Our Rights: The Southern Negro Youth Congress, 1937-1949. <u>Phylon</u> 48 (March 1987):38-50.

Jayco, Margaret. How Socialists Scored Victory Against FBI. <u>Militant</u> April 1, 1988. [Socialist Workers Party and Young Socialist Alliance].

Jayko, Margaret (ed.) <u>FBI</u> <u>on</u> <u>Trial:</u> <u>The</u> <u>Victory</u> <u>in</u> <u>the</u> <u>Socialist</u> <u>Workers</u> <u>Party</u> <u>Suit</u> <u>Against</u> <u>Government</u> <u>Spying</u>. New York: Pathfinders Press, 1988.

Judge Holds F.B.I. Misused U.S. Jury. <u>New</u> <u>York</u> <u>Times</u> December 4, 1988.

Keller, William W. <u>The</u> <u>Liberals</u> <u>and</u> <u>J.</u> <u>Edgar</u> <u>Hoover:</u> <u>Rise</u> <u>and</u> <u>Fall</u> <u>of</u> <u>a</u> <u>Domestic</u> <u>Intelligence</u> <u>State</u>. Doctoral dissertation, Cornell University, 1987. UMO # 8709001.

Keller, William W. <u>The</u> <u>Liberals</u> <u>and</u> <u>J.</u> <u>Edgar</u> <u>Hoover.</u> <u>Rise</u> <u>and</u> <u>Fall</u> <u>of</u> <u>a</u> <u>Domestic</u> <u>Intelligence</u> <u>State</u>. Princeton, NJ: Princeton University Press, 1989.

King, Wayne. F.B.I.s Papers Portray Inquiry Fed by Informer. <u>New</u> <u>York</u> <u>Times</u> February 13, 1988.

Koppes, Clayton R. and Gregory D. Black. Blacks, Loyalty, and Motion-Picture Propaganda in World War II. <u>Journal</u> <u>of</u> <u>American</u> <u>History</u> 73 (September 1986):383-406.

Kornweibel, Theodore, Jr. Black on Black: The FBI's First Negro Informants and Agents and the Investigation of Black Radicalism during the Red Scare. <u>Criminal</u> <u>Justice</u> <u>History</u> 8 (1987).

Kornweibel, Theodore, Jr. (ed.) <u>Federal</u> <u>Surveillance</u> <u>of</u> <u>Afro-Americans</u> <u>(1917-1925):</u> <u>The</u> <u>First</u> <u>World</u> <u>War,</u> <u>the</u> <u>Red</u> <u>Scare,</u> <u>and</u> <u>the</u> <u>Garvey</u> <u>Movement</u> [25 microfilm reels]. Frederick, MD: University Publications of America, 1987.

Lawrence, Ken. Mississippi Spies [Mississippi State Sovereignty Commission and its anti-black activities]. <u>Southern</u> <u>Exposure</u> 9 (Fall 1981):82-86.

Levine, Jack. Racism in the FBI. <u>Liberator</u> 2 (November-December 1962).

Marx, Gary T. <u>Undercover.</u> <u>Police</u> <u>Surveillance</u> <u>in</u> <u>America</u>. Berkeley, CA: University of California Press, 1989.

Matthiessen, Peter. <u>In</u> <u>the</u> <u>Spirit</u> <u>of</u> <u>Crazy</u> <u>Horse</u>. New York: Viking, 1983. [The FBI at the Pine Ridge Reservation, Wounded Knee, SD].

McCombs, Phil. After Agent's Racism Charges, Introspection in the FBI. <u>Boston</u> <u>Globe</u> April 3, 1988. [Reprinted from <u>Washington</u> <u>Post</u>].

McKnight, Gerald D. A Harvest of Hate: The FBI's War Against Black Youth - Domestic Intelligence in Memphis, Tennessee. <u>South</u> <u>Atlantic</u> <u>Quarterly</u> 86 (Winter 1987):1-19.

McKnight, Gerald D. The 1968 Memphis Sanitation Strike and the FBI: A Case Study in Urban Surveillance. South Atlantic Quarterly 83 (Spring 1984):138-56.

Morgan, Richard E. Domestic Intelligence: Monitoring Dissent in America. Austin: University of Texas, 1980.

Navasky, Victor. Kennedy Justice. New York: Atheneum, 1971.

Neier, Aryeh. Surveillance by the F.B.I. Index on Censorship 10 (April 1981):42-47.

Nelson, Jack and Jack Bass. The F.B.I. and Orangeburg [S.C.]. New South 25 (Fall 1970):2-17. [Police shooting of black students at South Carolina State College, February 1968].

New York State Senate. Revolutionary Radicalism. Report of the Joint Legislative Committee Investigating Seditious Activities. Propoganda Among Negroes, pp. 1476-1520, Part 1, Vol. II, Filed April 24, 1920.

The Official and Confidential Files of FBI Director J. Edgar Hoover [5 reels of microfilm]. Wilmington, DE: Scholarly Resources, 1988.

O'Reilly, Kenneth. The FBI and the Civil Rights Movement During the Kennedy Years: From the Freedom Rides to Albany. Journal of Southern History 54 (May 1988):201-32.

O'Reilly, Kenneth. The FBI and the Politics of the 1960s' Riots. Journal of American History 75 (June 1988):91-114.

O'Reilly, Kenneth. "Racial Matters." The FBI's Secret File on Black America, 1960-1972. New York: Free Press, 1989.

O'Reilly, Kenneth. The Roosevelt Administration and Black America: Federal Surveillance Policy and Civil Rights During the New Deal and World War II Years. Phylon 48 (March 1987):12-25.

Pawa, J. M. Black Radicals and White Spies: Harlem, 1919. Negro History Bulletin (October 1972):129-33.

Powers, Richard S. Secrecy and Power: The Life of J. Edgar Hoover. New York: Free Press, 1987.

Records of the Subversive Activities Control Board, 1950-1972. Part II: Communist-action and Communist-front Organizations [72 microfilm reels]. Frederick, MD: University Publications of America, 1988.

Richards, David. Played Out: The Jean Seberg Story. New York: Random House, 1981.

Sanford, Delacy W., Jr. Congressional Investigation of Black Communism, 1919-1967. Doctoral dissertation, State University of New York at Stony Brook, 1973.

Schlesinger, Arthur M., Jr. Robert Kennedy and His Times. Boston: Houghton Mifflin, 1978.

Schultz, Bud and Ruth Schultz. It Did Happen Here. Recollections of Political Repression in America. Berkeley, CA: University of California Press, 1989.

Sheldon, Rose M. Tinker, Tailor, Caesar, Spy: Espionage in Ancient Rome. Doctoral dissertation, University of Michigan, 1987. UMO # 8720338.

Shenon, Philip. Black F.B.I. Agent's Ordeal: Meanness that Never Let Up [Racial harassment within the FBI]. New York Times January 25, 1988.

Shenon, Philip. F.B.I. Agent Admits Harassing Black. New York Times July 5, 1988.

Smith, Baxter. FBI Plot Against the Black Movement. New York: Pathfinder Press, April 1974.

Smith, Philip T. Policing Victorian London: Political Policing, Public Order, and the London Metropolitan Police. Westport, CT: Greenwood, 1985.

Snyder, Robert E. Spying on Southerners: The FBI and Erskine Caldwell. Georgia Historical Quarterly 72 (Summer 1988):248-81.

Taylor, Flint and Margaret Vanhouten. Counterintelligence: A Documentary Look at America's Secret Police. Chicago: National Lawyer's Guild Task Force on Counterintelligence and the Secret Police, 1978.

Theoharis, Athan. Spying on Americans. Political Surveillance from Hoover to the Huston Plan. Philadelphia, PA: Temple University Press, 1978.

Theoharis, Athan and John Stuart Cox. The Boss: J. Edgar Hoover and the Great American Inquisition. Philadelphia, PA: Temple University Press, 1987.

Tilsen, Ken. The FBI, Wounded Knee and Politics. Iowa Journal of Social Work (Fall 1976).

Ungar, Sanford J. FBI. Boston: Little Brown, 1975.

Ungar, Sanford J. The F.B.I. on the Defensive Again. New York Times Magazine May 15, 1988. ["Overzealousness and racism"].

U.S. Congress, 66th, 1st session, Senate. Investigative Activities of the Department of Justice, Radicalism and Sedition Among the Negroes as Reflected in Their Publications. Senate Documents 12 (1919).

U.S. Congress, session, Senate, Select Committee to Study Government Operations. The FBI's Covert Program to Destroy the Black Panther Party. Washington, D.C.: GPO, 1976.

U.S. Congress, session, Senate, Select Committee to Study Government Operations. _The FBI's Covert Program to Destroy the Black Panther Party_. Washington, D.C.: GPO, 1976.

U.S. Congress, 94th, 1st session, House of Representatives, Select Committee on Intelligence. _Hearings on Domestic Intelligence Programs_. Washington, D.C.: GPO, 1975.

U.S. Dept. of Justice. Youth Marches for Integrated Schools. Federal Bureau of Investigation, Numerical file number 62-105187.

United States, Federal Bureau of Investigation. _COINTELPRO: The Counterintelligence Program of the FBI_ [30 microfilm reels]. Wilmington, DE: Scholarly Resources, 1978.

United States, Federal Bureau of Investigation. _Communist Infiltration of the SCLC: FBI Investigation File_ [9 microfilm reels]. Wilmington, DE: Scholarly Resources, 1983.

United States, Federal Bureau of Investigation. _Martin Luther King, Jr. FBI Assassination File_ [25 microfilm reels]. Wilmington, DE: Scholarly Resources, 1978.

U.S. Military Intelligence Reports: Surveillance of Radicals in the United States, 1917-1941 [34 microfilm reels]. Frederick, MD: University Publications of America, 1987.

Using the Freedom of Information Act, 1987 edition. Fund for Open Information and Accountability, 145 W. 4th St., New York, NY 10012.

Washburn, Patrick S. J. Edgar Hoover and the Black Press in World War II. _Journalism History_ 13 (Spring 1986):26-33.

Washburn, Patrick S. _A Question of Sedition: The Federal Government's Investigation of the Black Press During World War II_. New York: Oxford, 1986.

Wechsler, James. The FBI's Failure in the South. _Progressive_ 27 (December 1963):20-23.

Wesley, David. _Hate Groups and the Un-American Activities Committee_. New York: Emergency Civil Liberties Committee, 1961.

Wheaton, Elizabeth. _Codename GREENKILL: The 1979 Greensboro Killings_. Athens, GA: University of Georgia Press, 1987.

Whited, Charles. _Chiodo: Undercover Cop_. Chicago: Playboy Press, 1973.

Wilkins, Roy and Ramsey Clark. _Search and Destroy. A Report on the Commission of Inquiry into the Black Panthers and the Police_. New York: Metropolitan Applied Research Center, 1973.

Wise, David. _The American Police State_. New York: Random House, 1976.

[See also sections 12, 17, 18, 20, 32, 34, 50, 55, and 82]

79. Tests and Measurements

*There is no more reason for teaching Negro children a certain
kind of arithmetic, or reading, or history, on the basis of
their lower scores taken in the gross than there would be to
have a special curriculum for the white rural children of the
South as compared to the urban white children of the section of
the North.*

- Horace Mann Bond, The Education of the Negro in the
American Social Order, p. 329.

Afram Associates, Inc. Black Experience Test. New York: Afram
  Associates, Inc., 1970.

Alne, Denise J. Evidence of Bias in the WAIS: A Comparison of Blacks and
  Whites. Doctoral dissertation, City University of New York, 1984.
  UMO # 8423050.

Beckwith, James P., Jr. Constitutional Requirements for Standardized
  Ability Tests Used in Education. Vanderbilt Law Review 26 (May
  1973):789-821.

Behnke and others. Testing Results for Minority Isolated Schools. San
  Diego, CA: San Diego City Schools Planning, Research and Evaluation
  Division, 1985.

Behrendt, A. and others. Selectivity Bias and the Determinants of SAT
  Scores. Economics of Education Review 5 (1986).

Bickelhaupt, Susan. Home a Key to Test Scores [Mass.]. Boston Globe
  October 24, 1986.

Blasik, Katherine A. and Robert J. Simpson. Standardized Testing: Policy
  Implications for Employment in Education. Journal of Law and
  Education 17 (Spring 1988):243-80.

Browne, Duana B. WISC-R Scoring Patterns among Native Americans of the
  Northern Plains. White Cloud Journal of American Indian Mental
  Health 2 (1984):3-16.

Burrus, Porter B., II. Effects of Examiner Race on Black Highschoolers'
  WISC-R IQ and Test Anxiety Scores. Doctoral dissertation, University
  of San Francisco, 1986. UMO # 8616574.

Conway, James M. Title VII and Competitive Testing. Hofstra Law Review
  15 (Winter 1987):299-322.

Crouse, James and Dale Trusheim. The Case Against the S.A.T.. Chicago,
  IL: University of Chicago Press, 1988.

Cummins, Jim. Psychological Assessment of Minority Students: Out of
  Context, Out of Focus, Out of Control? Journal of Reading, Writing,

and Learning Disabilities International 2 (1986):9-19.

Dahlstrom, W. Grant. MMPI Patterns of American Minorities. Minneapolis, MN: University of Minnesota Press, 1986.

Daniels, Lee A. Groups Charge Bias in Merit Scholarship Testing. New York Times June 29, 1988.

Dometrius, N. C. and L. Sigelman. The Cost of Quality: Teacher Testing and Racial-Ethnic Representativeness in Public Education. Social Science Quarterly 69 (March 1988).

Elmer, Muriel I. Intercultural Effectiveness: Development of an Intercultural Competency Scale. Doctoral dissertation, Michigan State University, 1986. UMO # 8625019.

First, Joan M. and José Cárdenas. A Minority View on Testing. Educational Measurement: Issues and Practice 5 (Spring 1986):6-11.

Fiske, Edward B. America's Test Mania. New York Times Education Life April 10, 1988.

Hackett, Rachelle K. and others. Test Construction Manipulating Score Differences Between Black and White Examinees: Properties of the Resulting Tests. Princeton, NJ: Educational Testing Service, 1987.

Hickman, Julia A. and Cecil R. Reynolds. Are Race Differences in Mental Test Scores an Artifact of Psychometric Methods? A Test of Harrington's Experimental Model. Journal of Special Education 20 (Winter 1986-87):409-30.

Hoover, Mary. The Politics of Education: Illiteracy and Test Bias. National Black Law Journal 10 (Winter 1987):64-72.

Hoover, Mary R. and others. Bias in Reading Tests for Black Language Speakers: A Sociolinguistic Perspective. Negro Educational Review (April-July 1987):81-98.

Long, Howard H. Test Results of Third-Grade Negro Children Selected on the Basis of Socio-Economic Status. Journal of Negro Education 4 (April 1935):192-212.

Lopez, Richard E. and Julian Samora. George Sánchez and Testing. In: Americo Paredes (ed.), Humanidad. Essays in Honor of Goerge I. Sanchez, pp. 107-115. Los Angeles, CA: Chicano Studies Center, University of California, 1977.

Mackler, Bernard and Dana Holman. Assessing, Packaging, and Delivery: Tests, Testing, and Race. Young Children 31 (July 1976):351-64.

Maheody, Larry and others. Minority Overrepresentation in Special Education: A Functional Assessment Perspective. Special Services in the Schools 1 (1984):5-19.

Medina, Noe and D. Monty Neill. Fallout from the Testing Explosion: How

100 Million Standardized Exams Undermine Equity and Excellence in
America's Public Schools. Cambridge, MA: Fair Test, 1988.

Miller, Kent S. and Ralph M. Dreger (eds.) Comparative Studies of Blacks
and Whites in the United States. New York: Seminar Press, 1973.

Mills, Roger and Miriam M. Bryan. Testing... Grouping: The New
Segregation in Southern Schools. Atlanta: Southern Regional
Council, 1976.

Neill, D. Monty and Noe J. Medina. Standardized Testing: Harmful to
Educational Health. Phi Delata Kappan 70 (May 1989):688-97.

Olson, Lynn. Tests Found Barring Thousands of Minority Teacher
Candidates. Education Week November 23, 1988.

Owen, David. The S.A.T. and Social Stratification. Journal of Education
(Boston) 168 (1986):81-92.

Pitt, David E. After New York Test, Most New Sergeants in Police are
White. New York Times January 13, 1989.

Powell, B. and L. C. Steelman. Equity and the LSAT. Harvard Educational
Review 53 (1983):32-45.

Prasse, David P. and Daniel J. Reschly. Larry P.: A Case of Segregation,
Testing, or Program Efficacy? Exceptional Children 52 (January
1986):333-46. [Racial Bias in IQ Tests].

Reschly, Daniel J. and others. Multifactored Nonbiased Assessment:
Converged and Discriminant Validity of Social and Cognitive Measures
with Black and White Regular and Special Education Students.
November 1984. ERIC ED 252 034.

Reynolds, Cecil R. and Robert T. Brown (eds.) Perspectives on Bias in
Mental Testing. New York: Plenum, 1984.

Roberts, Eileen and Richard De Blassie. Test Bias and the Culturally
Different Early Adolescent. Adolescence 18 (Winter 1983):837-44.

Sale, Robert P. Reclassification of Black Students Initially Classified
as Mildly Mentally Handicapped. Doctoral dissertation, University of
Georgia, 1986. UMO # 8621683.

Sedlacek, William E. Test Bias and the Elimination of Racism. Journal of
College Student Personnel 18 (January 1977):16-19.

Sokal, Michael M. (ed.) Psychological Testing and American Society,
1840-1930. New Brunswick, NJ: Rutgers University Press, 1987.

Taylor, Orlando L. and Dorian L. Lee. Standardized Tests and African-
American Children: Communication and Language Issues. Negro
Educational Review (April-July 1987):67=80.

Thomas, R. Murray. Fiddling the Data: Vested-Interest Influence on

Educational Evaluation. 1981. ERIC ED 254 551.

Valencia, Richard R. and Richard J. Ranskin. Evidence of Content Bias on the McCarthy Scales with Mexican American Children: Implications for Test Translation and Nonbiased Assessment. Journal of Educational Psychology 77 (1985):197-207.

Watson, Bernard C. The Social Consequences of Testing: Another View. New Directions for Testing and Measurement 9 (1981):39-51.

Williams, Robert L. and others. Psychological Tests and Minorities. Washington, D.C.: GPO, 1977.

Williams, Robert L. and others. The War Against Testing: A Current Status Report. Journal of Negro Education 49 (Summer 1980):263-73.

Williams, T. S. Some Issues in the Standardized Testing of Minority Students. Journal of Education 165 (1983):192-208.

Winters, Clyde A. Psychology Tests and Black Police Recruits. Labor Law Journal 39 (September 1988):634-36.

Wood, Frank H. and others. The Lora Case: Nonbiased Referral, Assessment, and Placement Procedures. Exceptional Children 52 (January 1986):323-31.

Wyatt, Gail E. Alternatives to the Use of Standardized Tests with Afro-American Children. In: Barbara Ann Bass and others (eds.), The Afro-American Family, pp. 119-35. New York: Grune and Stratton, 1982.

Zirkel, Perry A. Spanish-speaking Students and Standardized Tests. Urban Review (1972):32-40.

Tests and Measurements Bibliography

Cameron, Colin (comp.) Discrimination in Testing Bibliography. Revised edition. 1973. ERIC ED 086 736.

80. Undoing Personal Racism

Race prejudice can't be talked down; it must be lived down.

-Francis James Grimké, Stray Thoughts and Meditations, (1914-1934).

Adams, Paul L. Dealing with Racism in Biracial Psychiatry. Journal of the American Academy of Child Psychiatry 9 (1970):33-43.

Balch, Philip and Karen Paulsen. Strategies for the Modification and Prevention of Racial Prejudice in Children: A Review. 1978. ERIC ED 178 805.

Beasley, Lou. A Beginning to Eradicate Racist Attitudes. Social Casework 53 (January 1972):9-13.

Bellucci, Jo-Ann E. and Nisim M. Elbaz. Gentle Doses of Antiprejudice. Elementary School Guidance and Counseling 16 (February 1982):202-209.

Billings, Charles. Racism and Prejudice. Hayden, 1977.

Boas, Franz. Changing the Racial Attitudes of White Americans. In: George Stocking (ed.), A Franz Boas Reader. Chicago: University of Chicago Press, 1974.

Bowser, Benjamin P. and Raymond G. Hunt. Afterthoughts and Reflections, In: Benjamin P. Bowser and Raymond G. Hunt (eds.), Impacts of Racism on White Americans, pp. 245-259. Beverly Hills, CA: Sage, 1981.

Challenging Racism. London: ALTARF, 1984. [Room 216, 38 Mount Pleasant, London Wcl, England].

Coffin, Gregory C. Combating Racism in the Junior High School. Middle School/Junior High Principal's Service February, 1971.

Comer, James P. Are Our Children Less Prejudiced Today? Parade December 2, 1984.

Della-Sora, Delmo. The Schools Can Overcome Racism. Educational Leadership 29 (February 1972):443-449.

Dhondy, Farrukh. Overtly Political Focus. Times Educational Supplement November 2, 1973. [The missing political element in race relations instruction].

Dodgson, P. and D. Stewart. Multiculturism or Anti-racist Teaching: A Question of Alternatives. Multiracial Education 9 (1981):40-51.

Dummett, Ann. RAT, ART or WHAT? New Society (October 10, 1986). [On Racism Awareness Training].

Edler, James M. White on White: An Anti-Racism Manual for White Educators in the Process of Becoming. Doctoral dissertation, University of Massachusetts, 1974. UMO # 74-15008.

Education and Racism: An Action Manual. Washington, D.C.: National Education Associates, 1973.

Fuentes, Luis. The Fight Against Racism in Our Schools. New York: Pathfinder Press, 1974.

Gaertner, Samuel L. and John F. Dovidio. Racism Among the Well-Intentioned. In: Edwin G. Clausen and Jack Bermingham (eds.), Pluralism, Racism, and Public Policy. The Search for Equality. Boston: Hall, 1981.

Goldstein, Carol G. and others. Racial Attitudes in Young Children as a Function of Interracial Contact in the Public Schools. American Journal of Orthopsychiatry 49 (January 1979):89-99.

Green, Andy. In Defense of Anti-Racist Teaching. Multiracial Education (Spring 1982).

Gross, Peter W. [White Racism]. Making Up for It. Civil Rights Digest Summer 1969.

Gurnah, Ahmed. The Politics of Racism Awareness Training. Critical Social Policy (London) 11 (1984):6-20.

Guyton, Jane M. A Developmental Counseling Approach to Alter Self-Concept and Racial Prejudice in Elementary Children [5th-6th graders]. Doctoral dissertation, University of Arkasas, 1987. UMO # 8718814.

Hall, Stuart. Teaching Race. Early Child Development and Care. 10 (1983):259-73.

Harper, Frederick D. The Student Personnel Worker's Commitment to Eliminating Racism. February 1970. ERIC ED 043 910.

Height, Dorothy I. The YWCA's One Imperative: Eliminate Racism, 1971. National Board, YWCA, 600 Lexington Ave., New York, NY 10022.

Holland, K. and G. Parbin. Reversing Racism: Lesson from America. London: Social Affairs Unit, 1984.

Hooks, Bell. Overcoming White Supremacy. Zeta Magazine 1 (January 1988):24-27.

Hunter, John M. Teaching to Eliminate Black-White Racism: An Educational Systems Approach. Journal of Geography 71 (February 1972):87-95.

Institute of Race Relations. Antiracist Not Multicultural Education. Race and Class 22 (Summer 1980):81-83.

Johns, Rupert G. Racism and Its Elimination. New York: U.N. Institute for Training and Research, 1981.

Johnson, A. Lee. The Self-Esteem Conspiracy: Liberating Your Personal
     Power. Strategic Learning Systems, 1987.

Karp, Joan B. The Emotional Impact and a Model For Changing Racist
     Attitudes. In: Benjamin P. Bowser and Raymond G. Hunt (eds.),
     Impacts of Racism on White Americans, pp. 87-96. Beverly Hills, CA:
     Sage, 1981.

Katz, Judy H. A Systematic Handbook of Exercises for the Re-education
     of White People with Respect to Racist Attitudes and Behaviors.
     Doctoral dissertation, University of Massachusetts, 1976. UMO # 76-
     14695.

Katz, Judy H. White Awareness: A Handbook for Anti-Racism Training.
     Norman, OK: University of Oklahoma Press, 1978.

Katz, Judy H. and Allen Ivey. White Awareness: The Frontier of Racism
     Awareness Training. Personnel and Guidance Journal 55 (April
     1977):485-489.

Katz, Judy H. and Cresencio Torres. Combatting Racism in Education.
     Early Child Development and Care 10 (1983):333-344.

Katz, Maude White. End Racism in Education: A Concerned Parent Speaks.
     Freedomways Fall 1968.

Katz, Phyllis A. Developmental Foundations of Gender and Racial
     Attitudes. In: Robert L. Leahy (ed.), The Child's Construction of
     Social Inequality, pp. 41-78. New York: Academic Press, 1983.

Katz, Phyllis A. Racism and Social Science: Towards a New Commitment.
     In: Phyllis S. Katz (ed.), Towards the Elimination of Racism, pp. 3-
     18. New York: Pergamon, 1976.

Katz, Phyllis A. and Sue R. Zalk. Modification of Children's Racial
     Attitudes. Developmental Psychology 14 (September 1978):447-61.

Kehoe, John and Frank Echols. Educational Approaches for Combatting
     Prejudice and Racism. In: S. Shapson and V. D'Oyley (eds.),
     Bilingual and Multicultural Education: Canadian Perspectives, pp.
     130-139. Clevedon, Avon: Multilingual Matters, 1984.

Kranz, Peter L. Confronting Bigotry Brings It Home. Civil Rights Digest
     5 (Summer 1973):37-38.

Levin, Shalom. Combating Racism in the Classroom - the World's Teachers
     Cooperate. Patterns of Prejudice 18 (April 1984):35-38.

Lindsay, Ouida. Breaking the Bonds of Racism. 1974. ETC Publications,
     Dept. L, 18512 Pierce Terrace, Homewood, IL 60430.

Love, Barbara J. Combating Racism through Teacher Training. Doctoral
     dissertation, University of Massachusetts, 1972. UMO # 73-05246.

Lyman, Phillip C. Race Relations Seminars. Handbook for Moderators, Coordinators, and Commanders. Fort Benning, GA: Race Relations Coordinating Group, August 1971.

MacDonnell, Joan Benson. Cross Cultural Impact, 1972. Division of Youth Activities, United States Catholic Conference, 1312 Massachusetts Ave., N.W. Washington, D.C. 20005. [Holding workshops on racism].

Mayer, Steven E. and Charles Buckman-Ellis. Evaluation of the Tillman Seminar on White Racism, September 1980. ERIC ED 199 131.

McCrory, John B. White Racism, Freedom from It. Civil Rights Digest Summer 1969.

McLean, Deckle. Education Bears the Burden of Eliminating Racism. Boston Globe October 19, 1971.

Moore, Robert B. A Rationale, Description and Analysis of Racism Awareness and Action Training Program for White Teachers. Doctoral dissertation, University of Massachusetts, 1974. UMO # 74-15032.

Mukherjee, Tuku. Collusion, Conflict or Constructive Antiracist Socialization. Multicultural Teaching 1 (1983):24-25. [Great Britain].

Mullard, Chris. The Educational Management and Demanagement of Racism. Education Policy Bulletin 10 (1982):21-40.

National Union of Teachers. Combating Racism in Schools. London: NUT, 1983.

Oden, Chester W., Jr. and W. Scott MacDonald. Human Relations Training in School Settings. In School Crime and Disruption: Prevention Models, pp. 103-114. Washington, D.C.: GPO, June 1978.

Palmer, Frank (ed.) Anti-racism: An Assault on Education and Value. London: Sherwood Press, 1986.

Prunty, Howard E., Terry L. Singer and Lindsay A. Thomas. Confronting Racism in Inner City Schools [Pittsburgh]. Social Work 22 (May 1977):190-194.

Pumphrey, Peter D. Some Reflections on Racism Awareness Training. New Community 12 (Winter 1985):485-489.

Race in the Classroom, Teaching Against Racism in the Primary School. All London Teachers Against Racism and Fascism (ALTARF), c/o Lambeth Teacher's Centre, Santley Street, London SW 4, England. (1981).

Rooney-Rebeck, Patricia and Leonard Jason. Prevention of Prejudice in Elementary School Students. Journal of Primary Prevention 7 (Winter 1986):63-73. [1st and 3rd grades].

Ruddell, David. Racism Awareness: An Approach for Schools. Remedial

<u>Education</u> 18 (1983):125-129.

Sedlacek, William E. and Glenwood C. Brooks, Jr. <u>A</u> <u>Procedure</u> <u>for</u>
    <u>Eliminating</u> <u>Racism</u> <u>in</u> <u>Our</u> <u>Schools</u>. August, 1973. ERIC ED 085 649.

Sedlacek, William E. and Glenwood C. Brooks, Jr. Eliminating Racism in
    Educational Settings. <u>In</u>: Oscar A. Barbarin and others (eds.),
    <u>Institutional</u> <u>Racism</u> <u>and</u> <u>Community</u> <u>Competence</u>, pp. 223-229.
    Washington, D.C.: GPO, 1982.

Sedlacek, William E. and Glenwood C. Brooks, Jr. <u>Racism</u> <u>in</u> <u>American</u>
    <u>Education:</u> <u>A</u> <u>Model</u> <u>for</u> <u>Change</u>. Chicago: Nelson-Hall, 1976.

Sege, Irene. He Found Fears Fading as Friendships Were Formed [White
    student graduating from Boston public high school]. <u>Boston</u> <u>Globe</u>
    April 27, 1986.

Shaw, John W. and others (eds.) <u>Strategies</u> <u>for</u> <u>Improving</u> <u>Race</u> <u>Relations.</u>
    <u>The</u> <u>Anglo-American</u> <u>Experience</u>. Manchester: Manchester University
    Press, 1986.

Sherwood, Tom and Mary Batticata. Race Relations in Virginia: No
    Desegregation of the Heart Yet. <u>Washington</u> <u>Post</u> February 1, 1985.

Sivanandan, Ambelavenar. RAT [Racism Awareness Training] and the
    Degradation of Black Struggle. <u>Race</u> <u>and</u> <u>Class</u> 26 (Spring 1985).

Staub, Ervin. Promoting Positive Behavior in Schools, in other
    Educational Settings, and in the Home. <u>In</u>: P. Rushton and R.
    Sorrentino (eds.), <u>Altruism</u> <u>and</u> <u>Helping</u> <u>Behavior</u> <u>II</u>. Erlbaum
    Associates, 1981.

Stevens, William K. White Philadelphian, 13, Is a Model to Those Combating
    Racist Incidents. <u>New</u> <u>York</u> <u>Times</u> November 24, 1986.

<u>Taking</u> <u>Racism</u> <u>Personally:</u> <u>White</u> <u>Anti-racism</u> <u>at</u> <u>the</u> <u>Crossroads</u>. London:
    Peace News, 1978.

Taylor, Bill. Anti-racist Education in Noncontact Areas: The Need for a
    Gentle Approach. <u>New</u> <u>Community</u> 13 (Autumn 1986):177-184.

<u>Teaching</u> <u>and</u> <u>Racism</u> (second edition, 1979). All London Teachers Against
    Racism and Fascism (ALTARF), c/o Lambeth Teacher's Centre, Santley
    Street, London SW 4 England.

Tillman, James , Jr. and Mary Norman Tillman. <u>What</u> <u>Is</u> <u>Your</u> <u>Racism</u>
    <u>Quotient?</u> <u>A</u> <u>Laymen's</u> <u>Guide</u> <u>for</u> <u>Detecting</u> <u>and</u> <u>Treating</u> <u>Racism</u>.
    Syracuse, NY: Tillman Associates, 1968.

Troyna, Barry and Wendy Ball. Styles of LEA Policy Intervention in
    Multicultural/Antiracist Education. <u>Educational</u> <u>Review</u> 37
    (1985):165-173.

United Nations. A Program Against Racism. <u>Integrateducation</u> 12
    (November-December 1974):32-35.

United Nations, Division of Human Rights. Seminar on the Dangers of Recrudescence of Intolerance in All its Forms and the Search for Ways of Preventing and Combating it. UN document ST/TAO/HR/44. August 24-6, 1971.

UNESCO. Race, Science and Society. New York: Columbia University Press, 1976.

UNESCO. Statement on Race and Racial Prejudice. International Social Service Bulletin XX No. 1 (1968). [Adopted in Paris, September 1967].

Vachon, Robert. The Fight Against Racism. Could Our Assumptions Be Racist? Rikka 7 (Summer 1980):18-25.

Weinberg, Meyer. Racism: Its Ubiquity and Antiquity. Equal Education in Massachusetts: A Chronicle 4 (May 1983):11-12.

Weiss, Joan C. and Paul H. Ephross. Group Work Approaches to 'Hate Violence' Incidents. Social Work 31 (March-April 1986):132-36.

[White Racism]. Strategies Against It. Civil Rights Digest (Summer 1969).

Wilson, Geraldine L. The Word Nigger Is What's Not Allowed. Interracial Books for Children Bulletin 11, Nos. 3-4 (1980).

Wilson, Maggie. White Student Black World: A Handbook for Action Against Racism. Oxford: Third World First, 1978.

[See also sections 3, 6, 10, and 14]

81. Unemployment

*We have young people in our black communities of thirty years or
so who have never held a job. We are thereby developing a
permanent, jobless subsociety, the implications of which are far
too dangerous to imagine.*

- Andrew Billingsley, New York Times, August 3, 1976.

Anderson, Bernard E. Tragedy of Black Teen-age Joblessness. Los Angeles
Times September 25, 1975.

Bernick, Michael. Urban Illusion: New Approaches to Inner City
Unemployment. New York: Praeger, 1987.

Bowers, Norman. Tracking Youth Joblessness: Persistent or Fleeting?
Monthly Labor Review 105 (February 1982):3-15.

Bowers, Norman. Young and Marginal: An Overview of Youth Unemployment.
Monthly Labor Review (October 1979):4-18.

Cherry, Robert. Black Youth Employment Problems. In: Robert Cherry and
others (eds.), The Imperiled Economy, Vol 2. New York: Union for
Radical Political Economics, 1988.

Cogan, John. The Decline in Black Teenage Employment, 1950-70. American
Economic Review 72 (September 1982):621-39.

Comptroller General of the U.S. Labor Market Problems of Teenagers Result
Largely from Doing Poorly in School. Washington, D.C.: General
Accounting Office, 1982.

Darden, Joe T. Racial Differences in Unemployment: A Spatial
Perspective. Review of Black Political Economy 12 (Spring 1983).

De Freitas, G. A Time-Series Analysis of Hispanic Unemployment. Journal
of Human Resources 21 (Winter 1986).

Di Prete, Thomas A. Unemployment Over the Life Cycle: Racial Differences
and the Effect of Changing Economic Conditions. American Journal of
Sociology 87 (September 1981):286-307.

Downing, Douglas A. Teenage Employment: Personal Characteristics, Job
Duration, and the Racial Unemployment Differential. Doctoral
dissertation, Yale University, 1987. UMO # 8729050.

Dressler, William W. Unemployment and Depressive Symptoms in a Southern
Black Community. Journal of Nervous and Mental Diseases 174
(November 1986):639-45.

Du Boff, R. Unemployment in the United States: A Historical Summary.
Monthly Review 29 (November 1977):10-24.

569

Farley, J. E. Disproportionate Black and Hispanic Unemployment in U.S. Metropolitan Areas: The Roles of Racial Inequality, Segregation and Discrimination in Male Joblessness. American Journal of Economics and Sociology 46 (April 1987).

Flaim, P. O. Unemployment in 1982: The Cost to Workers and Their Families. Monthly Labor Review 107 (February 1984).

Fosu, Augustin K. Black-White Unemployment Patterns in Michigan, 1971-1986. In: Frances S. Thomas (ed.), The State of Black Michigan: 1987, pp. 41-44. East Lansing, MI: Urban Affairs Program, Michigan State University, 1987.

Freeman, Richard B. The Relations of Criminal Activity to Black Youth Employment. Review of Black Political Economy 16 (Summer-Fall 1987).

Freeman, Richard B. and Harry J. Holzer (eds.) The Black Youth Employment Crisis. Chicago: University of Chicago Press, 1986.

Garcia, Philip and Aida Hurtado. Joblessness among Hispanic Youth: 1973-1981. Literature Review and Statement of Problem. January 18, 1982. ERIC ED 245 028.

Gibbs, Jewelle T. Young, Black, in Critical Condition. Los Angeles Times May 29, 1988, part 5, p. 6.

Gilroy, Curtis L. Black and White Unemployment: The Dynamics of the Differential. Monthly Labor Review 97 (1974):38-47.

Glasgow, Douglas G. The Black Underclass: Poverty, Unemployment and Entrapment for Ghetto Youth. London: Jossey-Bass, 1980.

Hernandez, Jose. Puerto Rican Youth Employment. Maplewood, NJ: Waterfront Press, 1983. [1976 data].

Holzer, H. J. Informal Job Search and Black Youth Unemployment. American Economic Review 77 (June 1987).

Interface, Inc. Youth Unemployment in New York City: The Cost of Doing Nothing. June 1983. ERIC ED 251 531.

Magura, M. and E. Shapiro. The Black Dropout Rate and the Black Youth Unemployment Rate: A Granger-Causal Analysis. Review of Black Political Economy 15 (Winter 1987).

Malveaux, Julianne. Theoretical Explanations of the Persistence of Racial Unemployment Differentials. In: William A. Darity, Jr. (ed.), Labor Economics: Modern Views, pp. 91-118. Boston: Kluwer-Nijhoff, 1982.

Mangum, Garth L. and Stephen F. Seninger. Coming of Age in the Ghetto: A Dilemma of Youth Unemployment. Baltimore, MD: Johns Hopkins University Press, 1978.

Mare, Robert D. and Christopher Winship. Changes in the Relative Labor

Force Status of Black and White Youths: A Review of the Literature. Madison: Institute for Research in Poverty, University of Wisconsin, January 1980.

Mare, Robert and Christopher Winship. The Paradox of Lessening Racial Inequality and Joblessness Among Black Youth. American Sociological Review (February 1984):39-55.

Markey, J. P. The Labor Market Problems of Today's High School Dropouts. Monthy Labor Review 111 (June 1988).

Moss, J. A. Unemployment among Black Youth: A Policy Dilemma. Social Work 27 (January 1982):47-52.

Ogbu, John U. Cultural Boundaries and Minority Youth Orientation Toward Work. In: David Stern and Dorothy Eichorn (eds.), Adolescence and Work. Influences of Social Structure, Labor Markets, and Culture. Hillsdale, NJ: Erlbaum, 1989.

Ong, Paul M. Chinatown Unemployment and the Ethnic Labor Market. Amerasia Journal 11 (Spring-Summer 1984):35-54.

Perry, Carrolle. Black Unemployment in Philadelphia. In: The State of Black Philadelphia 1981, pp. 40-46. Philadelphia, PA: Urban League of Philadelphia, 1981.

Rees, Albert. An Essay on Youth Joblessness. Journal of Economic Literature 24 (June 1986):613-28.

Rosenberg, Sam. Reagan Social Policy and Labour Force Restructuring. Cambridge Journal of Economics 7 (1983):179-96.

Rouse, Walter V. Public School/Private Sector Partnerships for Creating Jobs for Disadvantaged Youth. Doctoral dissertation, University of Southern California, 1984.

Sampson, Robert J. Urban Black Violence: The Effect of Male Joblessness and Family Disruption. American Journal of Sociology 93 (September 1987):348-82.

Silberberg, E. Race, Recent Entry, and Labor Market Participation. American Economic Review 75 (December 1985).

Sing, Bill. Layoffs of Minorities Are Disproportionate [National scene]. Los Angeles Times June 2, 1983.

Sparks, Randy J. 'Heavenly Houston' or 'Hellish Houston'? Black Unemployment and Relief Efforts, 1929-1936. Southern Studies 25 (Winter 1986):352-66.

Stephenson, Stanley P., Jr. Labor Market Turnover and Joblessness for Hispanic American Youth. September 1982. ERIC ED 246 161.

Stutz, Terrence. School of Hard Knocks. Unemployment Rate Among DISD Graduates Is Record High. Dallas Morning News May 15, 1982.

[School-by-school unemployment rates].

Swinton, David H. and Lawrence C. Morse. The Source of Minority Youth Employment Problems. May 1983. ERIC ED 254 573.

U.S. Conference of Mayors. Youth Unemployment in the Summer of '82. A Survey of the 125 Cities. April 26, 1982. ERIC ED 219 587.

U.S. Congress, 96th, 1st session, House of Representatives, Committee on Education and Labor, Subcommittee on Elementary, Secondary, and Vocational Education, Subcommittee on Employment Opportunities. Problems of Youth Unemployment. Washington, D.C.: GPO, 1980.

U.S. Congress, 98th, 1st session, House of Representatives, Committee on Education and Labor, Subcommittee on Labor Standards. Impact of Unemployment on Children and Families: Hearings.... Washington, D.C.: GPO, 1984.

Williams, Donald R. Labor Force Participation of Black and White Youth. Ann Arbor, MI: University of Michigan Research Press, 1987.

Williams, Donald R. Racial Differences in the Labor Force Participation of Male Teenagers. Doctoral dissertation, Northwestern University, 1984. UMO # 8502454.

Unemployment Bibliography

Cameron, Colin and Anila B. Menon. Hard Core Unemployment: A Selected Annotated Bibliography. 1969. ERIC ED 039 323.

Reid, Ira De A. (comp.) Negro Youth, Their Social and Economic Backgrounds: A Selected Bibliography of Unpublished Studies, 1900-1938. Washington, D.C.: American Youth Commission of the American Council on Education, 1939.

82. Violence Against Minorities

In the years from 1900 to 1922 there has been an average of a race riot in the United States every year, half of them in the South and half in the North. ... In these same years, 1,563 Negroes have been lynched; since the war [1st World War, 1914-1918] thirty four Negroes have been burned alive at the stake.

- W. E. B. Du Bois, 'Hosts of Black Labor," 1923.

Alberts, William E. The White Magic of Systematic Racism. Crisis 85 (November 1978):295-308. [Violence in Boston].

Amann, Peter H. Vigilante Fascism: The Black Legion as an American Hybrid. Comparative Studies in Society and History 25 (July 1983):490-524.

Applegate, Rex. Riot Control - Material and Techniques. Harrisburg, PA: Stackpole, 1969.

Asian American Resource Workshop. To Live in Peace ... Responding to Anti-Asian Violence in Boston. Boston: The Workshop, 1987.

Bancroft, Nancy. American Fascism: Analysis and Call for Research. Phylon 43 (June 1982):155-66.

Barnes, Brooks M. The Onancock Race Riot of 1907. The Virginia Magazine of History and Biography 92 (July 1984):336-51.

Beasley, Maurine H. The Muckrakers and Lynching: A Case Study of Racial Thinking. August 1983. ERIC ED 229 769.

Beeber, Dorothy. Race Riot in Columbia, Tennessee, February 25-27, 1946. Tennessee Historical Quarterly 39 (Spring 1980):49-61.

Belknap, Michael R. Federal Law and Southern Order. Racial Violence and Constitutional Conflict in the Post-Brown South. Athens, GA: University of Georgia Press, 1987.

Bendal, Mary-Ann. Speaking Out: Vigilante Attitudes Haven't Died Out Yet. USA Today (March 13, 1986). [Interview with John Henry Faulk].

Bermanzohn, Paul C. and Sally A. Bermanzohn. The True Story of the Greensboro Massacre. New York: C. Cance, 1980. [November 3, 1979].

Bernstein, Iver C. The New York City Draft Riots of 1863 and Class Relations on the Eve of Industrial Capitalism. [2 vols.] Doctoral dissertation, Yale University, 1985. UMO # 8619060.

Blain, William T. Challenging the Lawless: The Mississippi Secret Service, 1870-1871. Journal of Mississippi History 40 (May 1978):119-31.

Bogardus, Emory S. Anti-Filipino Race Riots: A Report Made to the
     Ingraham Institute of Social Studies of San Diego. San Diego, CA:
     1930.

Bond, Horace Man. What Lies Behind Lynching. Nation 128 (March
     1929):370-71.

Brown, Richard M. Strain of Violence. Historical Studies of American
     Violence and Vigilantism. New York: 1975.

Burran, James A., III. Racial Violence in the South During World War II.
     Doctoral dissertation, University of Tennessee, 1977.

Button, James W. Black Violence: Political Impact of the 1960s Riots.
     Princeton, NJ: Princeton University Press, 1978.

Cameron, James. From the Inside Out: A Lynching in the North [Marion,
     Indiana]. Fairbanks, AL: That New Pub. Co., 1980.

Capeci, Dominic J., Jr. The Lynching of Cleo Wright: Federal Protection
     of Constitutional Rights During World War II. Journal of American
     History (March 1986):850-87.

Carpenter, John A. Atrocities in the Reconstruction Period. Journal of
     Negro History 47 (October 1962):234-47.

Careoll, Murray L. Governor Francis E. Warren, The United States Army and
     the Chinese Massacre at Rock Springs. Annals of Wyoming 59 (Fall
     1987):16-27.

Center for Research on Criminal Justice. The Iron Fist and the Velvet
     Glove: An Analysis of the U.S. Police. Berkeley, CA, 1975.

Chadbourn, James H. Lynching and the Law. Chapel Hill, NC: University
     of North Carolina Press, 1933.

Cohen, Robert C. Black Crusader: A Biography of Robert Franklin
     Williams. Secaucus, NJ: Lyle Stuart, 1972.

Cooper, John L. The Police and the Ghetto. Port Washington, NY:
     Kennikat Press, 1979.

Cortner, Richard C. A Mob Intent on Death: The NAACP and the Arkansas
     Race Riots. Middletown, CT: Wesleyan University Press, 1986.

Crouch, Barry A. A Spirit of Lawlessness: White Violence; Texas Blacks,
     1865-1868. Journal of Social History 18 (Winter 1984):217-32.

Crowe, Charles. Racial Massacre in Atlanta, September 22, 1906. Journal
     of Negro History 54 (April 1969):150-73.

Crowe, Charles. Racial Violence and Social Reform - Origins of the
     Atlanta Riot of 1906. Journal of Negro History 53 (July 1968):234-
     56.

Cutler, J. E. Lynch Law. Longmans, 1905.

Cutler, James E. Lynching in the United States. South Atlantic Quarterly (April 1907).

Daniels, Roger (ed.) Anti-Chinese Violence in North America. New York: Arno, 1979.

Dauphine, James G. The Knights of the White Camelia in Louisiana, 1867-1869. Master's thesis, University of Southwestern Louisiana, 1983.

Davis, Angela. Violence Against Women and the Ongoing Challenge to Racism. Latham, NY: Kitchen Table : Women of Color Press, 1988.

Davis, Thulani. But Who's Counting? Violent Racial Incidents Add Up. Village Voice July 14, 1987.

De Witt, Howard A. The Watsonville Anti-Filipino Riot of 1930: A Case Study of the Great Depression and Ethnic Conflict in California. Southern California Quarterly 61 (Fall 1979):291-302.

Du Bois, W. E. B. The Lynching Industry. Crisis (February 1915).

Du Bois, W. E. B. Mob Tactics. Crisis 34 (August 1927):204. [Blacks' self-defense].

Dulaney, William M. Black Shields: A Historical and Comparative Survey of Blacks in American Police Forces. Doctoral dissertation, Ohio State University, 1984. UMO # 8504005.

Duster, Alfreda M. (ed.) Crusade for Justice: The Autobiography of Ida B. Wells [Leader in anti-lynching movement]. Chicago: University of Chicago Press, 1970.

Ellsworth, Scott. Death in a Promised Land: The Tulsa Race Riot of 1921. Baton Rouge: Louisiana State University Press, 1981.

Fede, Andrew. Legitimized Violent Slave Abuse in the American South, 1619-1865. American Journal of Legal History 29 (April 1985):93-150.

Fedo, Michael. They Was Just Niggers [Lynching of blacks in Duluth, 1920]. Ontario, CA: Brasch and Brasch, 1979.

Feldberg, Michael. The Philadelphia Riots of 1844: A Study of Ethnic Conflict. Westport, CT: Greenwood, 1975.

Fitzsimmons, Theodore B. The Camilla Riot. Georgia Historical Quarterly 35 (March 1951):116-25.

Franklin, John Hope. The Militant South. Cambridge, MA, 1956.

George, Paul S. Policing Miami's Black Community, 1896-1930. Florida Historical Quarterly 57 (April 1979):434-450.

575

Gilje, Paul A. **Mobocracy:** **Popular** **Disorder** **in** **New** **York** **City,** **1763-1834**. Chapel Hill, NC: University of North Carolina Press, 1987. [Chapter 6 deals with the anti-black violence of 1834].

Governor's Task Force on Civil Rights. **Report** **on** **Racial,** **Ethnic** **and** **Religious** **Violence** **in** **California** **1982**. [2 vols.] Sacramento, CA: State and Consumer Services Agency, December 10, 1982.

Granada, Ray. Violence: An Instrument of Policy in Reconstruction Alabama. **Alabama** **Historical** **Quarterly** 30 (Fall-Winter 1968).

Green, Philip. Can It [Fascism] Happen Here? **New** **York** **Times** **Magazine** September 20, 1970.

Grimké, Francis J. **The** **Lynching** **of** **Negroes** **in** **the** **South**. Washington, D.C., 1899.

Grimshaw, Allen D. (ed.) **Racial** **Violence** **in** **the** **United** **States**. Chicago: Aldine, 1969.

Gross, Bertram. **Friendly** **Fascism:** **The** **New** **Face** **of** **Power** **in** **America**. Bosotn: South End Press, 1982.

Gurr, Ted Robert (ed.) **Violence** **in** **America**. [2 vols.] (third edition). Newbury Park, CA: Sage, 1989.

Hackney, Sheldon. Southern Violence. **American** **Historical** **Review** 74 (February 1969):906-25. [See below, Albert C. Smith].

Hair, William I. **Carnival** **of** **Fury:** **Robert** **Charles** **and** **the** **New** **Orleans** **Riot** **of** **1900**. Baton Rouge: Louisiana State University Pres, 1976.

Harding, Leonard. The Cincinnati Riots of 1862. **Cincinnati** **Historical** **Society** **Bulletin** 25 (1967):229-39.

Harris, Trudier. **Exorcising** **Blackness:** **Historical** **and** **Literacy** **Lynching** **and** **Burning** **Rituals**. Bloomington, IN: Indiana University Press, 1984.

Harry, Margot. Attention MOVE! This is America. **Race** **and** **Class** (Spring 1987).

Hartley, Robert W. A Long, Hot Summer: The St. Augustine Racial Disorders of 1964. Master's thesis, Stetson University, 1972.

Haynes, Robert V. **A** **Night** **of** **Violence:** **The** **Houston** **Riot** **of** **1917**. Baton Rouge: Louisiana State University Press, 1976.

Hennessey, Melinda M. Racial Violence During Reconstruction: The 1876 Riots in Charleston and Cainhoy. **South** **Carolina** **Historical** **Magazine** 86 (April 1985):100-12.

Hennessey, Melinda M. **To** **Live** **and** **Die** **in** **Dixie:** **Reconstruction** **Race** **Riots** **in** **the** **South**. Doctoral dissertation, Kent State University,

1978.

Higgenbotham, Charimon. The Danville Riot of 1883. Master's thesis, Virginia State College, 1955.

Higginbotham, A. Leon, Jr. Labor Union Racial Violence. In: Gilbert Ware (ed.), From the Black Bar. Voices for Equal Justice, pp. 255-61. New York: Putnam's, 1976.

Higuchi, Hayumi. White Supremacy on the Cape Fear: The Wilmington Affair of 1898. Master's thesis, University of North Carolina, 1980.

Hirsch, Arnold. Race and Housing: Violence and Communal Protest in Chicago, 1940-1960. In: Melvin G. Holli and Peter d'A. Jones (eds.), The Ethnic Frontier, pp. 331-68. Grand Rapids, MI: Erdmans, 1977.

Holmes, William F. The Leflore County Massacre and the Demise of the Colored Farmers' Alliance. Phylon 34 (1973):267-74.

Holmes, William F. Whitecapping in Mississippi: Agrarian Violence in the Populist Era. Mid-America 55 (1973):134-48.

Howard, Gene L. Death at Cross Plains: An Alabama Reconstruction Tragedy [Lynching of a teacher of black railroad workers in Cross Plains]. University, AL: University of Alabama Press, 1984.

Howard, Walter T. Vigilante Justice and National Reaction: The 1937 Tallahassee Double Lynching. Florida Historical Quarterly 67 (July 1988):32-51.

Howard, Walter T. Vigilante Justice: Extra-legal Execution in Florida, 1930-1940 [Lynchings in Florida]. Doctoral dissertation, Florida State University, 1987. UMO # 8711723.

Hyser, Raymond M. and Dennis B. Downey. 'A Crooked Death': Coatesville, Pennsylvania and the Lynching of Zachariah Walker. Pennsylvania History 54 (August 1987):85-102.

Ingalls, Robert P. Lynching and Establishment Violence in Tampa, 1858-1935. Journal of Southern History 53 (November 1987):613-44.

Ingalls, Robert P. Urban Vigilantes in the New South. Tampa, 1882-1936. Knoxville, TN: University of Tennessee Press, 1988.

James, George. [Black] Assault Victims Liken [White] Attackers to 'Wolf Pack'. New York Times December 29, 1987.

James, George. Reports of Racial Assaults Rise Significantly in New York City. New York Times September 23, 1987.

James, William. A Strong Note of Warning on the Lynching Epidemic. Springfield Daily Republican (Mass.) July 23, 1903, p. 11.

Kelly, William R. and David Snyder. Racial Violence and Socioeconomic

Changes among Blacks in the United States. Social Forces 58 (March 1980):739-760.

Kerber, Linda K. Abolitionists and Amalgamators: The New York City Race Riots of 1834. New York Historical Society Quarterly 48 (1967).

Kester, Howard. Revolt Among the Sharecroppers [Violence by planters against the Southern Tenant Farmers Union]. New York: Arno Press, 1969 reprint.

Kilgo, John C. An Inquiry Concerning Lynchings. South Atlantic Quarterly 1 (January 1902):4-13.

Klotman, Phyllis R. Tearing a Hole in History: Lynching as Theme and Motif. Black American Literature Forum 19 (Summer 1985):55-63.

Knowlton, Clark S. Violence in New Mexico: A Sociological Perspective. California Law Review 58 (October 1970).

Lane, Roger. Roots of Violence in Black Philadelphia, 1860-1900. Cambridge, MA: Harvard University Press, 1986.

Leinen, Stephen. Black Police, White Society. New York: New York University Press, 1984.

Levstik, Frank R. The Toledo Riot of 1862: A Study of Midwest Negrophobia. Northwest Ohio Quarterly 54 (Fall 1972).

Lovett, Bobby L. Memphis Riots: White Reaction to Blacks in Memphis, May 1865-July 1866. Tennessee Historical Quarterly 38 (Spring 1979):9-33.

Lupo, Alan. Liberty's Chosen Home: The Politics of Violence in Boston. Boston: Beacon Press, 1988, orig. 1977. [Contains new epilogue].

Marable, Manning. The Meaning of Racist Violence in Late Capitalism. In: How Capitalism Underdeveloped Black America, pp. 231-53. Boston: South End Press, 1983.

Marriott, Michel. In Jersey City, [Asian] Indians Face Violence. New York Times October 12, 1987.

Martin, Louis. Prelude to Disaster: Detroit. Common Ground (Autumn 1943):21-26.

McCullom, Rod. Racial Harassment Continues to Rise: Severity of Local Incidents Increases [Chicago metropolitan area]. Chicago Reporter 17 (February 1988).

McDuffie, Jerome A. Politics in Wilmington and New Hanover County, 1865-1900: The Genesis of a Race Riot. Doctoral dissertation, Kent State University, 1979.

McFadden, Robert D. and others. Brawley Case: Stubborn Puzzle, Silent Victim. New York Times February 29, 1988. [Tawana Brawley of

Wappinger Falls, New York].

McGovern, James R. Anatomy of a Lynching: The Killing of Claude Neal.
    Baton Rouge: Louisiana State University Press, 1982.

Menard, Orville D. Tom Dennison, the Omaha Bee, and the 1919 Omaha Race
    Riot. Nebraska History 68 (Winter 1987):152-65.

Messner, William F. Black Violence and White Response: Louisiana, 1862.
    Journal of Southern History 41 (1975):19-38.

Mitchell, John L. Many Blacks Fear Police Are the Enemy. Los Angeles
    Times August 27, 1982. [Los Angeles].

Monti, Daniel J. Intergroup Conflict and Collective Violence: The Case
    of New York City, 1960-July 1964. Journal of Political and Military
    Sociology 6 (Fall 1978):147-162.

Moore, Michael. Pride and Prejudice [Asian Americans]. San Francisco
    Examiner Image November 15, 1987.

Moton, David R. Southern Violence: An Analysis of Lynchings in the
    South-Central Region of the United States from 1889 to 1918.
    Master's thesis, Northern Illinois University, 1986.

Mullen, Brian. Atrocity as a Function of Lynch Mob Composition: A Self-
    Attention Perspective. Personality and Social Psychology Bulletin 12
    (June 1986):187-97.

NAACP. Burning At Stake in the United States. New York: NAACP, June
    1919.

NAACP. Thirty Years of Lynching in the United States. New York: Negro
    Universities Press, 1969 (orig. 1919).

O'Brien, G. Return to 'Normalcy': Organized Racial Violence in the Post-
    World War II South. In: Ted R. Gurr (ed.), Violence in America,
    vol. 2 (third edition). Newbury Park, CA: Sage, 1989.

Osofsky, Gilbert. Race Riot, 1900: A Study of Ethnic Violence. Journal
    of Negro Education (Winter 1963):16-24.

Overend, William. The '43 Zoot Suit Riots Re-examined. Los Angeles Times
    May 9, 1978.

Phillips, Charles D. Exploring Relations Among Forms of Social Contact:
    The Lynching and Execution of Blacks in North Carolina, 1889-1918.
    Law and Society Review 21 (No. 3, 1987):361-74.

Pickens, William. The American Congo: Burning of Henry Lowry. In:
    Nancy Cunard (ed.), Negro: An Anthology. New York: Frederick
    Ungar, 1970.

Porter, Bruce D. and Marvin Dunn. The Miami Riot of 1980: Crossing the
    Bounds. Lexington, MA: Lexington Books, 1984.

Prather, H. Leon. We Have Taken a City: Wilmington Racial Massacre and
     Coup of 1898. Cranbury, NJ: Fairleigh Dickinson University Press,
     1984.

Prindle, Janice. New York's Whitest. Village Voice October 15, 1980.
     [Minorities on the NYC police force].

Rabinowitz, Howard N. The Conflict Between Blacks and the Police in the
     Urban South, 1865-1900. Historian 39 (1976):62-76.

Rable, George C. But There Was No Peace: The Role of Violence in the
     Politics of Reconstruction. Athens, GA: University of Georgia
     Press, 1984.

Randolph, A. Philip. Lynching: Capitalism Its Cause, Socialism Its Cure.
     Messenger (March 1919).

Raper, Arthur F. The Tragedy of Lynching. Chapel Hill, NC: University
     of North Carolina Press, 1932.

Redekep, David. The Lynching of Willie Earle. Master's thesis, Clemson
     University, 1987.

Report of Governor's Dade County Citizens' Committee. Tallahassee, FL:
     The Office of the Governor, October 30, 1980.

Robinson, Richard R. Racism as an Aspect of the Violent History of the
     State of Texas in the 1830s and 1840s. Master's thesis, Kean College
     of New Jersey, 1978.

Rorty, James and Winifred Rauschenbush. The Lessons of the Peekskill
     Riots: What Happened and Why. Commentary (October 1950):309-23.

Rousey, Dennis C. Black Policemen in New Orleans During Reconstruction.
     Historian 49 (February 1987):223-43.

Rudwick, Elliot M. Race Riot at East St. Louis, July 2, 1917. Cleveland,
     OH: Meridian Books, 1966.

Rudwick, Elliot (ed.) The East St. Louis Race Riot of 1917 [8
     microfilm reels]. Frederick, MD: University Publications of
     America, 1987.

Runcie, John. 'Hunting the Nigs' in Philadelphia: The Race Riot of 1834.
     Pennsylvania History 39 (1972):187-218.

Ryan, James G. The Memphis Riots of 1866: Terror in a Black Community
     during Reconstruction. Journal of Negro History (July 1977):243-57.

Salter, John R., Jr. Civil Rights and Self-Defense. Against the Current
     3 (July-August 1988):23-25.

Schonbach, Morris. Native American Fascism during the 1930s and 1940s: A
     Study of Its Roots, Its Growth, and Its Decline. New York: Garland,

1985.

Scott, Elsie L. _Violence Against Blacks in the United States, 1979-1981_. Washington, D.C.: Mental Health Research and Development Center, Institute for Urban Affairs and Research, Howard University, n.d.

Senechal, Roberta H. _In Lincoln's Shadow: The Springfield, Illinois Race Riot of 1908_. Doctoral dissertation, University of Virginia, 1986. UMO # 8705716.

Shapiro, Herbert. _White Violence and Black Response. From Reconstruction to Montgomery_. Amherst, MA: University of Massachusetts Press, 1988.

Singletary, Otis A. _Negro Militia and Reconstruction_. Austin: 1957.

Sitkoff, Harvard. Racial Militancy and Interracial Violence in the Second World War. _Journal of American History_ (December 1971):661-81.

Slotkin, Richard. _The Fatal Environment: The Myth of the Frontier in the Age of Industrialization 1800-1890_. New York: Atheneum, 1985. [Custer's last stand].

Slotkin, Richard. _Regeneration through Violence_ [White violence against American Indians]. 1973.

Smead, Edwin H., Jr. _The Lynching of Mack Charles Parker in Poplarville, Mississipppi, April 25, 1959_ [Last lynching in Mississippi]. Doctoral dissertation, University of Mississippi, 1979. UMO # 8017000.

Smead, Howard. _Black Justice: The Lynching of Mack Charles Parker_. New York: Oxford University Press, 1986.

Smith, Albert C. 'Southern Violence' Reconsidered: Arson as Protest in Black Belt Georgia, 1865-1910. _Journal of Southern History_ 51 (November 1985):527-64. [See, above, Sheldon Hackney].

Spofford, Tim. _Lynch Street: The May 1970 Slayings at Jackson State College_. Kent, OH: Kent State University Press, 1988.

Suarez, Manuel. _Requiem on Cerro Maravilla: The Police Murders in Puerto Rico and the U.S. Government Coverup_. 1987. Waterfront Press, 52 Maple Ave., Maplewood, NJ 07040.

Terrell, Mary Church. Lynching from a Negro's Point of View. _North American Review_ (June 1904):853-68.

Toy, E. V., Jr. Right-Wing Extremism: From the KKK to the Order, 1915 to 1988. _In_: Ted R. Gurr (ed.), _Violence in America_, vol. 2 (third edition). Newbury Park, CA: Sage, 1989.

Tucker, David M. Miss Ida B. Wells and Memphis Lynching. _Phylon_ 32 (1971):112-22.

581

Tuttle, William M., Jr. Labor Conflict and Racial Violence: The Worker in Chicago, 1894-1919. Labor History 10 (Summer 1969):408-32.

Tuttle, William M., Jr. Race Riot: Chicago in the Red Summer of 1919. New York: Atheneum, 1972.

U.S. Commission on Civil Rights. Intimidation and Violence. Racial and Religious Bigotry in America. Washington, D.C.: The Commission, January 1983.

U.S. Commission on Civil Rights. Recent Activities Against Citizens and Residents of Asian Descent. Washington, D.C.: The Commission, 1986.

U.S. Congress, 96th, 2nd session, House of Representatives, Committee on the Judiciary, Subcommittee on Crime. Increasing Violence Against Minorities: Hearings. ... Washington, D.C.: GPO, December 9, 1980.

U.S. Congress, 97th, 1st session, House of Representatives, Committee on the Judiciary, Subcommittee on Criminal Justice. Racially Motivated Violence: Hearings. ... Washington, D.C.: GPO, 1983.

U.S. Federal Bureau of Investigation. Prevention and Control of Mobs and Riots. Washington, D.C.: FBI, 1967.

Utley, Robert M. Frontier Regulars. The United States Army and the Indian, 1886-1891. Lincoln: University of Nebraska Press, 1984.

Vandal, Giles. The New Orleans Riot: The Anatomy of a Tragedy. Doctoral dissertation, College of William and Mary, 1978.

Vandal, Giles. The New Orleans Riot of 1866: Anatomy of a Tragedy. Lafayette, LA: 1983.

Vennochi, Joan. When a Crime Is Something More. Boston Globe November 22, 1982. [Boston Police Community Disorders Unit].

Waller, Altina L. Community, Class and Race in the Memphis Riot of 1866. Journal of Social History 18 (Winter 1984):233-46.

Washington, Booker T. Future of the American Negro, 1899. [Lynching, pp. 185-99].

Washington Lawyers' Committee for Civil Rights Under Law. Civil and Criminal Remedies for Racially and Religiously Motivated Violence in Maryland, Virginia, and the District of Columbia. Washington, D.C.: The Committee, June 1983.

Werner, John M. "Reaping the Bloody Harvest": Race Riots in the United States during the Age of Jackson, 1824-1849. New York: Garland, 1987.

West, Louis Jolyon. The Psychology of Racial Violence. Archives of General Psychiatry June 1967.

Wheaton, Elizabeth. Codename GREENKIL. The 1979 Greensboro Killings.

582

Athens, GA: University of Georgia Press, 1987.

White, Walter F. Rope and Faggot. New York: Knopf, 1929.

White House Interagency Task Force. Report on Civil Disturbance in Miami-Dade County, Florida. Washington, D.C.: The Task Force, 1981.

Whitfield, Stephen J. A Death in the Delta. The Story of Emmett Till. New York: Free Press, 1988.

Wickenhaver, Janet. Racial Terror on the Gold Coast [Violence against Asian Indians in New Jersey]. Village Voice January 27, 1988.

Widick, B. J. Detroit: City of Class and Race Violence. Chicago, IL: Quadrangle, 1972.

Wieder, Alan. The New Orleans School Crisis of 1960: Causes and Consequences. Phylon 48 (June 1987):122-31.

Williams, Robert F. and Mark Schleiffer. Negroes with Guns. Chicago: Third World Press, 1973.

Wilson, Charles E. The System of Police Brutality. Freedomways (Winter 1968).

Wise, Leah. The Elaine Massacre. Southern Exposure 1 (1974):9-10.

Wortman, Roy T. Denver's Anti-Chinese Riot, 1880. Colorado Magazine 42 (Fall 1965):275-91.

Wylie, Irvin G. Race and Class Conflict on Mississippi's Cotton Frontier. Journal of Southern History (May 1954):183-96.

Wynne, Lewis N. and Milly St. Julien. The Camilla Race Riot and the Failure of Reconstruction in Georgia. Jr. S.W. Georgia History 5 (Fall 1987):15-37.

Yedinak, Mary. Cicero: Why It Rioted. Bachelor's thesis, University of Illinois-Urbana, 1967.

Zangrando, Robert L. The NAACP Crusade against Lynching, 1909-1950. Philadelphia, PA: Temple University Press, 1980.

Zeskind, Leonard. They Don't All Wear Sheets [Violence against minorities, 1980-1986]. Atlanta: Center for Democratic Renewal, 1987.

Violence Against Minorities

The Lynching Records at Tuskegee Institute; with Lynching in America: A Bibliography. In: Daniel T. Williams (comp.), Eight Negro Bibliographies. New York: Kraus Reprint Co., 1970.

King, William M. (comp.) <u>Urban</u> <u>Racial</u> <u>Violence</u> <u>in</u> <u>the</u> <u>U.S.:</u> <u>An</u>
     <u>Historical</u> <u>and</u> <u>Comparative</u> <u>Bibliography</u>. Monticello, IL: Council of
     Planning Libraries, 1974.

Whitlock, Sherry (comp.) <u>Prejudice</u> <u>and</u> <u>Violence,</u> <u>An</u> <u>Annotated</u>
     <u>Bibliography</u> <u>of</u> <u>Selected</u> <u>Materials</u> <u>on</u> <u>Racial,</u> <u>Religious,</u> <u>and</u> <u>Ethnic</u>
     <u>Violence</u> <u>and</u> <u>Intimidation</u>. 1985. National Institute Against
     Prejudice and Violence, 525 W. Redwood Street, Baltimore, MD 21201.

[See also sections 6, 14, 18, 20, 29, 32, 40, 55, 69, and 75]

83. Wealth and Income

*To be a poor man is hard, but to be a poor race in a land of
dollars is the very bottom of hardships.*

W. E. B. Du Bois, "Strivings of the Negro People," 1897.

America, R. (ed.) Race, Restitution and Public Policy: The Present Real
    Value and Benefits from Slavery and Discrimination. New York:
    Praeger Press, forthcoming.

Birnbaum, Harvard and Rafael Weston. Homeownership and the Wealth
    Position of Black and White Americans. Review of Income and Wealth
    20 (March 1974).

Bonekemper, Edward H., III. Negro Ownership of Real Property in Hampton
    and Elizabeth City County Virginia, 1860-1870. Journal of Negro
    History 55 (1970):165-81.

Brimmer, Andrew F. Income, Wealth, and Investment Behavior in the Black
    Community. American Economic Review 78 (May 1988).

Browne, Robert S. Wealth Distribution and Its Impact on Minorities.
    Review of Black Political Economy 4 (1974).

Campbell, Colin D. (ed.) Income Redistribution. Washington, D.C.:
    American Enterprise Institute, 1977.

Cohn, E. and B. F. Kiker. Socioeconomic Background, Schooling, Experience
    and Monetary Rewards in the United States. Economica 53 (November
    1986).

Currie, Elliot and others. The New Immiseration. Socialist Revolution 5
    (October-December 1975)7-29.

Danziger, Sheldon and Peter Gottschalk. Earnings Inequality, the Spatial
    Concentration of Poverty, and the Underclass. American Economic
    Review 77 (May 1987)211-15.

Darity, William A., Jr. and S. L. Myers, Jr. Changes in Black-White
    Income Inequality, 1968-78: A Decade of Progress. Review of Black
    Political Economy 10 (Summer 1980):384-90.

Darling, Marsha Jean. The Growth and Decline of the Afro-American Family
    Farm in Warren County, North Carolina, 1910-1960. Doctoral
    dissertation, Duke University, 1982. UMO # 8313257.

Datcher-Loury, L. Racial Differences in the Stability of High Earnings
    among Young Men. Journal of Labor Economics 4 (July 1986).

De Canio, Stephen. Productivity and Income Distribution in the Post-
    Bellum South. Journal of Economic History 34 (1974):422-46.
    [Southern agriculture, 1880-1910].

Du Bois, W. E. B.   The Freedmen and Their Sons.   Independent   53 (November
    14, 1901):2709.

Du Bois, W. E. B.   Georgia Negroes and Their Fifty Millions of Savings.
    World's Work   18 (May 1909):11550-4.

Du Bois, W. E. B.   Negro Property.   World Today   19 (August 1910):905-6.

Du Bois, W. E. B.   The Savings of Black Georgia.   Outlook   69 (September
    14, 1901):128-30.

Du Bois, W. E. B.   Violations of Property Rights.   Crisis   2 (May
    1911):28-32.

Du Bois, W. E. B.   Wealth and Power.   Amsterdam News   November 11, 1931.

Dunson, B. H. and P. Jackson.   The Distributional Aspects of Inflation.
    Quarterly Review of Economics and Business   26 (Winter 1986).   [On
    blacks and whites].

Fareed, A. E. and G. D. Riggs.   The Human Wealth of White and Nonwhite
    Men.   Review of Business and Economic Research   15 (Winter 1980).

Farley, Reynolds and Suzanne Biandi.   The Growing Gap between Blacks.
    American Demographics   5 (July 1983).

Felder, Henry.   The Changing Patterns of Black Family Income.

Felder, Henry.   The Economic Status of Black Americans: A New Look at the
    Data.   Washington, D.C.:   Joint Center for Political Studies, 1983.

Fisher, James S.   Negro Farm Ownership in the South.   Annals of the
    Association of American Geographers   63 (1973):478-89.

Franklin, Stephen D. and J. D. Smith.   Black-White Differences in Income
    and Wealth.   American Economic Review   67 (1977):405-9.

Greene, Larry A.   Blacks.   In: Encyclopedia of American Economic History,
    III.   New York: Scribner's, 1980.

Gwartney, J.   Changes in the Non-White/White Income Ratio 1939-1967.
    American Economic Review   60 (December 1970).

Harris, Donald J.   Capital Accumulation and Income Distribution.
    Stanford, CA: Stanford University Press, 1978.

Harris, Donald J.   Economic Growth, Structural Change, and the Relative
    Income Status of Blacks in the U.S. Economy, 1947-1978.   Review of
    Black Political Economy   12 (Spring 1983):75-92.

Haulman, Clyde A.   Changes in Wealth Holding in Richmond, Virginia, 1860-
    1870.   Journal of Urban History   13 (November 1986):53-71.

Henretta, John C.   Race Differences in Middle Class Lifestyle: The Role of Home Ownership. Social Science Research 8 (1979):63-78.

Higgs, Robert. Accumulation of Property by Southern Blacks before World War I. American Economic Review 72 (September 1982):725-37.

Higgs, Robert. Accumulation of Property by Southern Blacks Before World War I: Reply. American Economic Review 74 (September 1984). [See, Margo, below].

Higgs, Robert. The Wealth of Japanese Tenant Farmers in California, 1909. Agricultural History 53 (April 1979):488-93.

Lebergott, Stanley. The Submerged Tenth: Color and Ethnic Group Income, 1900-1970. In: The American Economy. Income, Wealth, and Want, pp. 44-52. Princeton, NJ: Princeton University Press, 1976.

Lebergott, Stanley. White and Non-White Income Distributions: 1900-1970. In The American Economy. Income, Wealth, and Want, pp. 299-309. Princeton, NJ: Princeton University Press, 1976.

Lee, B. S. Analytical Comparisons of Internal, External and Differential Indices of Income Inequality between Black and White for 1964-1977. American Economist 28 (Fall 1984).

Levy, Frank. Dollars and Dreams. The Changing American Income Distribution. New York: Basic Books, 1988. [1973-1984].

Lundsten, Lorman L. and Harold Black. The Impact of Race and Other Variables on the Composition and Value of Individual Portfolios. Review of Black Political Economy 8 (Summer 1978).

Margo, Robert A. Accumulation of Property by Southern Blacks before World War I: Comment and Further Evidence. American Economic Review 74 (September 1984):768-81.

McPherson, Robert S. Ricos and Pobres: Wealth Distribution on the Navajo Reservation in 1915. New Mex. Hist. Rev. 60 (October 1985):415-34.

Miller, Herman. Race, Creed, and Color - The Income of Minorities. Chapter 6 of Rich Man, Poor Man. New York: Crowell, 1964.

Oblinger, Carl D. Alms for Oblivion: The Making of a Black Underclass in Southeastern Pennsylvania, 1780-1860. In: John E. Bodnar (ed.), The Ethnic Experience in Pennsylvania, pp. 94-119. Lewsiburg, PA: Bucknell University Press, 1973.

O'Hare, William P. Wealth and Economic Status: A Perspective on Racial Inequality. Washington, D.C.: Joint Center for Political Studies, 1983.

Rasmussen, D. A Note on the Relative Income of Non-White Men 1948-64. Quarterly Review of Economics 84 (February 1970).

Schaefer, Donald F. A Model of Migration and Wealth Accumulation: Farmers at the Antebellum Southern Frontier. Explorations in

Economic History 24 (April 1987):130-57.

Schwartz, S. Earnings Capacity and the Trend in Inequality among Black
    Men. Journal of Human Resources 21 (Winter 1986).

Silk, Leonard. Now, to Figure Why the Poor Get Poorer. New York Times
    December 18, 1988.

Smith, James P. Race and Human Capital. American Economic Review 74
    (September 1984).

Sterner, Richard. The Negroes' Share: A Study of Income, Consumption,
    Housing, and Public Assistance. New York: Harper, 1943.

Sum, Andrew. Declining Earnings of Young Men. Washington, D.C.:
    Children's Defense Fund, 1987.

Terrell, Henry S. Wealth Accumulation of Black and White Families: The
    Empirical Evidence. Journal of Finance 26 (May 1971):363-77.

Tsukada, Mamoru. Income Parity through Different Paths: Chinese
    Americans, Japanese Americans, and Caucasians in Hawaii. Amerasia
    Journal 14 (1988):47-60.

Winnick, A. J. The Changing Distribution of Income and Wealth in the
    U.S., 1960-1985: An Examination of the Movement Toward Two
    Societies, Separate and Unequal. In: Patricia Voydanoff and Linda
    C. Majka (eds.), Families and Economic Distress. Newbury Park, CA:
    Sage, 1988.

Work, Monroe N. A Half Century of Progress: The Negro in America in 1866
    and 1922. Missionary Review of the World 45 (June 1922).

Work, Monroe N. Two Generations Since Emancipation. Missionary Review
    of the World 59 (June 1936):289-90.

84. Whites

The discovery of personal whiteness among the world's peoples is a very modern thing - a nineteenth- and twentieth- century matter, indeed. The ancient world would have laughed at such a distinction. ... Today ... the world in a sudden, emotional conversion has discovered that it is white and by that token, wonderful!

- W. E. B. Du Bois, "On Being Black," 1920.

Anderson, Ernest Leon. Scraping By: A Field Study of Semirural Poverty in the Texas Hill Country [Poor whites]. Doctoral dissertation, University of Texas, 1987. UMO # 8728508.

Bardnt, Joseph. Liberating Our White Ghetto. Minneapolis, MN: Augsburg Publishing House, 1972.

Berlin, Ira. White Majority. Social History 5 (May 1977):653-59.

Bingham, Robert. An Ex-Slave Holder's View of the Negro Question in the South. Harpers Monthly Magazine (European ed.) (July 1900):8-15.

Brown, Bertram S. Racism and Our Ethnic Minorities. In: Frank F. Montalvo (comp.), White Working Class Culture. Patrick Air Force Base, FL: Defense Race Relations Institute, 1975.

Brown, David. The White Man's Problem. African Methodist Episcopal Zion Quarterly 4 (April 1894):268-74.

Buck, Paul H. The Poor Whites of the Ante-Bellum South. American Historical Review 31 (1925):41-54.

Cecil-Fronsman, Bill. The Common Whites: Class and Culture in Antebellum North Carolina. Doctoral dissertation, University of North Carolina, 1983. UMO # 8316586.

Churchill, Ward. White Studies: The Intellectual Imperialism of Contemporary U.S. Education. Integrateducation 19 (January-April 1981):51-57.

Clark, Kenneth B. Beyond the Dilemma [Effect of racism on whites]. In: Lester Thoussen (ed.), Representative American Speeches: 1969-1970. New York: Wilson, 1970.

Coles, Robert. Understanding White Racists. New York Review of Books 18 (December 1971):12-15.

Coles, Robert. The White Northerner. Pride and Prejudice. Atlantic Monthly June 1966.

Cook, Sylvia J. From Tobacco Road to Route 66: The Southern Poor White in Fiction. Chapel Hill, NC: University of North Carolina Press,

1976.

Cunnigen, Donald. Men and Women of Goodwill: Mississippi's White
Liberals. Doctoral dissertation, Harvard University, 1988. UMO #
8820540.

Danzig, David. Rightists, Racists, and Separatists: A White Block in the
Making? Commentary August 1964.

Davis, George A. The Hypocrisies of White Racism. In: George A. Davis,
Donald S. Smith, and Carlyle Johnson, Black Issues. Patrick Air
Force Base, FL: Defense Race Relations Institute, 1975.

Dennis, Rutledge M. Socialization and Racism: The White Experience. In:
Benjamin P. Bowser and Raymond G. Hunt (ed.), Impacts of Racism on
White Americans, pp. 71-85. Beverly Hills, CA: Sage, 1981.

Dent, Elizabeth. The Salience of Prowhite/Antiblack Bias. Child
Development 49 (December 1978):1280-86.

Ekrich, A. Roger. Bound for America: The Transportation of British
Convicts to the Colonies. 1718-1775. New York: Oxford University
Press, 1987.

Feagin, Joe R. White Separatists and Black Separatists: A Comparative
Analysis. Social Problems 19 (Fall 1971):167-180.

Fellman, Michael. Getting Right with the Poor White. Canadian Review of
American Studies 18 (Winter 1987):527-39.

Garcia, Jesus. The White Ethnic Experience in Selected Secondary U.S.
History Textbooks: A Comparative Investigation. Social Studies 77
(July-August 1986):169-75.

Gitlin, Todd and Nance Hollander. Uptown: Poor Whites in Chicago. New
York: Harper and Row, 1970.

Gordon, A. H. Some Disadvantages of Being White. Messenger 10
(1928):79.

Guthrie, Robert V. White Racism and Its Impact on Black and White
Behavior. Journal of Non-White Concerns in Personnel and Guidance 1
(April 1973):144-149.

Jackson, Agnes Moreland. Challenge to All White Americans or, White
Ethnicity from a Black Perspective. Sounding (Spring 1973)

Johnson, Christopher S. Identifying the Antebellum Southern Poor White:
A Preliminary Study of Sources and Methods. Southern Historian 8
(Spring 1987):54-63.

Johnson, Christopher S. Poverty and Dependency in Antebellum Mississippi
[Poor whites]. Doctoral dissertation, University of California,
Riverside, 1988. UMO # 8817524.

King, Larry L. Confessions of a White Racist. Harper's Magazine January 1970.

King, Larry L. Confessions of a White Racist. New York: Viking, 1971.

Killian, Lewis. White Southerners (second edition). Amherst, MA: University of Massachusetts Press, 1985.

Levy, Charles J. Voluntary Servitude: Whites in the Negro Movement. New York, 1968.

Lieberson, Stanley. Unhyphenated Whites in the United States. Ethnic and Racial Studies 8 (January 1985):159-80.

MacLeod, Jay. Aint' No Makin' It [Poor white youth]. Boulder, CO: Westview Press, 1987.

Morrill, Peter B. Becoming a White Racist: A Study in the Social Ascription of Responsibility. Doctoral dissertation, New York University, 1979. UMO # 79-18984.

Morris, Richard B. White Bondage in Ante-Bellum South Carolina. South Carolina Historical Magazine (October 1948).

Morrison, Iris. White Studies. Forum for the Discussion of New Trends in Education 20 (April 1977):5-8.

Newby, I. A. Plain Folk in the New South. Social Change and Cultural Persistence, 1880-1915 ["Impoverished white working class"]. Baton Rouge: Louisiana State University Press, 1989.

Rafter, Nicole H. White Trash: The Eugenic Family Studies, 1877-1919. Boston: Northeastern University Press, 1988.

Rogin, Michael. Wallace and the Middle Class: The White Blacklash in Wisconsin. Public Opinion Quarterly Spring, 1966.

Rubin, Lillian. The Racism of Liberals. Trans-action September, 1968.

Schuyler, George S. Our White Folk. American Mercury 12 (1927):385-92.

Shannon, Barbara E. Implications of White Racism for Social Work Practice. Social Casework 51 (1970):270-276.

Terry, Robert W. For Whites Only (Revised edition). Grand Rapids, MI: Eerdmans, 1975.

Terry, Robert W. The Negative Impact on White Values. In: Benjamin P. Bowser and Raymond G. Hunt (eds.), Impacts of Racism on White Americans, pp. 119-151. Beverly Hills, CA: Sage, 1981.

Tourgee, Albion W. Shall White Minorities Rule? Forum 27 (April 1899):143-55.

Towle, Joseph and Colin Turnbull. The White Problem in America. Natural

History June, 1968.

Wayson, William W. White Racists in America: We Have Met Them and They
     Are Us. _In_: G. K. Verma and Christopher Bagley (eds.), _Race and
     Education Across Cultures_. Stamford, CT: Greylock Publishers, 1975.

White House Conference on Whites. _Ebony_ (July 1966). [The need for
     holding such a conference].

Whittaker, Elvi. _The Mainland Haole: The White Experience in Hawaii_.
     New York: Columbia University Press, 1986.

Wilcox, Preston. Social Policy and White Racism. _Social Policy_ May-June
     1970.

Whites Bibliography

Pohl, David L. (comp.) The Impact of Racism on White Americans: A
     Bibliography. _Sage Race Relations Abstracts_ 5 (May 1980).

85. Women, Minority

*Dear Husband ... My master has sold [our son] albert to a trader
... and the other child is for sale also. ... I want you to tell
dr. Hamelton and your master if either will buy me ... I don't
want a trader to get me they asked me if I had got any person to
buy me and I told them no. ... I am heartsick. ... I am and ever
will be you kind wife.*

- Maria Perkins, a slave wife, writing in 1852 to her slave
husband, Richard Perkins, U. B. Phillips, Life and Labour in the
Old South, p. 212.

Abramowitz, Mimi. Regulating the Lives of Women. Social Welfare Policy
from Colonial Times to the Present. Boston: South End Press, 1988.

Acosta-Belen, Edna and Elia H. Christensen. The Puerto Rican Woman. New
York: Praeger, 1986.

Albelda, Randy. 'Nice Work If You Can Get It': Segmentation of White and
Black Women Workers in the Post-War Period. Review of Radical
Political Economics 17 (1985):72-85.

Aldridge, Delores. Black Women in the Economic Marketplace: A Battle
Unfinished. Journal of Social and Behavioral Sciences 21 (Winter
1975):48-62.

Allen, Paula G. The Sacred Hoop: Recovering the Feminine in American
Indian Tradition. Boston: Beacon, 1987.

Allen, Ruth A. Mexican Peon Women in Texas. Sociology and Social
Research (November-December 1931):131-42.

Almeida [Engram], Eleanor de. Whose Values? Racial Chauvinism in
Research on Black Families. Black Sociologist 6 (1977):9-24.

Almquist, Elizabeth M. Minorities, Gender and Work. Lexington, MA:
Heath, 1979.

Almquist, Elizabeth M. Untangling the Effects of Race and Sex: The
Disadvantaged Status of Black Women. Social Science Quarterly 56
(1975):129-42.

Andersen, Margaret. Denying Difference: The Continuing Basis for the
Exclusion of Race and Gender in the Curriculum. Memphis, TN: Center
for Research on Women, Memphis State University, 1987.

Apodoca, Maria L. The Chicana Woman: An Historical Materialist
Perspective. Latin American Perspectives 4 (Winter-Spring 1977):70-
89.

Aptheker, Bettina. Woman's Legacy: Essays on Race, Sex, and Class in
American History. Amherst, MA: University of Massachusetts Press,

1982.

Aquino, Belinda A. The History of Pilipino Women in Hawaii. _Bridge_ 7
     (Spring 1979):17-21.

Artis-Gordwin, Sharon E. _Professional Barriers and Facilitators for_
     Minority Women in Educational Research. Doctoral dissertation,
     Harvard University, 1986. UMO # 8620685.

Bataille, Gretchen M. and Kathleen M. Sands. _American Indian Women:_
     Telling Their Lives [Analysis of autobiographies]. Lincoln:
     University of Nebraska Press, 1984.

Bellush, Jewel. Room at the Top: The Case of District Council 37 of the
     American Federation of State, County and Municipal Employees in New
     York City [Black women leadership]. _Sage_ 3 (Spring 1986):35-40.

Better, Shirley J. _Black Working Women: Role Perception, Role Strain,_
     and Life Satisfaction. Doctoral dissertation, University of
     California, Los Angeles, 1987. UMO # 8803670.

Bianchi, Suzanne M. _Household Composition and Racial Inequality_.
     Boulder, CO: Westview Press, 1981.

Blackwelder, Julia K. Race, Ethnicity, and Women's Lives in the Urban
     South. _In_: Randall M. Miller and George E. Pozzetta (eds.), _Shades_
     of the Sunbelt. Westport, CT: Greenwood, 1988.

Blackwelder, Julia K. _Women of the Depression: Caste and Culture in San_
     Antonio, 1929-1939. College Station: Texas A and M Press, 1984.

Blount, Melissa. Surpassing Obstacles: Black Women in Medicine. _Journal_
     of the American Medical Women's Association. 39 (1984):192-5.

Blackburn, Regina. In Search of the Black Female Self: African-American
     Women's Autobiographies and Ethnicity. _In_: Estelle Jelinke (ed.),
     Women's Autobiography, pp. 133-148.

Bracey, John H., Jr. Afro-American Women: A Brief Guide to Writings from
     Historical and Feminist Perspectives. _Contributions in Black Studies_
     8 (1986-1987):106-10.

Brady, Marilyn D. Kansas Federation of Colored Women's Clubs, 1900-1930.
     Kansas History 9 (Spring 1986):19-30.

Brady, Victoria. Resist! Survival Tactics of Indian Women. _California_
     History (1984):140-51.

Brewer, Rose M. Black Women in Poverty: Some Comments on Female-Headed
     Families. _Signs_ 13 (Winter 1988):331-39.

Brown, Andolyn V. _Black Female Administrators in Higher Education - A_
     Survey of Demographic Data, Previous Work Experiences,
     Characteristics of Present Positions and Characteristics of Employing
     Institutions. Doctoral dissertation, Bowling Green State

University, 1980. UMO # 8100307.

Brown, Anita and others. A Review of Psychology of Women Textbooks:
Focus on the Afro-American Women. <u>Psychology of Women Quarterly</u> 9
(March 1985):29-38.

Brown, Lillian M. <u>The Contemporary Black Woman: Her Labor Market Status</u>.
Master's thesis, New York State University, Binghampton, 1981.

Bryan, Louis C. Modjeska M. Simkins - Profile of a Legend. <u>Sage</u> 3
(Spring 1986):56-7.

Burnham, Linda. Has Poverty Feminized in Black America? <u>Black Scholar</u>
16 (March-April 1985):14-24.

Buss, Fran L. <u>Dignity. Lower Income Women Tell of Their Lives and
Struggles</u>. Ann Arbor, MI: University of Michigan Press, 1985.

Cannon, Lynn W. and others. <u>Race and Class Bias in Research on Women: A
Methodological Note</u>. Memphis, TN: Center for Research on Women,
Memphis State University, 1987.

Cash, Floris L. B. <u>Womanhood and Protest: The Club Movement among Black
Women, 1892-1922</u>. Doctoral dissertation, State University of New
York at Stony Brook, 1986. UMO # 8704374.

Cheng, Lucie. Free, Indentured, Enslaved: Chinese Prostitutes in
Nineteenth-Century America. <u>In</u>: Lucie Cheng and Edna Bonacich
(eds.), <u>Labor Immigration Under Capitalism</u>, pp. 402-34. Berkeley,
CA: University of California Press, 1984.

Chin, Ai-li S. Adaptive Roles of Chinese Women in the U.S. <u>Bulletin,
Chinese Historical Society of America</u> 14 (January 1979).

Christensen, Kimberly E. L. <u>Accounting for the Relative Income Gains of
Black Females: 1955-1982</u>. Doctoral dissertation, University of
Massachusetts, 1986. UMO # 8622659.

Clark, Darlene and Kate Wittenstein. Female Slave Resistance: The
Economics of Sex. <u>In</u>: Filomina C. Steady (ed.), <u>The Black Woman
Cross-Culturally</u>, pp. 289-300. Cambridge, MA: Schenkman, 1981.

Clark-Lewis, Elizabeth. <u>From "Servant" to "Dayworker": A Study of
Selected Houshold Service Workers in Washington, D.C., 1900-1926</u>.
Doctoral dissertation, University of Maryland, 1983. UMO # 8429912.

Clark-Lewis, Elizabeth. <u>This Work Had a End: The Transition from Live-in
to Day Work</u>. Memphis, TN: Center for Research on Women, Memphis
State University, 1985.

Clegg, Brenda F. <u>Black Female Domestics During the Great Depression in
New York City 1930-1940</u>. Doctoral dissertation, University of
Michigan, 1983. UMO # 8324157.

Coley, Soraya M. <u>And Still I Rise: An Exploratory Study of Contemporary</u>

Black Private Household Workers. Doctoral dissertation, Bryn Mawr College, 1981.

Collier-Arrington, Betty J. and Louis Williams. The Myth of Economic Superiority of the Black Female. Urban League Review 5 (Summer 1980):66-70.

Colson, Elizabeth (ed.) Autobiographies of Three Pomo Women. Berkeley, CA: Department of Anthropology, University of California, 1974.

The Combahee River Collective Statement: Black Feminist Organizing in the Seventies and Eighties. Latham, NY: Kitchen Table: Women of Color Press, 1988.

Commission on Civil Rights of Puerto Rico. La Iqualdad de Derechos y Opportunidades de la Mujer Puertorriquena. San Juan: The Commission, 1972.

Conference on the Educational and Occupational Needs of American Indian Women, October 12-13, 1976. Washington, D.C.: GPO, 1980.

Conklin, Nancy F. and others. The Culture of Southern Black Women: Approaches and Materials [Curriculum guide]. University, AL: Archive of American Minority Cultures and Women's Studies Program, University of Alabama, 1983.

Cooper, Anna Julia. A Voice for the South. New York: Oxford University Press, 1988, orig. 1892.

Davis, Angela Y. Radical Perspectives on the Empowerment of Afro-American Women: Lessons for the 1980s. Harvard Educational Review 58 (August 1988):348-53.

Davis, Angela Y. Reflections on the Black Woman's Role in the Community of Slaves. Black Scholar 3 (December 1971):2-15.

Davis, Frank. Black Community's Social Security. Washington, D.C.: University Press of America, 1978.

Davis, Marianna W. (ed.). Contributions of Black Women to America. [2 vols.] Columbia, SC: Kenday Press, 1982.

Demirturk, Emine L. The Female Identity in Cross-Cultural Perspectives: Immigrant Women's Autobiographies. Doctoral dissertation, University of Iowa, 1986.

Deutsch, Sarah. No Separate Refuge: Culture, Class, and Gender on an Anglo-Hispanic Frontier in the American Southwest, 1880-1940. New York: Oxford University Press, 1987.

Dickson, Lynda F. The Early Club Movement Among Black Women in Denver: 1890-1925. Doctoral dissertation, University of Colorado, 1982. UMO # 8221063.

Dill, Bonnie T. Across the Boundaries of Race and Class: An Exploration

of the Relationship Between Work and Family Among Black Female
Domestic Servants. Doctoral dissertation, New York University, 1979.
UMO # 8010339.

Donovan, Rebecca and others. Unemployment among Low-income Women: An
Exploratory Study. Social Work 32 (July-August 1987):301-05.

Dougherty, Molly C. Becoming a Woman in Southern Black Culture.
Nashville: Vanderbilt University Press, 1978.

Douglas, Priscilla H. Black Working Women. Doctoral dissertation,
Harvard University, 1981. UMO # 8125477.

Douglas, Priscilla H. Black Working Women: Factors Affecting Labor
Market Experience. Wellesley College Center for Research on Women,
Working Paper, March 1980.

Du Bois, W. E. B. The Burden of Black Women. Crisis 9 (November 1914).

Du Bois, W. E. B. The Work of Negro Women in Society. Spelman Messenger
18 (February 1902):1-3.

Elsasser, Nan and others. La Mujeres: Conversations from a Hispanic
Community. Old Westbury, NY: Feminist Press, 1981.

Enabulele, Arlene B. and Dionne Jones. A Resource Guide on Black Women in
the United States. Washington, D.C.: Institute for Urban Affairs
and Research, Howard University, 1978.

Evans, Mari (ed.) Black Women Writers (1950-1980): A Critical
Evaluation. Garden City, NJ: Doubleday, 1984.

Figueira-McDonough, Josefine. Gender, Race, and Class: Differences in
Levels of Feminist Orientation. Journal of Applied Behavioral
Science 21 (1985):121-42.

Fisher, Dexter (ed.) The Third Woman: Minority Women in the United
States. Boston: Houghton Mifflin, 1980.

Fox-Genovese, Elizabeth. Within the Plantation Household: Black and
White Women of the Old South, Chapel Hill: University of North
Carolina Press, 1988.

Fuchs, Victor. The Feminization of Poverty? Working Paper No. 1934.
Cambridge, MA: NBER, May 1986.

Garcia, Mario T. The Chicana in American History: The Mexican Women of
El Paso, 1880-1920: A Case Study. Pacific Historical Review 49
(May 1980):315-37.

Garcia Ramis, Magali. Women's Tales [in Puerto Rico]. In: Asela
Rodriguez de Laguna (ed.), Images and Indentities. The Puerto Rican
in Two World Contexts, pp. 109-15. New Brunswick, NJ: Transaction
Books, 1987.

Gillas, Cheryl L. T. *Living and Working in a World of Trouble: The Emergent Career of the Black Woman Community Worker*. Doctoral dissertation, Northeastern University, 1979. UMO # 8006385.

Glenn, Evelyn N. *Issei, Nisei, War Bride: Three Generations of Japanese American Women in Domestic Service*. Philadelphia, PA: Temple University Press, 1986.

Glenn, Evelyn N. Occupational Ghettoization: Japanese American Women and Domestic Service, 1905-1970. *Ethnicity* 8 (October 1981):352-86.

Gonzales, Rosalinda M. Chicanos and Mexican Immigrant Families 1920-40: Women's Subordination and Family Exploitation. In: Lois Scharf and Joan M. Jensen (eds.), *Decades of Discontent. The Women's Movement, 1920-1940*. Westport, CT: Greenwood, 1983.

Gonzales, Sylvia. The White Feminist Movement: The Chicana Perspective. *Social Science Journal* 14 (April 1977).

Gordon, Vivian V. *Black Women, Feminism and Black Liberation: Which Way?* Chicago: Third World Press, 1984.

Green, Mildred Denley. *Black Women Composers: A Genesis*. Boston: Hall-Twyane, 1983.

Greene, Helen. Black Women in the Criminal Justice System. *Urban League Review* 6 (Fall 1981):55-61.

Gregory, Chester W. Black Women in Pre-Federal America. In: Mabel E. Deutrich and Virginia C. Purdy (eds.), *Clio Was a Woman: Studies in the History of American Women*, pp. 53-70.

Griswold del Castillo, Richard. *La Familiar: Chicano Families in the Urban Southwest, 1848 to the Present*. Notre Dame, IN: University of Notre Dame Press, 1984.

Gundersen, Joan R. The Double Bonds of Race and Sex: Black and White Women in a Colonial Virginia Parish. *Journal of Southern History* 52 (August 1986):351-72.

Gwartney-Gibbs, Patricia A. and Patricia A. Taylor. Black Women Workers' Earnings Progress in Three Industrial Sectors. *Sage* 3 (Spring 1986):20-25.

Hamilton, Tullia K. B. *The National Association of Colored Women, 1896-1920*. Doctoral dissertation, Emory University, 1978. UMO # 7912743.

Hardy, D. Antoinette. *Black Women in American Bands and Orchestras*. Metuchen, NJ: Scarecrow Press, 1980.

Harley, Sharon L. Federal Job Training and Economically Disadvantaged Women. In *Women and Work 1: An Annual Review*, pp. 282-310. Beverly Hills, CA: Sage, 1985.

Harley, Sharon L. and Rosalyn Terborg-Penn (eds.) *The Afro-American*

Women. In Women and Work 1: An Annual Review, pp. 282-310. Beverly
    Hills, CA: Sage, 1985.

Harley, Sharon L. Mary Church Terrell: Genteel Militant. In: Leon
    Litwack and August Meier, (eds.), Black Leaders of the Nineteenth
    Century. Urbana, IL: University of Illinois Press, 1988.

von Hassell, Malve. Issei Women Between Two Worlds: 1875-1985. Doctoral
    dissertation, New School for Social Research, 1987. UMO # 8715863.

Hawks, Joanne V. and Sheila L. Skemp. Sex, Race, and the Role of Women in
    the South. Jackson: University Press of Mississippi, 1983.

Helmbold, Lois R. Beyond the Family Economy: Black and White Working-
    Class Women during the Great Depression. Feminist Studies 13 (Fall
    1987):629-55.

Helmbold, Lois R. Downward Occupational Mobility during the Great
    Depression: Urban Black and White Working Class Women. Labor
    History 29 (Spring 1988):135-72.

Hesse-Biber, Sharlene. The Black Woman Worker: A Minority Group
    Perspective on Women at Work. Sage 3 (Spring 1986):26-34.

Higginbotham, Elizabeth. Employment for Professional Black Women in the
    Twentieth Century. Memphis, TN: Center for Research on Women,
    Memphis State University, 1985.

Higginbotham, Elizabeth. Work and Survival for Black Women. Memphis, TN:
    Center for Research on Women, Memphis State University, 1984.

Hine, Darlene Clark. Lifting the Veil, Shattering the Silence: Black
    Women's History in Slavery and Freedom. In: Darlene Clark Hine
    (ed.), The State of Afro-American History: Past, Present, and
    Future. Baton Rouge: Louisiana State University Press, 1986.

Hine, Darlene Clark. When the Truth Is Told: A History of Black Women's
    Culture and Community in Indiana, 1875-1950. Indianapolis, IN:
    Indianapolis Section, National Council of Negro Women, 1981.

Hirata, Lucie C. Chinese Immigrant Women in Nineteenth-Century
    California. In: Carol R. Berkin and Mary Beth Norton (eds.), Women
    of America: A History. Boston: Houghton Mifflin, 1979.

Holleran, Philip M. and Margaret Schwartz. Another Look at Comparable
    Worth's Impact on Black Women. Review of Radical Political Economy
    16 (Winter 1988):97-102.

Hooks, Bell. Straightening Our Hair. Zeta Magazine 1 (September
    1988):33-37.

Horton, James Oliver. Freedom's Yoke: Gender Conventions among
    Antebellum Free Blacks. Feminist Studies 12 (Spring 1986):51-76.

Jackson, Jacquelyne J. Black Women in a Racist Society. In: Charles

Willie and others (eds.), <u>Racism</u> <u>and</u> <u>Mental</u> <u>Health</u>, pp. 185-268.
Pittsburgh: University of Pittsburgh Press, 1973.

Jameson, Elizabeth. Toward a Multicultural History of Women in the
Western United States. <u>Signs</u> 13 (1988):761-91.

Janiewski, Dolores E. Flawed Victories: The Experiences of Black and
White Women Workers in Durham during the 1930s. <u>In</u>: Lois Scharf and
Joan M. Jensen (eds.), <u>Decades</u> <u>of</u> <u>Discontent:</u> <u>The</u> <u>Women's</u> <u>Movement,</u>
<u>1920-1940</u>. Westport, CT: Greenwood, 1983.

Janiewski, Dolores E. <u>Sisterhood</u> <u>Denied:</u> <u>Race,</u> <u>Gender,</u> <u>and</u> <u>Class</u> <u>in</u> <u>a</u>
<u>New</u> <u>South</u> <u>Community</u>. Philadelphia: Temple University Press, 1984.

Jensen, Joan M. and Darlis A. Miller (eds.) <u>New</u> <u>Mexico</u> <u>Women:</u>
<u>Intercultural</u> <u>Perspectives</u>. Albuquerque: University of New Mexico
Press, 1986.

Jones, Barbara A. P. The Economic Status of Black Women. <u>In</u> <u>The</u> <u>State</u> <u>of</u>
<u>Black</u> <u>America,</u> <u>1983</u>. New York: National Urban League, 1983.

Jones, Beverly W. Race, Sex, and Class: Black Female Tobacco Workers in
Durham, North Carolina, 1920-1940, and the Development of Female
Consciousness. <u>Feminist</u> <u>Studies</u> 10 (1984):441-51.

Jones, J. P., III. Work, Welfare, and Poverty among Black Female-Headed
Families. <u>Economic</u> <u>Geography</u> 63 (January 1987).

Jones, Jacqueline. <u>Labor</u> <u>of</u> <u>Love,</u> <u>Labor</u> <u>of</u> <u>Sorrow:</u> <u>Black</u> <u>Women,</u> <u>Work,</u>
<u>and</u> <u>the</u> <u>Family</u> <u>from</u> <u>Slavery</u> <u>to</u> <u>the</u> <u>Present</u>. New York: Basic Books,
1985.

Kawachi, Kazuko. Feminists of Color and their Diverse Participation in
the U.S. Women's Movement. <u>American</u> <u>Review</u> (Tokyo) 20 (1986):114-
40.

Kilson, M. Black Women in the Professions, 1890-1970. <u>Management</u> <u>Labor</u>
<u>Review</u> (May 1977):38-41.

Kim, Bok-Lim C. Asian Wives of U.S. Servicemen: Women in Shadows.
<u>Amerasia</u> <u>Journal</u> 4 (1977):91-115.

King, Lourdes M. Puertorriqueñas in the United States: The Impact of
Double Discrimination. <u>Civil</u> <u>Rights</u> <u>Digest</u> (September 1974):20-27.

Kulis, S. and others. Minorities and Women in the Pacific Sociological
Association Region: A Five-year Progress Report. <u>Sociological</u>
<u>Perspectives</u> 29 (1986):147-70.

Ladner, Joyce. Racism and Tradition: Black Womanhood in Historical
Perspectives. <u>In</u>: Berenice A. Carroll (ed.), <u>Liberating</u> <u>Women's</u>
<u>History:</u> <u>Theoretical</u> <u>and</u> <u>Critical</u> <u>Essays</u>. Urbana, IL: University
of Illinois Press, 1976.

Lanker, Brian. <u>I</u> <u>Dream</u> <u>a</u> <u>World:</u> <u>Portraits</u> <u>of</u> <u>Black</u> <u>Women</u> <u>Who</u> <u>Changed</u>

America. New York: Stewart, Tabori & Chang, 1989.

Lavender, Abraham D. Ethnic Women and Feminist Values: Toward a "New" Value System. University Press of America, 1986.

Lawson, Ellen N. and Marlene D. Merrill (eds.) The Three Sarahs: Documents of Black Antebellum College Women. New York: E. Mellen Press, 1984.

Lefkowitz, R. and A. Withorn. For Crying Out Loud: Women and Poverty in the United States. New York: Pilgrim, 1986.

Leashore, Bogart R. Black Female Workers: Live-in Domestics in Detroit, Michigan, 1860-1880. Phylon 45 (June 1984):111-20.

Lebsock, Suzanne. Free Black Women and the Question of Matriarchy: Petersburg, Virginia, 1784-1820. Feminist Studies 8 (Summer 1982).

Lewis, Shelby. The Meaning and Effect of the UN Decade for Women on Black Women in America. Women's Studies International Forum 8 (1985):117-20.

Loewenberg, Bert J. and Ruth Bogin (eds.) Black Women in Nineteenth-century American Life: Their Words, Their Thoughts and Their Feelings. Pennsylvania State University Press, 1976.

Longcope, Kay. Black Professional and Female. Boston Globe January 5, 1983.

Lopez, Iris. Social Coercion and Sterilization among Puerto Rican Women. Sage Race Relations Abstracts 8 (August 1983):27-40.

Lorde, Audre. Apartheid U.S.A. Latham, NY: Kitchen Table: Women of Color Press, 1988.

Lyles, Barbara D. The Black Woman: Person or Non-Person. Crisis (May 1975):163-66.

Lykes, M. Brinton. Discrimination and Coping in the Lives of Black Women. Journal of Social Issues 39 (1983):79-100.

Lynch, Robert N. Women in Northern Paiute Politics. Signs 11 (Winter 1986):352-66.

Majors, Monroe A. Noted Negro Women. New York: Arno, 1982 (orig. 1893).

Malveaux, Julianne. Current Economic Trends and Black Feminist Consciousness. Black Scholar 16 (March-April 1985):26-31.

Malveaux, Julianne. The Economic Interests of Black and White Women: Are They Similar? Review of Black Political Economy 18 (Summer 1985):5-27.

Malveaux, Julianne and Susan Englander. Race and Class in Nursing Occupations. Sage 3 (Spring 1986):41-45.

Mann, Susan A. Social Change and Sexual Inequality: The Impact of the
    Transition from Slavery to Sharecropping on Black Women. Memphis,
    TN: Center for Research on Women, Memphis State University, 1986.

Marable, June M. The Role of Women in Public School Administration as
    Perceived by Black Women Administrators in the Field [Ohio].
    Doctoral dissertation, Miami University, 1974. UMO # 75-14316.

Marable, Manning. Grounding with My Sisters: Patriarchy and the
    Exploitation of Black Women. In: How Capitalism Underdeveloped
    Black America, pp. 69-103. Boston: South End Press, 1983.

McCann, Carole R. Race, Class and Gender in U.S. Birth Control Politics,
    1920-1945. Doctoral dissertation, University of California, Santa
    Cruz, 1987. UMO # 8810866.

McCrate, Elaine. The Myth of 'Children Having Children.' Boston Globe
    October 12, 1986.

McCrate, Elaine. Trade, Merger and Employment: Economic Theory of
    Marriage. Review of Radical Political Economic 19 (1987):73-89.

McDougald, Elise J. The Double Task. The Struggle of Negro Women for Sex
    and Race Emancipation. Survey Graphic 6 (March 1925):689-91.

McGeary, Michael and Lawrence Lynn (eds.) Inner City Poverty in America.
    Washington, D.C.: National Academy Press, 1988.

Mirande, Alfredo and Evangelina Enriquez. La Chicana: The Mexican-
    American Woman. Chicago: University of Chicago Press, 1979.

Mirikitani, Janice (ed.) Third World Women. San Francisco, CA: Third
    World Communications Press, 1973.

Mora, Magdalena and Adelaida R. Del Castillo (eds.) Mexican Women in the
    United States. Struggles Past and Present. Los Angeles: Chicano
    Studies Research Center, University of California, 1980.

Moraga, Cherrie and Gloria Anzaldua (eds.) This Bridge Called My Back:
    Writings by Radical Women of Color. New York: Kitchen Table, Women
    of Color Press, 1983.

Moses, Yolanda T. Black American Women and Work: Historical and
    Contemporary Strategies for Empowerment. Women's Studies
    International Forum 8 (1985):351-9.

Mossell, N. F. (Mrs.). The Work of the Afro-American Woman. New York:
    Oxford University Press, 1988 reprint.

Murray, Pauli. The Liberation of Black Women. In Mary Lou Thompson
    (ed.), Voice of the New Feminism, pp. 88-102. Boston: Beacon Press,
    1970.

Myers, Lena Wright. Black Women, Do They Cope Better? Englewood Cliffs,

NJ: Prentice-Hall, 1980.

National Commission for Employment Policy. Increasing the Earnings of
    Disadvantaged Women. January 1981. ERIC ED 215 084.

Neverdon-Morton, Cynthia. Afro-American Women of the South and the
    Advancement of the Race, 1895-1925. Knoxville, TN: University of
    Tennessee Press, 1988.

Neverdon-Morton, Cynthia. The Black Woman's Struggle for Equality in the
    South, 1895-1925. In: Sharon Harley and Rosalyn Terborg-Penn
    (eds.), The Afro-American Woman: Struggles and Images, pp. 43-57.
    Port Washington, NY: Kennikat Press, 1978.

Newsome, Imani-Sheila. Work My Soul Must Have: A Three-Generational
    Study of Black Women in Ministry. Sage 3 (Spring 1986):50-52.

Nelson, Charmeynne D. Myths about Black Women Workers in Modern America.
    Black Scholar 6 (1975):11-15.

Niethammer, Carolyn. Daughters of the Earth: The Lives and Legends of
    American Indian Women. New York, 1977.

Nivens, Beatryce. Black Woman's Career Book. Garden City, NY: Anchor
    Press, 1982.

Nord, S. An Analysis of the Effects of Higher Education on Wage
    Differentials between Blacks and Whites by Gender in the United
    States. Applied Economics 18 (February 1986).

Oates, Mary Louise. Black Sororities: A Long History of Service and
    Loyalty. Los Angeles Times APril 11, 1981.

Parkhurst, Jessie W. The Role of the Black Mammy in the Plantation
    Household. Journal of Negro History 23 (July 1938):349-69.

Payton, Carolyn R. Addressing the Special Needs of Minority Women. New
    Directions for Student Services 29 (March 1985):75-90.

Perdue, Theda. Southern Indians and the Cult of True Womanhood. In:
    Walter J. Fraser, Jr. and others (eds.), The Web of Southern Social
    Relations: Women, Family, and Education. Athens, GA: University of
    Georgia Press, 1985.

Perdue, Theda. The Traditional Status of Cherokee Women. Furman Studies
    26 (December 1980):19-25.

Perkins, Carol O. Pragmatic Idealism: Industrial Training, Liberal
    Education and Women's Special Needs. Conflict and Continuity in the
    Experiences of Mary McLeod Bethune and Other Black Women Educators,
    1900-1930. Doctoral dissertation, Claremont Graduate School and San
    Diego State University, 1987. UMO # 8709295.

Pidgeon, Mary E. Women in the Economy of the United States of America: A
    Summary Report. Women's Bureau Report No. 155. Washington, D.C.:

GPO, 1937.

Pinderhughes, Elaine B. Minority Women: A Nodal Position in the Functioning of the Social System. Family Therapy Collections 16 (1986):51-63.

Plato, Ann. Essays. New York: Oxford University Press, 1988, orig. 1841.

Pleck, Elizabeth H. A Mother's Wages: Income Earning Among Married Italian and Black Women, 1896-1911. In: Nancy Cott and E. Pleck (eds.), A Heritage of Her Own. New York: Simon and Schuster, 1979.

Powers, Marla N. Oglala Women. Myth, Ritual, and Reality. Chicago: University of Chicago Press, 1986.

Press, Pat. Black Women, Alone [Middle-class Black women]. Washington Post March 18, 1984.

Ramos, Maria C. A Study of Black Women in Management. Doctoral dissertation, University of Massachusetts, 1981. UMO # 81218037.

Reich, Michael. Black-White Income Differences. In: Robert Cherry and others (eds.), The Imperiled Economy, Vol. 2. New York: Union for Radical Political Economics, 1988.

Reid, C. E. The Effect of Residential Location on the Wages of Black Women and White Women. Journal of Urban Economics. 18 (November 1985).

Rexroat, Cynthia A. Racial Differences in Wives' Labor Force Participation. Doctoral dissertation, University of Illinois, 1980. UMO # 8108635.

Richardson, Marilyn (ed.) Maria W. Stewart, America's First Black Woman Political Writer. Bloomington, IN: Indiana University Press, 1987.

Riley, Glenda. American Daughters: Black Women in the West. Montana 38 (Spring 1988):14-27.

Rollins, Judith. The Social Psychology of the Relationship between Black Female Domestic Servants and their White Female Employers. Doctoral dissertation, Brandeis University, 1983. UMO # 8318241.

Ryan, A. S. Asian-American Women: A Historical and Cultural Perspective. In: A. Wieck and S. T. Vandiver (eds.), Women, Power, and Change, pp. 78-88. Washington, D.C.: National Association of Social Workers, 1982.

Saavedra-Vela, Pilar. The Dark Side of Hispanic Women's Education. Agenda (May-June 1978).

Safa, Helen I. Female Employment and the Social Reproduction of the Puerto Rican Working Class. International Migration Review 18 (Winter 1984):1168-87.

Safilios-Rothschild, Constantine. The Case of Black Women: Race and Sex
    Discrimination. In: Sex Role Socialization and Sex Discrimination:
    A Synthesis and Critique of the Literature, pp. 91-93. Washington,
    D.C.: National Institute of Education, October 1979.

Saiki, Patsy S. Japanese Women in Hawaii: The First 100 Years. 1985.
    920 Prospect St., Honolulu, HI 96822.

Sanchez Korrol, Virginia E. Survival of Puerto Rican Women in New York
    before World War II. In: Clara E. Rodriguez and others (eds.), The
    Puerto Rican Struggle, pp. 47-57. New York: Puerto Rican Migration
    Research Consortium, 1980.

Sandefur, G. D. and A. Sakamoto. American Indian Household Structure and
    Income. Demography 25 (February 1988).

Sanders, J. Staying Poor: How the Job Training Partnership Act Fails
    Women. Metuchen, NJ: Scarecrow Press, 1988.

Santana Cooney, Rosemary and Alice Colon. Work and Family: The Recent
    Struggle of Puerto Rican Females. In: Clara E. Rodriguez and others
    (eds.), The Puerto Rican Struggle, pp. 58-73. New York: Puerto
    Migration Research Consortium.

Sawhill, Isabel V. Poverty in the U.S.: Why Is It So Persistent?
    Journal of Economic Literature 26 (September 1988):1073-1119.

Scott, Patricia Bell. Schoolin' 'Respectable' Ladies of Color: Issues in
    the History of Black Women's Higher Educaiton. Journal of the NAWDAC
    43 (Winter 1980):22-28.

Seder, Jean. Voices of Another Time: Three Memories [Three Black
    southern women]. Philadelphia, PA: Institute for the Study of
    Human Issues, 1985.

Segura, Denise. Labor Market Stratification and Chicanos. Berkeley
    Journal of Sociology 29 (1984).

Seller, Maxine. The Education of the Immigrant Woman, 1900-1935. Journal
    of Urban History 4 (May 1978):307-30.

Sellers, Valita. As Black Women Rise in Professional Ranks Marriage Gets
    Chancy. Wall Street Journal May 16, 1986.

Shammas, Carole. Black Women's Work and the Evolution of Plantation
    Society in Virginia. Labor History 26 (Winter 1985):5-28.

Shebala, Marley. Progress Made for Navajo Women. Navajo Times January
    5, 1984.

Sheparson, Mary. The Status of Navajo Women. American Indian Quarterly
    6 (Spring 1982):149-69.

Shepherd, Gloria. The Rape of Black Women During Slavery. Doctoral dissertation, State University of New York at Albany, 1988. UMO # 8805389.

Shortlidge, Richard L. The Hypothetical Labor Market Response of Black and White Women to a National Program of Free Day Care Centers. Columbus, OH: Center for Human Resources Research, Ohio State University, August 1977.

Sidel, Ruth. Women and Children Last: The Plight of Poor Women in Affluent America. New York: Viking, 1986.

Simms, Margaret C. and Julianne Malveaux (eds.) Slipping through the Cracks: The Status of Black Women. New Brunswick, NJ: Transaction Books, 1986.

Sims, Naomi. All About Success for the Black Woman. Garden City, NY: Doubleday, 1982.

Slaughter, Diana and Carol Walcer. Expressed Values of Lower Socioeconomic Status Black American Women. June 1980. ERIC ED 197 853.

Smith, A. and A. Stewart. Approaches to Studying Racism and Sexism in Black Woman's Lives. Journal of Social Issues 39 (July 1983):1-15.

Smith, Carol. A Study of Images of Black Women, a Content Analysis of Black Women in Ebony Magazine, 1965 through 1977. Master's thesis, Purdue University, 1978.

Smith, Eleanor. Black American Women and Work: A Historical Review - 1619-1920. Women's Studies International Forum 8 (1985):343-50.

Smith, Elsie J. The Career Development of Young Black Females: The Forgotten Group. Youth and Society 12 (March 1981):277-312.

Special Issue on Black Women. Black Collegian 11 (April-May 1981):entire issue.

Solow, Katherine with Gary Walker. The Job Training Partnership Act Service to Women. 1986. Grinker, Walker and Associates, 130 W. 42nd St., New York, NY 10036.

Stack, Carol B. The Culture of Gender: Women and Men of Color. Signs 11 (Winter 1986):321-24.

Stepanek, Michael. The Liberated Woman in the Oneida Community: 1840- 1872. Educational Perspectives 16 (March 1977):22-26.

Stephens, Lenora C. Black Women in Film. Southern Quarterly 19 (Spring- Summer 1981):164-170.

Sterling, Dorothy (ed.) We Are Your Sisters: Black Women in the 19th Century. New York: Norton, 1984.

Stetson, Erlene. Black Feminism in Indiana, 1893-1933. Phylon 44

(December 1983):292-98.

Stevans, L. K. and others. Race and the Discouraged Female Worker: A
    Question of Labor Force Attachment. Review of Black Political
    Economy 14 (Summer 1985).

Stewart, Irene. A Voice in Her Tribe: A Navajo Woman's Own Story.
    Edited by David D. Dowdy. Socorro, NM: Bellera Press, 1980.

Sway, Basma K. Palestinian Women in the U.S.: Reality and Constraints.
    Master's thesis, Iowa State University, 1986.

Taylor, Patricia A. and others. Changes in the Structure of Earnings
    Inequality by Race, Sex and Industrial Sector, 1960-1980. Research
    in Social Stratification and Mobility 5 (1986):105-38.

Terrell, Mary Church. The Duty of the National Association of Colored
    Women to the Race. New York Age January 4, 1900.

Terrell, Mary Church. First Leader Recalls Early Days of Colored Women's
    Group. Washington Star July 28, 1946.

Tienda, M. and J. Glass. Household Structure and Labor Force Participation
    of Black, Hispanic, and White Mothers. Demography 22 (August 1985).

Tilly, Chris. Regenerating Inequality: The Distribution of U.S Family
    Income and Individual Earnings in the 1980s. In: Robert Cherry and
    others (eds.), The Imperiled Economy, Vol. 2. New York: Union for
    Radical Political Economics, 1988.

Tobin, McLean. The Black Female Ph.D.: Education and Career Development.
    Washington, D.C.: University Press of America, 1980.

Trennert, Robert S. Indian Women and the Non-reservation Boarding
    Schools, 1879-1934. Tucson: Southwest Institute for Research on
    Women, University of Arizona, 1980.

Tyson, Roberta S. A Descriptive Study of Factors Influencing the
    Professional Mobility of Black Female Administrators in Public
    Education in Louisiana between 1952 and 1978. Doctoral dissertation,
    George Peabody College for Teachers, 1980. UMO # 8105451.

Underhill, Ruth M. The Autobiography of a Papago Woman [Maria Chona].
    American Anthropological Association Memoirs 31 (1936).

U.S. Bureau of the Census. Families Maintained by Female Householders
    1970-1979. Washington, D.C.: GPO, 1980.

U.S. Commission on Civil Rights. Child Care and Equal Opportunity for
    Women. Washington, D.C.: The Commission, June 1981.

U.S. Commission on Civil Rights. A Growing Crisis, Disadvantaged Women
    and their Children. Washington, D.C.: The Commission, May 1983.

U.S. Commission on Civil Rights. Social Indicators of Equality for

Minorities and _Women_. Washington, D.C.:   GPO, 1978.

U.S. Women's Bureau. _Employment_ and _Economic_ Issues of _Low-Income_ Women.
Washington, D.C.: Women's Bureau, 1978.

Van Steen, Marcus. _Pauline Johnson._ Her _Life_ and _Work_ [Mohawk poet].
Toronto: Hodder and Stoughton, 1965.

Vaughn, Doris C. Stress and the American Black Woman: Analysis of
Research. _International_ _Journal_ _for_ _the_ _Advancement_ _of_ _Counselling_
9 (1986):341-50.

Vazquez Nuttall, Ena. The Support System and Coping Patterns of the
Female Puerto Rican Single Parent. _Journal_ _of_ _Non-White_ _Concerns_   7
(April 1979):128-37.

Wald, Karen. A Revolutionary Exile's Life Story [Assata Shakur (formerly
Joanne Chesimard), one-time activist in Black Panther Party].
Guardian February 10, 1988.

Wallace, Michele. Homelessness Is Where the Heart Is.   _Zeta_ _Magazine_   1
(July-August 1988):59-63.

Walton, Hanes, Jr. _Black_ _Women_ at _the_ _United_ States: The Politics, a
Theoretical _Model,_ and _the_ _Documents_ [Afro-American women
diplomats]. San Bernadino, CA: Borgo Press, 1987.

Washington, Mary A. Anna Julia Cooper: The Black Feminist Voice of the
1890s. _Legacy_ 4 (Fall 1987):3-15.

Washington, Mary Helen. _Inverted_ _Lives._ _Narratives_ _of_ _Black_ _Women_ _1860-_
_1960_. Garden City, NY: Ancho-Doubleday, 1987.

Weiner, Marli F. _Plantation_ _Mistresses_ and _Female_ _Slaves:_ Gender, Race,
and _South_ _Carolina_ _Women,_ _1830-1880_. Doctoral dissertation,
University of Rochester, 1986.   UMO # 8610879.

West, Guida. The _National_ _Welfare_ _Rights_ _Movement:_ The _Social_ _Protest_ _of_
Poor _Women_. New York: Praeger, 1981.

White, Deborah Gray. _Aren't_ _I_ _a_ _Woman?_ Female Slaves in _the_ _Plantation_
South. New York: Norton, 1985.

White, Deborah Gray. Female Slaves: Sex Roles and Status in the
Antebellum Plantation South. _Journal_ _of_ _Family_ _History_ 8 (Fall
1983):248-61.

White, Gloria M. Mary Church Terrell: Organizer of Black Women.
Integrateducation 17 (September-December 1979):2-8.

White Supremacy within the Women's Movement. _In:_ _Women's_ _Liberation_ _and_
Imperialism. San Francisco, CA: Prairie Fire Organizing Committee,
November 1977.

Wilkie, Jane R. _The_ _Decline_ _in_ _Occupational_ _Segregation_ _Between_ _Black_ _and_

White Women. September 6, 1982. ERIC ED 223 767.

Wilkinson, Doris Y. Afro-American Women and their Families. Marriage and Family Review 7 (1984):125-42.

Williams, Susan M. and Jenice L. View. The Economic Status of American Indian Women: A Navajo Study. The Brown Papers: A Publication of the National Institute of Women of Color 2 (January 1984).

Woo, Deborah. The Socioeconomic Status of Asian American Women in the Labor Force. Sociological Perspectives 28 (July 1985):307-38.

Woo, Merle. Our Common Cause: Freedom Organizing in the Eighties. Latham, NY: Kitchen Table: Women of Color Press, 1988.

Woodson, Carter G. The Negro Washerwoman: A Vanishing Figure. Journal of Negro History 15 (July 1930).

Woody, Bette and Michelene Malson. In Crisis: Low Income Black Women in the U.S. Workplace. 1984. ERIC ED 248 316.

Wright, Mary. Economic Development and Native American Women in the Early 19th Century. American Indian Quarterly 33 (1981):525-36.

Yamanaka, Keiko. Labor Force Participation of Asian American Women: Ethnicity, Work, and the Family. Doctoral dissertation, Cornell University, 1987. UMO # 8725833.

Yancy, Dorothy C. Dorothy Bolden Organizer of Domestic Workers: She Was Born Poor but She Would Not Bow Down. Sage 3 (Spring 1986):53-55. [1920-   ].

Young, Mary E. Women, Civilization, and the Indian Question. In: Mabel E. Deutrich and Virginia C. Purdy (eds.), Clio Was a Woman: Studies in the History of American Women, pp. 98-110. Washington, D.C.: Howard University Press, 1980.

Yu, Eui-Young and Earl H. Phillips (eds.) Korean Women in Transition: At Home and Abroad. Los Angeles: Center for Korean-American and Korean Studies, California State University, 1987.

Yung, Judy. Chinese Women of America: A Pictorial History. Seattle: University of Washington Press, 1986.

Zavwella, Patricia. Women's Work and Chicano Families: Cannery Workers of the Santa Clara Valley. Ithaca, NY: Cornell University Press, 1987.

Zinn, Maxine B. and others. The Costs of Exclusionary Practices in Women's Studies. Signs 11 (Winter 1986):290-303.

Annotated Bibliography. Asian Women pp. 131-43. Berkeley, CA: University of California, Asian-American Studies Center, 1971.

Bataille, Gretchen (comp.) Bibliography on Native Women. Concerns: The Newsletter of the Modern Language Association's Women's Caucus (1980):16-27.

Cabello-Argandona, Roberto and others (comps.) The Chicana: A Comprehensive Bibliography Study. Los Angeles, CA: Aztlan Publications, 1976.

Cole, Johnnetta B. (comp.) Black Women in America: An Annotated Bibliography. Black Scholar 3 (December 1971):41-53.

Davis, Lenwood G. (comp.) The Black Woman in American Society: A Selected Annotated Bibliography. Boston: G.K. Hall, 1975.

Davis, Lenwood G. (comp.) Black Women in the Cities, 1872-1972: A Bibliography of Published Works on the Life and Achievements of Black Women in the Cities of the U.S. (second edition). [Exchange Bibliographies Nos. 751/752.] Monticello, IL: Council of Planning Librarians, 1975.

Erhart, Julie K. and Elizabeth Johnson (comps.) Minority Women's Organizations and Programs: A Partial Annotated List. Washington, D.C.: Project on the Status and Education of Women, Association of American Colleges, 1984.

Gonsalves, Sandra V (comp.) Bibliography on Fear of Success in Black Women: 1970-1982. Psychological Reports 53 (1983):1249-50.

Green, Rayna (comp.) Native American Women: A Contextual Bibliography. Bloomington: Indiana University Press, 1983.

Jackson, Jacqueline J. (comp.) A Partial Bibliography on or Related to Black Women. Journal of Social and Behavioral Science 21 (Winter 1975):90-135.

Klotman, Phyllis R. and Wilmer H. Baatz (comps.) The Black Family and the Black Woman: A Bibliography. New York: Arno, 1978.

Koehler, Lyle (comp.) Native Women of the Americas: A Bibliography. Frontiers 6 (Fall 1981):73-101.

Miyano, Yumiko and Sumi Nakazawa (comps.) Bibliography on Japanese Women in American and Japan. Berkeley, CA: Japan Pacific Resource Network, 1988.

Native American Women. A Selected Bibliography. The Newsletter [of the Center for Research on Women, Memphis State University]. 6 (Fall 1987):7.

Oshana, Maryann. Women of Color: A Filmography of Minority and Third World Women. New York: Garland, 1985.

Portillo, Cristina and others (comps.) Bibliography of Writings on La Mujer. Berkeley, CA: University of California, Chicano Studies Library, December 1976.

Selected Bibliography of Social Science Readings on Women of Color in the United States. Rev. ed. Memphis: Center for Research on Women, Memphis State University, February 1988.

Sims, Janet (comp.) Black Women in the Employment Sector. Public Administration Series No. 243. Monticello, IL: Vance Bibliographies, 1979.

Sims, Janet (comp.) The Progress of Afro-American Women: A Selected Bibliography and Resource Guide. Westport, CT: Greenwood Press, 1980.

Stevenson, Rosemary M. (comp.) Black Women in the United States of America: A Bibliographical Essay. Sage Race Relations Abstracts 8 (November 1983):1-19.

Stone, Pauline C. T. and Cheryl L. Brown (comps.) The Black American Woman in the Social Science Literature. Ann Arbor, MI: University of Michigan, Women's Studies Program, 1978.

Terborg-Penn, Roslyn M. (comp.) The Historical Treatment of Afro-Americans in the Women's Suffrage Movement, 1900-1920: A Bibliographical Essay. Current Bibliography on African Affairs 7 (Summer 1974):245-59.

Williams, Ora (comp.) American Black Women in the Arts and Social Sciences: A Bibliographical Survey. Rev. ed. Metuchen, NJ: Scarecrow Press, 1978.

Yellin, Jean Fagan (comp.) Afro-American Women, 1800-1910: Excerpts from a Working Bibliography. In: Gloria T. Hill and others (eds.), All the Women Are White. All the Blacks Are Men. But Some of Us Are Brave. Black Women's Studies, pp. 221-44. Old Westbury, NY: Feminist Press, 1982.

86. General

... If this is a Great Society, I'd hate to see a bad one.

- Fannie Lou Hamer, The Worker, July 13, 1975.

Allen, Ernest. The Cultural Methodology of Harold Cruse. Journal of Ethnic Studies 5 (1977):26-50.

Allen, James P. and Eugene J. Turner. We the People. An Atlas of America's Ethnic Diversity. New York: MacMillan, 1987.

Anderson, Glenn B. and Frank G. Bowe. Racism Within the Deaf Community. American Annals of the Deaf 117 (December 1972):617-619.

Baxter, Paul and Basil Sansom (eds.) Race and Social Difference. Selected Readings. Baltimore, MD: Penguin, 1972.

Besag, Frank P. Social Darwinism, Race, and Research. Educational Evaluation and Policy Analysis 3 (January-February 1981):55-59.

Biddiss, Michael D. Fascism and the Race Question: A Review of Recent Historiography. Race January 1969.

Black Racism Project. Critique of the Black Nation Thesis, 1975. P.O. Box 3026, South Berkeley Station, Berkeley, CA 94703.

Black Revolution and White Backlash. National Guardian July, 1964. [Verbatim transcript of forum; participants included Lorraine Hansberry, David Suskind, Paule Marshall, Leroi Jones, Ossie Davis, Ruby Dee, Charles E. Silberman, John Killens, and James Wechsler.]

Blauner, Bob. Black Lives, White Lives. Three Decades of Race Relations in America. Berkeley, CA: University of California Press, 1988.

Boas, Franz. Problem of the American Negro. Yale Review 10 (1921):384-95.

Browne, Robert S. The Economic Case for Reparations to Black America. American Economic Review 62 (May 1972):39-46.

Cabbell, Edward J. Black Invisibility and Racism in Appalachia: An Informal Survey. In: William H. Turner and Edward J. Cabbell (eds.), Blacks in Appalachia. Lexington, KY: University of Kentucky Press, 1985.

Campbell, Ernest L. (ed.) Racial Tensions and National Identity. Nashville, TN: Vanderbilt University Press, 1972.

Carnoy, Martin. Education as Cultural Imperialism. New York: David McKay, 1974.

Childs, John Brown. Leadership, Conflict and Cooperation in Afro-American

Childs, John Brown. Leadership, Conflict and Cooperation in Afro-American Social Thought. Philadelphia, PA: Temple University Press, 1989.

Dewart, Janet (ed.) The State of Black America 1987. New York: National Urban League, 1987.

Dewey, John. Racial Prejudice and Friction. Chinese Social and Political Science Review 6 (1921):1-17.

Dickeman, Mildred. Thoughts on the Dominant American. Massachusetts Review 15 (Summer 1974):405-418.

Dorn, Edwin. Rules and Racial Equality. New Haven, CT: Yale University Press, 1979.

Du Bois, W. E. B. and Guy B. Johnson. Encyclopedia of the Negro. Prepartory Volume with Reference Lists and Reports. New York: Phelp-Stokes Fund, 1945.

Dunbar, Leslie W. Minority Report: What Has Happened to Black, Hispanics, American Indians, and Other American Minorities in the Eighties. New York: Pantheon, 1984.

Eckhardt, A. Roy. Black-Woman-Jew. Three Wars for Human Liberation. Bloomington, IN: Indiana University Press, 1989.

Ehrlich, Howard J. Some Criteria for Radical Social Research. Research Group One, 2743 Maryland Ave., Baltimore, MD 21218.

Frazier, E. Franklin. The New Negro. Nation July 7, 1956.

Gobetz, Giles Edward. 'Race' Differences in Attitudes and Ability Among the Geriatric Blind. Journal of Negro Education 41 (Winter 1972):57-61.

Hacker, Andrew. American Apartheid. New York Review of Books December 3, 1987.

Heiligman, Avron C. Racism in United States: Drug Legislation and the Trade-Off Behind It. Drug Forum: The Journal of Human Issues 7 (1978-1979):19-25.

Horne, Frank. I Am Initiated into the Negro Race. Opportunity 6 (1928):137-38.

Jackson, Derrick Z. Please Don't Call Me Black [Prefers "African American"]. Boston Globe January 15, 1989.

Johnson, Charles S. To Stem This Tide: A Survey of Racial Tension Areas in the United States. Boston, MA: Pilgrim Press, 1943.

Johnson, James Weldon. Negro Americans, What Now? New York: Viking, 1934.

The Kerner Report: The 1968 Report of the National Advisory Commission on

Civil Disorders. New York: Pantheon Books, 1988.

King, Anita (ed.) *Quotations in Black*. Westport, CT: Greenwood, 1981.

Kurokawa, Minako (ed.) *Minority Responses: Comparative Views of Reactions to Subordination*. New York: Random House, 1970.

La Vega, M. I. de. *El racismo en los Estados Unidos - una vision latin-americana del problema*. Bogota: Ediciones Centro de Estudios Colombianos, 1970.

Lapides, L. R. and D. Burrows. *Racism: A Casebook*. 1971.

Leavy, Walter. What's Behind the Resurgence of Racism in America? *Ebony* (April 1987):132-133, 136.

Lewis, Michael. *The Culture of Inequality*. Amherst, MA: University of Massachusetts Press, 1978.

Low, W. Augustus and Virgil A. Clift (eds.) *Encyclopedia of Black America*. New York: McGraw Hill, 1981.

Manicas, Peter T. The Foreclosure of Democracy in America. *Hist. Pol. Thought* 9 (Spring 1988):137-60.

Martinez, William. A Mexican American Talks about White Supremacy. *Bulletin for Interracial Books for Children* (Spring 1970).

Myrdal, Gunnar. *An American Dilemma: The Negro Problem in Modern Democracy* New York: Harper and Row, 1944.

National Institute of Mental Health (comp.) *Bibliography on Racism* Washington, D.C.: U.S. Department of Health, Education, and Welfare, n.d.

Oaks, Priscilla (comp.) *Minority Studies: A Selective Annotated Bibliography*. Boston: Hall, 1975.

O'Hare, William P. Black Demographic Trends in the 1980s. *Millbank Quarterly* 65 (1987):35-55, supplement 1.

Olsen, Edward G. What Shall We Teach About Race and Racism? *Kansas Teacher* December 1968.

Patterson, William L. (ed.) *We Charge Genocide*. New York: International Publishers, 1970.

Perkins, Joseph (ed.) *A Conservative Agenda for Black Americans*. Washington, D.C.: Heritage Foundation, 1987.

Perry, Ronald W. and Alvin H. Mushkatel. *Minority Citizens in Disasters*. Athens, GA: University of Georgia Press, 1986.

Pettigrew, Thomas F. Modern Racial Prejudice in America: Social Psychological Dimensions and Political Modelling. *Patterns of*

<u>Prejudice</u>   22 (Winter 1988):3-12.

Pettigrew, Thomas F. New Black-White Patterns: How to Best Conceptualize
    Them? <u>Annual</u> <u>Review</u> <u>of</u> <u>Sociology</u> 11 (1985):329-46.

Pickens, William. The Negro Problem in America. <u>Review</u> <u>of</u> <u>Nations</u> 1
    (1927):147-53.

Rosenfelt, Deborah S. (ed.) <u>Cross-Cultural</u> <u>Perspectives</u> <u>in</u> <u>the</u>
    <u>Curriculum.</u> <u>Resources</u> <u>for</u> <u>Change</u>. 1982. Office of the Chancellor,
    California State Unviersity, Academic Program Improvement, 400 Golden
    Shores Drive, Long Beach, CA 90802. [Principally a valuable
    comprehensive bibliography].

Shirdan, Althris W. <u>"Wasn't</u> <u>Born</u> <u>Yesterday,</u> <u>Didn't</u> <u>Get</u> <u>Here</u> <u>Last</u> <u>Night"</u>
    <u>(An</u> <u>Exploratory</u> <u>Study</u> <u>of</u> <u>Black</u> <u>Working</u> <u>Class</u> <u>Men)</u>. Doctoral
    dissertation, Bryn Mawr College, 1988. UMO # 8819186.

Sivanandan, Ambelavenar. Culture and Identity. <u>Liberator</u> June, 1970.

Sowell, Thomas. <u>Ethnic</u> <u>America:</u> <u>A</u> <u>History</u>. New York: Basic, 1981.

Sowell, Thomas and Lynn D. Collins (eds.) <u>American</u> <u>Ethnic</u> <u>Groups</u>.
    Washington, D.C.: Urban Institute, 1978.

Stanfield, John H. The Cracked Back Door: Foundations and Black Social
    Scientists between the World War. <u>American</u> <u>Sociologist</u> 17 (November
    1982):193-204.

Stanfield, John H. Northern Money and Southern Bogus Elitism:
    Rockefeller Foundation and the Commission on Interracial Cooperation
    Movement, 1919-1929. <u>Journal</u> <u>of</u> <u>Ethnic</u> <u>Studies</u> 15 (Summer 1987):1-
    22.

Stevenson, Rosemary M. <u>Index</u> <u>to</u> <u>Afro-American</u> <u>Reference</u> <u>Resources</u>.
    Westport, CT: Greenwood, 1988.

Strickland, William. The Road Since <u>Brown</u>: The Americanization of the
    Race. <u>Black</u> <u>Scholar</u> 11 (1979).

Szwed, John F. Race and the Embodiment of Culture. <u>Ethnicity</u> 2
    (1975):19-33.

Tabb, William K. Race Relations Models and Social Change. <u>Social</u>
    <u>Problems</u> 18 (Spring 1971):431-444.

Turner, Lou. Black Thought and Black Reality: A Critical Essay. <u>Ufahamu</u>
    10 (Spring 1981):101-13.

U.S. Native Hawaiians Study Commission. <u>Native</u> <u>Hawaiians</u> <u>Study</u>
    <u>Commission:</u> <u>Report</u> <u>on</u> <u>the</u> <u>Culture,</u> <u>Needs,</u> <u>and</u> <u>Concerns</u> <u>of</u> <u>Native</u>
    <u>Hawaiians</u>. [2 vols.] Washington, D.C.: U.S. Department of the
    Interior, 1983.

Welsing, Frances L. On 'Black Genetic Inferiority.' <u>Ebony</u> 29 (July

1974):104-105.

White, Barbara W. (ed.) Color in a White Society. Silver Springs, MD:
National Association of Social Workers, 1984.

Wilhelm, Sidney H. Can Marxism Explain America's Racism? Social Problems
28 (December 1980):98-112.

Wilhelm, Sidney H. Equality: America's Racist Ideology. In: J. David
Colfax and Jack L. Roach (eds.), Radical Sociology, pp. 246-262. New
York: Basic Books, 1971.

Williams, Janice B. A Perspective of Racism. Doctoral dissertation,
Rutgers University, 1980. UMO # 8105063.

Wright, David. The Geography of Race [Analysis of racism in two
textbooks on human geography]. Times Educational Supplement July
15, 1983.

Wright, Gerald C. Racism and Social Welfare Policy in America. Social
Science Quarterly 57 (March 1977):718-730.

87. Bibliographies, General

[Monroe N.] Work labored hardest at providing other scholars with
the tools for waging battle against erroneous stereotypes and
unjustified discrimination. He considered his greatest
contribution to be his bibliography [Bibliography of the Negro in
Africa and America, 1928] ...
> — Linda O. McMurry, Recorder of the
> Black Experience. A Biography of Monroe Nathan Work, p. 145.

Analytical Guide and Indexes to 'The Crisis': A Record of the Darker Races
  1910-1960 [3 vols.]. Westport, CT: Greenwood, 1975.

Cabbell, Edward J. (comp.) Like a Weaving: References and Resources on
  Black Appalachians. Black Diamonds 7 (1984):1-69.

DuBois, W.E.B. (comp.) A Select Bibliography of the Negro American.
  Atlanta: Atlanta University Press, 1905.

Gubert, Betty K. (comp.) Early Black Bibliographies, 1863-1918. New York:
  Garland, 1982.

Haddad, Yvonne Y. (comp.) Muslims in America: A Select Bibliography.
  Muslim World 76 (April 1986):93-122.

Kittelson, David J. (comp.) The Hawaiians: An Annotated Bibliography.
  Honolulu: Social Science Research Institute, University of Hawaii,
  1985.

McPherson, James M. and others (comps.) Blacks in America: Bibliographic
  Essays. Garden City, NJ: Doubleday, 1971.

Miller, Elizabeth W. (comp.) The Negro in America: A Bibliography.
  Cambridge, MA: Harvard University Press, 1966.

Miller, Wayne and others (comp.) A Comprehensive Bibliography for the Study
  of American Minorities [2 vols.]. New York: New York University
  Press, 1976.

Momeni, Jamshid A. (comp.) Demography of the Black Population in the United
  States: An Annotated Bibliography with a Review Essay. Westport, CT:
  Greenwood, 1983.

Newman, Richard (comp.) Black Access: A Bibliography of Afro-American
  Bibliographies. Westport, CT: Greenwood, 1984.

Newman, Richard (comp.) Black Index: Afro-American in Selected Periodicals,
  1907-1949. New York: Garland, 1981.

Sanford, Marvin (comp.) A Bibliography on the Revolutionary Approach to the Negro Question in America. Mena, AR: Commonwealth College Library, 1937.

Stevenson, Rosemary M. (comp.) Index to Afro-American Reference Resources. Westport, CT: Greenwood, 1988.

Thompson, Edgar T. and A. M. Thompson (comps.) Race and Region: A Descriptive Bibliography Compiled with Special Reference to the Relations between Whites and Negroes in the US. Chapel Hill, NC: University of North Carolina Press, 1949.

U.S. Information Agency. Afro-American Life, History and Culture. Washington, D.C.: Collections Development Branch, 1985.

Wade, Jacqueline (comp.) American Racism Bibliography. Philadelphia, PA: School of Social Work, University of Pennsylvania, 1981.

Westmoreland, Guy T., Jr. (comp.) An Annotated Guide to Basic Reference Books on the Black American Experience. Wilmington, DE: Scholarly Resources, 1974.

Work, Monroe N. (comp.) A Bibliography of the Negro in Africa and America. New York: H. W. Wilson, 1928.

Index

Alcock, D. G., 252
Aldrich, M., 153, 490
Aldridge, D., 593
Aleander, R. P. 86
Alegado, D. T., 304, 325
Alers, J. O., 234
Alexander, A., 180
Alexander, B., 392
Alexander, C. C., 318
Alexander, G. W., 509
Alexander, M., 53
Alexander, P. 495
Alexander, R., 60
Alexander, R. J., 53
Alexander, Roberta S., 400
Alexander, V. M., 237
Alford, T., 404
Algarin, Miguel, 373
Alho, O., 509
Ali, M., 30
Aljeaid, M. O., 541
Alkimat, A., 450
Allen, B. P., 486
Allen, E., Jr., 252, 325, 612
Allen, G. E., 299
Allen, I. L., 112, 350
Allen, J. A. V., 280
Allen, J. E., 234
Allen, J. P., 612
Allen, J. S., 133
Allen, M. B., 355
Allen, P. G., 593
Allen, R. A., 593
Allen, R. L., 153, 252, 495
Allen, Rosemary, 157
Allen, S., 482
Allen, T., 252
Allen, T. H., Jr., 180
Allen, W. G., 467
Allen, W. L., 180
Allen, Walter R., 142, 211, 217
Allen, William B., 24
Allen, Zita, 304
Alley-Claiborne, J. G., 494
Allison, K., 180
Allsup, Carl, 86, 157
Almaguer, T., 91, 444
Alman, E., 180
Almeida [Engram], E. de, 593
Almirol, E. B. 304
Almquist, E. M., 520, 593
Alne, Denise J., 559
Alston, Jacqelyn G., 433
Alter, J., 404
Altman, S., 295

Altschuler, G. C., 75
Alurista, 373
Alvarez, D., 511
Alvarez, R., 119, 252
Alvarez Gonzalez, J. J., 67
Alves, M. J., 112
Alvirez, David, 128, 137
Aly, J., 102
Amann, P. H., 503, 573
America, R., 585
van Amersfoort, J. M. M., 480
Amin, K., 385
Amin, R., 280
Amott, T., 1
Andersen, J. C., 149
Anderson, A. B., 67
Anderson, B. E., 137, 313, 569
Anderson, C. E., 420
Anderson, C. W., Jr., 355
Anderson, E., 252
Anderson, E. L., 589
Anderson, G. B., 612
Anderson, J. D., 157, 252, 260
Anderson, Jervis, 30
Anderson, K., 482
Anderson, M., 181, 593
Anderson, R., 234
Anderson, R. V., 524
Anderson, Ruth B., 30
Anderson, S., 252
Anderson, S. E., 75, 181
Ando, F. H., 53
Andres, B., 181
Andrew, M. G., 325
Angelou, Maya, 30
Anstey, R. T., 524
Anthony, A. A., 253
Anthony, C., 313
Anthony, Clara B., 295
Anthony, E., 181
Anzaldua, G., 602
Aoki, E., 181
Aoyagi, K., 211
Apodoca, M. L., 593
Apostle, R. A., 463
Appel, John, 16, 541
Appel, Selma, 16, 541
Applebone, P., 234, 355, 450
Applegate, J. R., 181
Applegate, R., 573
Aptheker, B., 593
Aptheker, Herbert, 13, 133, 135,
   136, 181, 253, 433, 471, 506
Aquino, Belinda A., 594
Arata, Esther S., 387

620

623

627

Carlisle, D. K., 420
Carlisle, R., 54
Carlisle, R. P., 433
Carlquist-Hernandez, K., 184
Carlson, Leonard A., 139
Carlson, N., 189
Carlson, Shirley J. M., 255
Carlton, R. L., 390
Carmack, R. M., 474
Carmichael, Stokely, 68
Carmines, E. G., 299
Carmody, Deirdre, 159
Carnegie, M. E., 437
Carnoy, M., 612
Caro, M., 420
Caron, N. P., 184
Carpenter, J., 159
Carpenter, J. A., 574
Carpenter, J. N., 185
Carper, N. G., 218
Carr, E. W., 159
Carrasquilla, A. L., 305
Carrion, J. M., 76, 433
Carroll, Diahann, 32
Carroll, J. M., 421
Carrott, M. B., 357
Carruthers, I. E. J. W., 496
Carson, Clayborne S., Jr., 47, 68, 105
Carson, E. D., 76, 86
Carter, Dan T., 255, 357
Carter, E., II, 65
Carter, G. F., 467
Carter, G. L., 230
Carter, L. H., 185
Carter, M., 189
Carter, Robert L., 160, 357
Carter, S. L., 357
Carter, T. P., 120, 160
Carter, Thyra, 256
Cartwright, J. H., 256
Cartwright, W. J., 299
Casas, J. M., 542
Casey, J., 185
Casey, J. A., 113
Cash, F. L. B., 595
Cash, R., 437
Cashmore, E. E., 467, 474
Casper G., 363
Casserly, M. D., 160
Cassity, M. J., 256
Casso, H., 185
Castro, A., 185
Castro, M., 374
Castro, R., 496

Casuso, J., 291
Cataldo, E., 114
Cattan, P., 327
Caudill, H. M., 256
Causey, Virginia, 256
Cauthern, N. R., 542
Cavalli-Sforza, L. L., 299
Cavanagh, T. E., 452
Cavanaugh, G. F., 316
Cawthon, R., 185
Cayton, H. R., 32, 185, 327
Cecil-Fronsman, B., 589
Cerroni-Long, E. L., 490
Cervantes, F. A., 447
Chachere, B., 490
Chacon, R., 327
Chadbourn, J. H., 574
Chafe, W. H., 400
Chaliard, G., 474
Chalk, O., 24
Chalmers, D. M., 318
Cham, M. B., 405
Chamberlain, M. K., 185
Chambers, B., 375
Chambers, E. W., 68
Chambers, F., 207
Chametzky, J., 375
Chan, A., 482
Chan, J., 375
Chan, J. P., 542
Chan, R. K., 542
Chanbers, Kimberly, 388
Chandler, C. R., 86
Chandler, Robert J., 68
Chandler, T., 185
Chandrasekhar, S., 305
Chaney, E. M., 311
Chang, E., 452
Chang, H., 76
Chang, W. B. C., 76
Chapman, A. E., 230
Chapman, Dorothy, 387
Chapman, G. D., 471
Chapman, P. D., 300
Chapman, T. H., 520
Char, T-y., 357
Charles, C., 32
Charles, J. P., 375
Chase, A., 299, 490
Chavers-Wright, M., 54
Chavis, B. F., Jr., 452
Cheboksarov, N. N., 92
Cheek, D., 484
Chen, S., 552
Cheng, L., 595

Cohn, A., 256
Cohn, E., 585
Cohn, R. L., 525
Colasanto, D., 76, 463
Colburn, D. R., 68, 115, 165, 236, 256, 393
Colby, D. C., 452
Colby, I. C., 231
Cole, B., 186
Cole, C. L., 153
Cole, F. A., Jr., 54
Cole, J., 474
Cole, Johnnetta B., 351, 610
Cole, J. R., 54
Cole, O., Jr., 231
Coleman, J. E., 2
Coleman, L., 51
Coleman, R. G., 257
Coleman-Puckett, A., 113
Coles, R., 452, 589
Coley, G. J., 405
Coley, S. M., 595
Colgan, C. A., 17
Colker, R., 357
Collier, B., 444
Collier, B. J., 139, 487
Collier, Eugenia, 11
Collier-Arrington, B. J., 596
Collins, Amy, 186
Collins, C., 139
Collins, K. E., 226
Collinbs, L. D., 130, 615
Collins, M., 521
Collins, S., 76
Collins, Sharon M., 54, 76
Collins, Sheila D., 452, 543
Collins, T. W., 327
Colon, A., 605
Colon, J., 375
Colonnese, T., 387
Colorado, Pamela, 92
Colson, E., 596
Comanor, W., 121
Comarmond, Patrice de, 496
Combs, M. W., 2
Comer, James P., 2, 32, 61, 212, 487, 496, 563
Compton, D., 305
Compton, J., 395
Comstock, G., 405
Conant, R. R., 226
Conde, D., 382
Condran, J., 463
Conklin, N. F., 596
Conlen, Paul, 257

Conner, D. L., 237
Connolly, H. X., 226
Connor, L. A., 2
Connor, R. D. W., 319
Conrad, A. H., 525
Conroy, J., 415
Constantino, R., 474
Contant, F., 99
Conway, J. M., 559
Conway, L., 471
Conway, M. M., 452
Conyers, J. E., 438
Cook, B. A., 328
Cook, F. J., 553
Cook, J., 17
Cook, Katherine M., 179
Cook, S. J., 589
Cook, T. J., 76
Cook, W. W., 296
Cooke, G. J., 375
Cooke, M. A., 237
Cooks, H. C., 186
Cooley, J. R., 375
Coolidge, M. R., 305
Cooper, A. J., 596
Cooper, Annie, 161
Cooper, D. I., Jr., 421
Cooper, H. M., 113
Cooper, J. A., 186
Cooper, J. L., 574
Cooper, J. P., Jr., 68
Cooper, K. J., 391
Cooper, K. L., 3
Cooper, M. N., 475
Cooper, R., 237
Cooper, W. F., 32
Cope, N. R., 237
Copeland, E. J., 438
Coplon, J. R., 398
Coppin, F. J., 32
Coray, M. S., 212
Corbett, A., 475
Corbett, Katharine T., 257
Corbin, David A., 161, 328
Cordasco, F., 161, 312
Corley, R. G., 389
Cormier, Agnes T., 396
Cornely, P. B., 237
Cornford, D. A., 328
Cortes, Carlos E., 257
Cortese, A. J., 186
Cortez, Gregoria P., 390
Cortner, R. C., 574
Cose, E., 405
Costa, F. A., 183

Gerber, D. A., 18
Gerber, J. B., 163
Gerhardt, G., 503
Gerlach, E., 69
Gerlach, L. R., 319
Gershenfeld, W. J., 209
Gershman, Carl, 78
Gershoni, Y., 475
Gerson, L. L., 65
Gerteis, L. S., 261
Gertz, E., 18
Geschwender, J. A., 330, 497
Gesensway, D., 100
Ghareeb, E. A., 475, 544
Ghassemlou, A. R., 475
Giampetro, Andrea, 4
Gibbs, Jewelle T., 61, 570
Gibbs, P. J., 544
Gibbs, T., 239
Gibson, A. M., 261
Gibson, D. B., 377
Gibson, J., 97
Gifford, Bernard R., 160
Gilber, R., 185
Gilbert, A., 18
Gilbert, A. L., 55, 59
Gilbert, G., 401
Gilbert, N., 483
Gilbert, R., 482
Gilbreath, Kent, 55
Gilbroy, P., 475
Giles, Michael, 114
Giles, M. W., 464
Giles, N., 189
Gilfoyle, T. J., 554
Gilje, P. A., 576
Gill, F., 416
Gill, G. P., 422
Gill, R. L., 360
Gilliam, R., 69
Gillas, C. L. T., 598
Gillenkirk, J., 97, 391
Gillerman, G., 163
Gillespie, D. A., 189
Gillette, H., Jr., 282
Gilliam, Dorothy, 544
Gillis, Katherine A., 422
Gills, D., 450
Gilman, H. J., 122
Gilman, S. L., 544
Gilman, S. C., 518
Gilman, S. I., 475
Gilmore, Al-Tony, 528
Giloth, R. P., 418
Gilroy, C. L., 570

Ginagerich, R., 91
Ginger, A. F., 360
Gingras, L., 34
Ginsberg, E., 239
Ginsberg, R., 189
Ginsberg, Y., 48
Ginzburg, A., 163
Girdner, A., 101
Giroux, V. A., Jr., 34
Gisst, F. W., 416
Gitelman, H. M., 122
Gitlin, T., 590
Gittell, M., 46, 438
Glaberman, M., 330
Gladwin, T., 61, 93
Glanz, R., 296
Glasgow, Douglas G., 78, 570
Glasrud, B. A., 528
Glass, B., 518
Glass, J., 607
Glassberg, 142
Glasser, I., 468
Glazer, Nathan, 4, 399
Glen, John M., 69
Glenn, E. N., 598
Glenn, N. D., 122, 154
Glick, B., 554
Glock, C. Y., 18
Cloor, P-A., 497
Gloster, R., 43.
Glott, C. S., 483
Go, R., 406
Gobetz, G. E., 613
Godwin, John L., 69
Göbel, T., 330
Goering, John M., 4
Goetting, A., 105
Goggin, Jacqueline, 261
Goings, K. W., 261
Goins, J. B., 314
Gold, A. R., 283
Gold, D. E., 122
Goldberg, K., 190
Goldberg, M., 476
Goldberg, R. A., 319, 402
Goldberg, Stephanie, 105
Goldberg, Steven, 25
Golden, D., 25
Goldfarb, R. A., 331
Goldman, A. H., 4
Goldman, Peter, 34
Goldsby, R. A., 300
Goldschmid, M., 497
Goldstein, Carol G., 564
Goldstein, I., 283, 284

Goldstein, R. J., 360, 544
Goleman, D., 300
Gollnick, D. M., 447
Gomex, J., 190
Gomez-Quinones, J., 190, 261, 331
Gong, T., 377
Gonsalves, S. V., 610
Gonzales, P. B., 190
Gonzales, R. M.
Gonzales, S., 598
Gonzalez, C., 518
Gonzalez, G. C., 163
Gonzalez, N. L., 306
Gonzalez, R. J., 351
Gonzalez Diaz, E., 454
Gonzalez-Gomez, J., 163
Good, P., 154
Goode, V., 122
Goodrich, Linda S., 261
Goodfriends, Joyce D., 528
Goodman, E., 554
Goodman, J., 483
Goodman, P., 487
Goodstein, Anita S., 261
Goodwin, M., 26
Goodwin, S., 438
Gopal, S., 261
Gordils, J., 377
Gordon, A. H., 590
Gordon, D. M., 122
Gordon, L., 142
Gordon, M. H., 306
Gordon, P., 476
Gordon, V. V., 598
Gorman, K. L., 34
Gorner, P., 142, 154
Gornick, Vivian, 18
Goror, L., 163
Gortmaker, S. L., 239
Goss, K. A., 190
Gossett, T. F., 261
Goston, M., 97
Gottlieb, M., 347
Gotsch-Thomson, S., 142
Gottlieb, P., 331, 416
Gottschalk, M. O., 190
Gottschalk, Peter, 77, 140, 585
Gould, K. H., 544
Gould, S. H., 4
Gould, W. B., 331
Gould, W. S., 422
Gowing, P. G., 476
Grabiner, G., 360
Grable, S. W., 284
Graebener, J., 78

Graham, G., 331
Graham, J. D., 90
Graham, L., 222
Graham, Maryemma, 377
Graham, Renee, 397
Graham, Thomas, 377
Granada, R., 576
Granat, D., 392
Granfield, Michael E., 57
Granger, G., 231
Granger, Lori, 284
Grant, C. A., 431, 521
Grant, D. L., 87
Grant, G., 163
Grant, J. A. C., 360
Grant, L., 163
Grant, R. B., 416
Gratus, J., 528
Gravely, W. B., 262
Graves, J. W., 390
Gray, A. T., 143
Gray, H., 406
Gray, R., 528
Graymont, B., 34
Greeley, A. M., 464
Green, A., 438
Green, Andy, 564
Green, C., 517
Green, D. G., 454
Green, D. S., 78
Green, E., Jr., 331
Green, J. R., 114, 331, 344
Green, L. C., 434
Green, M. D., 598
Green, Nancy L., 48
Green, P., 576
Green, R., 610
Green, R. L., 26, 163
Green, Raya, 521
Green, S. M., 331
Green, T. L., 55
Green, T. S., 26
Green, W. J., 163
Greenberg, B. S., 407
Greenberg, J., 360
Greenberg, Jack, 106
Greenberg, R. S., 239
Greenberg, S. B., 55, 231
Greenbag, S. W., 284
Greene, H., 598
Greene, J., 319
Greene, J. P., 528
Greene, Kathanne W., 4
Greene, L., 528
Greene, L. A., 586

Hall, E. R., 438
Hall, F. D., 143
Hall, G. M., 360
Hall, H. R., 237
Hall, K. L., 319, 320, 271
Hall, Linda, 351
Hall, P. A., 372
Hall, R. L., 434
Hall, Stuart, 61, 93, 564
Hall, Thomas, 93
Hallberg, C. V., 320
Haller, J. S., Jr., 491
Halliburton, J., 428
Halliburton, R., Jr., 428, 529
Halliday, T. Y., 59
Halloran, R., 422
Halperin, M., 554
Halter, M. B., 306
Halter, S. F., 422
Hambley, J., 519
Hamburg, Jill, 284
Hamilton, Charles V., 70, 93, 143, 454
Hamilton, F. D., 440
Hamilton, K. M., 43, 44
Hamilton, R. L., 416
Hamilton, T. K. B., 598
Hamlin, W. R., 396
Hammerback, J. C., 404, 434
Hammerman, H., 4
Hammett, H. B., 332
Hamps, S., 190
Hanafin, Teresa M., 123, 284
Hanchett, C. M., 34
Hancock, H. B., 222
Hancock, I. F., 476
Hancock, L., 164
Handlin, Mary F., 19
Handlin, Oscar, 19, 154, 399
Handy, E. S., 213
Handy, T., 58
Handy, J. W., III, 55
Handy, K. M., 79
Haney, J. B., 282
Hanft, R. S., 239
Hanger, K. S., 222
Hangt., R. S., 439
Hanks, L. J., 454
Hannah, T. S., 106
Hanneman, G. J., 407
Hannerz, U., 227
Hannon, J. U., 123, 143
Hansberry, L., 227
Hansen, A. A., 101
Hansen, Kristine, 351

Hansson, R. O., 190
Hapgood, Norman, 19
Harap, Louis, 48, 378
Harari, H., 544
Hardaway, R. D., 213
Hardee, B. B., 464, 468
Hardin, C. L., 190
Hardin, S. C., 70
Harding, L., 576
Harding, R. R., 123
Harding, S., 70
Harding, Vincent, 34, 87, 136, 262, 360, 512
Hardy, D. A., 598
Hare, Bruce R., 143
Harer, M. D., 106
Hargrave, E., 190
Hargrove, H. B., 422
Harkey, I., 407
Harlan, Louis R., 35, 164
Harley, Sharon L., 35, 598, 599
Harlow, N., 262
Harmetz, A., 439
Harmon, J. H., 55
Harmon, L., 287
Harmon, R., 494
Harmon, W., 439
Haro, R. P., 372
Harold, R., 190
Harper, C., Jr., 529
Harper, Frederick D., 564
Harper, F. E. W., 378
Harpole, Patricia C., 398
Harrie, Dan, 19
Harington, Michael, 65, 154
Harrington, R., 407
Harris, Abram L., 44, 55, 62, 154, 314, 332, 341, 416, 538
Harris, Art., 398
Harris, Barbara, 521
Harris, C. V., 164, 231
Harris, D. J., 143, 227, 332, 586
Harris, E. E., 164
Harris, Fred R., 143
Harris, H., 209
Harris, J. T., 407
Harris, J. W., 529
Harris, L., 243, 262, 445, 463, 464
Harris, R. L., Jr., 262
Harris, T., 576
Harris, Trudier, 378
Harris, V. J., 136
Harris, W., 213
Harris, W. H., 332

642

Keil, H., 334
Keil, T. J., 320
Keir, S. S., 214
Keiser, J. H., 334
Keith, D. J., 124, 362
Keith, S. N., 6
Keller, E. T., 423
Keller, G., 408
Keller, G. D., 380
Keller, S., 446
Keller, William W., 555
Kelley, R. D. G., 538
Kelley, V., 192
Kelley-Hawkins, Emma D., 380
Kellman, Steven G., 19
Kellner, B., 380
Kellog, J., 417
Kellogg, C. F., 87
Kellogg, J., 285
Kellogg, Peter J., 264
Kellough, James E., 6
Kelly, Ernece B., 380
Kelly, M. E., 166
Kelly, W. J., 264
Kelly, W. R., 577
Kelsey, G. D., 512
Kelso, D. R., 251
Kelway, A. J., 218
Kemp, K. A., 80
Kempf, K. L., 107
Kempton, Murray, 107
Kendal, 447
Kendrick, E. A., 241
Kennedy, D., 285
Kennedy, L., 264
Kennedy, Louise V., 419
Kennedy, Lisa, 408
Kennedy, M., 98
Kennedy, R. L., 362, 363
Kennedy, Randall, 6
Kennedy, T. R., 214
Kenney, C., 44, 192
Kennicott, P. C., 456
Kenny, C., 397
Kenny, S., 402
Kenschaft, P. C., 439
Kent, C. A., 154
Kent, G. O., 19
Kenyatta, M. I., 214
Kerber, L. K., 578
Kerbo, H. R., 193
Kernek, L., 193
Kernodle, R., 241
Kerr, P., 107, 241
Kessler, M. A., 145

Kessler, S., 334
Kessner, Carole, 380
Kester, H., 334, 578
Kettner, J. H., 65
Key, R. C., 439
Keyssar-Franke, Helene, 387
Kharif, W. R., 265
Kiah, Rosalie B., 380, 546
Kickinbird, K., 363
Kidd, F., 439
Kiefer, D., 145
Kiernan, L. A., 439
Kifner, J., 285
Kiker, B. F., 124, 585
Kilar, J. W., 315
Kilgo, J. C., 578
Killian, L. M., 468, 591
Kilson, Marian D. D'B., 80, 530
Kilson, Martin L., 6, 80, 151,
   193, 380, 600
Kim, B-L. C., 363, 600
Kim, C., 363
Kim, Elaine, 380
Kim, H-C., 265
Kim, Illsoo, 56
Kim, S. G., 539
Kimball, G. D., 403
Kimble, M., 26
Kimmel, M. S., 498
Kimmel, R. M., 223
Kimmich, M. H., 145
Kinder, D. R., 117, 391, 468
Kindred, D., 193
King, Allan, G., 124
King, Anita, 614
King, C. B., 315
King, Deborah K., 521
King, G. D., 483
King, H., 241
King, J., 285
King, L. L., 301, 423, 591
King, L. M., 600
King, M., 36
King, Mae C., 546
King, Mel, 98, 455
King, Martin Luther, Jr., 49
King, N., 6
King, Richard H., 66
King, V. H., 241
King, W. M., 166, 344, 584
King, Wayne, 320, 408, 504, 555
Kingston, Maxine Hong, 36, 380
Kinley-Cooper, Kimberly, 408
Kinlow, R. L., 403
Kinshasha, K. M., 265

MacGregor, M. J., 424, 425
McGuire, M. J., 348
McGuire, P., 424
McHugh, Cathy L., 337
McHugh, K. E., 417
McHugh, Maureen, 522
McIntosh, J. L., 243
McKay, C., 267
MacKay, K. L., 336
McKay, Nellie, 101, 381
McKay, R. B., 457
McKee, D. L., 267
McKelvey, B., 219
McKinney, E. R., 337
McKitrick, E., 526
McKiven, H. M., Jr., 389
McKnight, Gerald D., 555, 556
McLachlan, H. V., 445
McLaughlin, M. E., 309
McLaurin, M. A., 62, 337, 547
McLean, Deckle, 566
McLemore, S. D., 267
McLeod, J. W., 337, 591
McLouglin, W. G., 429
McLoyd, V. C., 62
McMahon, S., 243
McManus, E. J., 531
McMath, R. C., Jr., 337
McMillan, E. 88
MacMillan, M. E., 364
McMillen, N. R., 267, 396, 457
McMorris, R., 169
McMurray, L. O., 38, 519
McNamara, Jo Ann K., 521
McNealy, R. L., 403
McNeil, G. R., 38, 115, 364
McNeil, J. M., 148
McNeil, Teresa B., 169
McNichol, D., 195
McPartland, J. M., 2, 120
McPherson, D. A., 38
McPherson, James A., 71, 265, 288
McPherson, J. M., 424, 547, 617
McPherson, R. S., 587
McRae, F. F., 195
McRae, N., 223
McTigue, Geraldine, 288
McWhiney, G., 218
McWilliams, Carey, 20, 267
Ma, L. E. A., 56
Macaruso, V., 547
Machado, Deirdre, A. M., 266
Macher, David J., 107
Machnacki, D., 364
Macias, J., 431

Maciel, David, 261, 266, 331
Mackintosh, B., 518
Mackler, B., 560
Madden, R. L., 392
Maddex, J. P., Jr., 513
Madsen, Jane M., 62, 547
Madyun, G., 391
Magdol, E., 347
Magnet, Myron, 81
Magubane, Bernard, 12
Maguire, R. E., 396
Magura, M., 570
Mahan, Harold E., 267
Maharidge, D., 81
Maheody, L., 560
Mahon, J. K., 429
Mahoney, Kathryn L., 267
Main, G. L., 530
Maizlish, S. E., 252
Major, G. J., 81
Majors, M. A., 601
Makihara, K., 544
Maldonado, C. S., 194
Maldonado, E., 210
Maldonado-Denis, M., 417
Malgady, R. G., 243
Mallam, R. C., 167
Malloy, W. W., 124
Malon, L., 391
Malpass, Elizabeth D., 267
Malson, M., 609
Malveaux, Julianne, 6, 81, 145,
   570, 601, 606
Mamiya, L. H., 267, 513
Mandel, B. J., 37
Mandel, J., 364
Manes, J., 354
Maness, L. E., 424
Mangan, J. A., 27
Mangione, A. R., 449
Mangum, C. Jr., 364
Mangum, G. L., 570
Manicas, P. T., 614
Manis, A., M., 513
Mankoff, M., 188
Mann, S. A., 602
Manners, R. A., 448
Manning, K. R., 518
Manning, S. W., 336
Marable, J. M., 602
Marable, Manning, 56, 71, 81,
   107, 136, 154, 167, 194, 267,
   336, 347, 435, 456, 468, 513,
   539, 578, 602
Maran, P., 440

Mitchell, E. P., 514
Mitchell, G. S., 327
Mitchell, Gail G. J., 126
Mitchell, H. L., 338
Mitchell, J. L., 579
Mitchell, Roxanne, 499
Mitchell-Kernan, C., 60
Mitgang, N. R., 35
Miyano, Y., 610
Mizio, E., 94
Mjoseth, J., 195
Mkalimoto, E., 435
Mobley, J. A., 44
Modell, John, 101, 214
Modey, Y. F., 365
Modras, Ronald, 20
Mörner, M., 478
Moffatt, M., 195
Mogdil, C., 302
Mogdil, S., 302
Mogull, Robert G., 27
Mohl, Raymond A., 126, 146, 254, 268, 457
Mohr, C. L., 278, 531
Mohr, E. V., 382, 418
Moland, J., 297
Molek, M., 38
Molin, P. F., 169
Mollica, R. F., 244
Molnar, H., 440
Momaday, N. Scott, 382
Momeni, J. A., 294, 617
Moneyhorn, C. H., 268, 457
Monfort, Franklin, 116
Monk, D. H., 169
Monmaney, T., 244
Monroe, S., 440
Monroy, D. G., 457
Montagu, M. F. A., 20, 244, 302
Montague, W., 169
Montalto, N., 492
Montejano, D., 268, 338
Montejano-Enriquez, D., 126
Montgomery, E., 126
Monti, D. J., 579
Montiel, M., 214
Moody, Anne, 38
Mooney, B., 146
Mooney, Linda, 542
Mooney, R. J., 365
Moore, B. L., 424
Moore, Carlos, 499
Moore, D. E., 457
Moore, D. G., 196
Moore, E. G. J., 60

Moore, G., 314
Moore, G. W., 338
Moore, H., 338
Moore, H., Jr., 108, 365
Moore, J. B., 108
Moore, J. H., 531
Moore, J. T., 38, 88
Moore, Joan W., 81, 94
Moore, K., 457
Moore, L. J., 321
Moore, M., 579
Moore, R. B., 352
Moore, Robert B., 566
Moore, R. L., 539
Mora, M., 602
Moraberger, R. E., 382
Moraga, C., 602
Morais, N., 20
Morales, A., 488
Morales, J. Jr., 418
Morales, R. F., 88
Morales Carrion, A., 268
Moranian, S. E., 169
Morawski, Ewa, 309, 338
Moreland, L. B., 365
Moreland, L. W., 457
Moreland, P., 410
Morgan, D. R., .14
Morgan, E. S., 531
Morgan, G., 81, 338, 469
Morgan, Lynda J., 268
Morgan, P. D., 531
Morgan, Richard S., 556
Morgan, T., 63, 169
Morgan, W. D., 151
Morganfield, R., 196
Moriarity, J., 81
Morishima, J. K., 247
Moriyama, A. T., 309
Morrill, P. B., 410, 591
Morrill, R. L., 268
Morris, A., 88
Morris, A. A., 7
Morris, A. D., 71
Morris, C. E., 268
Morris, F. L., 302
Morris, J. S., 547
Morris, L., 196
Morris, R. B., 591
Morris, R. C., 169
Morris, R. J., 353
Morris, Thomas D., 108, 365
Morrissey, M., 81
Morrison, I., 591
Morrison, K. C., 126, 365

662

669

672

About the Compiler

MEYER WEINBERG was previously a Professor of History at the City College of Chicago. He is the author of several books including *The Search for Quality Integrated Education* (Greenwood Press, 1983) and *America's Economic Heritage* (Greenwood Press, 1983).